LATINO
HISTORY AND CULTURE
AN ENCYCLOPEDIA

Volume Two

David J. Leonard and Carmen R. Lugo-Lugo, editors

SHARPE REFERENCE

an imprint of M.E. Sharpe, Inc.

M.E. Sharpe, Inc.
80 Business Park Drive
Armonk, NY 10504

Library of Congress Cataloging-in-Publication Data

Latino history and culture: an encyclopedia / David J. Leonard and Carmen R. Lugo-
Lugo, editors.
    p. cm.
Includes bibliographical references and index.
ISBN 978-0-7656-8083-9 (hardcover: alk. paper)
1. Hispanic Americans—Encyclopedias. I. Leonard, David J. II. Lugo-Lugo, Carmen R.

E184.S75L3622 2009
305.868'07303—dc22   2008047796

Cover photos by Getty and the following (from top left corner): Doug Collier/AFP; Alex
Wong; Bob Parent/Hulton Archive; Tim Boyle; Kevin Mazur/WireImage.

Printed and bound in the United States of America

The paper used in this publication meets the minimum requirements of
American National Standard for Information Sciences
Permanence of Paper for Printed Library Materials,
ANSI Z 39.48.1984.

(c) 10 9 8 7 6 5 4 3 2 1

Publisher: Myron E. Sharpe
Vice President and Director of New Product Development: Donna Sanzone
Vice President and Production Director: Carmen Chetti
Executive Development Editor: Jeff Hacker
Project Manager: Laura Brengelman
Program Coordinator: Cathleen Prisco
Assistant Editor: Alison Morretta
Text Design: Carmen Chetti and Jesse Sanchez
Cover Design: Jesse Sanchez

Contents

iii

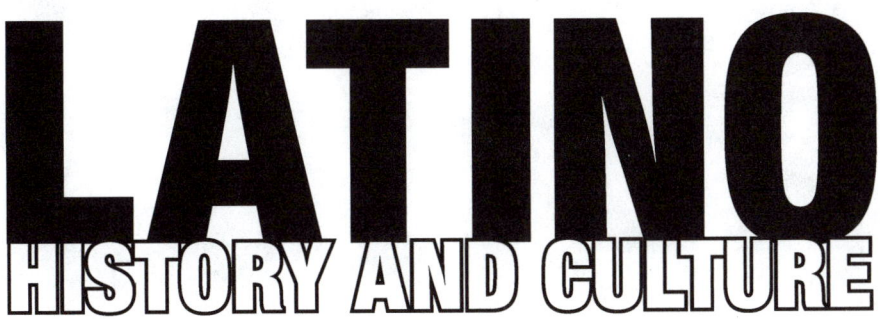

LATINO
HISTORY AND CULTURE

Volume Two

Macheteros, Los

Los Macheteros (the Machete Wielders) is a paramilitary organization that seeks the political and social independence of Puerto Rico from what it considers colonial rule by the United States of America. Also known as *El Ejército Popular Boricua* (the Puerto Rican Popular Army), Los Macheteros is committed to the defense of Puerto Rican culture, the establishment of a sovereign Puerto Rican nation, and the separation of Puerto Rico's legal system from that of the United States.

Established in 1976 by Puerto Rican nationalists Filiberto Ojeda Ríos, Juan Enrique Segarra Palmer, and Orlando Gonzalez Claudio, Los Macheteros remains a clandestine organization on the island, with membership of approximately 1,100 and cells reportedly active throughout the United States. Since 1977, Los Macheteros has claimed responsibility for numerous armed robberies and bombings, actions that have inspired other Puerto Rican nationalists. Statehood advocates and U.S. government officials, however, have branded Los Macheteros a terrorist organization—a label that members believe inadequately reflects the complex colonial relationship between Puerto Rico and the United States. Members of Los Macheteros regard their activities to be those of freedom fighters, dedicated to the sociopolitical liberation of Puerto Rico.

One of the first actions carried out by Los Macheteros took place on January 2, 1977, one day after Carlos Romero Barceló, a statehood advocate, was sworn in as governor of Puerto Rico. Members of the organization succeeded in placing two bombs at a U.S. ROTC (Reserve Officers Training Corps) building in San Juan. Although the bombs were detected and successfully dismantled by police, Los Macheteros counted the event—and the publicity of it—as a successful step toward securing Puerto Rico's independence.

Over the course of the next two decades, Los Macheteros claimed responsibility for a number of other attacks on the United States. A year after the attempted bombing of the ROTC building in San Juan, Los Macheteros stole 17,500 feet (5,300 meters) of detonation cord and 500 pounds (230 kilograms) of ammonium nitrate (used in explosives) from a government warehouse in Manati, Puerto Rico. In 1981, Los Macheteros destroyed nine planes at a Puerto Rican Air National Guard base, causing an estimated $45 million in damages. Members of the group recorded the event on film, later aired on Puerto Rican television news programs. Waving their emblematic machetes and Puerto Rican flags, members of Los Macheteros declared solidarity with El Salvador's struggle against U.S intervention and protested the incarceration of eleven Puerto Rican nationalists.

Other events carried out by Los Macheteros have included the 1981 bombing of the Puerto Rican Electrical Power Authority in Santurce; a 1982 retaliatory attack in response to U.S. military maneuvers on the island of Vieques the year before; and the 1985 bombing of the U.S. courthouse in Old San Juan.

Los Macheteros is perhaps best remembered, however, for an attack it organized on U.S. soil. On September 12, 1983, New York City native and Los Macheteros member Victor Gerena single-handedly stole $7 million from a Wells Fargo depository in West Hartford, Connecticut. In the operation, known as *Aguila Blanca* (White Eagle), Gerena, an employee of West Fargo at the time, attacked two coworkers and escaped with the money. He was placed on the Federal Bureau of Investigation's (FBI's) Ten Most Wanted list, charged with fourteen counts of aggravated robbery, aggravated robbery of federally insured bank funds, armed robbery, and conspiracy to interfere with commerce by robbery. In January 1985, two years after the robbery, Los Macheteros sponsored what it called the Three Kings giveaway, in which the group bought gifts for the poor using money from the Wells Fargo depository.

The FBI initially targeted nineteen Puerto Ricans alleged to have been involved in the robbery or the transfer of the money; all nineteen were arrested and charged with acts of fraud and robbery. They refuted the charges and accused the United States of violating UN Resolution 2621 (1970), which declared colonialism an international crime and reaffirmed the right of any colonized nation to utilize whatever tactics necessary to obtain its independence. Los Macheteros accused the U.S. government of crimes that included an excessive number of military bases in Puerto Rico, population control experiments that left one-third of all women in Puerto Rico sterile, the illegal bombing of Culebra and Vieques (two Puerto Rican islands used as target sites in military exercises), the secret testing of Agent Orange, and the infamous Dr. Rhoads cancer "treatments." (Cornelius P. Rhoads, a physician from the United States, admitted to injecting Puerto Ricans with cancer cells as part of an investigation conducted by the Rockefeller Institute for Medical Research, a New York–based research facility).

Los Macheteros continues its fight for Puerto Rican independence to the present day, athough the organization has suffered losses. On September 23, 2005, cofounder Ríos, 72, was gunned down by agents of the FBI who surrounded the house in Hormigueros, Puerto Rico, where he was hiding. Ríos, wanted by the FBI for his involvement in the West Fargo robbery, was killed under controversial circumstances on the anniversary of the 1868 rebellion for Puerto Rican independence known as El Grito de Lares. Gerena, still wanted by the FBI, remains a folk hero to many Puerto Ricans still advocating independence.

Brian Montes

See also: Nationalism; Puerto Ricans.

Further Reading

Fernandez, Ronald. *Los Macheteros: The Wells Fargo Robbery and the Violent Struggle for Puerto Rican Independence.* New York: Prentice Hall, 1987.
———. *Prisoners of Colonialism: The Struggle for Justice in Puerto Rico.* Monroe, ME: Common Courage, 1994.

Machismo

*M*achismo is a social attitude and belief system characterized by exaggerated masculinity, sexual bravado, and a belief in male domination over women and other men. Machismo is upheld by ideologies that dictate different social expectations and lifestyles for men and women. Conventional expectations of men, for example, include physical strength and emotional invulnerability. Expectations of women, by contrast, demand humility, physical weakness, and submission to males. In addition to these ideological expressions, machismo is reinforced by routine behavior and interactions that can be regionally and culturally specific. Through repeated practices and personal interactions, the system of machismo becomes treated as a social norm that is reproduced and perpetuated. While machismo is generally associated with Latino male behavior and attitudes, it can be observed in a spectrum of racial, ethnic, and national communities.

The word "machismo" is generally believed to derive from the Spanish *macho,* meaning "male." The term "macho" has roots in the classical Náhuatl language of the Aztecs of central Mexico, in which it meant "image" or "reflection of myself." Being macho is characterized by excessive virility through the illustration of masculine strength and sexual prowess. Displays of machismo in contemporary society may be a by-product of the humiliation experienced by indigenous men during colonization, given the violence and subjugation that occurred during that period. Some have argued that in order to compensate for physical and cultural defeat, indigenous men have taken on macho attitudes that would carry over into *mestizo* (mixed European and native) culture. As in earlier periods of Spanish conquest, machismo in the United States today may also have its roots in competition between men, of similar or different ethnic backgrounds, for valor and status earned by demonstrated dominance over women. For example, violence against women was commonplace during the Spanish invasion of California in the late eighteenth century. As invading soldiers systematically violated indigenous women, a standard of European racial superiority was instilled at the expense of in-digenous men who were not able to protect their female kin.

The everyday occurrence of machismo in U.S. Latino communities cannot be solely attributed to the legacy of conquest. It is impossible to universalize the root of contemporary manifestations of excessive masculinity, especially because the behaviors are not unique to Latino populations. As in earlier times of conquest, however, contemporary machismo is tied to a complex interplay of racial, class-based, and gender dynamics. Recent Latino immigrants, for example, may feel threatened by the relative lack of traditional, male-headed families in Anglo-American culture. Some Latino husbands, confronted with discrimination in the workplace and the new opportunities available to women, may seek to reclaim a measure of male privilege and domination by taking out their frustrations physically and emotionally against their wives.

Machismo can also be understood in the context of the customary roles of men and women in society at large, in the domestic setting, and in relationships with each other. Over time, the expected roles become perceived as "natural" attributes of each sex. In this context, special value is placed on characteristics, behaviors, and ideas that are typically, though not exclusively, associated with males. Despite societal changes that in some cultures have allowed these gender roles to shift and change, their primacy as social norms remains widely apparent.

Machismo in the United States Today

Modern examples of machismo can be found, among other places, in the Chicano Movement of the 1960s and 1970s. Women were initially sidelined in the struggle for Mexican American civil rights and empowerment, ostensibly because their gender-based concerns were tangential to the movement's ethnic nationalist focus. Pressured to support male counterparts in the movement unquestioningly, many Chicanas broke away to form separate groups free from patriarchal structure. These included the National Conference of Puerto Rican Women (NACOPRW),

established in 1972 to ensure that Puerto Rican and other Hispanic women secure equal rights under the law and to promote equitable social, economic, and political participation for Puerto Rican women. Similarly, female activists in 1980s Los Angeles encountered male resistance toward their neighborhood mobilization efforts, which included day-care centers, health clinics, and English as a Second Language (ESL) programs. Such efforts ultimately gained the acceptance of men in the community, provided their wives did not abandon their domestic household responsibilities.

In the 2000s, machismo is widely regarded as part of a supposed cultural ethic that includes chronic poverty, laziness, and other ethnic and class-based prejudices. In everyday life, the system of machismo is reinforced through repeated practices and behavior patterns, generally on the part of men toward women. To satisfy the macho image, for example, men should father as many children as possible (ideally male), appear fearless, and practice tight control, if not complete domination, over female relatives. While such attitudes and practices are strongly associated with men, women can act out their own *machista* attitudes by displaying emotional invulnerability, physical aggression, and sexual dominance. Still, many of the social spaces where such practices take place do not typically admit women, thereby reinforcing the idea that machismo mediates competition and structures power in the interest of men. In the United States, gang membership may provide a venue in which to practice the intermale competition that undergirds machismo.

Practices that perpetuate machismo vary according to the meaning of "macho" to particular groups of Latinos/as in the contemporary United States. Negative conceptions of machismo are generally associated with behavior that physically or psychologically harms women in the process of proving one's manhood. Such practices include domestic violence, lack of care for family members, and self-centeredness. Positive conceptions of a "macho" male, contrastingly, connote protectiveness toward one's family, standing up for one's rights, and meeting kinship obligations such as financial support. The associations vary regionally across the United States, as well as across generations and among national or cultural traditions. Younger U.S. Latinos/as may be more exposed to fluctuating gender roles in the course of their upbringing, thereby feeling less pressure to assert their masculinity by illustrating dominance over women.

In the twenty-first century, the ideology of machismo is challenged in a number of different realms. Industrialization and urbanization throughout the twentieth century influenced traditional gender roles, as more women began to work outside of the home. Accordingly, urban populations today tend to have more equitable gender roles, while the influence of machismo remains comparatively pervasive in rural communities. Factors such as ethnicity, nationality, and socioeconomic class also account for variations in expected gender roles. In addition, increased female migration from Latin America to the United States may lead to gradual shifts in social norms as women establish themselves in new communities. Nevertheless, women's advances in public arenas do not necessarily correlate with increased male responsibility in domestic spaces like the household. Instead of fundamental changes in gender roles, many women simply take on additional burdens with new formal and informal labor responsibilities. Rates of domestic violence, meanwhile, remain high in many U.S. Latino communities. Despite the advances of the twentieth century, understanding the system of machismo and challenging machista attitudes will remain a central challenge for future generations of women and men in the United States.

Heather E. Craigie

See also: Chicano Movement; Family and Community; Identity and Labels; Marianismo; Women.

Further Reading

Abalos, David T. *The Latino Male: A Radical Redefinition.* Boulder, CO: Lynne Rienner, 2002.

Chant, Sylvia, and Nikki Craske. *Gender in Latin America.* New Brunswick, NJ: Rutgers University Press, 2003.

Mirandé, Alfredo. *Hombres y Machos: Masculinity and Latino Culture.* Boulder, CO: Westview, 1997.

Pardo, Mary S. *Mexican American Women Activists: Identity and Resistance in Two Los Angeles Communities.* Philadelphia: Temple University Press, 1998.

Malinche, La (c. 1500–c. 1529)

La Malinche, also referred to as Malinali Tenepat, Malintzín, Doña Marina, and La Chingada, is a historical figure whose life took on legendary proportions. The precise details of her life are hard to pin down because most of what we know of her today has been handed down through legend and myth. A popular figure in Mexican and Chicano culture, La Malinche is popularly known as the mother of the Mexican people, a role she came to occupy as the native mistress of Hernán Cortés, the sixteenth-century Spanish conquistador of Mexico whose son she bore. La Malinche remains a complex and controversial figure, alternately portrayed as a tragic heroine, a betraying mother, and a violated or violating woman. Her life, meaning, and cultural relevance depend on who is telling the story.

In Mexican tradition, she is Doña Marina, the resourceful and loyal companion to Hernán Cortés. After the Mexican revolution of the early twentieth century and the nationalist cultural movement that accompanied it, Malinche was cast in the Mexican imagination as a traitor and a whore, a woman who betrayed her people, aided in their destruction, and bore the bastard son of their conqueror. In the contemporary Chicana feminist movement, by contrast, La Malinche has been reconstituted as a woman who succeeded in rising above patriarchy, negotiating and transcending the masculinist cultures that injured her.

Although the precise details of Malinche's life may be difficult to separate from her myth, the general outline of her story is consistent. Her shifting identity— her constant naming and renaming—is a product of the reconsideration of her myth by feminist and postcolonial scholars in the late twentieth century, who, through questioning the structure of patriarchal society, have reclaimed La Malinche as a feminist icon who transcends traditional nomenclature.

History

La Malinche's early life before the conquest is hard to discern. Because written records were rare in the period of the conquest, scholars have had trouble pinning down her birth and death dates, though it is clear that she was born around 1500 and died between 1527 and 1529. Much of what we know of La Malinche's early life comes from secondhand sources, such as Bernal Díaz del Castillo, a contemporary of Cortés whose eyewitness account, *The Conquest of New Spain,* provides much of what is known about both Malinche and the era of the conquest. According to Díaz's somewhat romanticized account, La Malinche was born into an upper level of Aztec society. After her father's death, her mother had another child—a son—by a second husband. In order to ensure that the son would be the sole inheritor of the family's power and influence, her mother gave Malinche as a slave to the invading Spanish. Because she was fluent in both Náhuatl (the Aztec language) and Mayan, Malinche acted as a link in the chain of translators, Náhuatl to Mayan to Spanish, for Cortés. In that capacity, she became Cortés's consort and bore him a son, Don Martín Cortés I. Born of two different worlds, a dying empire (the Aztec) on the one hand and a rising empire (Spain) on the other, Don Martín Cortés I became the symbol of a new, hybrid American identity. He was among the first *mestizos* (persons of indigenous and Spanish descent).

Masculinist Myth

Before the rise of the Mexican and Chicano cultural movements in the early years of the twentieth century, Mexican high culture emphasized its Euro-Iberian roots and its Spanish colonial past. In the context of Spanish conquest, La Malinche was better known through her Spanish name, Doña Marina. The indigenous name of Malintzín was likely replaced by the Spanish name Marina (derived from *mar,* the Spanish word for "sea") as a result of Christian baptism. During the conquest, it was regular practice for the Spaniards to baptize women in order to take them as mistresses. Whether or not this was the case, the emergence of Marina as both a name and an identity signals a shift of cultural emphasis away from a conquered indigenous culture to a conquering culture. Marina's inclusion in the culture of conquest is further evidenced by the addition of the title Doña in recognition of her role as Cortés's confi-

dante, lover, and translator. As Mexican, and later Chicano, sensibilities shifted in the twentieth century away from a predominantly Euro-Spanish cultural awareness and toward a more indigenous and mestizo-based cultural identification, the history, role, and reception of Malinche also changed.

By the time of the Mexican Revolution (1910), cultural sensibilities were moving away from European models of art, history, and culture, and focusing instead on the mestizo and indigenous roots of Mexican culture and nationhood. Within this context, the noble Doña Marina is derided as a cultural pariah. Her involvement with Cortés is understood as a betrayal of her own people. Malinche, in this interpretation, becomes little more than a whore, aiding in the destruction of her community and homeland for the love of a man. In Mexico, therefore, to be called a *Malinchista* is to be called a traitor or a lover of a foreigner. Cultural loyalty and feminine sexuality become political statements that are inseparable from one another and require that women (and their bodies) be carefully controlled; women, as the symbolic daughters of Malinche, are capable of betrayals that can destroy entire civilizations.

The presence of La Malinche as the whoring, betraying mother stands in stark contrast to the other image of idealized femininity in Mexican culture, the Virgin Mary. While the Virgin Mary is the loved, saintly, protecting, ever-sacrificing mother of the Americas, Malinche is the scorned, betraying, fallen, violated mother who exposed both her body and her people to invasion. The two images are often presented as the virgin/whore dichotomy, whereby women either have no control over their sexuality and their bodies (the Virgin birth indicating both an absence of sexuality and a yielding of bodily agency to higher, masculine power), or else possess and exercise a power that becomes equated with commercial exchange. It is in the latter context that La Malinche's name shifts yet again, as her identity becomes synonymous with La Chingada (one who is sexually taken or conquered).

By the 1970s, the Chicano nationalist movement was in full swing in the American West and Southwest. Drawing on the emphasis of indigenous culture in the Mexican nationalist movement and inspired by the American civil rights movement,

Chicanos/as began demanding both equal rights and a recognition of their status as a conquered people. Since the Treaty of Guadalupe Hidalgo in 1848 essentially ceded half of Mexico to the ever-expanding Anglo-American empire, Chicanos/as pointed to their disenfranchisement from mainstream U.S. culture as historically constructed and argued that they are the true owners and inheritors of the American Southwest. The emphasis of the Chicano movement on the indigenous, traditional culture of Mexico and the American Southwest (including the return to Atzlán and the creation of the "Cosmic Race") affirmed the role of La Malinche as one of traitorous sexuality. Writers, artists, and thinkers focused on what they regarded as the culturally betraying woman, casting Malinche as a modern-day Eve.

Feminist Reclamations

In response to their symbolic and actual disenfranchisement from the Chicano movement specifically, and their oppression within Chicano culture more generally, Chicana feminists began arguing that patriarchy, and not the feminine body, was the destructive force behind the conquest. In making their argument, they revisited the myth of La Malinche to reclaim her body and her legend as symbols of resistance and strength. Feminist critics such as Gloria Anzaldúa pointed to the consistent betrayal of women by both men and other women as the source of division within Chicano, Mexican, and Anglo culture. She contends that while Chicanos/as may be disenfranchised by both Mexican and Anglo cultures, all three of these cultures, by virtue of their patriarchy, have been violent and repressive toward women. For Anzaldúa and other feminists, Malinche is a prime example of this. Her own people betrayed her when she was given to Cortés, and her body was used as a medium of exchange to ensure the ascendancy of the male child. Thus, they argue, Malinche's involvement with Cortés was less a cultural betrayal than an exercise of her own agency and intellect, insofar as she was able to fight the patriarchal culture that betrayed her by using the very cultural tools (language) it provided. In this context, Malinche is less a traitorous whore than a revolutionary mother. Thrust into the crossroads of history by the betrayal of her own people, it was entirely appropriate that Malinche produced the mestizo nation from her own body.

All in all, La Malinche represents a culturally complicated intersection of feminine sexuality, intellect, power, and cultural loyalty. Her enduring presence in modern Mexican, Chicano, and Chicana culture indicates that the uneasy intersections she straddles are far from being resolved.

Lorna Perez

See also: Chicano Movement; Conquest of the Americas; Feminism; Marianismo.

Further Reading

Cypess, Sandra Messinger. *La Malinche in Mexican Literature: From History to Myth.* Austin: University of Texas Press, 1991.

Díaz del Castillo, Bernal, and Maurice Keatinge. *The True History of the Conquest of Mexico, Written in the Year 1568 by Captain Bernal Díaz Del Castillo, One of the Conquerors, and Translated from the Original Spanish by Maurice Keatinge, Esq.; with an Introduction by Arthur D. Howden Smith.* New York: R.M. McBride, 1938.

Paz, Octavio. *The Labyrinth of Solitude; The Other Mexico; Return to the Labyrinth of Solitude; Mexico and the United States; the Philanthropic Ogre.* New York: Grove, 1991.

Manifest Destiny

Manifest Destiny, first enunciated in the 1840s, is a doctrine which concluded that the United States occupied a special position in the world and had a righteous, preordained, God-given mission to expand its territorial holdings across the American continent to spread freedom and democracy. First invoked on the eve of the Mexican-American War as a justification for U.S. expansionism and exceptionalism, the doctrine of Manifest Destiny has had an enduring influence on historical understandings and political relations.

Although Euro-Americans have long regarded themselves as a chosen people, even before the establishment of the United States, the idea of a Manifest Destiny did not crystallize until the middle of the nineteenth century. In 1845, the New York editor and political commentator John O'Sullivan first used the term in the pages of the *United States Magazine and Democratic Review.* He meant for the term to encapsulate and celebrate the unique position of the United States as the ordained "nation of human progress." O'Sullivan introduced the concept of Manifest Destiny into the ongoing national discussion of territorial expansion and foreign relations. He initially used the concept to urge the annexation of Texas, and later that year he invoked it again in calling for the incorporation of Oregon. In the latter context, O'Sullivan clearly articulated what would become the common understanding of the phrase and its significance for the nation: "the right of our manifest destiny to overspread and to possess the whole continent which providence has given us for the development of the great experiment of liberty and federated self government." With these words, he captured the expansionist spirit of the day while identifying the unique blend of religiosity, fate, and nationalism central to U.S. policy from independence to the present day. On the one hand, Manifest Destiny pointed to a common belief in the unique character of the United States, celebrating its commitment to democracy, its youthful vigor, and its difference from Europe. On the other hand, it outlined the mission of the United States to expand and grow into its rightful position in the world and, more important, to bring freedom and civilization to its less fortunate neighbors.

Long before O'Sullivan coined the term, however, European immigrants to North America applied a doctrine of God-given right in their relations with native peoples. Violence, squatting, and treaties combined as powerful means of displacement and dispossession. Settlers and their state sponsors created a cycle of trade, debt, and land cessions. In the mid-nineteenth century, Manifest Destiny would come to describe and justify this cycle of encroachment, trade, dependence, spontaneous violence, provocation, military threat and invasion, and removal, which guided U.S. efforts to annex Texas, Oregon, and California. Later it would help fuel the movement to annex Mexico and Cuba, and it would remain an important element in expansionist projects at the end of century—most infamously in the Spanish-American War, which made Puerto Rico and the

Philippines American colonies. In each of these cases, advocates of Manifest Destiny spoke of America's obligation to humanity to spread liberty and uplift the unfortunate—calling for the spread of just government, civilization, and freedom. The natural growth of the United States was routinely spoken of as an extension of natural law.

As the United States expanded, it usurped the territory and sovereignty of established nations—both indigenous and Latino. Countless thousands of farmers as well as their families and communities were dispossessed as wealth and resources were transferred to foreign speculators, settlers, and soldiers. In turn, once proud people were disenfranchised as they were absorbed by the expanding nation. Worse, the United States brought with it legal codes and social institutions that imposed a rigid system of racial rule upon its new subjects—a system that worked to undermine local language, identity, and customs.

Not all Americans supported Manifest Destiny or the expansionism central to it. Many, in fact, voiced strong opposition to it. In the eyes of some politicians and commentators, Manifest Destiny brought unbearable financial and social burdens that threatened to overtax government resources and public goodwill. Others expressed deep concerns about the prospects of absorbing into the young republic alien peoples who were not white. Still others argued that it was contrary to the values of American democracy. Despite pronounced opposition, Manifest Destiny proved fundamental to American military and political exploits for decades.

Throughout the nineteenth century, the doctrine of Manifest Destiny knitted together political ideals, social values, white supremacy, and imperialism. Importantly, each informed the others, simultaneously justifying territorial expansion and racial hierarchy. While Manifest Destiny expressed an idealistic commitment to liberty and the rule of law—the growth of the nation would also increase freedom and democracy—in actuality it was driven by conquest and annexation. Much as it took territory from the state of Mexico, so it usurped land and resources from Latinos/as in Texas, California, and across the Southwest. It took away rights from Latinos/as incorporated into the United States after the Mexican War and disproportionately redistributed them among Anglo settlers. At the same time, the expansion undertaken in the name of Manifest Destiny hinged on the institution of slavery to ease the incorporation of people and places.

Manifest Destiny did not disappear with the close of the nineteenth century. Indeed, according to some historians and cultural critics, it has influenced American domestic and foreign policy ever since, as a justification for securing land, labor, resources, and markets.

C. Richard King

See also: Mexican-American War; Spanish-American War.

Further Reading

Horsman, Reginald. *Race and Manifest Destiny: The Origins of American Racial Anglo-Saxonism.* Cambridge, MA: Harvard University Press, 1981.

Stephanson, Anders. *Manifest Destiny: American Expansionism and the Empire of Right.* New York: Hill and Wang, 1995.

Marianismo

*M*arianismo, the female equivalent of *machismo,* refers to the exaggerated gender stereotype of the ideal woman in Latin America. Deriving from Catholic teachings regarding the Virgin Mary (María), marianismo imagines the most desirable women within Latin America as virgins and those mirroring the qualities of the Madonna. Women are viewed as semidivine, with moral clarity and authority over men. They possess the feminine qualities of spiritual superiority, moral righteousness, submissiveness, sexual purity, and an unending capacity for sacrifice. The respected woman is gentle, loving, selfless, and unequivocally committed to her family. She puts family needs above her own and is always there to support and forgive. Marianismo is not a religious practice, though the veneration of the Virgin Mary is a dominant theme in Roman Catholicism, the preeminent religion in Latin America since the Spanish conquest. This concept of the ideal woman has its roots in the Old World, before the wide-ranging explorations of the fifteenth century. The phenomenon,

however, reached its current proportions among the *mestizo* social classes in the New World—North and South America as viewed by the Europeans after the arrival of Christopher Columbus in 1492. Attributes of marianismo can be found in Italy and Spain, but only in Latin America has it reached full development.

The Latin American idea of womanhood is best understood in the broader context of gender roles. Machismo, the counterpart and complement of marianismo, embodies hypervirile male behavior. Men are admired for their physical strength, sexual prowess, self-assuredness, and aggressive advances toward women. They are expected to care for their female relatives and to protect them from the harsh realities of the public and political realms. In return, women are to submit to male desires while also acting as the moral guardians of home and family. Women are expected to maneuver around the aggressive nature of machismo and, because of their passive natures, to succumb.

Archetypes of Womanhood

Self-sacrificing, submissive, and morally pure, the ideal woman is often thought of as someone possessing the qualities of the Virgin Mary. The image of Mary is one of the most dominant and widespread in Latin American Christianity and a ubiquitous feature of Latin American culture in general. Devotion to a variety of regionally designated "virgins of mother-worship" is at the foundation of the social and religious organization of many Latin American communities. Festivals, icons, religious ceremonies, and parades draw national and international audiences. Annually, thousands of pilgrims and tourists visit provincial shrines and attend celebrations. The Virgin of Guadalupe, for example, is a major international attraction and a central figure in the Mexican national character. Local rituals related to protection and rebirth are also common, and the prevalence of the name María further reflects the importance of Mary. Although marianismo is not a religious practice or observance per se, Mary is said to represent the essence of true femininity—both the spiritual strength and power associated with womanhood and the sacredness attached to motherhood.

Many contemporary Latina women, however, are caught in a double bind between maintaining their womanhood and complying with male demands. They are viewed as accomplices, either willing or unwilling, to men's illicit activities, and they are associated with the image of victim or betrayer. This alternative female model, sometimes referred to as Marina or La Malinche, is based on the literary view of a sixteen-year-old Aztec named Malitzín, who became the interpreter and lover of the sixteenth-century Spanish explorer Hernán Cortés. As the legend goes, Marina came to the aid of the Spanish, giving them strategic information that undermined the Aztec emperor Moctezuma, ultimately contributing to the destruction of the Aztecs and their massive empire. In the end, Cortés gave Marina a small piece of property and married her to one of his men; she subsequently bore a child that had been conceived during her time with Cortés. Marina died at the age of twenty-five and has become a figure who symbolizes the tragedy of the fallen, violated woman.

The Mariana, the representation of a good, chaste woman, and the Marina, the quintessence of an unseemly, blemished woman, personify the dominant archetypes of womanhood in Latin America today.

Tenets of Marianismo

At the core of marianismo is a special emphasis on women's reproductive and familial roles. Stemming from the wonder attached to women's ability to bear children, images of fertility goddesses with pronounced breasts and accentuated bellies were common in ancient art. Rituals associated with planting and harvest seasons connected women to nature and were intricately linked to the social milieu of ancient communities. Though life-cycle events occurred throughout much of the world, the hyperfemininity attached to womanhood reached an exaggerated form in colonial Latin America. In response to the overstated, brash qualities associated with the adventuresome Spanish explorers of the sixteenth century, notions of manhood took on unrealistic propositions. A woman's antithetical position to this masculine archetype and her unyielding commitment to family emerged as central feminine attributes.

As a public display of family honor, mourning is an integral part of womanhood. In Latino culture, women are required to engage in an elaborate and extensive mourning process upon the death of a family member. The stereotypical image of a middle-aged woman draped in a black-clad mantilla kneeling before the altar reflects selfless devotion and suffering. Praying for the souls of loved ones, especially sinful men, echoes the woman's heartfelt affection for family. Although both women and men are expected to observe the passing of family members, a woman's grieving is more involved and can last a lifetime. She is obligated to wear a distinctive style of black dress and is prohibited from social and public displays of joy. The details of this practice depend on her relationship with the deceased. After the passing of a parent or husband, a woman is bound to wearing all-black clothing, including inner and outer garments, for the duration of her life. To mourn the death of sisters, brothers, aunts, and uncles, she is required to dress in full mourning garb for three years. Grieving for all other family members involves a shorter bereavement period, typically three months to one year. A woman is also to refrain from jovial festivities such as parties, watching television, or attending concerts and to avoid those who indulge in such frivolity. Men, however, experience a much less strict code of mourning, often donning only a black armband for a brief period.

There are also different standards of male and female sexual behavior. Before marriage, tradition dictates that middle- and upper-class women abstain from sexual activity. Society views women who flaunt their sexuality as bad and unfeminine—or as having taken on male attributes. Although virginity is the ideal, betrothed couples often disregard this rule. Once engaged to be married, it is socially acceptable for a woman and her fiancé to deviate from the norm and indulge in limited sexual relations. Because premarital chastity for women is cherished, a stigma is still attached to this conduct, and women frequently have their hymens surgically repaired. The practice goes back to fifteenth-century Spain, when midwives performed the operation to renew the virginal quality of the bride. Moreover, premarital sex is not considered an act of female pleasure, but a precautionary measure to ensure that the man does not stray. Even in marriage, women are not expected to enjoy sex but to engage in it only to procreate and oblige their husbands. Among peasants, the poor, and working classes, however, consensual unions are common without affecting a woman's reputation.

The Future of Marianismo

Throughout Latin America, there exists a long-standing and deeply engrained set of beliefs, behaviors, and attitudes associated with womanhood. A woman is expected to be caring, humble, submissive, chaste, and devoted to family. In exchange for upholding these high standards, she receives unwavering esteem and regard from others. Many women, however, are unable to fulfill the strict tenets of womanhood, and full-blown marianismo can only conceivably exist in the lifestyle of middle-aged, middle- and upper-class women. Moreover, as the younger generation of women receive formal education, exercise political rights, and seek employment outside the home, an internal struggle between maintaining the doctrine of the ideal woman, like that practiced by their mothers and grandmothers, collides with the yearning to adopt or the need to adapt to contemporary realities. The future of marianismo, thus, lies in the reconciliation of tradition with modernity.

E. Sue Wamsley

See also: Family and Community; Identity and Labels; Machismo; Malinche, La; Women.

Further Reading

Chaney, Elsa M. *Supermadre: Women in Politics in Latin America.* Austin: University of Texas Press, 1979.

Minas, Anne, ed. *Gender Basics: Feminist Perspectives on Women and Men.* 2nd ed. Belmont, CA: Wadsworth/ Thomson Learning, 2000.

Rodríguez, Victoria E., ed. *Women's Participation in Mexican Political Life.* Boulder, CO: Westview, 1998.

Stevens, Evelyn. "Marianismo: The Other Face of Machismo in Latin America." In *Female and Male in Latin America: Essays,* ed. Ann Pescatello. Pittsburgh, PA: University of Pittsburgh Press, 1973.

Yeager, Gertrude M. *Confronting Change, Challenging Tradition: Women in Latin American History.* Wilmington, DE: Scholarly Resources, 1994.

Mariel Boatlift

The Mariel Boatlift was a mass migration of Cuban nationals from the port city of Mariel to southern Florida between April 15 and early October 1980. The exodus began when Cuban President Fidel Castro temporarily lifted emigration restrictions and announced that all Cubans who wished to leave the island could do so by way of Mariel. By the time it was over, more than 125,000 refugees—nicknamed *marielitos*—had left the island and made their way across the Straits of Florida on small, overcrowded fishing boats.

The boatlift took place amid growing dissent in Cuba over economic problems, food shortages, and visits by exiled relatives (under a special arrangement with the U.S. government) that demonstrated the material advantages less than 100 miles (160 kilometers) away. To avoid political upheaval, Castro allowed the boatlift as a means of defusing dissent and providing those who were most disgruntled—and most likely to challenge the government—the opportunity to leave.

The specific events that precipitated the boatlift began on April 1, 1980, when a group of disaffected Cubans drove a bus through the gate of the Peruvian

Cuban refugees arrive in Key West, Florida, during the Mariel Boatlift in April 1980. By the time the mass exodus was over that October, more than 125,000 disaffected Cubans had made their way across the Straits of Florida. *(Tim Chapman/Miami Herald/Getty Images)*

Embassy in Havana, claiming sanctuary for themselves and 10,000 other asylum-seekers who followed them onto the embassy grounds. While the Peruvian government gave sanctuary and security to the Cubans, they solicited international assistance to resettle all 10,000 refugees. U.S. President Jimmy Carter agreed to accept up to 3,500, with priority given to released political prisoners, members of families already in the United States, and refugees seeking actual political asylum. Before transportation could be arranged, however, Castro declared the port of Mariel—located on the island's northwest coast—open to anyone who desired to leave. Thus began the mass migration, as thousands of Cubans crowded onto vessels or awaited departure, while Cuban exiles living in the United States secured boats and headed to Key West and Miami ports to pick up family and friends.

By the end of April, more than 7,000 Cubans had left from Mariel and arrived in the United States, followed by more than 86,000 in May and over 20,000 in June. By October, an estimated 125,000 marielitos had left the island in fewer than 2,000 small boats. The majority landed in Miami and other locations south to Key West. The influx quickly overburdened the U.S. Coast Guard and immigration processing centers, with the new arrivals temporarily housed in Florida refugee camps and military installations as far north as Pennsylvania and Wisconsin.

Some of the marielitos were held in federal prisons awaiting deportation hearings. This decision was driven in part by the sheer number of incoming refugees, but largely by the discovery that some number of them had been released from Cuban prisons and mental hospitals. Ultimately, about 2 percent of the incoming Cubans were identified as serious or violent criminals and therefore denied asylum.

Castro finally declared the port of Mariel closed on September 26, 1980, and the boatlift officially ended in October by mutual agreement between the Cuban and U.S. governments. For the marielitos who remained in U.S. refugee camps, the saga continued for many months. U.S. refugee policy was altered to provide most with refugee status and the opportunity to resettle permanently in America. Approximately 50 percent of Mariel immigrants came to reside permanently in Miami, yielding a 20 percent increase in the Cuban working population of the city and exerting pressure on the city's entire labor market.

Cheris Brewer Current

See also: Castro, Fidel; Cuban Refugee Center; Cuban Refugee Program; Cubans; Marielitos.

Further Reading

Ojito, Mirta. *Finding Mañana: A Memoir of a Cuban Exodus.* New York: Penguin, 2005.

Marielitos

Marielito is the term used to refer to each of the 125,266 Cubans who fled the island in 1980 from the Port of Mariel. The mass departure, the largest in the history of the island and one that would transform the city of Miami in the United States, was set in motion in April 1980, when six Cuban nationals drove a bus into the Peruvian embassy compound in Havana, desperately seeking permits to abandon the country. The situation was magnified when Peru agreed to grant them political asylum. Cuban President Fidel Castro responded by removing the security guards posted at the doors of the embassy, thereby allowing any and all Cubans to seek refuge inside.

In less than twenty-four hours, approximately 10,800 asylum seekers occupied the embassy and demanded permits to leave the country. Castro granted every citizen the right to leave the island freely from the Port of Mariel and invited any Cuban-Americans in Florida with relatives in Cuba to come to Mariel to pick them up. As a result, thousands of ships sailed from Cuba to the coast of Florida, while the so-called *flotilla libertadora* sailed in the opposite direction to rescue those waiting to be picked up at Mariel.

During the five months that Castro kept the port open to evacuation—from April 21 to September 26, 1980—the marielitos who arrived in Florida became part of what came to be known as the

"Cuban miracle" and changed the city of Miami forever. In the 1980s, only 35 percent of the population in Miami's Dade County was Latino; after the Mariel exodus, the figure rose to more than 60 percent. In Dade, thousands of volunteers greeted the newly arrived Cubans, who were offered food, clothes, and shelter while being scrutinized by the U.S. Immigration and Naturalization Service at Tamiami Park. Most of the marielitos did not conform, however, to the social, economic, and political traits of the Cubans already living in the city. While those who had migrated to the United States in 1959 were mainly supporters of the deposed dictator Fulgencio Batista, more than 70 percent of the marielitos belonged to the lower working classes. This was an embarrassment to Castro's government, which had also made use of the Mariel exodus to get rid of such "unwanted" social groups as criminals, prostitutes, homosexuals (including the writer Reinaldo Arenas), and patients from the Mazorra Mental Hospital in Havana. Castro's May Day Celebration Speech, in which he declared that those leaving from Mariel were "the scum of the country, welcome to leave Cuba if any country would have them," was just the first of the many false accusations against the Mariel group.

The Mariel migration, then, was partially responsible for an initial stigmatization of the Cuban population in the United States, and the term marielito was—and still is—charged with negative connotations. The large numbers of the new arrivals did not help the Cuban reputation, as the Miami community struggled to overcome a lack of appropriate housing and employment. The popular media had long since associated Cuban immigrants with criminal activities in the United States. In the 1980s, films such as Brian de Palma's *Scarface* (1983), which portrayed the marielitos as violent thugs, drug dealers, and smugglers, did further damage to the image of Cubans in particular and the Latino population in general. As a result of the hostility directed at the marielitos from Cuban Americans and the population at large, the U.S. government protested to the Cuban regime, which in 1984 agreed to the repatriation of approximately 2,500 nationals who had committed crimes in the United States.

On the other hand, the Mariel boatlift had positive consequences for the Latino community of the United States. The need to cope with the large number of marielitos and the increasing distrust of all Cubans forced the Cuban American community of Miami to organize politically. The large-scale migration was also directly responsible for the 1994–1995 immigration agreement between the United States and Cuba; this has been of crucial importance to the thousands of Cubans who cross the Florida Strait every year. Commonly referred to as the "dry feet/wet feet policy," the measure allows those Cubans who make it to U.S. soil to remain in the country and obtain a working visa after one year, whereas those intercepted at sea are repatriated. More important, the agreement calls for the granting of at least 20,000 visas to Cuban citizens every year and the commitment by the Cuban government not to take any legal action against those sent back by the United States. In this respect, the Mariel exodus was not only a blow to the Castro regime—which was forced to admit that many Cubans who had once supported the revolution now wanted to flee the island—but also the defining event and foundation of political influence for the Cuban exile community in Miami.

David Arbesú

See also: Cuban Refugee Center; Cuban Refugee Program; Cubans; Mariel Boatlift.

Further Reading

Gay, Kathlyn. *Leaving Cuba: From Operation Pedro Pan to Elian.* Brookfield, CT: Twenty-First Century Books, 2000.

Libal, Autumn. *Cuban Americans: Exiles from an Island Home.* Philadelphia: Mason Crest, 2005.

Peterson, Tiffany. *Cuban Americans.* Chicago: Heinemann, 2003.

McCarran-Walter Act (1952)

The McCarran-Walter Act—also known as the Immigration and Nationality Act of 1952—reinforced the restrictionist immigration policies first implemented in the 1920s. Despite its overall limitations, certain parts of the 1952 measure allowed for slight, but important, changes in U.S. immigration law. It was not until 1965 that the United States finally opened its doors to greater numbers of immigrants from various parts of the world, particularly from Asia and Latin America.

The Cold War led political leaders to revamp immigration laws. Under political pressure from the Truman administration and other officials, the Senate Judiciary Committee ordered an investigation of American immigration processes in 1947. The head of the committee was Senator Patrick A. McCarran (D-NV), who held a deep fear of communist infiltration of the United States and was the most ardent opponent of immigration reform in the Senate. In the House, McCarran's counterpart was Representative Francis E. Walter (D-PA), who likewise feared an influx of subversives.

The Judiciary Committee's investigation resulted in a 900-page report, released in 1950. The report concluded that it was in the political interest of the United States to preserve the national origins quota system, which favored the admission of immigrants from northern and western Europe. After Congress passed the act, President Truman vetoed it because he opposed ethnic and racial prerequisites to U.S. citizenship; he believed that such measures tarnished the reputation of the United States. Congressional supporters of the McCarran-Walter Act, however, obtained the two-thirds support in the Senate and House necessary to override the president's veto. The act became official in 1952.

While the McCarran-Walter Act endorsed the national origins quota system, it revised the law concerning deportation, subversion, and quota distribution and preferences. The deportation measures targeted undocumented workers from Mexico, making it easier for Border Patrol agents to search vehicles and increasing the Border Patrol's jurisdiction along the U.S.-Mexico border. Another deportation measure made harboring undocumented workers a felony, but a clause known as the "Texas Proviso," which stated that employing illegal immigrants was not "harboring" them, made this measure basically ineffective.

When it came to subversion, the act provided amnesty to immigrants who hailed from totalitarian nations who could prove that they had opposed this form of government for five years or that they had been coerced into subscribing to totalitarianism. The most stringent measure of this kind opposed temporary visitor visas to any foreigner deemed subversive by the United States.

With regard to quota distributions and preferences, the McCarran-Walter Act gave priority to immigrants from Europe who were highly trained and possessed skills sorely needed in the United States and to immigrants who had relatives in the United States who were citizens or resident aliens. Perhaps the most significant change was the removal of the category "alien ineligible to citizenship" from U.S. immigration law, a qualification that had been used to prevent large-scale immigration from Asian nations. The McCarran-Walter Act established a small quota—about 100 persons—for each Asian nation. One drawback was that any person of Asian descent who immigrated to the United States counted toward the quota of the Asian country his ancestors hailed from, even if such a person had been born or held citizenship in a non-Asian country. Though the small quotas for Asian nations seemed inconsequential, other provisions of the McCarran-Walter Act made it possible for slightly greater numbers of Asians to immigrate.

Special provisions, such as allowing spouses and children of U.S. citizens to enter the country as non-quota immigrants, meant that many more Asians came to the United States than were allotted by the quotas. The number of immigrants from Asian nations grew steadily after 1952, though they remained a tiny percentage of overall U.S. immigration. One other problematic aspect of the McCarran-Walter Act was that it placed European colonies in the Western Hemisphere under a quota system. Most of these colonies were located in the Caribbean, with predominantly black populations. This particular measure, therefore, limited the ability of black Caribbeans to migrate to the United States. Since the McCarran-Walter Act did not impose quotas on independent countries of the Western Hemisphere, the stage was set for a heavy increase in Latin American immigration.

The McCarran-Walter Act of 1952 largely preserved the racial and ethnic biases first established in the early 1920s. It was not until the mid-1960s—with the Immigration and Naturalization Act of 1965—that the United States made major changes to its immigration laws and ended the national-origins quota system.

Lisa Y. Ramos

See also: Immigration and Nationality Act of 1965; Immigration Enforcement.

Further Reading

Briggs, Vernon M., Jr. *Mass Immigration and the National Interest.* Armonk, NY: M.E. Sharpe, 1992.

Daniels, Roger. *Guarding the Golden Door: American Immigration Policy and Immigrants Since 1882.* New York: Hill and Wang, 2004.

Edwards, Jerome E. *Pat McCarran: Political Boss of Nevada.* Nevada Studies in History and Political Science. Reno: University of Nevada Press, 1982.

Reimers, David M. *Still the Golden Door: The Third World Comes to America.* 2nd ed. New York: Columbia University Press, 1992.

Medrano v. Allee (1972)

In June 1967, after witnessing their yearlong strike efforts collapse under the weight of harassment and repression by state and local officials, the United Farm Workers (UFW) in Starr County, Texas, turned to the federal courts in a last-ditch effort to revive unionization efforts, claiming that their civil rights had been violated. The Southern District Court of Texas took up the case, *Medrano v. Allee,* in 1972, with the U.S. Supreme Court weighing in on the case in 1974. Both courts declared that state and local officials had acted as biased participants in a labor-management dispute between farmworkers and fruit growers. The courts also held that five separate state laws governing unlawful assembly, breach of the peace, use of abusive language, mass picketing, and secondary boycotts were unconstitutional.

Starr County is located along the Mexican border in South Texas and was (and remains) one of the poorest counties in the nation. Agricultural wages in the area varied from forty cents an hour to eighty-five cents an hour, forcing many farmworkers to look to migrant labor as the only means of economic survival. Not surprisingly, Starr County sent a vast percentage of its total population into the agricultural

migration streams that annually moved north from the Rio Grande Valley. Eugene Nelson, a leader of the UFW, moved to Starr County in early 1966 after working with César Chávez in California. He soon established a union of farmworkers among the melon pickers in South Texas, and they organized a strike in the weeks before the summer harvest.

From the beginning, local officials made no secret of their goal of crushing the strike. Picketers were arrested and refused bond, charges were fabricated, and the Starr County Sheriff's Department violently harassed protestors. Things went from bad to worse for the strikers when the Texas Rangers were called into Starr County under the leadership of Captain Alfred (A.Y.) Allee, a cigar-chomping man notorious for his temper and willingness to resort to physical violence. Union officials and striking workers were repeatedly threatened with physical violence by the rangers and deputies. One union member, Magdaleno Dimas, was arrested on three separate occasions and was beaten each time. One month before the union filed its federal suit, Allee savagely beat Dimas, who suffered from a brain concussion and spinal trauma. Shortly thereafter, with local and state officials clearly more interested in crushing the strike than in maintaining peace, the union turned to the courts.

Francisco Medrano, Kathy Baker, David Lopez, Gilbert Padilla, Magdaleno Dimas, and Benjamin Rodriguez filed the federal case, claiming that state and local officials had violated their First Amendment rights of free speech and peaceful assembly. The defendants were five Texas Rangers, the Starr County sheriff, two deputy sheriffs, a special deputy, and the Starr County justice of the peace. First the District Court, and later the Supreme Court, found that the defendants had willfully and continually violated the civil rights of the striking workers by engaging in a pattern of behavior whose sole objective was the destruction of the union. In addition, and most important, the courts found that the laws under which the strikers were prosecuted were unacceptably vague. They gave the police and other officials too much leeway in defining activities that posed a threat to public order. The courts ruled that any laws with the potential of infringing upon First Amendment rights must outline specifically what entailed a threat to society. This was their attempt to eliminate bad-faith prosecutions, such as those undertaken by Starr County officials. Thus, the District Court struck down five Texas laws as unconstitutional, and the U.S. Supreme Court upheld the finding two years later.

The court's decision came too late for the growth of farm unionism in Texas. The UFW was never able to build a stable union structure among the massive number of Mexican and Mexican American farm laborers that moved in and out of South Texas. In the end, the intervention of the federal courts, while forcing the state of Texas to update its antipicketing laws, was too little too late. Farm unionism was never revived in any substantial way. Instead, the action of the federal courts in *Medrano v. Allee* only temporarily dampened Texas's long-standing tradition of violent opposition to unionization and its history of subjugation of Mexican American social movements.

John Weber

See also: Chávez, César; Migrant Workers; Unions, Industrial and Trade; United Farm Workers of America.

Further Reading

Fisch, Louise Ann. *All Rise: Reynaldo G. Garza, The First Mexican American Federal Judge.* College Station: Texas A&M University Press, 1996.

Montejano, David. *Anglos and Mexicans in the Making of Texas, 1836–1986.* Austin: University of Texas Press, 1987.

Melting Pot

See Acculturation and Assimilation

Mendez v. Westminster School District (1946)

The *Mendez v. Westminster School District* court case is one of the most important but least recounted events in Mexican American civil rights

history. The individuals involved in the case are rarely mentioned among the civil rights heroes discussed in history textbooks, even though the case represented the first legal challenge to the Jim Crow laws that legitimized segregation in the United States, and it set a precedent for the landmark U.S. Supreme Court decision in *Brown v. Board of Education* (1954).

The case began in the mid-1940s, when a group of Mexican Americans of the Westminster and Modeno school districts in Southern California, propelled by increased political activity at the end of World War II, filed a suit against four Orange County school districts. The suit alleged that the school districts, in facilitating the segregation of approximately 5,000 Mexican American children, were in violation of the U.S. Constitution.

The lawsuit began when Sylvia, Jerome, and Gonzalo Mendez, Jr., the children of Felícitas Méndez and Gonzalo Méndez, Sr., were not allowed to attend the Seventeenth Street School but were assigned instead to the Hoover School, which was designated as the "Mexican School" within the Westminster School District. Segregation of Mexicans and Mexican Americans was customary and pervasive throughout the Southwest during the first half of the twentieth century. By 1930, for example, nearly 90 percent of all school districts in the region were segregated. For Gonzalo Méndez, a native of Chihuahua, Mexico, who migrated to the United States in the 1920s, and Felícitas, a native of Puerto Rico, the refusal by the Westminster school to accept their children set off a series of legal proceedings that would eventually topple discriminatory laws affecting all Mexican Americans and other ethnic and racial groups throughout the country.

After meeting with the school board, Méndez was able to negotiate an agreement whereby the Westminster School District would grant the Méndez children special admission without overturning its policy of segregation. Méndez would soon abandon that agreement because he found the thought of other Mexican students attending separate, poorer schools unacceptable. The Méndez family hired David Marcus, a local attorney with experience with segregation cases; he had challenged segregation laws that prevented Mexicans from entering Los Angeles city pools and parks. Additional lawyers were provided by the League of United Latin American Citizens. The legal team quickly agreed that the school districts were in direct violation of the law. Segregation based solely on race, they maintained, was a violation of the constitutional guarantees of equal protection under the law as stipulated by the Fifth and Fourteenth amendments of the U.S. Constitution. With the help of his attorneys, Méndez was able to organize parents from Westminster and the nearby communities of El Modena, Santa Ana, and Garden Grove, where similar cases were beginning to spring up, and on March 2, 1945, a lawsuit was filed against them.

In court, Méndez's attorneys used the testimonies of students who attended the Mexican schools. During the early part of the twentieth century, school segregation was supported under the "separate but equal" doctrine—the principle, enunciated in the Supreme Court ruling of *Plessy v. Ferguson* (1896), that maintaining separate facilities or restricting access to public places based on race or national origin is legal so long as those places are similar and equal. The Méndez attorneys set out to challenge that doctrine, arguing that separate facilities were not only unlawful but detrimental to those using them. Relying on sociologists and educators who testified that putting some students in separate facilities made them feel inferior, the Méndez attorneys were able to convince the court that segregation was inherently unequal.

Ruling in favor of the complainants on March 21, 1945, federal court judge Paul McCormick concluded that segregation was illegal under both state statutes and the Equal Protection Clause of the Fourteenth Amendment. Segregation, he held, was socially unhealthy, as it denied Mexican American students the benefit of interacting in the classroom with children of different cultures. Moreover, he ruled, even separate schools with similar facilities failed to provide equal protection under the law. As a result, Judge McCormick ordered the school districts to eliminate all separate facilities.

California Governor Earl Warren, who would later serve as chief justice of the U.S. Supreme Court in the 1954 *Brown* decision, upheld the ruling, mandating the integration of all schools in the state. Soon thereafter, school districts throughout the Southwest would do the same. Almost immediately, however, the four school districts of Orange County, unwilling to accept the court's decision to desegregate, appealed McCormick's decision to the higher courts, arguing that their facilities were entirely equal and that the federal court had no jurisdiction in such matters. A year later, the Ninth U.S. Circuit Court of Appeals in San Francisco upheld the lower court's decision, agreeing that the school districts were in violation of the Constitution. In addition, the Ninth Circuit Court also instructed the Los Angeles federal grand jury to review the situation in Orange County for possible indictment of the school board members. The school districts finally agreed to comply with the court's ruling and slowly began to end segregation practices. Despite both rulings, however, segregation continued to be practiced in schools across America. Only after the continued efforts of activists and the Supreme Court ruling in *Brown* did school segregation begin to crumble nationwide. Although it took until the mid-1970s for the process to be complete, the seeds had been planted in 1945 by the small group of activists of the Westminster and Modeno school districts in California. Their successful legal challenge to segregation in schools based on language and cultural differences helped pave the wave for the dismantling of segregation based on race.

Jesse J. Esparza

See also: *Del Rio Independent School District v. Salvatierra* (1930); Education; League of United Latin American Citizens.

Further Reading

San Miguel, Guadalupe, Jr. *"Let All of Them Take Heed": Mexican Americans and the Campaign for Educational Equality in Texas, 1910–1981.* Austin: University of Texas Press, 1987.

Sanchez, George I. *Concerning Segregation of Spanish-Speaking Children in the Public Schools.* Austin: University of Texas Press, 1951.

Wollenberg, Charles. *All Deliberate Speed: Segregation and Exclusion in California Schools, 1855–1975.* Berkeley: University of California Press, 1977.

———. *"Mendez v. Westminster:* Race, Nationality and Segregation in California Schools." *California Historical Quarterly* 53:4 (Winter 1974): 317–32.

Mestizo/a

The term *mestizo/a* (from the Latin *mixticius,* meaning "mixed") came into use in the Spanish colonial empire to refer to people of mixed European and indigenous heritage in the Americas. Over time, the meaning has broadened to include the blend of Latino and mainstream culture in the United States and elsewhere.

An amorphous biological and cultural classification, mestizo refers to people whose parents were Spanish and indigenous (or spoke Spanish and a native language). The precise definition varies from culture to culture, with yet other terms used historically to designate persons with different proportions of European and indigenous blood/ancestry (such as *castizo, cuarterón de indio, cholo,* and *zambo*). Typically, however, in Latin American countries the term "mestizo/a" (or Portuguese counterpart, *mestiço*) implies that the person speaks Spanish or Portuguese, while an *indio* speaks an indigenous language. Nevertheless, under the Spanish caste system in America, mestizos were regarded as inferior to full-blooded Spanish-born persons, who could hold positions of power, own property, and generally access all the rights and privileges of Spanish citizenship. Mestizo/as, like Indians and Africans, held a lower status in general.

Many Mexicans and Mexican Americans consider Hernán Cortés, the Spanish explorer and conquistador, and La Malinche, his indigenous translator and adviser during the conquest of Mexico, as the parents of the first mestizo—Martín Cortés I, born in 1523. Martín lived in the shadow of his half brother—Martín Cortés II, who was born to Cortés and his Spanish wife—and treated as a second-class citizen.

It was not until the Chicano power movement of the twentieth century that scholars, activists, writers, and artists recast mestizo identity as a source of power and cultural strength rather than a stain of colonialism and cultural dilution. Efforts to reclaim and embrace a dual heritage became a path to reclaiming the forgotten or disparaged indigenous part of Latino culture. Additionally, the mestizo experience came to signify wide-ranging Latino efforts—political, social, and cultural—to adapt to and survive the history of conquest, colonization, and racism. Whereas in the past mestizo/a had signified inferiority and a cultural watering down, for many it came to represent empowerment and the ability to change with the circumstances. For others, however, mestizo continues to hold negative connotations. For example, members of the Mexica Movement, an organization founded in 1993 dedicated to liberating North America from European occupation, argue that *mestizo* will always be defined in colonial terms that imply inferiority and therefore reject the concept.

Thus, among contemporary Latinos/as, mestizo/a conveys both the oppression of colonialism and the expansiveness of the Latino experience in the United States. While the Latino community—and many individual members—is multiracial and multi-ethnic, mestizo/a remains a contested identifier because of its links to the history of European colonization.

Vibrina Coronado

See also: Chicano Movement; Conquest of the Americas; Identity and Labels; Malinche, La.

Further Reading

Alcoff, Linda. "Mestizo Identity." In *American Mixed Race: The Culture of Microdiversity,* ed. Naomi Zack. Lanham, MD: Rowman & Littlefield, 1995.

Anzaldúa, Gloria. *Borderlands/La Frontera: The New Mestiza.* 1987. San Francisco: Aunt Lute, 2007.

Elizondo, Virgilio. *The Future Is Mestizo: Life Where Cultures Meet.* Rev. ed. Boulder: University Press of Colorado, 2000.

Gruzinsk, Serge. *The Mestizo Mind: The Intellectual Dynamics of Colonization and Globalization.* New York: Routledge, 2002.

Vento, Arnoldo. *Mestizo: The History, Culture and Politics of the Mexican and the Chicano.* Lanham, MD: University Press of America, 1998.

Mexican American Legal Defense and Education Fund

Founded in 1968, the Mexican American Legal Defense and Education Fund (MALDEF) remains a prominent social justice organization dedicated to the protection and promotion of Latino civil rights. Since its inception, MALDEF has concentrated its efforts in the areas of education, employment, immigration, language rights, and political access. While critics have questioned its adherence to its mission statement—given its advocacy of open borders, free college education for illegal immigrants, and voting rights for criminals—MALDEF continues to represent itself as an organization committed to equal opportunity and empowerment for all Latinos/as in the United States. It remains dedicated, first, "to foster[ing] sound public policies, laws, and programs that safeguard the rights of Latinos/as"; and second, to "expanding the opportunities for Latinos/as to participate fully in society and to make a positive contribution toward its well-being."

Originally based in San Antonio, Texas, and now headquartered in Los Angeles, MALDEF was founded by Pete Tijerina, then civil rights chairman of the San Antonio branch of the League of United Latin American Citizens (LULAC). In the spirit of the political, racial, and social activism of the times, MALDEF grew out of a meeting between Tijerina, Albert A. Peña, Jr., Roy Padilla, and Bill Pincus in early 1968. Pincus, a representative from the Ford Foundation, informed the group that the New York–based philanthropy would be willing to fund a non-profit organization dedicated to the legal protection and advocacy of Mexican Americans. With this assurance, Tijerina was able to move forward in creating the group. With help from LULAC and the National Association for the Advancement of Colored People (NAACP), the organizers successfully completed a grant proposal for the Ford Foundation and created committees in Arizona, California, Colorado, New Mexico, and Texas. In May 1968, the Ford Foundation awarded a $2.2 million grant to be used over a five-year period, and MALDEF officially came into being. Tijerina served as its first president, with Mario Obledo appointed as general counsel.

MALDEF retained its headquarters in San Antonio until 1970, with a divisional office in Los Angeles and local committee offices throughout the Southwest. While the organization focused its energies on legal action, the leaders believed that safeguarding Latino civil rights called for involvement

in a variety of areas. It was during this period, for example, that MALDEF formed a scholarship fund to enhance its mission through education, training a generation of Chicano law students in the protection and advancement of civil rights.

In 1970, MALDEF underwent a restructuring to retain funding from the Ford Foundation. Specifically, the changes included the merger of the president and counsel positions, relocation of the headquarters to San Francisco, a shift from legal aid to the utilization of the judicial process, and the creation of community outreach programs. New branches were also added in Denver (1971), Albuquerque, New Mexico (1972), and Washington, D.C. (1972).

In 1973, Vilma Martinez—a MALDEF board member and former lawyer for the NAACP Legal Defense Fund—was named the organization's new president and general counsel. Under her direction, the organization enjoyed nationwide growth and notable institutional changes—including the creation of an intern/extern program, the Chicana Rights Program, and the Voting Rights Project. Developing favorable legal precedents on which to argue, the organization under Martinez's direction participated in several significant cases. In 1974, it represented the plaintiffs in *Serna v. Portales,* in which the federal circuit court upheld a ruling that the Portales (New Mexico) School District had engaged in discrimination against students with Spanish surnames, evidenced by low academic achievement and high dropout and truancy rates among Latino students. The court ordered the school district to implement a series of policies, ranging from bicultural and bilingual educational curriculums to the hiring of bilingual teachers and administration. Other cases in which MALDEF alleged civil rights violations by public schools and fought for improved educational opportunities for Latino youth include *Crofts v. Board of Governors* (1974), *Guerra v. Board of Trustees* (1975), *Bakke v. Regents of the University of California* (1978), and *Plyler v. Doe* (1982).

But the organization did not limit itself to educational protection. In 1974, for example, it successfully represented minority and female cannery employees at the California-based Basic Vegetable Company in a class-action lawsuit that alleged employment discrimination. In its ruling, the U.S.

District Court required the company to change its employment, hiring, training, and promotional practices in compliance with the Fourteenth Amendment and federal civil rights law. In another high-profile case, MALDEF alleged in 1978 that raids by the U.S. Immigration and Naturalization Service (INS) in California were unconstitutional. The court agreed, limiting the scope and magnitude of immigration raids conducted by that federal agency.

MALDEF continued its efforts on behalf of immigrant rights in 1994 by campaigning against California's Proposition 187, which sought to deny social services, health care, and access to public education to undocumented immigrants. One of the organization's biggest successes was the settlement it reached in the case of *Gregorio T. v. Wilson* (1995), when Governor Gray Davis and the State of California decided to withdraw their appeal of a district court ruling that in effect declared every section of Proposition 187 unconstitutional.

Since its formation in the late 1960s, MALDEF has pursued its objective of providing legal assistance to protect and extend the civil rights guaranteed to America's growing Latino population. In the more than forty years of its existence, the organization has fought diligently, if not always successfully, "to empower the Latino community to fully participate in our society."

In the early twenty-first century, MALDEF regards immigrant rights as the paramount issue for Latinos/as throughout the nation. In the pursuit of that cause and others, it has devoted ample resources and concerted efforts outside of litigation, promoting the development of Latino leaders, taking part in high-level policy commissions and local PTA groups, serving as a media advocate, and making higher education more accessible through its scholarship program. Since its inception, MALDEF has played a vital role on a range of legal issues—from employment and immigration rights to bilingual education and public-resource equity—and established itself as a stalwart within the Latino legal community. As of 2007, MALDEF had twenty-two full-time attorneys representing the interests and issues facing Latinos/as throughout the United States.

Rachel Sandoval and David J. Leonard

See also: Education; League of United Latin American Citizens; Peña, Albert A., Jr.; Proposition 187 (1994); Samora, Julian; Southwest Voter Registration Education Project.

Further Reading

Gonzales, Sylvia Alicia. *Hispanic American Voluntary Organizations.* Westport, CT: Greenwood, 1985.
Mexican American Legal Defense and Education Fund. http://www.maldef.org.

Mexican-American Movement

An offshoot of the Young Men's Christian Association (YMCA), the Mexican-American Movement (MAM) was a California-based organization founded in 1942 "to improve social, educational, economic, and spiritual conditions among Mexican Americans and Mexican people living in the United States." With the goal of helping Mexican immigrants become "better Americans," MAM encouraged higher education through financial aid to college students, promoted good citizenship and good relations with non-Mexicans, and organized local councils with the goal of becoming a national organization. Historians have pointed to MAM as the first Latino student organization in the United States.

Background

The influx of Mexicans to the United States in the early decades of the twentieth century, largely a consequence of the Mexican Revolution and the recruitment of workers by labor-strapped American farm owners, led to a nativist response among many Americans who began speaking of a so-called "Mexican problem." Few of the newly arrived children were able to complete elementary school—because of lack of access, the language barrier, or the need to work—but many Anglos regarded this as symptomatic of an inability to adapt to the American way of life. Labeled as ignorant, lazy, and conditioned to the wretchedness of poverty, Mexicans were subjected to the same kind of racial stereotyping and debasement

ANNUAL CONVENTION = Mexican American Movement
Nov. 23, 1947 = 12:30 p.m. = Edison Building = Los Angeles

THE BOARD OF DIRECTORS

PROGRAM

The schedule for the day will be as follows:

12:30 P. M.
1—Registration
2—Opening of the Convention and Presentation of Guests
—Arthur O. Casas
3—Reports of Permanent Committees—Chairman of Committees
4—Reports of Local Councils
—Secretaries or Presidents of Local Councils.
5—Entertainment—Anthony Candia
6—New Business:
Resolutions—Paul Coronel
Presentation of Charters—Arthur O. Casas
Report of Nominating Committee—Steven A. Reyes
Action of the report of the Nominating Committee and Election
of Officers.
Installation—A. B. Collins
Good and Welfare—Open period for all comments and questions
5:00 P. M.
7—Adjournment

The Mexican-American Movement, said to be the first Latino student organization in the United States, worked to help Mexican immigrants become "better Americans." The group was founded in 1942; shown here is the program for its 1947 convention. *(Supreme Council of the Mexican American Movement Collection. Urban Archives Center. Oviatt Library. California State University, Northridge)*

to which African Americans, Asians, and other minorities had been subjected.

As anti-Mexican sentiment reached a peak in the 1930s, however, second-generation Mexicans had become more settled and achieved greater social mobility. No longer viewing themselves as immigrants but as U.S. citizens, this new generation began asserting their political, social, and economic rights as full-fledged Americans. They began calling themselves "Mexican Americans," and, at the same time that they began to stake their claim in American society, they worked to change the image of Mexicans in the United States. The YMCA, a Protestant youth organization founded in Great Britain in 1844 and

the United States in 1851, proved especially active in efforts to Americanize Mexican immigrants. It sought to do so by promoting English-language instruction, U.S. citizenship, Protestant values, and free-market principles.

During the Great Depression of the 1930s, the YMCA of Los Angeles committed $30,000 to Mexican American youth in the city and hired social worker Tom García to set up a training and recreation program. In 1934, García organized the first Mexican Youth Conference, which focused on educational, training, and service opportunities for adolescent boys. YMCA officials forged contacts in higher education, opening the way to community outreach efforts, scholarship programs, and social networks for Latino youth seeking to continue their education beyond high school. As a direct offshoot of the YMCA campaign and Mexican Youth Conference, students at UCLA established the first-of-its-kind Mexican-American Movement in 1942. Although YMCA leaders at first were against the new organization, MAM promoted many of the Y's Protestant values to a largely Catholic membership and promoted its cause of Americanization.

Goals and Tactics

According to MAM's official handbook, the organization was to be politically nonpartisan and nonsectarian. It was committed to solving the problems of the Mexican American community and raising the quality of life through education, trust and participation in U.S. institutions, and full engagement in the American way of life. As the key to elevating the Mexican American community, education was preeminent among its goals. Shedding the image of immigrants and expressing their desire to become full-fledged Americans, according to MAM, could best be achieved by enabling the younger generation to continue their education beyond high school and earn higher degrees. Achieving professional success, said MAM leaders, would contribute to American society in a way that could only cast Mexican Americans in a positive light and overcome negative Anglo images of the first generation of immigrants.

MAM's attempts to further the integration of Mexican American youth were not universally accepted, however, as many young Chicanos/as were wary of the demands for conformity. With its emphasis on Americanization and the minimization of ties between Mexicans in the United States and those south of the border, MAM found diminishing support in Mexican American communities, especially after World War II. Advancement through education had proven to be a highly ambitious goal given social conditions in the Mexican American community during the 1930s. The completion rate among high school students was extremely low according to one study, which attributed the dropout rate to financial problems at home and lack of encouragement to pursue education as the means to a better life.

In the meantime, MAM promoted its principles through annual meetings—which began with Tom García's Mexican Youth Conference in San Pedro in 1934—and the publication of a newsletter. Called *The Mexican Voice,* an "inspirational/educational paper," it was published by students at UCLA beginning in 1938—making it the first Latino college student newspaper in the United States. Under founding editor Felix Gutierrez and his successors, *The Mexican Voice* articulated the cause and principles of MAM. To promote the cause of higher education in the Mexican American community, the paper periodically featured biographies of individual members of MAM as role models. Members were described as "New Modern Mexicans" to help overcome the fate and self-image implied by the slogan "A Mexican hasn't a chance."

1940s and Beyond

By the 1940s, especially after U.S. entry into World War II, the image of Mexican American youth had become increasingly negative. With the heightened sense of patriotism in mainstream America, the cultural pride and anticonformity being expressed by Chicano youth was anathema and a source of fear. Exemplifying the volatility of the times—and the difficult position of MAM—were the Zoot Suit Riots between U.S. servicemen and Latino youth in Southern California in 1942–1943. Named for the fashion sported by Mexican American young men—a flashy style featuring baggy, tight-cuffed pants, a wide-lapelled, shoulder-padded jacket, and a wide-brimmed hat—the street fighting became a source of media, police, and public hysteria.

Early accounts in Los Angeles newspapers, disregarding the events or circumstances that had led to the fighting, portrayed the zoot suiters as a local menace. While drunken sailors had ventured into their neighborhoods and randomly antagonized Latino youth, the press, police, and local officials gave lurid accounts of alleged crimes committed by zoot suiters. Chicanos/as were further attacked for not supporting the war effort, which further stoked the fears of the Anglo community. In keeping with its organizational goals and principles, MAM attempted to intervene.

Caught in the cultural and racial divide, the organization proved ineffectual in limiting the negative Anglo reaction to zoot suiters or quelling the anger of the embattled Mexican American community. Indeed, the negative effects of the Zoot Suit Riots largely derailed the organizational goals of Americanization and Anglo acceptance of Mexican American youth. Some MAM leaders even echoed the sentiments of their Anglo counterparts, ignoring the conditions of deprivation and inequality afflicting Chicano youth. The emphases on education and Americanization garnered little support among Mexican Americans, given the injustices being leveled on the community and the grim state of education.

Its ideology undermined by social and historical realities, MAM ran its course as a force of change during World War II. *The Mexican Voice* effectively ceased publication in 1944, changing its name to *The Forward* and shifting its focus to the wartime activities of former MAM members. When the fighting was over in Europe and Asia, MAM proved unable to recruit Latino veterans returning home from their tours of duty. MAM leaders had made it a point of emphasis to recruit returning veterans to engage in social activism, but few were interested in joining its efforts. Their hands were full with readjusting to civilian life, finding jobs, and assuming family responsibilities.

Final attempts to keep MAM afloat included the creation of a Youth Council to recruit the next generation of members. The "old blood" had not maintained the enthusiasm necessary to sustain the organization, however, and its goal of creating "better Americans" was out of step with the temper of the Mexican American community. By the early 1950s, MAM had ceased to exist as a viable organization.

Legacy

Whatever its deficiencies, the legacies and contributions of MAM include positive portrayals of Mexican American youth who became leaders in their own right. The creation of MAM came at an important time for the Mexican community in America, helping the second generation overcome their identity as an immigrant community and assert their social, economic, and political rights. With its emphasis on completing higher education, MAM had not only inspired some Chicano youth to find greater success in mainstream U.S. society, but had also helped—at least in some measure—overcome Anglo stereotypes of Mexican immigrants. Although short-lived and only marginally successful, MAM's goal of enhancing the image of Mexican Americans helped lay the foundation for the next generation's Chicano civil rights and cultural pride movement of the 1960s.

Paul López

See also: Education; Identity and Labels; Mexicans; Zoot Suit Riots.

Further Reading

Larralde, Carlos. *Mexican-American Movements and Leaders.* Los Alamitos, CA: Hwong, 1976
Muñoz, Carlos, Jr. *Youth, Identity, Power: The Chicano Movement.* New York: Verso, 1989.
Sánchez, George J. *Becoming Mexican American: Ethnicity, Culture, and Identity in Chicano Los Angeles, 1900–1945.* New York: Oxford University Press, 1995.

Mexican American Political Association

Founded in 1959 in California by a group of Chicano activists, the Mexican American Political Association (MAPA) was established with the goals of becoming the political voice of the Mexican American community and helping elect Chicano candidates to public office. Feeling excluded from the country's two-party system, a group of 150 Chicano leaders, including Bert Corona, Herman Gallegos, and Eduardo Quevedo, met in Fresno, California, to discuss what they could do to increase the political clout of Mexican Americans.

One of the earliest Mexican American groups to organize politically, MAPA has focused its efforts almost exclusively on Chicano issues, concentrating on seeking out, financing, and electing Chicano candidates, as well as increasing the power of the Mexican American vote. Utilizing a range of tactics, from traditional lobbying to grassroots organizing and public demonstrations, MAPA has worked to register voters, train campaign workers, identify candidates worthy of endorsement, and monitor judicial appointments. Although founded as a nonpartisan organization, MAPA has historically lent its support to the Democratic Party.

Perhaps most famous for its role as a Chicano political advocacy organization in the election campaign of Edward R. Roybal (D-CA) to the U.S. Congress in 1962, MAPA is also credited with securing the appointments of several Mexican American judges to state and municipal courts in California. Aware that Mexican Americans did not have equal representation among elected or appointed officials, MAPA cofounders Eduardo Quevedo and Bert Corona were at the forefront of Roybal's campaign as well as the election of other Mexican Americans to the California legislature, turning out the Mexican American vote in large numbers.

Less well known but equally important in MAPA's history has been its work to defend the civil rights of the Mexican American community, taking action against police brutality, poverty, discrimination in the schools, and other forms of social injustice. In 1966, for example, Quevedo and Corona met with President Lyndon B. Johnson to discuss the abysmal working conditions of migrant farmworkers and rampant poverty in the Latino community. The meeting resulted in Johnson's convening the White House Conference on Mexican American Affairs and creating the Inter-Agency Cabinet Committee on Mexican American Affairs, which directed various programs affecting Mexican Americans. By 1969,

Nativo López, president of the Mexican American Political Association, addressed rallies for improved worker benefits at the ports of Los Angeles and Long Beach, California, in spring 2006. He urged workers to participate in a national immigrant boycott on May 1. *(David McNew/Getty Images)*

this committee expanded its scope to include all Latinos/as, changing its name to the Cabinet Committee on Opportunities for Spanish-Speaking Peoples.

In the 1990s, MAPA continued to focus on these issues, playing an instrumental role in the campaign against Proposition 187, a 1994 California ballot initiative to deny health care and educational benefits to undocumented immigrants in the state; Proposition 209, a 1996 initiative that resulted in the end of affirmative action in the state by prohibiting public institutions from considering race, sex, or ethnicity as part of the admission's process; and Proposition 227, a 1998 initiative to eliminate bilingual education. As a strong advocate for affirmative action, bilingual education, and universal health care for all Latinos/as, MAPA coordinated opposition to these ballot initiatives. Although unsuccessful, with California voters ultimately voting in favor all three propositions (although Proposition 187 would be

overturned in the courts), MAPA played an instrumental role in educating and organizing Latino voters, while developing coalitions with organizations and minority communities throughout California.

The early success of MAPA inspired other activists to establish chapters throughout the Southwest. Despite efforts in the late 1970s to make MAPA a truly national organization, it remained essentially a California group. By the 1980s, it had a membership totaling more than 5,000 in roughly sixty chapters in California alone; there was at least one chapter in each of the state's districts. Internal divisions and the changing political atmosphere of the country, however, resulted in a considerable decline in MAPA's membership and political influence. As of 2009, MAPA has fourteen chapters in California as well as a presence in Chicago, New York City, Portland, Oregon, Washington, D.C., Phoenix, and in Washington State. Its remains active in politics and involved in a spectrum of activities including promoting Latino candidates, training campaign workers, raising campaign funds, testifying in favor of legislation that enhances the opportunities available to Latinos/as, participating in voter registration drives and educational programs within the Latino community, and otherwise pushing for improved political visibility and power for Latinos/as nationwide.

Jesse J. Esparza and David J. Leonard

See also: Chicano/a; Corona, Bert; Mexicans; Migrant Workers; Politics; Proposition 187 (1994); Proposition 209 (1996); Proposition 227 (1998); Roybal, Edward R.

Further Reading

Castro, Tony. *Chicano Power: The Emergence of Mexican America.* New York: E.P. Dutton, 1974.

García, Mario T. *Memories of Chicano History: The Life and Narrative of Bert Corona.* Berkeley: University of California Press, 1994.

Mexican American Political Association. http://www.mapa.org.

Mexican American Student Association

The Mexican American Student Association (MASA) promotes Mexican American cultural awareness, provides a support network to facilitate academic success, and promotes tolerance between and within Latino and other multicultural communities. Founded in 1966 amid an emerging Chicano movement at East Los Angeles Community College, MASA emerged out of a desire to enhance the opportunities and experiences available to Mexican Americans in U.S. higher education. Over the course of more than forty years, various universities across North America have adopted MASA as their active Mexican American organization. The University of Texas, University of Florida, and University of Nebraska–Lincoln are some of the state universities with which MASA is associated.

Activism among Mexican American university students in the mid-1960s stemmed from a quest for cultural identity and a shared desire to recapture what

had been lost through the socialization process imposed by American public institutions, especially schools. In 1966, student activists throughout the Southwest began forming distinct Mexican American student organizations on their campuses. The organization at St. Mary's College in San Antonio, Texas, was named the Mexican American Youth Organization (MAYO). The University of Texas at Austin established the Mexican American Student Organization (MASO), later changing its name to MAYO. In the Los Angeles area, chapters of the United Mexican American Students (UMAS) were formed at UCLA; California State College, Los Angeles; Loyola University, Long Beach; and San Fernando Valley State College. At East Los Angeles Community College, another group organized as the Mexican American Student Association (MASA). Although each organization had a unique view and interpretation of the Chicano movement, all were dedicated to the advancement of the community and the culture. And they all shared a common ideology: Higher education was essential to the survival of Chicano culture.

MASA soon became involved in the East Los Angeles Chicano movement. On the morning of March 3, 1968, the halls of East Los Angeles's Abraham Lincoln High School, a predominantly Chicano school, were filled with the voices of students protesting racist educational policies and teachers. They called for freedom of speech, the hiring of Chicano teachers and administrators, and classes on Mexican American history and culture.

To focus the progressive energy of Chicano youth on display in East Los Angeles, Chicano rights organizers, including members of MASA, held a Crusade for Justice Conference in Denver, Colorado. Out of the conference, attendees created El Plan Espiritual de Aztlán, a manifesto and practical plan to advance the Chicano cause. According to the plan, education should focus on the history, culture, and contributions of Chicanos; the community should control its own schools, teachers, administrators, counselors, and programs; and institutions should serve the Chicano population by providing the services necessary for self-determination and social mobility.

In 1969, a month after the Crusade for Justice Conference was held in Denver, the Chicano Coordinating Council on Higher Education (CCCHE) held a conference at the University of California, Santa Barbara. This was the first opportunity for young Chicanos who attended the Denver conference to implement the ideas of El Plan Espiritual de Aztlán. MASA members attended the conference with hopes of uniting the East Los Angeles Chicano responses to their plight with the rest of the nation's Chicano movement. Although California attendees voted to drop their original organizational names, such as MAYO and MASA, and adopt a new common name—Movimiento Estudiantíl Chicano de Aztlán (MEChA)—a number of universities in the Southwest chose to retain the MASA name and ideology. In the decades since its founding, MASA has been seen as a relatively moderate activist organization committed to cultural awareness. Unlike MEChA, politically charged and often chided for its radicalism, MASA focuses specifically on education and the effort to enroll Mexican Americans in U.S. universities and help them succeed, while preserving cultural identity and pride.

During the course of more than four decades, MASA has helped hundreds of Mexican American students attend and graduate from North American universities. By providing grants, scholarships, fellowships, and guidance, MASA has made it financially possible for many students to pay tuition and buy essential supplies. Many MASA groups raise funds for the Simon Orta Scholarship, which helps students dedicated to MASA and cultural promotion. By means of mentoring programs, awareness days, and special events, MASA promotes cultural awareness. MASA organizations also educate their surrounding communities about Latino culture and traditions. Each MASA group creates its own constitution and list of officers in accordance with university policies. What they and every member share is an enthusiasm for Latino culture.

Stefanie Tacata

See *also:* Chicano Movement; Movimiento Estudiantíl Chicano de Aztlán; Plan Espiritual de Aztlán, El.

Further Reading

Aguirre, Adalberto, Jr., and Ruben O. Martinez. "Chicanos in Higher Education: Issues and Dilemmas for the 21st Century." *ASHE-ERIC Higher Education Report, No. 3.* Washington, DC: George Washington University, 1993.

Sánchez, George J. *Becoming Mexican American: Ethnicity, Culture and Identity in Chicano Los Angeles, 1900–1945.* New York: Oxford University Press, 1995.

Mexican American Women's National Association

The mission of the Mexican American Women's National Association (MANA) is to create a cooperative community of Latinas working to develop leadership, community service, activism, and a higher quality of life. Blandina Cárdenas Ramírez founded MANA as a nonprofit advocacy organization for Mexican American women at the local, state, and national level in 1974. Ramírez wanted to address the needs of Latina women, specifically issues of reproductive freedom, educational opportunity, and equal pay, that were overlooked by traditional Anglo-American middle- and upper-class feminism of the 1970s. Thus, the acronym MANA is short for *hermana,* or "sister."

In Washington, D.C., MANA organizers lobby on behalf of Latina women's issues and better representation for Chicanas in the policy discussions, reports, and decision-making processes of the federal government. In turn, it emphasizes the concerns of Latina women through publication of economic status reports and policy analyses concerning health, education, and employment and then empowers them to effect change in their lives and communities. MANA advocates a family-oriented perspective, including issues of economic justice.

In 1994, MANA expanded to include more than Mexican Americans and officially changed its name to MANA, A National Latina Organization. It presents itself as the largest pan-Latina organization in the United States, encompassing Latinas of Mexican, Puerto Rican, Dominican, Cuban, Central American, South American, and Spanish decent. MANA has a current membership of more than 1,000. The membership comes from diverse professional backgrounds and age groups, and includes some men and Anglo-American women.

MANA values the empowerment of Latinas, and acts by sharing culture and heritage, taking positive risks, defining its own agenda, promoting community activism, upholding equality, encouraging creativity, and honoring Latinas who have made valuable contributions to society. In short, MANA promotes the social achievements of Latinas in the United States by raising the consciousness of Latina women while giving back to communities. It reaches its goals through chapter-based, local adult leadership and educational programs, such as the AvanZamos Ford Fellowship Program, as well as through national conferences.

Las Primeras (The Firsts) is a conference held annually in the nation's capital during Hispanic Heritage month. Every fall, MANA recognizes organizations and people who contribute to Latina achievements, at the same time raising awareness of Latina success and accomplishments. Honorees represent fields ranging from the arts, business, and communications to community service, leadership, the sciences, and sports. A sampling of past honorees includes former U.S. Surgeon General Antonia Novello, National Hispanic Council on Aging President Marta Sotomayor, Cuban American Olympic medalist Jennifer Rodriguez, Yvonne M. Shepard, CEO and president of AT&T Puerto Rico, and Tish Hinojosa, a composer and recording artist.

Independent university and local MANA chapters are found in virtually every major U.S. city, as well as smaller ones with strong Latina communities. While a national organization, chapters tend to focus on local issues. Whereas one city might focus on welfare programs and child passenger safety, another might concentrate on battered women or Latina health services, and still another on promoting technology literacy or addressing heart disease within the Latina community. MANA also sponsors educational programs and mentoring opportunities for adolescent girls, and provides several higher education scholarships each year. For example, Hermanitas (Little Sisters) is an antidropout program for Latinas aged eleven through eighteen. MANA offers educational opportunities through a Girl Scout Partnership program, local school initiatives, the National Hermanitas Summer Institute, and community service. Individual MANA members provide career counseling, encourage leadership, and help adolescent females prepare for higher education. MANA also bestows the HerMANO/HerMANA Award, which recognizes individuals who contribute to the Latina community, and the Cooperation of the Year award, for companies that recognize and collaborate with the Latina community.

MANA is also affiliated with other organizations to promote the advancement of the Latina community and women's leadership. Among these are the Hispanic Women's Network of Texas, the undergraduate and professional sorority Latinas Promoviendo Comunidad/Lambda Pi Chi Sorority, Inc., and the National Council of Women's Organizations (NCWO). Overall, MANA provides a network for a diverse group of Latina women, their families, and the larger Hispanic community, while working to promote and create a better quality of life for Latinas.

Howell Williams

See also: Education; Women.

Further Reading

Crocker, Elvira Valenzuela. *MANA, One Dream, Many Voices: A History of the Mexican American Women's National Association.* Washington, DC: Mexican American Women's National Association, 1991.

MANA, A National Latina Organization. http://www.hermana.org.

Ruíz, Vicki L. *From Out of the Shadows: Mexican Women in Twentieth-Century America.* New York: Oxford University Press, 2008.

Mexican American Youth Organization

In 1967, five students at St. Mary's University in San Antonio, Texas, formed what would be a short-lived but enormously influential Chicano civil rights organization. Despite its innocuous name, the Mexican American Youth Organization (MAYO) quickly emerged as a radical voice for the oppressed Chicano majority in San Antonio and South Texas. During its short existence, from 1967 until 1972, MAYO was able to challenge the electoral monopoly held by the local Democratic Party while bringing South Texas closer to the elusive but elementary goal of true democracy by forcing the established parties to acknowledge the political clout of the Chicano population.

The five founders of MAYO came into the organization with activist experience: José Angel Gutiérrez had been active in the 1963 Chicano political takeover of the town of Crystal City, Texas, while Mario Compeán, Willie Velasquez, Ignacio Pérez, and Juan Patlán were active in assisting striking farmworkers in the Lower Rio Grande Valley of Texas in 1966 and 1967. They viewed MAYO as a radical civil rights organization that sought to provide a voice for the Chicano majority of South Texas. This was largely accomplished through direct action, though MAYO also branched out into more traditional social services related to job training.

As their first target, the founders of MAYO sought to challenge the inequality and racism in the schools of South Texas. Unlike older Mexican American civil rights groups, however, MAYO shunned backroom discussions and litigation, instead looking to direct action. Their preferred tactic was the school boycott. In a number of cases, MAYO was able to force school districts to negotiate for change because funding was determined by the total number of school days attended. With their funding jeopardized, school boards were forced to, at the very least, listen to student complaints.

The most famous and successful of the walkouts occurred in Crystal City from December 1969 to January 1970. Crystal City was a strictly segregated town under the control of large growers who banded together in a rudimentary political machine. They had been able to win back control of the town in 1965, after ongoing legal and economic coercion helped bring down the five Chicano city councilmen elected in 1963. In the fall of 1969, students at Crystal City High School drew up a list of grievances—ranging from the lack of educational content dealing with Mexicans and Mexican Americans to the method by which cheerleaders were selected—and presented it to the school board. When the board refused to act on their grievances, the students began the boycott on December 9 under the direction

of MAYO. When some students were fired from their part-time jobs for taking part in the school boycott, the action expanded to include an economic boycott of several Anglo-owned businesses. Hundreds of students took part in the demonstrations, which extended from the end of the first semester into the Christmas holidays. Thanks to the combined efforts of the boycott and outside pressure from state and federal officials, the school board finally accepted the majority of student demands. The boycott ended on January 6, 1970.

The successful conclusion of the Crystal City school boycott was far from the end of MAYO's activities, however. It merely signaled the beginning of a new phase in the history of the organization. One of the tactics used to build upon the strike and cultivate support in the community was to send striking students around the Crystal City area to register voters. Thus, in 1970, Chicano voter registration was at an all-time high, and MAYO looked to capitalize on its momentum by attempting to garner political power within Crystal City and its nearby communities. Early in the year, the organization and its allies registered candidates in four South Texas counties under the name of La Raza Unida Party. By the end of 1970, *La Raza Unida* held political offices in Crystal City and the nearby towns of Cotulla and Carrizo Springs.

While the political events of 1970 marked the peak of success for MAYO, they also sowed the seeds of its dissolution, as La Raza Unida Party rapidly devoured the limited resources previously used to run a variety of programs in South Texas. By 1972, as La Raza Unida continued to expand operations, MAYO disappeared. Despite its short existence, however, the Mexican American Youth Organization was one of the most important Chicano civil rights organizations of the late 1960s. Not only did it give birth to La Raza Unida Party, but it forced the Anglo population of South Texas to recognize the political voices and desires of Mexican Americans.

John Weber

See also: Blowouts; Chicano Movement; Crystal City, Texas; Education; Gutiérrez, José Angel; La Raza Unida Party.

Further Reading

García, Ignacio M. *United We Win: The Rise and Fall of La Raza Unida Party.* Tucson: University of Arizona Mexican American Studies Research Center, 1989.

Gómez Quiñones, Juan. *Chicano Politics: Reality and Promise, 1940–1990.* Albuquerque: University of New Mexico Press, 1990.

Navarro, Armando. *Mexican American Youth Organization: Avant-Garde of the Chicano Movement in Texas.* Austin: University of Texas Press, 1995.

Mexican-American War

The Mexican-American War, fought during the years 1846–1848, was primarily the result of a U.S. military intrusion into disputed Mexican territory. The peace treaty that ended hostilities forced Mexicans to cede more than half of their national territory to the United States, dealing Mexico an economic blow from which it has never recovered. These lands, which vastly increased the size and mineral wealth of the United States, today encompass the states of California, New Mexico, Nevada, Utah, Arizona, and parts of Texas, Colorado, and Wyoming. In return, the United States paid Mexico the sum of $15 million and assumed responsibility for all unpaid claims previously filed by U.S. citizens against the Mexican government.

Events Leading to War

A number of conflicts arose between the United States and Mexico in the decades leading up to the Mexican-American War. Foremost among these was the one over the Mexican territory of Texas. Beginning in 1819, the Spanish government authorized Catholic citizens of the United States to settle in Texas under the leadership of Moses Austin, the founder of the American lead industry, who had received permission from the Mexican government to bring Anglo settlers into Texas. The Mexican Congress extended the authorization following Mexican independence from Spain in 1821, and, over the next decade, American speculators, criminals, and adventurers flooded into Texas. By 1830, the American population in Texas outnumbered the Mexican population by a ratio of ten to one.

In 1836, outraged by the Mexican government's attempts to enforce property laws, centralize government power, and curtail slavery (Mexico had abolished slavery in 1829), Texans called a convention and set up a provisional government. The Mexican government responded by dispatching two army divisions, led by President and General Antonio López de Santa Anna, in an attempt to put down the rebellion. Although U.S. government officials claimed a position of strict neutrality, they aided the Texas army by sending weapons, men, and ammunition. Santa Anna's forces defeated the rebels at the famous Battle of the Alamo in March 1836, but fell to Texas General Sam Houston at the Battle of San Jacinto the following month. Santa Anna himself was captured in the latter campaign and forced to sign a treaty acknowledging Texas's independence. Although Mexico insisted that Texas remained Mexican territory, the United States, France, and Great Britain all formally recognized the Lone Star Republic as an independent sovereign nation.

As early as September 1836, Texans voted for annexation by the United States. Congress delayed approval, however, because many representatives of the North opposed the extension of slavery into the area. In the 1844 presidential election, Democratic candidate James K. Polk thrust the issue to the forefront by running on a pro-expansionist platform that included the immediate annexation of Texas. Polk was swept into office by supporters who rallied under the cry "Polk, Slavery, Texas!" Polk's election coincided with the emergence of Manifest Destiny, the doctrine that the Anglos were destined to conquer and possess the entire North American continent.

Congress's decision to annex Texas transferred all of Texas's disputes with Mexico to the United States, including the ongoing disagreement regarding its southern border. Mexico insisted that the border was the Rio Nueces; Texans maintained that the border lay 130 miles (209 kilometers) farther south, along the Rio Grande. In June 1845, six months before officially admitting Texas into statehood, U.S. Secretary of War William Marcy ordered an army under General Zachary Taylor to occupy the disputed area between the Rio Nueces and Rio Grande. As Mexican forces assembled on the southern bank of the Rio Grande in anticipation of Taylor's arrival, Polk dispatched John Slidell to Mexico City to negotiate a resolution of the dispute—but the Mexican government was unwilling even to meet with him.

Any hopes of seeking a diplomatic resolution to the conflict were dashed on April 25, 1846, when a squadron of U.S. dragoons on a reconnaissance mission under Captain Seth Thornton was defeated by Mexican forces outside Port Isabel, a town near the mouth of the Rio Grande. Hostilities quickly escalated, and on May 8 and 9, 1846, Taylor routed the Mexican army at the Battles of Palo Alto and Resaca De Palma. Polk now had the pretext he needed to declare war. When he delivered his war message to Congress on May 11, 1846, it marked the first time in U.S. history that a president announced a war in progress prior to a congressional declaration. Although Thornton's dragoons had crossed into disputed Mexican territory, Polk claimed that Mexican forces had "shed American blood upon American soil." Within two days, Congress officially declared war. On July 7, the Mexican government answered in kind "in order to repel the aggression of the United States of America."

Major Campaigns

Colonel Stephen Watts Kearny was put in charge of invading and occupying the territory of New Mexico. Leading an army made up almost exclusively of volunteer soldiers, Kearny encountered little resistance from the impoverished, unarmed local population and easily captured the cities of Las Vegas, San Miguel, and Santa Fé. The only resistance he did face stemmed from local retaliation to the abuses committed by his own undisciplined volunteer soldiers.

In the Battle of Monterrey, September 21–23, 1846, U.S. troops under General Zachary Taylor forced the Mexican army to surrender, but then allowed it to withdraw. Still, this battle was considered an important U.S. victory in the Mexican-American War. *(MPI/Stringer/Hulton Archive/Getty Images)*

By the end of February 1847, less than eight months after the campaign began, New Mexico was securely in the hands of the United States.

The California campaign was conducted primarily by the U.S. Navy under Commodore John D. Sloat and his replacement, Commodore Robert Field Stockton. On July 2, 1846, Sloat anchored his naval squadron off the coast of Monterey, and within ten days his forces occupied the towns of Monterey, San Juan Bautista, and San Francisco. Due to poor health, he was replaced by Stockton, who went on to capture San Diego, Santa Clara, San Pedro, and Los Angeles. The Mexican forces in California did not stand a chance against the larger, better-armed U.S. forces, but they did continue to conduct guerrilla resistance for several months following the U.S. victories.

After defeating Mexico at the Battles of Palo Alto and Resaca De Palma in May 1846, Taylor pursued the retreating Mexicans across the Rio Grande. On May 18 he took the town of Matamoros, after which his army advanced on the Mexican town of Monterrey and captured it in a three-day battle that ended on September 23. As Taylor moved deeper and deeper into Mexican territory, General Santa Anna, who had recently returned to power after a period of exile in Cuba, prepared to lead a large Mexican force north to stop the Americans' advance. Santa Anna learned that much of Taylor's army had been diverted to the south and took the opportunity to engage the Americans in a weakened state. When the two armies met at the Battle of Buena Vista on February 22, 1847, Santa Anna had a significant numerical advantage but could not drive out the well-entrenched, better-armed American volunteers. Both Mexico and the United States claimed victory, but Santa Anna withdrew his men when he learned that Taylor had reinforcements on the way. Taylor's victories won him great popularity, so much so that he was elected president after the war's conclusion.

Meanwhile, General Winfield Scott led a U.S. campaign to take Mexico City, which began with the bombardment of the Port of Veracruz from March 22 to 26, 1847. U.S. Navy warships were equipped with state-of-the-art artillery, which allowed them to shell the city without risk of being reached by its antiquated armaments. Following the fall of Veracruz, Scott began his march to Mexico City. Santa Anna had returned there following the Battle of Buena Vista to find the city in the throes of revolution. Within a week of his return, he managed to put down the revolt, unite the politicians, install himself as president, and reorganize the army in preparation for Scott's advance. Santa Anna led his troops to await Scott's forces at the mountain pass of Cerra Gordo, but the Americans' superior weaponry and organization were too much for them. Santa Anna withdrew his troops and was pursued by Scott, who again defeated the Mexicans, at the Battles of Contreras and Churubusco on August 19 and 20, 1847.

This series of defeats forced the Mexicans to accept an armistice during which peace negotiations could ensue. After two weeks of futile negotiations, however, fighting resumed. From September 8 to 14, Scott's forces stormed the well-defended Mexican capital, winning decisive victories at the strongholds of Casa Mata, Molino Del Rey, and the great fortress of Chapultepec. Following the invasion and occupation of Mexico City, the Mexican government had no choice but to resume peace negotiations.

Legacy

The United States had won a relatively easy victory against a poorly defended, militarily inferior nation plagued by internal political divisions. Veteran diplomat Nicholas Trist represented the United States in the peace negotiations with Mexico. President Polk recalled him after the collapse of the first armistice, but, by the time he received the notification, Mexico City had fallen. Trist decided to go ahead with the peace negotiations, which ultimately resulted in the Treaty of Guadalupe Hidalgo of 1848. The treaty forced Mexico to cede more than half of its land to the United States in exchange for $15 million. The U.S. government also agreed to assume all claims for damages demanded of Mexico by Americans.

The victory over Mexico bolstered U.S. nationalism and confirmed Americans' belief in the theory of Manifest Destiny and the superiority of the Anglos. The sensationalized newspaper coverage of the conflict further fueled racist anti-Mexican sentiment. In Mexico, the war spawned a deep-seated distrust of the United States among politicians and the general populace that is still visible today. The acquisition of so much Mexican territory also thrust the U.S. government into bitter sectionalist debate over whether the territory should be slave or free. The resulting Compromise of 1850 made California a free state and established the principle of "popular sovereignty," whereby the residents of a particular territory would decide if the territory would accept or reject slavery. This policy soon became one of the underlying causes of the American Civil War.

Bretton T. Alvaré

See also: Alamo, Battle of the; Manifest Destiny; Mexicans; Military, Latinos in the; Taos Rebellion; Tejanos; Treaty of Guadalupe Hidalgo (1848).

Further Reading

Bauer, K. Jack. *The Mexican War 1846–1848.* Lincoln: University of Nebraska Press, 1974.

Martinez, Orlando. *The Great Landgrab: The Mexican-American War 1846–1848.* London: Quartet, 1975.

McCaffrey, James M. *Army of Manifest Destiny: The American Soldier in the Mexican War 1846–1848.* New York: New York University Press, 1992.

Robinson, Charles M., III. *Texas and the Mexican War: A History and a Guide.* Austin: Texas State Historical Society, 2004.

Vázquez, Josefina Zoraida. "Causes of the War with the United States." In *Dueling Eagles: Reinterpreting the U.S.-Mexican War, 1846–1848,* ed. Richard V. Francaviglia and Douglas W. Richmond. Fort Worth: Texas Christian University Press, 2000.

Mexicans

In the United States at the turn of the twenty-first century, according to the U.S. Census, 25 million people identified themselves as Mexican immigrants or Mexican Americans. Unlike the many Latino groups that migrated to the United States in large numbers during the twentieth century, Mexican Americans constitute one of the oldest communities in the nation. Indeed, Mexicans were already living in the southern and western regions of North America during the sixteenth and seventeenth centuries, founding, for example, the city of Santa Fe (now New Mexico) in 1609. Many more Mexicans migrated to the United States during the early and mid-twentieth century, and untold numbers continue to cross the Mexican-U.S. border in the 2000s. Mexico is the leading country of origin for migrant workers coming into the United States, both legally and illegally; in the 1990s, more legal immigrants came from Mexico than from all European countries combined. Mexican Americans comprise one of the most influential social and cultural groups in the United States, shaping the politics, language, culture, and daily life of America increasingly with time.

Early Immigration

The Treaty of Guadalupe Hidalgo not only ended the U.S.-Mexican War in 1848, but also allowed the United States to annex from Mexico all or parts of the present-day states of California, Arizona, New Mexico, Nevada, Colorado, Utah, and Wyoming. The United States also maintained control of Texas, which officially became a U.S. state in 1845. The residents of these territories thus became the first established Mexican American communities in the United States.

Although sizable Mexican communities developed in the Southwest throughout the second half of the nineteenth century, particularly in Texas, the large-scale migration of Mexicans to the United States began in the early twentieth century. From 1910 through 1929, more than 1 million Mexicans migrated to the United States; many entered as refugees fleeing the Mexican Revolution (1910–1920), while others were attracted by job opportunities available in the economic development of the Southwest. During World War I, U.S. businesses faced labor shortages as 4 million American men entered the armed forces. Consequently, large numbers of Mexicans were recruited as labor migrants. Most found employment in the agriculture, mining, and railroad industries of the Southwest. However, Mexicans also settled in cities throughout the Midwest, especially Chicago, Kansas City, and Detroit, and in the Pittsburgh area of western Pennsylvania, where many found work in steel mills. The single largest community, however, was established in Los Angeles. Prior to the 1920s, the Mexican American population was concentrated heavily in Texas, but rapid economic and industrial development in Southern California during the early decades of the twentieth century, fueled by the agricultural, petroleum, auto manufacturing, and motion picture industries, attracted Mexican job-seekers in large numbers.

Heavy Mexican immigration, both legal and illegal, continued until the Great Depression of the early 1930s. As the nation's unemployment rate climbed to 25 percent and millions of workers lost their jobs, many non-Latino U.S. citizens viewed Mexican immigrants and Mexican Americans as unwanted competitors for scarce labor opportunities and public relief programs, resulting in widespread calls for their repatriation. Between 300,000 and 500,000 Mexicans (some of whom were U.S. citizens) were sent back to Mexico during the 1930s, through both voluntary means and forced deportations.

With the labor shortages resulting from World War II, however, Mexican migration would increase during the 1940s. In 1942, the Franklin Roosevelt administration initiated the Bracero Program with the Mexican government, whereby tens of thousands of Mexicans came to the United States as temporary contract workers to fill the labor needs in agriculture, the railroad, and other specified industries. The Bracero Program, which last until 1964, contributed to the growth of Mexican communities throughout the United States, particularly in California.

Reception, Deportation, Assimilation

While the U.S. government and American businesses have historically encouraged the immigration of low-wage Mexicans workers, the policy has faced opposition from the American populace. Mexican immigrants have faced pervasive and ongoing racism, cultural stereotypes, and questions regarding their ability to assimilate into American society. In the early part of the twentieth century, public schools in many locations implemented "Americanization" programs that focused on teaching Mexican children English and eradicating the use of Spanish, as well as teaching Anglo-Protestant values. In the Southwest, Mexican children were ridiculed, punished, and even beaten for speaking Spanish in school.

Bringing native foods for lunch, such as tacos or tamales, was strictly forbidden. Eurocentric curricula and teacher biases were widespread, denigrating Mexican heritage and culture and channeling immigrant students into lower-level courses and manual labor jobs.

The U.S. economy entered a recession in 1953, which nearly doubled the unemployment rate. As during the Great Depression, Mexicans were once again seen as a threat to American prosperity and jobs. This time, the U.S. government responded with a massive deportation scheme, called Operation Wetback, in which almost 4 million undocumented Mexican immigrants were deported. Few were given a formal deportation hearing, and many of those deported were male heads of household who left wives and children in the United States.

Mexican Americans reacted to these conditions in different ways. Some sought to assimilate into the social and cultural mainstream, while others sought to maintain their ethnic identity. While full assimilation into the dominant Anglo-Saxon core was regarded in some circles as the best strategy against anti-Mexican prejudice and discrimination, full assimilation and acceptance was generally difficult and usually an option only to individuals with light skin and "European" features. In New Mexico and Texas, some identified themselves as "Hispanos" or "Hispanics" to emphasize their European roots and separate themselves from "Mexicans." During the 1960s and early 1970s, the Chicano Movement (or *El Movimiento*) flourished among Mexican American youth in the Southwest as an expression of cultural identity and empowerment. *Chicanismo* rejected assimilationist philosophies and asserted pride in the indigenous and mixed ancestry of Mexicans. The Chicano Movement thus proved active in protesting police brutality, the Vietnam War, and the poor educational facilities available to Chicano and Mexican American youth.

Recent Developments

The Mexican American population has grown rapidly since the 1970s, as a result of high levels of both legal and illegal immigration and a higher birthrate than the rest of the U.S. population. The increase in immigration has resulted primarily from the economic problems in Mexico and prospect of higher-paying jobs in the United States. By the twenty-first century, Mexican American communities could be found in all fifty states, with sizable Mexican populations not only in California, the Southwest, and large metropolitan areas such as Chicago and New York, but even in the South, particularly Georgia and North Carolina.

The rapid growth of the Mexican American population and the formation of new communities in areas that historically have had little or no Latino population have been met with backlash and resistance by some American citizens. Several state and local governments throughout the country have enacted "English as the Official Language" legislation due to the perceived threat posed by Spanish. A number of state and local governments, as well as the U.S. Congress, have sponsored bills aimed at cracking down on undocumented immigrants, largely Mexicans. In addition, several grassroots anti-immigrant and immigration control groups have sprung up since the early 1990s, some of which espouse explicitly anti-Mexican views.

Notwithstanding what some have identified as a heightened state of anti-Mexican sentiment, the early part of the twenty-first century has afforded increasing visibility to the Mexican American community. Mexican and Mexican American celebrities have gained prominence in American popular culture from television and movies to sports and music. Eva Longoria and Salma Hayek are two of the latest generation of Hollywood's leading ladies, while Mexican American actors Anthony Quinn and Edward James Olmos have enjoyed illustrious careers on the large and small screens. Popular Chicano comedians include Richard "Cheech" Marin, Paul Rodríguez, and George Lopez. Oscar de la Hoya won the gold medal in boxing at the 1992 Summer Olympics and has won world titles in five weight divisions as a professional fighter. Folk singer Joan Baez and rock musician Carlos Santana are Grammy Award–winning musicians of Mexican descent who have made contributions to America's musical landscape for decades.

As the population of Mexican Americans has grown since the mid-twentieth century, their political power and representation has also increased, particularly in California and Texas. Democrat Henry Cisneros served as the mayor of San Antonio from 1981 to 1989, and later as secretary of housing and urban development during the Clinton administration. New Mexico governor Bill Richardson, also a Democrat, served in the Clinton administration as ambassador to the United Nations and secretary of energy; in 2008 he sought the party's nomination for president. Other notable Mexican American politicians in the twenty-first century include California Congresswoman Loretta Sanchez (D-CA), Los Angeles Mayor Antonio Villaraigosa, and former California Lieutenant Governor Cruz Bustamante.

Justin D. García

See also: Bracero Program; Chicano Movement; Education; Film; Identity and Labels; Illegal Immigration; Immigration Enforcement; Migrant Workers; Politics; Repatriation; Treaty of Guadalupe Hidalgo (1848).

Further Reading

Meier, Matt S., and Feliciano Ribera. *Mexican Americans, American Mexicans: From Conquistadors to Chicanos.* New York: Hill and Wang, 1994.

Sánchez, George J. *Becoming Mexican American: Ethnicity, Culture, and Identity in Chicano Los Angeles, 1900–1945.* New York: Oxford University Press, 1995.

Vigil, James Diego. *From Indians to Chicanos: The Dynamics of Mexican-American Culture.* 2nd ed. Prospect Heights, IL: Waveland, 1998.

Miami

Sometimes referred to as "Havana USA," Miami has long been considered the heart of the Cuban exile community in America. While Cubans still dominate life in Miami in terms of their numbers as well as their political and economic power, the influx of other Latin Americans in recent decades has provided the city with a dynamic and even more diverse Latino community. This expansion of the Latino population has changed what has traditionally been considered a Cuban city and institutions. For instance, the annual Cuban festival Calle Ocho is now conceptualized as not only a Cuban event but also a generic "Hispanic" celebration.

Today, more than 63 percent of the city's population is Latino. The concentration is even higher in certain neighborhoods, such as Sweetwater, where 93 percent is Latino, and Hialeah, which has a Latino population of 88 percent. Little Havana became the center of Miami's exile community in the 1960s as the large influx of refugees settled along Eighth Street–Calle Ocho and built a rich ethnic neighborhood. While Little Havana remains the cultural center of Cuban life in Miami, a substantial number of its Cuban residents have moved to other neighborhoods in recent years, and Little Havana now boasts a growing pan-Latino population.

Compared to the rest of the nation and even the rest of the state of Florida, Miami is a relatively young city. Founded in 1896, it remained small and isolated until several real-estate barons developed the coast during the 1920s and 1930s, transforming an isolated, swampy backwater into a booming recreational center and tourist destination. The tourist industry made Miami the nation's playground and a prime vacation spot for many upper-class Latin Americans. Although Miami's Latino population is generally linked to the post-1959 immigration of Cuban refugees (following the success of the Castro revolution in Cuba and the installation of his socialist regime), the Latino presence in fact is much older. In 1957, about 85,000 Latin Americans resided in Miami; more than half were Cuban.

However, the Latino population in Miami climbed quickly with the inflow of Cuban refugees fleeing Castro's revolution. By 1970, there were just under 300,000 Cubans living in Miami; by 1980, a decade of immigration and the influx of *marielitos* brought the number of Cubans to just under 600,000. The sizable Cuban population has revolutionized the city's economy and culture, taking control of local government and the means of production as Miami grew from a seasonal resort town to a cosmopolitan metropolis. Because the city's Cubans generally regard themselves as exiles and not immigrants, maintaining their ethnic identity and cultural institutions has been important to them. With this is mind, they have reconstructed a "Havana in exile," with countless shops, restaurants, and other establishments that mirror those found in the Cuban capital.

In addition to Cubans, other sizable Latino groups call Miami home. These include Puerto Rican, Colombians, Nicaraguans, and Dominicans. During the 1980s and 1990s, political instability in Central America "pushed" many refugees and immigrants from Honduras, Nicaragua, and Panama northward. Attracted by the economic opportunities made available by Cuban-owned businesses and the bilingual education policies of Miami-Dade County public schools, many of the Central American immigrants chose to settle in Miami and have begun transforming the city into the "capital of Latin America."

The strong Cuban presence, however, has functioned as a double-edged sword for Miami's Latino community. While the financial success of the Cuban community has helped engender a broad range of other Latino businesses, Cuban-centric politics have overshadowed the needs of other Latinos/as. Cubans in Miami are thus positioned as both the saviors and the bane of the Latino community.

Cheris Brewer Current

See also: Cuban Refugee Program; Cubans; Mariel Boatlift; Marielitos.

Further Reading

García, María Cristina. *Havana USA: Cuban Exiles and Cuban Americans in South Florida, 1959–1994.* Berkeley: University of California Press, 1996.

Portes, Alejandro, and Alex Stepick. *City on the Edge: The Transformation of Miami.* Berkeley: University of California Press, 1993.

Stepick, Alex, Guillermo Grenier, Max Castro, and Marvin Dunn. *This Land Is Our Land: Immigrants and Power in Miami.* Berkeley: University of California Press, 2003.

Torres, María de los Angeles. *In the Land of Mirrors: Cuban Exile Politics in the United States.* Ann Arbor: University of Michigan Press, 1999.

Migrant Workers

Migrant workers are agricultural laborers who provide the labor input necessary for the production of fresh fruits and vegetables, and who relocate continuously according to seasonal labor demands.

In the United States, migrants have long represented one of the most impoverished and oppressed populations of workers. Historically, the overwhelming majority of migrant workers in America have been of Mexican descent. A number of attempts to improve their working conditions have been made by migrant workers themselves and those acting on their behalf. However, their often quasi-legal status has allowed migrant workers and their employers to subvert the limited protective regulations put in place by the U.S. government. As a result, migrant workers continue to be denied the basic legal rights afforded to workers in virtually every other employment sector in the U.S. economy.

The unreliable, dangerous, and labor-intensive nature of migrant work has historically impelled employers to recruit workers from the most vulnerable populations of U.S. society. The situation has varied from region to region: In the South, African American and poor white sharecroppers were exploited; in the East and Midwest, European immigrants were used; and in the West and Southwest, Chinese, Filipino, and Mexican immigrants were recruited into the migrant labor force. The first migrant workers were employed in the mid-1800s by California grain growers, who sought the cheapest, most vulnerable laborers they could find; hiring immigrant populations provided an ideal solution. The mindset of growers is summed up in an 1854 article from the *California Farmer,* which asked: "Then where shall the laborers be found? The Chinese! . . . Those great walls of China are to be broken down and that population is to be to California what the African has been to the South." With the passage of the Chinese Exclusion Act in 1882, however, Mexican immigrants began to eclipse Chinese as the primary providers of migrant labor. Since the turn of the twentieth century, Mexican immigrants have dominated the nation's migrant labor force, especially in the Southwest.

In the Midwest, unsustainable farming techniques, the displacement of buffalo herds, and severe droughts combined to create an agricultural crisis that peaked in the years following the Great Depression. The once-fertile soils of the plains regions were rendered dry and barren, resulting in massive dust storms and a sharp drop in the amount of arable land. Tens of thousands of American farmers and their families were forced to leave their homes in search of agricultural opportunities in California. Like their Mexican counterparts, these dust bowl migrants faced discrimination and brutality at the hands of police and bank officials as they moved from place to place, struggling to survive. In *The Grapes of Wrath* (novel, 1939; film, 1940), John Steinbeck brought to life the plight of these white migrant workers, referred to by the pejorative term "Okies."

The Bracero Program was instituted in 1942 in response to requests by farmers in the Southwest that the federal government allow the importation of temporary Mexican workers. The Mexican government, wary of the poor working and living conditions on U.S. farms, persuaded the American government to guarantee all contracts issued to Mexican migrant workers, or *braceros.* For the duration of World War II, the Bracero Program remained relatively small, accounting for fewer than 100,000 of the nation's 4 million farmworkers annually. Participants in the Bracero Program were outnumbered by illegal immigrants who, though working side by side, were not entitled to the protections of the federal government. Many were legalized after arriving and working in the United States, in a process that official government documents described as "drying out the wetbacks."

In 1951, at the request of growers, Congress enacted the Mexican Farm Labor Program, after which Mexican immigration to the United States soared, reaching nearly 500,000 in 1955. Patterns of migration remained relatively unchanged after the program was terminated in 1964, since millions of Mexican migrant workers already had personal relationships with U.S. growers who were willing to hire them if they continued to immigrate illegally.

With no laws to protect them, the Mexican migrant workers endured working conditions and standards of living that were among the poorest in the nation. They were plagued by complications from harmful pesticides, unsanitary facilities, dangerous working conditions, malnutrition, slave wages, and disease outbreaks of epidemic proportions. Efforts to improve the lot of migrant workers had been ongoing since the nineteenth century, but it was not until the decades following World War II that attempts to

Mexican cotton pickers near Corcoran, in California's Central Valley, went on strike for higher wages in October 1933. Facing vigilante violence and forced into a single labor camp, they won a raise of 75 cents per 100 pounds—but no union recognition. *(Library of Congress)*

organize migrant workers came to fruition. In the context of the political activism of the 1960s, the National Farm Workers Association (NFWA) was founded in order to fight for better wages and working conditions and the right to organize for farmworkers. Under the collaborative leadership of César Chávez and Dolores Huerta, the NWFA, which later became the United Farm Workers (UFW), secured the rights of farmworkers to unionize and engage in collective bargaining with growers. Huerta and Chávez organized one of the first successful multiethnic workers' rights movements in the nation's history when they joined forces with Filipino workers in a boycott of California grapes in 1965.

Despite the victories of the NFWA and UFW during and since the 1960s, migrant workers remain one of the most exploited groups of workers in the United States. As of 2002, some 83 percent of migrant workers identified themselves as "Hispanic," and more than half (53 percent) were in the country illegally, leaving them susceptible to exploitation and abuse.

Bretton T. Alvaré

See also: Bracero Program; Chávez, César; Grape Strikes and Boycotts; Huerta, Dolores; Mexicans; United Farm Workers of America.

Further Reading

Daniel, Cletus E. *Bitter Harvest: A History of California Farmworkers, 1870–1941.* Ithaca, NY: Cornell University Press. 1981.

"Findings from the National Agricultural Workers Survey (NAWS) 2001–2002: A Demographic and Employment Profile of United States Farm Workers." U.S. Department of Labor, Office of the Assistant Secretary for Policy. Office of Programmatic Policy. Research Report No. 9. March 2005.

Martin, Philip L., and David A. Martin. *The Endless Quest: Helping America's Farm Workers.* Boulder, CO: Westview, 1994.

Military, Latinos in the

According to the 2004 annual Department of Defense report *Population Representation in the Military Services* (generally referred to as the PopRep), there were 116,410 Hispanics enlisted personnel in the U.S. military, comprising 9.83 percent of the total enlisted force. The armed service with the largest percentage of Latinos/as was the Marine Corps with 14.55 percent; the branch with the lowest percentage was the Air Force, with 5.95 percent. In terms of raw numbers, the Army still had the most Latino enlistments, with 46,759. Given that civilian Latinos/as between the ages of eighteen and forty-four make up 16.41 percent of the population, it would appear that Latinos/as are underrepresented in the military.

If, however, one takes into account the educational qualifications (high school diploma or equivalent) and immigration status (legal resident) generally required for enlistment, the pool of eligible Latinos/as is dramatically reduced. According to fiscal year 2004 figures, only 62 percent (9,348,062) of all eighteen- to twenty-four-year-old Hispanics had a high school diploma or its equivalent. Thus, the percentage of Latino enlisted personnel (9.83 percent) is roughly comparable to that of the educationally qualified Latino civilian workforce (10.67 percent). Likewise, the 17,827 enlisted Latina women, accounting for 15.31 percent of all Latinos/as in the military, appear in nearly the same ratio (14.76 percent) as women overall in the enlisted force.

Differences are much more apparent in the officer corps. The service with the highest percentage of Latino officers is the Marine Corps (6.17 percent), while the Air Force had the lowest (3.66 percent). Although Latinos/as make up 9.83 percent of the overall enlisted force, only 4.66 percent of all officers are Latino/a.

It is important to keep in mind, however, that a college degree is the standard prerequisite for becoming a commissioned officer. As such, the percentage of Latino officers in the military is directly affected by the number of Latino civilian college graduates. If one compares the percentage of qualified Latino civilians (6.54 percent) with the overall percentage of Latino officers (4.66 percent), the representation gap is markedly narrower.

Even so, there is an undeniable underrepresentation of Latino officers at the highest ranks. Approximately 70 percent of all Latino officers are concentrated at the rank of captain (the equivalent of a Navy lieutenant) or lower, compared with 60 percent for the military as whole. In 2004, of the 880 flag rank officers (generals and admirals) only eleven were Latino. This select group accounted for only 1.25 percent of all flag rank officers.

Although Latinos/as continue to be underrepresented at the highest levels, there has been a notable increase both in overall numbers and in percentage representation in recent years. For most of the 1970s,

the total number of Latinos/as in the U.S. armed forces fluctuated between 78,000 and 83,000, and accounted for between 4.0 and 4.6 percent of all enlistees. During the mid-1980s, the total number of enlisted Latinos/as dropped to an average of approximately 73,000; because of a slight downsize in the military, however, they continued to represent on the order of 4.0 percent of all enlisted personnel. Following the end of the Cold War, the overall size of the military shrank from 1,775,000 in 1992 to 1,369,000 in 2001. This 23 percent drop in manpower stands in stark contrast to the 30 percent increase in the number of enlisted Latinos/as over the same period. During the 1990s, the total number of Latinos/as in the military surged from 90,600 to almost 118,000. In addition, whereas at the beginning of the 1990s Latinos/as accounted for 1.7 percent of all officers earning commissions in one of the nation's military academies, by 2001 the figure had risen to 4.1 percent. Correspondingly, Latinos/as as a percentage of total accessions to the officer ranks jumped from 2.78 percent in 1992 to 5.02 percent in 2004.

Early History

Data on the history of Latino participation in the U.S. military prior to the 1970s is woefully incomplete. It was not until after World War II that the Department of Defense even began acknowledging Hispanic American soldiers as a separate group from other Americans. Even then, during the course of the Korean War and the Vietnam War, the government did not maintain detailed records or reports on Latino participation in the military. Prior to 1976, the Department of Defense compiled statistics simply by counting the number of servicemen and servicewomen with Spanish-sounding last names. In that year, however, the Department of Defense began asking new recruits to designate their ethnic heritage in order to record the number of Latino servicemen and servicewomen. Although the government did not compile statistics regarding the specific number of Latino military personnel for most of the nation's history, historians have been able to gather the stories of many notable Latinos/as who made important contributions defending the United States in armed conflicts dating back to the eighteenth century.

FY 2004 Active Component Enlisted Members by Race/Ethnicity, Service, and Gender with Civilian Comparison Group

| Race/Ethnicity | MILITARY SERVICE | | | | | | | | | | 18- to 44-Year-Old Civilians | |
| | U.S. Army | | U.S. Navy | | U.S. Marine Corps | | U.S. Air Force | | Total Department of Defense | | | |
	Males	Females	Males	Females	Males	Females	Males	Females	Males	Females	Males	Females
a. Number												
Hispanic	39,370	7,389	24,251	4,604	21,184	1,855	13,778	3,979	98,583	17,827	8,827,608	5,552,060
Not Hispanic*	313,784	52,972	244,324	40,714	127,540	7,799	225,102	55,457	910,750	156,942	38,701,620	34,530,976
TOTAL	353,154	60,361	268,575	45,318	148,724	9,654	238,880	59,436	1,009,333	174,769	47,529,229	40,083,037
b. Percent												
Hispanic	11.15%	12.24%	9.03%	10.16%	14.24%	19.21%	5.77%	6.69%	9.77%	10.20%	18.57%	13.85%
Not Hispanic*	88.85%	87.76%	90.97%	89.84%	85.76%	80.79%	94.23%	93.31%	90.23%	89.80%	81.43%	86.15%
TOTAL	100.00%	100.00%	100.00%	100.00%	100.00%	100.00%	100.00%	100.00%	100.00%	100.00%	100.00%	100.00%

*Includes individuals who indicated non-Hispanic ethnicity or did not respond to ethnicity question. Also note that columns may not add precisely to totals due to rounding.
Source: Office of the Under Secretary of Defense, Personnel and Readiness, *Population Representation in the Military Services, Fiscal Year 2004*. Available at http://www.defenselink.mil.

FY 2004 Active Component Officer Accessions and Officer Corps by Race/Ethnicity and Service with Civilian Comparison Group

| Race/Ethnicity | MILITARY SERVICE | | | | | | | | | | Civilian College Graduates* | |
| | U.S. Army | | U.S. Navy | | U.S. Marine Corps | | U.S. Air Force | | Total Department of Defense | | | |
	#	%	#	%	#	%	#	%	#	%	#	%
Hispanic	3,410	4.97%	2,744	5.21%	1,033	6.17%	2,716	3.66%	9,903	4.66%	1,925,081	6.54%
Not Hispanic**	65,224	95.03%	49,963	94.79%	15,709	93.83%	71,588	96.34%	202,484	95.34%	27,494,372	93.46%
TOTAL	68,634	100.00%	52,707	100.00%	16,742	100.00%	74,304	100.00%	212,387	100.00%	29,419,453	100.00%

*Comparison group for accessions includes 21- to 35-year-old college graduates in the noninstitutional civilian population, October 2003–September 2004.
**Includes individuals who indicated non-Hispanic ethnicity or did not respond to ethnicity question. Also note that columns may not add to totals due to rounding.
Source: Office of the Under Secretary of Defense, Personnel and Readiness, *Population Representation in the Military Services, Fiscal Year 2004*. Available at http://www.defenselink.mil.

Many scholars trace the starting point of the history of Latinos/as in the U.S. military to the War of American Independence. As the war progressed, many Latin Americans and Spaniards played decisive roles on the battlefields. Notably, General Bernardo de Gálvez, Spanish governor of the Louisiana Territory, helped provision General George Washington's forces with weapons, ammunition, and supplies, and led troops against the British at Pensacola (present-day Florida), Mobile (present-day Alabama), Natchez (present-day Mississippi), Baton Rouge (present-day Louisiana), and Saint Louis (present-day Missouri). Another important figure was Jorge Farragut, who emigrated to America from the Spanish island of Minorca, where he was born, to help fight against the British. Farragut went on to become a captain in the U.S. Navy and commanded a gunboat during the War of 1812. General Bernardo de Gálvez and Captain Jorge Farragut are just two examples of a Latino presence in the U.S. military from the very beginning of the republic.

Nineteenth Century

As a consequence of the Mexican-American War, the United States obtained territories from Mexico that encompass much of the present-day Southwest, from Texas to California. The Treaty of Guadalupe Hidalgo, which settled the conflict in 1848, allowed Mexicans in the newly acquired lands to continue living in their communities and, if they so desired, to become U.S. citizens. The result was that by 1860, according to census figures, there were 27,466 Mexican Americans living throughout the United States.

With the onset of the Civil War, Mexican Americans, like all Americans, were forced to choose sides. Not surprisingly, Latino soldiers enlisted in both the Union and Confederate armies, though exactly how many served is unclear. Estimates range from several thousand to over 20,000. In recent years historians have begun to compile various profiles of Latino Civil War veterans. Major Salvador Vallejo, for example, commanded the First Battalion of Native Cavalry, one of four companies of Mexican American Californians who served with the Union forces. Likewise, Major Leonides M. Martin commanded the Tenth Texas Cavalry for the Confederate Army. And at least one Latina also took part in the fighting. Loretta Janeta Velazquez, a Cuban-born woman married to a Confederate soldier, reputedly disguised herself as a man, assumed the name of Harry T. Buford, and fought in the battles of Bull Run, Ball's Bluff, and Fort Donelson. After being detected as a woman, she was discharged—only to reenlist and fight at Shiloh before being detected again. The most famous Latino soldier of the Civil War remains Admiral David G. Farragut, the son of American Revolution veteran Jorge Farrugut. The first-ever admiral of the U.S. Navy, he is remembered in history textbooks for having shouted the phrase, "Damn the torpedoes! Full speed ahead!" during a skirmish at Mobile Bay, Alabama, on August 5, 1864. At least three more Latino Civil War veterans deserve mention as well. Philip Bazar (born in Chile), John Ortega (born in Spain), and Joseph H. De Castro all earned the Medal of Honor—the United States's highest award for military valor—for their actions.

When the U.S. military became involved in other nineteenth-century conflicts, Latinos/as continued to be present. During the Spanish-American War in 1898, several Spanish surnames appear among the list of Rough Riders, the First U.S. Volunteer Cavalry under the command of Colonel Leonard Wood and Lieutenant Colonel Theodore Roosevelt. Most notably, Captain Maximiliano Luna served as official interpreter for Colonel Wood after the latter was named military governor of Santiago, Cuba. In a separate conflict on the other side of the globe, Private France Silva, a Latino Marine born in California, earned the Medal of Honor for his actions during the 1900 Boxer Rebellion in China.

Twentieth Century

The United States entered World War I on April 6, 1917, and, over the course of a year and a half, nearly 4.8 million draftees and volunteers from around the country were mobilized into service. Among them were an estimated 200,000 Latinos. Although the majority of these were Mexican Americans, there was a significant Puerto Rican presence as well. Following passage of the Jones Act on March 2, 1917, all Puerto Ricans became U.S. citizens unless they specifically rejected citizenship. Some 18,000 Puerto

Ricans were organized into six segregated infantry regiments that served in military installations on the island and in the Panama Canal Zone. One notable Latino, Private Marcelino Serna, received the Distinguished Service Cross for single-handedly capturing twenty-four German soldiers. Another, David Barkley, was awarded the Medal of Honor posthumously for risking his life above and beyond the call of duty. Oddly, his Latino heritage was not formally recognized until 1989.

World War II proved to be a decisive turning point in the history of Latino participation in the military. Again, precise figures are unavailable, but scholars have estimated that approximately 500,000 Latinos served in the U.S. armed forces following the attack on Pearl Harbor in 1941. As in World War I, the vast majority were of Mexican descent. However, some 65,000 Puerto Ricans also served, including 200 Puerto Rican women in the Women's Army Corps. The total number of Puerto Ricans could have been even higher, for an additional 285,000 volunteers were never called into active duty. Still, the most remarkable statistic is that twelve of the 440 Medals of Honor awarded during the war went to Latino soldiers, making them the most decorated ethnic group in the U.S. armed forces.

Latinos/as continued to show the same willingness to serve and the same type of bravery throughout the Cold War era. During the Korean Conflict in the early 1950s, some 148,000 Latinos/as served in the U.S. military, earning nine of the 131 Medals of Honor awarded. Of the many Latinos/as who served, one group in particular deserves special mention. Puerto Rico's Sixty-fifth Infantry Regiment earned a Presidential Unit Citation, a Meritorious Unit Commendation, two Republic of Korea Presidential Unit Citations, the Gold Bravery Medal of Greece, several Distinguished Service Crosses, and hundreds of Silver Stars and Bronze Stars for valor.

Approximately 80,000 Latinos/as from across the nation served in the military during the United States's decade-long involvement in Vietnam and received thirteen of the 239 Medals of Honor awarded. In more recent conflicts such as Operation Desert Shield/Desert Storm, the Bosnia peacekeeping missions, the campaigns in Afghanistan, and the War in Iraq, Latinos/as have proven to be integral members of the U.S. armed forces at every level. For example, of the 425,000 soldiers deployed during Operation Desert Shield/Desert Storm in 1990–1991, some 20,000 were Latino/a. In the war in Afghanistan (Operation Enduring Freedom), Latino servicemen and servicewomen accounted for roughly 9 percent of all U.S. casualties as of the end of April 2006. In the War in Iraq (Operation Iraqi Freedom), the death toll for Latino soldiers reached 270 (or about 11.3 percent of all casualties) as of the end of April 2006.

Future Trends

Whereas Latinos/as accounted for 4.5 percent of the population in 1970, the figure increased to more than 13 percent by 2000. With Latinos/as continuing to be the fastest-growing minority group in the United States, the trend of increased Latino participation in the military is likely to continue for some time into the future. In 1983, only 4 percent of all new recruits were Latinos/as; by 2000, that number had climbed to 11.3 percent. Recent data suggests there are over 130,000 Latinos/as in the armed forces (including the Coast Guard), accounting for 9 percent of the total. Add to that approximately 70,000 in the reserve forces, and the final sum exceeds 200,000.

Douglas R. Keberlein Gutiérrez

See also: Mexican-American War; Spanish-American War; Treaty of Guadalupe Hidalgo (1848); Vietnam War.

Further Reading

Defense Equal Opportunity Management Institute. *Semiannual Demographic Profile of the Department of Defense and U.S. Coast Guard.* Statistical Series Pamphlet No. 05–1. Washington, DC: U.S. Government Printing Office, published annually.

———. *Twenty-Seven Year Demographic Trends: Active Duty Forces 1977–2004.* Statistical Series Pamphlet No. 04–5. Washington, DC: U.S. Government Printing Office, 2004.

Fischer, Hannah. "United States Military Casualty Statistics: Operation Iraqi Freedom and Operation Enduring Freedom." *CRS Report for Congress,* June 8, 2006.

Office of the Assistant Secretary of Defense. *Population Representation in the Military Services: Fiscal Year.* Washington, DC: U.S. Government Printing Office, published annually.

Rochin, Refugio I., and Lionel Fernández. *U.S. Latino Patriots: From the American Revolution to Afghanistan, An Overview.* Pew Hispanic Center, 2002. Available at http://pewhispanic.org.

United States Office of the Deputy Assistant Secretary of Defense for Military Manpower and Personnel Policy. *Hispanics in America's Defense.* Washington, DC: U.S. Government Printing Office, 1990.

Miscegenation

Miscegenation refers to marriage, cohabitation, or sexual relations between people of different racial categories. The term itself falsely implies that racial categories are based on real biological differences and that interracial relationships are therefore socially or biologically abnormal. The idea of miscegenation was invented during the colonial period of American history as a means of maintaining white privilege. Antimiscegenation legislation continued to prohibit interracial marriages and sexual relations in most states until the U.S. Supreme Court ruling in the case of *Loving v. Virginia* (1967) deemed such laws unconstitutional. While most miscegenation laws specifically prohibited black-white marriage and sexual relations, some states extended them to prohibit marriages between whites and Native Americans, Asian Americans, and Latinos/as as well.

Miscegenation in the United States

Miscegenation specifically refers to the "race-mixing" that results from interracial sexual relations, but from its inception, U.S. antimiscegenation legislation has primarily regulated interracial marriage. There are a number of reasons for this. When antimiscegenation laws were first written in the seventeenth century, sexual relations between males of Anglo-American slaveholding families and their female slaves were common and widespread, so keeping the legislation confined to interracial marriage allowed Anglo-American males to continue sexually exploiting their female slaves without fear of punishment. Second, the entire purpose of the legislation was to secure and protect Anglo-American privilege by preventing other groups from attaining social or economic status. By specifically addressing issues related to marriage and inheritance, antimiscegenation legislation tacitly sanctioned interracial sexual relations but prevented non-Anglo participants and any resultant illegitimate progeny from advancing themselves socially or economically.

The United States is the only nation in the world to have ever prohibited interracial marriage. Although the term "miscegenation" was not invented until 1864, legislation restricting marriage and sexual relations along racial lines dates back to the General Assembly of the Colony of Maryland in 1661. Intent on forging a legal system that would maintain European privilege while preventing people of color from attaining wealth and status, the assembly passed a law stating that if a white woman married a "negro," their children would be considered slaves who, along with their mother, would be required to serve their father's master for the remainder of his life. In 1691, Virginia passed similar legislation, followed by Massachusetts in 1705, North Carolina in 1715, and Pennsylvania in 1725. These laws predated the biological constructions of race that would rise to prominence in the decades surrounding the American Revolution, and were enacted to maintain an unequal social order rather than to avoid the not yet imagined dangers of racial mixing.

The first widespread discussion of interracial sex in U.S. history occurred in 1802, when Thomas Jefferson's political opponents alleged that he had fornicated with one of his female slaves, Sally Hemings. In the decades that followed, literary and pictorial depictions of interracial marriage and sexual relations, published by anti-abolitionists, aided the construction of racial stereotypes in the United States by portraying people of color as physically and socially inferior to "Anglos." In the 1840s, influenced by growing public opinion, scientists began arguing that "Negroes" and "Anglos" originated from completely separate species, elevating racial mixing from the realm of social unacceptability to being a violation of the very laws of nature. At the same time, the Mexican-American War sparked widespread anti-Mexican fervor in the United States. Mexicans, just like Irish, African American, and Chinese populations, were deemed racially inferior to Anglos, and states with significant Mexican populations extended their antimiscegenation laws to include them as well.

In 1864, "miscegenation" replaced "amalgamation" as the term used to refer to racial mixture when it appeared in an anonymous pamphlet titled, "Miscegenation: The Theory of the Blending of the Races, Applied to the American White Man and Negro." The pamphlet claimed to be the work of radical Republican abolitionists, but in fact it was an attempt by Democrats to scare voters by depicting a future American society controlled by blacks and mulattoes where whites were the slaves and servants. By the end of the Civil War, miscegenation, and the biological notions of race it implied, had become firmly rooted in American culture.

Eugenics

At the turn of the twentieth century, race theorists had convinced American and European societies that biologically distinct "races" were an evolutionary reality. They argued that the "Anglo race" was superior to all others in terms of both intellectual and physical ability and that efforts should be made to prevent its degeneration by prohibiting miscegenation. Their ideas about race and human evolution were extremely misguided, however, because they based their research on Mendelian laws of genetic inheritance, which they erroneously applied to human populations. Thus, they explained everything from criminality to poverty to promiscuity as the result of "bad genes." Humanity would be much better off, they argued, if these polluting genes could be bred out of existence.

To achieve this end, they devised the pseudoscience of eugenics. Funded by wealthy industrialists and government agencies, the eugenics movement aimed to improve the course of human evolution by encouraging the "well bred" to procreate, while simultaneously preventing "undesirables" from marrying and reproducing. In the United States, eugenics programs led to the involuntary sterilization of more than 60,000 citizens. Nazi Germany would take eugenics to the extreme, exterminating over 6 million Jews, Gypsies, homosexuals, and mentally disabled persons in the pursuit of racial purity. The discovery of the Nazi concentration camps was not enough to end involuntary sterilization programs in the United States, but it did inspire an anti-fascist, anti-racist rhetoric that made antimiscegenation legislation seem decidedly "un-American." Lawyers began challenging state laws restricting interracial sex and marriage, but pressure from segregationists in the South kept the U.S. Supreme Court from considering the constitutionality of antimiscegenation laws.

Perez v. Sharp

In 1948, California became the first state to rule antimiscegenation legislation unconstitutional. Andrea Perez, a woman of Mexican descent, filed a lawsuit against a Los Angeles county clerk who refused to issue a marriage license to her and her African American fiancé, Sylvester Davis. Los Angeles had one of the highest rates of interracial marriage in the country, with just under half of all Mexican marriages involving interracial couples. However, because Perez was legally classified as white, the clerk refused to issue her and Davis a marriage license.

Perez's lawyers argued that the state antimiscegenation laws were unconstitutional since they violated her right to equal protection under the law. The state had violated Perez's individual right to marry but not the rights of other white citizens who could marry whomever they wanted. They also claimed that the laws violated Perez's religious freedom since she and Davis were devout Roman Catholics and the church did not forbid interracial marriage. In a landmark decision, the court ruled in favor of Perez. California repealed its antimiscegenation laws shortly thereafter, but it would be another twenty years before the U.S. Supreme Court finally addressed the issue.

Loving v. Virginia

The *Loving v. Virginia* case of 1967 brought an end to antimiscegenation laws in the United States. In June 1958, Mildred Jeter and Richard Loving were married in Washington, D.C., and moved to Virginia shortly thereafter. In October 1958, a grand jury issued an indictment charging them with violating state antimiscegenation laws; the following June, the Lovings pleaded guilty and were sentenced to a year in prison. The decision of the state court judge embodied the biological constructions of racial difference born in the eighteenth and nineteenth centuries that continued to pervade American culture: "Almighty God created the races white, black, yellow, malay, and red and he placed them on separate continents. And but for the interference with His arrangement there would be no cause for such marriages. The fact that He separated the races shows that He did not intend for the races to mix." The judge agreed to suspend the Lovings' sentence on the condition that they leave Virginia and not return for twenty-five years. The couple refused to leave and instead took their case all the way to the U.S. Supreme Court, which ruled in their favor in 1967. The majority found that Virginia's laws violated the Equal Protection Clause of the Fourteenth Amendment because they rested "solely upon distinctions drawn according to race."

Legacy

Although antimiscegenation legislation ended some four decades ago, the specter of miscegenation still looms large in the American popular imagination. According to the 2000 Census, only 2 percent of all marriages in the United States can be considered interracial. While this is significantly higher than the 1960 figure of 0.4 percent, it shows that race remains a powerful factor when choosing one's spouse. However, race is much less of a factor for Latinos/as than for other U.S. minority groups. Because, historically, miscegenation theory and legislation were aimed primarily at restricting black-white marriage and sexual relations, Latinos/as have been much less affected by its legacy. Native-born Latinos/as are more likely to marry native-born whites than Asians or African Americans. Similarly, native-born whites are ten times more likely to marry Latinos/as than African Americans and twice as likely to marry Latinos/as than to marry Asians.

Paleontology and evolutionary biology have definitively proven that at no point in human history have separate, pure, biologically distinct races in geographic isolation from one another ever existed. Human populations have always intermingled. During the colonial period in North America, certain sexual and marital relationships were deemed "interracial," assigned a negative social stigma, and prohibited by law as part of a political scheme to prevent people of color from upsetting the social order, which in North America was based on Anglo-European supremacy. The process of racial mixing that miscegenation is meant to describe is a historical construction, not a biological reality.

Bretton T. Alvaré

See also: Race.

Further Reading

Gordon, Albert. *Intermarriage.* Boston: Beacon, 1964.

Lemire, Elise. *Miscegenation: Making Race in America.* Philadelphia: University of Pennsylvania Press, 2002.

Lubin, Alex. "'What's Love Got to do With It?' The Politics of Race and Marriage in the California Supreme Court's 1948 *Perez v. Sharp* Decision." *OAH Magazine of History* 18:4 (July 2004): 31–34.

Provine, William B. "Genetics and the Biology of Race Crossing." In *Mixed Race Studies,* ed. by Jayne O. Ifekwunigwe. New York: Routledge, 2004.

Raimon, Eva Allegra. *The "Tragic Mulatta" Revisited: Race and Nationalism in Nineteenth-Century Antislavery Fiction.* New Brunswick, NJ: Rutgers University Press, 2004.

Root, Maria P.P. "Within, Between, and Beyond Race." In *Mixed Race Studies,* ed. Jayne O. Ifekwunigwe. New York: Routledge, 2004.

Moraga, Cherríe (1952–)

Born on September 25, 1952, in Whittier, California, Cherríe Moraga emerged in the 1980s as one of the leading Chicana poets, playwrights, and feminist activists of her time. Having grown up in a mixed-race, working-class family in Whittier, she produced works that were shaped by the race and gender dynamics of her family and her neighborhood. Today she is known for the connections she makes in her creative work between sex and race, her development of the concept and hopes for a Queer Aztlán, and her scripting of plays that bring together issues of family, labor rights, sexuality, and Chicana power. Moraga has written several books, coedited anthologies, and written numerous plays. Her most influential works, however, remain some of her earliest: *This Bridge Called My Back* (1981), which was subtitled *Writings by Radical Women of Color,* is a feminist anthology she coedited with Gloria Anzaldúa; *Loving in the War Years* (1983) is an original work.

This Bridge Called My Back began as an attempt to speak back to white feminists, but quickly became something more. In the words of Moraga and Gloria Anzaldúa, "What began as a reaction to the racism of white feminists soon became an affirmation of women of color to our own feminism." The text included a number of essays that became classics, revolutionizing women across generations. Audre Lord's "The Master's Tools Will Never Dismantle the Master's House," for example, boldly claims that if women of color were to change the world, they must reject the violent competition that the dominant society takes for granted. Merl Woo's "Letter to Ma" and the Combahee River Collective's "Black Feminist Statement," also included in the volume, argue that the experiences of women of color provide them with unique knowledge and that what they experience every day provides tools for social transformation.

Loving in the War Years is a very different volume, and Moraga's own. A collection of poetry, coming-of-age stories, family history, and political theory woven together in a nonlinear narrative of resistance, it addresses lesbian Chicanas struggling to survive in a racist, homophobic, misogynist society. The poem "Loving in the War Years," for example, draws attention to the daily violence faced by lesbians of color, and "Pesadilla" argues that sometimes love is not enough—that the daily violence visited on lesbians of color sometimes crushes them, their families, and their relationships. Other essays in the book, such as the now famous "Long Line of Vendidas," draw on and challenge stories and histories that have been used to oppress Chicanas, including ones from the Chicano community itself. *Loving in the War Years* was the first explicitly Chicana lesbian volume published in the United States.

The daughter of a Chicana mother and Anglo father, Moraga could often pass for white. Her development was shaped by the experiences of her family—the other members of which could not pass for white—and by observing the differences in the way teachers treated her and the way they treated darker Chicanao/as. After earning her Bachelor of Arts degree from San Francisco State University in 1974, Moraga went on to teach high school and to take creative writing classes at the Women's Building in Los Angeles, founded by and for the women of Los Angeles for mutual support and empowerment. It was at the Women's Building that Moraga began to write poetry from both a lesbian and a Chicana point of view. In the late 1970s, she moved to the Bay Area to study for a master's degree in feminist studies at San Francisco State University. It was at that time that she began, with Gloría Anzaldúa, to compile and edit *This Bridge Called My Back.*

The 1980s were a watershed for Moraga and for Chicana literature. The publication of *This Bridge Called My Back* marked a particular turning point in publishing for women of color, as it was followed by a flurry of publications. In 1986, it received the prestigious Before Columbus Foundation American Book Award, a national literary award that acknowledges artistic excellence and seeks to promote multicultural literature. During this time, Moraga also cofounded the Kitchen Table Press, a New York collective dedicated to the empowerment of women of color in the works that it chose to publish and in its day-to-day operations. For the next twenty years, Kitchen Table Press continued to publish cutting-edge writing by women of color, including Barbara Smith's *Home Girls* (1983) and Mitsuye Yamada's *Desert Run* (1989).

Moraga later became known for her dramatic works and the concept of Queer Aztlán. Among her several plays performed throughout the United States are *Shadow of a Man* (1988) and *Giving Up the Ghost: Teatro in Two Acts* (1984). Queer Aztlán derives from the legendary ancestral home of the Aztec people somewhere north of Mexico City, perhaps in what is now the American Southwest. Aztlán is the dream of a better place, a brown country where community is valued over individualism and where Anglo violence is banished. The traditional concept of

Aztlán, as Moraga understood it, was an inherently patriarchal space, a land of brotherhood where women are an afterthought and there is no place for brown gays and lesbians. The idea of a Queer Aztlán, which Moraga explores in such works as *The Last Generation* (1993), a collection of poems and essays, and her play *The Hungry Woman* (2001), is a similarly idealized home, a place of safety, belonging, and freedom to express one's identity as a Latina lesbian.

Cherríe Moraga has been the recipient of a National Endowment for the Arts Theatre Playwright's Fellowship and a Fund for New American Plays Award from the Kennedy Center for the Performing Arts. In 2001 she received a Scholar's Award from the National Association for Chicana and Chicano Studies, acknowledging her influence in the field and her commitment to justice in U.S. society at large and in the queer and Chicana communities. Her work is read in women's centers and in Chicana and women's studies classrooms throughout the nation, and a new generation of Chicana scholars, among them Yvonne Yarbro-Bejarano and Paula M. Moya, has begun to critique and to build upon her work. Moraga's writings have helped move Chicana studies and women's studies in new directions, articulating the unique struggles of a generation of queer Chicanas.

Linda Heidenreich

See also: Chicanisma; Chicano/a; Feminism.

Further Reading

Ikas, Karin Rosa. *Chicana Ways: Conversations with Ten Chicana Writers.* Reno: University of Nevada Press, 2002.

Moraga, Cherríe. *Loving in the War Years: lo que nunca pasó por sus labios.* 1983. Cambridge, MA: South End, 2000.

Moraga, Cherríe, and Gloria E. Anzaldúa, eds. *This Bridge Called My Back: Writings by Radical Women of Color.* 1981. Berkeley, CA: Women of Color, 2002.

Moya, Paula. "Postmodernism, Realism, and the Politics of Identity." In *Feminist Genealogies, Colonial Legacies, Democratic Futures.* New York: Routledge, 1997.

Yarbro-Bejarano, Yvonne. "De-constructing the Lesbian Body: Cherríe Moraga's *Loving in the War Years.*" In *Chicana Lesbians: The Girls Our Mothers Warned Us About.* Berkeley, CA: Third Woman, 1991.

Morales, Iris (?–)

A community activist, lawyer, educator, and documentary filmmaker, Iris Morales has spent her life working for the establishment of social and economic justice for the poor, women, and people of color. As a leader of the Puerto Rican nationalist group the Young Lords (YLs) and later as an organizer of grassroots service and support organizations, she has been a driving force behind efforts to empower and provide opportunities for the Hispanic community.

A native of New York City, Iris Morales was the first child of immigrant parents, who came to the United States during the Puerto Rican migration of the 1940s. Her father, a former sugarcane cutter, worked as an elevator operator in New York hotels; her mother worked in the garment industry as a sewing machine operator. As the eldest child, Iris became the translator, interpreter, and negotiator for her parents and other Puerto Rican families in the community. She would accompany the adults to hospitals, schools, and government offices to serve as an intermediary in obtaining medical treatment, Social Security benefits, welfare, workers' compensation, and other services. These activities provided a first-hand view of how immigrants—especially the poor, people of color, and persons who did not speak English—were treated by official institutions.

Living in New York City during the 1960s exposed her even more to the social injustices experienced by minorities in the United States and made her more politically active. While still a teenager, she attended youth meetings of the Student Nonviolent Coordinating Committee (SNCC) and the National Association for the Advancement of Colored People (NAACP) and marched against the Vietnam War. She also studied African American history and the teachings of Malcolm X. After graduating from high school, she became a tenant rights organizer with the West Side Block Organization in New York City, a group of Columbia University students and community members who advocated for better housing conditions.

Even as she dedicated her energies to empowering disenfranchised communities through organizing, education remained important to Iris and her family. In 1965, she enrolled in the City College of New York (CCNY), where she studied political science and economics. At the time, City College did not offer any Latino/Puerto Rican studies courses and had no Puerto Rican or Latino on-campus organizations. This led Morales to join ONYX, an African American student organization, and to study Latino history informally with other students. As the number of Puerto Ricans on campus increased, however, she helped organize CCNY's first Puerto Rican group, called Puerto Ricans in Student Action. She also continued her community work, teaching at the Academy for Black and Latin Education, a storefront school that offered an alternative way for young people to complete their high school equivalency diploma; participating in the cultural activities in Harlem; and helping to produce a play performed by the East Harlem Gut Theater, a Puerto Rican street performance theater group. In 1968, Morales joined a busload of Latinos/as and African Americans on a trip through the Midwest to the Crusade for Justice Conference in Denver, Colorado, where she met José "Cha Cha" Jimenez and other members of the Young Lords of Chicago, a Puerto Rican street gang that had transformed itself into a group advocating social justice, political action, and basic human rights for all Americans.

When a New York branch of the YLs formed the following year, Iris joined the group and remained a member until 1975. She immersed herself in the work of the organization, focusing on a medical testing program for Puerto Ricans in New York, promoting Puerto Rican independence, and organizing educational conferences. She also played an instrumental role in the Young Lords' effort to take over a church in Spanish Harlem that would not provide space for a free breakfast program for welfare mothers. The church was transformed into a community resource where food, clothing, and medical care could be obtained. As a leader of the YLs, she served as deputy minister of education and minister of information, and became one of the primary feminist influences in the organization. She advocated successfully for the addition of women to the Central Committee, the governing body of the organization, and helped form the Woman's Union, an organization of Latinas devoted to child care and health issues.

In 1972, the Young Lords reconstituted itself as the Puerto Rican Revolutionary Workers Organization, resulting in greater adherence to Maoist principles, a focus on interracial coalition-building as part of a global working-class revolution, and the establishment of a branch in Puerto Rico. Morales joined with a faction of other YL members who opposed the name change and shift in ideology, which she believed detracted from the organization's ability to help Puerto Ricans struggling in New York City. The Central Committee considered their opposition a violation of the organization's principles and, in an effort to distance the dissenters from one another, sent them to different branches outside New York. Morales was sent to Philadelphia, where she worked from 1972 to 1974. She helped organize the Philadelphia membership against police brutality and racism, and united them with such other activist groups as the Black Panther Party and the I Wor Kuen, an organization of Chinese American activists. Returning to New York and demoralized by the infighting, she resigned from the Puerto Rican Revolutionary Workers Organization in 1975.

Morales attended New York University law school, where she was a Root-Tilden scholar, and graduated in 1979. Nine years later, a group of former YL members held a meeting and discussed the importance of studying the organization's history. Morales took the lead in producing a video about the YLs' experience, founded the Latino Education Network Service, and became the producer-writer-director of *¡Palante, Siempre Palante! The Young Lords,* a historical documentary. The film was broadcast nationally on public television in 1996 and has been used as an educational and organizing tool by grassroots organizers in the years since.

Channeling her experience as an activist, attorney, and organizer, Morales in the early 1990s cofounded and directed the New Educational Opportunities Network, a nonprofit organization providing media and educational services to minority youths. In 1996, she became the director of education programs for the Puerto Rican Legal Defense and Education Fund. And in 1997, she became director of the New York Networks for School Renewal (NYNSR), which promoted the establishment of small public schools. While at the NYNSR, Morales helped found the Coalition of Latinos/as for the Advancement of Visionary Education, organizing educators and parents to advocate for the public education needs of Latino children and their families, and providing training workshops for parent groups in low-income neighborhoods. Since 1998, she has continued her work in community activism as director of the Union Square Awards, which provides funding and support to grassroots activists in local communities throughout New York City.

Joann E. Donatiello

See also: Education; Puerto Ricans; Women; Young Lords.

Further Reading

López, Adalberto, ed. *The Puerto Ricans, Their History, Culture and Society.* Cambridge, MA: Schenkman, 1980.

Morales, Iris. "¡Palante, Siempre Palante! The Young Lords." In *The Puerto Rican Movement: Voices from the Diaspora,* ed. Andrés Torres and José E. Velázquez. Philadelphia: Temple University Press, 1998.

The Young Lords Party and Michael Abramson. *Palante: Young Lords Party.* New York: McGraw-Hill, 1971.

Moreno, Rita
(1931–)

Rita Moreno, a Puerto Rican actress and singer, is the only Latino entertainer to have won the four most prestigious awards in American music, film, and stage performance—the Emmy, Tony, Oscar, and Grammy.

She was born Rosa Dolores Alverio on December 11, 1931. Although she was born to rural farmers in Humacao, Puerto Rico, by an early age she was already working in show business. By the time she was eleven, Moreno was dubbing Spanish voice-overs for American films. She made her debut on Broadway two years later, costarring with Eli Wallach in *Skydrift* (1945) and earning stellar reviews for her performance. Still, despite the praise, Moreno found difficulty securing additional roles.

Her signing with the movie studio MGM in 1946 not only resulted in greater opportunity, but also precipitated her transformation from Rosa Dolores Alverio to "Rita Moreno" (a more marketable figure). Still, she found herself limited to stereotypical roles such as an Indian maiden or "hot-blooded" Latinas. Finally in 1956, she ventured into new territory, playing Tuptim in the film version of *The King and I.* She received outstanding reviews for her passionate portrayal of the literate slave who befriends Anna (a schoolteacher who had recently moved to Siam to teach English). However, it was not until her performance as Anita in the film version of *West Side Story* (1961), some twenty-five films later, that Moreno became a star. Her performance earned an Oscar for best supporting actress at the 1962 Academy Awards. And while *West Side Story* was a cultural landmark— the first mainstream feature film portraying Puerto Ricans—Moreno was the only actual Puerto Rican to play a major role.

In 1962, Moreno moved to London and was featured in Hal Prince's stage production of *She Loves Me.* After returning to New York, she won a Grammy Award in 1972 for her work on the Electric Company Album, based on a popular comedy-variety television show that attempted to teach basic reading to children between the ages of seven and ten.

Moreno earned a Tony Award for best supporting or featured actress (dramatic) for her 1975 stage performance in *The Ritz,* a comedic mob farce in which she played bathhouse entertainer Googie Gomez; she also starred in the 1976 film version. Now a mainstream star and a household name, Moreno went on to receive an Emmy Award in 1977 for a guest appearance in an episode of "The Muppet Show" and again in 1978 for a role in "The Rockford Files." In 1995, at the unveiling of her star on the Hollywood Walk of Fame, Moreno dropped to her knees and began to weep, admitting later that she had been dreaming of that moment since the age of six. In 2004, President George W. Bush awarded her the Presidential Medal of Freedom, the highest civilian honor in the United States.

Although Moreno's performances have earned much critical acclaim as well as honors and awards, they have also been the source of criticism. Some have criticized Moreno for perpetuating stereotypes of Latinas. Yet others seem to understand Moreno's place in history, acknowledging the times and societal conditions in which she forged her career, and accepting her stereotypical roles as symptomatic of the limited opportunities that existed for women of color in Hollywood and in American popular culture as a whole.

Dinorah Caridad Nieves

See also: Film; Music; *West Side Story* (1957, 1961).

Further Reading

Gerner, Fawn. *Hard Won Wisdom: Today's Extraordinary Women Mentor You to Find Self-Awareness, Balance, and Perspective.* New York: Berkeley, 2001

Stone, Deborah. *Rita Moreno.* Castro Valley, CA: Quercas, 1990

Suntree, Susan. *Hispanics of Achievement: Rita Moreno.* New York: Chelsea House, 1992.

Mothers of East L.A.

Mothers of East L.A., or Madres del Este de Los Angeles-Santa Isabel (MELA-SI), is a grassroots organization of women in Santa Isabel, California, whose activist work aims to raise awareness about injustices facing the community. Its self-declared goals and objectives cover a broad range of issues, all of which focus on the empowerment of families within the Latino community: "To promote the environmental, political, and educational awareness, advancement, and well-being of the Latino population within (but not limited to) the East Los Angeles community." The organization describes itself as follows:

> Not economically rich, but culturally wealthy, Mothers of East L.A. works for the empowerment of Latinos/as within their East Los Angeles community and beyond. Not politically powerful, but socially conscious; not mainstream educated, but armed with the knowledge, commitment, and determination that only a mother can possess.

The Mothers of East L.A. was organized in 1984 as part of a campaign to challenge the construction of a prison in the Boyle Heights neighborhood of the city. After knocking on doors and calling a meeting

Organizer Juana Gutiérrez (at microphone) and other members of the community activist group Mothers of East L.A. conduct a 1992 press conference on water conservation, one of a number of local environmental and social issues this group has addressed. *(Mothers of East Los Angeles Papers. Urban Archives Center. Oviatt Library. California State University, Northridge)*

to discuss the impact of the proposed prison, neighborhood resident Juana Gutiérrez and other Neighborhood Watch captains began organizing the Mothers of East L.A. Not only did the organization successfully block the building of the proposed prison in the Boyles Heights neighborhood, but it also successfully lobbied the city government to pass a bill banning the construction of any prisons within Los Angeles County.

The initial success inspired subsequent activist efforts on the part of the MELA-SI, including a campaign against municipal city decisions regarding the location of public waste facilities. The group contended that the plans constituted environmental racism, because they called for the location of potentially harmful facilities in neighborhoods inhabited by Latinos/as and other people of color. MELA-SI's protest efforts focused specifically on a number of projects: the construction of a municipal waste incinerator and an oil pipeline three feet below an East Los Angeles junior high school, a chemical treatment plant across the street from one of the largest high schools in the Los Angeles Unified School District, two more incinerators, and a dump site.

The success of MELA-SI activities has been partly a function of coalitions with other organizations and constituencies. For example, it joined forces with students from Huntington High School in 1989 to stop the construction of a plant that would have treated hazardous chemicals in close proximity to several schools. MELA-SI also employs high school students in its Lead Poison Awareness Program and its Graffiti Abatement Program, while maintaining a scholarship fund that assists continuing college students with aid ranging from $300 to $1,000.

The Mothers of East L.A. employs a variety of tactics in the effort to reach across geographic, ethnic, and class lines within the community. These tactics include door-to-door educational campaigns, picketing, coalitions with churches and other organizations within the community, lobbying city and state government, media campaigns, and candlelight vigils. Most of all, it has dedicated itself to keeping government institutions accountable to local citizens, protecting East Los Angeles from environmental hazards and political corruption. In addition, as an organization that promotes environmental, political, and educational awareness, MELA-SI also supports the advancement and well-being of Latinos/as across the United States through protests, get-out-the-vote campaigns, lobbying, a biannual newsletter, and educational programs that provide information to Latinos/as on important social issues, politics, or specific concerns within local communities.

While MELA-SI has remained focused on empowering East Los Angeles, its influence has been felt in other communities as well. The Graffiti Abatement Program is internationally known, and the water conservation program has provided a model for similar efforts in seventeen U.S. cities as well as in South Africa. In this program, low-flush toilets are given to customers, reducing the water usage and saving thousands of gallons of water every year. The old toilets are recycled, and the money is used to fund other programs.

Sarah Hentges

See also: East Los Angeles.

Further Reading

Minkoff, Debra C. *Organizing for Equality: The Evolution of Women's and Racial-Ethnic Organizations in America, 1955–1985.* Arnold and Caroline Rose Monograph Series of the American Sociological Association. Newark, NJ: Rutgers University Press, 1995.

Pardo, Mary S. *Mexican American Women Activists: Identity and Resistance in Two Los Angeles Communities.* Philadelphia: Temple University Press, 1998.

Movimiento Estudiantíl Chicano de Aztlán

Established in 1969 at the University of California, Santa Barbara, Movimiento Estudiantíl Chicano de Aztlán (Chicano Student Movement of Aztlán, or MEChA) is a national organization that works to promote Chicano unity and empowerment through political action and education. Today there are more than 400 MEChA chapters in high schools, colleges, and universities throughout the United States, especially in the Southwest and Midwest.

Roots

MEChA traces its origin to the Chicano Movement of the late 1960s and early 1970s, which sought political empowerment and civil rights for Mexican Americans. In March 1969, students from across the Southwest and Midwest assembled in Denver, Colorado, for the First National Chicano Youth Liberation Conference, convened by activist Rodolfo "Corky" Gonzales. Conference participants adopted *El Plan Espiritual de Aztlán* (the Spiritual Plan of Aztlán), a manifesto for the cause of Chicano activism and identity. A few weeks later, in April 1969, the Chicano Coordinating Council on Higher Education (CCCHE), a collective of students, faculty, staff, and community leaders, met at the University of California, Santa Barbara, and drew up a comprehensive blueprint for implementing the concepts articulated in El Plan Espiritual de Aztlán, through higher education and political action. The latter document became known as El Plan de Santa Barbara. Although the name Movimiento Estudiantil Chicano de Aztlán was already in use by a few local student groups, conference attendees officially adopted the name MEChA and were charged with ensuring compliance with the goals of the plan.

El Plan de Santa Barbara expressed the frustrations of Chicanos/as over decades of inequality and exclusion from the democratic promises of the United States and from the protections of the Treaty of Guadalupe Hidalgo, signed in 1848 at the end of the Mexican-American War. The Santa Barbara manifesto also expressed the hope and militancy necessary to create social change to rectify lifetimes of injustice. Chicanos/as at the conference considered education and community development to be the most pressing needs.

Education had long been regarded by the Mexican American community as a primary avenue of personal enrichment and community advancement. Thus, MEChA called upon those in higher education to provide leadership and mentoring to enhance the accessibility and success of young members of the Mexican American community, and to increase the number of educated and socially active Chicanos/as. Leadership came in the form of the Educational Opportunity Program (EOP), for example, which benefited not only Chicanos/as, but also other disadvantaged groups excluded from higher education and the opportunities it opened up.

El Plan de Santa Barbara also created a master plan for Chicano curriculum, as it was deemed insufficient to have more people in higher education without changing the content of instruction to reflect the diverse histories and life experiences of ethnic American groups. MEChA chapters across the country helped create Chicano studies programs and departments in colleges, universities, and high schools, including California State University at Northridge (CSUN) in 1969, the University of California at Santa Barbara (UCSB) in 1971, and the University of Texas at El Paso (UTEP) in 1972. Student members also actively promoted the hiring of Chicano faculty and staff for the classroom and support services.

The organization went beyond higher education as well, promoting leadership in Latino communities, or barrios, and devising programs to enlist the help and resources of schools and universities. Thus, students in MEChA served as a bridge between existing educational and community organizations, establishing and expanding Chicano social networks. Political awareness and participation was another

primary goal articulated in El Plan de Santa Barbara, leading in 1970 to the formation of La Raza Unida Party, a Chicano political organization that won important electoral victories in the early 1970s. MEChA raised awareness of Chicano issues and promoted political action through organized walkouts, sit-ins, self-education programs, community meetings, and voter-registration drives. It trained young people in organization and leadership, helping them graduate from college and assume active roles in the community.

Organizational Growth and Challenges

MEChA has gone through alternating periods of success and decline. In the 1980s, like other organizations of the Chicano Movement, such as the United Farm Workers (UFW), MEChA suffered a drop-off in overall membership as well as the visibility and viability of individual chapters. Much like La Raza Unida Party, which split over ideological differences of separatism versus assimilation, MEChA students fought internally about strategy and philosophy, debating levels of militancy, nationalism, and Marxism, and the speed at which to demand change.

MEChA's popularity surged again in the early 1990s, however, as young people studying Chicano history came to recognize that many of the problems that had given rise to the activist movement of the previous generation were still present: high student drop-out rates; high student push-out rates (those who are counseled or forced out of school prior to graduation); police brutality in the barrios; and socioeconomic inequality. Older Chicano activists joined younger counterparts in the 1990s in becoming more radicalized and militant after the complacency of the previous decade.

A number of events in the early 1990s reminded Chicanos/as that persistent vigilance was necessary to maintain the civil and human rights gains of the Chicano Movement. In the intellectual climate of the times, Chicano studies was labeled as an exercise in "political correctness" and identity politics, devoid of academic merit and rigor. Meanwhile, eugenicist ideologies resurfaced in discussion of the intelligence "bell curve," suggesting that Chicanos/as were racially inferior and unsuited to higher education. In April 1992, Los Angeles erupted in race riots following the videotaped beating of African American motorist Rodney King and the acquittal of the police officers who committed the beating, highlighting ethnic tensions in the city and the socioeconomic results of exclusion and inequality.

Also in the early 1990s, the MEChA chapter at the University of California at Los Angeles (UCLA) protested an attempt by the administration to eliminate the school's Chicano studies program. After a three-year struggle by MEChA members, Mexican American activists, and other community leaders, including a student hunger strike in 1993, UCLA established the César E. Chávez Center for Interdisciplinary Instruction in Chicana/o Studies, which gave rise to a full-fledged academic department in 2004.

MEChA Today

In the twenty-first century, MEChA has faced attacks from conservatives. In his book *The Death of the West* (2002), conservative politician and commentator Pat Buchanan singled out MEChA as an organization of hatred, exclusion, and "brown supremacy." During the 2003 California gubernatorial recall campaign pitting incumbent Gray Davis against Arnold Schwarzenegger and Lieutenant Governor Cruz Bustamante, a Latino, conservative pundits criticized Bustamante for being a member of MEChA when he was a student at Fresno State, including suggestions that he was involved in a militant Chicano plot to take over the state. In 2005, Los Angeles mayoral candidate Antonio Villaraigosa, seeking to avoid the same fate as Bustamante, renounced his leadership of a MEChA chapter while a student at UCLA.

Despite its critics and internal struggles, MEChA has remained a vital and successful part of the continuing Chicano struggle for civil and human rights. Although the organization has been the subject of government surveillance and membership has become a disadvantage for anyone seeking public office, young people continue to join and work on behalf of their own opportunities and their communities. Each year, statewide and national MEChA conferences attract thousands of young Chicanos/as, as well as other ethnic students who seek to promote education and political activism as means of actualizing social change.

Susan Marie Green

See also: Aztlán; Chicano/a; Chicano Movement; Chicano Studies; Gonzales, Rodolfo "Corky"; La Raza; La Raza Unida Party; Mexican American Student Association; Plan de Santa Barbara, El; Plan Espiritual de Aztlán, El.

Further Reading

Acuña, Rodolfo. *Occupied America: A History of Chicanos.* 5th ed. New York: Pearson Longman, 2004.

MEChA. http://www.nationalmecha.org.

Muñoz, Carlos, Jr. *Youth, Identity, Power: The Chicano Movement.* New York: Verso, 1989.

Mujeres Activas en Letras y Cambio Social

Mujeres Activas en Letras y Cambio Social (Women Active in Letters and Social Change, or MALCS), an organization dedicated to Chicana/Latina women in higher education, was founded in 1983 at the University of California, Berkeley (UC Berkeley). Its goals include recruiting and supporting Latinas in higher education and advanced studies; developing and strengthening regional and local chapters to involve Latinas at all levels of the educational ladder; encouraging and promoting the distribution of research on Latinas; and promoting the development and institutionalization of Latina studies classes and departments. MALCS membership is open to all Chicanas, Latinas, and Native American women working toward the support, education, and dissemination of Latina and Native American women's issues, including faculty, staff, graduate students, undergraduates, and community members.

Although Latinas were active in the civil rights movement of the 1960s and the Chicano movement of the mid-1960s and early 1970s, they were rarely given equal standing with men in either one. "Sensing a collective loss of voice, feeling highly isolated, eager to extend their knowledge to other women, and desiring to change society's perceptions," according to the group's official history, a group of Chicana/Latina academics gathered at UC Davis in April 1982. The group established an informal organization at the meeting, declaring the official formation of MALCS a year later at the Berkeley campus. From the outset, members dedicated themselves to unifying their collective aims as Latina/Chicana academics through community activism.

"We are the daughters of Chicano working-class families involved in higher education," declared MALCS's founding declaration. "We were raised in labor camps and barrios, where sharing our resources was the basis of survival. . . . Our purpose is to fight the race, class, and gender oppression we have experienced in the universities. Further, we reject the separation of scholarship and community involvement."

The new organization welcomed the participation of Chicanas supportive of its values and its efforts to create a professional and support network, a space to share scholarship, and a place to strategize scholarly and community activism. Its insistence on maintaining a connection between the academy and the community, between scholarship and activism, was grounded in both the Chicano Movement and the women's movement. MALCS drew on both sources in the creation of its unique response to sexism and racism against Chicanas/Latinas.

Although MALCS remains active into the twenty-first century, its mission and *declaración* have changed, reflecting the more prominent Chicana/Latina identity in higher education specifically and society in general. According to the mission statement in use since 1991, MALCS is an "organization of Chicanas/Latinas and Native American women working in academia and in community settings with a common goal: to work toward the support, education and dissemination of Chicana/Latina and Native American women's issues." Thus, one of the aspects of the organization that has changed from the early days is the notion that members are united in class background and experience, and that Chicanas are inherently equivalent to Latinas in general. Another shift in emphasis seen in the revised declaration is the explicit connection between Chicana/Latina heritage and Native American heritage. Members of the latter group are welcomed as equal participants in the organization (even if not heavily represented in some chapters).

With headquarters in Berkeley, MALCS encourages the formation of local chapters—which by the early 2000s included an area chapter in San Antonio, Texas, and two in greater Los Angeles—one at the University of California at Los Angeles (UCLA) and one at California State University at Los Angeles (CSULA). All official MALCS documents and conference papers are archived at UCLA.

The organization began publishing academic papers of Latina scholarship in *Trabajos Monograficos* in 1985, which later became the peer-reviewed biannual journal *Chicana/Latina Studies: The Journal of Mujeres Activas en Letras y Cambio Social.* Historically supported by the Chicana Studies Department at UC Davis, the journal came to be edited, published, and hosted by the Chicana/o Studies Department at Loyola Marymount University in Los Angeles. The journal welcomes interdisciplinary contributions, reviews, creative work, and commentary in both English and Spanish, making it unique in the field of feminist/women's studies. *Noticias,* the official MALCS newsletter, is also published biannually.

In 1985, MALCS established an annual four-day summer institute of research and creative presentations, workshops, and training sessions open to faculty, staff, and students at all levels, as well as members of the community at large. Held at a different member campus each year, the institute provides a place both for scholarly research in Chicana/Latina and Native American studies and for general empowerment and networking opportunities, seeking to bridge the gaps among university faculty, staff, undergraduate and graduate students, and community members through joint discussion. The institute's central themes from year to year have reflected the general changes in women of color studies: Sexual Politics; *Violencia y la Mujer* (Women and Violence); Ethics; Resistance and Celebration: *La Fuerza de las Mujeres* (Women's Power); Heterogeneity of Chicana Feminism: Problems and Possibilities; *Solidaridad* (Solidarity): Collaborating Across Identities, Communities and Boundaries; *Los Recuerdos del Porvenir* (Remembrances of Things to Come); *¡Activismo! Académicas, Artistas, Científicas y más . . .* (Activism! Academics, Artists, Scientists and more . . .); *Reflexiones y Visiones* (Reflections and Visions: MALCS Building the Future); Cyber Imaginaries: Decolonizing the Future; *Sabiduría y Acción: La Fuerza de las Mujeres* (Wisdom and Action: Women's Power); and *Transfronteras* (Transborders), Geographies and Generations.

Numerous internationally and nationally known scholars in Chicana/Latina and Native American studies as well as women of color studies have marked their passage into the field through MALCS. Thus, it continues to be an important touchstone and support system that reflects the interests and concerns of Chicanas/Latinas and Native American women in higher education.

Ellen M. Gil-Gómez

See also: Chicano Movement; Chicano Studies; Feminism.

Further Reading

MALCS, Mujeres Activas en Letras y Cambio Social. http://www.malcs.net.

Pesquera, Betriz M., and Denise A. Segura. "There is No Going Back: Chicanas and Feminism." In *Chicana Feminist Thought: The Basic Historical Writings,* ed. Alma M. García. New York: Routledge, 1997.

Mulataje

In the strictest sense, *mulataje* is a Spanish word used during the colonization of the Americas to refer to the intermixing of blacks (Africans) and whites (Europeans). Today, however, the term is a little more difficult to define, as it has acquired distinct but related concrete and conceptual meanings. Sometimes mulataje is used in a similar fashion to the term *mestizaje,* referring to the process of interbreeding between people of different so-called races (usually white and nonwhite), as well as to the blending or juxtaposition of cultures and identity that results from it.

For the most part, however, mulatto (*mulato* in Spanish and Portuguese) designates a person who is the offspring of a European parent and an African parent, most strictly the first-generation children. For a variety of historical reasons—including the scarcity of Spanish and Portuguese women in the colonies at the beginning of the colonization period (early 1500s to early 1600s) and the granting of lim-

ited rights for indigenous people and slaves—Spanish and Portuguese colonial powers encouraged intermarriage and sexual relationships between indigenous peoples, Europeans, and Africans. Historically, then, as a process, mulataje usually involved relations between European men and African women, which were far more socially acceptable than relations between European women and African men. The colonial governments of Spain and Portugal thus pursued a policy of assimilation by degree, based on the rationale that continual intermixing would unfailingly lead to light-skinned subjects. This threw mixed-race persons into complicated social hierarchies where the pinnacle of advantage remained European. While the social and legal situation of mixed-race subjects was more complex than in North American colonies, it was hardly less racist, inequitable, or even violent.

Perhaps racism is reflected in the very term "mulatto," which most dictionaries say is derived from the Old Spanish word for mule, *mulo,* the offspring of a male donkey and a female horse; such offspring are sterile. It was in the late seventeenth century that European scientists and thinkers began to construct the modern notion of biological race. Indeed, the very process of colonialism and the mixing of races in the colonies informed the scientific effort; the concept of race as it emerged at the time supported political efforts to classify people and helped account for (and morally justify) vast social inequalities.

In some contexts, mestizaje and mulataje are used in an explicitly evaluative sense, either to glorify or to denigrate the people and cultures evidencing historical mixing. For example, the nineteenth-century Argentine statesman and writer Domingo F. Sarmiento considered racial mixing an obstacle to social progress. On the other hand, the twentieth-century Mexican educator and statesman Jose Vasconcelos followed, for a time at least, the example of nineteenth-century revolutionary leader Simón Bolívar in claiming for Latin America a new, positive identity based on the mixing of races and cultures. For Vasconcelos, the mixing of races would lead to what he called a "cosmic race," formed from the best elements of the existing races. Some politicians and writers, particularly in Caribbean countries during the nineteenth and twentieth centuries, preferred to use mulataje instead of mestizaje in constructing specific regional and national identities. In this respect, mulataje is sometimes connected with the project of *mulatez*—which can be defined as a glorification of mulattoes and mulattoness. In contrast to widespread assumptions of mulataje as less acceptable than mestizaje—even as a sign of virulent moral corruption and an unstable force threatening social unity—some Caribbean thinkers began to celebrate racial and cultural ambiguity and hybridity. The Cuban political thinker and poet José Martí can be placed in this camp. Likewise, the Puerto Rican poet Luis Palés Matos, Cuban poet Nicolás Guillén, and Dominican poet Manuel del Cabral all celebrated mulataje and mulattoes (more precisely, mulatta women) and reflected on mulatto identity. Some literary critics read literary mulataje and mulatez poetry as a vindication of blackness, while others argue that celebrating mulataje promotes social practices of covering over black identity, "whitening" it so as to make it more acceptable. More recently, some thinkers, particularly in North America, have invoked mulataje and similar notions—such as "hybridity," "creolization," and "plurality"—to challenge strict, taken-for-granted understandings of race—that it is either white or black, and an unchangeable human trait.

Agnes B. Curry

See also: Chicano Movement; Chicano Studies; Feminism. Miscegenation; Mulatto/a.

Further Reading

"Afro-Americans: A Hemispheric Perspective." Excerpted by Vernellia R. Randall from Cottrol, Robert J. "Shadow: Law, Liberalism, and Cultures of Racial Hierarchy and Identity in the Americas." *Tulane Law Review* (November 2001).

Buscaglia-Salgado, José F. *Undoing Empire: Race and Nation in the Mulatto Caribbean.* Minneapolis: University of Minnesota Press, 2003.

Martinez-Echazabal, Lourdes. "Mestizaje and the Discourse of National/Cultural Identity in Latin America, 1845–1959." *Latin American Perspectives* 25:3 (May 1998).

Miller, Marilyn Grace. *The Rise and Fall of the Cosmic Race: The Cult of Mestizaje in Latin America.* Austin: University of Texas Press, 2004.

Mulatto/a

Mulatto/a is a term used to identify people of mixed African and European ancestry. In response to the long history of European colonialism, a number of terms have been created to classify people of mixed ancestry, among them mulatto, *mestizo, zambo,* and half-breed. Mulatto remains a controversial term because it reinforces a false biological construction of racial difference. Furthermore, it designates only a small segment of the population as having mixed racial heritage, belying the fact that most residents of the United States are the product of centuries of racial and ethnic mixing.

Given the differences in conquest and governance by the European colonizers of the New World, the treatment and status of mulattoes was different in the American Southwest, controlled by Spain and Mexico, and in the Southeast, under the colonial rule of the British. Early Spanish colonization was an almost exclusively male affair, in that only males ventured to the New World. As a result, Spaniards (black, white, and mulatto) were encouraged by the crown to intermarry with local Amerindian populations so as to cultivate amicable relations between Spain and its new subjects. The products of Spanish-Amerindian unions were called mestizos, while the children resulting from sexual encounters between Africans and Amerindians were referred to as zambos.

The Spanish and those in service of the Spanish crown, including Christopher Columbus himself, initially attempted to use American Indians for slave labor in the gold mines and sugar plantations of New Spain. However, Indians' tendencies to escape from slavery or fall victim to European diseases obliged the colonizers to look to Africa for free labor. In 1505, motivated by the financial possibilities of an expanded production of sugar, the Spanish began importing slaves from West Africa to the Caribbean on a large scale. Amid the increasing number of African slaves in the Spanish colonies, sexual encounters—many of them violent and forcible—increased, resulting in the rapid growth of the mulatto population. Mulattoes achieved a higher social status than their mothers and were much more likely to be employed in domestic service or trained as artisans than were dark-skinned Africans, who were confined to more laborious work in the field.

In Mexico, slavery was equally commonplace, although the slave population consisted of both Africans and American Indians. These populations intermingled with the Spanish and with one another to forge a *mestizaje* (mixed race) society. Thus, skin color alone could not be used to identify race, resulting in racial classification on the basis of religion, culture, and behavior, rather than physical appearance. When Mexico gained independence from Spain in 1821, the new government encouraged and embraced the mestizaje population, hoping to establish a nation without racial division that celebrated its heterogeneous and hybrid national identity. In northern Mexico (present-day California, Nevada, New Mexico, Arizona, and Utah), Mexican migrants adopted Amerindian forms of agriculture and combined them with Mexican and Amerindian adaptations of Spanish culture and religion to form a unique, syncretic society and culture that persists to this day.

British settlers came to North America with the purpose of establishing a new, permanent social order modeled on the English system. Many were religious and political refugees or commoners in search of land ownership and other economic opportunities and therefore were looking to relocate permanently. British colonial settlers tended to migrate with their entire families intact, unlike the exclusively male Spanish colonizers of Mexico and the Caribbean. Far from embracing or encouraging mestizaje, British colonists excluded Native Americans from the dominant social order and displaced them, rather than integrating them into colonial society. The large-scale importation of Africans as slaves led to the creation of a social order organized strictly along racial and class lines. Racial mixing, while common, was taboo, and interracial marriage was illegal in most states. The mulatto population that resulted from such mixing challenged the social structure that governed the American colonies and the early U.S. republic. In the seventeenth and eighteenth centuries, mulattoes comprised a separate class, above dark-skinned slaves, and, as in Mexico, they were

more likely to be employed as domestic servants or artisans than field hands. In the second half of the nineteenth century, however, following the emancipation of slaves in the United States, many states, especially in the South where the collapse of an economic system based on slavery threatened to dissolve the entire social order, began to change their definitions of race to prevent all people of color, including mulattoes, from achieving equality with whites. In eighteenth-century Virginia, for example, anyone less than one-quarter black was considered white. In 1910, the fraction was lowered to one-sixteenth, and in 1930, the state legislature adopted the "one-drop rule," whereby a single drop of African blood made one legally black. While Spain and later Mexico embraced mestizaje, social and political exclusion on the basis of race remained ingrained in U.S. society.

The different character of slavery and colonialism in the Southwestern versus the Southeastern United States also led to different attitudes toward and among mulattoes in these two areas. While "mulatto" remains synonymous with "black" in much of the Southeast, it has a very different, more complex cultural meaning in the Southwest. Indeed the designation is a source of pride among Latino/as who embrace their mestizaje heritage. The ever-growing mulatto population continues to challenge the validity of U.S. racial categories, but at the same time reinforces those categories by validating biological constructions of race in the eyes of those who wish to retain them.

Bretton T. Alvaré

See also: Conquest of the Americas; Identity and Labels; Miscegenation; Mulataje; Race.

Further Reading

Bost, Suzanne. *Mulattas and Mestizas: Representing Mixed Identities in the Americas, 1850–2000.* Athens: University of Georgia Press, 2003.

Conniff, Michael L., and Thomas J. Davis. *Africans in the Americas.* New York: St. Martin's, 1994.

Esteva-Fabregat, Claudio. *Mestizaje in Ibero-America.* Trans. John Wheat. Tucson: University of Arizona Press, 1987.

Williamson, Joel. *New People: Miscegenation and Mulattoes in the United States.* New York: Free Press, 1980.

Muñoz Marín, Luis
(1898–1980)

Luis Muñoz Marín was twentieth-century Puerto Rico's most prominent politician, as well as a published poet and journalist. He was elected as the island's first popularly elected governor in 1948 and served for four consecutive four-year terms (1949–1965).

He was born José Luis Alberto Muñoz Marín on February 18, 1898, in San Juan, Puerto Rico. He was the only son of Amalia Marín and Luis Muñoz Rivera, an influential journalist and statesman who led the movement for autonomy from Spain and representation in the Spanish Parliament, which was granted in December 1897. Much to Muñoz Rivera's regret, however, Puerto Rico's experience as an autonomous Spanish possession did not last long. The island was ceded to the United States in the Treaty of Paris that ended the Spanish-American War in 1898—the year of Muñoz Marín's birth.

Muñoz Marín grew up in both Puerto Rico and the United States, where from 1901 to 1904 his father edited New York City's *Puerto Rican Herald* and from 1910 to 1916 served as Puerto Rico's resident commissioner to the U.S. House of Representatives. Muñoz Marín attended Georgetown University Law School, but left without earning a degree after his father died in 1916. He was working as secretary to Puerto Rico's resident commissioner in Washington, D.C., when the Jones Act of 1917 granted U.S. citizenship to residents of Puerto Rico. During the 1920s, he supported Puerto Rican independence and was a member of Puerto Rico's Socialist Party, which was affiliated with the Socialist Party in the United States. Traveling back and forth between Puerto Rico and the New York City literary scene, Muñoz Marín published books of poetry and contributed articles on arts and politics to various U.S. publications. In 1926, he became editor of *La Democracia,* a newspaper that had been founded by his father in 1889.

Advocating independence and the rights of *jíbaros,* Puerto Rico's rural smallholders and landless peasants, Muñoz Marín was elected to the Puerto Rican Senate as a member of the Liberal Party in 1932. An ardent supporter of the New Deal, President Franklin D. Roosevelt's legislative program for rescuing the United States from the Great Depression, Muñoz Marín gained political prestige by securing for Puerto Rico millions of dollars in U.S. aid to enhance transportation, communication, education, health facilities, and energy infrastructure.

In 1938, Muñoz Marín founded the Partido Popular Democrático (Popular Democratic Party), which came to dominate island politics by setting aside the issue of independence or statehood and focusing instead on economic and social issues. Under the party motto, "Bread, Land, and Liberty," Muñoz Marín campaigned vigorously in the November 1940 elections, promoting land reform, improved working conditions, and public works projects. The Partido Popular Democrático had an impressive turnout, and Muñoz Marín became president of the Puerto Rican Senate. Serving in that position from 1941 to 1948, he collaborated with Roosevelt-appointed Governor Rexford G. Tugwell, who supported the Partido Popular Democrático's agenda. Thousands of acres of land were redistributed, numerous public housing projects were built, agricultural and industrial development projects were initiated, and low-cost electricity, water, and transportation cooperatives were formed.

In 1948, after the U.S. Congress made the Puerto Rican governorship an elective office, Muñoz Marín became Puerto Rico's first democratically elected governor. In his inaugural address, he announced the creation of Operation Bootstrap, which sought external financing for industrialization projects on the island. The program attracted U.S. capital investment by offering new industries tax exemptions, assistance with labor problems, and support for plant construction. Private investment from U.S. subsidiaries willing to invest in the island boomed, transforming Puerto Rico into a modern, urban, industrialized society. At the same time, however, the high rate of economic growth was accompanied by correspondingly high levels of unemployment and emigration.

In 1950, the U.S. Congress passed Public Law 600, which enabled Puerto Ricans to draft their own constitution. Desiring to remain within the U.S. federal system, Muñoz Marín promoted Puerto Ri-

Luis Muñoz Marín, who became the first freely elected governor of Puerto Rico in 1948, campaigns (successfully) for his fourth term in 1960. A promoter of economic development and commonwealth status, he came to be called the "father of modern Puerto Rico." *(Hank Walker/Stringer/ Time & Life Pictures/Getty Images)*

can commonwealth status as opposed to statehood or independence. He believed that commonwealth status would both safeguard Puerto Rico's unique Caribbean culture and provide economic security and viability. It would also guarantee the island's fiscal and cultural autonomy, while retaining for Puerto Ricans the advantages of U.S. citizenship, federal aid, and market access. After Puerto Ricans ratified their first constitution by popular vote in 1952, Muñoz Marín inaugurated the Estado Libre Asociado de Puerto Rico (Associated Free State of Puerto Rico), a commonwealth in free association with the United States. Winning reelection as governor in 1952, 1956, and 1960, Muñoz Marín retired from office after completing his fourth term—but not before receiving the Presidential Medal of Freedom, the highest civilian award in the United States, from U.S. President Lyndon B. Johnson in 1963. Muñoz Marín remained active in Puerto Rican politics, serving in

the Senate until 1970 and continuing as spokesman for maintaining commonwealth status until his death in San Juan on April 30, 1980.

David M. Carletta

See also: Jones Act (1917); Muñoz Rivera, Luis; Operation Bootstrap; Puerto Rican Literature; Puerto Ricans.

Further Reading

Aitken, Thomas, Jr. *Poet in the Fortress: The Story of Luis Muñoz Marín.* New York: New American Library, 1964.
Mathews, Thomas G. *Luis Muñoz Marín: A Concise Biography.* New York: American R.D.M., 1967.

Muñoz Rivera, Luis (1859–1916)

Luis Muñoz Rivera—a late-nineteenth-century politician, poet, and journalist—struggled for the political autonomy of Puerto Rico and became a key voice in helping liberate his country from Spain in 1897. In addition to his political activities, he published two collections of political poetry, *Retamas* in 1891 and *Tropicales* in 1902.

He was born on July 17, 1859, in Barranquitas, Puerto Rico, the eldest son of Luís Ramon Muñoz Barrios, a Conservative Party leader, landowner, and merchant, and Monserrate Rivera Vasquez. The young Muñoz Rivera attended the local elementary school in his town, where he became an avid reader of Spanish and French literature and developed an interest in Puerto Rican social and political history. After his mother died when he was twelve, he took on the task of tutoring his nine younger brothers. Largely self-taught, Muñoz Rivera wrote several patriotic poems; a newspaper in Ponce, *El Pueblo,* published one of them, "Adelante!" (Forward!), in 1882. He later became interested in journalism.

In 1883, Muñoz Rivera joined the short-lived Barranquitas Liberal Party, under whose banner he ran for membership in the provincial assembly. Although he lost, his fledgling interest in politics continued, and in 1887 he helped found the Autonomist Party, which sought independence for the island within the Spanish colonial system. To provide a voice for the party, Muñoz Rivera founded the newspaper *La Democracia* (*The Democracy*), in which he expressed support for the cause of autonomy and for the party. Many of his articles dealt with subjects that affected the daily lives of Puerto Ricans, including poor education, illiteracy, poverty, suppression of newspapers, and lack of municipal self-government. His controversial editorials angered the Spanish administration and gave rise to several lawsuits, but Muñoz Rivera continued to speak out for autonomy and for alliance with a liberal political party in Spain, the Liberal Fusion Party, led by Práxedes Mateo Sagasta.

In 1895, Muñoz Rivera traveled to Spain to learn about national politics and better understand the workings of the country's government. Upon his return, he helped draft the Plan de Ponce, which sought political identity and administrative autonomy for the people of Puerto Rico. In late 1896, he returned to Spain as part of a four-member commission that met with political leader Práxedes Mateo Sagasta, who signed an agreement stating that if he and the liberals were to come to power in Spain, he would grant Puerto Rico autonomy. In November 1897, after being installed as prime minister, Sagasta granted the Autonomist Charter; Muñoz Rivera was appointed secretary of state and chief of the cabinet of the newly independent government of Puerto Rico. He served in this position until early 1899, after the U.S. invasion of Puerto Rico and the consequent establishment of a military government.

In the months that followed, Muñoz Rivera's devotion to social conditions in Puerto Rico led him to found a newspaper *El Territorio* (*The Territory*) in which he voiced the problems of the island landowners. As a result of the U.S.-imposed trade blockade, the farmers were unable to export their goods. Also in 1899, Muñoz Rivera traveled to the United States in an unsuccessful attempt to reach a free trade agreement for the island.

Opposing the Foraker Act—the 1900 U.S. law that established a limited popular (civilian) government in Puerto Rico—Muñoz Rivera organized the Federal Party and launched *El Diario de Puerto Rico* as its organ in 1900. After *El Diario* printed an editorial denouncing the Republican mayor of San Juan,

an angry mob destroyed the paper's offices and printing press. Muñoz Rivera moved to New York, where he hoped to be in a better position to gauge U.S. sentiment toward Puerto Rico and to gain ammunition for his fight to restore Puerto Rican independence.

In 1901, while living in New York, Muñoz Rivera established the *Puerto Rican Herald,* a bilingual newspaper. In the first issue, Muñoz Rivera wrote an open letter to President William McKinley where he characterized the Foraker Act as a disgrace to both the United States and Puerto Rico. Three years later, he returned to Puerto Rico and became one of the founders of the Unionist Party, a merger of the Federal and Republican parties. In 1906, he was elected to the Puerto Rican House of Delegates as a Unionist. Reelected two years later, he served until 1910, when he was elected resident commissioner to the U.S. House of Representatives, the island's official spokesperson in Washington. While serving in that capacity, he continued writing articles for *La Democracia* as a means of reporting U.S. political events to the people of Puerto Rico.

In Congress, Muñoz Rivera continued his crusade against the Foraker Act. He studied English in the evenings in order to successfully present his arguments to Congress and the president, with whom he met to discuss a change in the political status of the island. President Woodrow Wilson stated that the Unionist Party would have to abandon the goal of independence to get the administration's approval to amend the Foraker Act. Muñoz Rivera conceded, and from that moment autonomy became the goal of the Unionist Party.

Muñoz Rivera's efforts culminated in passage of the Jones Act, which President Wilson signed into law on March 2, 1917. In addition to granting full U.S. citizenship to Puerto Ricans, the legislation also granted the island greater autonomy by establishing a two-chamber legislative assembly—a nineteen-member Senate and a thirty-nine-member House of Delegates, elected by universal male suffrage.

Muñoz Rivera did not live long enough to see the fruits of his labor, as he returned to Puerto Rico in September 1916, ill with cancer, and died on November 15 in San Juan. Thousands turned out for his funeral. In 1949, his son, Luis Muñoz Marín—

also a politician, poet, and journalist—became the first democratically elected governor of Puerto Rico and continued the work of his father to promote self-rule.

Anita Damjanovic

See also: Foraker Act (1900); Jones Act (1917); Muñoz Marín, Luis; Puerto Rican Literature; Puerto Ricans.

Further Reading

Norris, Marianna. *Father and Son for Freedom.* New York: Dodd, Mead, 1968.
Sterling, Philip, and Maria Brau. *The Quiet Rebels: Four Puerto Rican Leaders: José Celso Barbosa, Luis Muñoz Rivera, José De Diego, Luiz Muñoz Marín.* Garden City, NY: Doubleday, 1968.

Mural Art

Mural art in North and Central America has a history extending back at least 2,700 years to the Olmec site in present-day Mexico known as Grutas de Oxtotitlan. Mural painting has been found at nearly every major archaeological site in Mexico, Guatemala, Honduras, and Belize. The rich imagery of murals found at sites such as Bonampak, Palenque, El Tajín, Monte Alban, and Teotihuacán depicts a variety of mythological, religious, and historical scenes representing all of Mesoamerica's major civilizations, including the Olmec, Maya, Zapotec, Toltec, and Aztec cultures. Following the Spanish conquest of Mexico in the sixteenth century, indigenous artists were quickly recruited to transfer their skills in sculpture, architecture, and painting to the symbolism of the Catholic Church in its campaign of conversion. The murals they produced still adorn hundreds of churches and monasteries throughout Mexico, which help to maintain both the legacy of mural art and the mastery of its practitioners. This legacy is inescapable wherever one travels in the Mesoamerican world, not only in murals, but also in mosaics, sculpture, and ceramics. Mesoamerica's long history of mural painting was revitalized during the early twentieth-century revolutionary period in Mexico, as a new national *mestizo* identity was being celebrated and promoted in the arts.

The writer and politician Jose Vasconcelos, who served as minister of public education in the early 1920s, initiated a program of "indigenism" in mural painting to enshrine what he called *la raza cósmica* (the cosmic race) on the walls and ceilings of Mexico's colonial buildings. The work of *los tres grandes*—Diego Rivera, José Clemente Orozco, and David Alfaro Siqueiros—quickly spread their influence across the border during the 1920s, 1930s, and 1940s, as the United States initiated Depression-era public art projects through the Works Progress Administration (WPA) in post offices, hospitals, schools, and other government buildings. Hundreds of ethnically and racially diverse artists were employed by WPA's Federal Art Project (formerly known as the Public Works of Art Project) to create works of art throughout the nation. African American artists were particularly instrumental in bringing the tradition of mural painting to the United States because of the stark parallels they saw between the struggles of indigenous peoples in Mexico and those of black Americans. Indeed, leaders of the Harlem Renaissance modeled many of their strategies after what was called the Mexican School, a movement that began in 1922. Artists like Elizabeth Catlett and Charles White traveled to Mexico to study with artist groups such as the Taller de Gráfica Popular, founded in 1937 in Mexico City. Notable Latino mural artists who worked for the WPA included Roberto Vallangca, Xavier Gonzales, and Miguel Covarrubias.

Given the long tradition of mural painting in Mesoamerica and its revival in postrevolution Mexico, much of the mural art in the modern United States directly corresponds to the efforts of Chicanos/as to bolster pride and cohesion in their communities. By the 1960s, as the cultural revolution took shape within Mexican American communities, local activists began using public mural art to foment a sentiment of resistance and affirmation. Resisting the pressures of assimilation and affirming the inherent value of their cultural heritage, students and activists in California and around the country founded *El Movimiento* (the Chicano social and civil rights movement) and the Chicano Arts Movement. The depiction in murals of the mythical Aztec homeland Aztlán (considered by many Chicanos/as to be

Mural art, as exemplified by this themed painting in Chicago's Little Village neighborhood, has a long tradition in Latino culture—from ancient Mesoamerican civilizations to twentieth-century Mexican masters and contemporary street artists in urban America. *(Tim Boyle/Getty Images)*

located in the Southwest region of the United States) embodied the desire to build a sense of community and pride in barrios and neighborhoods throughout the Southwest, especially in California, where the largest concentration of public mural art is found. Especially influential in the Chicano Arts Movement and the creation of murals throughout the country were the Centro Cultural de la Raza of San Diego, founded in 1970; the Royal Chicano Air Force, founded in Sacramento in 1969; the Bay Area's Galería de la Raza, founded in 1970; and Self Help Graphics and Art, founded in Los Angeles in 1972.

Mural art has deep connections to other forms of public art, such as posters and silk screens, used to further the collective spirit of Chicano and Latino cultural identity. Such public expressions also heavily influenced the emergence of graffiti throughout urban America. These various types of public art have continued to flourish throughout the country wherever Latino communities have arisen. Since 1976, the Social and Public Art Resource Center (SPARC) in Venice, California, founded by muralist Judith Baca, painter Christina Schlesinger, and filmmaker Donna Deitch, has continued the tradition of public art that originated in Mexico and was embraced by artists in the United States. No longer exclusively associated with Chicano and Latino community identity, SPARC is "committed to producing and promoting work that reflects the lives and concerns of America's ethnically and economically diverse populations including: women, the working poor, youth, the elderly and newly arrived immigrant communities."

At its core, mural art has always been about political advocacy for those without voices. For nearly a century, this unique form of public art has inspired critical thought, collective action, and social unity in diverse communities across the United States and

Mexico. Its legacy has had a vital role in strengthening identity, exposing inequities, and building pride in the Latino community.

Jeremy Hockett

See also: Baca, Judith F.; Chicano Art; Chicano Movement; Gonzalez, Jose-Luis; Graffiti; Indigenismo.

Further Reading

Barnett, Alan W. *Community Murals: The People's Art.* Philadelphia: Art Alliance, 1984.

Barnett-Sanchez, Holly, and Eva Sperling Cockcroft, eds. *Signs from the Heart: California Chicano Murals.* Albuquerque: University of New Mexico Press, 1993.

Broid de Marek, Elizabeth. *Chicano Muralism.* El Paso: University of Texas Press, 1985.

Gaspar de Alba, Alicia. *Chicano Art Inside/Outside the Master's House: Cultural Politics and the CARA Exhibition.* Austin: University of Texas Press, 1998.

Gerace, Gloria. *Urban Surprises: A Guide to Public Art in Los Angeles.* Princeton, NJ: Architectural Press, 2006.

Kim, Sojin, and Peter Quezada. *Chicano Graffiti and Murals: The Neighborhood Art of Peter Quezada.* Jackson: University Press of Mississippi, 1995.

Social and Public Art Resource Center. http://www.sparcmurals.org.

Murrieta, Joaquín
(c. 1829–1853)

Widely known as the "Robin Hood of El Dorado," "The Ghost of Sonora," and "The Patriot," the nineteenth-century figure of Joaquín Murrieta has been widely romanticized in modern myth and media. A legendary Mexican bandit associated with the California Gold Rush of the 1850s, he is portrayed as a chivalric outlaw who took justice into his own hands and played an important role in the Mexican resistance to the U.S. invasion of that territory. Fiercely loyal to his countrymen, Murrieta and his band of desperadoes avenged the invaders' abuse of defenseless Latino miners. Wanted by foreign authorities, Murrieta obtained the legendary status of such other frontier men as Davy Crockett, Daniel Boone, Wyatt Earp, and Billy the Kid.

Joaquín Murrieta, or Murieta, was born around 1829 either in Sonora, Mexico, or in Chile. During the Gold Rush of the early 1850s, he moved to California, and he worked in the abundant Stanislaus mining fields to seek his fortune. In 1852, the Foreign Miners' Tax was levied on Chinese and Mexican miners, who were accused of having amassed fortunes that belonged to Anglo Americans. When Murrieta refused to pay the three-dollar monthly payment to keep his mine, he was expelled from his claim. Dispossessed of his only source of income in the region, he joined other rebellious miners to form his own group of Mexican bandits and prey upon the tyrannical possessors of the land. For the next two years, together with his fellow bandits, Murrieta attacked U.S. traders, killed Chinese mine workers, robbed stores, and stole cattle and more than $100,000 in gold throughout the length and breadth of the mother lode area.

To put an end to this reign of terror, on May 11, 1853, California Governor John Bigler signed a measure to authorize Captain Harry Love, deputy sheriff of Los Angeles and a former Texas Ranger, to organize a company of mounted men to capture Murrieta. Promised a generous monthly salary of $150 and a $5,000 bonus for the capture of Murrieta dead or alive, Love and his Rangers combed the vast lands on which the bandits' attacks occurred. On July 25, 1853, they encountered a number of Mexican riders near Panoche Pass in San Benito County, about 100 miles (160 kilometers) from the mother lode and 50 miles (80 kilometers) away from Monterey on the coast. Their chance encounter led to an armed confrontation, in the course of which the Mexicans were killed.

Seeking the reward money, the Rangers identified their victims as Joaquín Murrieta and his right-hand lieutenant, Manuel "Three-Fingered Jack" García. As the purported evidence of their mission, they produced a head said to be Murrieta's and a hand said to be García's in two jars of brandy. Although the deaths of the banditos were confirmed by thousands of spectators who visited the public expositions of the jars in Mariposa County, Stockton, and San Francisco, a young woman who said she was Murrieta's sister claimed not to recognize the head because it did not carry her brother's scar. She accused Captain Love and his Rangers of fabricating the evidence and spreading false rumors in displaying the jars. The identity of the head remained a mystery, and the jar was lost in the 1906 San Francisco earthquake.

But by no means did Murrieta's "disappearance" cast him into oblivion. The legend of the Mexican thief had already begun to be forged in 1854, with the publication of John Rollin Ridge's *The Life and Adventures of Joaquín Murrieta, the Celebrated California Bandit.* Despite Murrieta's criminal record, Ridge portrayed him as a graceful and handsome folk hero who had turned to crime after American miners raped his girlfriend Rosita and hanged his half-brother for an offense he had not committed. Watching his family dishonored, Ridge's Murrieta swore vengeance on the offenders and their country, and, becoming the leader of a band of desperadoes, he went on a bloody tirade. After that, virtually every robbery and murder that occurred anywhere in the mother lode region was attributed to Murrieta. Through a series of bank robberies, Murrieta is also believed to have accumulated a large sum of money. Well into the twentieth century, extensive treasure hunts were organized to find his treasure—none of them successful.

Based in part on the allure of Joaquín Murrieta, the Canadian writer Johnston MacCulley in 1919 created the avenging character of Diego de la Vega, widely known as "El Zorro," in serialized magazine stories. Like the romanticized Murrieta, Zorro is characterized by his charm, patriotic commitment, dexterity with a sword, and brazen efforts to free his countrymen from exploitive and corrupted tyrants, whom he brands with a "Z."

Indeed, the figure of Murrieta has inspired poets, film, directors and scriptwriters worldwide. His story has been told in the play *Fulgor y muerte de Joaquín Murrieta* (*Splendor and Death of Joaquín Murrieta,* 1967) by the great Chilean writer Pablo Neruda; in the Russian rock opera *Zvezda i smert' Khoakina Mur'ety* (*The Star and Death of Joaquín Murrieta,* 1967) by Alexei Rybnikov and Pavel Grushko, and in several Hollywood movies, such as D.W. Griffith's western *Scarlet Days* (1919) and Martin Campbell's *The Mask of Zorro* (1998) and *The Legend of Zorro* (2005).

Jorge Abril Sánchez

See also: Foreign Miners' Tax (1850).

Further Reading

Burns, Walter Noble. *The Robin Hood of El Dorado: The Saga of Joaquín Murrieta, Famous Outlaw of California's Age of Gold.* New York: Coward-McCann, 1932.

Etulain, Richard W., and Glenda Riley. *With Badges and Bullets: Lawmen & Outlaws in the Old West.* Golden, CO: Fulcrum, 1999.

Latta, Frank Forrest. *Joaquín Murrieta and His Horse Gangs.* Santa Cruz, CA: Bear State, 1980.

Varley, James F. *The Legend of Joaquín Murrieta: California's Gold Rush Bandit.* Twin Falls, ID: Big Lost River, 1995.

Museo del Barrio, El

In 1969, artist Raphael Montañez Ortiz, along with Puerto Rican activists, artists, teachers, and members of the Spanish Harlem community, established El Museo del Barrio in East Harlem's Spanish-speaking El Barrio, the neighborhood extending from Ninety-Sixth Street to the Harlem River and from Fifth Avenue to the East River on Manhattan's Upper East Side. El Museo del Barrio became New York's first museum dedicated solely to Puerto Rican art. Since its formation, El Museo has evolved into New York's leading Latino cultural institution, having expanded its mission to represent the diversity of art and culture in all of the Caribbean and Latin America. Its mission is to "present and preserve the art and culture of Puerto Ricans and all Latin Americans in the United States."

Amid the 1960s civil rights movement, Ortiz and Harlem's community activists founded El Museo del Barrio because they felt that mainstream New York City museums, such as the Metropolitan Museum of Art and the Museum of Modern Art, did not adequately represent Puerto Rican culture and that their own neighborhood needed a dedicated expression of Puerto Rican art and culture. Initially El Museo operated in a public-school classroom as an adjunct to the local school district, and then in brownstones in Spanish Harlem. From 1969 to 1976, El Museo was located in a succession of storefronts on Third and Lexington avenues, in the heart of El Barrio. In 1977, it found a permanent home in the neoclassical Heckscher Building at 1230 Fifth Avenue.

is a celebrated array of Pre-Columbian art (thirteenth to fifteenth centuries) and artifacts made by the indigenous peoples of the Caribbean and Puerto Rico. Highlights include approximately 2,000 examples of ceremonial and domestic objects made by the Arawak Taínos, the Caribs, and the Ingeris. Other features of the permanent collection include approximately 900 examples of folk and traditional arts, both secular and religious. In addition, El Museo boasts a special collection of 360 carved and painted Santos, devotional wooden figurines of saints for home worship. Orishas, spiritual figures representing the forces of nature in the Yoruba faith, illustrate the convergence of Christianity with Afro-Caribbean religion.

Paintings, works on paper, and sculpture are well represented at the museum. During the twentieth century, following the example of Mexican revolutionary artists, artists created prints and posters that reflected the social and civil struggles of the world around them. El Museo regularly presents the work of leading contemporary artists, helping launch, for example, the career of the celebrated sculpture, video, and installation artist Pepón Osorio.

In the 2000s, El Museo has presented more mainstream artists and exhibitions and fewer political artists and exhibitions than it did during the 1960s and 1970s. Meanwhile, other smaller, more experimental museums have taken on the mission once held by El Museo to present the more social and politically oriented exhibitions. For example, Alejandro Anreus curated "Albizu Lives! A Visual Commemoration," held at the Jersey City Museum, New Jersey, to mark the thirtieth anniversary of the death of the Puerto Rican nationalist Pedro Albizu Campos. When El Museo does mount more topical exhibitions, such as the prints of Afro-Puerto Rican artist Juan Sanchez, it is in the form of traveling exhibitions from other institutions or organized by an outside curator. As New York City's Latino population continues to change, El Museo no doubt will continue to evolve as well, redefining its mission, its exhibitions, and its collections along the way.

Diana L. Linden

See also: Puerto Ricans.

The annual *Día de los Reyes* (Three Kings Day) Parade is held at El Museo del Barrio in East Harlem, New York City. In addition to exhibiting art and artifacts, the museum sponsors educational programs, festivals, and other special events in its efforts to preserve Latino culture. *(AP Images/ Adam Nadel)*

During the 1980s, under the directorship of Susanna Torruella-Leval, El Museo began to broaden its reach to a more diversified Latino audience. This change reflected the dramatic population shifts in New York City, with more and more Latinos/as coming from the Dominican Republic, Mexico, and Central America. While the expansion of El Museo has been widely applauded, some have been critical, arguing that it is a redirection from its working-class Puerto Rican roots in favor of the more established and lucrative Latin American art market. Museum curators maintain that the move to upper Fifth Avenue allowed El Museo to maintain contact with its core community yet reach out to a wider non-Latino audience, now comprising some 40 percent of visitors.

At the heart of the museum is a permanent collection of approximately 8,000 objects. Central to it

Further Reading

El Museo del Barrio. http://www.elmuseo.org.

Smith, Edward Lucie. *Latin American Art of the Twentieth Century.* London: Thames & Hudson, 1993.

Voces y Visiones: Highlights from El Museo del Barrio's Permanent Collection. New York: El Museo del Barrio, 2006.

Music

Like other immigrant communities, Latinos/as brought their music with them when they came to the United States or, in the case of Puerto Rican and early Mexican American communities, when the United States incorporated part or all of their native lands in the nineteenth century. But while Latino music has been played in the United States for more than 150 years, it has gained increased popularity with the rising tide of Latino immigration after World War II, both within those communities and among the American population generally.

Latino music during the postwar period has gone through three general growth phases. It enjoyed its first wave of popularity in the 1940s and 1950s, as big bands, often led by Puerto Rican and Cuban conductors, played dance music in nightclubs, usually in Miami, New York, and other big northeastern cities where the first large wave of Caribbean immigrants settled. The second wave came in the 1960s and 1970s, with the birth of salsa among Caribbean immigrant communities in New York City. And the latest wave has been since the 1970s, with the rapid growth of Latino immigrant groups beyond Cubans, Mexicans, and Puerto Ricans, most notably, Dominicans, Colombians, and Central Americans.

Latin America and the Spanish-speaking Caribbean are two of the most musically rich and diverse regions of the world. Thus, with the sheer diversity

The famed Mexican singer Pedro Fernández performs with his mariachi band at the White House in 2002. Mariachi refers to a traditional Mexican genre and the ensembles that play it—originally street musicians. *(Paul J. Richards/AFP/Getty Images)*

of peoples immigrating to the United States from these regions has come an astonishing variety of musical genres: mariachi, *norteño, ranchera,* and others from Mexico; *bomba* and *plena* from Puerto Rico; *son cubano* and rumba from Cuba; merengue from the Dominican Republic; *cumbia* from Colombia and Central America; and the hybrid *reggaeton* from Panama. In addition, even those Latin American countries that have not sent many immigrants have exported their music, including bossa nova and samba from Brazil and the tango from Argentina.

Once in the United States, Latin music has undergone transformations. Just as Latino immigrants have mixed with other American populations, so their music has been inflected with the sounds of other American groups, producing or contributing to such hybrid styles as traditional Tejano music and the more contemporary *rock en español.*

Mexican American Music

Mexicans, the largest Latino immigrant group in the United States, have brought with them a number of musical forms, most of them based in the various regions of their native land. Perhaps the best known regional style of music is norteño, a type of ranchera music. As its name implies, norteño music originates in the northern reaches of Mexico, where most early Mexican immigrants to the United States came from, and those parts of the Southwestern United States that were once part of Mexico. A dance music related to polka—the influence comes from the German and, later, Slavic immigrants to the region—traditional norteño musical compositions featured accordions and an instrument known as the *bajo sexto,* an oversized twelve-string guitar. In more recent times, norteño has incorporated the saxophone and electric bass guitar, the latter in place of the bajo sexto. Closely related to norteño music is the style known as *tejano,* after the original Mexican inhabitants of Texas, though tejano is more influenced by American dance styles, particularly the big band swing music of the mid-twentieth century.

The most recognizable Mexican music, at least to non-Latinos, is mariarchi. Originating in the state of Jalisco in west central Mexico (home to Guadalajara, the country's second-largest city), mariachi is usually played by a small *conjunto,* or group, consisting of stringed instruments, including violins and guitars of various types. A mix of influences—including European, African, and Amer-Indian—mariachi music can include both *corridos,* or ballads, and waltz-like dance tunes.

While Mexican American music has long been a cultural staple in the American Southwest, it has come to be heard in Northeastern cities and Midwestern towns in recent decades, following the migration of Mexican immigrants to those regions of the country.

Music from the Caribbean and Central America

The East Coast of the United States has been more heavily influenced by music from the Spanish-speaking Caribbean and Colombia, as most of the immigrants from those regions have traditionally settled in the East.

Like other Spanish-speaking Caribbean musical forms, Puerto Rican styles are more heavily inflected with African rhythms than Mexican music, a legacy of the region's mass slave trade prior to the late nineteenth century. Perhaps the most famous Puerto Rican musical form is the danceable, percussion-based bomba. Similar to bomba is plena, another percussion-based musical style, which mixes Spanish and African influences and often features lyrics that comment on political and social themes. Salsa, while usually attributed to Puerto Ricans by non-Latinos is, in fact, a hybrid musical sound that originated in the mixed neighborhoods of New York City in the 1960s, where Latino immigrants came into contact with each other's music and with the musical forms of African Americans, including jazz, swing, and rhythm and blues. Now played throughout Latin America and around the world, salsa, with its fast-moving dance rhythms, is the most popular music form that originated among Latinos/as in the United States.

Like bomba and plena, rumba reflects the mixed heritage of the Spanish-speaking Caribbean, as it

Music on the island of Puerto Rico is characterized by a diversity of genres and styles—from drum-and-guitar *jibaro* folk music to *bomba*, salsa, *plena*, and contemporary *reggaetón*—with native, African, and Spanish influences. *(Amy Toensing/Getty Images)*

features European-influenced melodies and African-based rhythms. Originating in Cuba, rumba compositions usually consist of two parts, a beginning vocal performance, or *canto,* sometimes featuring rhythmic, meaningless syllables. As the singer vocalizes, he or she is accompanied by an ever more insistent drumbeat, after which the song breaks into a danceable instrumental piece with frequent solos. Perhaps the most popular musical Latino style in the United States, prior to the birth of salsa, rumba was introduced to the wider public by a number of Latino bandleaders, the most famous of which were Desi Arnaz and Xavier Cugat, in the 1940s and 1950s.

By the 1980s, large numbers of immigrants from the Dominican Republic were also coming into the United States, largely settling in New York City and other major urban centers of the Northeast. With them came their distinctive merengue music. A highly syncopated style heavily influenced by African rhythms, merengue features percussion instruments, both drums and hand-held instruments such as the maraca or the tambora, as well as brass horns.

Originally a folk dance music from Colombia, cumbia became popular throughout Central America over the course of the twentieth century. A mix of Amerindian and African musical forms, cumbia is yet another percussion-based musical form. Somewhat slower in tempo than the popular Caribbean musical styles, cumbia has caught on in the United States with the influx of Central American and Colombian immigrants since the 1980s.

Perhaps the most popular contemporary form of Central American music in the United States—as well as throughout Latin America—is reggaetón. Originating in Panama, reggaetón is, like its name, a hybrid. The word combines reggae, the Jamaican musical form, and *ton,* shortened Spanish for tune. In the early 1900s, thousands of Jamaicans came to Panama to work the canal. Remaining culturally distinct from the native Panamanian population, they continued to listen to the musical styles from their homeland, including, by the 1960s and 1970s, reggae. By the 1990s, Panamanians of all ethnic origins were fusing Colombia-originated cumbia music with Jamaican reggae and then overlaying it with urban hip-hop lyrics coming over the radio from the United States.

As reggaetón's development reveals, North America can also influence sounds south of the border, which then come back into the United States with new immigrants. Such has been the case with rock en español. Featuring traditional rock-and-roll instrumentals and vocals, rock en español—widely popular in Latin America but most associated with younger Mexicans, a result of that country's proximity to the United States—is inflected with Latino rhythms.

Latino musical influences in the United States are only likely to grow in the coming decades, say musicologists and cultural studies scholars, as mass Latino immigration continues and second-generation Latinos/as begin to settle outside their traditional urban enclaves. But unlike earlier immigrant groups, whose musical forms faded in popularity with the acculturation process—little played outside cultural festivals and with little appeal to the second and third generations of immigrant parents and grandparents—Latino music is probably destined, for several reasons, to have much wider popularity among both Latinos/as and other North Americans. First is the sheer size of this immigrant group. Second is mass communications, which brings the latest sounds from the homeland into the United States, and back again. Third is the fact that non-Latinos/as are much more open to cultural influences from abroad than were native-born Americans of generations past. And finally, Latin American music, with its infectious rhythms, is simply too enjoyable to ignore.

James Ciment

See also: Corridos; Mexicans; Popular Culture; Puerto Ricans; Tejanos.

Further Reading

Alava, Silvio H. *Spanish Harlem's Musical Legacy, 1930–1980.* Charleston, SC: Arcadia, 2007.

Madrid, Alejandro. *Sounds of the Modern Nation: Music, Culture, and Ideas in Post-Revolutionary Mexico.* Philadelphia: Temple University Press, 2008.

Morales, Ed. *The Latin Beat: The Rhythms and Roots of Latin Music from Bossa Nova to Salsa and Beyond.* Cambridge, MA: Da Capo, 2003.

Roberts, John Storm. *The Latin Tinge: The Impact of Latin American Music on the United States.* 2nd ed. New York: Oxford University Press, 1999.

Narváez, Pánfilo (c. 1470–1528)

The Spanish explorer and conquistador Pánfilo Narváez helped establish a permanent Latino presence in the Caribbean and the present-day southeastern United States. He is best known for an ill-fated expedition to settle Florida in 1528, a mission that he did not survive. The stories of the few sailors who did survive, however, led to further interest in Spanish settlement in the New World.

Narváez was born in the kingdom of Castile, Spain, around 1470. He traveled with the Spanish explorer Diego Velázquez de Cuéllar to Cuba in 1511 and participated in the conquest of the island. In 1520, he was ordered by Velázquez, then the governor of Cuba, to travel to Mexico, thwart the advance of Hernán Cortés, capture him, and return him to Cuba for disobeying orders. When Narváez and Cortés met in battle, however, Cortés won. Narváez lost an eye, was imprisoned for two years, and finally returned to Spain in defeat.

In 1526, the king of Spain named Narváez *adelantado,* or governor, of Florida and authorized him to settle the area of what is now the state of Florida and the Gulf Coast region. In June 1527, Narváez left Spain for the Americas with 600 men, including the expedition's treasurer and second in charge, Alvar Nuñez Cabeza de Vaca. The ships stopped at Santo Domingo—where a number of men abandoned the venture—and proceeded to Cuba, where a hurricane hit the island, and two ships were lost. After acquiring more men and ships, Narváez left Cuba for Florida.

The ships dropped off about 300 men and eighty horses in the area of Tampa Bay during the spring of 1528. Timucuan Indians in the vicinity met the expedition and convinced the Spaniards to travel by foot farther north and west to an area of gold and riches called Apalache, near present-day Tallahassee.

There Narváez and his men encountered Apalachee Indians, who were friendly at first but who later attacked the Spaniards after they kidnapped an Apalachee chief. With many of his men dead or ailing as a result of Indian attacks and disease, Narváez resolved to leave Florida. The expedition succeeded in building five ships from horsehair, clothing, plants, and trees.

In September 1528, 242 survivors of the original 300 set sail for the Gulf Coast near what is now Texas. Storms thrashed and separated the ships. Thirst was a serious problem, and some men died from drinking too much salt water. Narváez was one of the casualties of the trip. In November, however, Cabeza de Vaca's ship arrived in the area around present-day Galveston Island off the Texas coast, at which time, he and three remaining shipmates were enslaved by the Karankawa Indians. Having eventually freed themselves, Cabeza de Vaca and the others wandered for several years, finally being rescued by a band of Spanish slave hunters in northern New Spain, present-day Mexico, in 1536.

The four survivors of the Narváez expedition would come to tell their story when Cabeza de Vaca published his account in Spain in 1542. His descriptions of their adventures and the riches to be obtained contributed to Spain's interest in the northern areas of New Spain. Later that decade, Francisco Vásquez de Coronado led an expedition into the southwestern United States looking for the legendary Seven Cities of Cíbola, said to be places of gold and splendor.

Amy Meschke Porter

See also: Conquest of the Americas.

Further Reading

Cabeza de Vaca, Alvar Nuñez. *Adventures in the Unknown Interior of America.* Trans. and ed. Cyclone Covey. Albuquerque: University of New Mexico Press, 1997.

Marrinan, Rochelle A., John F. Scarry, and Rhonda L. Majors. "Prelude to de Soto: The Expedition of Pánfilo de Narváez." In *Columbian Consequences,* Vol. 2, *Archaeological and Historical Perspectives on the Spanish Borderlands East,* ed. David Hurst Thomas. Washington DC: Smithsonian Institution, 1990.

Weber, David J. *The Spanish Frontier in North America.* New Haven, CT: Yale University Press, 1992.

National Agricultural Workers Union

The National Agricultural Workers Union (NAWU) represented the final attempt to organize agricultural workers as a traditional labor organization before César Chávez founded the National Farm Workers Association (the precursor to the United Farm Workers of America) in 1962. The NAWU was actually the first labor organization to which Chávez belonged.

Attempts to organize farmworkers had begun during the Great Depression with the formation of the Southern Tenant Farmers Union (STFU). The STFU was founded as a biracial labor organization in Arkansas by Socialists H.L. Mitchell and Clay East in 1934, in part to gain a greater share of money from the Agricultural Adjustment Act. The STFU faced powerful resistance from local and state governments in the South because of its color-blind racial policy. That, combined with chronic funding problems, contributed to the union's failure to become a significant organizing force in the region. Economic changes and a population shift out of the South during World War II greatly diminished the number of tenant farmers and sharecroppers, and led the STFU to begin to organize farm laborers in the Southwest and California. To reflect its change in emphasis, the STFU, in 1946, became the National Farm Workers Union (NFWU). In 1955, just before the merger between the American Federation of Labor (AFL) and the Congress of Industrial Organizations (CIO), the NFWU again changed its name—to the National Agricultural Workers Union—to reflect the renewed effort to organize American farmworkers. The AFL-CIO failed to financially support these organizing efforts, however, and the NAWU continued to flounder.

Part of the reason for the failure of the NAWU was the fact that the organization was chronically underfunded. Farmworkers, like tenant farmers and sharecroppers during the early history of the organization, were extremely poor and often unable to pay even the minimal dues required by the union. Because other unions were unwilling to provide the necessary funds for effective organizing campaigns—or strike funds—the NAWU was never able to organize enough workers to win contracts from the large, well-funded agricultural firms that employed most farmworkers.

A second obstacle to organizing farmworkers in the postwar era was the increased use of *braceros* (temporary migrant workers under a U.S.-Mexican government program) and undocumented laborers from Mexico. The Bracero Program, which allowed U.S. growers and agricultural firms to hire workers from Mexico, was established in 1942 to resolve farm labor shortages due to the conscription of able-bodied American males in the war effort and their hiring in war-related industries. Agribusiness interests were able to send recruiters into Mexico to seek out workers willing to come to "el norte" as part of the guest-worker program, which remained in effect until 1964. Undocumented workers from Mexico also became an important source of farm labor—particularly after Congress passed legislation in 1952 that exempted growers from legal penalties for hiring undocumented workers.

Efforts to organize farmworkers had always been chronically underfunded, and the merger of the CIO with the AFL in 1955 did nothing to alleviate this condition. Traditional labor had shown little inclination to tackle the special problems of organizing agricultural workers. The postwar shift to a largely Latino labor force reinforced this attitude. In 1954, in fact, many AFL unions enthusiastically endorsed the government crackdown on undocumented workers—a program called "Operation Wetback," whereby undocumented workers were deported, but the growers who employed them were not penalized.

By the time of the final name change, then, the NAWU had become largely moribund. In 1959, when the AFL-CIO announced a campaign to organize farmworkers, it bypassed the affiliated NAWU and created the Agricultural Workers Organizing

Committee (AWOC)—despite the fact that the NAWU was already chartered with that responsibility. When the NAWU merged with the Amalgamated Meat Cutters and Butcher Workmen (who had rejected merger overtures from the Packinghouse Workers Union) in 1960, it ceased operating as an independent union and left the task of organizing farmworkers to other unions that proved more adept at addressing the concerns and problems of migrant farmworkers.

Gregory M. Miller

See also: Chávez, César; Migrant Workers; Unions, Industrial and Trade; United Farm Workers of America.

Further Reading

Galarza, Ernesto. *Farm Workers and Agri-Business in California, 1947–1960.* South Bend, IN: University of Notre Dame Press, 1977.

Meister, Dick, and Anne Loftis. *A Long Time Coming: The Struggle to Unionize America's Farm Workers.* New York: Macmillan, 1977.

Mitchell, H.L. *Mean Things Happening in This Land: The Life and Times of H.L. Mitchell, Cofounder of the Southern Tenant Farmers Union.* Montclair, NJ: Allanheld, Osmun, 1979.

National Association of Cuban-American Women

A service organization based in Washington, D.C., the National Association of Cuban-American Women of the United States (NACAW-USA) works to achieve equal education and training, meaningful work, and fair compensation for Latinas and other minority women in America. The organization was founded in 1972 by Ana Maria Perera, formerly a professor in Cuba, who immigrated to the United States in the 1960s, under its Spanish-language equivalent Assocación Nacional de Mujeres Cubanoamericanas de Estados Unidos. In 1994, the organization absorbed the National Association of Cuban Men and Women of the United States, increasing its membership to more than 5,000.

NACAW operates its most extensive programs in the eastern half of United States, in cities such as Union City, New Jersey, and Fort Wayne, Indiana, where it disseminates information on postsecondary educational opportunities and sources of financial aid. Chapters act as clearinghouses and referral centers, where they coordinate activities with national Latino organizations, respond to female concerns from minority populations, and encourage participation in legislative activities and professional endeavors.

One of the purposes of the organization is to promote and maintain Cuban traditions and practices within the United States. The organization's New Jersey chapter, for example, participates in the Three Kings Day celebration initiated by the National Cuban American Association in 1982. As part of the festivities, and in keeping with Cuban traditions, three organization members dressed as kings hand out gifts to community children at local parks. On Easter Sunday, chapter members and associates make a yearly hospitality visit to children in the Jersey City Medical Center and an AIDS group home.

The organization has established an award to recognize women who fight for human rights. Their award is named for the late Elena Mederos, who served as minister of social welfare in Fidel Castro's government in 1959 and left for the United States in 1961 to fight for human rights. In 1998, Univision talk show host Cristina Saralegui was awarded the Elena Mederos Award for her leadership in the Latino community. In 2002, Adriana Birne, principal of the Early Childhood Programs for the Union City (New Jersey) Board of Education, was named the winner for contributions to her community. And in 2007, a group of six Cuban political prisoners known as *Las Plantadas* ("the emplanted ones" or "firm ones") was honored with the award for their refusal to conform to the Castro government, for setting an example of "the dignity and courage of women," and for promoting the cause of a free Cuba. The six women—Gladys Campaneria, Genovena Felixgraw, Olga Morgan, Miriam Ortega, Clara Rodriguez, and Ana Lazara Rodriguez—had worked against the Cuban dictator during the 1950s and 1960s; this led to their imprisonment, torture, and eventual exile.

NACAW leaders work with other organizations that benefit Cuban American women, such as the

Cuban-American Legal Defense and Education Fund, a nonprofit organization that helps Cuban Americans and other Hispanics gain equal treatment and equal opportunity in the fields of education, employment, housing, politics, and criminal justice.

Erika Gisela Abad

See also: Cubans.

Further Reading

Coalition of Cuban-American Women. http://coalitionof cubanamericanwomen.blogspot.com.

Hispanic Heritage Foundation. http://www.hispanic heritage.org.

"National Women of Color Organizations." Ford Foundation Archives. http://www.fordfound.org.

"Remembering the 'Plantadas'—National Association of Cuban-American Women honors ex-political prisoners." *Hispanic Tips,* March, 27, 2007. http://www.hispanictips.com.

National Boricua Latino Health Organization

The National Boricua Latino Health Organization (NBLHO) is a Latino medical student group found at medical schools throughout the northeastern United States. Its mission is to recruit Latinos/as into the health professions, educate the public and the medical community about Latino health issues, advocate for increased Latino participation in all medical fields, and promote awareness about social, political, and economic issues as they relate to Latino health. It also serves as a support network for Latino students and health professionals.

The group was formed in 1972 at Harvard Medical School (HMS) by two students, Jaime "Gus" Rivera and Emilio J. Carrillo, who received their medical degrees in 1976. Having benefited from the support of Dr. Helen Rodriguez Trias, the chief of pediatrics at Lincoln Hospital in the Bronx, New York City, Rivera and Carrillo saw a need for a Latino support group in Boston. In 1972, there were few Latinos/as living on the East Coast and even fewer attending the three major medical schools in Boston (Harvard Medical School, Tufts

School of Medicine, and Boston University School of Medicine).

In the late 1960s, Harvard had begun an initiative to recruit minority students to its medical school. Alvin Poussaint, an African American physician from Mississippi and a veteran of the civil rights movement, was hired to lead the initiative, resulting in an increased number of medical students of color.

Minority students often faced a racially difficult climate. During their first year at Harvard Medical School, Rivera and Carrillo staged a sit-in in the dean's office to demand increased Latino representation in the student body and ultimately the ranks of faculty. In addition to serving on the HMS admissions committee, Rivera and Carrillo founded the Boricua Health Organization (BHO) in 1972 and hired a student recruiter, Carmen Troche Rivera, to increase the matriculation of Latino students at the three Boston medical schools.

In addition to cofounding the Boricua Health Organization, Carrillo started the *Journal of Latin Community Health* and the *Journal of Multicultural Community Health.* He has served on a number of state and federal advisory councils, and cofounded the Manhattan Cross Cultural Group, a training and research organization committed to improving health care for diverse patient populations and eliminating health disparities. He has also served as president and chief medical officer of the New York–Presbyterian Community Health Plan and as associate professor of clinical public health and medicine at the Weill Cornell Medical College.

Today, there are approximately twenty-four active medical school chapters of the NBLHO and 200 student members from Washington, D.C., to Maine. New chapters and members are being added every year. The organization focuses on recruitment and provides educational and career guidance for Latino high school and college students interested in becoming physicians. An annual conference brings together Latino college students, medical students, and physicians to focus on the prominent health care issues affecting the Latino community, such as language barriers, cultural competency, migrant health care, and community access programs. The NBLHO is a member of the National Network of Latin American Medical Students, a national partnership of regional Latino medical student groups.

Lenny Lopez

See also: Health and Health Care.

Further Reading

Aguirre-Molina, Marilyn, Carlos W. Molina, and Ruth Enid Zambrana. *Health Issues in the Latino Community.* San Francisco: Jossey-Bass, 2001.

National Boricua Latino Health Organization. http://www.nblho.org.

Smedley, Brian D., Adrienne Y. Stith, and Alan R. Nelson, eds. *Unequal Treatment: Confronting Racial and Ethnic Disparities in Health Care.* Washington, DC: National Academies, 2003.

National Chicano Moratorium

Held on August 29, 1970, in East Los Angeles, the National Chicano Moratorium was the largest anti–Vietnam War demonstration of Chicanos/as in the United States. By the late 1960s, many segments of American society were questioning the country's involvement in the Vietnam War. The Chicano National Moratorium was part of a series of demonstrations held by Chicanos/as from 1969 through 1970. At the time, Chicanos/as represented 8 to 12 percent of the Southwest population but accounted for 22 percent of the region's war casualties. Because of the infrequency of student deferments, the difficulties they faced finding employment, and other factors, America's poor and people of color were serving disproportionately in the armed forces. The National Chicano Moratorium sought to give voice to these inequities, denouncing the war as yet another imperial effort that put young men and women of color in harm's way. In message and tactics, the moratorium represented one effort in the broader Chicano movement for civil rights, national identity, and economic and political self-determination.

Rosalio Muñoz, a former student body president at the University of California, Los Angeles (UCLA); Sal Baldenegro of the University of Arizona; Ernesto Vigil of the Crusade for Justice in Denver; Manuel Gómez of Hayward State College; Lorenzo Campbell of the University of California, Riverside; and David Sánchez of the Brown Berets all refused induction into the military and began planning actions to protest the war during the late 1960s. Eventually, Muñoz met with Rodolpho "Corky" Gonzales, the founder of the Crusade for Justice, and held a series of meetings to plan a moratorium against the war. The Brown Berets formed the National Chicano Moratorium Committee, and two protests were held—on December 20, 1969, and on February 28, 1970—with thousands in attendance. Similar protests took place throughout the Southwest, and at the Second Annual Chicano Youth Conference a National Chicano Moratorium was planned for August of that year in Los Angeles.

To prevent violence, preparations for the National Chicano Moratorium were extensively rehearsed in a series of smaller marches that included members of the Mexican-American Unity Council, Movimiento Estudiantil Chicano de Aztlán, and Mexican American Political Association. The police kept close surveillance on all these antiwar activities, as did members of the Federal Bureau of Investigation's COINTELPRO unit (a counterintelligence program).

On the day of the moratorium, between 20,000 and 30,000 men, women, children, and seniors marched, sang, and eventually settled in Laguna Park for speeches, music, picnic lunches, and *ballet folklórico*. A minor skirmish at a local liquor store spilled over into the park, and police used the incident as a pretext to rush the area and break up the peaceful demonstration. Municipal and county law enforcement officers shot tear gas into the crowd; protestors threw rocks and debris to defend themselves against beatings. The injured and fleeing found refuge in nearby homes. A makeshift legal aid center was established to help those who had been arrested, and older activists directed the injured to a local medical center. The resulting stampede left sixty-one persons injured, led to the arrest of more than 400, damaged 158 buildings, and destroyed four, with over $1 million in property damage. The most tragic result was the death of news reporter Rubén Salazar and two others, including fifteen-year-old Brown Beret member Mark Ward.

After covering the day's events, Salazar had gone to relax at the Silver Dollar Bar with two KMEX-TV colleagues. Police claimed a suspect was hiding in the bar and shot a ten-inch tear gas projectile into the establishment. The projectile struck Salazar and killed him. Salazar had reported on the February 1970 Los Angeles moratorium with a column in the *Los Angeles Times*. He had painted a complex picture of the moratorium within the Chicano community, focusing on the generational divide regarding the war.

Chicanos/as found the death of Salazar suspicious because he was working on a series of stories titled "What Progress in Thirty Years of Police Community Relations?" The series followed on the heels of his coverage of the deaths of two Mexican nationals, cousins Guillermo and Beltran Sánchez, at the hands of Los Angeles detectives and the San Leandro police. Police had threatened Salazar, demanding that he tone down his coverage of the episode, as it was inciting the Chicano community. Salazar refused to do so, and police-community relations continued to deteriorate.

The Chicano community was enraged when the investigation into Salazar's death turned into an indictment of the National Chicano Moratorium itself, with the Los Angeles District Attorney's Office depicting protestors as Communists by pointing to "Viva Che" signs held by some. Although an inquest by the Los Angeles Coroner's Office ruled the death of Ruben Salazar a homicide, the Los Angeles district attorney concluded that the police acted in good faith, further angering the community.

A movie about the National Chicano Moratorium and the subsequent investigation and acquittal, which was titled *Requiem 29,* was produced in 1970 by East L.A. Thirteen member Moctezuma Esparza and directed by David García. It won a bronze medal at the Atlanta International Film Festival the following year.

Although the National Chicano Moratorium was crushed, the antiwar movement among Chicanos/as gained strength. Rubén Salazar was considered a martyr of the Chicano movement, dying unjustly in the fight for civil rights. Laguna Park in downtown Los Angeles was renamed Salazar Park in his honor.

Susan Marie Green

See also: Brown Berets; Chicano Movement; Gonzales, Rodolfo "Corky"; Mexican American Political Association; Movimiento Estudiantíl Chicano de Aztlán; Salazar, Rubén.

Further Reading

Acuña, Rodolfo. *Occupied America: A History of Chicanos.* 5th ed. New York: Pearson Longman, 2004.

García, Mario T. *Memories of Chicano History: The Life and Narrative of Bert Corona.* Berkeley: University of California Press, 1994.

Muñoz, Carlos, Jr. *Youth, Identity, Power: The Chicano Movement.* New York: Verso, 1989.

Salazar, Ruben. *Border Correspondent: Selected Writings, 1955–1970.* Ed. Mario T. García. Berkeley: University of California Press, 1995.

National Conference of Puerto Rican Women

In 1972, the National Conference of Puerto Rican Women (NACOPRW) was founded in Washington, D.C., as a nonprofit, nonpartisan organization to advocate for the civil rights of Puerto Rican women and other Latinas in the United States. The organization's goals are to ensure that Puerto Rican and other Latinas secure equal rights under the law; to promote equitable social, economic, and political participation for Puerto Rican women; to support the continuing development of leadership skills among Puerto Rican women; to strengthen communications among all Latinas in North America; and to foster continued awareness of the value of Puerto Rican cultural heritage.

NACOPRW was formed to address the needs of women at a time when early organizations and activist groups, such as the National Puerto Rican Forum and the Young Lords, were established to address the specific concerns of mainland Puerto Rican communities. Although such organizations had a positive impact on the sociopolitical power of the Puerto

Rican community, leadership was largely in the hands of men, and they lacked a specific focus on the needs of Puerto Rican women. It was not until 1972 that two organizations were established that had female leadership: the Puerto Rican Legal Defense and Education Fund and the National Conference of Puerto Rican Women. NACOPRW, however, was the first organization founded for the sole purpose of meeting the needs of women in Puerto Rican and other Latino communities, which it continues to serve in the 2000s.

Member participation takes place at both the local and the national levels. Seven members sit on the board of directors, and the organization has five standing committees with at least two members each. In addition to Washington, D.C., NACOPRW maintains a visible presence with twelve chapters across the United States: Miami, Florida; Orlando, Florida; Chicago and East Chicago, Illinois; Northern Illinois; Indiana; Tri-County Chapters, Maryland; Nassau-Suffolk (Long Island), New York; New York City; Philadelphia; California; and Northern Virginia. Voting rights and eligibility for local and national offices within the organization vary according to membership class; however, everyone who is a member of the organization has the opportunity to be heard at meetings. Members are kept up-to-date on events, issues, and other organizational information through a quarterly newsletter, *Ecos Nationales* (National Echoes), and an annual conference.

NACOPRW conferences serve above all as a networking tool, bringing together Latinas from throughout the United States who play significant leadership roles in their respective communities. As of 2008, NACOPRW had held a total of twenty-eight annual conferences, emphasizing the training and education of Latinas from all demographics. Themes discussed have included health care, leadership training, economic development, education, technology, mentoring, and political empowerment. Perennial conference highlights include exhibit booths provided by federal and state government agencies, which inform participants of the services they provide and job openings.

The national organization supports local communities by providing scholarships to Latina students in the area. Local chapters organize and participate in events meaningful to Latina culture and education, including family picnics and food events featuring Puerto Rican cuisine, youth-leadership groups, and networking events with other Puerto Rican civic organizations. Under President Anaida Colón-Muñiz, the national headquarters in Washington, D.C., works with like-minded advocacy groups as a political lobbying force and promotes the creation of local chapters.

Vanessa Esther Martinez-Renuncio

See also: Puerto Ricans; Young Lords.

Further Reading

Hernandez, Aileen C. "National Women of Color Organizations: A Report to the Ford Foundation." Ford Foundation, Women's Program Forum, 1991.
National Conference of Puerto Rican Women. http://www.nacoprw.com.

National Congress for Puerto Rican Rights

The National Congress for Puerto Rican Rights (NCPRR) is an activist, grassroots organization founded in the South Bronx, New York City, in 1981 to address the social injustices experienced by Puerto Ricans in the United States. It was established by Juan González, Richie Perez, and Vicente "Panamá" Alba—all former members of the disbanded Young Lords Party, a 1960s Puerto Rican nationalist youth organization—who organized a convention to form a human rights group that would address the needs of local Puerto Ricans. A number of the early members of NCPRR were also former members of the Young Lords Party.

Dedicated to pursuing full equality and ending discrimination, NCPRR advocates for the human and civil rights of Puerto Ricans; educates members and the community about the conditions affecting the Puerto Rican and Latino communities, such as poverty and lack of jobs; and recommends ways of improving them. The organization supports affiliated organizations and local groups by bringing citywide and national support to their local efforts.

It also develops new leadership, with an emphasis on youth and women; informs elected representatives and public officials about problems in the U.S. Puerto Rican community and offers ways of addressing them; organizes local and national campaigns; serves as a voice for other Puerto Ricans who cannot speak out because they work in agencies or community groups dependent on government funding; and mentors new activists. The group's student networking committee provides a forum and support group for student activists and seeks to foster community and campus activism in the New York City area.

Before establishing the NCPRR, González, Perez, and Alba had extensive backgrounds in community organizing. As the principal organizers of the Young Lords Party, they called upon their experience and their extensive ties in the Puerto Rican community to launch NCPRR. As head of the NCPRR's Justice Committee, Perez focused his efforts on the issues of racial profiling and police brutality in Puerto Rican neighborhoods and as an advocate against recruitment of impoverished Puerto Rican youth by the U.S. armed forces. Alba also played a strong role in the creation of the Justice Committee and was instrumental in organizing various protests with fellow Young Lords cofounder Miguel "Mickey" Melendez, who wrote of the Young Lords experience in his memoir, *We Took the Streets: Fighting for Latino Rights with the Young Lords* (2003).

NCPRR publishes a biennial *Status Report on Puerto Ricans in the U.S.,* which presents an unvarnished and up-to-date picture of the living conditions of Puerto Ricans in cities across the United States; other publications include a series of national and local newsletters. The organization also engages in activities such as dinners, marches, and rallies that seek to preserve the Spanish language and Puerto Rican culture. It seeks progressive coalitions with other people of color, such as Mexican Americans and African Americans, and groups fighting discrimination. The NCPRR is perhaps best known for its organizing against environmental racism, police abuse and brutality, racially motivated violence, unemployment, and other forms of discrimination; its work in support of local communities and issues affecting Puerto Ricans on the island; and its campaigns

to hold elected and appointed officials accountable. The group also works with New York area groups, such as the Community Service Society, to increase Puerto Rican voter registration in the city. Chapters throughout the United States, including ones in Philadelphia, Boston, and San Francisco, remain active in addressing these and specific local issues.

Erika Gisela Abad

See also: Puerto Ricans; Young Lords.

Further Reading

Melendez, Miguel "Mickey, and José Torres. *We Took the Streets: Fighting for Latino Rights with the Young Lords.* New York: St. Martin's, 2003.
National Congress for Puerto Rican Rights. http://www.columbia.edu/~rmg36/NCPRR.html.

National Council of Hispanic Women

Founded in 1984, the National Council of Hispanic Women (NCHW) is a nonprofit organization located in Washington, D.C., whose main concern is to empower Hispanic women. The NCHW has two primary goals: to integrate Hispanic woman into mainstream American society through collaboration with universities and corporations, and to achieve a greater representation of Hispanic women in policy making through their leadership in business and government.

NCHW accomplishes these goals by running outreach programs for young Hispanic women, attending conferences with other Hispanic American organizations, sponsoring workshops that teach entrepreneurial skills to Hispanic American women, conducting studies on government initiatives that affect the lives of Hispanic American women, and establishing a scholarship fund to assist Hispanic American women in achieving their goals of higher education.

Although the organization focuses primarily on the integration and success of Latinas, members also work with and for individuals regardless of race, creed, nationality, and religion. To that effect, the NCHW has been actively involved and has consistently collaborated with a diverse group of organizations pursuing similar goals, such as the American Association of University Women, a 100,000-member organization that advances equality for women and girls through advocacy, education, and research, and the National Council of La Raza (NCLR), a nonprofit organization dedicated to reducing poverty and discrimination and improving opportunities for Hispanic Americans.

NCHW's office is located in Washington, D.C., but members span the country, working closely with the NCLR and other institutions whose mission complements theirs, such as the Small Business Administration, the U.S. Administration on Aging, and the National Association of State Units on Aging. The council has also endorsed political campaigns of candidates who work to further the goals of Hispanics.

NCHW is a partner organization of the Hispanic Heritage Foundation and its Hispanic Heritage Award, which recognizes the achievements of Hispanic Americans and offers youth mentorship programs. In addition to collaborating with such national organizations and programs, individual NCHW chapters also work to sponsor local events. In 2006, for example, Martha Steinkamp of the Florida chapter of NCHW presented a documentary of Florida first ladies at the Broward County celebration of Women's History Month. Marti Arci, a trustee of NCHW and vice president of the Hispanic Council for Reform and Educational Options, worked in support of the No Child Left Behind Act of 2001, training parents on the specific guidelines of the law and its initiatives for improving the performance of U.S. primary and secondary school students.

NCHW's collaborative efforts with a wide range of government offices, other Hispanic not-for-profit organizations, and universities demonstrate its commitment to political and ideological impartiality. This speaks specifically to the goal of integrating Hispanics into leadership roles and participation in mainstream U.S. society. Toward that end, the organization has honored such women role models as New York State Supreme Court Justice Irma Vidal and former Mayor Dora Alcala of Del Rio, Texas. Likewise it has recognized Hispanic women who have served in the U.S. armed forces, those who have held local

and state offices, and those who have dedicated their lives to social advocacy and education.

In 1999, NCHW President Evangelina Elizondo participated in the Congreso Internacional de la Mujer Hispana in Guadalajara, Jalisco, Mexico, with representatives from Mexico and other Latin American countries. Economist Velma Montoya, who worked as an expert economist for the federal government, served in 2004 as president of NCHW, on the Steering Committee for "Bush-Cheney '04 W Stands for Women," and on the advisory board for the University of California's Outreach Board in 1999. Education has been one of the main concerns of women and men involved in NCHW, who regard it as an important way of securing socioeconomic mobility and political participation.

The Online Archive of California's collection on the National Council of La Raza includes information on NCLR's efforts in assisting various national organizations, including the National Council of Hispanic Women. Other documentary information on the NCHW can be found in the Irene I. Blea Papers at the University of New Mexico's Southwest Research Center.

Erika Gisela Abad

See also: Education; National Council of La Raza; Politics.

Further Reading

National Council of Hispanic Women. http://www.nch women.org.

National Council of La Raza

Billed as the largest national Latino-based civil rights and advocacy group in the United States today, the National Council of La Raza (NCLR) is a private, nonprofit, nonpartisan, tax-exempt organization headquartered in Washington, D.C. Founded in 1968, the NCLR has, since its establishment, worked at both the state and local levels to increase opportunities for the Latino community.

Janet Murguía, president and chief executive officer of the National Council of La Raza, speaks at the inauguration of the organization's new headquarters in Washington, D.C., in June 2005. *(Alex Wong/Getty Images)*

With the help of a $630,000 grant from the Ford Foundation, the NCLR was founded as the Southwest Council of La Raza, a service-oriented organization in Phoenix, Arizona. The Ford grant was used to finance an unprecedented study of Mexican American society. Part of the funds was used to hire three Mexican American activists—Julian Samora, Herman Gallegos, and Ernesto Galarza—to travel throughout the Southwest and consult with local leaders about the needs of the Mexican American community. The study revealed that Mexican Americans faced a number of obstacles in their way toward achieving a secure place in American society; the most notable was chronic poverty. Organization leaders also identified a clear need for more local, grassroots advocacy and for a national organization to promote the cause of Mexican Americans and other Latinos/as in the United States.

The Southwest Council of La Raza emerged as a leading umbrella organization in the fight to end the exclusion of Mexican Americans from the U.S. mainstream and became a unifying voice of the community. From its inception, the group worked to strengthen community-based Chicano organizations throughout the Southwest, providing them with advice, support, and financial contributions for housing and economic development programs. By 1972, after steadily expanding its field of social and political activity, the Southwest Council moved its main offices to Washington, D.C., and changed its name to the National Council of La Raza.

A central goal of the NCLR was to narrow the gap between Chicano and mainstream Anglo society. Another major focus of its efforts was to promote the work of community organizations—making a special effort to raise money for civil rights groups such as the Mexican American Legal Defense and Education Fund (MALDEF), a program dedicated to protecting the civil rights and liberties of Mexican Americans through the legal system, and the Southwest Voter Registration Education Project, a program founded in 1947 by Willie Velasquez of San Antonio, Texas, which focuses on registering Mexican Americans to vote. La Raza Investment Corporation, a Mexican American company widely known for providing loans and managerial assistance to barrio businesspeople, was an extension of the NCLR's plan to provide Mexican Americans with seed funds to ensure their success.

With civil rights veteran Raul Yzaguerre taking over as president from Henry Santiestevan in 1974, the NCLR emerged as an influential national organization. Under Yzaguerre's leadership, the NCLR became one of the largest Latino-based umbrella organizations in the country, with more than 300 affiliate groups, 35,000 members, and an annual budget of more than $40 million. Its activities expanded commensurately. In 1975, Yzaguerre used the NCLR to organize the Forum of National Hispanic Organizations, which brought Puerto Rican and Cuban groups into the fold. Over the course of the next three decades, the NCLR has provided invaluable support to an extensive list of community organizations, fighting for better educational opportunities, for improved housing, against discrimination, and for the greater inclusion of Mexican Americans in U.S. society.

The NCLR has also lent its support to voter registration campaigns, playing a key role in giving Mexican Americans and other Latinos/as a stronger voice in government at every level. The National Council of La Raza thus ranks with such other major civil rights organizations as the League of United Latin American Citizens (LULAC), the oldest Mexican American civil rights group in America; the American GI Forum, founded in 1949 by Hector P. García and made up mostly of Chicano veterans; and the Mexican American Legal Defense and Education Fund (MALDEF). From its headquarters in the nation's capital, the NCLR continues to play a major role in the development of community programs and other civil rights issues, including job discrimination,

voting rights and gerrymandering, and bilingual education. Current activities emphasize research and analysis, technical assistance to local organizations in program development, funding, and operation.

Jesse J. Esparza

See also: American GI Forum; La Raza; League of United Latin American Citizens; Mexican American Legal Defense and Education Fund; Poverty.

Further Reading
Gonzales, Sylvia Alicia. *Hispanic American Voluntary Organizations.* Westport, CT: Greenwood 1985.
National Council of La Raza. http://www.nclr.org.
"State of Hispanic America." Washington, DC: National Council of La Raza, 1998.

National Farm Labor Union

The National Farm Labor Union (NFLU), originally called the Southern Tenant Farmers' Union (STFU), was founded in 1934 to help tenant farmers and sharecroppers in the South secure better working conditions. The organization was unique in its time, as it sought to organize both white and black workers. The STFU changed its name to the National Farm Labor Union on December 12, 1945, in order to include the agricultural areas of the West Coast and Southwest, and expand its efforts to the national level. The organization, led by Ernesto Galarza, became especially important to Latinos/as during World War II, when farm labor shortages were brought on by a combination of military conscription and the mass migration of black and white Southerners to the North and West in search of industrial jobs. This led large planters in the South to mechanize cotton cultivation, and agribusiness interests in other regions to turn to the government for assistance in recruiting farm labor. To meet the labor shortage, chiefly in the agricultural sector, the U.S. and Mexican governments reached an agreement in 1942 that established the Bracero temporary-worker program. The STFU opposed the Bracero Program, arguing that farm jobs should go to its members, many of whom had migrated to California and parts of the Southwest, rather than to Mexican nationals.

After the war, the renamed and reorganized NFLU attempted to organize workers employed by large agribusiness firms in California, many of whom were Mexican Bracero Program workers, known as *braceros*. The initial target was the DiGiorgio Corporation based at the Arvin Ranch near Bakersfield, perhaps the strongest foe of unionization among California growers. After two months of organizing, however, the NFLU had successfully signed up a majority of full-time workers at DiGiorgio. Later in 1948, following the company's refusal to recognize the union or bargain with its leaders, the NFLU called the workers out on strike. On the first day of the job action, more than 1,000 workers—white and Mexican American, joined by 130 braceros—formed picket lines that extended 20 miles (36 kilometers) around the Arvin Ranch site.

The DiGiorgio company turned for assistance to the U.S. Department of Agriculture and the consul of Mexico; braceros who refused to report were threatened with immediate deportation and the loss of their bracero status. The U.S. government, meanwhile, brought in additional braceros to replace the strikers. Despite provisions in the Bracero Program agreement that barred workers in the program from being used as strikebreakers, Kern County sheriff's deputies escorted the new arrivals through the picket lines.

Notwithstanding government efforts to break the will of the union, the strikers remained on the picket line. In addition, members of the Teamsters Union and winery workers refused to handle grapes picked by strikebreakers in a secondary boycott action. And as a third tier of resistance, the NFLU called upon the general public to boycott all DiGiorgio products. Although the momentum of the strike was cause for optimism among workers and the union, a federal examiner ruled that the National Labor Relations Act of 1935, which guaranteed the right of collective bargaining, did not cover farmworkers in regard to secondary boycotts, making those tactics illegal. The ruling of the National Labor Relations Board contributed to the dissolution of the strike in 1950.

Large growers and agribusinesses relied increasingly on braceros, who had no rights as U.S. citizens, to undermine union job actions and keep workers in line—to use them, in effect, as strikebreakers or replacements. To counter this practice, Ernesto Galarza, a prominent NFLU organizer, dedicated himself to exposing and challenging the abuse of the program and breaches of the original agreement.

Because of the perceived abundance of cheap labor from Mexico—both braceros and undocumented workers—the NFLU was largely unsuccessful in organizing farm labor in the United States. That is, braceros and undocumented workers proved difficult to organize in the 1940s, because most were migrants and because they were offered few legal protections under U.S. law. A young Chicano named César Chávez, who in 1962 founded a successor to the NFLU, the National Farm Workers Association (NFWA)—later the United Farm Workers (UFW)—took up the cause of farm labor in America again.

Gregory M. Miller

See also: Bracero Program; Unions, Industrial and Trade; United Farm Workers of America.

Further Reading

Galarza, Ernesto. *Farm Workers and Agri-Business in California, 1947–1960.* South Bend, IN: University of Notre Dame Press, 1977.

Meister, Dick, and Anne Loftis. *A Long Time Coming: The Struggle to Unionize America's Farm Workers.* New York: Macmillan, 1977.

Mitchell, H.L. *Mean Things Happening in This Land: The Life and Times of H.L. Mitchell, Cofounder of the Southern Tenant Farmers Union.* Montclair, NJ: Allanheld, Osmun, 1979.

National Puerto Rican Coalition

The National Puerto Rican Coalition (NPRC), a Washington, D.C.–based advocacy group, works to improve the economic, political, and social well-being of Puerto Ricans both on the U.S. mainland and in Puerto Rico. As of 2007, the NPRC was the nation's leading Puerto Rican advocacy and policy organization, responsible for representing the interests of 7 million U.S. citizens through a network of more than 1,000 community-based organizations and leaders.

In 1976, the U.S. Commission on Civil Rights (USCCR) published a report titled *Puerto Ricans in the United States: An Uncertain Future,* which described the substandard employment, education, and income conditions facing Puerto Ricans residing in the continental United States. To improve this situation, the USCCR convened a meeting the following year in Washington, D.C., inviting forty Puerto Rican community leaders to discuss what could be done at the national level to effect change. At the meeting, the participants concluded that a national organization was necessary to effectively address the poverty and disenfranchisement issues plaguing the Puerto Rican community. Thus, the NPRC was established in 1977 to bring Puerto Rican community issues to the national level and engage in public policy decision-making.

In the 2000s, the NPRC achieves its goals through involvement in public policy-making, community building, and youth leadership formation. Public policy initiatives are aimed at educating public officials, community advocates, and the community at large on the social issues that affect the most vulnerable Puerto Ricans and other Latinos. The coalition does this by reporting on the impact of legislative changes on federally funded social interest programs and publishing demographic profiles on congressional districts with significant Puerto Rican populations. *The National Directory of Puerto Rican Elected Officials,* compiled by the NPRC, lists elected legislative officials of Puerto Rican background at the federal, state, and municipal levels. The NPRC's public policy analysis on issues affecting Puerto Ricans and Latinos in general provides invaluable input for national organizations and their advocates.

The Community Building Initiative is the NPRC's most significant community outreach program, through which it provides assistance to nonprofit civic groups in an effort to create and implement solutions to political, social, and economic issues. In cooperation with other community advocacy organizations, such as the National Hispanic Housing Council, the NPRC provides technical assistance for housing programs. All told, the NPRC has assisted more than 200 communities by providing financial backing for social interest housing and economic development projects.

To address the specific needs of Puerto Rican and other Latino students, the NPRC also runs the Puerto Rican/Latino Youth Development Initiative, involving students in the NPRC's annual conference and engaging them in public policy formulation and leadership skills development. The program strengthens connections between students nationwide through constant communication and meetings. The quarterly newsletter *Adelante* informs students about public-policy issues and actively encourages them to submit their viewpoints as articles for publication. To empower Latino youth with the employment skills needed to succeed, the NPRC offers training sessions and seminars through its College to Career Program.

The NPRC has played an active role in the struggle to end the U.S. Navy's occupation of Vieques, Puerto Rico. Activities have included participation in national protests to end the occupation and filing civil rights violations complaints with the U.S. Department of Justice against the Navy. In addition, the NPRC has been instrumental in lobbying the Environmental Protection Agency (EPA) to include Vieques in the list of Superfund sites, making it eligible to receive federal funds for cleanup and restoration of polluted areas.

Juan Declet and Tischa A. Muñoz-Erickson

See also: Education; Politics; Puerto Ricans; Vieques, Puerto Rico.

Further Reading

National Puerto Rican Coalition. http://www.bateylink.org.

Nationalism

Nationalism is a feeling of loyalty and devotion toward one's country, elevating its ideals and promoting its interests against those of other countries or interest groups that would resist, threaten, or deny them. It entails a sense of pride in national identity based on common origin, ethnicity, or cultural ties, and a commitment—individually or as part of a group or movement—to take action to achieve or sustain national self-determination. While fundamentally related, the nationalist struggles of each of the three major Latino immigrant groups in the United States—Mexican American/Chicano, Puerto Rican, and Cuban American—have been unique in ideology and practice. As each group entered the United States under different circumstances, for different reasons, and with a different relationship to the home country, their reception and strategies for maintaining cultural identity and political and economic power have varied. Latino nationalisms have evolved in stages, moving from assimilation and accommodation to armed resistance and separatism, with self-defense and mutual aid somewhere in between. All of these strategies have achieved a measure of success, ensuring that they will be revived in succeeding generations.

Nationalism for Latinos does not necessarily focus on a nation-state per se as a sovereign political entity, but on how a cultural and political community with a shared history and ideology represents itself and its interests; it is virtually synonymous in modern times with political consciousness. Although land ownership is often a central goal of national movements, Latino nationalists generally do not seek property and sovereignty per se, but rather a national identity, rights, and recognition in the context of broader U.S. society. Latino nationalisms thus are regarded as subsets of mainstream American nationalism, sometimes complementary but more often as a result of power struggle and contestation. The official or dominant nationalism of the United States is based largely on the experiences and histories of white, landed, Anglo-Saxon Protestant men. Latino nationalism often manifests itself when mainstream America fails to represent a particular group and its sociocultural, political, or economic interests, or when those interests move in a different direction. Historically, nationalist affiliations in America have been mutually exclusive. That is, individuals generally have not been able to be members of two nationalities at the same time; one could not be Cuban *and* American, but Cuban *or* American. Nor could

one be a person of color and be defined or identified within the confines of the white American nation.

Two events in U.S. history that have contributed especially to nationalist sentiments and movements in twentieth-century Latino communities are the Mexican-American War, which ended in 1848, and the Spanish-American War fifty years later, including the treaties and agreements that resulted from them. Both had an enduring influence on the variables that have shaped Latino nationalism in all its forms and expressions: race, membership in the community, geographic location, gender, time frame, demographics, and socioeconomic and political contexts. Among their legacies have been a history of disenfranchisement and the denial of other citizenship rights by means of poll taxes, separate but equal educational facilities, and English-only initiatives. Yet Latinos/as have not been powerless or voiceless, creating change through intermarriage, political organization and patronage, armed resistance, social banditry, mutual aid societies, and labor unions in the late nineteenth and early twentieth centuries. In addition to traditional political means and legal institutions, they have turned to civil rights organizations, veterans groups, the church, lobbying, and various means of protest and boycott to make their feelings known and to affect political outcomes.

Mexican American Nationalism

Chicano nationalism and the Mexican American experience in the United States are unique because they are based on both conquest and immigration to the contiguous forty-eight states. Chicanos/as were technically created and incorporated into the United States in 1848 with the Treaty of Guadalupe Hidalgo at the end of the Mexican-American War. They are a racially and culturally blended, *mestizo* population indigenous to the United States. There have also been major waves of Mexican migration during the twentieth century, from the early decades right up to the 2000s, and issues of acceptance, identity, and assimilation—or lack thereof—have continued to be part of the everyday Chicano experience. Likewise, the mutually exclusive experiences of conquest and immigration/assimilation have shaped Chicano nationalism.

Mexicans, Mexican Americans, and later Chicanos/as have taken part in a variety of nationalist movements focused on assimilation in mainstream America. These have included participation in organizations like the League of United Latin American Citizens (LULAC), which emphasized political advocacy, U.S. patriotism, citizenship, and the learning and use of English language; the Partido Liberal Mexicano (PLM), the major political organization of Mexican and Mexican American intellectuals who supported the Mexican Revolution (1910–1920) and operated in Texas during the first two decades of the twentieth century; and the Asociación Nacional Mexico-Americana (ANMA), an organization established in 1950 to prevent the separation of family members and the expulsion of Mexican immigrants during Operation Wetback, the U.S. government's program to systematically deport undocumented workers from 1950 to 1955. A separatist Chicano nationalism evolved with the formation of a third Chicano political party, La Raza Unida, established by Latino activists in 1970 in response to the exclusion of Latinos from both the Democratic and Republican parties.

Puerto Rican Nationalism

Among Latino groups, Puerto Ricans have enjoyed a unique status in the United States. Following the Spanish-American War in 1898 and the signing of the Jones Act in 1917, Puerto Rico became a commonwealth of the United States; Puerto Ricans were granted U.S. citizenship and the right of free movement between the island and the mainland—though neither island nor mainland residents have enjoyed the same freedoms and privileges as other U.S. citizens. In any event, the Puerto Rican nationalist struggle has been different from that of Mexican Americans and other Latino groups. While the tenor and goals of Puerto Rican nationalism have shifted focus over time, the central enduring question has been that of the island's official status: whether it should become the fifty-first U.S. state, remain a commonwealth, or move to become an independent nation.

In the 1930s, Pedro Albizu Campos, the head of the Puerto Rican Nationalist Party, led a movement

The cause of Puerto Rican nationalism fueled the most persistent—and at times violent—Latino independence movement of the twentieth century. *Independentistas* today are in a small minority. *(Library of Congress)*

against U.S. imperialism and in favor of Puerto Rican independence. Also in the 1930s, Luis Muñoz Marín, a senator (and later governor) in Puerto Rico's Popular Democratic Party, campaigned for independence in rural areas, emphasizing land reform and self-sufficiency. (Muñoz Marín later supported commonwealth status.) These early movements paved the way for Puerto Rican nationalist groups to form on the island and mainland in the late 1960s, such as the Young Lords. Established in 1969 in New York City, the Young Lords Party was an urban-based movement for Puerto Rican civil rights and self-determination, not unlike the Chicano student organization Movimiento Estudiantíl Chicano de Aztlán (the Chicano Student Movement of Aztlán, or MEChA). The Young Lords protested for better education, health, and sanitation for Puerto Ricans in major cities across the United States.

Puerto Rican nationalists took up a new cause in the 1970s, protesting the U.S. Navy's live-ammunition target practice and military exercises on the island of Vieques (appropriated during the 1940s), despite a previous agreement to vacate the island and restore it to residents. Relying on community mobilization and civil disobedience, Vieques residents and protestors from the mainland engaged in a struggle to halt the bombardment of the island. Unlike the Young Lords of the 1960s and 1970s, the Vieques protestors gained widespread attention and mainstream support among the American public, including Hollywood celebrities such as Martin Sheen. The U.S. government finally agreed to end the bombing on Vieques, and the Navy turned over the last of its land holdings there to the Department of the Interior in 2003; the impact zones were designated as wilderness preserves.

The struggles of both the Young Lords and the Vieques protestors reflected the limited power of Puerto Ricans in relation to the U.S. government and their long-frustrated attempts to gain economic and political change. At the same time, however, mutual aid societies—voluntary associations formed to provide aid, benefit, or relief—have been active, and often successful, in promoting Puerto Rican identity and culture through local schools, self-help programs, parades, and patriotic celebrations. Artists, musicians, performers, writers, and athletes have also extended Puerto Rican issues into the mainstream when traditional political avenues have been blunted.

Cuban Nationalism

Although Cubans began entering the United States after the Spanish-American War in 1898, the close proximity of the island to the United States (about 90 miles or 150 kilometers) and the waves of political asylum seekers after the Cuban Revolution in 1959 have made their experience in the United States different from that of other Latino groups. Over the decades, various groups and organizations in the United States (including the federal government) have attempted or supported the overthrow of Cuban leader Fidel Castro and the "liberation" of the island, among them the National Liberation Movement, Hermanos al Rescate (Brothers to the Rescue), and the Cuban American National Foundation. Numerous other organizations were founded to support those who had fled the island for the United States.

In Miami in 1972, a leader of the Cuban exile community, Mario Vizcaino, established the Cuban American National Council (CNC) in an effort to integrate Cuban exiles and their children into U.S. society and serve as an advocate for this population. The CNC thus began providing social services, such as direct job placement and student internships, conducting research and publishing policy analyses, and working with other like-minded Latino organizations, such as the National Council of La Raza (NCLR), the largest national Latino civil rights and advocacy organization in the United States. Since its inception, the CNC has provided a range of social services to low-income Latinos, particularly in South Florida, where Dominicans, Haitians, and others have joined Cuban exile communities.

Cubans generally have enjoyed more mainstream success in the United States than Mexican Americans or Puerto Ricans, in part because of their greater financial resources and in part because of the unifying effects of their patriotism, anti-Castro fervor, and community resources. Cuban Americans have been successful in electing local officials, judges, governors, and even U.S. representatives and senators, thus achieving much more success than other Latino groups in gaining popular and governmental support for their nationalist agenda. Moreover, Cuban immigrants have been generally more educated and professionally trained than their Mexican and Puerto Rican counterparts, helping them secure better jobs, start their own businesses, and generally achieve greater economic success.

Other Nationalist Campaigns

Other Latino groups have been involved in notable nationalist efforts in the United States. Organizations such as the Central American Resource Center (CARECEN) and the Coalition for Human Immigrant Rights of Los Angeles (CHIRLA) have combined human rights campaigns with political mobilization and public-policy work to create change on behalf of various national groups. CARECEN, founded in 1983 by a group of Salvadoran refugees whose mission is to secure legal status for the thousands of Central Americans fleeing civil war, has worked to support permanent resident status, family reunification, and active citizenship for Salvadorans in the United States. CHIRLA, established in 1986, serves as both a clearinghouse and information provider to agencies and individuals about immigration laws and rights.

In the spring of 2006, U.S. Latinos demonstrated their collective civil and political power to an unprecedented degree on behalf of undocumented workers and immigration legislation reform. More than 2 million immigrants and their supporters marched in cities across the United States in defiance of the Sensenbrenner Bill of 2005, which proposed tightening the U.S.-Mexico border and subjecting undocumented immigrants to long prison terms. These protests foreshadowed the political potential of the Latino community in the United States and perhaps the formation of a broader pan-Latino nationalism that transcends geography and national origin.

Susan Marie Green

See also: Albizu Campos, Pedro; Chicano/a; Cubans; Jones Act (1917); La Raza Unida Party; League of United Latin American Citizens; Macheteros, Los; Mexicans; Movimiento Estudiantíl Chicano de Aztlán; Muñoz Marín, Luis; Puerto Ricans; Spanish-American War; Young Lords.

Further Reading

Anaya, Rudolfo, and Francisco Lomeli. *Aztlán: Essays on the Chicano Homeland.* Albuquerque: University of New Mexico Press, 1991.

García, Ignacio M. *Chicanismo: The Forging of a Militant Ethos among Mexican Americans.* Tucson: University of Arizona Press, 1997.

Geron, Kim. *Latino Political Power.* Boulder, CO: Lynne Rienner, 2005.

Gutiérrez, David. *Walls and Mirrors: Mexican Americans, Mexican Immigrants, and the Politics of Ethnicity.* Berkeley: University of California Press, 1995.

Oboler, Suzanne. *Ethnic Labels, Latino Lives: Identity and the Politics of (Re)Presentation in the United States.* Minneapolis: University of Minnesota Press, 1995.

New York

Although they are widely perceived to be a relatively recent immigrant group, Latinos/as have been living in New York State since the early nineteenth century. By the late twentieth century and certainly today, they have represented a sizable and highly influential segment of the state population, especially in the greater metropolitan area of New York City. According to the 2000 Census, Latinos/as constitute 15.1 percent of the state population. The actual number remains difficult to ascertain, however, given that a significant number of Spanish speakers do not have legal status. Of the 2,867,583 Latinos/as counted in the 2000 U.S. Census, approximately 2.16 million reside in the New York City metro area. Elsewhere, significant Latino communities are found in Erie and Monroe counties in the western part of the state.

Nineteenth Century to World War II

The early nineteenth century brought a trickle of Latino immigration to New York, largely from the Caribbean region. From 1810 to 1860, Latinos/as in the state belonged predominantly to the merchant class. An informal census by Yale president Timothy Dwight in 1810 noted the presence of a small class of Spanish and Latino Caribbean merchants in New York City. These businessmen oversaw trade between New York ports and Spanish ports in the Caribbean and other parts of Latin America. The first official count of Latinos/as was made in the state census of 1845, which reported 508 Mexicans and South Americans living in the New York City area; academics believe they were mostly merchants and their employees. Thus, the earliest Latino community was relatively homogeneous and concentrated in the business sector.

By 1860, the socioeconomic composition of the Latino population in New York City began to change. Latinos/as now could be found managing and working in factories, grocery stores, pharmacies, barbershops, artisan shops, restaurants, and boardinghouses. Many semiskilled and skilled laborers and artisans

Spanish Harlem, or El Barrio, in upper Manhattan became New York's largest Puerto Rican enclave during the Great Migration of the late 1940s and 1950s. Still the city's largest Latino community, Spanish Harlem has taken on a Mexican personality in recent years. *(Roy Stevens/Time & Life Pictures/Getty Images)*

worked in the tobacco industry, whose production and trade flourished in the state between 1880 and 1920. Another notable class of Latino immigrants in New York City at the end of the nineteenth century was political exiles. Among the most notable figures of the émigré community were the Cuban freedom fighter José Martí, self-described "Afro-Puerto Rican" independence advocate Arturo Alfonso Schomburg, and Dominican nationalist Juan Pablo Duarte.

The Latino population of New York underwent its first major boom in the 1920s. From a total of 41,094, according to the 1920 census, the number of Latinos/as in the state shot up to 110,233 by 1930. Puerto Ricans emerged as the largest Latino community during this period. Of the hundreds of thousands of Puerto Ricans who arrived in New York in the first half of the twentieth century, most were working-

class and many were women. They worked mostly in the manufacturing and service industries of the New York City metropolitan area, though some were artisans or white-collar workers. Tensions between those of Spanish descent and those from the multiracial Caribbean islands began to grow after the 1920s. Clubs organized by Spanish New Yorkers, for instance, began to limit membership to Anglo Spanish-speakers only. As the overall Spanish-speaking population continued to grow, the problem of how they would define themselves in a country where all were minorities became ever more pronounced.

From the mid-1910s through the 1930s, most Latino immigrants to New York settled in Manhattan, primarily in the South Central and East Harlem areas, from 110th Street to 125th Street, between Fifth Avenue and Manhattan Avenue. Attracted by affordable housing and a large outdoor market, referred to as *la Marqueta,* that sold familiar Caribbean foods and spices, large segments of the Puerto Rican community settled in the neighborhood around 115th and 116th streets. In the successive waves of immigration that arrived in the city during the late eighteenth and early nineteenth centuries, Puerto Ricans came to replace the Jewish and Italian communities that had occupied the neighborhood before them. Although a significant number of Puerto Rican immigrants also settled in Brooklyn waterfront districts, such as Greenpoint, in the mid-1920s, more and more put down roots in Harlem. They called the neighborhood El Barrio, or *la colonia hispana.*

The wave of Puerto Rican and other Latino immigrants did not come without resistance from the established Anglo community. In 1926, a riot ensued in Harlem when long-term residents cast epithets and threw bottles at Puerto Rican and other Latino newcomers over fears that the neighborhood was being overrun. The Puerto Rican community turned to Carlos Tapia, a resident of the Brooklyn *colonia* whose reputation extended to Manhattan. A successful storeowner, Tapia had held a number of jobs and roles in the community, earning a reputation for standing up to such opposition. Tapia and a group of Puerto Rican followers arrived ready to confront the attackers, but the police moved in to block retaliation. Because many immigrants had settled in

New York City, especially in the period between 1880 and 1920, it was no surprise that tensions emerged as each group sought to create a community of its own.

Culturally and socially speaking, the Latino community founded a number of organizations that helped them to adjust to life on the U.S. mainland. Spanish-speaking New Yorkers prior to World War II turned to *La Prensa* for their news. Founded in 1913, *La Prensa* claimed to be the only Spanish and Hispano-American newspaper in the United States. In fact, there were about 400 Spanish-language periodicals in the country at the time, many published in the Southwest. Nevertheless, readers of *La Prensa* could find bona fide reporting on both domestic and international affairs, as well as local employment advertisements and calendars of upcoming cultural and social events. While smaller Spanish-language publications later emerged in the city, none enjoyed as wide a readership or was as influential as *La Prensa*.

Other ways in which Puerto Ricans kept their culture alive included participation in a variety of social organizations, such as neighborhood clubs made up of people from the same region in Puerto Rico, and political organizations, many of them in support of Puerto Rican independence. In casual neighborhood social clubs, Puerto Ricans ate, chatted, played music and games, and held activities for children. Religious clubs, primarily Catholic, also played a major role in helping Puerto Ricans adjust to life on the U.S. mainland. Mutual aid societies in the city, such as La Aurora, La Razón, and El Ejemplo, provided economic and social assistance to Puerto Rican immigrants in times of dire need. And trade unions, especially among Latinos/as in the tobacco industry, proved to be another source of crucial support. Thus, the Puerto Rican immigrant population in New York may have been far from home, but they found others like them struggling to adapt to a foreign land while maintaining close ties to their ancestral home.

Postwar Boom

From the 1940s through the 1960s, the Latino population of New York increased dramatically—from 61,463 in 1940 to 811,843 by 1970. Because the Puerto Rican immigrant population consisted largely of poor individuals from rural areas with little education and few job skills, those who were able to find work were generally relegated to low-paying blue-collar or service-industry jobs. The community in general thus faced difficulties in housing, education, and access to health care. But Puerto Ricans were hardly the only Latino group to arrive in New York in large numbers after World War II. Indeed, it was during this period that the Spanish-speaking community in the city became fully heterogeneous.

As a direct consequence of Fidel Castro's rise to power in Cuba, a mass exodus from the island brought literally hundreds of thousands of Cubans to U.S. shores, especially between 1960 through 1979. While most settled in Miami and other areas of Florida, the influx was heavy in the metropolitan area of New York as well. Most Cubans who arrived during the 1960s were from the urban working-class sector. Over the course of the next thirty years, many of these newcomers were able to improve their socio-economic status, thanks in large part to the U.S. government's Cuban Adjustment Act (1966), which has funded and provided resources to communities where Cubans have settled, bolstering education, welfare, hospital, and other public services.

During the same period, Dominicans also began arriving on U.S. shores in large numbers—especially in the New York area—as civil war in the homeland and the intervention of U.S. troops in the mid-1960s led to a vast migration. Like the Puerto Rican immigrant community, the Dominican newcomers were largely of mixed-race background. Those who arrived in the 1960s, however, differed from the Puerto Ricans who had arrived in the immediate postwar years, as they came largely from urban areas and possessed some job skills. Many of the Dominicans who came to New York settled in areas that had been dominated by Puerto Ricans, such as the South Bronx and the Lower East Side. To find employment and gain access to social services and cultural programs, they turned to established Puerto Rican organizations. Indeed, many who came to the United States as undocumented (illegal) immigrants posed as Puerto Ricans, who had citizen status, to avoid deportation.

The many Dominican immigrants who were undocumented actually constituted a desirable labor pool for area businesses, as they were willing to work for less than the minimum wage. Thus, over time, undocumented Dominican men and women came to replace Puerto Ricans in the New York area manufacturing industries. The total Dominican population of the New York metro area is more than 800,000, according to the U.S. Census, or about two-thirds of all Dominicans living in the United States. About half of Dominican Americans have arrived since the late 1980s, at which time the Dominican population of New York, which includes New York and parts of New Jersey and Connecticut, has become increasingly diverse and successful. In 1990, according to one study, Dominicans operated 70 percent of all Latino bodegas (grocery stores), three supermarket chains, and two television channels—irrefutable evidence of a new level of prosperity. The population center and cultural heart of the Dominican community of New York, with by far the highest concentration of Dominican residents, is the Washington Heights section of Manhattan, sometimes referred to as *Quisqueya* (Hispaniola) *Heights.*

Beginning in the 1970s, several Central and South American groups also began to arrive in New York in large numbers, fleeing economic hardship and the political violence that sometimes plagued their homelands. The Colombian and Ecuadorian populations of the metropolitan area increased most dramatically. Many immigrants from these and other countries settled heavily in the New York City borough of Queens—especially the Corona, Jackson Heights, and Elmhurst neighborhoods—where they set up restaurants, other small businesses, social clubs, and community-service organizations. Finally, the Mexican presence in the metropolitan area underwent a major surge in the 1990s, during which it constituted the fastest-growing immigrant population. Spanish Harlem, once overwhelmingly Puerto Rican, became steadily Mexicanized. Indeed, a single national or cultural group no longer dominates most Latino neighborhoods in New York City.

As the Spanish-speaking population continued to mushroom in the decades after World War II, Latinos/as exerted a greater and greater influence in city and state politics. It was a long climb. In 1949, New York Mayor William O'Dwyer created the Mayor's Commission on Puerto Rican Affairs (MCPRA) to help Puerto Rican immigrants assimilate more smoothly into U.S. society. The motives of the MCPRA, however, proved to be less than entirely benevolent, as the mayor's office was motivated by political expediency; the MCPRA, it was hoped, would diminish the influence of U.S. Congressman Vito Marcantonio, who represented East Harlem, where many Puerto Ricans lived. Marcantonio's ties to radical organizations and the Puerto Rican Nationalist Party made him a persona non grata among officials in the mayor's office. At the same time, however, the MCPRA proved to be effective in helping the Puerto Rican community in employment, education, and housing. The organization was disbanded in 1955, however, and replaced by the Commission on Intergroup Relations (COIR).

Other important Latino organizations to emerge in the city during the 1950s included the Desfile Puertorriqueño (the coordinating council for the Puerto Rican Day Parade), the Puerto Rican Association for Community Affairs, and El Congreso del Pueblo (The Council of Hometown Clubs). The Puerto Rican Forum, established in 1957 and today the oldest national Puerto Rican association in the United States, sought recognition as the primary organization for addressing Puerto Rican issues in the United States. Antonia Pantoja, who arrived in New York from Puerto Rico in 1944, led the organization at the outset, finding success on the strength of volunteer assistance and fund-raising. The Puerto Rican Forum also went on to support the activities of other, smaller Puerto Rican organizations. In 1961, Pantoja was a cofounder of ASPIRA, a nonprofit organization based in the city that proved both enduring and successful in promoting education and civic responsibility in the Latino community.

Dominicans, the other leading Latino group in metropolitan New York, have also exerted a growing political influence. In 1991, Guillermo Linares became the first Dominican to win elective office in the United States, gaining a seat on the New York City Council; in 2004, Mayor Michael Bloomberg appointed Linares commissioner of the city's Office of Immigrant Affairs. Meanwhile, Dominicans and Puerto Ricans alike have managed to gain representation in the New York City and New York State legislative bodies. And in 2005, Fernando Ferrer, a Puerto Rican who had served as Bronx borough president from 1987 to 2001, won the Democratic Party nomination for mayor. Although he fell short in the general election that November, Ferrer's candidacy underscored the readiness of the Latino community to attain the pinnacle of political power in New York.

In the social and cultural sphere, the Dominican Day Parade has become a major annual event in New York City since its inception in 1982, and a number of organizations have proven effective in addressing the needs of ethnic Dominicans in the metropolitan area—among them Alianza Dominicana, the Dominican Women's Development Center, and the Community Association of Progressive Dominicans. Thus, even as Latinos/as in the New York City area have grown increasingly diverse, with divergent histories and socioeconomic circumstances, the fact that so many speak Spanish and practice Catholicism continues to draw many of them together in political interests, social institutions, and cultural identity.

Lisa Y. Ramos

See also: Cubans; Puerto Ricans.

Further Reading

González, Juan. *Harvest of Empire: A History of Latinos in America.* New York: Viking, 2000.

Harvard Law Review Association. "The Cuban Adjustment Act of 1966: ¿Mirando por los Ojos de Don Quijote o Sancho Panza?" *Harvard Law Review* 114:3 (January 2001): 902–25.

Haslip-Viera, Gabriel, and Sherrie L. Baver, eds. *Latinos in New York: Communities in Transition.* South Bend, IN: University of Notre Dame Press, 1996.

Montes, Agustín Laó, and Arlene Davila, eds. *Mambo Montage: The Latinization of New York.* New York: Columbia University Press, 2001.

Sánchez Korrol, Virginia E. *From Colonia to Community: The History of Puerto Ricans in New York City.* Rev. ed. Berkeley: University of California Press, 1994.

Suárez-Orozco, Marcelo M., and Mariela M. Páez, eds. *Latinos: Remaking America.* Berkeley: University of California Press, 2002.

Nicaraguans

According to the 2000 U.S. Census, a total of 177,684 Nicaraguans live in the United States, of whom 44.5 percent reside in Florida, 29.2 percent in California, and 4.6 percent in New York, with smaller but still sizable populations in Texas and New Jersey. Nicaraguans in America are concentrated primarily in the urban areas of Miami, Los Angeles, and New York City. According to other sources, upwards of 250,000 Nicaraguans reside in the United States.

Most Nicaraguan immigration to the United States has occurred since the late 1970s. After more than four decades of dictatorship, the Sandinista National Liberation Front (FSLN) toppled the Somoza regime and formally took power in 1979. The Sandinistas introduced widespread political, economic, and social changes, but the country remained in turmoil, and by 1981 the Sandinistas began fighting a guerrilla war with counterrevolutionaries, or contras, backed by the United States. During this period of turmoil and warfare, between 1980 and 1982, many Nicaraguans associated with the Somoza regime, as well as wealthy elites, left the country. As the conflict affected all aspects of life in Nicaragua, professionals from many industries and members of the middle class emigrated as well. Throughout the 1980s, many who came to the United States filed for political asylum in hopes of securing refugee status.

Because of U.S. political interests in the region during the Cold War, Nicaraguans benefited from special treatment by the Immigration and Naturalization Service (INS). During the 1980s, more than 10,000 Nicaraguans were granted political asylum in the United States. The Immigration Reform and Control Act (IRCA) of 1986 further benefited Nicaraguans, as it included provisions for any immigrant who had arrived before 1982 and those employed in seasonal agricultural work for at least ninety days between May 1985 and May 1986 to remain in the country legally.

U.S. support for Nicaraguan immigration did not end with IRCA. In 1987, the INS established a new program to give Nicaraguans a second opportunity for legal residency. Through the Nicaraguan

Review Program (NRP), Nicaraguan immigrants could request a second review of their cases from the INS. Although the NRP was suspended in 1995, the 1997 Nicaraguan Adjustment and Central American Relief Act (NACARA) allowed all Nicaraguans and Cubans living in the United States since 1995 to acquire legal residency. Finally, after Hurricane Mitch ravaged Central America in 1998, Temporary Protected Status (TPS) was granted to Nicaraguans living in the United States; this status was later extended until July 2006.

The Nicaraguan community in the United States is highly diverse and consists of three large cultural groups. The most established Nicaraguan population consists mainly of Creoles of the Caribbean coast. In fact, many of those who entered the United States prior to the 1970s are Creole, a mixed race of people who tend to speak English because of the long-standing American influence on their region of origin. The largest Nicaraguan group is made up of *mestizos* of the Pacific coast. Most members of this community arrived in the United States after the 1979 Nicaraguan revolution and include many midlevel professionals. The third group is the Miskito population of the Rio Coco and the Puerto Cabezas areas of Nicaragua. Miskitos are considered an indigenous people of Nicaragua, although most are of mixed blood. Most members of this group arrived in the United States during the mid- to late 1980s. Although some are professionals, many work in the service sector in restaurants and hotels.

Nicaragua is a predominantly Catholic country, and many important festivals are centered around the patron saints of specific towns and villages or the Virgen de la Asunción, the patroness of Nicaragua. Even for those living in a foreign country, these festivals continue to be important, especially in areas with larger Nicaraguan communities. The festivals include processions, traditional dances, and church services. Many Nicaraguans maintain strong connections with their home country, and those who can visit for major festivals.

Traditional foods also play an important role in the life of Nicaraguans in the United States. Larger Nicaraguan communities have "Nica" groceries and small restaurants called *fritangas*. Because of the diverse cultural origins of Nicaraguan immigrants in the United States, the food is varied as well. Typical dishes include rice and beans, fried plantains, grain-based drinks, *vigoron* (fried pork rinds on a bed of boiled cassava, topped with cabbage and tomato salad), and tamales.

Nicaraguans have high rates of U.S. naturalization, even though they (unlike other Latin Americans) cannot hold dual citizenship; upon becoming U.S. citizens, Nicaraguans immediately lose their Nicaraguan citizenship. Despite their increasing presence in the United States and the high rate of naturalization, Nicaraguans continue to play an important role in the economic development of their birth country by sending back money to family members and friends. Foreign remittances account for an increasing portion of Nicaragua's gross domestic product (16.2 percent in 2002).

Despite their relatively recent arrival in the United States, Nicaraguans are making their presence felt in American society, especially in large urban areas. Ongoing economic difficulties in their home country suggest that their presence will only increase, as more Nicaraguans come to the United States in search of economic opportunity.

C. Alison Newby

See also: Immigration Reform and Control Act of 1986.

Further Reading

Fernández-Kelly, Patricia, and Sara Curran. "Nicaraguans: Voices Lost, Voices Found." In *Ethnicities: Children of Immigrants in America,* ed. R. Rumbaut and A. Portes. Berkeley: University of California Press, 2001.

Portes, Alejandro, and Ruben Rumbaut. *Legacies: The Story of the Immigrant Second Generation.* Berkeley: University of California Press, 2001.

Walker, Thomas. *Nicaragua.* 4th ed. Boulder, CO: Westview, 2003.

Norte, El
(1983)

Premiering in the United Kingdom in 1983 and released in New York City in January 1984, *El Norte* was the first full-length film by writer-director Gregory Nava, a classic of the Latin American immigrant experience and one of the acclaimed cinematic works of the 1980s. Although it was a huge critical success—becoming the first independent film to earn an Academy Award nomination for best original screenplay (1985) and being selected for the U.S. National Film Registry (1995)—it did not reach the status of a box-office hit. Nevertheless, it was one of the few independent films up to that time to reach mainstream audiences and left a lasting impression on many who viewed it for its combination of Latin American "magical realism"—the seamless merging of fantastic events and everyday experience—with the portrayal of immigrant lives and dreams.

The story focuses on two young Guatemalans—a brother and sister named Enrique (David Villalpando) and Rosa (Zaide Silvia Gutiérrez)—who are forced to leave their Quiché Mayan village and travel through Mexico to the United States (*el norte*) in search of new lives and opportunities. The narrative is divided into three sections, each covering the characters' emotional as well as physical journey. The first section covers the siblings' life in Guatemala, which they are forced to leave after their father Arturo (Ernesto Gómez Cruz) is killed by a government death squad while organizing villagers against greedy landowners, and their mother (Alicia del Lago) "disappears." This is followed by their journey north through Mexico and an illegal crossing into the United States through a rat-infested tunnel; in the final act Enrique and Rosa arrive in Los Angeles, where they become part of the large undocumented population working in the dangerous shadow economy. After initial success and hope of reaching their dream, their tale ultimately ends tragically with Rosa's death and Enrique's acceptance of his role as an exploited laborer.

The influence of *El Norte* was significant in several respects. From Hollywood's perspective, the film—following the lead of Luis Valdez's *Zoot Suit* of 1981—made clear that a Chicano filmmaker could make a critical hit with a relatively small budget. Presenting a film's narrative either partially or solely in subtitles was a source of apprehension among U.S. film studios and theater owners, but the success of Nava's film proved that with the right film it could be tolerated by audiences. The success of *El Norte* also encouraged other Chicano

artists in Hollywood. The so-called "Decade of the Hispanic" (1980s) was marked by the rise of other Chicano filmmakers, resulting in the production of a number of films focusing on the Chicano experience.

Mainstream critics praised *El Norte* for its artfulness and poetry, and for its original focus on the immigration story directly through the eyes of Latin American immigrants, without apology. It was applauded as a break from the genre of docudrama or minority "message" films. Indeed, the popular film critic Roger Ebert stated in his review that *El Norte* succeeds in spite of its political story and precisely for its emphasis on poetic imagery and its representation of the humanity of its characters.

In the Chicano film community, meanwhile, there has been little consensus as to whether *El Norte* is, in fact, a Chicano film at all. Many contend that it is geared toward a mainstream Anglo audience, as an "art film" rather than in the tradition of true Chicano cinema. This perception is supported by the reviews of mainstream critics such as Ebert, who have focused on its dreamlike and supernatural imagery rather than its political and social commentary. Many Chicano critics argue further that by foregrounding the disjointed narrative-mythic structure, the film ultimately allows the protagonists to remain as mysterious natives rather than political émigrés. Others feel that Nava deftly embeds a strong political content into the mythic structure of the story. Thus, *El Norte* not only represents a particular moment in film history, but also brings to the fore the entire question of what Chicano film is in theme, content, and audience reception.

Ellen M. Gil-Gómez

See also: Film; Guatemalans; Illegal Immigration; Valdez, Luis.

Further Reading

Barrera, Mario. "Story Structure in Latino Feature Films." In *Chicanos and Film: Representation and Resistance,* ed. Chon A. Noriega. Minneapolis: University of Minnesota Press, 1992.

Fregoso, Rosa Linda. *The Bronze Screen: Chicana and Chicano Film Culture.* Minneapolis: University of Minnesota Press, 1993.

North American Free Trade Agreement

A comprehensive and still controversial trade pact between Canada, Mexico, and the United States, the North American Free Trade Agreement (NAFTA) was symbolically signed by representatives of these three nations in October 1992, and it was signed into U.S. law by President Bill Clinton in December 1993. The agreement officially went into effect on January 1, 1994.

Conceived as an expansion to the free trade agreement signed by the United States and Canada in January 1988, NAFTA called for the removal of most barriers to trade and investment among the United States, Canada, and Mexico over a fifteen-year period, creating the world's largest free-trade zone. The result was the formation of a market of more than 440 million people and a combined gross domestic product (GDP) of $7.7 trillion. Since NAFTA, overall trade between the three countries has grown from $297 billion in 1993 to $883 billion in 2006, an increase of 198 percent, according to the U.S. Department of Commerce. Despite these statistics, the treaty has been variously criticized for not improving the life standards of the majority of the inhabitants of the three countries; for not producing the rapid economic development of Mexico that was predicted by advocates of the original treaty; and, in both the United States and Mexico, for causing the demise of various industries and job markets.

Key Elements

The stated goals of NAFTA were the phasing out of all tariffs and other trade barriers among the participating countries, leading to their elimination within fifteen years. Other important goals included the clarification and protection of intellectual property rights, such as copyrights, patents, and trademarks; the elimination of restrictions on investment by citizens of the signatory countries; the elimination of impediments to the free flow of capital, such as demands that profits be reinvested in the country where they were generated; and environmental and worker protection. In contrast to other regional treaties, like the one that gave rise to the European Union, NAFTA explicitly avoided issues pertaining to the workers of member nations, such as labor laws and regulations, while offering extraordinary protection to investors.

Given NAFTA's aim to reduce and ultimately do away with tariffs on goods produced in the territory of the partner countries, it was imperative for the treaty to clarify the meaning of "origin." Therefore, NAFTA established rules to determine whether a product can be said to originate in North America, so as to prevent extending the benefits of reduced tariffs to products made with components from elsewhere and only minimally processed in signatory countries. In order to facilitate the transit of goods across the borders of the three partners, NAFTA calls for the establishment of uniform customs procedures and documentation. Furthermore, recognizing the important role of services in overall commerce, the treaty extends protections to cross-border trade in services as well as goods. (Air and water transportation, as well as telecommunications, are among the few specific services excluded from NAFTA's protection.)

In the 1940s, Mexico adopted a policy of so-called "import substitution," allowing it to substi-

Left to right, rear: Mexican President Carlos Salinas de Gortari, U.S. President George H.W. Bush, and Canadian Prime Minister Brian Mulroney look on as diplomats from their respective nations sign the draft of the North American Free Trade Agreement in October 1992. *(Dirck Halstead/Time & Life Pictures/Getty Images)*

tute locally produced products in place of imported products, including finished goods. The import substitution was aimed at protecting the development of Mexico's fledgling industry in order to achieve self-sufficiency by means of protective tariffs against imports. NAFTA called for the elimination of this and other protectionist practices, such as those limiting investment in Mexican territory by U.S. and Canadian citizens, conditioning imports to a certain level of exports, demanding that foreign industries doing business in Mexico transfer their technology to Mexican competitors, or limiting the rights of foreign companies to repatriate profits and capital.

Under NAFTA's provisions, most disputes between partners regarding dumping (in which a manufacturer in one country exports a product to another country at a price that is either below the one it charges at home or below the costs of production) and illegal subsidies (financial support by the government to a particular company or industry) are to be settled by direct consultation between the parties. Only the most serious cases are adjudicated by a panel of experts from the countries in conflict, without any possibility of appeal to national courts.

Mexico's Road to NAFTA

By the early 1980s, Mexico's economy was in a period of decline attributed by many, at least in part, to rampant corruption, mismanagement, and cronyism after five decades of PRI (Partido Revolucionario Institucional) government. A decline in the price of oil, Mexico's largest single source of revenue, compounded the economic woes. With the devaluation of the peso, inflation out of control, and the nation in need of new loans to pay the interest on its virtually unpayable debt, Mexico was forced to accept the "structural adjustments" demanded by the powerful financial organizations that had been providing financial support: the International Monetary Fund (IMF) and the World Bank. It was perhaps no coincidence that Mexico's Harvard-educated president, Miguel de la Madrid Hurtado, being a great advocate of neoliberalism (economic liberalism as a means of promoting economic development and securing political liberty), was sympathetic to the demands of those lenders: reduction of agricultural subsidies,

privatization of state-owned firms, and reduction of education and social services budgets. Under de la Madrid, Mexico joined the General Agreement on Tariffs and Trade (GATT), the predecessor of the World Trade Organization (WTO), in 1986.

De la Madrid's handpicked successor was his minister of the economy, Carlos Salinas de Gortari, also Harvard-educated, who had been instrumental in the implementation of neoliberalist policies. Salinas's general vision of Mexican agriculture—implicit in his policies—is particularly relevant for an understanding of why Mexico would sign a trade agreement in which it was asked to give up farm subsidies while the United States was allowed to keep them. His policies suggested a belief that in order to modernize, Mexico would have to "weed out" those farmers still working the land in "inefficient," traditional ways. This would pave the way for industrial agriculture, capable of economies of scale. An important step in that direction was the substantial modification of Mexico's constitutional Article 27, long regarded as a triumph of the Mexican Revolution of 1917. Article 27 recognized the preconquest form of collective land ownership in Mexico called *ejido.* Since communally owned lands (*ejidos*) could not be sold or mortgaged, they offered a guarantee of minimal subsistence for millions of poor Mexicans. The modification of Article 27 in 1992 made ejidos no less sellable than any private piece of property.

Effects after First Decade

In order to understand the effects of NAFTA, it is important to bear in mind the profound asymmetries of power among the players: in 1995, Mexico's $250 billion GDP constituted 3.2 percent of North America's combined GDP, Canada's $569 billion amounted to 7.3 percent, and the United States's $6.952 trillion constituted 89.5 percent. According to David Márquez Ayala, a Mexican analyst, NAFTA has been a statistical reality "but an economic fallacy," since it masks the fact that Mexico's economy has functioned as little more than a giant *maquiladora,* or "platform for the commerce of foreign companies." The majority of commercial transactions reflected under the rubric of Mexico's international commerce are carried out between foreign firms outside of Mexico and their own Mexican subsidiaries or other foreign companies. Thus, according to Márquez Ayala, "the Mexican content of Mexico's exports has dropped drastically: in 1993, out of each U.S. dollar exported, 88 cents were Mexican input (labor, services, raw materials, components and others); in 1994 the ratio was only 42 cents and today, ten years after NAFTA, the ratio is less than 25 cents." From 1994 to 2003, Mexico's average gross national product (GNP) growth was 2.7 percent per year, whereas from 1935 to 1982, the period preceding neoliberalism, that growth rate had been 6.1 percent per year. These figures provide a textbook example of what economists call "growth without development," in which an increase in exports does not represent a healthy development for a country's economy.

Minimum wage in Mexico has lost 69 percent of its purchasing power since 1982, when neoliberal experimentation began. Nowhere are the devastating effects of NAFTA on Mexican workers reflected more clearly than in the figures regarding Mexico's dependence on subsidized U.S. agricultural products, which jumped from $2.7 billion per year in 1980–1982 to $10.8 billion in 2000–2002. The profound and speedy transformation of Mexican agriculture has caused massive domestic migration to urban areas and, logically, transnational migration to the huge labor market of the United States as well.

World Bank Vision

The World Bank has been instrumental in promoting commercial treaties aimed at fostering "free" trade. According to the World Bank, NAFTA has had a positive impact on the region, particularly Mexico, which for some time has been the largest exporter in Latin America (albeit with the largest trade deficit in the region). According to that institution, without the treaty, global exports from Mexico would have been 25 percent smaller. Commerce between the United States and Mexico has played a significant role in that regard. In 2005, the sale of Mexican commodities amounted to approximately $17 billion, or 426 percent more than in 1993. Exports from Mexico to Canada, while much smaller, also showed accelerated growth, reaching a record $12 billion in 2005.

Similarly, according to the World Bank, direct foreign investment in Mexico would have been 40 percent smaller had Mexico not joined NAFTA. Direct foreign investment reached $17.8 billion in 2005, more than three times the amount in 1993. Nevertheless, as the World Bank acknowledges, participation in the treaty does not in itself guarantee the economic growth a country requires in order to overcome the serious social problems it faces. According to the bank, in order to achieve sustained growth, Mexico needs to put in place a series of reforms: improve the country's legal system to reassure investors, step up the war against corruption, and develop an educational system that truly contributes to raising national productivity.

Opposition

NAFTA met with criticism even before it went into effect. In an article published in 1993, the American linguist and international critic Noam Chomsky warns that the treaty would above all benefit the multinational corporations that dominate the world economy, supported as they are by multilateral institutions such as the World Bank. Chomsky also points out that treaties such as NAFTA negate the rights of workers and other citizens, who are not entitled to vote on the provisions of the treaties even though they inevitably have serious domestic repercussions. In addition, according to Chomsky, prior to the signing of the agreement, the Labor Advisory Committee (LAC), which represents U.S. labor unions, denounced the unwillingness of the U.S. government to debate with organized labor the implications of the agreement for the domestic labor force. The LAC claims that NAFTA prevents democratically elected government agencies of each of the signatory countries from imposing regulations that would go against its provisions in areas such as environmental protection, health, and workers' rights. As a result, the LAC demanded the renegotiation of NAFTA.

Opposition to NAFTA was also reflected in the rebellion by Mexico's Zapatista National Liberation Army (Ejército Zapatista de Liberación Nacional, EZLN), which erupted in the southern state of Chiapas on January 1, 1994, the same day that the trade agreement went into effect. Neo-Zapatistas described

NAFTA as a "death certificate" for indigenous *campesinos* and other small Mexican farmers, who are unable to compete against the flood of U.S. agricultural goods produced with government subsidies. Other political forces have also expressed their opposition to NAFTA. The Partido de la Revolución Democrática (PRD) has pointed out that NAFTA does not include measures to diminish Mexico's developmental lag behind the United States—in contrast to the situation in the European Union, whose richer members routinely provide support to poorer partners in areas such as infrastructure development in order to reduce their disadvantages.

The initiative spearheaded by the United States to extend NAFTA to the rest of the Americas (except Cuba) has not succeeded, although Washington has signed trade agreements with several countries of the region, including Chile and a number of Central American countries. In 1994, thirty-four heads of state agreed to conclude negotiations to form the Free Trade Agreement of the Americas (Acuerdo de Libre Comercio de las Americas, or ACLA) no later than 2005, though there were no indications that such an agreement would become a reality any time soon. On the contrary, at the Summit of the Americas in November 2005 in Mar del Plata, Argentina, the heads of state of countries comprising Mercosur (Mercado Común del Sur, or Common Market of the South, integrated by Brazil, Paraguay, Uruguay, and Argentina) questioned the benefits that their nations could gain from joining ALCA. Instead, the leaders reiterated their support for Mercosur, which includes not only the free circulation of merchandise but also the free circulation of workers among member nations. In the framework of that summit, President Hugo Chávez of Venezuela declared: "In Mar del Plata lies the grave of the ACLA." Chávez reiterated his commitment to push for the Alternativa Bolivariana para los Pueblos de América (Bolivarian Alternative for the Peoples of the Americas), which differs from ALCA in that it would seek "a truly liberating integration" based on justice and equality.

Impact in Mexico

With the passing of time, the negative consequences of a trade agreement under such disparate conditions as those of NAFTA have become more and more evident. The accomplishments made since the signing of the treaty are much more modest than anticipated, especially for Mexico. Income for the vast majority of Mexicans has not improved substantially. In addition, the abrupt opening of the Mexican economy came as a heavy blow to many industrial sectors of the country, some of which have practically vanished, giving rise to severe unemployment. The United States and to a lesser extent Canada, meanwhile, have continued to apply protectionist measures to support their agriculture, as well as other sectors. Such protectionist measures are evident in the obstacles still facing the Mexican sugar and truck industries, which are prohibited from circulating products north of the Mexican border.

With the commercial disputes generated by these and many other restrictions far from being resolved, Mexico, in the eyes of many other Latin American countries, is no longer an example worth following. Brazil, Argentina, and other nations thus rejected calls for joining ALCA, at least under the same conditions that Mexico joined NAFTA. By contrast, they propose mechanisms of commercial integration that will guarantee equal benefits for each country.

Alberto Hernández-Lemus and
Juan Carlos Hernández-Lemus

Further Reading

Cameron, Maxwell A., and Brian W. Tomlin. *The Making of NAFTA: How the Deal Was Done*. Ithaca, NY: Cornell University Press, 2002.

Chomsky, Noam. "The Masters of Mankind: Notes on NAFTA." *The Nation*, March 29, 1993.

Fernández-Kelly, Patricia, and Jon Shefner, eds. *NAFTA and Beyond: Alternative Perspectives in the Study of Global Trade and Development*. Thousand Oaks, CA: Sage, 2007.

Finbow, Robert G. *The Limits of Regionalism: NAFTA's Labor Accord*. Burlington, VT: Ashgate, 2006.

Lederman, Daniel, et al. *Lessons from NAFTA for Latin America and the Caribbean Countries*. Washington, DC: World Bank, 2003.

"Mexico Country Brief." World Bank. http://www.world bank.org/mx.

Odell, John S. *Negotiating Trade: Developing Countries in the WTO and NAFTA*. New York: Cambridge University Press, 2006.

Novello, Antonia
(1944–)

Having experienced the pain and the desperation of a patient who cannot pay the cost of her health care, the Puerto Rican–born doctor and public health official Antonia Coello Novello has devoted her life to medicine and the needs of the weak and powerless. As surgeon general of the United States from 1990 to 1993, she brought to her work a strong empathy for people who—like herself as a child—suffered from the apathy and injustice of a society that fails to address the medical needs of the poor. Witnessing the havoc AIDS was causing in her native Puerto Rico, Novello concentrated her efforts on alleviating the suffering of HIV-infected women and children and on alerting the population to the danger of the most lethal disease of the twentieth century.

Born Antonia Coello in the small town of Fajardo, Puerto Rico, on August 23, 1944, she suffered misfortunes in her youth that would affect her life forever. She was diagnosed at birth with a chronic illness of the colon that, while not life-threatening, required her to undergo surgery. Her family was unable to afford the procedure, however, and she was hospitalized every summer during her adolescence to control the condition. Although she finally had the operation at age eighteen, complications resulted in new health problems. When she turned twenty, Antonia traveled to the United States to have surgery at the prestigious Mayo Clinic in Rochester, Minnesota, where she finally received effective treatment.

If her physical handicap was difficult, the death of her father, when she was only eight years old, was a major turning point in her life. Yet, her mother, Ana Delia Coello, who worked as a teacher and a high school principal, would have a significant impact on her, pressing upon her the importance of education. Antonia set her sights on an advanced degree at an early age. She graduated from high school at age fifteen and enrolled at the University of Puerto Rico at Río Piedras, where she completed a Bachelor of Science degree in 1965. She transferred to the School of Medicine of the University of Puerto Rico at San Juan and in 1970 became a doctor of medicine.

Also in 1970, she was married to Joseph R. Novello, a U.S. Navy flight surgeon. The couple gained residencies at the University of Michigan Medical Center at Ann Arbor, where she satisfied the requirements for an internship and residency in pediatric nephrology, and worked for two years with children who suffered from kidney disease. Her professionalism and medical abilities also earned her a yearlong fellowship in the Department of Pediatrics at Georgetown University Hospital in Washington, D.C. In 1976, after her work there, she opened a private practice in pediatrics in nearby Springfield, Virginia.

Novello began her career in public health in 1978, joining the U.S. Public Health Service Commissioned Corps (the uniformed division of the Public Health Service, or PHS). As a member of that body, she traveled extensively to impoverished areas of the country, such as Indian reservations, where there was a scarcity of medical personnel. The following year, she joined the PHS's National Institutes of Health (NIH) in Bethesda, Maryland, as a project officer in the Institute of Arthritis, Metabolism and Digestive Diseases. Her uncommon dedication and skills as both a doctor and administrator catapulted her to even higher levels of success. During the following years at NIH, Novello held several positions, ranging from deputy director of the National Institute of Child Health and Human Development (NICHD) to coordinator for AIDS Research at NICHD. Although her responsibilities at NIH kept her busy, Novello continued her studies, and in 1982 she earned a master's degree in public health at Johns Hopkins University's School of Hygiene and Public Health in Baltimore. She also became a clinical professor of pediatrics, teaching at Georgetown University in 1986.

With her growing reputation in both medicine and administration, Novello also became involved in politics in the early 1980s. As an adviser to Congress, she made major contributions to the drafting and enactment of the Organ Transplantation Procurement Act of 1984 and, while serving the Senate Committee on Labor and Human Resources, lobbied for mandatory warning labels on cigarette packaging. Novello's impressive curriculum vitae and strong ideas on medical-legal issues caught the attention of

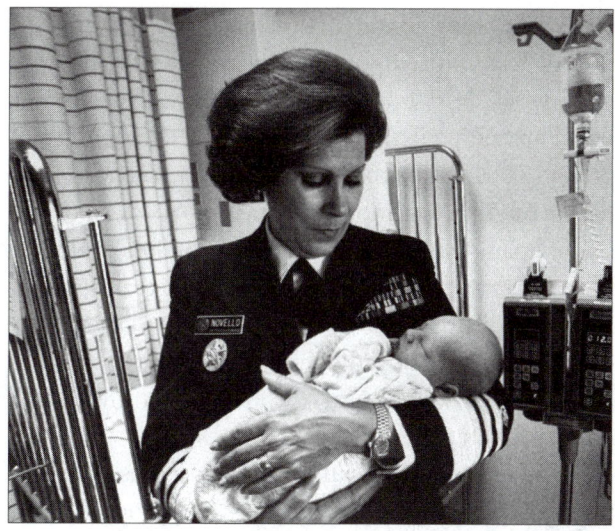

The first Latina and first woman to hold the position of surgeon general of the United States (1990–1993), Antonia Novello was born, raised, and educated in Puerto Rico. *(Taro Yamasaki/Stringer/Time & Life Pictures/Getty Images)*

the White House, and in the fall of 1989 President George H.W. Bush nominated her to be surgeon general of the United States. She became the first woman and the first Latino/a to hold this important position.

As surgeon general, Novello focused her efforts on the health of women and children, especially in poor communities of color, which she visited often in order to increase public awareness of the dangers of underage drinking, smoking, and AIDS. During her three-year tenure, Novello emphasized the need to treat women with AIDS, and she educated women on the risks of neonatal transmission of HIV. She also played an important role in promoting the immunization of children and in reducing drug use among adolescents. With the nation's children in mind, she launched the Healthy Children Ready to Learn Initiative (a multi-agency program to ensure that children arrive in school healthy enough to focus on learning), met with major beer and wine producers to convince them to help end the sale of liquor to minors, and repeatedly criticized the tobacco industry for appealing to the youth market through the use of cartoon characters.

After leaving office in 1993, Novello continued her work in public health in other capacities. For the next three years, she served the United Nations

Children's Fund (UNICEF) as special representative for health and nutrition. In 1993, Novello also made her debut as an author, publishing a book on Latino health entitled *The Surgeon General's Regional Meeting on Hispanic/Latino Health.* In 1996, she became a visiting professor at the Johns Hopkins School of Hygiene and Public Health.

Antonia Novello's work has been applauded throughout her career and has earned her widespread recognition. In 1998, for example, Novello received the Award for Leadership at the Hispanic Heritage Awards in Washington, D.C. She was named commissioner of health for the State of New York in 1999, with the specific goals of providing health care for uninsured children and improving hospital care in low-income areas. In 2002, Novello was awarded both the James Smithson Bicentennial Medal and the Legion of Merit Medal by U.S. Secretary of State Colin Powell, an honor rarely conferred on civilians. Courted by Republican insiders to run against Democratic Senator Hillary Rodham Clinton in the 2006 New York senatorial election, she chose instead to continue pursuing her goals as the state's health commissioner.

Jorge Abril Sánchez

See also: AIDS/HIV; Health and Health Care; Puerto Ricans.

Further Reading

Fernández, Mayra, and Rick Villarreal. *Antonia Novello, Doctor.* Cleveland, OH: Modern Curriculum, 1994.

Hawxhurst, Joan C. *Antonia Novello, U.S. Surgeon General.* Brookfield, CT: Millbrook, 1993.

Marsh, Carole. *Antonia Novello: First Hispanic U.S. Surgeon General.* Peachtree City, GA: Gallopade International, 2002.

Nuyorican

"Nuyorican" is a Spanglish term that refers to a New York City Puerto Rican. Originally pejorative, the term was used to designate a population, which, like the word itself, was a cultural hybrid between Spanish-speaking Puerto Rico and the Anglo-American urban mainland.

While Puerto Rican emigration to the mainland United States had been taking place since the late nineteenth century, the granting of U.S. citizenship to Puerto Rican residents in 1917, together with government programs in both Puerto Rico and the United States, gave new encouragement to relocation as a way of addressing problems of overpopulation and unemployment on the island. The thirty-year span from 1940 to 1970 witnessed a massive population shift that resulted in the relocation of more than a third of the island's inhabitants to the U.S. mainland, mostly to urban centers like Chicago and New York City. The shift created a new set of cultural complications, since Puerto Ricans could no longer be defined as a group that was dominantly from or living in Puerto Rico. Moreover, the migration corresponded to a period in Puerto Rico when, thanks in large part to the industrialization projects of Operation Bootstrap, traditional Puerto Rican life was being drastically transformed from rural peasantry to urbanization. Along with the efforts at Americanization initiated by the U.S. government—such as English-only programs in elementary schools and the granting of citizenship—it became increasingly clear that the meaning of being Puerto Rican was changing dramatically.

One of the ways that this began to manifest itself was through widespread questions about authenticity, specifically what qualities or characteristics constituted and signaled Puerto Rican identity and who could properly make claim to it. Within the context of colonization, citizenship alone could not be a sufficient measure; as a result, geographic location—where one lived—became one of the common measures of Puerto Rican-ness. The term Nuyorican, for example, came to be used by mainland Puerto Ricans in reference to those living in New York, as opposed to "real" Puerto Ricans living on the island.

This distinction, however, glosses over the cultural flux in which mainland Puerto Ricans found themselves. The problems faced by newly arrived and first-generation Puerto Ricans in mainland society were enormous, including language barriers, racial and ethnic discrimination, poverty, and urban alienation. As mainland Puerto Ricans struggled to accommodate to a new and less than welcoming so-

cial order, they found little solace in returning to Puerto Rico, since upon their return they were often considered "less" Puerto Rican than those who never left. For many circular migrants and their children, prolonged absence from the island, the predominant use of English, an imperfect grasp of Spanish, or the use of Spanglish all have been seen as a loss of Puerto Rican-ness and an acceptance, reluctant or otherwise, of U.S. culture. The term "Nuyorican," then, was used to signify not only a physical remove from the island but also cultural distance from the "real" Puerto Rican experience.

The term "Nuyorican," loaded as it was with implications of inauthenticity, was reappropriated in the late 1970s and 1980s, when writers and intellectuals like Miguel Algarín, Miguel Piñero, Bob Holman, Jesús Colón, and Pedro Pietri adopted it as a kind of battle cry and transformed the term's pejorativeness into an indictment of racism, sexism, bigotry, class discrimination, and, what was for many, the broken American Dream. The promises of emigration—that a better life awaits on the other side—turned into a nightmare for many Puerto Ricans, because, unlike European immigrants with similar aspirations, Puerto Ricans constituted a colonial minority. Part of the assumed benefit of continued colonization was that it could afford Puerto Ricans, by virtue of their U.S. citizenship, greater opportunities on the mainland. The reality, however, was that in addition to the racism, disenfranchisement, poverty, and urban blight that many Puerto Ricans confronted, they also faced rejection and stigmatization by their own people.

The writers of the Nuyorican Poets Café, located on Manhattan's Lower East Side, began drawing attention to this divide. Certainly, if they were less Puerto Rican by virtue of their American experiences, then they also were not American by virtue of their Puerto Rican identity. This double exclusion left the group somewhere in the middle of these seeming polarities, and their writings insisted on mutual recognition of the privilege, violence, and elitism that alienated and marginalized them. As a result, they began to produce art characterized by a grittily realistic depiction of urban decay. Their poems and plays explored such subjects as gang violence, poverty, HIV/AIDS, prison life, rape, and discrimination. The Nuyorican Poets Café was the nucleus of this creative movement, which wed the beats and rhythms of hip-hop with the flow of Spanglish and subject matter such as cultural alienation and disenfranchisement. The impact of the movement continued to grow, and many credit the Nuyorican Poets Café with the popularity of spoken word poetry and poetry slams in the 1990s and 2000s.

The Nuyorican poets also recognized the double-edged sword associated with their cultural status. On the one hand, they indicted American society for its racism and ethnocentrism; on the other hand, they criticized Puerto Rican culture for its insularity and abandonment. In this context, the term "Nuyorican" became a reaffirmation of cultural difference that existed on both sides of the island-mainland divide. For many, embracing the divide allowed for a radical critique of both island and mainland society while participating actively in both.

Lorna Perez

See also: Circular Migration; Nuyorican Poets Café; Puerto Ricans; Spanglish.

Further Reading

Algarín, Miguel, and Bob Holman, eds. *Aloud: Voices from the Nuyorican Poets Cafe.* New York: Henry Holt, 1994.

Flores, Juan. *Divided Borders: Essays on Puerto Rican Identity.* Houston, TX: Arte Público, 1993.

Negrón-Muntaner, Frances, and Ramón Grosfoguel, eds. *Puerto Rican Jam: Rethinking Colonialism and Nationalism.* Minneapolis: University of Minnesota Press, 1997.

Nuyorican Poets Café

The Nuyorican Poets Café is a multidisciplinary arts venue located on the Lower East Side of New York City and founded in the early 1970s by Puerto Rican poet and Rutgers University professor Miguel Algarín. It served as the center of the burgeoning Nuyorican literary and cultural movement, and as a venue for many of its leading poets and playwrights, including Algarín, cofounder Miguel Piñero, Pedro Pietri, Sandra María Esteves, and Tato Laviera. It continues to be an important cultural

space for New York City's Puerto Rican and Latino communities and an influential arts organization in general, renowned as a forum for innovative music, spoken word, visual and performing arts, comedy, and theater.

The group began informally, with Algarín inviting writers to his Loisaida ("Lower East Side" in local Puerto Rican dialect) apartment for mutual support, friendship, and an opportunity to share their writing. Helping Algarín gather these writers were poet Pietri and playwright Piñero, best known for his Obie Award–winning play *Short Eyes* (1974). Departing from the conventional view that poetry belongs to the highly educated, should aspire to refined language, and should concern itself only with contemplative topics such as nature and beauty, the Nuyorican Poets Café sought to bring poetry to the people of

Poet, writer, and professor Miguel Algarín, pictured here in 2005, started the Nuyorican Poets Café as a living room writers' salon in his East Village, New York City, apartment in the early 1970s. *(AP Images/Bebeto Matthews)*

El Barrio, or Spanish Harlem, in the northeastern part of Manhattan. The writers of the Nuyorican Poets Café made their neighborhood the subject of their poetry and encouraged other residents to write about their own lives in their own language.

While "Nuyorican" had been a derogatory term used by Puerto Ricans on the island to refer to their New York counterparts, Algarín and Piñero appropriated it to signify the distinctive culture and artistic expressions of New York Puerto Ricans. In an effort to dispel the false myth that Puerto Ricans could not be poets, Algarín and Piñero in 1975 published *Nuyorican Poetry: An Anthology of Words and Feelings*. Critics praised the book, which caught the attention of many people who had never traveled to Spanish Harlem, nor had thought of Puerto Ricans as artists and writers.

In the late 1970s, the gathering moved from Algarín's crowded apartment to a local bar, and again in 1980 to 236 East Third Street. The café closed in 1982 and reopened in 1989, a year after Piñero's death from cirrhosis. The 1990s brought a new wave of popularity, and the venue aligned itself with other racial and ethnic minorities, including politically progressive Euro-Americans. It was during this period that poet, performer, and entrepreneur Bob Holman helped the café develop "poetry slams," a high-energy, urban, hip-hop, freestyle form of the art. Poetry slams are competitions in which poets dramatically perform their work and are graded by the audience. By the mid-1990s, the Nuyorican Poets Café had become the hub of a nationwide poetry renaissance, and a few breakout stars had emerged from the slam scene, among them Edwin Torres, Reg E. Gaines, Tracie Morris, and Paul Beatty. The new generation of poets included many non–Puerto Ricans, especially African Americans and Asian Americans; the café's increasingly multicultural orientation was evident in the Algarín-Holman anthology *Aloud: Voices from the Nuyorican Poets Cafe* (1994), which won an American Book Award.

Dubbed "the minister, part-time mayor, and full-time poet-laureate of Loisaida," Algarín sits on the café's board of directors to the present day. From a small casual gathering of poets, the Nuyorican Poets Café has grown to become one of the hallmarks of the arts in New York City, serving a dual function as Puerto Rican community space and multicultural arts organization.

Diana L. Linden

See also: Algarin, Miguel; New York; Nuyorican; Puerto Rican Literature; Puerto Ricans.

Further Reading

Algarín, Miguel, and Bob Holman, eds. *Aloud: Voices from the Nuyorican Poets Cafe.* New York: Henry Holt, 1994.

Algarín, Miguel, and Miguel Piñero, eds. *Nuyorican Poetry: An Anthology of Puerto Rican Words and Feelings.* New York: William Morrow, 1975.

Nuyorican Poets Café. http://www.nuyorican.org.

Operation Bootstrap

Operation Bootstrap (*Operación Manos a la Obra*), spearheaded by Puerto Rican politicians Teodoro Moscoso and Luis Muñoz Marín, was an ambitious post–World War II economic development program aimed at transforming Puerto Rico from an agriculture-based society to an industrial one. Established and operated by the commonwealth government of Puerto Rico and the U.S. federal government, Operation Bootstrap was launched in 1948 and continued well into the 1970s. Its effects are still felt today.

Objective and Function

The objective of Operation Bootstrap was to move Puerto Rico into the "modern world" through rapid industrialization, while maintaining a focus on the welfare of the people. The plan relied on U.S. capital and markets, seeking to entice mainland corporations to relocate through tax incentives and benefit programs. The latter included, but were not limited to, subsidized factory space, recruitment of trained personnel, and loan assistance. The idea was that U.S. corporations would borrow money from the commonwealth to invest in labor-intensive island manufacturing. Raw materials would be imported and products would be manufactured in Puerto Rico; the finished goods then would be exported for sale in the United States. American corporations, moreover, would feel compelled to set up shop in Puerto Rico because of the availability of a large labor pool willing to work for low wages and a government that would be willing to accommodate the demands of foreign capital.

Operation Bootstrap brought more than 1,000 manufacturing plants to Puerto Rico between 1948 and 1965, attracting more than one-fifth of the largest U.S. corporations. Tax incentives were the primary attraction. The first tax exemption bill was passed in Puerto Rico as early as 1947, allowing qualified corporations to operate freely on the island without having to pay local taxes for a fixed period of time. Because U.S. corporations were already receiving exemptions from federal taxes, the idea of receiving exemptions from local taxes made Puerto Rico even more enticing. By 1957, Operation Bootstrap had made Puerto Rico a model of how an agriculture-based nation could be transformed. The success of the program was touted as an "economic miracle," and the island was nicknamed "Showcase of the Caribbean."

Leadership

The two most notable leaders of the program were Luis Muñoz Marín and Teodoro Moscoso. Muñoz Marín served as governor of the island from 1949 to 1965 and developed a government agency called Fomento to oversee economic development. Fomento later became synonymous with Operation Bootstrap in its efforts to industrialize Puerto Rico. Moscoso, the chief architect of Operation Bootstrap, was a pharmacist by training but a political activist with extensive government experience. He had been brought into government by Governor Rexford G. Tugwell in 1941 and served in a variety of high-level positions, including head of the Agency for Economic Development (1942–1961), U.S. ambassador to Venezuela (1961–1962), and U.S. coordinator of the Alliance for Progress, a program to support Latin American economies through industrialization.

Moscoso pushed for a Puerto Rican development program with the help of PDP (Partido Popular Democrático, or Popular Democratic Party) leader Muñoz Marín. The two men began to work closely in their efforts to promote Puerto Rican industrialization. Moscoso believed that such a program would have to depend on U.S. investors and firms because the island did not have the necessary resources to industrialize on its own.

Impact

During the more than two decades of Operation Bootstrap's existence, the government of Puerto Rico undertook a number of initiatives to improve conditions on the island. Improvements, big and small, were made in the infrastructure of the island's transportation, energy, and communications systems; the education and health systems; drinking water; public electricity and sewage systems; and food and clothing. A massive public housing program improved living conditions for people across the island, reducing the number of shantytowns, or *arrabales,* and shrinking the existing ones.

Operation Bootstrap thus proved successful on many levels. It not only brought many industrial companies to Puerto Rico—and with them thousands of new jobs—but it also transformed Puerto Rico from an underdeveloped island into a more prosperous one for residents. At the same time, however, the transformation weakened Puerto Rico's agricultural production, and the island stopped growing most of its own food. It was left with no choice but to import necessities from the United States. Moreover, many of the corporations that relocated did so simply for the cheap-wage labor and tax incentives; contributing to the internal well-being of Puerto Rico was not part of their agenda. Urbanization and the vast expansion of the middle class altered the political landscape for Puerto Rico, giving rise to a true two-party system. The New Progressive Party (Partido Nuevo Progresista, or PNP) was certified in January 1968 and defeated the PDP in national elections that November.

Operation Bootstrap did achieve its goal of transforming the Puerto Rican economy and raising the standard of living. By 1965, Puerto Ricans had the highest average individual income in Latin America. The benefits did not extend to all island residents, however, as unemployment actually increased from 1947 to 1960. Up to 70 percent of the island's families remained under the poverty line. One problem was that many U.S. corporations simply left once their tax breaks expired. Many residents were forced to leave their homes and migrate to cities in search of work, only to find that jobs had dried up as companies shut down. As a result, many Puerto Ricans migrated to the mainland to find jobs. The duration of Operation Bootstrap was marked by waves of immigration to the mainland and back to Puerto Rico, coinciding with trends in the economy.

Demise

By the mid-1960s, Operation Bootstrap began to lose its effectiveness as corporate tax exemptions and other incentive programs were coming to an end. At the same time, Puerto Rican workers began to demand higher salaries. In the mid-1970s, the U.S. economy itself went into decline, with rising unemployment rates. The recession proved severe, resulting in fewer consumer purchases and corporate investments. In addition, global inflation had made imported goods considerably more expensive. Because of U.S. minimum wage laws, Puerto Rico was unable to compete with other countries for labor-intensive, low-capital industries. As a result of these factors, Puerto Rico became less appealing for U.S. corporations—which began closing up shop on the island and seeking low-wage labor elsewhere.

Since the 1970s, Operation Bootstrap has retained a powerful legacy in Puerto Rican society and politics, and among policy makers. Economic administrator Antonio J. Colorado, one of Moscoso's protégés, sought to revive Operation Bootstrap in the 1980s, but the effort died when he lost the election for resident commissioner in 1992. Finally, in 1995, the U.S. Congress amended the Small Business Job Protection Act and eliminated Section 936 (tax incentive program for corporations), giving existing industries on the island ten years to phase out the benefits program. The legislation also raised the minimum wage in Puerto Rico.

Example for the Future?

A number of economic planners and political theorists have regarded Operation Bootstrap as an early and exemplary model of industrialization based on foreign investment through transnational corporations. Other economic programs based on export-led industrialization have been established in the decades since—among them the United Nations' Point Four, the Alliance for Progress, the Caribbean Basin Initiative, and the *maquiladoras* (assembly plants) along the Mexico-U.S. border. The shortcomings and inequities of Operation Bootstrap are not overlooked, however, leading international economic institutions, governments, and local leaders to reconsider its tenets and seek new models of growth and development.

Melissa-Ann Yeager

See also: Muñoz Marín, Luis; Puerto Ricans.

Further Reading

Dietz, James L. *Puerto Rico: Negotiating Development and Change.* Boulder, CO: Lynne Rienner, 2003.

Fernandez, Ronald. *The Disenchanted Island: Puerto Rico and the United States in the Twentieth Century.* Westport, CT: Praeger, 1996.

Fernandez, Ronald, Serafín Méndez Méndez, and Gail Cueto. *Puerto Rico Past and Present: An Encyclopedia.* Westport, CT: Greenwood, 1998.

Maldonado, A.W. *Teodoro Moscoso and Puerto Rico's Operation Bootstrap.* Gainesville: University Press of Florida, 1997.

Meléndez, Edwin, and Edgardo Meléndez. *Colonial Dilemma: Critical Perspectives on Contemporary Puerto Rico.* Boston: South End, 1993.

Santana, Déborah Berman. *Kicking Off the Bootstraps: Environment, Development, and Community Power in Puerto Rico.* Tucson: University of Arizona Press, 1996.

Operation Wetback

In the 1950s, the changing American economy, Cold War fears of invasion, and continuing racism prompted public sentiment to urge removal of illegal immigrants from the United States. In 1954, Operation Wetback—a U.S. federal program conducted in cooperation with the Mexican government—targeted tens of thousands of illegal Mexican immigrants in Arizona, California, and Texas and forcibly removed them back across the border. The program also persuaded hundreds of thousands of undocumented immigrants to return to Mexico before being captured. Although statistics vary, by the end of 1954 when the program ceased, an estimated 125,000 Mexican nationals had been deported.

Background

Mexican laborers in the years after World War II struggled to make a living. Many migrated to the southwestern United States to toil on large farms and for industrial companies that sought cheap labor. Few of these workers were able to enter the United States through legal channels; most were able to sneak across the unguarded border and evade capture by the U.S. Immigration and Naturalization Service (INS). These undocumented workers—pejoratively nicknamed "wetbacks" on the assumption that they swam across the Rio Grande into the United States—generally lived in substandard conditions and were paid extremely low wages.

By 1954, both the Mexican and American governments came to believe that unregulated immigration involved too many dangers to be tolerated. The U.S. Labor Department had long demanded border controls, both to protect American workers from Mexican competition and to support the Bracero Program—a politically popular contract-labor program instituted by the government in 1942, which allowed U.S. farmers to hire Mexican workers, known as *braceros,* at low wages for the agriculture labor market. Mexico believed that illegal emigration was detrimental to Mexican citizens, to the Bracero Program, and to relations with the United States. Texas growers had been removed from participation in the Bracero Program on the grounds that they had violated contracts, discriminated against workers, and violated the civil rights of Mexicans by having them arrested for petty offenses. However, Mexico was unable and unwilling to put an end to the outward flow of undocumented workers from its borders because of inadequate enforcement resources, legal technicalities guaranteeing the free movement of its citizens, the need to have a safety valve for its unemployed population, and the fear of adverse reaction. Thus Mexico agreed to let the U.S. government assume the initiative with Operation Wetback.

Operation

Led by retired U.S. Army general and Commissioner of Immigration Joseph M. Swing, Operation Wetback targeted only undocumented workers. The government did not seek to punish employers who hired them, chiefly because of political fears about the power of growers and reluctance to target Anglos. Growers were assured that an adequate supply of legal labor in the form of braceros would continue to be available for those who applied for such workers. Additionally, the INS appeased farm groups by targeting illegal workers in the industrial sector.

Undocumented workers throughout the Southwest were urged to avoid apprehension and deportation by leaving before the operation actually got under way. Press reports about the program greatly overestimated the size of the 500-man Operation Wetback force, prompting many aliens to flee across the border to evade what they believed to be certain arrest and harsh treatment. INS officials estimated that more than 400,000 undocumented workers in California alone left voluntarily; in Texas, the government believed that more than 63,000 illegal aliens returned to Mexico of their own accord.

The drive to round up undocumented aliens officially began on June 10, 1954, in southern California and western Arizona. Only a small portion of the 2,000-mile (3,200-kilometer) border with Mexico was covered. The start date coincided with the harvest season because U.S. Border Patrol officials believed that the timing offered the best chance of capturing illegal immigrants. In addition, to prevent illegal aliens already in the borderland from fleeing farther inland, the Border Patrol set up roadblocks north of the frontier.

By June 19, 1954, the Border Patrol forces in California were exceeding 1,000 apprehensions per day. Between July 1 and July 26, however, the number of apprehensions declined to 670 per day. In California, the main focus of the operation was Los Angeles, with help from the Los Angeles Police Department and the Los Angeles County Sheriff's Office. By July 25, the daily number of apprehensions in California had declined to about 400. By the end of the state roundup, a total of 51,784 aliens had been deported. The Arizona phase of the operation was not as intensive, because the harvest season there had effectively ended when the drive began. The Arizona roundup operation, which apprehended 23,222 aliens, was mainly concentrated in the Salt River Valley and in Yuma County. In mid-July, Operation Wet-

back shifted its focus to Texas and New Mexico, redeploying many of the Border Patrol officers to these states. By July 27, a total of 52,374 Mexican aliens in Texas had been apprehended and expelled.

Once captured, Mexican immigrants were transported across the border by bus and airplane (usually the former). The deported workers were forced to pay $10 toward the cost of travel if they possessed more than $13. The Mexican government then used railroads to transport detainees into the interior in the belief that it would be more difficult for them to return to cross the border.

Problems with the program appeared almost immediately. The Mexican government lacked the funds and the railway cars needed for the daily transportation of large numbers of people into the interior. The populations of border towns such as San Luis and Mexicali had been swelled by the arrival of thousands of Mexicans who had either been repatriated or had fled across the border to avoid capture. Many were without food and shelter, and little was being done to meet their needs.

In response, Mexico's Interior Department asked the U.S. State Department for help in convincing the INS to recruit as many of the illegal workers as possible for the Bracero Program. It is not known how many workers were actually converted to braceros, but the ranks of the latter did increase dramatically in 1954—from 201,380 to 309,033 in one year. After the 1954 campaign, the number of braceros contracted nationwide continued to increase annually until the end of the program in 1964. Abuses of braceros were common enough that many Mexicans viewed the program as a form of legalized slavery. Preferring the freedom of undocumented status but wanting to avoid deportation, many hid in their residences until the raids stopped. By mid-September 1954, the INS had exhausted the funds set aside for Operation Wetback. The roundup ceased, and the Border Patrol returned to routine operations along the frontier.

Assessment

Government officials at the state and federal levels pronounced Operation Wetback a success. California and Texas both reported that many jobs previously held by undocumented workers had been made available to citizens. According to Border Patrol records, however, 30 to 40 percent of those bus-lifted were unemployed at the time of their apprehension—offsetting claims that the undocumented aliens had been depriving U.S. workers of jobs. (The estimates themselves were suspect, moreover, because the Border Patrol was not an impartial collector of statistics and because immigrants who were being deported were not likely to confide honestly about their employment status.) Among other positive economic gains attributed to the roundup were reports that retail sales in areas of high concentrations of undocumented workers increased sharply after the illegals had been removed. In addition to helping reduce outlays for public services, several Southwestern states reported significant reductions in crime and disease rates.

Despite such claims of success, the intensive targeted approach of Operation Wetback was generally abandoned in subsequent years, as support for such measures waned. In the twenty-first century, however, rising fears of unchecked immigration have prompted discussion of resurrecting such a program.

Caryn E. Neumann

See also: Bracero Program; Illegal Immigration; Immigration Enforcement; Mexicans; Migrant Workers; Repatriation.

Further Reading

Calavita, Kitty. *Inside the State: The Bracero Program, Immigration, and the I.N.S.* New York: Routledge, 1992.

Garcia, Juan Ramon. *Operation Wetback: The Mass Deportation of Mexican Undocumented Workers in 1954.* Westport, CT: Greenwood, 1980.

Kirsten, Peter N. *Anglo Over Bracero: A History of the Mexican Workers in the United States from Roosevelt to Nixon.* San Francisco: R and E Research Associates, 1977.

Opinión, La

La Opinión is a Spanish-language newspaper published daily in Los Angeles and distributed in six Southern California counties. With a daily circulation of more than 121,000, according to 2007 figures, it is the largest Spanish-language newspaper in the United States and the second–most read newspaper in Los Angeles, after the *Los Angeles Times.* In November 2007, *La Opinión* ranked number one in net daily paid circulation growth among the 200 largest newspapers in America, providing both a source of information and cultural pride for the Latino community.

Ignacio Lozano, Sr., whose family migrated to San Antonio, Texas, from Mexico in 1908, founded and published the first issue of *La Opinión* on Mexican Independence Day, September 16, 1926. Lozano also opened Libreria Lozano, a bookstore specializing in Spanish-language books and newspapers. Lozano began his publishing career in 1913 by launching the Spanish-language daily *La Prensa* in San Antonio, where the family had settled after migrating. After his death in 1953, Lozano was succeeded at *La Opinión* by his son, Ignacio Lozano, Jr. His mother, Alicia Elizondo de Lozano, managed *La Prensa.* Lozano, Jr., published *La Opinión* until 1986.

As a start-up daily newspaper serving the needs of a small but growing Mexican community in Los Angeles, *La Opinión* built its popularity on the successes of previous Spanish-language newspapers, which appealed to local Latino communities throughout the United States. As early as the 1850s, Spanish-language sections had appeared in newspapers in the southwestern United States. From 1855 to 1859, Francisco Ramirez, a reporter for the Spanish section of the *Los Angeles Star,* published *El Clamor Público,* which exposed the exclusion of Mexicans from the United States and the racism they faced at the hands of newly arriving Anglo-American settlers. It was the first of many Spanish-language papers that were local in distribution and short-lived in duration, but presented a Latino point of view on issues, not just a reprinting of local news in a different language. By the mid-1870s in Tucson, Arizona, Spanish-language papers included *Las Dos Repúblicas, El Fronterizo,* and *El Tucsonense.* Much like *El Clamor Público,* they not only reported news but also protested negative stereotypes of Mexicans and advocated for the protection of their civil rights. By the 1890s, Cubans in Florida had several Spanish-language newspapers, such as *La Igualdad* and *La Fraternidad.*

Like *El Clamor Público* and other early newspapers, *La Opinión* attempted not only to present the news, but also to serve a function in the community, providing in-depth local and national articles on subjects such as voting, immigration, and health care. It was one of the few newspapers to provide comprehensive coverage of the deportations and repatriations of Mexicans during the 1930s as well as the Zoot Suit Riots of the 1940s, during which servicemen and civilians attacked Mexican American youth. In 1999 and 2000, the National Association of Hispanic Journalists recognized *La Opinión* for its excellence in publishing.

One of the challenges that *La Opinión* has faced over the years is the changing demographics of the market it serves in Los Angeles. Lozano, Jr., summarized the need for *La Opinión* to adapt in 1970: "Our mission was no longer to be a Mexican newspaper published in Los Angeles, but an American newspaper that happens to be published in Spanish." With the continued influx of Latino immigrants from Central and South America, *La Opinión* has broadened its perspective in an attempt to reach Spanish speakers emigrating from the Latino Diaspora. The paper has diversified its coverage from a purely Mexican American focus to include issues relevant to the Central American, South American, Cuban, and Puerto Rican populations that have grown in Los Angeles since the 1970s.

Spanish-language newspaper circulation in the United States has tripled since 1990, a trend that runs contrary to the ongoing decline among mainstream newspapers. In an effort to capitalize on the continuing influx of Latinos to America, in 2004 *La Opinión* merged with New York City–based *El Diario/La Prensa*, the oldest Spanish-language newspaper in the United States, to form ImpreMedia. In addition to its publication of *La Opinion* (Los Angeles), this news and information company publishes several Spanish-language newspapers in New York (*El Diario/La Prensa*), Chicago (*La Raza*), San Francisco (*El Mensajero*), Houston (*Rumbo Houston*), and Miami (*El Nuevo Herald*). All together, its print and online news sources reach 11 million readers each month, serving markets in which 72 percent of U.S. Latinos reside.

Susan Marie Green

See also: Los Angeles; Spanish Language.

Further Reading

ImpreMedia. http://www.impremedia.com.

La Opinión Digital. http://www.laopinion.com.

Romo, Ricardo. *East Los Angeles: History of a Barrio.* Austin: University of Texas Press, 1983.

Truax, Eileen. "La Comunidad Alienta a 'La Opinion': Ignacio E. Lozano, Jr." *La Opinión,* April 30, 2006.

Wilson, Clint, II, Felix Gutierrez, and Lena Chao, eds. *Racism, Sexism, and the Media: The Rise of Class Communication in Multicultural America.* Thousand Oaks, CA: Sage, 2003.

Pachuco

The term *pachuco* is most commonly used in reference to groups of Mexican American young people who lived in Los Angeles during the 1940s. They were distinguished by a preference for zoot suits, the use of a form of slang that combined Spanish and English terms, and other markers such as distinctive hairstyles and tattoos. Variants of the style could be found in many other parts of the Southwest after World War II. Many Latinos/as today believe pachucos were social rebels against Anglo society, representing a culture neither purely Mexican nor American, outside the mainstream values of both.

The origin of pachuco style is somewhat obscure. According to various accounts, the pachuco emerged in South Texas during the 1920s, as the first massive waves of Mexican immigration arrived in the Southwest borderlands. The Mexican Revolution (1910–1921), labor shortages in the United States, and the expansion of railroads between the United States and Mexico prompted significant increases in immigration. Faced with poverty, segregation, ill treatment from police and white residents, and limited economic opportunity, Mexican barrio communities developed subcultures often associated with crime. Some residents made extra cash by bootlegging or selling opium, with the narcotics trade centered in El Paso and other border towns. Early pachucos are thought to have been involved in contraband smuggling along the U.S.-Mexican border during this period.

The limited opportunities in border towns resulted in a mass migration of Mexicans from the Southwest to Los Angeles during the course of the 1920s. The Mexican population of Los Angeles swelled to more than 100,000 by 1930. Through this migration process, newly arrived residents brought with them cultural attributes and styles that had developed within the violent border areas of Texas. In later years, Mexican American residents of Los Angeles recounted how some migrants from El Paso in the late 1920s and early 1930s styled their hair in an "Argentine ducktail" (slicked back from the sides, piled on top, and a small tail at the back) and wore flared pants, pegged at the bottoms. They also spoke *Caló,* the traditional slang of the old Spanish and Mexican underworlds, said to have arrived with Gypsy migrants to colonial New Spain (Mexico). In the early twentieth century, the dialect was used by a community of workers referred to as *Tirilis* or *Tirilones,* who were also known to wear cross-shaped tattoos on their foreheads. The El Paso newcomers to Los Angeles influenced younger, alienated Mexican Americans who later adopted the zoot suit as a badge of hip social defiance. They called themselves pachucos after the older migrants they admired from El Paso. (The term originated as local slang for residents of that city.)

Pachucos became nationally known in the aftermath of the Zoot Suit Riots in Los Angeles during the summer of 1943, when Chicano youth culture caught the wrath of mainstream Los Angeles society during World War II. Pachucos were well known for sporting the zoot suit—featuring a long "fingertip" coat, pegged baggy pants, and wide-brimmed felt hat. Girls, called *pachucas* or *cholitas,* wore short skirts and high pompadour hairdos. Like Chicano street youth of today, Los Angeles pachucos spoke a mixture of Caló and African American slang, and were comfortable dancing to both Mexican and swing music. At the same time, young Mexican Americans in Los Angeles—much like blacks in many locations—felt the brunt of their second-class status, exposed to the hostility of police, school segregation, and signs designating segregated public facilities.

During the riots of 1943, young zoot-suited men and boys were stripped of their clothing by groups of servicemen, with the endorsement of white onlookers and local newspapers, who labeled the pachucos "baby gangsters" and other derogatory terms. They would become legends among later generations of Mexican Americans who came out of the same Los Angeles neighborhoods and who paid tribute to their rebellion against Anglo society by adopting similar dress and slang.

By the late 1940s, people identifying themselves as pachucos could be found all over the western United States. During the 1950s, they wore creased khaki workpants with suspenders and "French toe" pointed shoes. They tattooed their hands with the "radiant cross" (a small cross surrounded by four protruding lines). Women wore khaki pants and tattooed dots to resemble "beauty marks" on their faces. By the late 1960s and early 1970s, a newer generation of barrio youth adopted the cholo style, derived from the old pachucos. Standard cholo dress for male youth included a plaid shirt buttoned at the top and well-creased khaki trousers. Also borrowed from the old pachuco culture was the use of Caló slang. Although there are no modern pachucos per se, they will be remembered forever among modern Latinos/as as the victims of racial violence during the Zoot Suit Riots of the 1940s and as icons of a distinctive Chicano culture.

E. Mark Moreno

See also: Identity and Labels; Zoot Suit Riots.

Further Reading

Barker, George C. *Pachuco: An American-Spanish Argot and Its Social Functions in Tucson, Arizona.* Tucson: University of Arizona Press, 1950, 1970.

García, Mario T. *Desert Immigrants: The Mexicans of El Paso, 1880–1920.* New Haven, CT: Yale University Press, 1981.

Griffith, Beatrice. *American Me.* Boston: Houghton Mifflin, 1948.

Mazón, Mauricio. *The Zoot-Suit Riots: The Psychology of Symbolic Annihilation.* Austin: University of Texas Press, 1984.

McWilliams, Carey. *North from Mexico: The Spanish-Speaking People of the United States.* 1949. Updated by Matt S. Meier. New York: Praeger, 1990.

Pagán, Eduardo Obregón. *Murder at the Sleepy Lagoon: Zoot Suits, Race, and Riot in Wartime L.A.* Chapel Hill: University of North Carolina Press, 2003.

Padilla, José
(1970–)

José Padilla is a U.S. citizen who was arrested in May 2002 for allegedly supporting Al-Qaeda terrorist activities, detained in a military prison without trial for the next five years as an "enemy combatant," and finally convicted in August 2007. A Puerto Rican originally from Brooklyn, New York, Padilla became a source of heated controversy and judicial wrangling over the terms of his detention (no formal criminal charges were filed against him for years) and the conduct of various legal proceedings associated with his case.

Born in Brooklyn on October 18, 1970, José Padilla—later known as Abdullah al-Muhajir—moved to Chicago with his mother, brother, and two sisters at an early age. He grew up in the poor, predominantly Latino district of Logan Square, where he attended Darwin Elementary School and Sunday Mass at Saint Sylvester Church. As a youth, Padilla was extremely popular in the neighborhood, known for his love of baseball and his impeccable manners. At the age of fourteen, he joined the (Maniac) Latin Disciples or Kings, a predominantly Puerto Rican street gang. Following a number of arrests and several stints in jail, Padilla attempted to reintegrate himself into society in 1992, taking a job at a fast food restaurant in Davie, Florida. It was there that he met Mohammad Javed, a Pakistani immigrant who became a kind of spiritual mentor. Having been exposed to the teachings of the Prophet Muhammad while in prison, Padilla turned to Javed for guidance in his conversion to Islam. He began to attend the Darul Uloom Islamic Institute in Pembroke Pines, Florida, and the Masjid al-Iman Mosque in nearby Sunrise, at which time he changed his legal name to Ibrahim, began wearing a red-and-white kaffiyeh, or headdress, and became increasingly militant politically.

In the mid-1990s, Padilla traveled to Egypt, Saudi Arabia, Pakistan, and Afghanistan as part of his religious conversion. Now using the name of Abdullah al-Muhajir ("Abdullah the Immigrant"), according to reports, he moved to Lahore, Pakistan, where he joined an Al-Qaeda cell. In 2001, Padilla is reported to have met with Osama Bin Laden's senior lieutenant, Abu Zubaydah, in Afghanistan. According to U.S. government allegations, during this meeting Padilla proposed a plan to build and detonate a radiological dispersal device, commonly known as a "dirty bomb," on American soil, probably in Washington, D.C. In 2002, it is believed, he received explicit directions to return to the United States to conduct reconnaissance work for future attacks on hotel rooms and gas stations.

On May 8, 2002, federal authorities apprehended Padilla at Chicago O'Hare Airport, after Zubaydah, who was in federal custody, informed U.S. investigators that Padilla was indeed a member of al-Qaeda. On June 9, 2002, President George W. Bush ordered that Padilla be held indefinitely as an "enemy combatant" and that he be transferred to a South Carolina naval base. Critics of the Bush administration argued that holding Padilla—still a U.S. citizen—for so long without charging him was a direct violation of the Constitution.

Padilla's legal defense team filed a motion with the Second U.S. Circuit Court of Appeals in Richmond, Virginia, demanding that he be formally charged or released. In response, the court ruled on December 18, 2003, that the Bush administration lacked the authority to designate a U.S. citizen arrested on U.S. soil as an "illegal enemy combatant" without clear congressional authorization; Padilla was ordered to be released from military custody within thirty days. The government appealed the ruling to the U.S. Supreme Court, which heard the case—*Rumsfeld v. Padilla*—in April 2004. On June 28, the justices ruled that the case had been improperly filed and dismissed the petition for appeal. Padilla remained in prison.

On June 13, 2005, the U.S. Supreme Court denied Padilla's petition to have his case heard directly by the court. Three months later, on September 9, the Fourth U.S. Circuit Court of Appeals ruled that President Bush had the authority to keep Padilla detained without charges. And on November 22, Padilla was indicted by a federal grand jury on charges of "conspiring to murder, kidnap and maim people overseas." There was no direct mention of al-Qaeda or a dirty bomb; indeed, none of the reasons previously given for his detainment and his removal to

solitary confinement in 2002 were included in the indictment. According to Padilla's lawyers and other critics of the administration, the decision to proceed with criminal prosecution was intended to avert an impending Supreme Court hearing on the legality of his detention. The government's shift in tactics was criticized in December 2005 by a federal appeals court, which temporarily denied transfer to civilian custody.

Padilla was removed from military custody on January 3, 2006, after the Supreme Court granted the Bush administration's request to transfer him to a federal prison in Miami. Finally, on August 16, 2007—more than five years after his arrest—José Padilla was found guilty of all charges against him by a federal jury, which concluded that he had, in fact, conspired to kill people in an overseas jihad and to fund and support overseas terrorism. Federal prosecutors requested a prison term of thirty years to life. On January 22, 2008, the judge sentenced Padilla to seventeen years, four months. Despite the verdict—and in part because of it—some members of the legal community, political establishment, media, and general public have continued to point to the Padilla case as an example of the Bush administration's willingness to compromise civil liberties and the judicial system to enhance government authority in America's domestic war on terror. Members of the Puerto Rican community in Chicago, where he grew up, were alternately perplexed as to how one of their own could become involved in the jihadist cause, uneasy at his treatment by the legal system, and concerned that portrayals of Padilla and his background could cast an unfair, unfavorable light on them.

Jorge Abril Sánchez

See also: Puerto Ricans.

Further Reading

Amnesty International. *USA Appealing for Justice: Supreme Court Hears Arguments against the Detention of Yaser Esam Hamdi and José Padilla.* London: International Secretariat, 2004.

Musch, Donald J. *Balancing Civil Rights and Security: American Judicial Responses Since 9/11.* Dobbs Ferry, NY: Oceana, 2003.

Panamanians

Although there is little information about the first wave of Panamanian migration to the United States—the U.S. Census Bureau did not begin tabulating separate statistics for Central American people until 1960—their presence can be traced at least to the early 1900s. Panamanian migration to the United States historically has been connected to the Panama Canal, on which work began in 1904. Most emigration occurred as a result of U.S. participation in the construction of the canal, its ongoing presence in the free trade zone, and the operation of U.S. military bases in Panama. Such connection created a regular flow of migrants going to the United States, linked to marriages with American citizens, work relationships with U.S. companies and families, and, later, political ties with opposition groups and U.S. interests.

By the 1970s, most Panamanians in the United States were nonwhite, with New York City numbering 17,000 mestizo, black, and Indian Panamanians. There were more women than men by about one-third, and female immigrants were predominantly between the ages of twenty and forty-nine. Many worked as domestics or low-paid, white-collar workers and sent much of what they earned to family in Panama. To the present day, the percentage of employed newcomers who are domestic workers has remained high, ranging from 15 to 28 percent.

Panamanian emigration has differed from that of other Central American countries, where political and economic upheaval forced a heavy outflow in the latter decades of the twentieth century. Whereas more than 1 million Guatemalans, Nicaraguans, and Salvadorans left their homelands for the United States after the Immigration Act of 1965—which set a quota of 120,000 per year for the Western Hemisphere—relatively few were Panamanians. The number of Panamanians living in the United States tripled in the last three decades of the twentieth century, reaching 91,723 in the 2000 U.S. Census. The latter figure represented a mere 0.3 percent of the total U.S. Latino population. According to the census, however, Panamanians were the most educated sub-

group of Central American immigrants; 20 percent were university graduates. Panamanians also represented a mere 1.59 percent of deportations from the United States, the second lowest by country of origin in Central America. Another distinguishing characteristic of Panamanian immigrants is their high rate of naturalization compared to other Central Americans. Panamanians are also more scattered geographically than other Central American immigrant subgroups, with no specific areas of high concentration. Relatively large presences are found in the states of New York (20,055), Florida (15,117), California (10,688), and Texas (7,076). Other regions with notable Panamanian communities include New Jersey, Arizona, and Illinois.

Many first-wave immigrants managed to obtain and hold jobs. Encouraged by their parents, the second generation of Panamanian Americans placed more emphasis on vocational training and college education. Thus, since the 1980s, many Panamanians have embraced professional careers and other white-collar jobs. The most recent generation has progressed even further in their educational and professional pursuits. In the twenty-first century, some 60 percent of Panamanian women in the U.S. workforce occupy midlevel occupations; another 15 percent are employed in management and professional positions. Among Panamanian men, occupational attainment has been strong in managerial, professional, technical, sales, and administrative support positions. Panamanians who have made conspicuous contributions to American culture include the salsa singer, songwriter, and actor Rubén Blades, Hall of Fame baseball player Rod Carew, and journalist Juan Williams.

Like other immigrant groups, Panamanian Americans have remained proud of their homeland and have kept close ties with family and friends left behind. According to World Bank statistics, remittances from Panamanians in the United States to their homeland total about $20 million per year. Because cultural ties between the two countries are strong, many Panamanians come to the United States for higher education and advanced training, and then launch business ventures in their homeland. There is also a steady flow of scholarly exchanges between Panama and the United States, in which Panamanian

Americans take an active role through academic organizations.

Pride for the native land is also expressed in holiday celebrations. In addition to U.S. holidays, Panamanians celebrate Independence Day of Panama on November 3 and Mother's Day on December 8. Many of their festivities feature traditional attire (*pollera* and *montuno*) and folk dances such as the *tamborito*, using drums originally brought to Panama by slaves from Africa and the West Indies. Popular Panamanian foods served at such events include *sancocho*, a soup made with meat and vegetables, and *tasajo*, grilled meat covered with tomato sauce. Other popular dishes are ceviche (raw fish cured in lime juice), empanadas, tortillas, and *carimañolas* (each made with ground beef stuffed in cornmeal or flour dough).

Social interaction between Panamanian Americans and other Latino groups in the United States defies generalization. Ties with other Latino groups are facilitated by a shared language, religion, and lifestyle, despite variations in national culture. These distinctions are permeable and flexible, except for the rigid respect to class and race differences in some groups. On the one hand, the assimilation of Panamanians into mainstream U.S. society has been hastened by a proliferation of mixed marriages. On the other hand, recent years have seen an opposite migratory movement of U.S. citizens to Panama. Many former Panama Canal Zone employees and their families have returned to Panama and encourage other U.S. citizens to do so as well. Between 1990 and 2000, the number of U.S. citizens obtaining pensioner visas increased by 136 percent. U.S. retirees are fond of Panama as a place to settle because of the relatively low cost of living, low property tax, affordable health care, stability of the banking system, pleasant climate, and general quality of life.

Aurora Fiengo-Varn

Further Reading

Dixon, Daniel, and Julie Murray. *America's Emigrants: U.S. Retirement Migration to Mexico and Panama.* Washington, DC: Migration Policy Institute, 2006.

Hassig, Susan. *Panama.* New York: Marshall Cavendish, 1997.

Sharp Dean, Rosetta. "Panamanian Americans." In *Multicultural America.* http://www.everyculture.com.

Paraguayans

Paraguayan Americans are immigrants of Paraguay or their descendants. According to the 2000 U.S. Census, there were 8,769 Paraguayan Americans living in the United States at the beginning of the twenty-first century. Thus, although it is relatively common for most Americans to have some daily or cultural contact with Latinos, particularly those residing in major metropolitan cities, it is far less common for them to have frequent, if any, interactions, or cultural/communal understanding of Paraguayan Americans—a fact not surprising given both the small size and relatively recent history of this group inside the United States.

Although the first documented Paraguayans living in the United States arrived sometime between 1841 and 1850, the initial wave of immigrants did not arrive until 1947. In reality, however, the wave was little more than a ripple. After a period of political instability and violence that ended with the seizure of power by General Alfredo Stroessner in 1954, Paraguayans began immigrating to the United States in hopes of a more prosperous and stable life. By the early 1960s, 25 percent of Paraguay's population lived outside the country; a majority emigrated to Brazil, Uruguay, and Argentina, with only a small percentage coming to the United States.

By the early 1970s, as a result of General Stroessner's repressive policies and the shrinking economic opportunities in Paraguay, emigration was on the rise, with more and more of the disaffected seeking residence in the United States. In 1979 alone, 11,000 Paraguayans entered the United States; within three years, the number declined to 4,000. In addition to those seeking a respite from poverty and political repression, this wavelet of Paraguayan immigration included a number of young people in search of better education, job training, or professional opportunity. As many of these youth arrived in the United States alone and without a job, many intended to return to Paraguay upon the completion of school—a trend confirmed by U.S. Census figures in 2000. The 1980s and 1990s, meanwhile, witnessed another noteworthy trend—an upsurge in the number of Paraguayan infants adopted by American families: 254 in 1989, rising to 405 in 1993 and 351 in 1995.

The prospects of a good education, job training, and improved income have led a majority of Paraguayans to settle in major metropolitan cities, such as New York, Miami, Dallas, Texas, and Atlanta. For Paraguayan men in search of unskilled service-sector work, and for women looking for domestic and service jobs, Chicago, New York, New Jersey, and Minneapolis have become popular destinations. Additionally, a sizable number of Paraguayans have immigrated to the United States in search of work in the agricultural industry, settling especially in California and Kansas. In the latter state, a nonprofit organization called Partners of the Americas has brought in Paraguayan farmers to cultivate wheat and raise cattle as part of an exchange program. In all, the Paraguayan community remains very small, even with its long history of immigration and presence within the United States.

Despite the class and educational diversity of the Paraguayan American community, and as evidenced by its low level of public assistance (less than 0.5 percent receive such aid), the community has been economically successful. As of 1990, the average household income of a Paraguayan American was $32,981, with nearly 1 percent of its population (141 out of 1,773 households) earning more than $100,000 dollars annually. Because the population remains quite small and many young Paraguayans return home, the Paraguayan community has had relatively limited direct influence on the political, social, and cultural mainstream of America.

David J. Leonard

Further Reading

Cooney, Jerry W. *Paraguay: A Bibliography of Immigration and Emigration.* Longview, WA: J.W. Cooney, 1996.
Miller, Oliver. "Paraguayan Americans." In *Multicultural America.* http://www.everyculture.com.
Whigham, Thomas, and Jerry W. Cooney. *A Guide to Collections on Paraguay in the United States.* Westport, CT: Greenwood, 1995.

Peña, Albert A., Jr.
(1917–2006)

While often remembered for his political activism in San Antonio, Texas, Albert A. Peña, Jr., devoted his entire life to fighting for Chicano civil rights, working as a municipal judge and promoter of liberal causes both inside Texas and nationally through the 1950s and 1960s. In Texas, Peña was co-chair of the Viva Kennedy Clubs in the early 1960s, which garnered support in the Mexican American community for the election of Democratic presidential candidate John F. Kennedy. His other state activities included organizing the Loyal American Democrats and the Bexar County Democratic Coalition, playing a key role in the Crystal City revolt of 1963—in which Mexican American voters succeeded in gaining a majority on the city council and formed La Raza Unida Party. Peña was also a cofounder of the Mexican American Legal Defense and Education Fund (MALDEF) and participated in such other national organizations as the League of United Latin American Citizens (LULAC) and the American GI Forum.

Born on December 15, 1917, in San Antonio, Peña attended San Antonio Tech High School, where he was encouraged to become an automobile mechanic. Like many Mexican American youths at the time, he was set on a course of vocational training through the practice of education tracking and a general lack of higher educational opportunity. Peña set his sights on college, however, but first joined the Navy and fought in World War II.

After his honorable discharge in 1945, Peña took advantage of his benefits under the GI Bill of Rights by attending St. Mary's University in San Antonio, where he earned his bachelor's degree and then enrolled in St. Mary's Law School. Gaining a reputation as a troublemaker for his involvement in student civil rights groups, he was forced to transfer to South Texas School of Law in Houston.

After earning his law degree in 1950, Peña joined the American GI Forum and LULAC, working to secure civil rights for Mexican Americans. In 1951, his determination to facilitate equality for Mexican

Americans led him to take on a case in Hondo, Texas, in which he successfully litigated against the city's segregation policies. The following year, he helped to organize the Loyal American Democrats in an effort to wrangle political power away from the conservative wing of the Democratic Party in San Antonio. In 1956, he became the first Mexican American to be elected to the Bexar County Commission.

As county commissioner, Peña faced an uphill battle promoting his agenda in the city's political arena, which had a history of excluding Mexican Americans through a poll tax and at-large voting districts (whereby a candidate could be elected from any part of the city but not accountable to a particular community). Consequently, most politicians in San Antonio appealed to white voters and ignored members of the Mexican American and African American communities. To make things even harder for Peña, municipal politics were controlled by the Good Government League (GGL)—a political machine consisting mostly of affluent Anglos. Its members resisted the struggles for civil rights, avoiding any proposed legislation in that direction and opposing candidates who supported a civil rights platform.

The political landscape of Bexar County led Peña and others to form the Bexar County Democratic Coalition (BCDC) in 1960, a political organization that worked to elect liberal Anglos, Mexican Americans, and African Americans to the city council and the state legislature. The increased political power of communities of color through the BCDC resulted in a backlash by the Anglo community, and the coalition sustained heavy losses in that year's elections. Although his organization never again challenged the GGL for political power in the county, Peña remained in office until 1972, when he suffered his first electoral defeat. Five years later, he was appointed a municipal judge in San Antonio and presided until the 1990s.

Peña's work as a civil rights leader for Mexican Americans in South Texas was not limited to San Antonio. In 1960, he was appointed state cochairman of the Viva Kennedy Clubs. In 1968, he cofounded the Mexican American Legal Defense and Education Fund (MALDEF), which became the nation's preeminent Latino legal and civil rights organization.

The following year, he helped organize the Crystal City revolt of 1969, in which Mexican Americans led by José Angel Gutiérrez began La Raza Unida Party and took over the city council.

After his death on July 3, 2006, a former colleague at MALDEF summarized Peña's life and work: "Albert A. Peña, Jr. was instrumental in the empowerment of Mexican Americans in Central and South Texas. He spearheaded the efforts to desegregate local schools surrounding the San Antonio area; he championed the rights of low-income people; he aggressively promoted the implementation of civil rights laws to challenge the discriminatory treatment of Mexican Americans; and he was one of the founders of the Mexican American Legal Defense and Educational Fund."

Daniel Guzmán

See also: American GI Forum; Crystal City, Texas; La Raza Unida Party; League of United Latin American Citizens; Mexican American Legal Defense and Education Fund; Politics; Viva Kennedy Clubs.

Further Reading

Acuña, Rodolfo. *Occupied America: A History of Chicanos.* 6th ed. New York: Pearson Longman, 2007.

Rosales, Rodolfo. *The Illusion of Inclusion: The Untold Political Story of San Antonio.* Austin: University of Texas Press, 2000.

Pérez, Emma
(1954–)

Emma Pérez is a Chicana historian, feminist theorist, and creative writer, and part of a larger community of Chicana scholars whose work challenges dominant ways of writing history and Eurocentric ways of understanding the world. As such, she is a strong symbol of Chicana history, struggles, and presence in the United States. An advocate of the philosophy that "the personal is political," Pérez was a cofounder of Mujeres Activas en Letras y Cambio Social (MALCS), an organization founded in 1982 by and for Chicana, Latina, and indigenous women for the purpose of mutual support in scholarly and community work.

Born on October 25, 1954, in El Campo, Texas, Pérez grew up in southeastern Texas in the 1950s and 1960s, experiencing racial segregation as part of the culture in which she was raised. When she was twelve, her family left the small town of El Campo for Pasadena, a suburb of Houston, where she lived before leaving home for college.

At the University of California at Los Angeles (UCLA), Pérez earned her bachelor's degree in political science and women's studies in 1979, a master's degree in history in 1982, and a PhD in history in 1988. She went on to teach Chicano history, women's history, and Chicano studies at a number of institutions—including the University of Minnesota, California State University at Los Angeles, and Pomona College—before returning to Texas to teach in the Department of History at the University of Texas, El Paso. In 2003, she joined the Department of Ethnic Studies at the University of Colorado at Boulder as an associate professor.

Pérez is best known for developing two key concepts that shape the work of many Chicana historians and theorists today: that of *sitio y lengua* (space and language) and that of "decolonial imaginary." Together these two concepts have shifted the way scholars frame and examine the lives and histories of Chicanas and other people of color in the United States. She introduced the former concept to the academic community in 1990 at a plenary session of the National Association of Chicana and Chicano Studies and expanded the theory in a 1991 article that appeared in Carla Trujillo's anthology, *Chicana Lesbians: The Girls Our Mothers Warned Us About* (1991). According to Pérez, all work comes from a specific *sitio y lengua*—or cultural context; thus, she argues, Chicanas and other women of color should create their ideas and works in a way that addresses and speaks to Chicana experience and that challenges the white male histories, language, and laws that dominate U.S. society. Without *sitio y lengua,* she contends, women are left vulnerable to the violence of colonizing men. Pérez believes it is important for historians to examine the past to find the spaces and words that communities of Chicanas have created, as well as the times in history when, due to the material and historical circumstances of the time, women were not able to create such spaces.

Pérez followed her theory of *sitio y lengua* with another concept said to have shaped much of Chicana history and postcolonial scholarship—that of the decolonial imaginary. According to her argument, most history in the past has been written from the perspective of a "colonial imaginary," a figurative space created by those in power that maintains the status quo. Even contemporary Chicana historians, she maintains, sometimes write from a colonial imaginary, using terms such as "the West" instead of "Greater Mexico," or the "U.S. Mexican War" instead of the "U.S. Invasion." Instead of referring to Chicano scholarship as "postcolonial," she says, one must acknowledge that people exist in a space *between* the colonial and the postcolonial, which she refers to as the decolonial. In this in-between space, she argues, one can disrupt dominant and linear ways of telling history. In fact, Pérez believes that if historians want to create work that is useful to both students and mainstream society, they have to imagine ways of writing that do not normalize linear models of time.

Another concept that Pérez stresses in her writings is that of intersectionality—the ways in which race, place, class, sex, sexuality, and gender weave in and out of people's lives. According to this theoretical approach, a middle-class Chicana from a Midwestern college town would have dramatically different life experiences from the daughter of Mexican farmworkers from a poor rural area. Such intersectionality is evident in Pérez's creative writings as well as her scholarship, dramatized in the novel *Gulf Dreams* (1996), for example.

Gulf Dreams was among the first Chicana lesbian novels to be published in the United States. While much white lesbian literature of the 1990s was dominated by "coming out" stories, *Gulf Dreams* tells a complex story of a working-class lesbian Chicana struggling against multiple oppressions in a small rural town in Texas. Rather than romanticize the protagonist's life, the novel realistically depicts the intersections of racism, homophobia, classism, sexism, and sexual violence both in Euro-American culture and in Chicana communities. And rather than offer up a happy ending, it suggests tools for survival in a racist and patriarchal society.

Perez's forthcoming novel, *Forgetting the Alamo, Or, Blood Memory,* scheduled for publication in 2010, explores the Anglo Texas colonial landscape of the mid-nineteenth century by showing how a Mexican family survived the battles of the Alamo and San Jacinto.

Linda Heidenreich

See also: Chicano/a; Chicano Studies; Feminism; Mujeres Activas en Letras y Cambio Social.

Further Reading

Pérez, Emma. *The Decolonial Imaginary: Writing Chicanas into History.* Bloomington: Indiana University Press, 1999.

———. *Gulf Dreams.* Berkeley, CA: Third Woman, 1996.

Torres, Lourdes. "Violence, Desire, and Transformative Remembering in Emma Pérez's *Gulf Dreams.*" In *Tortilleras: Hispanic and U.S. Latina Lesbian Expression,* ed. Lourdes Torres and Inmaculada Pertusa. Philadelphia: Temple University Press, 2003.

Trujillo, Carla, ed. *Chicana Lesbians: The Girls Our Mothers Warned Us About.* Berkeley, CA: Third Woman, 1991.

Performance Art, Solo

The term "Latino Performance" refers to a loose category of live stage art that draws on two strong traditions of Latino cultural production: theater and stand-up comedy. Emerging solo artists and collaborative theater collectives draw from the tradition and tactics established in the Chicano Movement's efforts to reach a wider audience through activist theater companies such as El Teatro Campesino beginning in the 1960s. In more recent productions by Guillermo Gómez-Peña and John Leguizamo, for example, performance art combines avant-garde goals and theatrical experimentation with established cultural forms, such as stand-up comedy. Latino performance artists also use the mass media of television and Broadway to present shows that both entertain and challenge audiences to think critically about cultural stereotypes. A number of Latino artists have become widely known and popular performers whose works are presented on Broadway, cable television, college campuses, and other venues across the country.

One influential example is John Leguizamo's off-Broadway stage shows such as *Mambo Mouth* (1991), *Spic-O-Rama* (1993), and *Freak* (1998, and later an HBO special), which garnered popular and critical praise for their humorous presentation of Latino family life and ethnic identity, often utilizing the very stereotypes that have been directed at Latinos/as to highlight his funny and sometimes painful insights about gender roles, family dynamics, and ethnic and immigrant histories. Leguizamo and other Latino artists such as Carmelita Tropicana, Marga Gómez ("Los Big Names" and "All Around the Block"), and Gómez-Peña have been especially influential in creating hybrid works that are both highbrow and popular, in which the voices of people of color are heard in new ways and by new audiences.

Also referred to as "solo performance art," these productions rely on autobiographical material and humor to soften and lure an audience into thinking about subjects they might otherwise ignore. In loose narratives of family and community history, many portraying the trials and absurdities of growing up Latino, the shows focus on societal questions in a personal context. It is this narrative cohesion and underlying seriousness of purpose, often delivered with a critical edge, that separate the autobiographical stage shows of Latino performance artists from the more fragmented pieces and purposes of mainstream stand-up comedy.

Latino performance artists working in less widely known venues have also had a significant impact, especially in the genre known as "border performance." Border performance plays on an understanding of "borders" as entities that are simultaneously geographical or national, like the U.S.-Mexican frontier, and those that are more symbolic, such as the invisible borders between ethnic groups, men and women, different generations, recent immigrants and long-time U.S. residents, and the like. While the "border" concept is most familiar to academics and intellectuals, the contributions of groundbreaking border performance artists from the United States, Mexico, Cuba, and Chile, among others, have transformed Latino theater and generated increased awareness of both performance art and the transnational role of artists.

One of the early border performance groups, working in Mexico and California during the 1980s, Taller de Artes Fronteriza is especially known for its most famous member, Guillermo Gómez-Peña, who

Colombian-born actor and stand-up comic John Leguizamo—seen here performing in his 1998 one-man Broadway show (and later film) *Freak*—brings a unique blend of comedy, social commentary, and character acting to Latino solo performance art. *(Jeff Christensen/Getty Images)*

moved to the United States and embarked on a successful solo career as a performer and writer. Developing characters called the "Mexterminator" and the "Border Brujo," Gómez-Peña has since joined such other Latino artists as Luis Cifuentes and the Cuban cultural critic and artist Coco Fusco in advancing border performance. Fusco and Gómez-Peña brought the genre to film with *The Couple in the Cage* (1997), which documents their 1990s performance art piece that parodies natural history museums and the "presentation" of Native Americans in U.S. popular and academic culture. At its best, border performance integrates both the insights of cultural criticism and the more comic, poignant, and visceral experiences of U.S. national and imaginary borders—all to illustrate the complexities of identity and belonging, as well as nation-state politics, economics, and popular culture.

The symbolic understanding of the border has been especially important to artists exploring the personal and political effects of differences in sexual identity and gender in what is often called "queer performance." Latinas and Latinos have made a significant impact in this subculture of popular entertainment through their work in a number of films and theater productions that have traveled across the United States and internationally, and in independent theater and club spaces. In works by Monica Palacios (*Latin Lezbo Comic: A Performance about Happiness, Challenges, and Tacos*) and Carmelita Tropicana (*Leche de amnesia/Milk of Amnesia* and *Carmelita Tropicana: Your Kunst Is Your Waffen*), humor and a sense of artistic experimentation combine to create pieces that highlight the connections among autobiography, culture, and sexuality. Artists such as Tropicana came out of both avant-garde stage traditions and a growing clarity about the intersections of ethnic and racial identities with class and sexuality. Queer and border performance, as well as the unique work of other Latino artists, have become lively fields of study for critics and students in academic fields other than theater arts, such as literary studies, ethnic studies, queer studies, feminism, and transnational cultural studies.

Katherine Sugg

See also: Chicano Movement; Teatro Campesino, El.

Further Reading

Arrizón, Alicia. *Latina Performance: Traversing the Stage.* Bloomington: Indiana University Press, 1999.

Fusco, Coco, ed. *Corpus Delecti: Performance Art of the Americas.* New York: Routledge, 2000

———. *English Is Broken Here: Notes on Cultural Fusion in the Americas.* New York: New Press, 1995.

Gómez-Peña, Guillermo. *Dangerous Border Crossers: The Artist Talks Back.* New York: Routledge, 2000.

Habell-Pallán, Michelle, and Mary Romero, eds. *Latino/a Popular Culture.* New York: New York University Press, 2002.

Peruvians

Peruvians in the United States have gone largely unnoticed on the political, economic, and cultural landscape because of their small number relative to other Latino immigrant groups, yet their significance in the nation's history and the present day transcend the limited size of the community.

The 2000 census registered 233,926 Peruvians residing in the United States; other estimates put the figure as high as 1 million. A majority live in five cities: Paterson, New Jersey; Miami; Los Angeles; Chicago; and New York. According to the existing data, Paterson hosts the largest number of Peruvian immigrants. At the beginning of the twentieth century, largely because of subsidiary manufacturing plants located in Peru, Paterson attracted immigrants to work in the silk industry. Peruvian migration to this city has been steady ever since. Otherwise, Peruvians have tended to settle where other Latino communities have already been established.

As early as 1849, records indicate that the first Peruvians came to the United States to work in the gold mines of California; there is little indication, however, as to whether they settled there permanently or returned to Peru. After World War II, there is a record of increasing numbers of Peruvians migrating to the United States and remaining there. The number of Peruvian immigrants and their descendants has risen steadily since the 1980s due to economic hyperinflation and political instability in the homeland. Data from the Integrated Public Use Microdata Series (IPUMS) show that 63 percent of the Peruvians who immigrated without U.S. citizenship arrived in the United States in the 1990s.

Like many other voluntary migrants, Peruvians have migrated to U.S. shores seeking employment, a better education, and improved living conditions. However, they tend to differ from many other Latino immigrants in terms of socioeconomic background and have—on the whole—more formal education. As of 2000, 37 percent of Peruvians in America had completed high school; 48 percent had either attended college for one to three years or had earned a college diploma. Some researchers have argued that, because of their educational background, Peruvians mirror the immigrant community from Western European countries and Canada. However, their higher educational level for the most part has not translated into better jobs. Most Peruvians hold jobs on the lower rungs of the employment ladder.

Statistical averages conceal the diversity of the Peruvian immigrant community and its place in American society and job market. Since the 1970s, for example, American sheep ranchers in California, Oregon, Nevada, Colorado, Idaho, Montana, and Wyoming have actively recruited Peruvian male laborers, who entered the country on H-2A visas as sheepherders. In their native country, they had worked on the haciendas and in the peasant communities of Peru's central highlands. Peruvian women, most of them uneducated and originally from the highlands, were brought to the United States to work as domestics beginning in the 1950s. Since that time, these women have built a network that helps recruit women from Andean villages to Miami and other cities in North America.

Another important group includes those from the middle class, who often arrive without legal status, language skills, or employment sponsorship. Lacking these resources, many have experienced instability in employment and downward economic mobility. As a result, they tend to view their situation in the United States as temporary, seeking legal status and working to regain the social standing they held in Peru.

At all levels of the socioeconomic scale, social networks have played an important role in choice of settlement site. Most Peruvian immigrants have access to family or friends already living in the United States, who provide them with an optimistic version of life in America, a community of which to be a part, a cultural milieu, and in some cases even prospects for employment. Like many other Latino immigrants, Peruvians are more likely to organize themselves in cultural rather than political spaces. One type of cultural organization revolves around religion, which in turn is linked to national identity. Peruvians in the United States are disproportionately Roman Catholic, the dominant religion of Peru itself. In recent years, however, there has been a rapid growth of evangelical Protestantism, particularly Pentecostalism, in the Peruvian American community. This conversion appears to play an increasingly important role in the construction of community and collective identity, combining liberation from the hierarchical world of Latin American Catholicism with Anglo values of freedom of conscience. In short, religion has been an important vehicle for Peruvian immigrants, enabling them both to integrate into U.S.

society and to break from the social hierarchies of their native country.

Erika Busse

Further Reading

Paerregaard, Karsten. 2008. *Peruvians Dispersed: A Global Ethnography of Migration.* Lanham, MD: Lexington.

Ruíz Baía, Larissa. "Rethinking Transnationalism: National Identities among Peruvian Catholics in New Jersey." *Christianity, Social Change and Globalization in the Americas.* Ed. Anna Peterson et al. New Brunswick, NJ: Rutgers University Press, 2001.

Sabogal, Elena. "Viviendo en la Sombra: The Immigration of Peruvian Professionals to South Florida." *Latino Studies* 3 (2005): 113–31.

Plan de Santa Barbara, El

In April 1969, the Chicano Coordinating Council on Higher Education organized a conference at the University of California, Santa Barbara, to discuss Chicano access to and experiences with higher education in the United States. The attendees formally recognized that education needed to be used strategically and that their future depended on an education that had values in common with those of the Chicano community. El Plan de Santa Barbara is a compilation of the recommendations made during that meeting, summarizing how colleges and universities can and should support their Chicano students. In its words, "We did not come to work for the university, but to demand that the university work for our people."

The document outlines ways to increase Chicano access to higher education. Together with El Plan Espiritual de Aztlán, drafted at the Chicano Youth Liberation Conference in Denver a month earlier, El Plan de Santa Barbara is acknowledged as one of the founding documents of the Movimiento Estudiantíl Chicano de Aztlán (MEChA), a national Chicano student organization.

El Plan de Santa Barbara begins with a manifesto that describes the conditions faced by Chicanos/as in the United States and draws attention to the need for grassroots activism regarding issues of so-cial justice, especially education. It gives Chicanos/as an opportunity to reckon with their history and to express a new consciousness and a new way of looking at the world and themselves. The manifesto emphasizes the value that the Chicano community places on higher education and highlights the importance of education in the personal advancement of Chicanos/as and the growth and development of the Chicano community. "Chicanos recognize the central importance of institutions of higher learning to modern progress, in this case, to the development of our community," it states. "But we go further; we believe that higher education must contribute to the formation of a complete man who truly values life and freedom."

Calling for self-determination and solidarity within the Chicano community, the plan advocates political and social action. It also describes the ongoing struggle of Chicanos/as in U.S. society and describes the costs of assimilation in pursuit of the American dream:

> For decades Mexican people in the United States struggled to realize the "American Dream." And some—a few—have. But the cost, the ultimate cost of assimilation, required turning away from *el barrio* and *la colonia*. In the meantime, due to the racist structure of this society . . . the barrio and colonia remained exploited, impoverished, and marginal.

Subsequent portions of El Plan de Santa Barbara provide a framework for organizing and coordinating the work of academic, social, and personal support services for Chicano students at colleges and universities in California. The plan demands that colleges and universities respond to the difficulties that Chicano students face while attending predominantly white schools by supporting and institutionalizing dedicated programs and services. It further demands that Chicano students, faculty, administrators, and staff be integral participants in the design and implementation of these programs. El Plan de Santa Barbara outlines a model for establishing Chicano studies programs. It also suggests steps for developing recruitment, admissions, and support services for Chicano students, emphasizing the critical role played by student organizations such as MEChA in this effort, and encourages students to become active and organized on campus as they work toward solidarity.

The document calls for the active recruitment and admission of Chicano students, faculty, administrators, and staff. Colleges are called on to address the academic and financial needs of their Chicano students. The plan states that colleges can begin to do this by sponsoring academic orientation programs that acknowledge students' cultural heritage. Colleges must also offer resources and support services to students, including access to free tutoring during their studies, and hire staff who can assist students with personal, academic, financial, and quality-of-life issues such as housing and transportation. In addition, advisers should be able to provide career counseling to students, helping them to focus on their lives after graduation.

An important aspect of El Plan de Santa Barbara is that it outlines the components of a Chicano studies curriculum and offers advice on issues related to courses, staffing, leadership, and organization. Chicano studies programs are characterized as evidence of the realization of Chicano power on college campuses. These programs, the plan argues, should be designed to allow students to major in Chicano studies and to study the Chicano cultural and historical experience in breadth and detail. The curriculum should include courses on Chicano, Mexican, and Anglo heritage, as well as classes addressing the history, economics, psychology, sociology, literature, politics, and education of Chicanos/as.

Colleges and universities are also asked to support and disseminate applied research projects to address the needs of the Chicano community. To this end, El Plan de Santa Barbara urges colleges to fund graduate fellowship programs for Chicano students so that they might gain experience in research and teaching while still in school. Colleges are also asked to provide opportunities for the creation and distribution of Chicano student scholarship, art, and other work related to their educational experiences.

The final sections of El Plan de Santa Barbara address student activism and campus organizing, underscoring the need for community, cultural, and social action centers. Colleges are described as having a responsibility to sponsor educational and cultural programming that is relevant to and involves the larger community in which they reside.

Billie Gastic

See also: Chicano/a; Chicano Studies; Movimiento Estudiantíl Chicano de Aztlán; Plan Espiritual de Aztlán, El.

Further Reading

Chicano Coordinating Council on Higher Education. *El Plan de Santa Barbara: A Chicano Plan for Higher Education.* Oakland, CA: La Causa, 1969.

Muñoz, Carlos, Jr. *Youth, Identity, Power: The Chicano Movement.* New York: Verso, 1989.

Plan Espiritual de Aztlán, El

Chicano activist Rodolfo "Corky" Gonzales announced *El Plan Espiritual de Aztlán* (The Spiritual Plan of Aztlán) on March 31, 1969, at the first annual Chicano Youth Liberation Conference in Denver, Colorado. The plan was drafted in an effort to provide direction to Chicano youth within the educational system. At the conference, Gonzales called for Chicanos/as to work together and to organize a new political party based on Chicano patriotism. In 1966, Gonzales founded the Crusade for Justice, one of the most successful civil rights organizations of the Chicano Movement, with the goal of creating a Chicano community independent of economic and political connections to the United States.

The weeklong National Chicano Youth Liberation Conference, which stressed the need for students and other youth to play a central role in the Chicano Movement, brought together, for the first time, activists from all over the country who were involved in both campus and community protest politics. El Plan Espiritual de Aztlán followed Gonzales's earlier program, *El Plan del Barrio,* issued during the 1968 Poor People's March on Washington, D.C., which called for greater cultural nationalism; better education, especially in the Spanish language; better housing; land reform, specifically the return of territories wrongfully taken from Mexico (and thus, from Mexican Americans); and the development of more Chicano-owned businesses.

The new plan, which would eventually become the framework of the broader Chicano Movement, urged unification and the creation of new civil rights organizations to ensure Chicano independence as well as ethnoracial patriotism. Breaking sharply with the integrationist goals of earlier Mexican American organizations, in El Plan Espiritual de Aztlán, the Crusade for Justice called for complete separation at all levels: political, economic, social, cultural, and educational. It further demanded that ancestral lands be restored to Chicanos/as. The Southwest region of the United States was designated as the original homeland, called Aztlán, in reference to the Aztecs' mythical place of origin. In Náhuatl, the language spoken by the Aztecs, *Aztlán* means "land to the north," referring to the American Southwest.

El Plan Espiritual de Aztlán outlined seven organizational goals for achieving Chicano liberation:

Unity: Folks would combine the barrios, the pueblos, the *campos* (countryside), and the poor, middle, and professional classes in hopes of liberating the community.

Economy: Anglos would be driven away from Chicano communities so that Chicanos/as could gain control of economic resources.

Education: It had to be specific to the history, contributions, and culture of Chicanos/as, that is to say, education about Chicano history and culture. Furthermore, Chicanos/as themselves had to be in control of the schools, serving as teachers, administrators, and counselors.

Institutions: They were to serve the people by providing services necessary for a full life, including compensation for past economic slavery, political exploitation, ethnic and cultural psychological damages, and the basic denial of civil and human liberties.

Self-defense: The barrios, the campos, the pueblos, and the ranchos would serve as the front line of defense against Anglo exploitation, with the youth serving as soldiers.

Preservation of culture: Chicano writers, poets, musicians, and artists needed to produce art that would be not only appealing to the people but also supportive of the advancement of the Chicano community. Corky Gonzales himself used art to further his cause. His 1965 poem "I Am Joaquin" dramatizes the experience of the Chicano people through history, evoking their indigenous roots while also expressing the repressed anger against racism and discrimination.

Political liberation: With the assumption that the American two-party system was corrupt, Chicanos/as were encouraged to create their own political party. This goal set the framework for the formation of various political organizations, the most popular of which was La Raza Unida Party (LRUP)—or united people's party—founded by Chicanos/as in South Texas in 1970. The LRUP was formed to organize unregistered voters into an independent political bloc that would be capable of electing candidates to office, especially in areas where Chicanos/as made up the majority of registered voters.

El Plan Espiritual de Aztlán lost its momentum after activist and LRUP founder José Angel Gutiérrez of Texas defeated Corky Gonzales in a national election within La Raza Unida Party. Nevertheless, with its emphasis on racial pride and a desire to create an independent and separate physical and social space for Chicanos/as, El Plan Espiritual de Aztlán became both the symbolic and the literal constitution of the Chicano Movement.

Jesse J. Esparza

See also: Aztlán; Chicano Movement; Gonzales, Rodolfo "Corky"; La Raza Unida Party; Mexican American Student Association; Plan de Santa Barbara, El; *Yo Soy Joaquín.*

Further Reading

Larralde, Carlos. *Mexican American Movements and Leaders.* Los Alamitos, CA: Hwong, 1976.
Marín, Christine. *A Spokesman of the Mexican American Movement: Rodolfo "Corky" Gonzales and the Fight for*

Chicano Liberation, 1966–1972. San Francisco: R and E Research Associates, 1977.

Meier, Matt S., and Margo Gutierrez. *Encyclopedia of the Mexican American Civil Rights Movement.* Westport, CT: Greenwood, 2000.

Platt Amendment (1901)

The Platt Amendment legally validated three decades of early twentieth-century U.S. supervision of Cuba. U.S. leaders who favored joining the late nineteenth-century European scramble for overseas imperial possessions were given their opportunity in 1895, after José Martí and Cuban rebels renewed long-standing efforts to win Cuban independence from Spain. At the time, Cuban trade accounted for 75 percent of all Latin American exports to the United States and more than half of all Latin American imports from the United States. With U.S. businessmen fretting about the protection of U.S.-owned property in Cuba, President William McKinley sent the battleship *Maine* to Havana's harbor. On February 15, 1898, the *Maine* exploded, killing 260 U.S. sailors. Said to have been caused by an underwater mine, the calamity broke the will of U.S. leaders who had resisted the pressure of those advocating war, a group that included Cuban lobbyists and readers stirred by newspaper reports. In the brief war that followed, the United States defeated the Kingdom of Spain.

Cuban rebels were excluded from participating in the December 1898 Treaty of Paris between Spain and the United States, which ended the Spanish-American War and the Spanish empire in the Western Hemisphere. Spanish sovereignty over Cuba was transferred to the United States. On January 1, 1899, Cuba was put under U.S. military occupation led by General John R. Brooke and his successor, General Leonard Wood. The victorious wartime deeds of the First Regiment of U.S. Cavalry Volunteers in Cuba, popularly known as the Rough Riders, helped their leader Theodore Roosevelt win the U.S. vice presidential nomination in 1900. Roosevelt became president the following year after an anarchist assassinated President McKinley.

Cuba became independent in May 1902, but only after a special U.S.-Cuban relationship was created in which Cuba became a protectorate of the United States. The Roosevelt administration approved Cuban independence but maintained control over Cubans (whom it considered unsuitable for self-government) through an amendment to the U.S. Army appropriations bill for fiscal year 1902 known as the Platt Amendment. Drafted by U.S. Secretary of War Elihu Root and named after its sponsor, Senator Orville H. Platt (R-CT), the amendment severely limited Cuba's autonomy. U.S. troops left the island only after Cuba's Constituent Assembly included the amendment's provisions as a codicil to the new Cuban Constitution of 1901. The Platt Amendment granted the United States the right to intervene in Cuban affairs to maintain "a government adequate for the protection of life, property, and individual liberty." Reflecting U.S. fear of European intervention in the Caribbean to collect on defaulted debts, the amendment stated that the Cuban government would not assume any extraordinary public debt. Cuba was also required to provide the United States with land for a naval base, subsequently constructed at Guantánamo Bay.

Incorporated into the U.S.-Cuban Permanent Treaty of 1903, the Platt Amendment compromised Cuban independence. Rival Cuban political factions repeatedly used the threat of U.S. intervention to attain or maintain power. In 1906, the disputed reelection of Cuba's first president, Tomás Estrada Palma, provoked an armed insurgency. Estrada Palma subsequently requested U.S. intervention and resigned his post. The U.S. military occupied Cuba from 1906 to 1909 and ruled through a provisional government headed by attorney and diplomat Charles E. Magoon. In 1912, U.S. Marines landed in Cuba to protect American property during an upheaval sparked by Afro-Cubans protesting political and social discrimination. In 1917, after President Mario García Menocal was reelected in contested balloting that triggered an uprising, U.S. troops landed and maintained a military presence in eastern Cuba until 1922.

Following the island's disputed presidential election of 1920, additional U.S. troops arrived in Cuba in January 1921 to prevent civil war. U.S. Special Envoy General Enoch H. Crowder resolved the electoral dispute in favor of Alfredo Zayas. U.S. forces remained in Cuba while Crowder pressured President Zayas to restructure the Cuban government, which the United States considered an oversized, corrupt, and nepotistic bureaucracy. Crowder's mission was aided by the power of the United States to block approval of a desired $50 million loan to Cuba from the J.P. Morgan banking firm pending the restructuring. Within weeks after receiving the loan, Zayas fired several cabinet members Crowder had pressured him to appoint. Disappointed, Crowder became the first U.S. ambassador to Cuba in 1923. That same year, U.S. forces were withdrawn from Cuba, marking the end of the U.S. military presence sanctioned by the Platt Amendment.

Cuba experienced a surge of nationalist sentiment in the 1920s. The Liberal Party platform called for the abrogation of the Platt Amendment during the presidential election of 1924, marking the first time such a policy was formally advocated by a major political party. Liberal Party candidate Gerardo Machado won the election, and in 1926 the League Against the Platt Amendment was organized in Havana. Two years later, the founding of the Anti-Imperialist League championed the same cause. Machado, who was reelected to a second presidential term in an uncontested 1928 election, assumed dictatorial powers to quell social unrest during the global depression of the early 1930s.

In May 1933, the new Franklin D. Roosevelt administration appointed Assistant Secretary of State Sumner Welles as the U.S. ambassador to Cuba. Welles tried unsuccessfully to convince Machado to resign. Fear of a U.S. military intervention led the Cuban army to move against Machado, who fled the country in August 1933. The U.S.-backed Carlos Manuel de Céspedes was selected to be the provisional president, but in September a military revolt headed by Sergeant Fulgencio Batista against the Cuban officer corps led to the establishment of a provisional government under the reform-minded leftist Ramón Grau San Martín. Grau's was the first government of the Republic of Cuba formed without U.S. sanction and support. Grau unilaterally nullified the Platt Amendment on the day of his inauguration in September 1933. The United States withheld recogni-

tion from the Grau administration and, in an effort to oust him, courted Batista. By year's end, Batista had been promoted to the rank of colonel and army chief of staff, and in January 1934, Batista led a military coup against Grau. Carlos Mendieta was installed as the provisional president, and the United States immediately recognized his government.

The Treaty of Relations with Cuba finally abrogated the Platt Amendment in May 1934, in accord with President Roosevelt's effort to improve relations with hemispheric neighbors known as the Good Neighbor Policy. According to the treaty, however, any agreements regarding the lease to the United States of Cuban land at Guantánamo Bay would remain in effect until annulled by both parties. Mendieta resigned the provisional presidency in December 1935, and Batista ruled Cuba for the rest of the 1930s behind puppet presidents. With the bilateral repeal of the Platt Amendment, the United States no longer had a constitutionally legitimated right to intervene at its own discretion in Cuba's domestic and international affairs.

David M. Carletta

See also: Spanish-American War.

Further Reading

Fitzgibbon, Russell H. *Cuba and the United States, 1900–1935.* New York: Russell & Russell, 1964.

Hernández, José M. *Cuba and the United States: Intervention and Militarism, 1868–1933.* Austin: University of Texas Press, 1993.

Hitchman, James H. *Leonard Wood and Cuban Independence, 1898–1902.* The Hague, The Netherlands: Martinus Nijhoff, 1971.

Pérez, Louis A., Jr. *Cuba Under the Platt Amendment, 1902–1934.* Pittsburgh, PA: University of Pittsburgh Press, 1986.

Politics

Although Latinos/as have consistently found themselves disenfranchised and politically powerless in the course of American history, they have fought continuously for inclusion and power. Since the signing of the Treaty of Guadalupe-Hidalgo, the 1848 treaty that ended the U.S. war against Mexico, Latinos/as have engaged in political struggles to secure and advance their interests. The two mainstream political parties, Republican and Democrat, have historically marginalized Latinos/as in the development of party platforms and selection of major candidates, while the practice of gerrymandering—the redrawing of electoral district boundaries for political advantage—has diluted Latino influence even in high-population regions. Thus, for centuries, the political aspirations of Latinos/as have been contained and their role in the mainstream political process limited. Indeed, the fight for Latino participation in the political process remains one of the oldest ongoing struggles for civil rights in America. Not until the late twentieth century would Latinos/as begin to gain positions of power at the national as well as state and local levels.

Early Participation

From the time the United States occupied Mexico's northern most territory, Latinos/as in that region found themselves victims of harassment and open discrimination. Contending that U.S. officials would not honor the stipulations of the Treaty of Guadalupe-Hidalgo that protected the civil liberties of Latinos/as living in the United States, several protest organizations were formed to protect those communities. Las Gorras Blancas was a secret organization established in northeastern New Mexico in the late 1880s to defend the old Mexican-Hispanic way of life and economy against Anglo land speculators and railroad companies. Building on the foundation established by Las Gorras Blancas, El Partido del Pueblo Unido was formed in 1890 to protect the rights of the Hispano community, although it ultimately proved ineffective against the Anglo political machine. Created by Nuevomexicanos (Hispanos) disillusioned with the two major parties, the Partido, while allied with the Populist Party at the national level, was successful only in county elections. By 1892, membership began to decline, and it was disbanded by the next election.

Despite such efforts and the improved economic and social standing of some members of the community, Latinos/as would remain largely on the fringes of the American political process, if not fully excluded. Following the end of the World War I, organizations such as the Order of Sons of America and the League of United Latin American Citizens were formed to promote Latino interests and participation in society. Yet most of these groups, at least during the 1920s and 1930s, were accommodationist rather than explicitly political organizations, seeking to influence existing mainstream parties but never fully part of the political process. The Order of Sons of America (OSA), or Orden Hijos de America, was founded in 1921 in San Antonio, Texas, by middle-class Latinos/as. The Sons of America moved beyond the efforts of mutualista-type organizations such as La Alianza de Sociedades Mutualistas of San Antonio, Texas, to a more political orientation. Thus, the OSA was more than a social support group seeking to protect its members from discrimination and economic privation; it also promoted efforts to eliminate discrimination. In 1929, at Corpus Christi, Texas, it banded together with several other organizations, including the League of Latin American Citizens, to form a new political organization—the League of United Latin American Citizens (LULAC). Emphasizing its belief in the American political system, LULAC would become the first umbrella political organization and the quintessential Latino civil rights group for years to come. During the World War II period, LULAC became increasingly activistic, seeking to secure a place for Latinos/as on juries and ending school segregation. To the present day, LULAC continues to be the most influential Latino organization and champion of civil rights for Spanish-speaking people in America.

Postwar Era: New Strategies, New Organizations

World War II marked a significant turning point in Latino political participation. As more Spanish-speaking people moved to urban centers, the possibility of organizing politically also increased. With the onset of the war, Latinos/as were motivated to form political organizations with new, more aggressive strategies. Moving beyond self-help organizations, a new generation of Latino leaders—such as Héctor P. García, Fred Ross, Albert Peña, and Bert Corona, to name a few—formed groups with the explicit goal of gaining political power. In California, for example, Latinos/as formed the Community Service Organization (CSO) in early 1940 with a particular focus on health, housing, political, and employment issues; it also went on to organize sweeping voter registration drives and political education projects. In 1948, Latinos/as in Texas established the American GI Forum (AGIF), made up largely of Mexican American World War II veterans. Founded by Héctor P. García, the AGIF emerged as a powerful legal and political organization.

In addition to veterans' rights and benefits for Latinos/as, the American GI Forum, like the CSO, organized voter registration drives and get-out-the-vote campaigns.

By the 1950s, Latino political participation was on the rise. Although elected and appointed political figures began to emerge on the scene, underrepresentation persisted. In 1959, Latino activists in California and Texas formed the Mexican American Political Association (MAPA), specifically dedicated to increasing political participation and influence. Founded by Eduardo Quevedo, Bert Corona, and others in Los Angeles, and by Albert Peña, the Bexar County commissioner in Texas, MAPA focused almost exclusively on Latino interests and issues. The organizational structure and resources were geared to lobbying for a Mexican American political agenda, promoting and financing Chicano candidates, influencing elections, and increasing the Latino vote. While a primary goal of MAPA was to get more Latinos/as (or candidates sensitive to Latino issues) into elective or appointed positions, it also functioned as a non-partisan pressure group that worked to communicate Latino demands to the two major political parties. MAPA showed its political strength in the 1958 Texas senatorial election, when it mounted a lobbying campaign and voter drives that helped Ralph Yarborough defeat conservative William Blakley in the Democratic primary election and Republican Ray Wittenburg in the general election. In 1964, even though its membership had declined, MAPA helped Yarborough defeat future president George H. W. Bush in the gubernatorial race. By 1960, however, most of MAPA's members would merge with other Latino activists to form a new, larger political organization—the Political Association of Spanish-Speaking Organizations, or PASO.

In the 1960 presidential election, Latinos/as, under the leadership of Héctor P. García and Carlos McCormick, both of the American GI Forum, along with Edward Roybal and Dennis Chavez, formed Viva Kennedy Clubs across the Southwest and in California and parts of the Midwest for the purpose of generating support for Democratic candidates John F. Kennedy and Texas native Lyndon B. Johnson. Many Latinos/as regarded them as sympathetic because of their endorsements of school desegregation, equal opportunities, fair housing, comprehensive legislation for migrant workers, and voting rights for Latinos/as, as well as their promise to appoint a Latino as an ambassador to Latin America during the 1960 Democratic National Convention. With the clubs especially active throughout the Southwest, Latinos/as became major participants in the electoral process and made a significant contribution to Kennedy's victory in a close race. The Viva Kennedy Clubs also constituted the first influential partisan group made up of Latinos/as. The Kennedy-Johnson ticket won 85 percent of the Latino vote nationwide and 91 percent in Texas. As a show of appreciation, President Kennedy held true to his

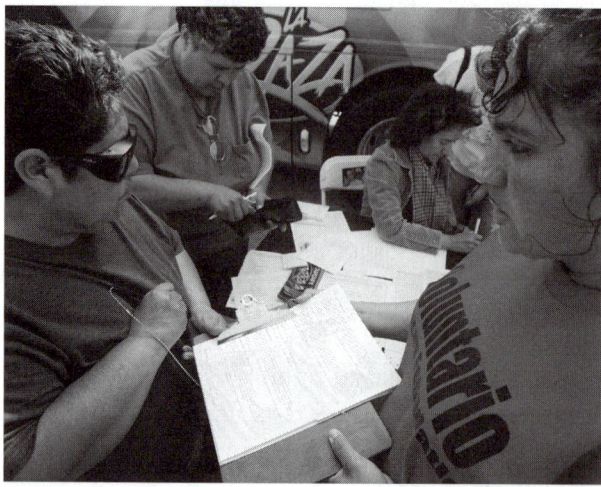

Organizers in California launch a voter registration and citizenship drive in 2006, with the goal of adding 1 million Latinos/as to the rolls. Voter registration and get-out-the vote campaigns have been central to Latino political mobilization efforts since the 1940s. *(David McNew/Getty Images)*

promise and appointed Raymond Telles as ambassador to Costa Rica, the first time a U.S. Latino had ever held such a position. In 1961, Kennedy was also instrumental in getting Henry B. Gonzalez elected to Congress, where he served for the next thirty-eight years. Importantly, the Viva Kennedy Clubs were instrumental in increasing Latino voter registration and turnout, thereby contributing to the success of Latino candidates at the local level.

With Kennedy in office, the possibility of increased political influence among Latinos/as seemed likely. Even after his death in 1963, Latinos/as were positive that their political clout would expand; after all, taking office following Kennedy was the new Latino champion in Washington, Lyndon Baines Johnson (LBJ). A Texan, Johnson was a longtime favorite of the Latino community. Before entering politics, he had been a teacher at an all Mexicano school in Cotulla, Texas, where he had become intimately aware of the needs of Latinos/as and the kinds of discrimination they faced. As a U.S. senator, he had won the affection of Latinos/as in 1949 by helping secure a burial with full military honors at Arlington National Cemetery for Private Felix Longoria, a Mexican American soldier who had been killed in the Philippines during World War II but denied a wake at his hometown's segregated cemetery in Texas. As Senate majority leader, Johnson also helped pass the first national civil rights legislation since Reconstruction—the Civil Rights Act of 1957, which established the Civil Rights Commission to root out voter discrimination based on race, color, creed, and national origin. Upon succeeding President Kennedy in the White House, Johnson pursued his predecessor's agenda and gained passage of the Civil Rights Act of 1964, which created the Equal Employment Opportunity Commission (EEOC) that worked to prevent job discrimination based on race, color, and gender. The legislation was cheered by Latinos/as, who for many decades had faced discrimination in the workplace or had been effectively barred from it entirely.

Nevertheless, some in the Latino community began to grow disgruntled with the Johnson administration, as employment discrimination against Latinos/as went largely unabated. In 1966, nearly fifty Latino activists and community leaders, represent-

ing such organizations as PASO, LULAC, and the American GI Forum, walked out of an EEOC conference held in Albuquerque, New Mexico, that was also attended by LBJ himself. Organized by Vicente Ximenes, Felix Garcia, and Ernesto Galarza, the walkout focused attention on the employment needs of Latinos/as and the persistent failures to resolve inequality. The group made several specific demands, including the appointment of Latinos/as to the EEOC, active recruitment of Latinos/as to other federal agencies, and a White House conference with President Johnson to discuss possible solutions. In response, Johnson named Ximenes to the EEOC and created the Inter-Agency Committee on Mexican American Affairs.

Adding to the disgruntlement of the Latino community was the country's involvement in the Vietnam War. Joining the growing antiwar movement over the aims and purposes of U.S. involvement, as well as the perceived dishonesty of the Johnson administration in the escalation of fighting, Latinos/as by 1968 were also angered by the inordinate number of poor minorities being drafted and shipped off to combat.

Meanwhile, the Political Association of Spanish-Speaking Organizations (PASO) had brought together leaders of various organizations who shared a desire for political unity within the Latino community. Their goal was to connect activists and political groups from throughout the Southwest in hopes of developing a solid Latino political bloc. Among those involved were leaders of both the Texas and the California MAPA organizations, the Community Service Organization, LULAC, and the American GI Forum. In the annals of Latino history, PASO is remembered largely for its efforts in Crystal City, Texas, in 1963, when it joined forces with the local Teamsters Union to elect Latinos to all five city council seats. The result was a sweep of the city council and the first time an all-Latino government body controlled a South Texas city. Despite this success, PASO suffered from persistent infighting between moderate and more radical members over the direction of the organization. While it attempted to replicate the Crystal City success in other locales, the infighting minimized its political clout beyond Texas. Never becoming the umbrella organization envisioned by its founders, PASO saw its membership go into decline. This was hastened by the emergence of La Raza Unida Party in 1970, a bona fide Latino political organization that took in many former PASO members.

All in all, MAPA, the Viva Kennedy Clubs, and PASO had significant success during the late 1950s and early 1960s in helping elect Latino candidates or those sympathetic to the Latino community. Beyond taking over the city council in Crystal City, helping elect President John Kennedy, and sending Henry B. Gonzalez and Edward Roybal to Congress, the leading Latino political organizations of this era were also successful in influencing the two major parties to pass legislation that benefited Latinos/as—for example, setting a minimum wage for migrant workers; creating welfare assistance for the elderly, widowed, and orphaned; and making available more federal aid opportunities for Latinos/as entering institutions of higher learning.

With all the progress, however, the Latino community remained underrepresented in the policy-making arena. Dissatisfied with the slow pace of advancement and aware of the political successes of African Americans, Latinos/as began to push for political power in new ways during the late 1960s and early 1970s. Embracing the confrontational model employed by African Americans in the pursuit of civil rights, the Chicano Movement of this period focused on political activism outside the "system." The leading organizations formed in the aftermath of World War II, the American GI Forum and the Mexican American Political Association, shifted their emphasis from conventional politics to more confrontational tactics. While lobbying for candidates, funding campaigns, and working to get out the vote were still part of their effort, participation in mainstream politics increasingly gave way to the organization of rallies, marches, walkouts, and other protest events. Indeed, as the Chicano Movement gained momentum, the country witnessed a series of demonstrations that shook its political foundation.

The Chicano Movement: Resurgence

The labor-organizing efforts of César Chávez and the farmworkers strike of 1965 were the sparks of expanded political consciousness and ethnic identity in the Spanish-speaking community of America. In the years that followed, colleges, high schools, and even elementary schools throughout the Southwest became increasingly active, with students forming loose community groups or larger organizations to promote educational equality and cultural identity. The Movimiento Estudiantíl Chicano de Aztlán (MEChA), Mexican American Youth Organization (MAYO), and United Mexican American Students (UMAS) were leading activist pressure groups for young Latinos/as in the late 1960s and early 1970s. Spanish-speaking youth in Texas and Southern California took part in school walkouts to protest the lack of educational resources and to demand a variety of reforms. Perhaps the most documented of the walkouts—or "blowouts"—were those in Los Angeles in 1968 and Crystal City, Texas, in 1972.

Also fueling the political activism of the Chicano Movement was Reies López Tijerina, who in New Mexico founded the Alianza Federal de Pueblos Libres to pressure the federal government to honor the Spanish and Mexican land grants of indigenous New Mexicans—a standoff that ended in violence. In Texas, meanwhile, José Angel Gutiérrez and MAYO both used the established political system as a means of change and organized protest marches and rallies in the streets to promote their cause. Established in 1967 in San Antonio by Willie Velásquez, Mario Compeán, Ignacio Pérez, Juan Patlán, and José Angel Gutiérrez, MAYO was made up largely of youth who criticized the two major parties for their lack of responsiveness to Latino needs. MAYO's influence in local politics was evidenced during the 1969 school walkouts, when it led a successful protest against discrimination in the schools of Crystal City. As a result of the incident, education officials were forced to make changes to curricula and make improvements to school facilities throughout the state. In San Antonio that same year, MAYO helped Mario Compeán in his campaign for mayor against Walter McAllister. Although McAllister ultimately prevailed, MAYO had begun empowering the Latino community and calling attention to its needs. Among the prospects raised by MAYO's efforts was political muscle through solidarity and the prospect of a third political party. It was this idea that would make the organization a key figure in the formation of La Raza Unida Party.

In Denver, meanwhile, Rodolfo "Corky" Gonzales's Crusade for Justice (CFJ), a nationalist organization dedicated to the creation of an independent Chicano nation, also aroused political activism. Founded in 1966 as a civil rights organization, CFJ championed the belief that Latinos/as needed to become completely independent of mainstream political ties and government agencies. In 1968, the Crusade for Justice also led a series of student walkouts and gained a measure of political influence at the local level. At the Chicano Youth Liberation Conference in Denver the following year, Gonzales and other activists drafted El Plan Espiritual de Aztlán, a manifesto that stressed the need for Latinos/as to control their own schools, communities, and political structures. The CFJ also demonstrated against and used its political clout to protest police brutality and the Vietnam War. Like MAYO, it organized a new political party based on Chicano nationalism. In 1970, Gonzales launched the Colorado-based La Raza Unida Party.

In all, the Chicano Movement pushed successfully for the creation of relief and welfare programs, the enactment of educational reform such as bilingual-bicultural instruction, the creation of job training programs, and the appointment of Latinos/as to positions of authority by major institutions. But perhaps the greatest political achievement for Latinos/as during the late 1960s and early 1970s was the establishment of various Raza Unida parties, which eventually united into one nationally based political organization.

Post-1960s Politics: Maturity

Although increasingly active, Latino political organizing remained limited in the absence of a unifying leader or political organization—at least until the founding of La Raza Unida Party (LRUP) in 1970. The concept came as a result of discussions held the year prior at the MAYO National Conference in Mission, Texas, where attendees endorsed the idea of an official Latino national party. In January 1970, La Raza Unida Party was officially constituted with the purpose of organizing unregistered voters and molding the Latino community into a solid, independent political bloc capable of electing Latino candidates to high-level positions. The initial strategy was to build on the successes of Latinos/as who had secured seats on local school boards and city councils in Texas, California, and Colorado. Soon, however, the organization began to shift its focus to electing candidates in areas where Latinos/as held majorities but were not well organized politically or widely registered to vote.

Immediately upon its formation, LRUP filed candidates for elections throughout the state of Texas. In 1970, it secured the election of Roel Rodriguez as commissioner of La Salle County. The next year, Latino candidates took control of the city council in San Juan in South Texas. In 1971, LRUP leaders meeting in San Antonio voted to organize and coordinate their efforts statewide. The party held its first national convention in El Paso the very next year and began running a multitude of candidates. Seeking a candidate for the Texas gubernatorial race, it enlisted attorney Ramsey Muñiz, a fellow LRUP member, with Alma Canales filling the ticket as his running mate for lieutenant governor. Although the Muñiz-Canales ticket fell far short of election, the campaign marked a new beginning of Latino politicking in the state. In Chicago, the LRUP endorsed Angel Moreno as its candidate for a congressional seat, though he, too, ultimately lost to the Democratic nominee. At the local level, meanwhile, the LRUP did score some notable successes. In Denver, it managed to get Sal Carpio elected to the city council, while in Arizona, it helped elect Alfredo Gutierrez as state senator.

In 1974, LRUP again entered the Texas governor's race, with Carlos Muñiz as its official candidate. Again LRUP posed no real threat to the incumbent, with the party's successes confined to local elections. In Crystal City, José Angel Gutiérrez was elected to a county judgeship, and in San Antonio the following year, Ciro Rodriguez was elected to the state legislature. Rodriguez had previously served as a member of the school board for the Harlandale Independent School District in San Antonio, joined by the LRUP's Pablo Escamilla. Even as far away as the District of Columbia, LRUP had its representatives elected to boards of education, as was Frank Shaffer-Corona in 1977.

The LRUP's clout began to wane in the late 1970s, especially after it began to lose state campaign funding. Even more damaging to its influence and future prospects, however, were the divided leadership and internal dissent among members. The infighting revolved primarily around the political goals and strategies of the party, as a result of which membership began to decline. In 1978, despite its diminishing influence, the LRUP ran yet another candidate in the Texas gubernatorial election. At the top of the ticket was Mario Compeán—who garnered a mere 2 percent of the statewide vote. As a result, the party lost all state funding and was effectively eliminated as an independent political party. It has remained in existence to the present day, operating as a voice of Latino interests within the two-party political system. By the early 1980s, with the Chicano Movement and political activism having waned, Latino political organizations generally abandoned rallies and protests, turned away from any organized national strategy and campaign support, and reverted back to working within the system. Still, there was no question that the political consciousness and ethnic pride of Latinos/as had been aroused and that they would continue their efforts to gain clout at every level of government and influence the nation's policy agenda.

Positions of Authority and Voter Influence

Despite the disappointments of the LRUP and many of its candidates, the election of Latinos/as to the U.S. Congress—beginning with Henry Gonzalez and Ed Roybal in the 1960s—was followed by others from far-flung constituencies and brought a consolidation of influence in that body. In 1968, Herman Badillo of New York won a seat in Congress and helped establish the first Hispanic Caucus on Capitol Hill.

Another rising star was Henry Cisneros, who began his political career in 1975 as a city council member in San Antonio, winning election as mayor in 1981. Cisneros went on to serve as U.S. secretary of the Department of Housing and Urban Development (HUD) from 1992 to 1997, under President Bill Clinton. In 1982, meanwhile, voters in New Mexico elected Bill Richardson to the U.S. House of Representatives,

where he served until 1997 and then was appointed, also by Clinton, as U.S. ambassador to the United Nations. The following year, Richardson returned to the cabinet as secretary of energy. With the end of the Clinton administration, Richardson returned home to New Mexico and won the race for governor in 2002. Six years later, he made history by entering the race for president of the United States—the first Latino ever to do so. Although he dropped out of the campaign early in the Democratic primary season, Richardson played a vital role in the candidacy of the party's eventual nominee, Senator Barack Obama of Illinois. As the most prominent Latino in American national politics, Richardson helped garner support for Obama in both the party primaries and the general election. In the aftermath of Obama's victory in November 2008, Richardson was tapped for a place in the new cabinet, as secretary of commerce, but he withdrew his nomination weeks later because of a federal investigation into his business dealings in New Mexico.

Other Latinos/as in high-profile positions have included Texas Supreme Court Justice Raúl A. Gonzalez (1984–1988), U.S. Surgeon General Antonia Novello (1990–1993), Secretary of Transportation and Secretary of Energy Federico Peña (1993–1997 and 1997–1998, respectively), and U.S. Senator Ken Salazar (D-CO, elected in 2004).

The two most notable figures among Latinos/as in politics during the twenty-first century are Antonio Villaraigosa, the widely popular mayor of Los Angeles elected in 2005, and Alberto Gonzales, the nation's first-ever Latino attorney general (2005–2007). Villaraigosa had previously served in the California State Assembly and on the Los Angeles City Council. Gonzales had served as White House counsel to President George W. Bush and, among other things, as a justice of the Texas Supreme Court.

In addition to appointing Latinos/as to positions of authority, politicians at the national level have been compelled by the ever-increasing Spanish-speaking population to actively court the Latino vote. Yet Latino voter turnout has remained relatively low. While people of "Hispanic" origin constituted some 14.4 percent of the total U.S. population according to the 2000 Census, Latinos/as represented only 5.5 percent of all votes cast in the national election that year. And with Latino population growth continuing to accelerate relative to the nation as a whole, Latino voter turnout rose to just over 6 percent in 2004. Of those who do vote, large majorities cast their ballots for Democratic candidates—49 percent in 2004, versus 27 percent for Republican candidates and 24 percent for independents. More traditional Latino communities tend to take conservative positions on social issues such as abortion and homosexuality, showing strong loyalty to the Roman Catholic Church. Under President George W. Bush, a Texan who made direct appeals to the Latino community in its native language, the Republican Party actively sought inroads with Latino voters. But with immigration policy the foremost issue in that constituency and with the White House taking a hard line on illegal immigration, the GOP fell from grace among many Latinos/as. The 2008 presidential election confirmed a major shift in party affiliation, as Latinos/as voted 67 percent for Democratic candidate Barack Obama and only 31 percent voted for Republican John McCain. Emerging as a mobilized Democratic voting bloc, Latinos/as contributed significantly to Obama victories in such battleground states as New Mexico, Nevada, and Colorado. Notable as well was the enormous Latino voter turnout in 2008. About 10 million Latinos/as went to the polls, marking a nearly 25 percent increase over 2004.

Jesse J. Esparza

See also: American GI Forum; Chávez, César; Chicano Movement; Cisneros, Henry; Community Service Organization; Corona, Bert; Crystal City, Texas; Galarza, Ernesto; García, Héctor P.; Gutiérrez, José Angel; La Raza Unida Party; League of United Latin American Citizens; Mexican American Political Association; Mexican American Youth Organization; Mexican-American War; Movimiento Estudiantíl Chicano de Aztlán; Peña, Albert A., Jr.; Plan Espiritual de Aztlán, El; Roybal, Edward R.; Tijerina, Reies López; Treaty of Guadalupe Hidalgo (1848); Villaraigosa, Antonio; Viva Kennedy Clubs.

Further Reading

Allsup, Carl. *The G.I. Forum: Origins and Evolution.* Austin, TX: Center for Mexican American Studies, 1982.
Cuellar, Robert. *A Social and Political History of the Mexican American Population of Texas, 1929–1963.* San Francisco: R and E Research Associates, 1974.
Garcia, Chris, and Rudolph O. de la Garza. *The Chicano Political Experience.* North Scituate, MA: Duxbury, 1977.
Garcia, Chris, ed. *La Causa Política: A Chicano Politics Reader.* South Bend, IN: University of Notre Dame Press, 1974.
García, Ignacio M. *United We Win: The Rise and Fall of La Raza Unida Party.* Tucson: University of Arizona Mexican American Studies Research Center, 1989.
Gómez-Quiñones, Juan. *Chicano Politics: Reality and Promise, 1940–1990.* Albuquerque: University of New Mexico Press, 1990.
———. *Roots of Chicano Politics, 1600–1948.* Albuquerque: University of New Mexico Press, 1994.
Gutierrez, David G. *Walls and Mirrors: Mexican Americans, Mexican Immigrants, and the Politics of Ethnicity.* Berkeley: University of California Press, 1995.
Guzman, Ralph C. *The Political Socialization of the Mexican American People.* New York: Arno, 1976.
Pew Hispanic Center. http://www.pewhispanic.org.
Shockley, John Staples. *Chicano Revolt in a Texas Town.* Notre Dame, IN: University of Notre Dame Press, 1974.
Vigil, Maurilio. *Chicano Politics.* Washington, DC: University Press of America, 1977.
Villarreal, Roberto E., and Norma G. Hernandez, eds. *Latinos and Political Coalitions.* Westport, CT: Greenwood, 1991.

Popular Culture

The term "popular culture" refers to the products and expressions of the commercial marketplace and mass media. In the United States today, it is exemplified by television shows, Hollywood movies, radio and recorded music, advertising, mass-circulation magazines, fashion trends, sporting events, video games, and other expressions of commonly shared tastes and values. Popular culture, typically contrasted with "highbrow" culture, is a relatively recent development in U.S. history. It did not fully emerge until the advent of the mass media and mass market in the early twentieth century.

For Latinos and Latinas, U.S. popular culture has presented two key problems virtually from the beginning. The first is the issue of *visibility,* or the extent to which Latinos/as are seen and embraced in the mainstream popular culture arena. The second is the issue of *representation,* or how Latinos/as are depicted in popular culture. Throughout the history

Pop singer Ricky Martin, born and raised in Puerto Rico, and actress-singer Jennifer Lopez, born in the South Bronx to Puerto Rican parents, epitomize the rise of Latino performers to the top echelon of mainstream pop culture in the 1990s and 2000s. *(Kevin Mazur/WireImage/Getty Images)*

of U.S. popular culture, there have been significant changes with respect to both issues. The problems of visibility and representation can be seen in the history of each of the major popular media arenas, including film, television, and music.

Film

From the turn of the twentieth century through the 1940s, with roles for Latino actors already severely limited, Hollywood resorted to stereotypes in the depiction of Latino characters. The choice facing Latinos/as in Hollywood was usually either to accept stereotypical roles or to have no acting work at all. Although the stereotypes predate Hollywood, they were certainly perpetuated and popularized by the

major movie studios. Westerns of the silent film era commonly depicted Mexicans as treacherous, morally corrupt, and uncivilized. Films such as *Indian Scout's Revenge* (1910), *Captured by Mexicans* (1914), and *Arizona Cat Claw* (1919) portrayed Mexicans as threatening the safety of Anglo settlers. The stereotype of the Mexican bandito became a mainstay of Western films for decades to come.

Other stereotypes were disseminated as well. Rudolph Valentino (who was actually Italian) became the famed "Latin Lover" of 1920s features, and much was made at the time of his ability to woo women with his suave demeanor. Portrayals of Latinas, when such roles appeared, similarly focused on the actresses' exotic sexual allure. It was often non-Latinas who played such roles, however, primarily because Latinas were largely excluded from the film industry and the industry feared interracial relations between white actors and those of color. Conversely, Latino actors and actresses who did find work were often made to conform to white standards of beauty. The screen legend and magazine pinup idol Rita Hayworth, who was born Margarita Carmen Cansino, was one such example. When studio producers discovered her talent, they feared that she looked "too Mexican" to appeal to white audiences and had her hair changed from brown to copper red and, ultimately, changed her name as well.

The decades immediately following World War II saw little change for Latino/as in Hollywood, with a continuation of the stereotypical representations and limited opportunities for Hispanic artists. It was during the 1950s and 1960s that the Western reached maturity as an original film genre, often including a struggle between white settlers and Native Americans or Mexican bandits as an element of the plot. Although Mexicans continued to be represented as bandits, exceptions to the rule were beginning to be seen. Film scholars have pointed to director Fred Zimmerman's 1952 classic, *High Noon,* as a feature film with a Mexican character portrayed as a heroine instead of a villain.

It was not until the cultural, social, and economic upheavals of the late 1960s and early 1970s, however, that Hollywood's failure to portray people of color in plausible and realistic ways finally came under serious attack. For Latinos/as, the Vietnam War protests, the United Farm Workers movement, and the Chicano student movement provided the contexts for a change in political consciousness. Hollywood, for its part, responded to the overall climate of the 1960s and 1970s by loosening its exclusionary practices. More Latino actors and actresses were able to play Latino roles. Comedian Cheech Marin and others became commercial successes with films in the 1970s and 1980s. Among Marin's successes was *Born in East L.A.* (1987), the story of a Latino factory worker who was native to East Los Angeles, yet wrongfully deported to Mexico when he failed to produce identification during a U.S. government raid. As Marin's character tries to make his way back to East Los Angeles from Tijuana, the film explores the complexities of the border experience and calls into question the meaning of "home" for Latinos/as living on the border.

The 1990s and early 2000s saw an even greater increase in Latino stars, in terms of both number and fame. Perhaps the greatest commercial success was that of pop singing idol Jennifer Lopez, whose film credits include *Selena* (1997) and *The Wedding Planner* (2001), as well as the box office bomb, *Gigli* (2003). Lopez became particularly adept in romantic comedy roles, playing opposite non-Latino actors. In movies such as *Maid in Manhattan* (2002) and *Monster-in-Law* (2005), her Latina background becomes at least tangentially important to the plot. In both films, her ethnicity is presented as a cultural difference that, while initially a problem, finally is overcome in the name of true love. Other Latina stars have been cast in similar situations in recent years, including Salma Hayek, who starred opposite Matthew Perry in *Fools Rush In* (1997), and Paz Vega, who played opposite Adam Sandler in *Spanglish* (2004).

Although such stars remain firmly on Hollywood's "A" list, they frequently receive parts that depict Latinos/as primarily in relation to whites rather than to other Latinos/as. Whether or not this has been a positive development has been a matter of disagreement. Some commentators have argued that portraying Latinos/as in such color blind ways trivializes the real-life importance of race to Latinos/as, particularly in their experiences of discrimination and racism.

Television

Latinos/as seeking entry into the television industry have experienced many of the same difficulties as Latinos/as in film: namely, struggles to receive parts and struggles to be depicted in nonstereotypical ways. Several systematic historical studies of U.S. television content have confirmed that Latino characters appear in numbers that are far out of proportion to the number of Latinos/as living in the United States. According to one such study, only 2 percent of all characters portrayed on television from 1955 to 1986 were identifiably "Hispanic." Moreover, most Latinos/as who appeared on television during this period had relatively minor roles and were seldom main characters.

One notable Latino artist who did transcend television's racial boundaries was the Cuban-born orchestra leader Desi Arnaz. After appearing in several minor Hollywood films, Arnaz rose to fame in the role of Ricky Ricardo in the long-running landmark TV series *I Love Lucy* (1952–1960). Arnaz played the husband of legendary comedienne Lucille Ball, who was also his real-life wife. As husband and wife, Arnaz and Ball established Desilu Productions, under which the live *I Love Lucy* show was produced from 1952 to 1960. Because television studio executives initially doubted that U.S. audiences would watch a sitcom about the marriage of a Latino man and a white woman, Arnaz and Ball had to finance the early production of *I Love Lucy* with their own money. The show remains immensely popular in syndication to the present day; with the global distribution of television programming, it has been estimated that *I Love Lucy* is aired on the small screen somewhere in the world at any given time of day.

In the late 1970s, the U.S. government issued a report that documented the exclusion of racial and ethnic minorities from popular television. Although the television industry has been known to respond to government and public pressure on a number of issues, responses of this sort typically have been modest and fleeting. Thus, progress in putting more

Latino faces on television has been slow. While Latinos/as continued to enjoy minor parts on television during the 1970s, starring roles were few and far between. One notable exception was Erik Estrada, who played the starring role of Frank "Ponch" Poncherello on the popular *ChiPs* (1977–1983), a weekly dramatic series about two California Highway Patrol officers. Another breakthrough was achieved by Ricardo Montalbán, who played the role of host on the popular series *Fantasy Island* (1978–1984).

The 1980s brought some new celebrity figures but no drastic changes. Studies of U.S. television content indicated that the proportion of Latino characters on TV during the decade was now up to 9 percent—an improvement in terms of visibility and opportunities for Latino artists, but still suggesting that Latinos/as were underrepresented relative to their population as a whole. New figures included celebrities in the blossoming talk-show genre, most notably Geraldo Rivera, who has had a steady presence on television since the early 1970s, most famously for his popular 1980s daytime talk show.

The 1990s brought the emergence of the reality TV genre, at the beginning led by MTV. From its inception, the cable network's *Real World* featured an ethnically and culturally diverse cast of twenty-somethings who were selected to live in a house together and have their lives taped over several months. In an early season of the show, Pedro Zamora, an openly gay Cuban immigrant and AIDS activist, became a visible symbol of the AIDS epidemic after his death in 1994.

Other Latino celebrities emerged on English-language U.S. television during the 1990s. Daisy Fuentes began her national television career as an MTV vj (video jockey) and became something of a sex symbol before going on to host various pageants and installments of *America's Funniest Home Videos*. Wilmer Valderrama gained widespread recognition starting with his role as Fez on *That 70's Show,* which premiered in 1998. Still, few shows on English-language television have featured Latinos/as as primary characters or figures. The few exceptions include *Resurrection Blvd.,* a drama about the dreams and ambitions of a Latino family living in East Los Angeles, which premiered on Showtime in 2000; PBS's *American Family,* a drama set in East Los Angeles and

featuring an all-Latino cast; and *The George Lopez Show,* a family comedy starring comedian George Lopez, which premiered on ABC in 2002. The show lasted until 2007, when it was replaced by *Cavemen* (which lasted only one season). When he learned about the cancellation of his show, Lopez asked: "So a Chicano can't be on TV, but a caveman can?"

While English-language television continued to be slow to adopt Latino-based show concepts, Spanish-language television in the United States began to meet the real and growing demand for entertainment among Latinos/as. Continuing immigration, rising affluence and purchasing power among Latinos/as, and a wider understanding among marketers of Latinos/as as a consumer group supported this surge in demand. The network Univision is the largest Spanish-language channel in the country and the fifth largest network overall. At any time of day, Univision attracts more of those who identify themselves as "Hispanic" than any other network, Spanish- or English-language. Univision is best known for its broadcast of the variety show *Sábado Gigante,* the talk show *Christina,* and a variety of *telenovelas.* Although the rise of Spanish-language television is a testament to the increased purchasing power of Latinos/as in the United States, it also reflects the extent to which Latinos/as are treated as a distinct and separate market segment by the television industry.

Music

Music emanating from Latino communities in the United States has always been in dialogue with musical forms emanating from European and African American cultures. In the realm of commercially recorded music, however, Latino artists have only recently begun to attain widespread "crossover" success (i.e., with works that appeal to listeners across racial and ethnic divides). Since the birth of the rock era, Latino crossover successes have been slow in coming. A significant example from the 1950s was Ritchie Valens's "La Bamba" (1958), the first song in Spanish to find major success with rock and pop audiences. Other breakthroughs occurred in the 1970s, with the successes of Carlos Santana's unique guitar riffs and Julio Iglesias's ballads.

The 1980s brought a number of Latino pop sensations. As a forerunner to the "boy band" phenomenon of the 1990s, the preteen pop group Menudo succeeded in selling records to a young audience during their short-lived career on the pop charts. Another one-hit wonder occurred during the decade with Gerardo's pop-rap success, "Rico Suave" (1991). However, the greatest commercial success of the decade was Cuban-born Gloria Estéfan's string of Top 40 hits, including "Conga" (1986), "Rhythm Is Gonna' Get You" (1988), and "Anything for You" (1988). Estéfan translated her music into a hugely profitable commercial enterprise, and her popularity continues to this day.

The 1990s brought the tremendously significant pop icon, Selena, to the U.S. popular music scene. Born in South Texas, Selena was, at the time of her death in 1995, poised to become "The Madonna of Latin Music," according to accounts in the popular press. Selena's music was rooted in the Tejano musical style of South Texas, but she was considered an innovator in her success at moving its stylistic elements to match the sensibilities of mainstream audiences in both Mexico and the United States. After her unexpected death at the hands of a possessive fan, she was celebrated in a biographical film, *Selena* (1997), with Jennifer Lopez playing the title role.

The latter half of the 1990s and the first years of the twenty-first century constituted a critical period for Latino artists seeking to obtain crossover appeal in the U.S. music market. A variety of Latino pop artists emerged during this time, including Ricky Martin, Marc Anthony, Jennifer Lopez, Enrique Iglesias, Christina Aguilera, and Shakira. Several of these artists, such as Shakira and Aguilera, made albums in both English and Spanish, attempting to solidify their appeal on both sides of the border. Most of the artists that emerged during this period were marketed as exotic sex symbols, whose perceived sensuality—particularly as it pertained to their dancing abilities—helped contribute to their crossover appeal with white audiences. Regardless, the sheer number of Latino pop artists that emerged during this time led to talk of a "Latin Explosion" in U.S. popular music. Although the popularity of "Latin" artists on the popular music scene certainly increased, this did not necessarily mean that Latinos/as were more welcome in American culture as a whole. Indeed, some commentators have noted a contradiction between the popularity of this music and the popularity of various anti-immigration and anti-Spanish language movements that continued throughout the late 1990s and early 2000s.

Past, Present, Future

Several relative trends are seen in the history of U.S. popular culture. First, the visibility of Latinos/as in popular culture has increased over the last half century, albeit modestly. Some media, such as commercial music, have commodified Latinos/as to a greater extent than other vehicles of popular culture, such as television. And second, representations of Latinos/as have undergone notable change in popular films and television shows. Latinos/as are generally depicted in ways that are less blatantly racist than a century—or even half a century—ago. Still, however, Latinos/as are often depicted primarily in relation to whites and not each other. Some scholars have questioned whether the trend toward color blindness in U.S. popular culture reflects a real improvement in how Latinos/as are represented, particularly because color blindness may negate the real importance of race in the everyday lives of audiences.

Analyses of the culture industries suggest that these dynamics are likely not the result of conscious racism on the part of corporate entertainment leaders. Rather, because decision makers in the culture industries are ultimately charged with making money for their companies, they inevitably favor film and television projects that they think will reach the widest and most lucrative audience. Many decision makers still believe that white media consumers will watch only certain types of movies or television shows. Moreover, predictions as to what sorts of programming will be commercially successful are based only on commonsense assumptions about race and other subjects—further contributing to the stereotyped portrayal of Latinos/as. In the long run, however, the fact that Latinos/as continue to grow in number and purchasing power in American society inevitably will alter how and the extent to which Latinos/as are depicted in the popular culture.

Stephen Zafirau

See also: Film; Identity and Labels; Music; Television; Univision.

Further Reading

Dávila, Arlene. "Mapping Latinidad: Spanish, English and 'Spanglish' in the Hispanic TV Landscape." *Television and New Media* 1 (2000): 73–92.

Fregoso, Rosalinda. *The Bronze Screen: Chicana and Chicano Film Culture.* Minneapolis: University of Minnesota Press, 1992.

Habell-Pallán, Michelle, and Mary Romero, eds. *Latino/a Popular Culture.* New York: New York University Press, 2002.

Hadley-Garcia, George. *Hispanic Hollywood: The Latins in Motion Pictures.* New York: Carol, 1993.

Rodríguez, Clara E. *Latin Looks: Images of Latinas and Latinos in the U.S. Media.* Boulder, CO: Westview, 1997.

Univision. http://www.univision.net.

Poverty

Although Latinos/as in the United States represent all socioeconomic classes, the U.S. Census Bureau reports that most Latino families live in poverty. According to the 2000 Census, 22.6 percent of Latinos/as live below the official poverty line, compared with 12.4 percent of the rest of the population. Of major Latino groups, Cubans are less likely to live in poverty (14.6 percent) than Dominicans (27.5 percent) or Puerto Ricans (25.8 percent). The generally high poverty level has been ascribed to various reasons, including immigration experience, occupational distribution and wages, educational attainment, and residential segregation.

Immigration Experience

Latinos, the second-largest ethnic minority group in the United States, represent a highly diverse group in many ways with varying job skills and educational backgrounds. Ever in search of better jobs and a better life for themselves and their children, most new Latino immigrants initially settle in cities where they can easily find work and affordable housing. For instance, many Mexicans who immigrated during the 1980s left cities and towns that had been rav-aged by their country's economic crisis, high inflation, and devaluation of the currency, the peso. Those leaving rural areas had lower occupational and educational skills, which put them at a disadvantage when they arrived in the United States. Thus, with much of the Mexican population living in poverty by the late 1990s, a higher percentage of city residents left the country to seek better opportunities in the barrios of Los Angeles and San Diego, California, and Abilene, Texas.

Puerto Ricans, on the other hand, began arriving in large numbers during their island's economic instability in the mid-1940s, facilitated by the affordability of commercial air travel. Many settled in metropolitan New York and other northeastern cities, finding jobs in the service and manufacturing sectors. By the 2000s—as a result of the nation's shrinking manufacturing sector, "revolving door" migration (back and forth between the mainland and island), and continuing patterns of discrimination, among other factors—the Puerto Rican community was more dispersed geographically and suffered high levels of poverty. Family structure was widely identified as both a cause and consequence of the overall trend. Puerto Rican households are more likely to be headed by single women with limited access to stable jobs, welfare assistance, and other financial support. The fact that Puerto Ricans are U.S. citizens and entitled to the rights, protections, and assistance programs available to all Americans makes their high poverty rate especially vexing to observers. Whatever the factors and explanations, the Puerto Rican community has not been as economically successful as other Latino subpopulations in the United States.

Contrary to popular perception, not all Latino immigrants or U.S-born Latinos/as are from rural extraction with limited skills and low educational attainment. Most Cubans, for example, came to the United States from a middle-class, professional background when they left the island in the 1960s. In contrast to other immigrant groups, they had better job skills and were able to start up businesses and establish strong support networks and social institutions. Especially in Florida, where most have settled, they have been able to establish economic networks and community groups that help maintain their socioeconomic status. Today, Cuban Americans enjoy education and income levels similar to those of the U.S. middle-class population at large. By comparison, although a majority of immigrants coming from South America in the 2000s are also highly educated and skilled professionals, their smaller numbers, less developed support network, and inability to speak English have made them more likely to remain underemployed and less likely to experience upward mobility.

Occupational Distribution and Wages

The immigration experience of Latinos/as from diverse cultural and socioeconomic backgrounds is another central factor in high poverty rates, which remain more a function of low wages than lack of employment. Many Latinos/as, especially those of rural extraction or with little schooling, lack the skills to compete in the new technology and global economies. Latino immigrants are more likely to work in blue-collar jobs, bringing in less income to support more family members. They often hold more than one job to support their families, with little time left to pursue an education, develop computer skills, or even learn English.

While Latino participation in the labor force is higher than for other groups, they earn less than the average non-Latino worker. In the United States, according to the 2000 Census, the median family income for the population as a whole was $50,046, compared to $34,400 for people of Hispanic/Latino origins. Among the latter, the figure was lowest for Dominicans ($28,729) and highest for Cubans and South Americans ($37,000). Mexicans are more likely to work as manual laborers, farmers, and service-industry workers, while Puerto Ricans are more likely to work in the clerical, service, and sales areas (17.1 percent). Nevertheless, Mexicans earned more than Puerto Ricans, an average of about $33,516 for the former and $32,791 for the latter. According to 2006 Census Bureau statistics, Latino men were highly concentrated in construction and maintenance occupations (31.3 percent), production and transpor-

tation jobs (22.1 percent), agriculture (20 percent), and service (19.2 percent); they are least likely to hold managerial or professional positions (14.6 percent) and sales jobs (14.8 percent). Latino women are overly represented in service jobs (30.6 percent) and office occupations (32.7 percent) compared to non-Latino women (18 percent). All in all, Latinos/as generally have little representation in high-skill, well-paying professions such as engineering, medicine, and law.

Low-wage employment and joblessness among Latinos/as are additional results of discrimination in hiring and workplace exploitation. Harboring negative assumptions about Latinos/as' immigration status, job experience, work ethic, and language skills, many employers pay inordinately low wages with few employment benefits. Often lacking the protection of U.S. citizenship makes untold millions of other Latinos/as even more vulnerable to exploitation. Finally, dark skin color may make even those with full citizenship subject to racist discrimination in the workplace.

Educational Attainment

As a general matter, both recently arrived Latinos/as and those born in the United States do not attain the same level of education as the rest of the American population. In this regard, the community is caught in a vicious cycle: low educational attainment is at once a cause and consequence of poverty. Many Latino youth are expected to work to help support their extended families, which conflicts with the need to pursue an education and job training. Low expectations, lack of financial support, lack of role models and mentors, and economic pressure to leave school are among the factors that quell the aspirations and potential of Latino youth today.

With a high school dropout rate of about 30 percent, only some 52 percent of Latinos/as over the age of twenty-five report earning a high school diploma—compared to 80 percent for the U.S. population as a whole. And while 24 percent of the overall U.S. population acquires a college degree, only 10 percent of Latinos/as report earning a diploma. While the latter figure represents a significant improvement over previous decades, Latinos/as who pursue higher education are more likely to choose community colleges over four-year institutions. The choice is based primarily on their ability to afford tuition while having the flexibility to work and earn a degree.

Residential Segregation

The cycle of poverty is further exacerbated by discrimination in housing. Life in the barrios isolates residents from better opportunities in society at large. Disruption of services, lack of development and investment, and limited economic opportunities make it all the harder for Latino families to get ahead. Segregation limits residential mobility even for those who have improved their socioeconomic status. And for the many Latino families that fall under the official poverty line ($19,300 per year for a family of four in 2004), the rising costs of housing, property taxes, and education in most large cities soar ever farther out of reach. Worsening economic conditions and neighborhoods facing rising crime rates and gang violence put even further pressure on families—especially youth.

The Future

Despite these adversities, some segments of the Latino community began to achieve a measure of prosperity in the 1970s and 1980s, rising to the middle class by starting businesses in the barrios, enabling them to purchase better homes in adjacent neighborhoods and towns. The trend has gained momentum in the 2000s, as advocates and social scientists have noted the continued growth of the Latino middle-class. Many U.S.-born, second-generation Latinos/as, especially Cubans and Mexican Americans, have achieved success as entrepreneurs, educators and other professionals, and even public officials. For those who have reversed the vicious cycle of poverty, economic empowerment has increased educational attainment. They have achieved the dream of owning a home and have seen their children pursue professional careers. Corporations and the media have focused increasingly on the Latino/Hispanic market as the community gains more economic power.

For many, however, poverty remains the reality as inordinate numbers of Latinos/as struggle to meet their basic housing, food, education, and health care needs. Access to a diversity of professions, job training programs, financial support, high quality education, sources of political empowerment, and command of the English language may help mitigate Latino poverty.

Madeline Troche-Rodríguez

See also: Circular Migration; Education; Poverty, Culture of.

Further Reading

Menanteau-Horta, Darío. "The Illusion of Inclusion: The Latino Experience in the United States." *Diálogo* 9 (Fall 2005): 36–41.

Ramírez, Roberto. "We the People: Hispanics in the United States." *Census 2000 Special Reports,* December 2004.

Suárez-Orozco, Marcelo M., and Mariela M. Páez, eds. *Latinos: Remaking America.* Berkeley: University of California Press, 2002.

Poverty, Culture of

The "culture of poverty" thesis was proposed by anthropologist Oscar Lewis in the mid-1960s to explain the social phenomenon of poverty in the United States—in particular its occurrence across generations—and how it conflicts with the common belief that America is a classless society in which anyone can achieve success. According to Lewis, who first used the term in his book *La Vida: A Puerto Rican Family in the Culture of Poverty* (1966), the culture of poverty represents a response by the poor to an economy characterized by high unemployment, low wages, and a failure by the mainstream to provide economic, social, or political organization for the poor. Those who have internalized the culture of poverty lack the tools needed to integrate effectively into the mainstream. Because they do not have access to economic opportunities within the mainstream, they are ultimately excluded from dominant institutions and services.

The culture of poverty is said to be characterized by several distinct social traits: female-headed households; passive, dependent, or absent males; poor housing conditions; chronic unemployment or underemployment; lack of familial stability; an absence of childhood; and marginality within the larger society. According to Lewis's thesis, behavioral patterns are handed down from generation to generation, resulting in cycles of poverty within particular families. By the age of six or seven, he contends, children have adopted these values, are ill-prepared to take advantage of educational opportunities, and develop an inability to escape or avoid dire economic situations. Both adults and children within the culture of poverty display a sense of resignation to their impoverishment and a lack of aspiration to overcome it. Nevertheless, Lewis maintained, the poor display an inordinate measure of resilience, vitality, and fortitude in the face of their circumstances. On the whole, he describes them as dignified, upstanding people capable of great kindness and generosity.

Each of Lewis's published works tests the culture of poverty thesis in a different ethnic or national context, demonstrating the value of family as a unit of analysis. In *Life in a Mexican Village* (1951), for example, he presents extensive anthropological research based on his studies of peasant life in Mexico and the roots and persistence of poverty. *Five Families* (1959) documents the daily lives of five Mexican families, and *The Children of Sanchez* (1961) examines the life of a family in the slums of Mexico City. In *La Vida: A Puerto Rican Family in the Culture of Poverty,* Lewis examines the Puerto Rican experience, both on the island and on the mainland, bringing the culture of poverty thesis into a U.S. context. In that book, he focuses particularly on cultural styles associated with Puerto Rican ghetto life, including migrant adjustment, economic obstacles, and related psychological problems.

Lewis's thesis sparked controversy from the moment it was unveiled. Some critics argued that his gender representations were not particular to those who live in poverty. Others contended that many of the cultural patterns (male dominance, female suffering, and broken homes) identified in *Children of Sanchez* could also be found in many Mexican families regardless of class status. Likewise in the case of *La Vida,* scholars, politicians, and Puerto Ricans both on the mainland and on the island regarded Lewis's portrayal of the typical family as exaggerated and misleading, questioning the class specificity of dysfunctions he ascribed to the poor. Indeed the text

was said to foster a negative stereotype of Puerto Ricans as lazy, hypersexual, and immoral. Moreover, the extreme marginalization of his protagonists, the Diaz family members, made them an atypical, nonrepresentative example of Puerto Rican life. All in all, scholars have continued to argue that poverty among Puerto Ricans (and any other group, for that matter) cannot be isolated from the problems of the communities in which they live. The effects of job displacement, poor housing and sanitation, pollution, low-performing schools, and violence cannot be overlooked.

In 1963, Nathan Glazer and Daniel Patrick Moynihan offered an update of Lewis's culture of poverty thesis in *Beyond the Melting Pot,* an influential work that argued that Italians, African Americans, Irish, Jews, and Puerto Ricans had not successfully assimilated into American society in part because of cultural choice. Their argument further stigmatized and pathologized Puerto Ricans living on the mainland with regard to education, culture, and economic mobility. Glazer and Moynihan equated a perceived weak and dysfunctional familial structure with a propensity by Puerto Ricans toward welfare dependency. In other words, the problems of the Puerto Rican community reflected a vicious circle—poverty bred by the culture of poverty, and vice versa. Glazer and Moynihan's version of the culture of poverty thesis has continued to shape media representations and public policy debates regarding not only Puerto Ricans, but Latino culture in general, to the present day.

According to a 2002 U.S. Census Bureau report, roughly 22 percent of Latinos/as live below the poverty line—a fact that elicits significant debate and discussion. Some argue that the number reflects the heavy influx of illegal immigrants, who lack the necessary jobs skills, education, and cultural attributes to succeed despite the opportunities available in America. The same voices tend to argue that the culture of poverty creates a chronic, long-term problem of dependency on health care and other social services provided by the government.

Many scholars and activists, on the other hand, have long disputed the culture of poverty theory, describing it as an effort to "blame the victims" while failing to recognize racism, social injustice, and disadvantage as causes of chronic, intergenerational poverty. Ruben Martinez, for example, argues that the culture of poverty thesis not only homogenizes Latinos/as, overlooking their diverse cultures, experiences, and class or professional status, but plays on racist stereotypes to exonerate society for its failures to provide equal opportunity for all groups.

Madeleine E. López and David J. Leonard

See also: Family and Community; Poverty.

Further Reading

Flores, Juan. *Divided Borders: Essays on Puerto Rican Identity.* Houston, TX: Arte Público, 1993.

Glazer, Nathan, and Daniel Patrick Moynihan. *Beyond the Melting Pot: The Negroes, Puerto Ricans, Jews, Italians and Irish of New York City.* Cambridge, MA: MIT Press, 1970.

Lewis, Oscar. *The Children of Sanchez: Autobiography of a Mexican Family.* New York: Random House, 1961.

———. *La Vida: A Puerto Rican Family in the Culture of Poverty—San Juan and New York.* New York: Random House, 1966.

———. *Life in a Mexican Village: Tepoztlan Restudied.* Urbana: University of Illinois Press, 1951.

Sánchez Korrol, Virginia E. *From Colonia to Community: The History of Puerto Ricans in New York City.* Berkeley: University of California Press, 1994.

Whalen, Carmen Teresa. *From Puerto Rico to Philadelphia: Puerto Rican Workers and Postwar Economies.* Philadelphia: Temple University Press, 2001.

Prinze, Freddie
(1954–1977)

The Puerto Rican American stand-up comedian and actor Freddie Prinze is one of only a handful of Puerto Rican Americans who has earned national prominence as a popular entertainer. He achieved fame and notoriety in his role as Chico Rodriguez in the 1970s television situation comedy *Chico and the Man* (1974–1978), for which he received a Golden Globe nomination for best TV actor in a musical or comedy (1976), before committing suicide at the age of twenty-two. His portrayal of a Latino character on prime-time television also sparked debate in the Latino community over issues of representation in the media.

He was born Frederick Karl Pruetzel on June 22, 1954, in the multi-ethnic New York City neighborhood of Washington Heights. His father was a German immigrant who worked as a tool and die maker, and his mother was a Puerto Rican factory worker. Playing on the word "Nuyorican" (a blending of the terms "New York" and "Puerto Rican," as some New York Puerto Ricans identify themselves), Prinze jokingly referred to himself as a "Hungarican" (even though his father was German by birth). In grade school, he started doing comedy routines in the restroom. "I started doing half-hour routines in the boys' room, just winging it," he later said. "Guys cut class to catch the act. It was, 'What time's Freddie playing the toilet today?' "

As a result of his talent and passion for entertaining, Prinze was accepted at Fiorello H. LaGuardia High School of the Performing Arts in New York, only to drop out to pursue a full-time career in show business. He began performing at comedy clubs throughout Manhattan, including the Improv Club on West 44th Street, where aspiring comics could try out their material. Prinze's comic wit, in the tradition of raw street humor, earned him a strong following. His routines often included impressions of ethnic minorities; one of his most famous routines centered on his Puerto Rican apartment building superintendent who, when asked to fix a problem in the building, would reply, "Eez not mai yob."

In 1973, after being noticed for his stand-up work, Prinze appeared on the *Tonight Show* with Johnny Carson, which led to an offer from NBC the following year to play the title role in *Chico and the Man*. In the weekly sitcom, Prinze formed a strong bond with Anglo co-star Jack Albertson, but struggled with the ethnic stereotypes presented in the show. The plot of *Chico and the Man* revolved around a curmudgeonly white racist widower and an energetic young Chicano. Albertson's character, Ed Brown, owned a filling station in Los Angeles and hired Chico to help him run it; Chico also lived there. The two bickered endlessly but, by the end of each episode, always came to understand each other or accept each other's differences.

Although he was of mixed race, Prinze played a Chicano on the show, as network executives attempted to capitalize on the popularity of barrio and

Freddie Prinze (center) starred as Chico Rodriguez in the 1970s TV sitcom *Chico and the Man.* It was the first U.S. television series to feature a Chicano lead character and setting. *(NBC Television/Hulton Archive/Getty Images)*

ghetto comedies during the 1970s. Chicano media activists, including the protest group Justicia, opposed the casting of a mixed-race Puerto Rican to play a Chicano and denounced the negative and distorted representations of Chicanos in the show. Prinze responded with his usual wisecracking humor—"If I can't play a Chicano because I'm Puerto Rican, then God's really gonna be mad when he finds out Charlton Heston played Moses." The show's producers nevertheless changed Prinze's character to half Puerto Rican and half Chicano.

In 1975, Prinze released a solo comedy album titled *Looking Good* and made appearances on such variety shows as *Dinah Shore* and *Tony Orlando and Dawn Show.* Despite his professional success, however, Prinze struggled with his personal demons, including drug and alcohol addiction. His substance abuse led to a drunk-driving arrest and divorce from his wife of fifteen months, Katherine Cochrane, who took custody of their infant son, Freddie Prinze, Jr.

Prinze made his final public appearance at President Jimmy Carter's Inaugural Ball in January 1977. On January 28, 1977, despondent over personal problems, Prinze killed himself by gunshot in front of his business manager, Martin Snyder.

Although his career was short-lived, Prinze's comedic contributions and example to the Latino community lived on. Comedians Jay Leno, David Brenner, and George Lopez all cited Prinze as an important influence in the development of their own careers. In 2004, Comedy Central named Prinze one of the 100 greatest stand-up comedians of all time. His son went on to success as a television and movie actor as well.

Susan Marie Green

See also: Identity and Labels; Television; Popular Culture; Puerto Ricans.

Further Reading

Oguss, Greg. "Whose Barrio Is It? *Chico and the Man* and the Integrated Ghetto Shows of the 1970s." *Television & New Media* 6:1 (February 2005): 3–21.

Rodríguez, Clara E. *Latin Looks: Images of Latinas and Latinos in the U.S. Media.* Boulder, CO: Westview, 1997.

Stack, Steven. "Celebrities and Suicide: A Taxonomy and Analysis, 1948–1983." *American Sociological Review* 52:3 (June 1987): 401–12.

Prison Gangs

Organized prison gangs in the United States, formed for protection and often engaging in criminal enterprises and violence against rivals, are a modern phenomenon of the U.S. penal system. The first Latino prison gangs were formed in California during the 1950s and 1960s, as the population of Latino inmates was increasing. Discrimination and poverty in life on the outside put higher education out of reach for most Latinos/as, while unemployment and drug abuse became common features of the barrio. Incarcerated Mexican Americans were a minority among established Anglo and African American populations at the time, so groups that may have been enemies on the streets banded together for self-preservation and the material interests of one another. The formation of Latino prison gangs led to the creation of gangs made up of black and white members during the 1970s, a time of intense violence in the California penal system.

Ethnic prison gangs were not unprecedented in American history. The Italian *Camorra,* organized in the prisons of southern Italy during the early nineteenth century, eventually expanded into criminal and political activities in Naples. With the first waves of migration in the mid-nineteenth century, the Camorra began spreading to the United States, where through bloodshed and changing times it became absorbed into what is now called the Mafia or Cosa Nostra by 1930.

In the late 1950s, with increases in the incarceration rates among Mexican American youth, a group of inmates from East Los Angeles housed at the Deuel Vocational Institute in Northern California organized the Mexican Mafia, or *La Eme*. Originally created as protection against white and black inmates, the gang became more organized and soon extended outside the prison system. In 1965, the gang's efforts to spread its influence among other Mexican American prisoners led to violence at the Soledad Correctional Training Facility in the Central Valley. Prisoners who considered themselves "independent" refused to be recruited into La Eme or to take part in violence or drug dealing on behalf of the gang. A series of attacks by the Mexican Mafia on "independent" Chicano prisoners led to the formation of a separate prison faction, called *Nuestra Familia* (NF), whose original members had come from a variety of locations in Los Angeles, Northern California, and the San Joaquin Valley.

A series of violent incidents over control of illegal activities in California prisons led to even more violence, both within prison walls and on the streets. These incidents also fed a growing gang lore that can be recited by California gang members even today. For example, in 1967 the "shoes" incident occurred when a Mexican Mafia member refused to give back shoes owned by an inmate from San Jose. This led to a cellblock-by-cellblock string of knife attacks that left several La Eme members, or *carnales,* injured but still alive. About four years later, Rodolfo "Cheyenne" Cadena, a highly respected leader of the Mexican Mafia, was murdered at Palm Hall in the state prison at Chino, California. This was considered an act of severe treachery, as Cadena was surprised by Nuestra Familia operatives in what was said to have been a peace meeting. Inmates who took part in the slaying were whisked away into protective custody, so grave was the threat to their lives.

Since the incident, gang members have regularly visited Cadena's gravesite in Los Angeles.

Throughout the 1970s, the two gangs committed bloody atrocities against each other. The gang wars soon took on racial overtones. Other inmates organized the "white pride" Aryan Brotherhood, which allied itself with La Eme, and the Black Guerilla Family, organized by African Americans who espoused radical politics, joined forces with the NF. The violence and rivalries became so severe that prisons were grouped into those "controlled" by one gang or another, with the Mexican Mafia taking over San Quentin prison and the NF controlling Deuel Vocational. Both gangs controlled much of the heroin traffic spreading into California barrios, which became rife with addiction. The gangs also owned legitimate businesses and in some cases infiltrated government programs aimed at Latinos/as. Although the ranks of the Mexican Mafia have always been more numerous, given the higher population of Latinos/as in Southern California, the intrastate rivalry has been consistently vicious and hateful.

In the 1980s, California law enforcement authorities curtailed many of the gangs' operations with a campaign of arrests, criminal convictions, and prison transfers, but the gangs were not destroyed. This became apparent with the release of the film *American Me* in 1992, in which Edward James Olmos both directed and starred as the Mexican Mafia leader Cadena (named Santana in the film). Members of La Eme disapproved of the representation and were suspected in the murder of Ana Lizarraga, a gang counselor and adviser on the film. That same year, a multiple indictment of Nuestra Familia members in San Jose resulted in several convictions for six murders. In 1997, twelve Mexican Mafia members were convicted on federal racketeering charges and seven counts of murder, including that of Lizarraga.

Between the years 2000 and 2006, leaders and members of both gangs were convicted and sentenced on a variety of charges in Southern and Northern California. The areas under gang influence have diminished since the 1970s, as more Latinos/as pursue higher education and move into the professional ranks, but lower-income and poor barrios continue to feel the presence of La Eme and the NF. Latino and Latina street gang members are still loosely aligned with the prison gangs: *Sureños* (Southerners) are generally associated with the Mexican Mafia, and *Norteños* (Northerners) claim allegiance to the Nuestra Familia.

Prison gangs are prevalent in other Latino communities of the United States and are not solely the creation of Mexican Americans. The Latin Kings was founded as a Puerto Rican street gang in Chicago during the 1940s. By the 1980s, it had spread through the East Coast and its prison systems, starting in Connecticut. Two inmates there wrote the *King Manifesto,* which emphasized spirituality and ritual—such as the recitation of special prayers at meetings—rules of protocol and discipline, and a commitment to secrecy within the organization. The document was adopted by a new branch of the Latin Kings at the Collins Correctional Institution in western New York State. The group soon spread throughout the state, claiming up to 5,000 members inside and outside prison walls. In the late 1990s, federal investigations resulted in hundreds of arrests, although the New York State Latin Kings (the Almighty Latin King and Queen Nation, or ALKQN) ordered members to foreswear violence against fellow Kings and Queens, and vowed to address social problems facing Latinos/as. Like its California counterparts, however, the Latin Kings remained active, with loosely linked branches in Chicago and on the East Coast. Although fragmented throughout these regions, it remains a powerful influence on young Puerto Ricans caught up in the economic and social hopelessness of the inner cities.

In 1981, the Ñeta Association—or *Asociación Ñeta*—was founded by Carlos "La Sombra" (The Shadow) Torres-Irriarte, a self-proclaimed revolutionary who advocated autonomy for Puerto Rico. The gang was formed in response to abuses by prison guards at the El Oso Blanco prison in Rio Piedras, PR. Rival gangs quickly formed as well, and one of its members succeeded in killing La Sombra in prison. Like Cadena in California, he became a martyr to his fellow gang members, and the Ñeta Association grew in numbers. During the 1980s, members who migrated to the United States founded branches in New York, New Jersey, and Connecticut. Members told new East Coast recruits that the gang sought to fight the injustices of the prison systems in

Puerto Rico and United States. By the 1990s, the power and influence of the Ñeta Association rivaled that of the Latin Kings. The former is unique in that women often have equal roles with men and share equal duties. An early U.S. member was said to be a woman known as "La Madrina" who escalated street recruitment in New York City. Although the gang was heavily involved in drug dealing, it also acted as an advocate for inmates' rights and became involved in programs aimed at Latino youths and various community projects. Law enforcement officials suspected that such efforts were aimed at recruitment rather than community service and cracked down on the gang beginning in 2000, sending many to prison—home territory for many Latino gangs.

E. Mark Moreno

See also: Chicago; East Los Angeles; Gangs; Prison Industrial Complex.

Further Reading

Barrios, Luis, and David C. Brotherton. *The Almighty Latin King and Queen Nation: Street Politics and the Transformation of a New York City Gang.* New York: Columbia University Press, 2004.

Davidson, Theodore R. *Chicano Prisoners: The Key to San Quentin.* New York: Holt, Rinehart and Winston, 1974.

Irwin, John. *Prisons in Turmoil.* Boston: Little, Brown, 1980.

Moore, Joan. *Homeboys: Gangs, Drugs, and Prison in the Barrios of Los Angeles.* Philadelphia: Temple University Press, 1978.

Morales, Gabriel C. *Varrio Warfare: Violence in the Latino Community.* Seattle, WA: Tecolote, 2000.

National Alliance of Gang Investigators Associations. http://www.nagia.org.

Padilla, Felix M. *Puerto Rican Chicago.* South Bend, IN: University of Notre Dame Press, 1987.

Sanchez, Reymundo. *My Bloody Life: The Making of a Latin King.* Chicago: Chicago Review, 2000.

Prison Industrial Complex

The "prison industrial complex" refers to the confluence of bureaucratic, economic, and political interests that promote increased spending on the construction, maintenance, and management of correctional facilities and inmates in the United States. The term, coined by journalist Eric Schlosser in a 1998 article in the *Atlantic Monthly,* was a kind of counterpart to the "military-industrial complex"—the growing U.S. network of armed forces, weapons and military services suppliers, and government agencies—against which President Dwight Eisenhower warned in his farewell address upon leaving office in January 1961. The emergence of the prison industrial complex, part of a broad restructuring and privatization of government functions over four decades or more, has followed changing perceptions about crime and race in the United States and coincided with a major increase in legal and illegal Latino immigration.

Background

The rise of prison privatization in the United States dates to the early 1970s, when conservative Republican politicians such as Barry Goldwater, Richard Nixon, and Nelson Rockefeller advocated a "tough on crime" policy to combat drug use in the wake of the Black and Chicano Power movements. In many criminal jurisdictions, virtually any drug offense—from dealing to mere possession of small quantities—was classified as a serious felony with mandatory prison time. The political and social sensibilities of the times thus contributed to a staggering increase in the U.S. prison population: from roughly 200,000 inmates in the 1970s to 1.4 million in 1994 and more than 2 million in 2003.

A variety of other complex causes and explanations underlies the trend, but the surge was abrupt and rapid. In the decades leading up to the 1970s, the incarceration rate in the United States had been relatively stable, hovering around 110 per 100,000 persons. The figure doubled in the 1980s, doubled again in the 1990s, and reached about 445 per 100,000 in the middle of the first decade of the twenty-first century. During the twenty-year period beginning in the mid-1980s, close to 1,000 incarceration facilities were built in the United States. Yet with the nation's prison population increasing by 50,000 to 80,000 each year, America's correctional facilities have become increasingly—and dangerously—overcrowded.

One reason for the dramatic increase in incarceration rates, according to some sociologists, has been large cutbacks in rehabilitation programs. Many nonviolent offenses, which in other countries are handled through drug rehabilitation, fines, or community service, carry mandatory prison time in the United States, a policy which some argue is a great financial and social burden on society, particularly in communities of color. Most of all, perhaps, the rapid expansion of the U.S. prison population has coincided with inordinately high rates of arrest for blacks and Latinos, the great influx of Spanish-speaking immigrants since the mid-1960s, and the concerted efforts of law enforcement and the prison industrial complex to capture and incarcerate—pending deportation—undocumented immigrants.

Racialization of Crime

The rise in U.S. incarceration rates has been accompanied by the widespread criminalization of youth of color, particularly blacks and Latinos. In 2007, according to a U.S. Department of Justice report, the incarceration rates for black and Latino males stood at 4.8 and 1.9 percent, respectively, while that for whites remained steady at only 0.7 percent. Among women, there were a total of 5,600 prisoners in state and federal facilities in 1970; by 1996, the figure had jumped to 75,000, and 60 percent of them were Latina and black. According to a Human Rights Watch survey of thirty-seven states published in 2002, under-eighteen Latino males in four states were incarcerated at seven to seventeen times the rate for white youth. Various reports and analyses cited the trends toward "three-strikes" laws, mandatory sentencing, and racial profiling as factors that increase long-standing racial and ethnic disparities in the corrections system.

In addition to the increase in absolute numbers of incarcerated people, the rates by ethnicity, gender, and age are also striking. A 2006 independent report indicates that—per 100,000 of U.S. population—2,468 of those incarcerated were black, compared to 1,038 and 409 who were Latino and white, respectively. Broken down by gender, per 100,000 people in the United States, 134 of those incarcerated were females, while 1,384 were males. The demographic of black males between twenty-five and twenty-nine years of age makes up the group with the highest rate of incarceration, at 11,695 per 100,000. Male Latinos in the same age cohort are imprisoned at a rate of 3,912 per 100,000, while male whites in that age group trail significantly at 1,685 per 100,000.

Incarceration of undocumented migrants awaiting deportation proceedings also drives the construction of federal prison facilities. From 1994 through 2001, the average daily population of immigrant detainees in the United States almost quadrupled, from 5,500 to 20,000. In 2003, the proposed federal budget included $50 million for new facilities for the Immigration and Naturalization Service—changed that year to U.S. Citizenship and Immigration Services (USCIS) and made part of the new Department of Homeland Security.

Private Prisons and Civil Rights Groups

Perhaps the single most dominant trend in the U.S. prison industrial complex—indeed its main defining characteristic—has been the spread of privately constructed and managed prison facilities. In rural locations across the country, private prisons have provided jobs, population stabilization, tax revenues, and economic growth. Although academics and politicians debate the long-term benefits of prison construction in a particular locale, more than 300 prisons were built in rural U.S. communities between the late 1980s and 2003. The prison industrial complex provides a cheap and readily available source of labor to private companies and public entities alike. Prisoner work crews are contracted to perform sanitation, garbage disposal, laundry, agricultural, and other service and maintenance tasks at a fraction of the cost of minimum-wage workers. Many small and rural communities around the country depend on prison labor to provide such services to their citizens.

Meanwhile, the Corrections Corporation of America (CCA), the nation's largest prison private enterprise, benefits from budgetary crises by contracting with states to transfer inmates to underserved prisons. Shuffling prisoners to far-flung facilities—to serve the supply-and-demand needs of the company—makes it difficult for family members to communi-

cate with or visit the inmates. Overcrowding is often another consequence of prisoner shuffling, creating dangerous environments and potentially explosive situations for both inmates and prison guards.

For these and other reasons, the U.S. prison industrial complex has come under the scrutiny of monitoring groups such as Human Rights Watch (HRW) and the American Civil Liberties Union (ACLU), which research and document the incarceration industry and its effects on Latinos as well as other communities of color. Grassroots organizations such as Critical Resistance and the Prison Moratorium Project conduct workshops to promote alternatives to incarceration. Nonprofits such as Building Blocks for Youth and the Youth Force Coalition focus their efforts on reducing overrepresentation of Latino youth and their brethren of color within the criminal justice system.

Juan Declet

See also: Illegal Immigration; Prison Gangs.

Further Reading

Evans, Linda, and Eve Goldberg. *The Prison Industrial Complex and the Global Economy.* Boston: Kersplebedeb, 1998.

Falk, Julie. "Fiscal Lockdown." *Dollars and Sense* (July/August 2003): 19–45.

Schlosser, Eric. "The Prison-Industrial Complex." *Atlantic Monthly,* December 1998.

Sudbury, Julia. *Global Lockdown: Race, Gender, and the Prison-Industrial Complex.* New York: Routledge, 2005.

Proposition 187
(1994)

Proposition 187, referred to by some as the "Save Our State" initiative, was a 1994 California referendum that sought to deny most publicly funded social services to undocumented immigrants and establish stricter penalties on individuals living in the state illegally. A referendum is a ballot initiative that contains a proposed law. Voters determine whether or not a referendum becomes law by voting to either approve or reject it. A referendum becomes law in California if at least 50 percent of voters vote in favor of the measure.

Specifically, Proposition 187 called for the denial of nonemergency medical care to undocumented immigrants and the exclusion of undocumented children from California's public schools. Other provisions advocated tougher criminal penalties for the manufacturing and use of false identification documents, and required public employees, such as teachers and police officers, to notify the California attorney general or the U.S. Immigration and Naturalization Service of individuals suspected of residing in the state illegally. California citizens were also encouraged to report anyone they suspected of being an undocumented immigrant.

On November 8, 1994, California voters approved Proposition 187 by a margin of 59 percent to 41 percent. Although it was slated to become state law on January 1, 1995, Proposition 187 never went into effect. Opponents of the measure immediately filed lawsuits against its implementation on the grounds that Proposition 187 was unconstitutional, and a federal judge enacted a restraining order that prevented the proposition from going into effect.

In the early 1990s, illegal immigration became one of the biggest political and social issues in California. More undocumented immigrants resided in California than any other state, and the backlash against *sin papeles* (those without papers) in the Golden State during the early 1990s coincided with a growing economic recession, rising unemployment, and annual state budget crises. Proposition 187's supporters argued that the measure was necessary because the large number of undocumented immigrants were overwhelming the state's public schools and hospitals. Such services, advocates maintained, should be reserved for U.S. citizens and legal immigrants. Many supporters of Proposition 187, including Republican Governor Pete Wilson, believed that access to social services was a "magnetic lure" that attracted undocumented immigrants to California. Since *indocumentados* (the undocumented) allegedly came to California in search of free social services, Proposition 187's backers argued that denial of such services would deter further illegal immigrants from settling in the state and encourage those already living in California to leave.

Opponents of the initiative included immigrant rights and human rights advocates, Latino civil rights organizations, and leaders from the agriculture, law enforcement, education, and medical professions. Civil rights organizations argued that Proposition 187 scapegoated undocumented immigrants by tapping into nativist and racist sentiments. Some feared that Proposition 187 would promote a hostile climate and lead to an increase in harassment against Mexican Americans and other Latinos/as, both foreign- and U.S.-born. The text of Proposition 187 created anxiety among some, invoking the phrase "reasonably suspects" seven times in reference to a citizen's suspicions that an individual was illegally residing in California. For example, public employees and private citizens were called upon to report people they "reasonably suspect" of being illegal immigrants to authorities, but the proposition's text did not define what criteria constituted "reasonable suspicion." In other words, citizens were not provided guidelines with which to conclude or "reasonably suspect" that someone was an illegal immigrant. Some civil rights advocates worried that such criteria would be based on accent, name, ethnicity, linguistic ability, or "looking foreign."

Other arguments against Proposition 187 focused on whether the various provisions of the measure were even constitutional. As a federal issue, immigration law is to be determined and enforced by the national government, rather than by state or local government. Also, in the case of *Plyler v. Doe* (1982), the U.S. Supreme Court had ruled that states could not exclude undocumented children from schools. These two criteria served as the basis for much of the legal action taken against Proposition 187 following its passage by voters.

Few political initiatives in recent decades have produced the degree of emotional and passionate debate as Proposition 187. The intensity ran deep among supporters and opponents alike. Critics of illegal immigration saw Proposition 187 as an opportunity to express their anger and concern over the impact of undocumented immigrants on social services, the economy, crime, and jobs. In addition, cultural fears that heavy immigration, particularly from Mexico and Latin America, posed a threat to the preservation of American culture factored into the atmosphere surrounding Proposition 187. Related rhetoric frequently utilized the term "invasion," and some grassroots organizations that supported Proposition

187 referred to illegal immigration from Mexico as *la reconquista,* implying that undocumented Mexicans were attempting to reconquer California and return the land to Mexico.

Such cultural fears intensified with televised demonstrations against Proposition 187 in which Chicano protesters were seen clenching their fists and waving Mexican flags. The racial divide over Proposition 187 was evident. Two-thirds of whites voted in favor of Proposition 187, while African American and Asian voters were fairly evenly divided in their votes, and over 70 percent of Latinos voted against the referendum.

Several prominent political figures took stands regarding Proposition 187. Governor Wilson, Speaker of the House Newt Gingrich, and presidential candidate Patrick Buchanan all expressed their support for the measure. President Bill Clinton, Vice President Al Gore, Texas Governor George W. Bush, and former secretary of the Department of Housing and Urban Development Jack Kemp voiced their opposition to Proposition 187.

In July 1999, California's new governor, Gray Davis, ended the nearly five-year legal battle over Proposition 187 by withdrawing the measure from the court system, an act that enraged its supporters. An attempt to place a Proposition 187–like referendum, nicknamed "Son of 187," on the 2004 California ballot failed to materialize due to a failure to garner sufficient citizens' signatures for the referendum's petition.

Proposition 187's legacy is twofold. First, the measure marked a dramatic policy shift in immigration reform. While immigration control measures themselves are not new, the aim of such measures historically has been to increase border patrol enforcement or deportation of undocumented migrants. Proposition 187 sought to crack down on illegal migration through denial of social services such as education and medical care. Throughout the 1990s and into the 2000s, several political figures and initiatives aimed at controlling immigration focused on denial of rights or privileges for undocumented immigrants, such as public and higher education, health care, driver licenses, or citizenship to U.S.-born children of undocumented immigrants. Second, Proposition 187 foreshadowed the emergence of grassroots

involvement with immigration policy, on both sides of the issue. Since the early 1990s, numerous anti-immigration organizations have emerged in several states—some of which invoke overtly racist rhetoric. Anti-immigration and pro-immigration rallies have also become common since the early 1990s, with demonstrators on both sides sometimes clashing with one another. In 2005, a private citizens group calling itself the "Minuteman Project" began patrolling the U.S.-Mexico border. Proposition 187's acrimonious debate also rekindled the Brown Berets and the Chicano movement in general, both of which had been in decline since the early 1970s.

Justin D. García

See also: Education; Health and Health Care; Illegal Immigration; Immigration Enforcement.

Further Reading

Chavez, Leo R. *Shadowed Lives: Undocumented Immigrants in American Society.* 2nd ed. Orlando, FL: Harcourt Brace, 1998.

Fox, Geoffrey. *Hispanic Nation: Culture, Politics, and the Constructing of Identity.* Tucson: University of Arizona Press, 1996.

Maharidge, Dale. *The Coming White Minority: California's Eruptions and the Nation's Future.* New York: Times, 1996.

Proposition 209
(1996)

Proposition 209, a California ballot initiative, amended the state's constitution to prohibit discrimination in public contracting, hiring, and education. According to the official text, the "state shall not discriminate against, or grant preferential treatment to, any individual or group on the basis of race, sex, color, ethnicity, or national origin in the operation of public employment, public education, or public contracting." In November 1996, 54 percent of voters cast their ballots in favor of Proposition 209, effectively ending affirmative action programs in the state.

In 1992, the Department of Education completed a study on the admission practices of the University of California at Berkeley's Boalt Hall School of Law. The study concluded that Boalt's admissions procedures violated federal law because it grouped qualified applicants by racial designation. While refusing to admit any misconduct, the school agreed to alter its admissions procedures, ceasing to separate its applicants by race. Shortly thereafter, California Governor Pete Wilson (R) argued in a speech titled "The Minority-Majority Society" that "affirmative action can no longer be justified." Accordingly, Wilson declared, "What we owe the people is not to ignore the unfairness and pretend it doesn't exist. We owe them the leadership and courage to change what's wrong and set it right. The question shouldn't be, how can we justify the current quagmire of race and gender-based preferences? The question should be, how can we reset our moral compass and get back on the road to quality and fairness under the law?" With this speech, the governor vowed to work to end affirmative action within public employment and college admissions.

Although affirmative action in California encompassed a spectrum of programs, including goals and timetables, fears about quotas and accusations of discrimination against whites and males for the sake of diversity and opportunity for less-than-qualified Latino, African American, and Native American applicants guided much of the debate.

On July 20, 1995, by a vote of 15–10, the Board of Regents of the University of California adopted Regents Resolutions SP-1 and SP-2. The former declared that race, religion, sex, color, ethnicity, and national origin could not be considered in the university admissions decision process. SP-2 eliminated consideration of the same attributes in hiring and contracting decisions made by the University of California (UC) system.

Hoping to extend the elimination of affirmative action beyond the university system, UC Regent

Students at the University of California, Berkeley, seek support for overturning Proposition 209, a 1996 ballot initiative that ended affirmative action in the state. At Berkeley and other college campuses, the measure brought a sharp decline in minority admissions. *(Lara Jo Regan/Liaison/Getty Images)*

Ward Connerly and others formed the California Civil Rights Initiative Campaign, an organization that would help draft Proposition 209, which would appear on the November 5, 1996, ballot. Supporters of Proposition 209 effectively argued that affirmative action was originally intended to ensure equal treatment for all Americans. In their estimation, however, special-interest groups undermined the intent of the legislation, resulting in an emphasis on racial quotas rather than equal treatment for all. More important, they claimed, discrimination against non-minorities and males in favor of minorities and females was just as wrong as racial discrimination.

Opponents argued that the state's affirmative action programs ensured social equality by funding tutoring, mentoring, outreach, and recruitment programs for minorities and women. These programs were created to address under-representation in schools and certain areas of public employment. Rather than facilitate equality, opponents of Proposition 209 contended, the elimination of affirmative action would result in the elimination of programs designed to encourage girls to pursue careers in science and math, tutoring for first-generation college students, and outreach programs for government-funded contracts. In essence, they maintained, passage of Proposition 209 would not "even out the playing field" for all races, but would legalize discrimination. Opponents were equally critical of the measure because, they contended, it was written to confuse voters through ambiguous language; although it would put an end to affirmative action programs, the specific term "affirmative action" did not appear in the title or the description. By noting that language of the proposition, which stated that the law would "prohibit discrimination and preferential treatment," opponents argued that the authors gathered support from liberal voters (who otherwise would vote in favor of affirmative action policies) as well as conservative ones through misleading rhetorical devices.

With almost 9 million Californians voting in the 1996 election, the proposition passed by a margin of 54–46. Latino voters, numbering more than 1 million, were overwhelmingly opposed to the measure, by a ratio of 3:1. The large turnout of Latino voters was attributed to the increase in Latino residents who had become naturalized citizens since 1992. (Approximately half a million Latinos/as were naturalized and became eligible to vote in 1995 alone; the figure reached 1 million the following year.) Indeed, according to Arturo Vargas, president of the National Association of Latino Elected and Appointed Officials (NALEO), many new Latino voters became citizens specifically to "fight racism" and "vote against Pete Wilson," contributing to a significant erosion of support for Republicans among Latino voters. Although Latino civic and community leaders mobilized to inform the community about Proposition 209, even the heavy Latino voter turnout could not defeat the measure.

On November 27, U.S. District Court Judge Thelton Henderson blocked the initial enforcement of Proposition 209, although the U.S. Court of Appeals for the Ninth Circuit later overturned his ruling, paving the way for the end to affirmative action in California. As a result, the University of California has seen dramatic declines in the admission of Latino, African American, and Native American students. Proposition 209 had an especially significant impact on the most prestigious campuses in the UC system (Berkeley and UCLA). In 1995, Latino, African American, and Native American students together had accounted for 26.1 percent of Berkeley's admission offers; by 2004, the figure had declined to 14.8 percent. The impact was also evident in UC professional and graduate schools. For the academic year 1997–98, the School of Law Boalt Hall enrolled only one African American student, compared to twenty the previous year; the admission of Latino law students dropped 50 percent. At UCLA, the enrollment of Latino, African American, and Native American students dropped 36 percent (from 2,121 to 1,358). While the impact of Proposition 209 was most visible at UC Berkeley and UCLA, it was seen throughout the UC system. In 1997–98, the number of Latino, African American, and Native American freshman declined 57 percent; Latino undergraduate enrollment specifically dropped by 33 percent. Whereas Latino, African American, and Native American students represented 21 percent of freshmen at all eight UC campuses in 1995, they accounted for 18 percent in 2004.

The passage of Proposition 209 in California has sparked similar efforts throughout the nation, with

Ward Connerly successfully leading efforts to end affirmative action in Michigan and Washington State. In 2008, voters in Nebraska passed similar legislation, while an effort in Colorado failed. Efforts to get similar initiatives on the 2008 ballot failed in Arizona, Missouri, and Oklahoma, although plans for future elections appear to be in place. The ongoing battle over affirmative action, with all its implications for educational and employment opportunities for people of color, has remained an issue that galvanizes Latino voters and affects relations among ethnic groups throughout the United States.

Marisa Hernández

See also: Education.

Further Reading

Ball, Howard. *The* Bakke *Case: Race, Education, and Affirmative Action.* Lawrence: University Press of Kansas, 2000.

Castellanos, Jeannett. *The Majority in the Minority: Expanding the Representation of Latina/o Faculty, Administrators and Students in Higher Education.* Sterling, VA: Stylus, 2003.

Crosby, Faye J. *Sex, Race, and Merit: Debating Affirmative Action in Education and Employment.* Ann Arbor: University of Michigan Press, 2000.

Guerrero, Andrea. *Silence at Boalt Hall: The Dismantling of Affirmative Action.* Berkeley: University of California Press, 2002.

Kirwan, William E. *What Makes Racial Diversity Work in Higher Education: Academic Leaders Present Successful Policies and Strategies.* Sterling, VA: Stylus, 2003.

Laird, Bob. *The Case for Affirmative Action in University Admissions.* Point Richmond, CA: Bay Tree, 2005.

Proposition 227 (1998)

Proposition 227, a California ballot initiative overwhelmingly approved by state voters in June 1998, abolished most bilingual education in public schools. Specifically, Proposition 227 required that children in public primary schools be instructed in English, while also providing parents the option of seeking a waiver to allow continued education in a bilingual setting when a sufficient number of parents (20 percent within one grade) make the request.

Background

Proposition 227 represented the culmination of a decades-long struggle over California's language education requirements. In 1973, the Dymally-Alatorre Bilingual Services Act was signed into law, thereby eliminating language barriers in the state and guaranteeing equal access to public services. One year later, the California legislature passed the Chacón-Moscone Bilingual-Bicultural Education Act, which institutionalized bilingual education programs in an effort to meet the needs of "limited English-proficiency" (LEP) students. In 1981, the state's commitment to bilingual education was further strengthened with passage of the California Bilingual Act, which clarified the obligation of school districts to meet the needs of LEP students. In 1996, however, government support for bilingual education suffered a setback when Governor George Deukmejian vetoed bill AB 2813, which would have extended the California Bilingual Act. The issue became the subject of community action later that year, as Latino parents from Los Angeles Unified School District's Ninth Street Elementary School initiated a boycott. Protesting the failure of the program to focus sufficiently on English proficiency, they refused to allow their children to attend until more English immersion classes were offered at the school.

From the late 1980s to the late 1990s, language education in California was hotly contested in the court system and state legislature. In 1996, the State Board of Education granted waivers to four school districts, exempting them the California Bilingual Act and allowing for the establishment of "sheltered English-immersion programs" and the dismantling of bilingual education programs. The following year, in the case of *Quiroz et al v. State Board of Education,* plaintiffs, arguing that district waivers violated the rights of LEP students, sued the Orange Unified School District. In March 1998, Sacramento County Superior Court Judge Ronald Robbie ruled in *Quiroz* that school districts have an obligation to provide primary education so as to ensure equal opportunity for academic achievement, and that the Board of Education does not have the right to grant waivers. The future of bilingual education was thus cast into question.

In the midst of the legal battles, and after learning of the Los Angeles boycotts, Ron Unz, a physicist and software developer turned politician, founded an organization called English for the Children in 1997, which sought a ban on bilingual education and established the basis for what would later become Proposition 227. Joined by Gloria Matta Tuchman, an elementary school teacher from Santa Ana and a long-time advocate of bilingual education reform, members of English for the Children drafted Proposition 227, which appeared on the June 1998 ballot slate. The measure would (1) require all educational instruction in English; (2) establish "intensive sheltered English immersion programs" for LEP students and transition them from bilingual classrooms to "traditional" classes; (3) allow enforcement lawsuits by parents and guardians; and (4) allow for parent-initiated waivers.

Pros and Cons

Supporters of Proposition 227 argued that it would help children learn English and enhance the economic and social status of all communities, particularly Latino immigrants. Citing high dropout and low literacy rates among California's immigrant groups, supporters described the state's bilingual educational efforts as a dramatic failure in need of major change. In their eyes, Proposition 227 would facilitate that change. Citing media reports and polls, supporters focused on the will of the Latino voters and pointed to the boycott in Los Angeles as a wakeup call to what parents wanted: English instruction rather than bilingual education. Newspaper opinion polls regularly showed a high number of Latinos/as in favor of English instruction.

Opponents argued that Proposition 227 was not really about empowering Latino parents, but yet another attack on immigrants and people of color. They also questioned the proposition's lack of reform at the instructor level, which they cited as the main reason for the shortcomings of bilingual education. The language mainstreaming of minority children,

in their view, amounted to enforced assimilation. Finally, opponents argued, the ballot initiative would undermine the creativity and academic freedom of teachers. According to one provision, school board members, administrators, and teachers could be held personally liable if they used a language other than English to assist a child.

Outcome and Consequences

A week before the June primary, Bill SB 6, which proposed that language education and services be determined by local school districts, was vetoed by Governor Peter Wilson. On June 2, 1998, voters in the state cast their ballots overwhelmingly (61 percent) in favor of Proposition 227; despite opinion polls and expert predictions to the contrary, an even larger majority (63 percent) of Latinos voted against the initiative. The Mexican American Legal Defense and Educational Fund (MALDEF) attempted to thwart implementation by legal injunction, but Proposition 227 became law in August 1998.

The effects of Proposition 227 have remained a matter of dispute, with supporters citing evidence of increased educational opportunities and others pointing to a variety of problems resulting from the end of bilingual education in the state. In 2000, Professor Eugene Garcia, dean of the Graduate School of Education at the University of California, Berkeley, concluded that Proposition 227 had resulted in considerable disruption to the educational experiences of minority students, while offering no substantive improvements in terms of learning, teaching, and educational environment.

Notwithstanding these findings, Arizona voters followed the lead of California in 2000, passing state Proposition 203, requiring that "all children in Arizona public schools shall be taught English as rapidly and efficiently as possible." While similar measures were rebuffed in Colorado and Massachusetts, the legacy of Proposition 227 transcends debate over educational impact, according to some. In the first decade of the twenty-first century, activists and scholars point to it as evidence of the increased hostility faced by the Latino community.

Rachel Sandoval and David J. Leonard

See also: Bilingualism; Education; Mexican American Legal Defense and Education Fund.

Further Reading

Garcia, Eugene E., and Julia E. Curry. "The Education of Limited English Proficient Students in California Schools: An Assessment of the Influence of Proposition 227 in Selected Districts and Schools." *Bilingual Research Journal* 24:1/2 (Winter/Spring 2000): 15–35.

Gibbs, Jewelle Taylor, and Teiahsja Bankhead. *Preserving Privilege: California Politics, Propositions, and People of Color.* Westport, CT: Praeger, 2001

Orellana, Marjorie Faulstich, Lucia Ek, and Arcelia Hernandez. "Bilingual Education in an Immigrant Community: Proposition 227 in California." *International Journal of Bilingual Education* 2:2 (1999).

San Miguel, Guadalupe, Jr. *Contested Policy: The Rise and Fall of Federal Bilingual Education in the United States, 1960–2001.* Denton: University of North Texas Press, 2004.

Puente, Tito
(1923–2000)

Jazz bandleader, percussionist, and composer Tito Puente was a driving force in the Latin music craze of the 1940s and 1950s. Known especially for mambo and salsa dance music, he created a fusion of jazz, Latin, and Afro-Cuban sounds. *(Frank Driggs Collection/Hulton Archive/Getty Images)*

The most influential salsa composer and performer of the twentieth century, five-time Grammy Award winner Tito Puente is known for his enduring contributions to the world of Latin music. He is popularly known as the King of Mambo and *El Rey del Timbal*—or "King of the Timbal," the percussion instrument for which he was most famous, although he also played piano, congas, bongos, alto saxophone, clarinet, and won acclaim as a composer and bandleader.

Born Ernesto Antonio Puente, Jr., in Spanish Harlem (New York City) on April 20, 1923, he began piano lessons at the age of seven. His idol became the drum player Gene Krupa, however, and Puente soon gave up the piano for drums and percussion. He also took dancing classes with his sister Ana, an activity for which he was awarded numerous prizes. His talent for music led him to drop out of school and join an orchestra in Miami Beach. There he began experimenting with Caribbean music, "mambo," "son," and "cha cha cha," although he was to return later to Manhattan in order to play with such important salsa players as José Curbelo, Charlie Benante, and the famous Noro Morales.

His first great opportunity came during World War II, when he joined the famous Machito Afro-Cuban band, although he was away for three years serving with the U.S. Navy in the South Pacific. During his stint in the military, he learned to play the alto saxophone and arrange music. When the war was over, Puente attended the Juilliard School of Music in New York City under the GI Bill, completing his studies there in 1947 at the age of twenty-four.

At the same time that he was pursuing his studies of orchestration, composition, and music theory, Puente was also learning from his band partner, Machito, his mentor into the late 1950s. The time Puente spent with the Machito band was one of the most creative of his career, and it was there that he learned how to play mambo, guajiras, and the mixture of Afro-Cuban rhythms with jazz. It was also at this time that he began experimenting with what is known as "Latin jazz."

By the mid-1950s, Puente was on the rise as a bandleader and composer, recording a number of dance hits and helping to launch the ballroom craze for the mambo. His next orchestra, The Picadilly Boys, performed regularly at the famous Palladium Ballroom in New York City, the city's unofficial mambo headquarters. Puente's band was one of the top three at the time, along with those of Machito and Tito Rodríguez, and his later associations with artists such as "La Lupe" and Celia Cruz were to prove highly successful. With Cruz, who in the words of Puente himself was the most important Latin artist of the time, he recorded the albums *The Mambo King Meets the Queen of Salsa* (2000) and *Tito Puente y Celia Cruz* (2002). It was during the 1950s, however, that Puente composed the album for which he was best known, *Dance Mania* (1958). Formal recognition would not come until 1979, when Puente was awarded his first Grammy Award, for *Homenaje a Beny,* a tribute to the Cuban musician Beny Moré. His other four Grammy Awards came in 1983 for *On Broadway;* in 1985 for *Mambo Diablo;* in 1990 for *Goza mi timbal;* and in 2000 for *Mambo Birdland.*

Puente died on May 31, 2000, at the age of seventy-seven, after undergoing heart surgery. He was survived by his wife, Margie, a daughter, Audrey, and two sons, Ronnie and Tito, Jr. In more than half a century of musicianship, he recorded over 100 albums and released over 400 themes. Among his last albums were *The Best of Dance Mania* (1994), *El rey de la salsa* (1996), *El rey del timbal* (1996), *Percussion's King* (1997), *The Complete RCA Recordings* (2001–2002), and *King of Kings: The Very Best of Tito Puente* (2002).

Puente's achievements were not confined strictly to the world of music. In 1968 he hosted his own television show, *Tito Puente's World,* and he was a guest star on *The Cosby Show, The David Letterman Show,* and in movies such as Woody Allen's *Radio Days* (1987) and—with Celia Cruz—*The Mambo Kings* (1992). He endowed the Juilliard School of Music with the Tito Puente Scholarship Fund for Latin percussionists in the United States, was granted a star on Hollywood's Walk of Fame, and was awarded degrees from Columbia University (1999), Old Westbury College (1980), and Hunter College (1992), all

in New York State. In addition, Puente received the national Medal of Arts from President Bill Clinton in 1997 and was cited by the Library of Congress as a Living Legend in April 2000.

David Arbesú

See also: Cruz, Celia; Music; Popular Culture.

Further Reading

Loza, Steven J. *Tito Puente and the Making of Latin Music.* Urbana: University of Illinois Press, 1999.

Schnabel, Tom. *Rhythm Planet: The Great World Music Makers.* New York: Universe, 1998.

Puerto Rican Day Parade

The Puerto Rican Day Parade began in New York City in 1958 as a celebration of Puerto Ricans and Puerto Rican heritage. Today the parade is held annually in cities with sizable Puerto Rican communities throughout the United States. In addition to New York, major metropolises that host a Puerto Rican Day Parade include Philadelphia, Chicago, and Cleveland; such smaller cities as Jersey City and Atlantic City (New Jersey) and Allentown and Lancaster (Pennsylvania) also sponsor yearly events. In the more than five decades since the inception of this event, it has become one of the largest, most publicized, and best-known ethnic cultural festivities in the country.

The first Puerto Rican Parade was held on April 12, 1958, in the East Harlem section of Manhattan, home of the largest Puerto Rican community in the continental United States and affectionately known as "El Barrio" to its residents. Community members Victor López and José Caballero served as the parade's president and coordinator, respectively. The official title of the celebration was the New York Puerto Rican Day Parade, a designation that would be used for the next thirty-seven years. Numerous celebrities from Puerto Rico, including several mayors from different towns and cities on the island either marched in or watched the parade. Altogether the celebration featured an estimated 20,000 participants and 125,000 spectators.

Actors Jimmy Smits (left) and Rosie Pérez (center) ride a float along New York's Fifth Avenue in the 2006 Puerto Rican Day Parade. Held on the second Sunday in June, the annual event attracts more than 2 million spectators. *(Donald Bowers/ Stringer/Getty Images)*

The New York Puerto Rican Day Parade originated in one of the most socially and politically significant eras for the Puerto Rican community. During the 1950s, approximately 20 percent of Puerto Rico's population left the island and migrated to the mainland United States; the largest contingent settled in New York City. A combination of factors compelled this migration, but perhaps the two most prominent reasons revolved around economic and population issues. As American corporations and mechanized labor gained a foothold on the island as part of Operation Bootstrap, large numbers of sugarcane and other subsistence agricultural workers became displaced, causing unemployment in Puerto Rico to increase. At the same time, overpopulation took hold on the island as a result of declines in infant mortality and death rates. Government officials in Puerto Rico and the mainland United States promoted migration as a way of alleviating these social problems, and, lured by the prospect of earning higher wages and the establishment of inexpensive

airlines from New York City to San Juan, many *Boricuas* (Puerto Ricans) left the island and took up residence in New York, Philadelphia, and Chicago.

Two significant political events also highlighted this era in Puerto Rican history. Luis Muñoz Marín became the first democratically elected governor of the island in 1948; until that time, the governor had been appointed by the president of the United States. Second, Puerto Rico became a commonwealth of the United States in 1952, its official status designated as *estado libre asociado* (free associated state). Along with its new political status, Puerto Rico adopted a constitution in 1952; also that year, Marín won reelection as governor.

In Philadelphia, the 1950s brought a large influx of Puerto Ricans, especially to the area surrounding Twentieth Street and Spring Garden Avenue. This neighborhood quickly become known as Philadelphia's barrio, although today that designation has shifted to the neighborhood between Fifth Street and Lehigh Avenue in North Philadelphia—now the heart of Philadelphia's Puerto Rican community. Philadelphia hosted its own Puerto Rican Day Parade in 1964 as part of Puerto Rican Week Festival. The event is now an annual celebration, held on the final Sunday in September. The parade begins near John F. Kennedy Boulevard in Center City and progresses along Benjamin Franklin Parkway toward the Philadelphia Museum of Art.

In 1995, the New York Puerto Rican Day Parade changed its official title to the National Puerto Rican Day Parade. The celebration now includes representatives and participants from thirty-one states and is one of the largest annual parades in the United States. Each year over 2 million spectators attend the National Puerto Rican Day Parade, which progresses from Forty-Fourth Street to Eighty-Sixth Street along Fifth Avenue.

The Puerto Rican Day Parade has become a staple of life in New York City and has even entered the popular culture. The latter fact was evidenced by a controversial episode of the popular NBC sitcom *Seinfeld,* titled "The Puerto Rican Day Parade," in May 1998. The episode featured the program's four main characters—Jerry (Jerry Seinfeld), George (Jason Alexander), Kramer (Michael Richards), and Elaine (Julia Louis-Dreyfus)—getting stuck in traffic on their way home from a baseball game; the streets are clogged because of the Puerto Rican Day Parade. In the ensuing mayhem, Kramer accidentally sets a Puerto Rican flag on fire, throws it to the ground, and stomps on it an attempt to quash the flames. An angry group of Puerto Rican spectators chases Kramer and shakes Jerry's vehicle, to which Kramer responds, "It's like this every day in Puerto Rico." Amid protests and criticism from the Puerto Rican community, NBC issued a public statement denying that the episode had a harmful intent or negative effect on perceptions of Puerto Ricans, since the program is a comedy.

As an example of ethnic pride and community organizing, the Puerto Rican Day Parade thus has attained a level of awareness within mainstream culture that signals a growing recognition of the space occupied by the Puerto Rican culture in American society at large.

Justin D. García

See also: New York; Puerto Ricans.

Further Reading

Cruz, Wilfredo. *Puerto Rican Chicago (Images of America).* Charleston, SC: Arcadia, 2005.

National Puerto Rican Day Parade. www.nationalpuerto ricandayparade.org.

Whalen, Carmen Teresa. *El Viaje: Puerto Ricans of Philadelphia (Images of America).* Charleston, SC: Arcadia, 2006.

———. *From Puerto Rico to Philadelphia: Puerto Rican Workers and Postwar Economies.* Philadelphia: Temple University Press, 2000.

Puerto Rican Literature

The emergence of Puerto Rican literature in the United States is a relatively recent phenomenon, originally defined by a group of outspoken poets in the 1960s and 1970s who depicted the harsh realities of life in the barrio, or inner-city Spanish-speaking neighborhoods. These Nuyorican ("New York" and "Puerto Rican") writers worked to establish a voice for *Boricuas* (Puerto Ricans), expressed their bicultural identities, and decried the racism, poverty, and alienation that Latino underclasses endured in the United States. Since that time, Puerto Rican literary expression has expanded to include more writers, broader themes, and a wider spectrum of topics, while still emphasizing the ambiguities and challenges to identity that come with living torn between two languages and two cultures. In the first decade of the twenty-first century, as American literature has embraced a wider range of multiethnic authors, and as Latino literature in general has received more mainstream acceptance among the reading public, Puerto Rican writing has won a firm place in the canon.

Early Voices

Puerto Ricans have been living and writing in the United States since the nineteenth century. Early immigrants from the island traveled to the United States to escape Spanish colonial rule, and those who wrote of the experience produced mainly journalistic

Pedro Pietri has been called the "poet laureate of the Nuyorican Movement." With Miguel Algarín, Miguel Piñero, and other members, he used his writing to explore cultural identity and evoke the gritty realities of New York City street life. *(Lawrence Lucier/Stringer/Getty Images)*

accounts and revolutionary diatribes. The U.S. accession of Puerto Rico after the Spanish-American War in 1898 and the granting of U.S. citizenship to island residents under the Jones Act in 1917 prompted a heavy influx of Puerto Ricans to the United States, and to New York City in particular. Many of the new immigrants wrote letters, diaries, poems, and newspaper articles about their experiences in the United States, but most of the accounts were written in Spanish and largely for audiences on the island.

The first significant Puerto Rican writer to capture the immigrant experience in the United States was the journalist, poet, and short story writer Jesús Colón, who arrived in New York City in 1917 at age sixteen. Colón was a social activist who wrote articles and sketches about New York's working class, depicting the lives of immigrants who came as U.S. citizens yet still faced harsh discrimination. Colón wrote

for both English- and Spanish-language newspapers and consequently was able to depict the Puerto Rican experience in New York for a large audience. A collection of his writings, *A Puerto Rican in New York and Other Sketches* (1961), is believed to be the first English-language book published by a Puerto Rican in the United States.

Colón was a kind of literary founding father of the Nuyorican movement, the next generation of Puerto Rican writers to emerge in New York City in the 1960s and 1970s. These writers were primarily the children of immigrants from Puerto Rico who came to the United States during the large migration after World War II. Among the notable early figures of the movement was Piri Thomás, who in 1967 published the autobiography *Down These Mean Streets.* Raised in "El Barrio" of New York City's Spanish Harlem, Thomás chronicled the struggle of a young man growing up in a neighborhood devastated by racism and poverty. His honest, painful look at life in the barrio and the struggle for cultural identity met with immediate critical success and became a model for subsequent Puerto Rican authors and for ethnic autobiography.

Other Nuyorican writers, including Miguel Algarín, Miguel Piñero, Pedro Pietri, and Tato Laviera, used the short story, novel, verse, and drama to explore their cultural identities and to affirm ethnic consciousness. Their works convey the sensibility and flavor of the urban, working-class streets of New York and often depict the gritty lives of the city's underclass, including crime and drug use. In the early 1970s, Algarín, with Piñero and Pietri, began an informal literary salon in his Lower East Side living room, where young writers and poets could come together to share their work and ideas. By 1975, with Puerto Rican literary expression gaining ground and the salon having outgrown Algarín's living room, he bought a bar in the neighborhood that became the permanent home to the Nuyorican Poets Café. The café served as a forum for live readings and a phenomenon called the poetry "slam"—a raw, freestyle form of recitation, sometimes competitive. Into the twentieth century, the Nuyorican Poets Café remains an important venue for multi-ethnic poetry, theater, music, hip-hop, and visual arts. Algarín has published more than ten books of verse and has written for the theater, television, and film. He has also coedited several critically acclaimed anthologies, including *Nuyorican Poetry: An Anthology of Puerto Rican Words and Feelings* (1975), which helped establish the Nuyorican movement and carve a place for Puerto Rican literature in the critical canon.

In addition to coediting *Nuyorican Poetry* with Algarín, Miguel Piñero produced several well-received works as a playwright and poet. As a young teen, Piñero was a gang leader, junior high school dropout, and felon, serving time in New York's Sing Sing Prison. While behind bars for armed robbery in 1972, he wrote the critically acclaimed play *Short Eyes* (prison slang for child molester). Premiering off-Broadway in 1974, *Short Eyes* won the New York Drama Critics Award (Obie) for best American play and was produced as a movie, with Piñero appearing in a small role, in 1977. The life and work of the author were documented in a major Hollywood release of 2001, *Piñero,* starring Benjamin Bratt in the title role.

Pedro Pietri likewise was instrumental in the development of Puerto Rican literature in the United States, specializing in overtly political protest poetry—passionate, angry, irreverent, and humorous—intended to be read aloud to mass audiences. Pietro wrote a total of twenty books of verse and drama and became best known for his poem "A Puerto Rican Obituary" (1973), a critique of American capitalism and a mock epic of the Puerto Rican community in the United States. Tato Laviera, another central figure of the Nuyorican poetry movement, drew inspiration from the rhythms and street language of daily life in New York, oral traditions from Puerto Rico, and Afro-Caribbean music and culture. Laviera's verse mixes English and Spanish, sometimes combining words and phrases from the two languages into Spanglish. In such collections as *La Carreta Made a U-Turn* (1979) and *AmeRícan* (1985), Laviera explores the cultural mixing and ambiguities of being Puerto Rican in the United States today.

Beyond the Nuyorican Poets Café

The artists associated with the Nuyorican Poets Café were heavily influenced by folk traditions and oral storytelling, drawing from American popular cul-

ture, jazz, and the Beat poets of the 1950s. Their work, and especially their poetry, is largely bilingual and became known for its depictions of the violence, drugs, and poverty of New York's barrio—images that became stereotypes of the city's Puerto Rican community. Other writers, including Nicholasa Mohr, wanted to offer a different view of the barrio. Her award-winning novel *Nilda* (1974), for example, depicts life in the Bronx through the eyes of a ten-year-old girl who is a second-generation Puerto Rican. Mohr's more than thirteen novels and short stories, many written for young adults, are told primarily from the point of view of a young child, emphasizing the family dynamics and personal relationships of characters living in the barrio. Mohr's novels for adult audiences, including *Rituals of Survival: A Woman's Portfolio* (1985), explore the role of women in a traditionally male-dominated Puerto Rican culture.

Another woman who found a voice among Nuyorican writers is the poet Sandra María Esteves, a political activist working for civil rights and Puerto Rican independence who began performing her poetry during the 1970s in support of these causes. Esteves was part of "El Grupo," a collective of Nuyorican socialist poets, performers, and musicians committed to protesting for civil rights throughout the eastern United States. Her collections of poetry, including *Yerba Buena* (1980) and *Finding Your Way* (2001), express the conflicts of living between two languages and two cultures, as well as being a Puerto Rican woman in a country dominated by Anglo males.

Among the most acclaimed contemporary Puerto Rican authors is the poet, novelist, and essayist Judith Ortiz Cofer. Having traveled back and forth between Puerto Rico and New Jersey as a child, Cofer explores issues of cultural identity in much of her poetry, collected in *Peregrina* (1986), *Reaching for the Mainland* (1987), and *Terms of Survival* (1987). Cofer's best-known work, however, is *Silent Dancing: A Partial Remembrance of a Puerto Rican Childhood* (1990), a series of autobiographical vignettes and poems that contains conflicting memories of her childhood. In all of her work—including the critically acclaimed *The Latin Deli* (1994) and *The Year of Our Revolution* (1998)—Cofer explores bicultural identity and the differing roles of women in Puerto Rico and the U.S. mainland.

Two other notable Puerto Rican poets are Martín Espada and Gloria Vando. The former is a poet, essayist, editor, and translator whose work explores Puerto Rican history, identity, and poverty, particularly the daily oppression of working-class Puerto Ricans by corporations, landlords, and the police. His poetry collection *Imagine the Angels of Bread* (1996) won the prestigious American Book Award. Gloria Vando, a poet writing in English and in Spanish, has published two notable collections of poetry, *Promesas: Geography of the Impossible* (1993) and *Shadows and Supposes* (2002), which won the Latino Literary Award for Best Poetry. She is also the cofounder and editor of Helicon Nine Editions, a small nonprofit press in Kansas City, Missouri.

The novelist Esmeralda Santiago received much popular acclaim with her memoir *When I Was Puerto Rican* (1993)—the first in a trilogy that also includes *Almost a Woman* (1998) and *The Turkish Lover* (2004)—about her early childhood in Puerto Rico, migration to the United States at age thirteen, and identity formation. Santiago's writings, which also include children's books and anthologies, portray the challenges of immigration and coming-of-age issues in teenage girls.

Although Puerto Rican poets, novelists, and essayists of the twentieth and twenty-first centuries offer distinctive personal perspectives and writing styles, they have several themes in common. Perhaps most notable among these are bicultural identity and the experience of circular migration on the U.S. mainland and in Puerto Rico, which revitalizes language, culture, and the ties between them in both locations. Women's voices have contributed yet other insights into the Puerto Rican experience, with those from particular communities—in New York, Los Angeles, Chicago, and elsewhere—adding a local perspective. Whether produced primarily in English, Spanish, or some combination of the two, Puerto Rican literature in the United States has become an integral and growing part of the American multicultural experience.

Molly Metherd

See also: Algarín, Miguel; Cofer, Judith Ortiz; Levins Morales, Aurora; Muñoz Marín, Luis; Muñoz Rivera, Luis; Nuyorican; Nuyorican Poets Café; Puerto Ricans; Santiago, Esmeralda; Thomás, Piri.

Further Reading

Algarín, Miguel, and Bob Holman, eds. *Aloud: Voices from the Nuyorican Poets Cafe.* New York: Henry Holt, 1994.

Colón, Jesús. *A Puerto Rican in New York and Other Sketches.* New York: Mainstream, 1961.

Esteves, Sandra María. "The Feminist Viewpoint in Poetry of Puerto Rican Women in the United States." In *Images and Identities: The Puerto Rican in Two World Contexts,* ed. Asela Rodríguez de Laguna. New Brunswick, NJ: Transaction, 1985.

Fernández, Roberta, ed. *In Other Words: Literature by Latinas of the United States.* Houston, TX: Arte Público, 1994.

Marzán, Julio, ed. *Inventing a Word: An Anthology of Twentieth-Century Puerto Rican Poetry.* New York: Columbia University Press, Center for Inter-American Relations, 1980.

Mohr, Eugene. *The Nuyorican Experience: Literature of the Puerto Rican Minority.* Westport, CT: Greenwood, 1982.

Santiago, Roberto, ed. *Boricuas: Influential Puerto Rican Writings—An Anthology.* New York: Ballatine, 1995.

Puerto Rican Revolutionary Workers Organization

The Puerto Rican Revolutionary Workers Organization (PRRWO) was one of many 1970s groups that contributed to the fight for equal rights for minorities in the United States. These rights included but were not limited to equal opportunities in employment, fair labor wages, and equal access to education. The work of the PRRWO represented one of the strongest contributions to the struggle for freedom and equality by the Puerto Rican community. The group's efforts focused on the needs of Puerto Ricans specifically, and it worked to win them equal access to education and health services, and to secure fair wages for Puerto Rican laborers. The PRRWO organized rallies to protest police brutality, the lack of adequate health care, and the presence of drug dealers in the Puerto Rican community. It even incited riots in hopes of forcing the city to collect garbage in Puerto Rican neighborhoods. Although its work started at the grassroots community level, the PRRWO considered itself a revolutionary political party fighting for the liberation of all oppressed peoples. One of its long-term goals was to convert America into a socialist society.

In conjunction with their organizing efforts on the mainland, the PRRWO focused on the conditions faced by Puerto Ricans still living on the island. Although the struggle for political independence was led by such other organizations as the Armed Forces for National Liberation of Puerto Rico (FALN), the Movement for National Liberation (MLN), and the Puerto Rican Independence Party (PIP), the PRRWO demonstrated its support for their efforts through rallies and educating the public on the plight of Puerto Ricans throughout their diaspora.

The PRRWO came into existence in July 1972, when the Young Lords Party (YLP), which had been at the forefront of the Puerto Rican movement on the mainland through the late 1960s and early 1970s, changed its name to the Puerto Rican Revolutionary Workers Organization. This change reflected the YLP's shift in focus from organizing within the Puerto Rican community to mobilizing Puerto Rican workers. The leaders of the organization concluded that addressing the needs of the working class in particular would allow for a more effective challenge to the capitalist and the American power structures. At the same time, it abandoned the original YLP emphases on campus organizing, community service, feminist and queer liberation, and antiwar activities. In establishing collaborative relationships with organizations involved in the labor movement and working with community organizations dedicated to empowering the working class and seeking to inspire a larger revolution, the PRRWO worked increasingly with organizations like the Communist Party USA (CPUSA), the Revolutionary Union (RU), and the Trotskyite Communist League (CL) and its National Continuations Committee (NCC). This ideology and organizational shift, however, resulted in a dramatic erosion of support from the Puerto Rican community.

Having transformed itself from an organization—the Young Lords Party—dedicated to the empowerment of all Puerto Ricans, securing the independence of Puerto Rico from the United States, and providing basic needs and services for Puerto Ricans to a radical group dedicated to organizing

workers in preparation for a revolution against capitalism, PRRWO found its support dwindling during the 1970s. Likewise, by its abandonment of civil disobedience and community-based demonstration for the sake of education and participation in conferences, the PRRWO no longer commanded attention within the Puerto Rican movement. By the late 1970s, it had disappeared from sight. Although its most significant contribution may have been creating a bridge between the Communist Party and Puerto Rican neighborhoods in East Coast cities, its ultimate historic importance rests with its failure to continue the efforts of the Young Lords Party, transforming what was a powerful agent of social change into a less significant revolutionary labor organization.

Timothy P. Gaster and David J. Leonard

See also: Puerto Ricans; Young Lords.

Further Reading

Torres, Andrés, and José E. Velázquez. *The Puerto Rican Movement: Voices from the Diaspora.* Philadelphia: Temple University Press, 1998.
Zavala, Iris M., and Rafael Rodriguez. *The Intellectual Roots of Independence: An Anthology of Puerto Rican Political Essays.* New York: Monthly Review, 1980.

Puerto Rican Studies

Puerto Rican studies is an interdisciplinary academic field that focuses on the experiences and issues affecting Puerto Ricans. The field draws from various disciplines in the social sciences and humanities, including but not limited to anthropology, sociology, political science, education, history, religion, and literature. Puerto Rican studies documents and conducts research on the history, culture, and contemporary social and political issues that affect the lives of Puerto Ricans in Puerto Rico and the United States.

Sharing a similar history with such other academic fields as Latino studies, African American studies, and Caribbean studies, Puerto Rican studies emerged in the 1960s and 1970s out of a movement comprising students, professors, and activists concerned with the conditions and underrepresentation of ethnic minority groups in American colleges and universities. Puerto Rican studies is equally concerned with circumstances that distinguish Puerto Ricans from other disadvantaged minority groups in the United States, such as the history of colonialism in Puerto Rico, the political status and relationship of Puerto Rico to the United States, migration to the United States, and the quality of life and political representation of Puerto Rican communities. The field has evolved to employ a variety of perspectives and methodologies, such as archival resources, ethnographic studies, quantitative and qualitative data, and literary and artistic sources.

While Puerto Rican studies covers a myriad of social, economic, and political aspects of the Puerto Rican experience, the field has distinguished itself for developing a depth of knowledge about the formation of Puerto Rican cultural and political identity, and about the factors related to the migration of Puerto Ricans to the United States. The theme of identity is explored through research on the history and culture of the Puerto Rican people, such as the contribution of Taíno, African, and Spanish ethnicities to the formation of contemporary cultural identity, the role of identity in shaping political representation and power, and the historical and contemporary expression of identity in literature, theater, the visual arts, and other aesthetic forms in Puerto Rico and the United States.

Studies on the diasporic experience of Puerto Ricans address the socioeconomic and political circumstances influencing migration between Puerto Rico and the United States, the social and political obstacles that Puerto Rican communities face in the United States as they struggle to achieve economic prosperity, and how this minority group has organized and become engaged in American politics. The field has historically analyzed the impact of U.S. policies on Puerto Rico, the experiences of returning migrants, and the contributions of the Puerto Rican community to U.S. society.

Puerto Rican studies has been the subject of criticism in some circles for its emphasis on cultural identity. Some scholars regard the appropriate field of study as more pluralistic than commonly understood, focusing increasing attention on contempo-

rary issues such as gender, health, education, labor, and environmental justice. Scholars are also engaging in comparative studies among Hispanic and other minority groups, and the ways these groups interface with the political sphere to promote social change and community empowerment.

A number of research and teaching programs that support scholarship on Puerto Rican studies have remained active into the twenty-first century. In the United States, the City University of New York (CUNY) was the first institution to establish a Puerto Rican Studies Department in 1969, after students petitioned and picketed to have courses relative to their experiences and cultures offered at the university. The Centro de Estudios Puertorriqueños (Center for Puerto Rican Studies–CENTRO) at Hunter College, CUNY, is a research institution known for its archival and library resources on Puerto Rican history and culture, as well as for the publication of the *Centro Journal,* which provides a vehicle for scholarship and research in Puerto Rican studies. Other U.S.-based research institutions include the Institute of Puerto Rican and Latino Studies at the University of Connecticut. In Puerto Rico, the Centro de Estudios Avanzados de Puerto Rico y El Caribe (Center for Advanced Puerto Rican and Caribbean Studies) disseminates scholarship on and grants advanced degrees in Puerto Rican studies. The number of undergraduate degrees in Puerto Rican studies is also rapidly increasing, with dozens of universities and colleges offering courses and bachelor degrees in the subject.

Research in Puerto Rican studies is also disseminated to the academic community through scientific journals, books, media, and conferences. The Puerto Rican Studies Association (PRSA), an international organization, holds a conference every two years for scholars to share and encourage the research, teaching, and community empowerment of Puerto Ricans. PRSA has a membership of several hundred active participants and issues a newsletter, membership directory, and other publications.

Puerto Rican studies is a burgeoning academic field, but scholars are also increasingly concerned with communicating the research to the broader public, influencing policy, and raising awareness on the issues that affect Puerto Ricans. In this way, the field engages in generating information, providing insight, and establishing resources that help produce social change and community empowerment.

Tischa A. Muñoz-Erickson and Juan Declet

See also: Latino Studies; Puerto Ricans.

Further Reading

Centro de Estudios Avanzados de Puerto Rico y El Caribe (Center for Advanced Puerto Rican and Caribbean Studies). http://www.prtc.net/~centro.
Centro de Estudios Puertorriqueños (Center for Puerto Rican Studies–CENTRO). http://www.centropr.org.
Puerto Rican Studies Association (PRSA). http://www. puertorican-studies.org.

Puerto Ricans

As of early 2008, according to the U.S. Census Bureau, the number of Puerto Ricans living in the continental United States was just under 4 million, or less than 10 percent of the total Latino population. Nevertheless, Puerto Ricans occupy a central place in the Latino community, itself the largest minority group in the country, for several reasons. First, the Puerto Rican homeland has been a U.S. possession since the Spanish-American War in 1898, and, since the Jones-Shafroth Act of 1917, Puerto Ricans are U.S. citizens by birth. Unlike other Latino groups, such as Mexican Americans, Dominicans, and Central Americans, Puerto Ricans do not have a sovereign nation they call home. Thus, their destiny is inextricably linked to the United States, whether on the island or on the mainland. Finally, for the first time, the number of Puerto Ricans living on the mainland exceeds those living on the island, raising new and unexplored dynamics in national and social identity.

Historians generally divide the migration of Puerto Ricans to the U.S. mainland into three historic periods. The first, from about 1900 to 1945, is referred to as "pioneer migration" and brought a modest influx of industrial workers to New York and agricultural laborers to Florida, New Jersey, and Hawaii.

In the years following World War II, especially with the advent of affordable commercial air travel, Puerto Ricans began traveling to the continental United States in rapidly increasing numbers. During the years 1946–1964, a period called "the great migration," certain areas in the United States for the first time experienced large-scale migration of persons whose primary language was Spanish and who were racially mixed. Arriving by the tens of thousands, they established the Puerto Rican barrios of New York City, such as Spanish Harlem (East Harlem in upper Manhattan) and the Lower East Side (Loisaida). Although the city benefited greatly from the expanded labor pool and social commentators observed a new spirit and personality in the urban environment, it was during this time that the so-called "Puerto Rican problem" began to be discussed. The problem, it was said, stemmed from the fact that the mainland Puerto Rican community was thin in tradition and cultural heritage. They did not bring their own religious institutions and clergy, for example, to the same extent that European immigrants had done throughout history. Furthermore, it was said, Puerto Ricans were not assimilating into U.S. society as well as Europeans had and were overtaxing the welfare system. What this view did not take into account, others pointed out, was the racial and ethnic discrimination faced by the new arrivals.

The third stage in migratory movement dates from 1965 to the present, a period characterized by "the revolving door migration." According to this new pattern, Puerto Ricans migrate to and from the mainland to Puerto Rico. They generally come to the United States in search of economic opportunity, returning to the island after varying periods of time to tend to family needs and for other personal reasons; some remain permanently, others go back to the States. The frequent coming and going has created a complex diaspora, unique in character and experience.

Initially, Puerto Ricans settled primarily on the East Coast of the United States. The earliest arrivals concentrated in New York City, with large numbers soon following in such major metropolises as Philadelphia and Chicago; Puerto Rican communities also began appearing in such smaller cities as Hartford,

Connecticut; Camden, New Jersey; and Lawrence, Massachusetts. With increasing mobility and the diversification of economic opportunity, Puerto Ricans in subsequent decades settled throughout the rest of the continental United States. Today, a majority of the Puerto Rican population still resides on the East Coast, heavily clustered in the Boston–New York–Washington corridor, though that majority continues to decline. States with the largest Puerto Rican populations are (in alphabetical order) California, Connecticut, Florida, Illinois, Massachusetts, New York, New Jersey, and Pennsylvania.

Most Puerto Ricans in the United States who live in urban enclaves define themselves as *Boricua* and face such challenges as substandard housing, a low standard of living, underfunded school systems, and elevated school drop out rates. Health concerns are also of great importance, with low rates of health insurance and high rates of AIDS/HIV infection and other diseases.

The complex relationship between Puerto Ricans living in the United States (sometimes called Nuyoricans, because of the early concentration in New York) and those who still reside on the island is characterized by ongoing efforts to define Puerto Rican identity and culture in ever-changing social circumstances. The proliferation of Puerto Rican Day parades in cities across the East Coast and Midwest represents one way for mainland Puerto Ricans to reaffirm their cultural identity. Another traditional celebration brought to U.S. soil is Día de los Reyes (Three Kings Day, or Epiphany), celebrated on January 6. Public and domestic celebrations of culture, religious traditions, foodways, and arts and crafts further reaffirm a unique heritage—part Spanish, part Taíno Indian, part African, and part American—reflecting the provenance of the majority of Puerto Rican people regardless of where they reside. The spirit of shared identity and cultural pride is summed up in a slogan issued by the Puerto Rican government: "We are one people, separated by the sea and integrally united by our culture."

The pride of the Puerto Rican community—and hope for an empathetic ear at the highest level of the legal system—found particular expression upon President Barack Obama's nomination of Sonia Sotomayor to the U.S. Supreme Court in 2009. A second-generation Nuyorican, Sotomayor rose from modest beginnings in the Bronx, New York, to become the first Latino/a named to the high court.

María Pabón López

See also: AIDS/HIV; Albizu Campos, Pedro; Boricua; Chicago; Circular Migration; Identity and Labels; Jones Act (1917); New York; Nuyorican; Puerto Rican Day Parade; Puerto Rican Literature; Puerto Rican Revolutionary Workers Organization; Puerto Rican Studies; Spanish-American War.

Further Reading

Acosta-Belén, Edna, ed. *Adiós, Borinquen Querida: The Puerto Rican Diaspora, Its History, and Contributions.* Albany: State University of New York Center for Latino, Latin American and Caribbean Studies, 2000.

Duany, Jorge. *The Puerto Rican Nation on the Move: Identities on the Island and in the United States.* Chapel Hill: University of North Carolina Press, 2002.

Fitzpatrick, Joseph P. *Puerto Rican Americans: The Meaning of Migration to the Mainland.* Englewood Cliffs, NJ: Prentice Hall, 1971.

Glazer, Nathan, and Daniel Patrick Moynihan. *Beyond the Melting Pot: The Negroes, Puerto Ricans, Jews, Italians and Irish of New York City.* Cambridge, MA: MIT Press, 1970.

Pérez y González, María E. *Puerto Ricans in the United States.* Westport, CT: Greenwood, 2000.

U.S. Commission on Civil Rights. *Puerto Ricans in the Continental United States: An Uncertain Future.* Washington, DC, 1976.

Quinceañera

The term *quinceañera* refers to a special celebration for Latinas when they turn fifteen, and to the young woman who is being honored. Also referred to as a "cotillion" or "quince años," quinceañera combines the Spanish words for "fifteen" (*quince*) and "years" (*años*). It is an important religious and cultural occasion for many Latinas in the United States and across Latin America. Quinceañera is a coming-of-age celebration in which a girl officially becomes a woman, is welcomed into the adult community, observes valued traditions, receives instruction on her adult duties, and makes promises to fulfill them. Much like a wedding, the quinceañera often takes months of planning and can cost thousands of dollars. Some compare it to the Jewish *bat mitzvah* or the coming-out parties for debutantes in the United States.

Traditionally, quinceañera marked the moment at which a young woman became eligible for courtship. Before that time, she was not allowed to wear makeup, dance, or date young men. The rite of passage is believed to have roots in a pre-Colombian Aztec ritual in Mexico, in which a fifteen-year-old girl left the care of her parents and teachers to become either a priestess or wife. After the Spanish conquest, the quinceañera became an important decision point in the life of a young woman—whether to enter service to the Church or to remain in society and marry. Today it is not only a social event, but also a religious ceremony in which the young woman receives instruction on her Catholic faith and its importance in adult life. Quinceañeras are celebrated differently in various Latin American cultures (and not celebrated at all in others).

The quinceañera usually involves a special religious Mass (or *Misa*) celebrated in the young woman's honor, followed by a party. In Cuba, however, there is only an elaborate ball and no Mass.

The similarities between a wedding and a quinceañera go beyond their common functions as religious ceremonies of duty and promise, and rites of passage. For example, the quinceañera wears an elaborate, often costly, dress (*vestido*) made of satin, organza, beading, and lace, and a crown (*corona*) made of rhinestones, pearls, or flowers. The dress resembles a wedding dress and is usually white, especially in Mexican quinceañeras where the tradition is strongest. However, the vestido in Salvadoran quinceañeras is typically pink because many Salvadorans believe that white should be reserved for brides.

Quinceañeras, like brides, carry a bouquet (*ramo*), usually made of artificial flowers, ribbon, or special dough. They also require shoes, jewelry, a rosary (*rosario*), a prayer book (*libro*), a ring (*anillo*), and a special cushion (*cojín*) on which to kneel at the altar during the Mass. All of these items become treasured keepsakes of the quinceañera's special day.

The quinceañera has a court (*corte de honor* or just *corte*), consisting of *damas* (ladies) and their male *chambelanes* (escorts) or *caballeros* (gentlemen). The members of the corte are usually teenagers who are close friends or relatives of the quinceañera. Sometimes, the damas help suggest chambelanes to serve as their escorts. The quinceañera also has a male escort, called the *chambelán de honor,* or honor escort. The damas wear matching formal dresses (different from the quinceañera's), and the chambelanes wear tuxedos. The size of the corte varies from only a few damas, to a small number of couples up to the traditional number of fourteen couples.

One of the duties of the corte is to rehearse and perform a choreographed dance, usually a waltz (*vals*). Traditionally, this performance is the first public dance of the honoree. The European waltz was added to the traditional ceremony after the Austrian archduke Maximilian and his wife Carlota became emperor and empress of Mexico in the 1860s. Under their influence, lavishness and European culture—especially in music, dance, dress, and architecture—found their way into Mexican society.

It is not necessary for the quinceañeras to be held exactly on the young woman's fifteenth birthday, but usually on a Saturday close to it. On the day of her quinceañera, the honoree spends hours on her hair, makeup, and wardrobe before being escorted to church by her family, sometimes in a rented limousine.

At church, she joins her corte and the guests, who have received formal invitations to the event, and is escorted down the aisle by her father or both parents. During Mass, the priest and sometimes family, *padrinos* (sponsors), or members of the corte, read passages from the Bible. The priest calls the padrinos forward to bless their gifts to the quinceañera. Then he gives instructions to the young woman and sometimes says a few words to the congregation in her honor—such as memories of her youth, or comments about her achievements or community activities. The young woman says a prayer of dedication to God, and all present receive Holy Communion. Sometimes a mariachi band plays during or after the Mass. Before leaving church, the quinceañera places a natural bouquet at the feet of an image of the Virgin Mary (the Vírgen de Guadalupe if the quinceañera is of Mexican descent), and she says a private prayer.

All then proceed to the *fiesta* (party), held either at a private home or in a rented hall. The corte is seated together at the head table, and everyone has dinner—usually traditional foods served buffet style, sometimes prepared by family members. There is a toast (*brindis*), music, and the performance of the vals by the corte. The quinceañera may also dance with her father, other male relatives, and the chambelanes. In some traditions, she throws a special doll, or *muñeca*, made for the occasion to represent her last childhood toy, for the younger guests to catch. Her father then changes her "little girl" shoes for her first pair of adult high heels. Another important element of the quinceañera celebration is the cake, or *pastel*. Like a wedding cake, it is typically elegant and white, often very costly. Guests receive *recuerdos*—mementos or special party favors—which are often handmade by female relatives and personalized with the date and the quinceañera's name. A photographer records the entire event, including formal poses

A young woman in Pico-Union, a predominantly Central American neighborhood in Los Angeles, basks in the moment during her *quinceañera*—the traditional Latina coming-of-age celebration at age fifteen. *(Gilles Mingasson/Getty Images)*

by the corte and the quinceañera alone, and may even record a video. The fiesta usually lasts well into the night with dancing, eating, talking, laughing, and reminiscing.

Many Latinas, especially those of Mexican descent, dream of their quinceañeras as little girls. However, not all Latino families can afford the extravagant celebration. Some manage with the financial help of *padrinos,* literally "godparents," but some are simply "sponsors" who are asked or offer to pay for part of the quinceañera. For example, the *padrinos del ramo* or "sponsors of the bouquet," pay for the bouquet and are recognized for their contribution during the celebration. Some Latino families go into debt or spend their entire savings on their daughter's quinceañera, with the feeling that it is worth every penny.

Despite its excitement, symbolism, and importance within many Latino communities, the quinceañera also can be controversial. There may be disagreements about which aspects of a quinceañera are "traditional" and what the "proper" elements and rituals ought to be. Some express concern with the apparent mixed messages concerning the young woman's sexuality. On the one hand, the social celebration implies that she is now sexually available to men, while on the other hand she is implicitly told during the religious ceremony to preserve her "virtue," "purity," and "dignity" (that is, remain a virgin) until marriage. Feminists also point out how the quinceañera ritual reinforces patriarchy and encourages female submission. The honoree is encouraged toward a life of service to others rather than toward independence, exploration, education, self-knowledge, or pursuing her own interests and needs. She is bound to the male-dominated church, and to her family, and she is under the watchful eye of her father until she is married, when she is put under the watchful eye of her husband. At a critical time in a young woman's life, just following puberty, great expectations about being a virgin, heterosexual, wife, and mother (in perpetual service to others) are placed on her through the quinceañera—and without making the same requirements of young men.

Like most human rituals, however, the quinceañera endures because it continues to play an important role in creating personal, cultural, gender, and religious identity for many Latinas and the Latino community. It will likely continue to evolve over time, as it has for centuries, but will not disappear anytime soon.

Susana Rinderle

See also: Family and Community.

Further Reading

Hoyt-Goldsmith, Diane. *Celebrating a Quinceañera: A Latina's Fifteenth Birthday Celebration.* New York: Holiday House, 2002.

Jeter, Sylvia. *The Quinceañera Planning Guide.* Frankfort, IL: Quinceanera-Boutique.com, 2002.

King, Elizabeth. *Quinceañera: Celebrating Fifteen.* New York: Dutton, 1998.

Quintanilla, Selena
See Selena

Race

Race is one of the most widely discussed, yet misunderstood, concepts in contemporary American society. The media and academic community frequently point out how the racial composition of the United States is rapidly changing, while a number of colleges require students to take a course in race studies as part of the curriculum. Backlashes against affirmative action, bilingual education, and immigration are frequently cited as reflections of the racial tension that persists in modern American life. Indeed, few topics have inspired such intense and conflicting emotions as race.

Biological and Social Dimensions

Race has both a biological and social connotation, although recent scientific research has questioned its validity as a legitimate biological concept. Physical anthropologists have raised four major arguments against race as a scientific construct. First, there has never been any agreement within the scientific community regarding the number of human races. Some have argued that there are only a few distinct races of human, from three to five. Those who take this position, known as "lumpers," tend to classify races by continents. Others, known as "splitters," have argued that there are several dozen or even hundreds of human races. Thus, one of the arguments against the scientific concept of race itself is that the number should have been settled long ago; if indeed there are discrete and distinct races, there should be little disagreement as to how many.

Second, most human variation is continuous (representing a continuum or spectrum) rather than clearly demarcated and capable of being classified into discrete units. One example of this is skin color. Human skin color is continuous, representing a spectrum from very light to very dark, with every possible shade in between. Third, it is argued, most human genetic variation is nonconcordant. This means that genes for skin color do not correspond with genes for hair texture, eye shape, hair color, or other genetic traits. Despite common misconception, sickle cell anemia is not concordant with skin color and is not a "racial" trait; the sickle cell allele is found in several areas of the world with high rates of malaria, including West Africa, Mediterranean Europe, parts of Arabia, and parts of India. Finally, analysis of DNA reveals that there is actually much more genetic diversity within members of the same socially defined racial groups than between members of different socially defined racial groups.

Although most scientists today do not consider race a valid biological concept, it remains a very powerful social construct. Race as a social construction refers to the fact that different societies establish different categories of people and different methods of classifying them. For example, according to the rule of hypodescent in the United States, people with any trace of African ancestry are automatically classified as "black." In Brazil, however, people are not automatically classified as "black" simply because they have African ancestry. Thus, race is socially constructed differently in the United States and Brazil.

For census taking and other purposes, the United States officially recognizes four racial categories: White, Black, Asian or Pacific Islander, and Native American Indian. Most official government forms also include an "other race" category, for individuals who do not identity themselves as a member of one of the four officially recognized racial categories. The U.S. Census Bureau does not recognize Latinos/as as a "race," but rather as an "ethnic group," pointing out that Latinos/as "can be of any race." In the 1990 and 2000 censuses, respondents were first asked to indicate whether or not they were Latino/a; then they were asked to identify their race. In both censuses, millions of Latino respondents identified themselves as being of an "other race," indicating that they were not satisfied with the four officially recognized racial categories.

Shifting Categories

The place of Latinos/as in the North American system of racial classification has changed over time. For example, the 1930 U.S. Census counted Mexicans as a separate, distinct racial group (like whites and blacks). From 1940 to 1960, however, the Census officially recognized Mexicans as "white," unless they displayed strong black or Native American physical features. Mexican American civil rights organizations at the time endorsed the classification of Mexicans as white in order to combat anti-Mexican racism through a philosophy of integration and assimilation. During the turbulent 1960s and early 1970s, many young people of Mexican ancestry living in the United States began embracing a nonwhite *Chicano* racial identity. Chicanos/as stressed pride in their indigenous roots and rejected the earlier generation's idea that Mexicans are "white."

Puerto Ricans and other Latinos/as have had similar experiences with U.S. racial categories. During the 1950s, Puerto Ricans, like Mexicans, were classified as "white" unless they were visibly black or Native American. However, the vast range in skin color and physical features among Latinos/as often confuses Americans and complicates Latinos' position in the U.S. racial system. Individuals who are either very light-complected or fairly dark-complected are often told that they "do not look Latino." Experiences of disgust and alienation with mainstream U.S. racial categories have been a popular theme in Nuyorican literature for several decades.

In 1980, the U.S. government introduced the "Hispanic" category on its census forms, although this was distinguished as an ethnic, rather than a racial, category. Respondents were asked to identify whether or not they were of Hispanic origin, in addition to identifying their race. The U.S. Census Bureau still uses these criteria to gather statistics on racial and ethnic demographics.

The various peoples of Latin American ancestry living in the United States do not all agree on how they wish to be identified. Some object to the umbrella term "Hispanic" because it was created by the American government and/or acknowledges only the European aspect of their heritage. The labels "Chicano" and "Mexican American" may be considered offensive, depending on one's personal or political ideologies. Puerto Ricans may prefer to be called *Nuyoricans* (if they reside in New York) or *boricuas*. Some people prefer to identify themselves by their national ancestry rather than by collective terms like "Hispanic" or "Latino," while others identify themselves simply as "American." Clearly, race can be an emotional issue not only between different groups of people, but even among people who share the same ancestral backgrounds.

Justin D. García

See also: Identity and Labels; La Raza; Latino/a; Miscegenation.

Further Reading

Haney-López, Ian F. *Racism on Trial: The Chicano Fight for Justice.* Cambridge, MA: Harvard University Press, 2003.

Relethford, John. *The Human Species: An Introduction to Biological Anthropology.* 5th ed. New York: McGraw-Hill, 2002.

Rodríguez, Clara E. *Changing Race: Latinos, the Census, and the History of Ethnicity in the United States.* New York: New York University Press, 2000.

Thomás, Piri. *Down These Mean Streets.* 1967. New York: Vintage Books, 1997.

Religion

As the fastest-growing minority in the United States, Latinos/as have had an increasing impact on all aspects of American life. Organizations of virtually every kind, including religious denominations and institutions, have created programs and established congregations to attract and incorporate a growing Spanish-speaking population.

History

Christopher Columbus and the Spanish explorers who followed him saw advantages in the so-called New World for economic gain and control. They

Peruvian Catholics march in a New York City procession honoring St. Martin of Porres, the first black saint of the Americas. The Catholic Church, as it has for centuries, continues to play a central role in the life and identity of the Latino community. *(Mario Tama/Getty Images)*

also believed that they were a superior people and that it was their responsibility to convert the natives. The military and the church thus worked together to enslave the original Americans and to impose new religious standards. With all the death and change wrought by the Spanish conquerors, however, native peoples also had a reverse effect on the Spanish and their way of life. Thus, for example, while Catholic missionaries established settlements in Florida, New Mexico, Texas, and California, they were forced to construct buildings that matched the local architecture. Native peoples and the European settlers alike developed folk traditions that became part of their Catholic practice.

One enduring example is the Virgin of Guadalupe. Two years after Hernán Cortés conquered the Aztecs in 1519, Fray Bernardino de Sahagún and other Franciscan monks arrived in Mexico. One of their earliest converts was given the Christian name of Juan Diego. Traveling to Mass on December 9, 1531, he had a vision of the Virgin Mary. Although doubt-

ful at first, Catholic leaders accepted his claims after the Virgin's image appeared on his cape, and the bishop ordered a church built on the site of the vision. (The original church was replaced with larger buildings in 1709 and 1976.) The Vatican accepted the miracle in 1745 and, every year on December 12, this church and others dedicated to the Virgin of Guadalupe celebrate Diego's vision.

For centuries, American Latinos/as practiced the Roman Catholic religion with special adaptations. Life rotated around the practice of the faith from baptism to last rites. First Communion, holidays, and marriages all had a religious element. Lent, Holy Week, Easter, and Christmas were especially celebrated in Latino communities.

Other denominations also established missions to share their Christian message. The first Protestant conversions occurred in the 1820s. In 1900, the Azusa Street Revival in Los Angeles attracted some Latinos/as to new Pentecostalism. During the next several years, the Apostolic movement continued to grow among Latinos/as. In 1925, twenty-seven Pentecostal pastors met in the Los Angeles area to discuss doctrine, requirements for ministers, and organization. After rapid initial growth, the movement's membership declined because of economic depression and internal dissent.

Other non-Catholic religions also created programs to attract Latinos/as Americans in the United States. The Methodist and Presbyterian churches trace their Latino missionary beginnings in Southern California to the 1850s. The Presbyterian Church, for example, established the Forsythe School for Mexican Girls in Los Angeles in 1884, and it continued to operate until the 1930s. The Mexican Methodist Church started a "Mexican Hotel" for young men working in Pasadena. Despite the Protestant churches' best efforts, though, only an estimated 5 percent of Mexicans and Mexican Americans converted to Protestantism between the first efforts and 1940 in Southern California.

Although such conversions were meager throughout the United States, the Catholic Church made adjustments when its Latino members started to join other churches between 1900 and 1940. In New Mexico, the Jesuits published an attack on Protestant doctrine. The Church recruited clergy and encouraged women's participation in education, and incorporated more Latino culture and popular religion into the Mass and other Catholic worship. As a result, Catholic communities began developing in Texas and New Mexico. During the 1930s, the Catholic Church established programs that proved critical in helping the Mexican American community and others survive the deprivations of the Great Depression.

Changes in the 1960s and 1970s

Grassroots organizations were started after World War II to encourage more assistance from the Catholic Church. In 1957, the Cursillo Movement promoted liturgies, folk music, and cultural traditions from Spain. Through workshops and programs, the Cursillo Movement called for lay involvement in worship and development of faith. By 1967, there were 8,000 Cursillistas in New York City alone. As the first major attempt by Latinos/as to adapt the activities of the Church, the Cursillo Movement was widely regarded as the community's single greatest influence on Catholicism in America.

César Chávez, a Cursillista and labor organizer in California, became a kind of Martin Luther King, Jr., figure for Mexican Americans when he helped organize the Delano grape strike and the United Farm Workers of Americo (UFW) in the 1960s. Mexican Americans also demanded changes in their relationship with the Catholic Church. As in the Cursillo Movement, they formed groups calling for more involvement and a stronger voice. Such groups included the Católicos por La Raza, the Chicano Priests Organization, Padres, and Las Hermanas. For example, Las Hermanas, a feminist group started in 1971, sponsored two surveys that revealed a lack of Latino ministry programs and complained about the role of women as domestics in Catholic parishes. In 1978, Mexican-born lay people in El Monte, California, formed Jóvenes Para Cristo, which also called for changes in the role of Latinos/as in the Church.

The Catholic Church itself recognized the need for change. In 1945, it created a Spanish-speaking organization to examine the specific needs of the Latino community. In 1971 and 1977, the U.S. Catholic Church sponsored events called National Encounters, at which clergy and lay members discussed the needs of Latino Catholics. Regional meetings such as the Hispanic Encuentro for Catholics from New Mexico, Arizona, Colorado, Wyoming, and Utah in 1985 addressed similar questions. In 1983, a pastoral letter titled "The Hispanic Presence: Challenges and Commitment" recognized the importance of faith within the Latino community and thus promoted the training of priests through a Latino ministry that worked with Spanish-speaking Catholics. Yet, as of 2004, only 3.8 percent of Catholic priests were Latino.

The Catholic Church was not the only one to undergo changes with respect to Latino participation. During the Latino Religious Resurgence of the 1960s and 1970s, Protestants and Pentecostals began to focus efforts on providing assistance to Latinos/as rather than demanding their Americanization and adaptation of the majority language and culture. Like the Catholic clergy, non-Catholic leaders responded to the call for minority civil rights in the 1960s. Latino members were granted greater control over religious worship in such areas as language and ritual.

Ongoing Change

Historically, Latinos/as Americans have predominantly been members of the Roman Catholic Church, and the majority still claim that faith. In 2001, the American Religious Identification Survey reported that 57 percent of Latinos/as identified themselves as Catholic—but that figure represented a decline from 66 percent in 1990. During the same time period, the percentage of Latinos/as who claimed no religion rose from 6 percent to 13 percent.

Other studies in the 1990s reported slightly different figures. The sociologist and Catholic priest Andrew Greeley reported that 23 percent of Latinos/as were not Catholic; most of these belonged to evangelical denominations. According to the Pew Hispanic Center's National Survey of Latinos, 70 percent identified themselves as Catholic, 20 percent as "Evangelical or Born Again," 2 percent as "Other Christian," and 8 percent as having "No Religion." The study found a difference, though, between foreign-born and native-born Latinos/as: 76 percent of foreign-born Latinos/as were members of the Catholic Church, compared with only 59 percent among the native-born.

The Catholic Church has continued to adapt to the needs of the expanding Latino population, and not only in urban areas. In Dalton, Georgia, ninety miles north of Atlanta, the St. Joseph's Parish built a $4.5 million, 30,000-square-foot church, more than doubling the space of the downtown facility where latecomers had to watch Mass via closed-circuit television. The pastor is bilingual and the associate is Mexican. When the first church was built in 1957, there were about 150 to 200 Catholic families. Today, of the 1,500 registered members, 1,000 are Latino/a. Meetings now focus on religious celebrations such as Holy Week, and weekday Masses are scheduled to accommodate Latino parishioners who work long hours and on Sundays.

The communities of Provo and Orem, Utah, located south of Salt Lake City, experienced similar changes. In the 1990s, the congregation outgrew its historic St. Francis church in downtown Provo and moved to a larger facility in neighboring Orem. Latinos/as accounted for most of the growth, with 60 percent of the parish's families being Latino/a. The priest spoke some Spanish, and the associate was a native of El Salvador who grew up in Mexico and trained for the seminary in California. Masses were held in English and Spanish. Spanish cultural activities include the singing of *Las Mañanitas,* a song usually sung at birthday parties, during the Lady of Guadalupe festival and *las posadas,* a nine-day celebration that precedes Christmas. Before the new church was completed, the parish celebrated Midnight Mass in English and Spanish at the Mormon Church's Provo tabernacle.

Non-Catholic churches are also trying to attract and serve Latino/as. The Evangelical churches are growing because they actively encourage Latino participation. The Spanish Seventh Day Adventist Church in Hillsboro, Oregon, is one example. On Saturday mornings, the Reverend Roger Hernandez leads the members in worship, including 125 new members in 2003. According to Hernandez, "When people come to the United States, they come looking for a change in their lives" and that includes a more informal, participatory form of worship. The church also offers English classes, a food bank, Bible studies, and small group social activities.

Mainline Protestant churches are also targeting Latinos/as. The North American Mission Board of the Southern Baptist Convention formed a Hispanic Task Force in 2003 to encourage Latino participation in Southern Baptist congregations. The church is also encouraging Latino seminary students. Southwestern Baptist Theological Seminary in Fort Worth, Texas, hired a Latino vice president, and the Southern Baptist Theological Seminary in Louisville, Kentucky, offers a master's degree of divinity in Spanish. In Birmingham, Alabama, the Dawson Memorial Baptist Church offers Spanish worship services and runs a variety of community outreach programs.

Religious groups that do not follow the mainline Protestant and Evangelical traditions, such as the Jehovah's Witnesses and the Church of Jesus Christ of Latter-day Saints (Mormons), are also experiencing growth in Latino membership. According to one study, more Latinos/as are Mormons than United Methodists. Mormon leaders formed the first Spanish-speaking congregation in Salt Lake City in 1925, and church leaders formed other Spanish congregations there as part of a regional mission in the 1950s. By 2005, Spanish Mormon wards and branches were thriving throughout the United States. The Serrano Ward in Provo, Utah, for example, provides a community for Latino members and sponsors more social activities than do most English-speaking wards.

The Serrano Ward provides an example of how Latinos/as and Anglos approach religion differently. For Anglo Americans, a yearly meeting (referred to as a "ward conference") is a time for those in charge on a stake level (similar to a diocese) to visit the local congregation, give speeches, and check on progress. The Serrano Ward, by contrast, treats the ward conference as an occasion for celebration, and organizes concerts and joint family activities.

There is also a growing Latino Muslim presence in the United States, with Latino mosques in New York, Southern California, and Chicago. The Islamic Society of North America established a Latino Co-ordinating Committee in 2003. As with other religions, the exact number of Latino Muslims is difficult to determine; the numbers suggested range from 25,000 to 60,000. Some Latinos/as were raised Muslim, but many are converts from Catholicism, finding connections between the Spanish and Islamic traditions and eschewing the hierarchy of the Catholic Church.

Although an increasing number of Latinos/as claim no religion, many still profess to be spiritual. In one survey, 53 percent of those with no formal religious affiliation still said that they "strongly believe" in God; only 4 percent had a "strong disbelief." These figures generally follow a national trend. According to national surveys, more Americans are "unchurched" than ever before but still believe in God and life after death.

Common Concerns

Recognizing common concerns, thirty-three church leaders from nineteen denominations met in Durham, North Carolina, in 2002 to exchange ideas about Latino churches. The group discussed the need for more Latino lay and ordained leaders and the problem of declining participation by second- and third-

generation youth. As the Reverend Justo Gonzalez explained, "Horizons have been shattered. Whatever their denomination, people discovered at this meeting that the commonality of issues they face is greater than they had thought. People realized that Latinos/as in other denominations face many of the same problems."

One common concern has to do with welcoming newcomers to the United States. Both undocumented workers and immigrants who come legally struggle to meet their daily needs, such as housing and medical care. They are discriminated against at work as they struggle to learn English and a new way of life. Recognizing the obstacles, the Catholic Church offers services to Latino/as. Nurses from the Sisters of the Holy Cross, for example, visit Latino/as working in hotels in Wendover, Nevada. Dioceses like the one in Atlanta, Georgia, offer help through Catholic Social Services. A website in Spanish and English provides lawyers and legal services.

Other churches offer similar services. In 1971, the Northern (American) Baptist Church established the Hispanic Urban Center in Los Angeles to provide education and social services. The International Pentecostal Holiness Church actively encourages members to learn about and understand ethnic groups, including "Hispanic Americans." After explaining some cultural aspects, a website encourages members to meet Latinos/as, provide religious and other classes, and establish congregations.

A Challenge for the Future

From 1492 to the present, European and American churches have adjusted to the needs and concerns of native and Spanish-speaking peoples. Yet, churches and other institutional religious groups almost never made the changes necessary to convince Latinos/as that they have been fully accepted by the majority. In the twentieth century especially, the Latino community clamored for more religious leaders, more Spanish services, more participation in policy making, and more involvement in services. Although the majority of Latinos/as are Catholic, many have formed non-Church organizations to push for a stronger role. Meanwhile, a minority of Latinos/as converted to Protestant and Muslim faiths during the twentieth century. These denominations have faced the same challenges as the Catholic Church in serving a growing Spanish-speaking population. In the broadest terms, at least, the prospects for the future seem clear. Latinos/as remain a religious people whose evolving needs and expectations from generation to generation will demand to be served.

Jessie L. Embry

See also: Conquest of the Americas; Spirituality.

Further Reading

Cortes, Carlos E., ed. *Protestantism and Latinos in the United States.* New York: Arno, 1980.

Crane, Ken R. *Latino Churches: Faith, Family, and Ethnicity in the Second Generation.* New York: LFB Scholarly Publishing, 2003.

Diaz-Stevens, Ana Maria, and Anthony M. Stevens-Arroyo. *Recognizing the Latino Resurgence in U.S. Religion: The Emmaus Paradigm.* Boulder, CO: Westview, 1998.

Dolan, Jay P., and Allan Figueroa Deck. *Hispanic Catholic Culture in the U.S.: Issues and Concerns.* South Bend, IN: University of Notre Dame Press, 1994.

Dolan, Jay P., and Gilberto M. Hinojosa. *Mexican Americans and the Catholic Church, 1900–1965.* South Bend, IN: University of Notre Dame Press, 1994.

Embry, Jessie L. *"In His Own Language": Mormon Spanish-Speaking Congregations in the United States.* Provo, UT: Charles Redd Center for Western Studies, 1997.

Holland, Clifton L. *The Religious Dimension in Hispanic Los Angeles: A Protestant Case Study.* Pasadena, CA: William Carey Library, 1974.

Maldonado, David. *Crossing Guadalupe Street: Growing up Hispanic and Protestant.* Albuquerque: University of New Mexico Press, 2001.

Medina, Lara. *Las Hermanas: Chicana/Latina Religious-Political Activism in the U.S. Catholic Church.* Philadelphia: Temple University Press, 2004.

Sandoval, Moises, ed. *Fronteras: A History of the Latin American Church in the USA Since 1513.* San Antonio, TX: Mexican American Cultural Center, 1983.

Repatriation

Most scholarly attention on the movements of Mexican and Mexican American populations has focused on immigration into the United States. Far less attention has been paid to the emigration of Mexicans and Mexican Americans from the United States to different countries. Still less attention has been given to the efforts of other countries, such as Mexico, at repatriating or reacquiring former nationals. In this context, repatriation refers to the assistance provided by the Mexican government to nationals living in the United States but who want to return across the border. Although the term is most often used to refer to specific periods, such as the massive movements of the early 1930s and the mid-1950s, repatriation efforts have actually been in existence since the signing of the Treaty of Guadalupe Hidalgo in 1848, ending the Mexican-American War. The treaty also stipulated that Mexico cede all of its northern territories to the United States, including all or parts of the present-day states of Texas, California, Nevada, Arizona, New Mexico, Utah, Colorado and Wyoming. In an effort to help its citizens living in these areas, the Mexican government offered numerous incentives to encourage them to return to Mexico. The government openly offered land and agricultural equipment to anyone willing to repatriate—that is, to return home. In 1855 it offered lands to Mexicans in California, and again during the 1870s it offered material encouragement to repatriate. In all, between 1,000 and 2,000 Mexicans repatriated.

Following World War I, the United States saw a heavy surge in repatriation, as an economic recession forced some 200,000 unemployed Mexicans back across the border. For its part, the Mexican government spent nearly $2.5 million in transportation costs to return its citizens to their hometowns and villages.

The next surge occurred during the Great Depression of the 1930s. Although exact figures are hard to determine, as many as 500,000 Mexican nationals were rounded up and deported back across the border during that period. Some left voluntarily, for a variety of reasons, but loss of work and the difficulty of finding a new job was the most common reason for repatriation. Based on census figures, historians have calculated that the number of persons born in Mexico but living in the United States dropped from 640,000 in 1930 to 377,000 in 1940—a decline of more than 40 percent. In many cases, the American-born children of Mexican nationals were also pushed across the border. Due mainly to the spread of nativism—attitudes and policies favoring the interests of those considered the true citizens of the United States (Anglos)—and the racial intolerance that swept the country, many of the people who were forced to leave were victims of human and civil rights violations. To help prevent any further abuses of Mexican nationals, the Mexican government again initiated a repatriation program that occurred in several phases.

In the first phase, from 1929 to 1930, Mexicans largely repatriated themselves. Most emigrated from Texas and California, but they also left other areas such as the Great Lakes region and scattered enclaves throughout much of the East also witnessed an exodus of Mexican nationals. With unemployment on the rise, the number of repatriates increased to as many as 85,000. By 1931, the second phase, the United States was swept by a hostile attitude toward Mexicans. Ignited by the belief that the removal of Mexicans from the country would free up jobs for American citizens and thereby help end the Depression, the federal government implemented anti-alien drives—campaigns to physically round up and deport all those in the country without the proper documentation. The problem with this campaign was that many legal residents and even American citizens of Mexican descent were deported. Although only a few undocumented workers were actually caught, the fear of harassment or incarceration helped drive out thousands of Mexicans—as many as 75,000 by 1932. In places like Los Angeles, government authorities adopted free-train-ride campaigns for families willing to undergo repatriation. This was essentially a series of train trips scheduled to carry Mexicans back to Mexico. The campaigns were short-lived and had only a minor impact on deportation efforts. By the late 1930s—the third phase—repatriation totals began to decline.

It was in 1939 that the Mexican government sponsored another campaign to attract Mexicans living in the United States, albeit with little success. The number of repatriates began to decline as the Depression wore on, but the deportation and repatriation efforts continued well into the mid-1940s. Although President Franklin Roosevelt's New Deal programs would begin to alleviate the unemploy-

ment crisis, it was the U.S. involvement in World War II that brought the country out of the Depression—effectively halting all deportation and repatriation efforts. After the U.S. entry into World War II, attitudes toward Mexicans changed; many who had fled or were expelled under hostile conditions now found it relatively easy, even inviting, to return north. Attracted by the availability of jobs in wartime industry, the massive flow of Mexicans southward came to a near standstill.

When the war was over, however, the United States was swept by a new wave of nativist sentiment. Deportation drives were implemented once again, only this time, the effort was meant to intimidate undocumented workers into leaving on their own as much as it was to deport them. One program, organized in the mid-1950s by the U.S. Immigration and Naturalization Service (INS) and officially designated Operation Wetback, was designed to return illegal Mexican workers to their homeland, and involved the massive roundup and deportation of undocumented Mexicans workers. Most of the workers had been invited into the country under the Bracero Program, based on a 1942 agreement between the Mexican and U.S. governments to bring in cheap labor for American agribusiness and border factories during and after World War II.

The Cold War of the 1950s ushered in a climate of suspicion and hostility in the United States, and once more the federal government supported roundup and deportation campaigns for anyone considered a threat. Invoking Cold War ideology against undocumented Mexicans, the U.S. government cited Communist infiltration as the main reason for the roundups and deportations; undocumented workers were labeled Communists and thrown out of the country. In all, an estimated 3.7 million Mexican workers were deported between 1950 and 1955. As in the 1930s, the Mexican government again initiated repatriation programs to help Mexican workers in the face of civil rights violations.

Historically, then, the Mexican government has initiated several repatriation programs for its citizens in other countries, especially the United States. Creating jobs and promising land, the government did its part in trying to ensure the return of its citizens. But its efforts were largely unsuccessful, as it lacked the ability to absorb the numbers of those moving south. The result in many cases was that the repatriated workers ended up returning to the United States within a few years of their arrival.

Jesse J. Esparza

See also: Bracero Program; Illegal Immigration; Mexican-American War; Operation Wetback.

Further Reading

Balderrama, Francisco E., and Raymond Rodríguez. *Decade of Betrayal: Mexican Repatriation in the 1930s.* Albuquerque: University of New Mexico Press, 2006.

Garcia, Juan Ramon. *Operation Wetback: The Mass Deportation of Mexican Undocumented Workers in 1954.* Westport, CT: Greenwood, 1980.

Hoffman, Abraham. *Unwanted Mexican Americans in the Great Depression: Repatriation Pressures, 1929–1939.* Tucson: University of Arizona Press, 1974.

Kiser, George C., and David Silverman. "Mexican Repatriation During the Great Depression." *Journal of Mexican American History* 3 (1973): 139–64.

Reisler, Mark. *By the Sweat of Their Brow: Mexican Immigrant Labor in the United States, 1900–1940.* Westport, CT: Greenwood, 1976.

Resident Commissioner, Puerto Rico

The resident commissioner is the delegate elected every four years by the people of Puerto Rico to represent them in the U.S. House of Representatives. (Originally the commissioner was elected to two-year terms, like full members of the U.S. Congress.) Given Puerto Rico's status as a Commonwealth of the United States (its official Spanish name is *estado libre asociado*—free associated state) since 1952, the Puerto Rican commissioner does not have a final floor vote on legislation. The resident commissioner is allowed to serve on congressional committees, however, and functions in every other way as an elected representative. Candidates for governor and resident commissioner of Puerto Rico have historically campaigned on a single ticket, although the law does not require voters to elect candidates from the same party.

On April 2, 1900, President William McKinley signed into a law the Foraker Act, which established a civil government in Puerto Rico. Under that legislation, the island's governor and cabinet members were to be appointed by the U.S. president, but Puerto Ricans would elect a chamber of delegates and one representative in Congress. Federico Degetau of the Puerto Rican Republic Party was elected as the first resident commissioner in 1900 and returned to office in 1902. During his tenure, Degetau introduced a bill to make Puerto Ricans citizens of the United States; the measure was not approved. Degetau also worked to obtain sufficient revenues to run a civil government and for the construction of public buildings. Tulio Larrinaga of the Unionist Party was elected in 1904 as the next resident commissioner, winning reelection in 1906 and 1908. Like his predecessor, Larrinaga introduced a bill to grant Puerto Ricans U.S. citizenship—again unsuccessfully; he also came out against the Foraker Act, which he believed did not go far enough in granting self-government for the island.

In 1911, Luis Muñoz Rivera, the founder of the Unionist Party and a strong critic of the Foraker Act, became the third resident commissioner. His work in Congress was instrumental in gaining passage of the Jones Act, signed into law by President Woodrow Wilson in 1917, which finally granted U.S. citizenship to Puerto Ricans, separated the insular government into three branches, and created an elective bicameral legislature. Felix Cordova Davila, a Unionist who served from 1917 to 1932, extended a variety of U.S. laws and programs that benefited Puerto Ricans, such as vocational education, construction of rural post roads, and welfare for mothers and children. He also introduced a bill that would have allowed for the election of the Puerto Rican governor by popular vote; the effort proved unsuccessful.

In 1946, President Harry S. Truman appointed Jesús T. Piñero, who had been commissioner for two years, as the first Puerto Rican governor of the island. Piñero named as his replacement a former cardiologist and Popular Democratic Party (PDP) cofounder, Antonio Fernós-Isern, who represented the island for nineteen years (1946–1965) and was the longest-serving resident commissioner. Fernós-Isern played an important role in promoting legislation that gave Puerto Ricans the right to elect their own governor (the so-called Crawford Project, signed into law by President Truman in 1947) and to establish their own constitutional government (Public Law 600, in 1950). Fernós-Isern also served as president of the convention that formulated the constitution of the Puerto Rican Commonwealth in 1952.

In 1968, Jorge Luis Córdova Díaz, a strong supporter of Puerto Rican statehood, became the island's first resident commissioner affiliated with the New Progressive Party (Partido Nuevo Progresista, PNP), which he had helped establish. Since the conclusion of his term in 1973, all Puerto Rican delegates to Congress have been members of either the PDP (supporters of the current Commonwealth status and of U.S. Democrats) or the PNP (advocates of statehood and Republicans in United States). In 1992, Antonio Colorado was appointed resident commissioner to fill the vacancy resulting from the resignation of Jaime Fuster, who was appointed associate justice of the Supreme Court of Puerto Rico. Colorado's bid for election later that year brought the possibility of a resident commissioner and a governor from opposing parties, as Colorado garnered more votes than the PDP gubernatorial candidate, Victoria Muñoz Mendoza, the first woman nominated for that office, but lost to Carlos Romero Barceló, the first former governor elected resident commissioner (1993–2001). It was not until 2004 that Puerto Ricans elected a PNP candidate, Luis Fortuño, as resident commissioner, and a PDP candidate, Aníbal Acevedo Vilá (who had been resident commissioner since 2001), as governor. As of 2008, the resident commissioner remained a non-voting delegate in the House of Representatives.

Roberto Carlos Ortiz

See also: Foraker Act (1900); Muñoz Rivera, Luis; Puerto Ricans.

Further Reading

Córdova, Gonzalo F. *Resident Commissioner, Santiago Iglesias and His Times.* Río Piedras, Puerto Rico: Editorial de la U.P.R., 1993.

Hispanic Americans in Congress. www.loc.gov/rr/hispanic/congress/.

Revolving Door Migration
See Circular Migration

Rodriguez, Alex
(1975–)

While by no means the first Latino/a to succeed in Major League Baseball, Alexander Emmanuel Rodriguez, widely known as "A-Rod," has earned a unique place in baseball history for his exceptional skills, his accomplishments on the diamond, his celebrity status, and his contract signed in 2000—at $252 million over ten years, the richest in the annals of American professional sports. (The contract was renegotiated in December 2007 for $275 million over ten years—still the largest in American sports.)

Born of Dominican parents on July 27, 1975, in New York City, Alex Rodriguez spent his early years in the Big Apple, where his family owned a shoe store in Washington Heights. In 1979, Alex and his family—including his parents, Victor and Lourdes, and his elder siblings, Suzy and Joe—moved back to their native country, where they opened a pharmacy in Santo Domingo. Although the drugstore was initially successful and provided them with a comfortable lifestyle, it soon went out of business. The family returned to the United States in 1983 and settled in Miami, where Alex's mother worked at an immigration office during the day and waited on tables at night; his father headed north to look for work and never came back.

Alex later revealed the emotional effects of losing his father, a situation that also drove him to take responsibility for supporting the family. That ambition coincided with the dream of becoming a professional player like his idols, Keith Hernandez, Dale Murphy, and Cal Ripken, Jr. In 1984, Alex met Juan Diego Arteaga, who coached a youth-league baseball team at Everglades Elementary School in Miami. Arteaga became Alex's mentor and, under his guidance, Rodriguez perfected his skills. In 1990, he

Baseball superstar Alex Rodriguez, born in the Brooklyn Heights section of New York City and raised partly in the Dominican Republic, became the highest-paid athlete in American sports. *(Jim McIsaac/Getty Images)*

with the Mariners in the spring of 1994, at age eighteen becoming one of the youngest players ever to play American professional baseball. In 1996, his first full season with the Mariners, he batted .358 (highest in the American League), with 36 home runs and 123 runs batted in (RBIs), and finished second in voting for the league's Most Valuable Player (MVP) award.

Although the Mariners did not often make it to the playoffs, Rodriguez built his reputation over the next several seasons as one of the best power-hitting shortstops in the history of the game. In 1998, he became only the third player ever to hit 40 home runs and steal 40 bases in a single season. He maintained his high level of performance in 1999 (42 home runs and 111 RBIs) and 2000 (.316, with 42 home runs and 132 RBIs).

Becoming a free agent after the 2000 season, A-Rod was courted by a number of teams before signing his record contract with the Texas Rangers. Despite the pressure that inevitably falls on an extravagantly paid superstar, Rodriguez achieved personal bests in the next two seasons, hitting 52 home runs and collecting 135 RBIs in 2001, followed by 57 home runs and 142 RBIs in 2002. The greatest honor came after the 2003 season, when he was elected as the American League's MVP. Rodriguez's personal feats, however, did not translate into success for his team, which continued to finish low in the standings—to the exasperation of its star player.

Frustration and discontent made Rodriguez realize that money and fame were not everything in sport, and in February 2004 he agreed to be traded to the New York Yankees—a team with a winning tradition.

Although his contract was preserved intact, the move to New York involved a series of important changes for Rodriguez; he moved from shortstop to third base, and changed the number on his jersey from 3 (retired by the Yankees in honor of Babe Ruth) to 13. The sacrifices proved well worth it, as the Yankees reached the 2004 American League Championship Series (ALCS)—in which they fell to the rival Boston Red Sox, four games to three. In 2005, A-Rod's second season with the Yankees, his numbers improved: a .321 batting average, with 48 home

attracted the interest of Westminster Christian High School coach Rich Hofman, who offered him financial aid to attend the private institution and be part of the Warriors, one of Florida's top high-school baseball programs. At Westminster, Rodriguez quickly became a star, playing shortstop and leading his team to the 1992 national championship in his junior season. The following year, Rodriguez confirmed his dominance on the field, leading his team to a number one national ranking by *USA Today.* Then in his senior year, he batted an astonishing .505, with 9 home runs, 36 runs batted in, and 35 stolen bases. He won the USA Baseball Junior Player of the Year award and was named to the U.S. national team for the World Junior Championships in Mexico, where he batted .425.

Rodriguez's remarkable statistical record caught the attention of professional scouts, and in 1993 he was picked first in the Major League amateur draft and signed to a three-year, $1.3 million contract by the Seattle Mariners. Rodriguez made his debut runs and 130 RBIs. He also set several marks for power: a new team record for home runs by a right-handed hitter in a season, a personal record for a minimum of 100 runs scored for the tenth straight year, and a tie for the most homers in one season by a third baseman. Although the Yankees lost the Division Series against the Anaheim Angels, these numbers earned Rodriguez his second American League MVP Award and his nomination to the Major League Baseball Latino Legends Team.

Although A-Rod's statistics for 2006 were embarrassing by no one else's standards (.290 batting average, 35 home runs, 121 RBIs), some New York Yankee fans expressed disapproval at his disappointing results in post-season play and perceived failures in "clutch" situations. As he continued to pursue his first World Series championship, he added to his growing record of personal accomplishments. By the time his career is over, according to many baseball experts, he was expected to be the holder of the game's most cherished records.

Ever controversial, Rodriguez disappointed fans when it was revealed in February 2009 that he had tested positive for performance-enhancing drugs in 2003. A-Rod confessed publicly and apologized for having taken substances he could not name for three years, covering the 2001–2003 seasons. Some baseball fans immediately counted Rodriguez among the game's stars whose past performance and future records would be permanently tarnished.

Despite his enormous success and celebrity, Alex Rodriguez has never forgotten the mean streets he walked in his youth. In 1996, he founded a program called Grand Slam for Kids to encourage youngsters to read, practice sports, and be good citizens. Two years later, he established the Alex Rodriguez Foundation, a charitable organization that works closely with the Boys and Girls Clubs of Miami, and built a $1 million education center in that city. In October 2002, Rodriguez donated $3.9 million to the University of Miami to fund an annual scholarship and to renovate the university's baseball stadium, which was renamed Mark Light Field at Alex Rodriguez Park.

Jorge Abril Sánchez

See also: Baseball.

Further Reading

Stewart, Mark. *Alex Rodriguez: Gunning for Greatness.* Brookfield, CT: Millbrook, 1999.

Stout, Glenn, and Matt Christopher. *On the Field with . . . Alex Rodriguez.* Boston: Little, Brown, 2002.

Wendel, Tim. *The New Face of Baseball: The One-Hundred Year Rise and Triumph of Latinos in America's Favorite Sport.* New York: HarperCollins, 2004.

Rodríguez, Luis J. (1954–)

The Chicano poet, novelist, public speaker, journalist, and critic Luis J. Rodríguez has written compellingly of his youth in East Los Angeles and the ordeals and injustices of the Latino experience in novels, children's books, fictionalized memoirs, and what he has called "poetry with a sense of social engagement."

Born in El Paso, Texas, on July 9, 1954, Rodríguez grew up in the Watts section of East Los Angeles. At the age of eleven, he became involved in local street gangs, and by his eighteenth birthday he had lost over twenty-five friends to violence. Rodríguez realized the need to change his life, and with the help of mentors who saw potential in him—teachers, a home school coordinator, and a community organizer—he was able to find an outlet. Since childhood, he had often taken refuge in reading and his interior life. In his teens, public murals in the neighborhood sparked his creativity, and he began writing vignettes and poetry about his experiences on the streets. After winning honorable mention in a Berkeley writing contest, with a prize of $250, he began to dedicate more time to his writing all the while holding down blue-collar day jobs and starting a family. By 1980, he was working full-time as a journalist and photographer for Los Angeles newspapers, while crafting his own literary works on the side.

Rodríguez's writings have focused on youth, prisons and prisoners, juvenile offenders, the homeless, labor, musicians, artists, communities, gang violence, families, and friends. His published works include *Poems Across the Pavement* (1989); *Trochemoche: Poems* (1989); *America Is Her Name* (1998), a children's book; *It Doesn't Have to Be This Way: A Barrio Story*

(1999); *The Republic of East L.A: Stories* (2002); *My Nature Is Hunger* (2005), another poetry collection; and *Music of the Mill* (2005), a novel about a second-generation mill worker named Johnny who battles oppression, other workers, unions, and corporate bosses.

His book *Heart and Hands: Creating Community in Violent Times* (2001) is a call to parents, children, and communities to discuss the brutality of young people in society today, from the Columbine killings to gang violence. Mixing his own history of violence with stories of others, he calls on society to find a way to give youth a vision for a better future and to engage them in the arts, science, religion, political, and cultural awareness. Also, examining working class and poverty issues that often lead to violence, Rodríguez asks readers to consider what their goals and aims are for the world they live in and whether they want to accept violence or change it.

His best-known work, *Always Running, La Vida Loca: Gang Days in L.A.* (1993), is an autobiographical novel, which won the prestigious Carl Sandburg Literature Award and is one of the most censored books in high schools libraries across America. Written for his fifteen-year-old son, who had joined a gang in Chicago, the novel recounts his own experiences on the streets of Los Angeles—the violence, family struggles, poverty, and other factors that contributed to his own choices and the persistent violence in the Latino community.

Although not as well known, his most significant work of poetry is a collection titled *The Concrete River* (1991), which contains a range of pieces that document his childhood, his life's struggles, and his experiences as a community leader. The collection is emblematic of what he has described as "barrio poetry." Intermingled with the English-language verse are Spanish words that evoke a sense of pride in his community and his people. In such poems as "Watts Bleed," "Death Watch," "Running to America," and "First Day of Work," he addresses the community of individuals everywhere who struggle with everyday issues ranging from hunger, injustice, imprisonment, absent parents, and segregation, or who face the universal struggles of being a husband and father, succeeding when others are trying to bring one down, reconciling with one's past, settling in a new culture, and reimagining one's place in the community at large.

As of 2006, Rodríguez has published eight books, including works of short fiction, nonfiction, poetry, and two children's stories. His many prizes and honors include a Paterson Poetry Prize, Skipping Stones Honor Award, Parent's Choice Book Award, the 1989 Poetry Center National Book Award of San Francisco, the Pen Josephine Miles Literary Award, *Foreword* Magazine's Silver Book Award, an Unsung Heroes of Compassion Award, awarded personally by His Holiness the Dalai Lama, and a 2006–2007 City of Los Angeles Individual Artist Fellowship. As a critic, Rodríguez has written for *The Nation, The Los Angeles Weekly, America's Review, The Chicago Reporter, Hispanic Link,* and *The Progressive.* His poetry is widely anthologized and has been performed at the Firehouse Theater and Club Lower Links in Chicago.

Rosa E. Soto

See also: Chicano/a; East Los Angeles; Gangs.

Further Reading

Rodríguez, Luis J. *Always Running: La Vida Loca, Gang Days in L.A.* New York: Simon and Schuster, 2005.

————. *The Concrete River.* Willimantic, CT: Curbstone, 1991.

————. *Heart and Souls: Creating Community in Violent Times.* New York: Seven Stories, 2001.

Schwartz, Michael. *Luis J. Rodríguez.* Contemporary Hispanic American Series. Austin, TX: Steck-Vaughn, 1998.

Rodriguez, Richard
(1944–)

Idolized by adherents and harshly censured by critics, the essayist and cultural critic Richard Rodriguez has cemented a reputation as one of the most controversial of contemporary Chicano writers. He is best known for his memoir *Hunger of Memory: The Education of Richard Rodriguez* (1981) and his award-winning commentaries on the Public Broadcasting Service (PBS). An opponent of affirmative action and bilingual education, he has openly embraced cultural assimilation, emerging as a spokesman for mainstream American culture.

Born of working-class Mexican immigrants on July 31, 1944, in San Francisco, he moved, as a preschool child with his parents and three siblings to Sacramento, California. In the state capital, Rodriguez entered first grade at Sacred Heart School, a Roman Catholic institution run by Irish nuns. His limited command of English restricted his ability to communicate at school, where he often kept silent and listened to his classmates interact with teachers. Growing weary of the solitude imposed by his parents' language, Rodriguez resolved to give up Spanish and pursue his dreams of getting a full education. His timidity vanished, and Richard became an exemplary student, eventually earning a bachelor's degree in English at Stanford University (1967), a master's degree in philosophy at Columbia University (1969), and a PhD in English renaissance literature at the University of California, Berkeley (1975).

Although he had achieved academic success and had satisfied his hunger for integration through education, Rodriguez still felt a sense of insecurity about his identity. Entering the job market in 1976, he found himself besieged with doubt as to whether the many tenure-track lecturing positions he had been offered were the result of his long years of effort or simply the universities' desire to fill their quotas for faculty of color. Rather than accept any of these offers, Rodriguez resolved to go his own way. He abandoned academia, and supported himself through freelance writing and various temporary jobs. Since then, he has traveled around the world working as an essayist, broadcast journalist, lecturer, and editor and writer for such prestigious periodicals as *The New York Times, The Wall Street Journal,* and *The New Republic.* Rodriguez has also written a trilogy of memoirs in which he tries to come to terms with the process and consequences of his Americanization. In addition to *Hunger of Memory,* the trilogy comprises *Days of Obligation: An Argument with My Mexican Father* (1992) and *Brown: The Last Discovery of America* (2002).

Hunger of Memory is a lengthy account of what he regards as a personal rite of passage—the journey from disadvantaged minority to fully assimilated scholarship student. In it he describes the suffering of his early schooling, in which he felt obliged to reject his family's Spanish culture and language for the sake of social acceptance, cultural assimilation, and academic success. Rodriguez's narrative earned the praise of conservative readers and critics, who held him up as a student of color who benefited from affirmative action but who, in the end, rejected such programs as unfair. At the same time, therefore, it earned him the repudiation of some Mexican Americans, who called him *"pocho"*—a person who repudiates his heritage and betrays his people.

To explain his views on these controversial issues, Rodriguez published *Days of Obligation: An Argument with My Mexican Father,* a diverse collection of essays in which he goes back to the Río Grande of the nineteenth century in a kind of dialogue with his Hispanic heritage and ethnicity. The narrative describes the poverty and decay that led many Mexicans to head north in search of a better life and explores the California territory as it evolved. *Days of Obligation* was nominated for a Pulitzer Prize.

Rodriguez ends his trilogy with an examination of racial categories in the United States, in *Brown: The Last Discovery of America.* In this work, he analyzes the fictive notions of "Hispanic" and "Latino," and describes "the browning of America"—the mixing of multiple cultures and ethnicities in contemporary society, the increase in cultural diversity, and the response of the diminishing white majority.

Rodriguez has appeared frequently as a commentator on the PBS programs *MacNeil/Lehrer News Hour* and *The News Hour with Jim Lehrer.* He is also an editor of *Harper's* magazine, *U.S. News & World Report,* and the Sunday "Opinion" section of the *Los Angeles Times.* His many honors include a George Foster Peabody Award (for outstanding achievement in broadcast and cable television) in 1997 for his work on *News Hour,* the Frankel Medal from the National Endowment for the Humanities in 1993, and the International Journalism Award from the World Affairs Council of California.

Jorge Abril Sánchez

See also: Acculturation and Assimilation; Chicano/a; Identity and Labels.

Further Reading

Bloom, Harold. *Hispanic-American Writers.* Philadelphia: Chelsea House, 1998.

Couser, G. Thomas. *Altered Egos: Authority in American Autobiography.* New York: Oxford University Press, 1989.

Guajardo, Paul. *Chicano Controversy: Oscar Acosta and Richard Rodriguez.* New York: Peter Lang, 2002.

Rodríguez de Tió, Lola (1843–1924)

The Puerto Rican nationalist and poet Lola Rodríguez de Tió is a celebrated figure in both Cuban and Puerto Rican history. An ardent feminist, she also believed in the abolition of slavery and was committed to the independence of Puerto Rico. She was the first Puerto Rican woman to publish a book of poems, producing three collections—*Mis Cantares* (1876), *Claros y Nieblas* (1885), and *Mi Libro de Cuba* (1893)—all of which were characterized by strong patriotic themes. She was also known for her eulogies to several Latin American notables, including the Cuban poet José Martí, the Chilean poet Gabriela Mistral, and the Puerto Rican poet José Gautier Benítez.

Born on September 14, 1843, in San Germán, Puerto Rico, into the island's ruling class, Rodríguez de Tió was the daughter of Don Sebastian Rodríguez de Astudillo, dean of the Magistracy of Puerto Rico, and Doña Carmen Ponce de León, a descendant of the explorer Ponce de León. Her mother, who encouraged her love of literature, facilitated her education through religious schools and by private tutors. Rodríguez de Tió showed promise as a poet from a young age.

Rodríguez de Tió moved with her family to Mayagüez, Puerto Rico, where she met the young journalist Bonocio Tió Segarra; the couple was married in 1863. Tió Segarra wrote and spoke out against the oppression of the Spanish colonial regime, and the couple's home became a salon where Puerto Rico's leading intellectuals, including the patriot Eugenio María de Hostos, discussed politics and called for revolution. It was during this period that Rodríguez de Tió published her first book of verse, *Mis Cantares,* which sold 2,500 copies. In addition, she wrote revolutionary lyrics to the melody *La Borinqueña,* which stated in part, "Awake from your sleep, for it's time to fight!" For encouraging revolutionary activ-

ity, the couple was exiled in 1877 and fled to Caracas, Venezuela, where they remained until 1885.

Upon their return to Puerto Rico, the couple became active in the independence movement, which fought for full island sovereignty. Rodríguez de Tió joined fellow patriots in their meetings to discuss politics and the possibility of independence from Spain. Fearing an insurrection, the Spanish governor, General Romualdo Palacios, had many of the participants of these meetings arrested, including abolitionist and Liberal Party member Ramón Baldorioty de Castro. Rodríguez de Tió committed herself to freeing these political prisoners and, through a letter-writing campaign to the Spanish authorities, managed to secure the freedom of several colleagues. Her 1887 poem "Nochebuena" was a tribute to political prisoners; she was exiled to Cuba two years later.

Rodríguez de Tió's home in Cuba became a gathering place for intellectuals, politicians, and other Puerto Rican exiles. After writing *Mi Libro de Cuba* and continuing her revolutionary activities, Rodríguez de Tió was deported from Havana as well in 1892. She and her husband relocated to New York, where they joined in the overseas campaign for Cuban independence, creating the Cuban Revolutionary Party in 1895.

Rodríguez de Tió finally was able to return to Cuba in 1899, where she fought for the social conditions of women, but visited Puerto Rico only a few times during the next twenty-five years. In 1910, she helped found the Cuban Academy of Arts and Letters and the following year formed the Galician Beneficent Society. She died in Havana on November 10, 1924. To some, Lola Rodríguez de Tió is remembered as the person who proposed that the Puerto Rican flag follow the design of the Cuban flag, only with the colors reversed—a kinship that reflects her own dual nationalism.

José Anazagasty-Rodríguez and Gina Misiroglu

See also: Cubans; Feminism; Nationalism; Puerto Ricans.

Further Reading

Babin, Maria Teresa, and Stan Steiner. *Borinquen: An Anthology of Puerto Rican Literature.* New York: Vintage Books, 1974.

Marques, Rene. *The Docile Puerto Rican.* Philadelphia: Temple University Press, 1976.

Roybal, Edward R.
(1916–2005)

The community activist and Democratic politician Edward Roybal spent his life representing and defending Latinos/as, other people of color, and the poor. His election to the U.S. House of Representatives in 1962 made him the first Latino from California to serve in Congress since Romualdo Pacheco (1877–1878, 1879–1833). Roybal's commitment to social change and his service in government made him an historic figure in Latino politics and culture.

Edward Ross Roybal was born on February 10, 1916, in Albuquerque, New Mexico. At the age of six, after his father lost his job in a railroad strike, Roybal and his family moved to Boyle Heights, a racially diverse and ideologically left-leaning neighborhood in East Los Angeles. Following his graduation from Roosevelt High School in 1934, he joined the Civilian Conservation Corps, a public works organization created as part of Franklin D. Roosevelt's New Deal. He attended the University of California at Los Angeles, where he studied business administration, and later Southwestern University in Los Angeles, where he studied law. After serving in the U.S. Army (1944–1945) during World War II, he became director of health education for the Los Angeles County Tuberculosis and Health Association, an organization dedicated to thwarting the epidemic of tuberculosis within the Mexican American community.

After an unsuccessful bid for the Los Angeles City Council in 1947, Roybal helped create the Community Service Organization (CSO), a Los Angeles group set up to fight discrimination against Mexicans in housing, employment, and education. Under the leadership of Roybal and community organizer Fred Ross, the CSO conducted voter registration and get-out-the-vote campaigns that would help propel Roybal's political career in Los Angeles. In 1949, he was elected to the Los Angeles City Council, a position he held until 1962 (including president pro tempore in his last term). Among the issues for which he became known was the "Battle of Chavez Ravine" during the 1950s, in which he opposed development plans that would remove Mexican Americans residents from their community to make room for a new baseball stadium.

In 1963, running as a liberal Democrat, Roybal was elected to the U.S. Congress representing California's twenty-fifth district (including East Los Angeles, his childhood home of Boyle Heights, and parts of Hollywood). Serving fifteen terms and nearly thirty years, Roybal became a prominent voice for the Latino community, other minorities, the elderly, and the disabled. In 1967, he introduced the first bilingual education bill, a measure that would provide funding and federal support for local schools that offered bilingual education programs. In 1968, he helped to create a cabinet committee on Opportunities for Spanish-Speaking People. In 1976, driven by

A prominent voice for Latinos/as in twentieth-century politics, Democrat Edward R. Roybal served thirteen years on the Los Angeles City Council (1949–1962) and fifteen terms in the U.S. Congress (1963–1993). *(Library of Congress)*

his commitment to political empowerment and communal representation for the Latino community, Roybal became a founding member of the Congressional Hispanic Caucus. During his tenure, he pushed legislation that outlawed age discrimination, required bilingual court proceedings, offered equal protection and benefits to the physically challenged, and supported funding for AIDS research.

Roybal declined to run for reelection in 1992 and was succeeded in office (for a redrawn district) by his daughter, Lucille Roybal-Allard. Retired to Pasadena, Edward Roybal died at age eighty-nine on October 24, 2005.

David J. Leonard and Carmen R. Lugo-Lugo

See also: Community Service Organization; Congressional Hispanic Caucus; Mexican American Political Association; Politics; Viva Kennedy Clubs.

Further Reading

Burt, Kenneth C. "The Power of a Mobilized Citizenry and Coalition Politics: The 1949 Election of Edward R. Roybal to the Los Angeles City Council." *Southern California Quarterly* 85 (Winter 2003).

Diaz, Katherine A. "Congressman Edward Roybal: Los Angeles Before the 1960s." *Caminos* 4:7 (July–August, 1983): 15–17, 38.

Escobar, Edward J. *Race, Police, and the Making of a Political Identity: Mexican Americans and the Los Angeles Police Department, 1900–1945.* Berkeley: University of California Press, 1999.

Lazarus, William. *Edward R. Roybal, Democratic Representative from California.* Citizens Look at Congress/Ralph Nader Congress Project. New York: Grossman, 1972.

Ruiz de Burton, María Amparo
(1832–1895)

María Amparo Ruiz de Burton has been identified as the first Mexican American writer to publish novels in English, writing about the Mexican-American War, U.S. racial politics, and the unfilled promise of American democracy. She spent her adult life fighting to keep her land, lobbying the U.S. Congress for Californio (Spanish-Speaking residents of California) rights, and writing novels that criticized the injustices experienced by Mexicans living in the United States.

Born on July 3, 1832, in La Paz, Baja California, María Amparo Ruiz de Burton was the daughter of Isabel Ruiz Maitorena and Jesús Maitorena. As part of an influential family—her grandfather served as governor of Baja California from 1822 to 1825, and both her grandfather and great-uncle received large land grants as a result of military service—she was a member of a segment of society that benefited from its willingness to help to colonize northern Mexico. Additionally, because of her family's class status, Ruiz de Burton had access to the best education available in Baja California; her parents hired a tutor from Spain during her early life. At the age of fifteen, she moved with her family to Monterey in Alta California, where she attended a local school and studied English.

In 1849, a year after the end of the Mexican-American War, she married Henry S. Burton, a captain in the U.S. Army. Burton's military career required him to travel extensively, and Ruiz de Burton joined him, first in San Diego and then in Washington, D.C. It was in the American capital that she socialized with the Anglo elite, including Mary Todd Lincoln. Moving among the leading politicians of her time, she met many men whom she would later lobby for Californio rights. She also witnessed a significant amount of government corruption, a topic she would write about in her 1885 novel, *The Squatter and the Don.*

Following the death of her husband in 1869, Ruiz de Burton returned to San Diego to oversee their ranch. Like other Californio women, however, she had lost many of her rights as a result of the U.S. war with Mexico and the resulting Treaty of Guadalupe Hidalgo (1848). As a female Mexican citizen, she previously had the right to control her own property, to litigate, and to retain ownership of any property she brought into a marriage. Under U.S. law, however, she was not entitled to any of these rights. Going to court to secure the right to manage her own property was the first, and one of the few, legal battles that Ruiz de Burton would win on U.S. soil.

In 1851, the U.S. Congress had passed the Land Act, which allowed Anglo settlers to set up homes ("squat") on land owned by Californios while they challenged the title, or legal ownership of the property, in court. Californios, for their part, had to go to court and prove that they owned their land. While most Californios were able to prove ownership of title, many eventually lost property to squatters because of legal fees. Because most landholding Californios did not have large savings but were part of a land-based economy, many were forced to sell portions of their land to pay their lawyers; indeed some of the lawyers charged exorbitant fees or took tracts of land as payment for services they did not deliver. María Amparo Ruiz de Burton faced a similar experience. In 1876, she won title to Rancho Jamul, the property she owned in Southern California, but by that time most of the land itself had been lost to squatters. Her situation was similar to that of many Californios in the late nineteenth century. Because the U.S. government encouraged squatters to settle on Californio land, many refused to leave even after the owners cleared their title. Only those families with the resources to force armed squatters from their property and to pay them for "improvements" they had made on the property, were able to reclaim their land.

Ruiz de Burton's struggle to keep her property demonstrated the resistance that landed Californians engaged in following the U.S. invasion. Her most important legacy, however, rests with her novels, *Who Would Have Thought It* (1872) and *The Squatter and the Don*, which expose the racism of the U.S. government and many of its citizens in the treatment of Mexican Americans. With insight as much as criticism, the two novels do not depict Anglos in broad, indiscriminate strokes; both include Euro-American characters who are allies to the Californios and themselves victims of government greed and corruption.

The *Squatter and the Don,* the work which Ruiz de Burton is best known for, is subtitled *A Novel Descriptive of Contemporary Occurrences in California.* Set in California after the Mexican-American War, it follows the fate of the Alamar family as they lose their land to squatters. In the novel, the Alamars fight to prove their title and attempt to reason with the squatters who are settling on their land. In the end, they lose because of the corruption of government officials who are more interested in their own profit than the rights of either the Californios or the squatters. Published in 1885, the novel is also a critique of monopoly capitalism and the collusion of the government and the railroads in the development and exploitation of the American Southwest.

Ruiz de Burton died in 1895, yet more than a century later her work continues to be read by students of Chicano and California history. Although she was not able to stop the displacement of Californios, she challenged Euro-American views of the invasion with an insight and power that have endured to the present day. Her work is regarded as a precursor to the Chicano resistance literature that emerged and flourished in the 1970s and 1980s.

Linda Heidenreich

See also: Mexican-American War.

Further Reading

Haas, Lisbeth. *Conquests and Historical Identities in California, 1769–1936.* Berkeley: University of California Press, 1995.

Ruiz de Burton, María Amparo. *The Squatter and the Don.* 1885. Houston, TX: Arte Público, 1997.

Sánchez, Rosaura, and Beatrice Pita. "María Amparo Ruiz de Burton and the Power of Her Pen." In *Latina Legacies: Identity, Biography, and Community,* ed. Vicki L. Ruíz and Virginia E. Sánchez Korrol. New York: Oxford University Press, 2005.

S

Salazar, Rubén
(1928–1970)

Chronicles of Los Angeles Chicano history would be incomplete without citing the events surrounding the death of journalist Rubén Salazar in August 1970. Known for exposing the unfair treatment of minorities by police officers in Los Angeles, Salazar was killed by a deputy sheriff during a National Chicano Moratorium March against the Vietnam War in East LA.

The tragic killing of the controversial and popular journalist made him a martyr of the Chicano Movement of the late 1960s and early 1970s, which sought Mexican American empowerment by countering discrimination in the public school system and negative ethnic stereotypes in the media. Salazar was the first Mexican-American journalist to work for the *El Paso Herald-Post,* the first Mexican-American journalist to have a column in a major English-language newspaper, the *Los Angeles Times,* and one of the first Latino journalists to cross into mainstream English-language journalism.

Salazar was born on March 3, 1928, in Ciudad Juárez, Chihuahua, Mexico. Less than a year after his birth, his parents, Luz and Salvador Salazar, moved the family across the border to El Paso, Texas, where they enjoyed a middle-class lifestyle through the elder Salazar's employment at a jewelry store. Rubén Salazar became a naturalized citizen and graduated from El Paso High School. After two years in the U.S. Army (1950–1952), he enrolled at Texas Western College (now the University of Texas at El Paso), where he majored in journalism and wrote a few pieces for *El Burro,* the campus paper.

After graduating from Texas Western with a bachelor's degree in journalism in 1954, he worked as a reporter for the *El Paso Herald-Post.* He soon became known for his sensational, first-person accounts of dangerous situations and sensitive issues, such as the treatment of Mexican Americans in Texas prisons. An avid journalist and in-depth investigator, Salazar explored jail conditions in El Paso, going so far as getting arrested on a phony drunkenness charge to get inside. He also witnessed and wrote about heroin addicts buying from dealers and shooting up.

From 1956 to 1958, Salazar worked for two Northern California newspapers, *The Santa Rosa Press Democrat* and then the *San Francisco News.* After relocating to Southern California and a brief stint at the *Los Angeles Herald-Express,* he accepted a job as city reporter for the *Los Angeles Times* in 1959. For the *Times,* he covered the Mexican American community and issues related to the U.S.–Mexico border, including the Bracero Program, which since World War II had brought thousands of Mexican contract laborers over the border to work in California agricultural fields. During the summer of 1963, Salazar reported on Mexican American leaders in Los Angeles who openly criticized the Kennedy administration for failing to address the lack of jobs, educational opportunities, and upward mobility in the Mexican American community. He also reported on the growing tension between Mexican Americans and African Americans over the division of federal allotments and competition for jobs and educational opportunities.

In April 1965, Salazar was sent to the Dominican Republic to cover the U.S. invasion and peacekeeping effort after a military coup and outbreak of civil war. Later that year, the *Times* sent him to Vietnam to report on the escalation of American military intervention in that country. In 1966, he was named the paper's bureau chief in Mexico City, where he covered events throughout Central America and the Caribbean, including Cuba. Two years later, while reporting on the election of Arnulfo Arias as president of Panama, he was captured and briefly held by rebel forces who accused him of being a Central Intelligence Agency (CIA) agent and a puppet of the U.S. State Department.

Salazar returned to Los Angeles in late 1968 to cover the growing tension in the city's Chicano communities, including the climax of the Chicano Movement and the activities of the Brown Berets, a Chicano youth organization that protested the cultural and racial discrimination they experienced in school, at the hands of police, and in the court system.

In 1969, he was hired as news director by KMEX-TV, a growing Los Angeles Spanish-language television station, while he continued to write a weekly column for the *Times* that served as a kind of mouthpiece for the East LA Chicano community. "Instead of writing blank descriptions of Mexican-American family life," *Newsweek* said of him in 1970, "Salazar regularly turns in hard-hitting weekly columns attacking 'Anglo' racism and voicing serious Mexican-American grievances." Criticizing the Los Angeles Police Department (LAPD) for targeting Mexican Americans, Salazar became the object of investigations by the LAPD and Federal Bureau of Investigation (FBI). Pressure was put on him to tone down his rhetoric.

Salazar's death came on August 29, 1970, while on assignment at a Chicano Moratorium protest against the disproportionate number of Chicanos being killed in Vietnam. As the demonstration became more violent, Salazar and two coworkers from KMEX sought refuge in the Silver Dollar bar on Whittier Avenue. Police officers, who claimed there had been an armed individual in the establishment, shot a tear-gas projectile into the bar that struck Salazar in the head; a second shot filled the bar with gas. The coroner's report ruled the shooting a homicide. State legislators urged an investigation, but none was undertaken. Members of the Chicano community concluded that the police had targeted Salazar as an "accidental" victim in revenge for his written attacks on police integrity.

In the aftermath of his death, a succession of tributes and commemorations ensured that Salazar's contributions to the Chicano community would not be forgotten. In 1971, he was awarded a special Robert F. Kennedy Journalism Award. The site of the 1970 protest rally, Laguna Park, was later renamed

Los Angeles journalist Rubén Salazar, a martyr of the Chicano Movement after his death at the hands of county law enforcement while reporting on an anti–Vietnam War protest in 1970, was honored with a U.S. commemorative postage stamp in 2007. *(AP Images/USPS)*

Salazar Park. And in 2007, Salazar was one of five journalists honored with a U.S. postage stamp for covering turbulent events of the twentieth century.

Glenda M. Flores and Gina Misiroglu

See also: Los Angeles; National Chicano Moratorium.

Further Reading

Chicano! The History of the Mexican American Civil Rights Movement. Dir. Galán Productions and NLCC. Video. NLCC Educational Media, 1996.

Del Olmo, Frank. "Rubén Salazar, Misunderstood Martyr." *Media Studies Journal* 11:2 (Spring 1997): 58–67.

Salazar, Rubén. *Border Correspondent: Selected Writings.* Ed. M. García. Berkeley: University of California Press, 1995.

Salvadorans

In what historians have called the greatest "refugee crisis of the Western Hemisphere," the influx of Salvadorans into the United States since the early 1980s has transformed the Latino community and American culture at large. The majority of Salvadorans—up to 1 million men, women, and children—arrived during the civil war between 1979 and 1993. Until about 1960, the Salvadoran American population had been extremely small, numbering no more than about 10,000 residents. By the turn of the twenty-first century, according to the U.S. Census, 802,743 Salvadorans were living in the United States.

Leftist rebels took up arms in 1979 against the Salvadoran government, whose economic policies and ties to the United States they believed had failed the people of El Salvador. Supported by the United States with money, weapons, and training, the Salvadoran government clashed violently with rebels for more than a decade, resulting in the deaths of an estimated 75,000 people and the displacement of thousands more. As a result of the rampant poverty and political chaos, between 20 and 30 percent of the citizenry left the country, with about half—between 500,000 and 1 million—immigrating to the United States. Because of the close U.S. relations with El Salvador's ruling military government, Washington initially denied political asylum to Salvadoran refugees, who were relegated to undocumented or illegal status.

The dramatic upsurge in the Salvadoran immigrant population, especially given the persistent flow of immigrants from Mexico and other parts of Latin America, not only resulted in significant changes to the Salvadoran community in the United States, but also led to a shift in U.S. foreign policy. Some historians have argued that the Salvadoran refugee crisis—along with the end of the Cold War—forced the U.S. government to reevaluate its role in Central America, as well as its overall policy on refugees, ultimately contributing to decreased levels of support for the Salvadoran regime. This, in turn, led to the peace accord of 1993.

Although most Salvadoran refugees had lived in rural communities, they became widely dispersed in the United States and settled heavily in such metropolitan centers as Los Angeles, San Francisco, and Santa Ana in California; New York City and Long Island in New York; and Chicago, Washington D.C., Boston, and Houston and Dallas, Texas. By the 1990s, Salvadoran communities had sprouted in such other urban centers as Atlanta, Las Vegas, and Greensboro and Raleigh, North Carolina.

On May 20, 1999, U.S. Immigration and Naturalization Service (INS) eased the rules for allowing illegal immigrants, specifically those who had fled Central America and Eastern Europe during the Cold War, to apply for permanent residence. And in 2001, following two devastating earthquakes in El Salvador, the George W. Bush administration announced that Salvadorans awaiting deportation would be granted an eighteen-month reprieve, meaning that they could continue to live and work in the United States regardless of their status as residents.

The dramatic increase in the Salvadoran American population led to significant changes in the existing community. In cities across the country, its influence can be seen in the wider availability of Salvadoran food (such as *pupusa, salpico,* or *chicha*) and the presence of street food vendors selling pupusas and mango slices in Salvadoran neighborhoods. Likewise, in many communities, Salvadoran organizations have emerged that are dedicated to cultural events, such as parades, feasts celebrating the patron saint, and festivals. While their small numbers and short history in the United States have resulted in relatively limited political and civic influence, Salvadoran Americans have contributed significantly to political decisions and debates regarding immigration, particularly legislation concerning refugees.

At the local level, Salvadoran leaders have played an important role in mediating racial and ethnic tensions, mostly based on struggles for resources and jobs, with Mexicans in Los Angeles and with African Americans in Washington, D.C. Indeed, the increased levels of violence that have occurred in El Salvador since the end of the civil war also have taken root in the Salvadoran American community. Perhaps the most notorious of the Salvadoran gangs are the Maras, whose membership has spread elsewhere in Central America and the United States as well. When Salvadoran youth in Los Angeles were denied membership in Mexican gangs, they created their own gang, Mara Salvatrucha, also known as MS-13.

Reflecting the circumstances of their departure from the homeland and their nonasylum status upon arrival, Salvadoran immigrants were funneled into various low-income service-sector jobs, rather than the agricultural work done by many Mexican American migrants. A majority of Salvadoran American men were employed in hotels, restaurants, and as day laborers; women took work as maids, nannies, and janitors. In addition to contributing to the American economy by servicing corporations, the business elite, and the entrepreneur class, Salvadoran immigrant workers have played an instrumental part in union battles for fair wages and conditions—for instance, the Los Angeles janitors' strike of April 2000.

Language barriers, combined with discrimination in jobs and housing, limited educational opportunities, and restrictions on social services have made poverty a vicious cycle among Salvadoran Americans. Community organizations and churches have provided assistance and support as they can.

The circumstances of leaving El Salvador and of life in the United States have led to a significant gender imbalance in the Salvadoran American community; a vast majority of the immigrants are men. Given that, as concluded by a 1990 *Los Angeles Times* poll, 70 percent of Salvadoran Americans plan to stay in the United States, an inordinate number of Salvadoran children who remain in the homeland not only face a life of poverty, but one without a father. Many Salvadorans living and working in the United States send money and commodities (such as televisions) back to their country. Researchers estimate that Salvadoran Americans send approximately $800 million each year to friends and family back home, which amounts to about $1,000 per person. Thus, an estimated 15 percent of the Salvadoran national economy derives from remittances by Salvadorans living in the United States. In 2001, therefore, the nation converted its official currency to the United States dollar.

Rachel Sandoval and David J. Leonard

Further Reading

Mahler, Sarah J. *Salvadorans in Suburbia: Symbiosis and Conflict.* Boston: Allyn and Bacon, 1995.

Montes, Segundo, Juan Jose, and García Vásquez. *Salvadoran Migration to the United States: An Exploratory Study.* Washington, DC: Center for Immigration Policy and Refugee Assistance, Georgetown University, 1988.

Suárez-Orozco, Marcelo M. *Central American Refugees and U.S. High Schools.* Palo Alto, CA: Stanford University Press, 1989.

Salvadoran refugees seek shelter at Casa Romero, a religious sanctuary near Brownsville, Texas, in 1989. Up to 1 million Salvadorans fled to the United States during the civil war of 1979–1993. *(Shelly Katz/Time & Life Pictures/ Getty Images)*

Samora, Julian
(1920–1996)

Long before there was an academic discipline called Chicano Studies, there was a handful of pioneering scholars whose work focused on the social problems associated with the Mexican American community. Among them was Julian Samora. Recognizing the important role social-science research plays in changing public policy and the conditions that affect the disadvantaged, Samora dedicated his career to cultivating a generation of social scientists who would help Mexican Americans overcome socioeconomic barriers. Rather than focusing on abstract theory, Samora's work always had a practical dimension with clear policy implications.

Samora was born in Pagosa Springs, Colorado, on March 2, 1920. His early life was marked by repeated experiences of racial discrimination. He was forced to repeat first grade because of his lack of command of the English language; in high school he ran for student-body president but lost by one vote because he was a Mexican. During his college years, Julian lost his mother to breast cancer and found himself alone at age nineteen.

In 1942, Julian started a family of his own, marrying Betty Archuleta, with whom he would raise five children. After completing his bachelor's degree at Adams State Teacher's College in Alamosa, Colorado that same year, Julian went on to earn his master's degree in sociology at Colorado State University in 1947. In 1953, he became the first Mexican American to earn a PhD in sociology and anthropology at Washington University in St. Louis.

His first academic appointment was at the University of Colorado School of Medicine in 1955. As an assistant professor of Preventive Medicine and Public Health, Samora was instrumental in developing the field of medical anthropology, the study of health, disease, and illness from an anthropological perspective—that is, with an awareness of the biological, cultural, linguistic, and historical similarities and differences among populations. His early studies of folk medicine and the role of ethnicity in sickness and health broke new ground.

Following his conviction to help others who were less fortunate, Samora embarked on a mission to deliver medical services for—and specifically tailored to—Mexican Americans in Colorado. Through his research and teaching, he developed a model for doctors to improve treatment by taking into account their patients' cultural background. From 1957 to 1958, he held an appointment at Michigan State University, where he taught sociology and anthropology. By 1959, he accepted a tenured position at the University of Notre Dame, where he went on to serve as head of the Department of Sociology and Anthropology from 1963 to 1966, founder and director of the Mexican American Graduate Studies program from 1972 to 1985, and director of Graduate Studies from 1981 to 1984.

It was at Notre Dame that Samora became a scholar of national prominence. Among his many accomplishments there was the establishment of the Mexican American Graduate Studies program. From 1972 through his retirement in 1985, he mentored and trained more than fifty students who earned advanced degrees in sociology, economics, law, political science, psychology, and history.

Samora wrote or edited six books in Chicano Studies, as well as countless research articles and public policy reports. Among his most notable books is *Los Mojados: The Wetback Story* (1971), one of the first to chronicle the undocumented immigration of Mexicans in the United States. Among his other accomplishments was being a cofounder of the Southwest (now National) Council of La Raza, the largest national Latino civil rights and advocacy organization in the United States. He was also a founding member in 1968, of the Mexican American Legal Defense and Education Fund (MALDEF), the leading non-profit Latino litigation, advocacy, and educational outreach institution in the United States. MALDEF's goal is to cultivate public policies, laws, and programs that safeguard Latino civil rights and empower the Latino community to fully participate in American society.

Samora served on a number of influential boards and as a consultant to a variety of national, state, and local organizations, including the U.S. Commission on Civil Rights (1962–1963), the President's Commission on Rural Poverty (1966–1967), the National Endowment for the Humanities (1969–1976), and the National Science Foundation (1979–1981). Perhaps his most prestigious award came in 1990, when the Mexican government bestowed upon him *El Orden del Águila Azteca* (the Order of the Aztec Eagle) Medal, its highest civilian award given to non-Mexican citizens. In tribute to Samora's contribution to the field of Chicano Studies, Michigan State University named its new research institute in his honor in 1989. The Julian Samora Research Center thus became the first major university research facility in America to be named for a Latino. Julian Samora died of a nervous system disorder on February 2, 1996, at the age of seventy-five.

Paul López

See also: Chicano Studies; Mexican American Legal Defense and Education Fund.

Further Reading

Samora, Julian, with Patricia Vande Simon. *A History of the Mexican American People.* Notre Dame, IN: University of Notre Dame Press, 1993.

———. *La Raza: Forgotten Americans.* Notre Dame, IN: University of Notre Dame Press, 1966.

———. *Los Mojados.* Notre Dame, IN: University of Notre Dame Press, 1972.

Samora, Julian, Joe Bernal, and Albert Pena. *Gunpowder Justice: A Reassessment of the Texas Rangers.* Notre Dame, IN: University of Notre Dame Press, 1979.

Santiago, Esmeralda
(1948–)

Esmeralda Santiago has emerged as one of today's preeminent Latina authors, acclaimed for her memoirs, which cover a wide array of political, social, ethnic, and cultural issues. Her personal stories are cast in a larger context of the political history between the United States and Puerto Rico, the tensions between island-born Puerto Ricans and Nuyoricans in New York, the struggles of immigration, and the coming-of-age issues faced by teenage girls.

Born on May 17, 1948, in San Juan, Puerto Rico, the eldest of eleven children, Santiago experienced firsthand how the unique commonwealth relationship between the United States and Puerto Rico affects the island populace. As a girl, she was part of the "Americanization" programs in the Puerto Rican educational system and witnessed the difficulties her mother faced as a single parent and sole wage earner for their family.

In 1961, when Esmeralda was thirteen, her mother moved the family from their shack in Macún to the mainland United States in hopes of achieving upward social mobility. All she could afford, however, was a decaying tenement in Brooklyn, New York. Despite her mother's employment in a bra factory, the family continued to struggle financially.

Esmeralda's first published memoir, *When I Was Puerto Rican* (1993), chronicles her early childhood in Puerto Rico, migration to the United States, and struggle to form a cultural identity. In it, she describes at length how that identity coalesced after a return visit to the island. "I was told I was no longer Puerto Rican because my Spanish was rusty, my gaze too direct, my personality too assertive," she wrote. "Yet in the United States, my darkness, my accented speech, my frequent lapses into confused silence between English and Spanish identified me as foreign, non-American. In writing the book I wanted to get back to that feeling of Puertoricanness I had before I came here."

Santiago's second memoir, *Almost a Woman* (1998), expands on her experiences in New York City and presents a more mature narrative, grappling with issues of social class, sexuality, and familial relations. The book begins with her admittance to New York City's High School of Performing Arts at age fifteen, where she majored in drama and dance. It narrates the acculturation process facilitated by the American educational system, which resulted in a strained relationship with her mother. After her high school graduation and eight years of part-time study at community colleges, she was admitted on a full scholarship to Harvard University, where she studied film production and graduated magna cum laude in 1976. She obtained a Master of Fine Arts degree in fiction writing from Sarah Lawrence College in 1992.

Santiago's third memoir, *The Turkish Lover* (2004), narrates the most oppressive years of her life, beginning in 1969, when at the age of twenty-one, she ran away from her domineering mother. She began a relationship with a Turkish immigrant filmmaker who was seventeen years her senior. Although he seemed to offer Esmeralda what seemed at the time to be the only route to her independence, she came to recognize her error and left him in 1976.

Santiago's memoirs have been both critically and commercially well received. Upon publication of her first memoir, she was acclaimed as "a welcome new voice, full of passion and authority" by the *Washington Post.* Her second memoir received several "Best of Year" mentions and won an American Library Association Alex Award for one of the Top Ten adult books for teenagers. In 2002, it was adapted into a television film that aired on the Public Broadcasting System, and won a CineSol (Latino Film Festival) SOL Award for Excellence. Since its release in English in 2004, Santiago's third memoir has sold more than 21,000 copies.

Aside from memoirs, Santiago also writes fiction and has coedited several collections. In 1996, she published *America's Dream,* a novel about a domestic servant who, in hoping to break the cycle of early pregnancy and domestic violence in which she is caught, leaves Puerto Rico to become a nanny in upscale Westchester County, New York. The book has been published in six languages. Santiago also coedited the anthologies *Las Christmas: Favorite Latino Authors Share Their Holiday Memories* (1998), in which Latino authors describe their fondest holiday memories, and *Las Mamis: Favorite Latino Authors Remember Their Mothers* (2000), a collection of fourteen essays by Latino/a authors—including Marjorie Agosín and José Vasconcelos—that capture the authors' relationships with their mothers. Her first venture into children's writing in both English and Spanish, *Una muñeca para el Día de Reyes* (*A Doll for Navidades*), appeared in 2005. Santiago's essays and opinion pieces have appeared in *The New York Times, The Boston Globe, Good Housekeeping,* and *VISTA Magazine.* She has received honorary doctor of letters degrees from Trinity University, Pace University, and Metropolitan College.

With her husband, documentary filmmaker Frank Cantor, Santiago formed a film production company based in Boston, Cantomedia, which coproduced *Writing a Life,* an hour-long documentary that profiles the author's life and work. Her films, like her books, have won several notable awards.

Glenda M. Flores

See also. Circular Migration; Nuyorican; Puerto Rican Literature.

Further Reading

Esmeralda Santiago Homepage. http://www.esmeralda santiago.com/index.html.

López, Adriana. "When I Was Esmeralda Santiago." *Críticas Magazine* (November 11, 2005).

Santiago, Fabiola. "Mad Love." *Latina Magazine* 2 (September 2004): 102–104.

Selena
(1971–1995)

The Mexican American singer Selena Quintanilla-Pérez, widely known as Selena, has also been referred to as the "queen of Tejano music." A popular recording artist by the time she was a teenager, Selena became an internationally renowned performer and a cultural icon in Latino communities across North America by the early 1990s. Her murder on March 31, 1995, was mourned by millions of fans—Latino and otherwise—around the world.

Selena was born on April 16, 1971, in Lake Jackson, Texas, of Mexican American parents, Marcella and Abraham Quintanilla, Jr., who owned a restaurant called Papagallos. The family business hosted Selena's first performances when she was a young girl. Her precocious talent and unusual self-confidence convinced her father to start an amateur group called Selena y Los Dinos (Selena and The Guys), made up of nine-year-old Selena, her brother Abraham Quintanilla III (on the bass), and her sister Suzette (on drums). When the restaurant went out of business, the family moved to Corpus Christi, Texas, and Selena y Los Dinos turned professional, playing everywhere they could to support the family.

Because Selena was constantly touring around the country, her father felt obliged to pull her out of school in eighth grade. Aware of the importance of getting an education, however, he did not allow Selena's musical career to jeopardize her future and encouraged her to take classes through the American School of Correspondence, a distance-learning institution for artists, and at Pacific Western University as a correspondence student in business.

Having grown up in the United States, Selena was educated in English; she could understand Spanish but could not speak it. That inability caused problems in her singing, as all the songs on her first Tejano records were written in Spanish. To get through them, she pronounced the lyrics phonetically. (By the time of her death, Selena was fluent in Spanish and singing in both languages.)

Known as the "queen of Tejano music," Selena began her singing career in the family business, a small-town restaurant in southeast Texas. By the time of her murder in March 1995, she had sold 18 million albums and won thirty-four Tejano Music Awards. *(Pam Francis/Time & Life Pictures/ Getty Images)*

Selena recorded her first album, *Mis Primeras Grabaciones* (My First Recordings), under the Freddie label in 1983, although the album was not released until after her death. Despite going almost unnoticed for several years, she did not give up her dream of stardom, and in 1986 recorded her second album, *Alpha,* which earned her Female Vocalist of the Year and Performer of the Year awards at the Tejano Music Awards in 1987. With the help of Rick Trevi, the founder of the Tejano Music Awards, and Johnny Canales, a Tejano musician and television personality, Selena released her third and fourth records under the titles of *Preciosa* (Beautiful) and *Dulce Amor* (Sweet Love) in 1988. These two albums established Selena's success, and in 1989 she signed with the Capitol/EMI Latin label.

Her new professional contract meant the rebirth of Selena y Los Dinos, which welcomed Pete Astudillo as a backup singer and songwriter in 1989 and her future husband, Chris Pérez, as a lead guitarist in 1990. With its new members, the band quickly produced several highly successful albums—*Ven Conmigo* (Come With Me; 1990), *Entre A Mi Mundo* (Come Into My World; 1992), and *Quiero* (I Love; 1993). The albums included a number of songs that became Selena classics—including "Baila Esta Cumbia" (Dance This Cumbia), "Como La Flor" (Like A Flower), "Siempre Estoy Pensando En Tí" (I'm Always Thinking About You), and "La Carcacha" (The Old Car)—and she became an international star. Before traveling abroad, Selena released a collection of her greatest hits in concert, titled *Selena Live,* for which she won a Grammy in 1993 for Best Mexican American Performance. In 1994, Selena y Los Dinos toured New York, Los Angeles, Argentina, and Puerto Rico, and released their eighth album, *Amor Prohibido* (Forbidden Love), which included such hits as "Bidi Bidi Bom Bom," "Fotos y Recuerdos" (Photos and Memories), "No Me Queda Más" (I've Got Nothing Left), and "El Chico del Apartamento 512" (The Boy in Apartment 512). The success of that record, which went gold, finally opened the doors to American pop mainstream success. In 1995, *Dreaming of You,* her first album in English, was released posthumously. It became an instant hit and conferred superstar status on Selena after her death.

In the early 1990s, with her popularity on the rise, Selena opened Selena Etc., a clothing manufacturing business, made her acting debut in the movie *Don Juan de Marco* (1994), and began the Selena Fan Club with Yolanda Saldívar, the manager of her boutique in San Antonio. Over the course of the next few years, Saldívar began to show signs of obsessiveness in her relationship with Selena and to fail in her duties as president of the fan club. When money began to disappear from Selena's business, the Quintanilla family decided to fire Saldívar. On March 31, 1995, at a motel room in Corpus Christi, the singer agreed to meet with Saldívar to retrieve some papers. Distraught over the idea of being separated from her idol, the thirty-four-year-old Saldívar fatally shot Selena in the back. Saldívar was later convicted and sentenced to a minimum of thirty years in prison.

At the time of her death, Selena had become the best-selling Latin artist of the 1990s, selling approximately 18 million albums. As popular as she became, however, she never forgot her roots. Her commitment to the Latino/a community was reflected in the hours she spent volunteering as a spokesperson for D.A.R.E. (Drug Abuse Resistance Education) and AIDS awareness programs, as well as participating in campaigns against battered women. In the aftermath of her death, which shocked the entire Latino/a community, Texas Governor George W. Bush declared April 16, her birthday, "Selena Day" in the state. The Selena Museum, with a life-sized bronze statue of her, was later opened in Corpus Christi.

Jorge Abril Sánchez

See also: Music; Popular Culture; Tejanos.

Further Reading

Arrarás, María Celeste. *Selena's Secret: The Revealing Story Behind Her Tragic Death.* New York: Fireside, 1997.
Mavis, Barbara. *Selena.* New York: Mitchell Lane, 2003.
Novas, Himilce. *Remembering Selena: A Tribute in Pictures & Words.* New York: St. Martin's Griffin, 1995.
Valdez, Carlos. *Justice for Selena: The State vs. Yolanda Saldivar.* New York: Trafford, 2005.

Serra, Junípero
(1713–1784)

The Spanish Catholic priest and missionary Father Junípero Serra personally established nine Franciscan missions—followed by thirteen more under his leadership—in Alta California (the present-day state of California) in the 1760s and 1770s. The chain of religious outposts along the Pacific coast was founded to spread Christian doctrine among local Native Americans, while confirming Spanish claims to the area. Known as the "Apostle of California," Serra left a complex legacy of selfless missionary work and personal conviction on the one hand, and the denial of native culture and devastation of indigenous life on the other. His efforts marked the beginning of white European culture on the Pacific coast and the origin of Spanish California.

He was born Miguel José Serra on Mallorca, a Spanish island in the Mediterranean, on November 24, 1713. Although he did not come from a wealthy family, he had a strong religious education and displayed his intellectual ability from a young age. He entered the Franciscan order in 1730 and lectured in

one of its schools before being ordained as a priest in 1738. He took the name Junípero in honor of St. Juniper, one of the original followers of St. Francis of Assisi (founder of the Franciscan order). Upon earning his doctorate at Lullian University in Palma, Mallorca, Father Serra taught theology and philosophy there for much of the next decade. In 1749, he gave up his prestigious academic post to seek converts and a martyr's death in the Americas.

Serra's arrival in Mexico was remarkable for the fact that he insisted on walking from the port at Vera Cruz to Mexico City. During the 1750s, Serra worked at various jobs in and around the colonial capital, including missionary work and teaching. The expulsion of the Jesuits from New Spain, and especially their arrest and removal from Baja California, landed the Franciscan Serra an appointment as head of new missions in 1767. Two years later, Serra accompanied Captain Gaspar de Portolà on a military expedition to Alta California. Establishing settlements for New Spain to colonize native peoples and to block any land claims by other foreign settlers, Serra managed the religious aspects of colonization while Portolà attended to military and other secular matters. In 1769, Serra and Portolà founded their first two missions at San Diego and Monterey.

Even in the late eighteenth century, Europeans had little understanding of the geography of the interior of North America. As such, England, Spain, Holland, and Russia all maintained claims to the continent's Pacific coast. Of these nations, Russia posed the most immediate and serious threat to Spanish expansion in the region. In the late 1760s, therefore, Serra's Franciscans and Portolà's soldiers struck out to the north in an effort to gain native converts and stop Russian encroachment. Over the course of the next several years, Serra founded seven more missions along the coast: at San Antonio, San Gabriel, San Luis Obispo, San Francisco, San Juan Capistrano, Santa Clara, and San Buenaventura. A total of twenty-one missions eventually were founded in the Alta California chain.

Serra was legendary for his unyielding religious convictions, following a severe form of Catholic observance in the tradition of Franciscan abnegation: he wore coarse shirts with bits of metal that irritated his skin, flogged himself until he drew blood, burned himself with a candle, and insisted on walking everywhere, aggravating his ulcerous legs. He also suffered from asthma and generally poor health.

Like other Spanish colonizers before and after him, Father Serra failed to grasp the subtleties and sophistication of native culture, especially concerning the importance of gifts and reciprocity. To bring them into line with the new mission order, Serra insisted on intimidating indigenous peoples, resorting to such heavy-handed tactics as whippings, burnings, and executions to achieve his goals. Far more damaging to native life, however, were the effects of European diseases, which spread rapidly with the concentration of indigenous people in mission settlements. Native populations dropped precipitously, as native cultures declined in the face of religious conversion. The Catholic missions of Alta California, intending to help—even save—native peoples, had disastrous effects. In 1775, Ipai-speaking Indians of San Diego responded by murdering their priest and burning his mission. Other native communities followed suit.

By the time of Serra's own death (from a snake bite) in 1784, his missions accounted for nearly all cattle and grain production in California and boasted a native population of nearly 5,000. He is also credited with founding *pueblos* (towns) at San José and Los Angeles, and administering to the churches there as well as those at the *presidios* (royal forts) of Monterey, San Francisco, Santa Barbara, and San Diego.

Father Serra was beatified (the first step toward sainthood) by Pope John Paul II in 1988, despite the objections of many Native Americans and others. The official position of the Catholic Church is that he offered protection and divine salvation to indigenous Californians; other supporters say he was simply a man of his times. Regardless of the strong opinions on both sides, the pervasive Spanish influence in California today is a constant reminder of Serra's central role in North American history. His dedication to the California mission movement is commemorated by statues throughout the state, parks, and other facilities named in his honor, and with a U.S. postage stamp.

Matthew Jennings

See also: Conquest of the Americas; Religion.

Further Reading

Costo, Rupert, and Jeannette Henry Costo, eds. *The Missions of California: A Legacy of Genocide*. San Francisco: Indian Historian, 1987.

Tinker, George E. *Missionary Conquest: The Gospel and Native American Cultural Genocide*. Minneapolis, MN: Fortress, 1993.

Weber, David J. *The Spanish Frontier in North America*. New Haven, CT: Yale University Press, 1992.

Sleepy Lagoon Case

The Sleepy Lagoon Case was a 1942 murder trial of twenty-two Latino young men in Los Angeles that came to be regarded as one of the most egregious abuses of civil rights in modern U.S. legal history and a landmark event for the Latino community in Southern California.

The episode began early on Sunday August 2, 1942, when a twenty-two-year-old Mexican American man named José Díaz was found beaten and stabbed to death at a reservoir in southeast Los Angeles. Amid racial hysteria stirred by sensationalist press coverage, police round-ups led to the arrest of more than 600 Mexican American youths said to be connected to the incident. A total of twenty-two went on trial for murder later in the year; despite minimal evidence, twelve were convicted of murder and five were convicted of assault. The trial rallied support from the Latino community, and the convictions triggered outrage. The Sleepy Lagoon Case, in fact, is seen by historians as one of the precursors of the outbreak of violence that broke out the following year known as the Zoot Suit Riots. In October 1944, the U.S. District Court of Appeals overturned the convictions of all seventeen Sleepy Lagoon defendants on the grounds that they had been deprived the due process of law.

Events and Arrest

On the night of August 1, 1942, Díaz attended a birthday party for Eleanor Delgadillo Coronado at the home of her parents at the Williams Ranch, a largely Mexican American housing development near the Los Angeles County city of Maywood. The Delgadillos, neighbors of the Díaz family, lived in a bunkhouse near a reservoir known as the Sleepy Lagoon. A quiet man who hesitated to attend parties, Díaz wanted to see his friends and neighbors one last time before reporting to the U.S. Army recruitment center for his induction on Monday. The party ended by 1:00 a.m. Sunday, and an intoxicated Díaz began the short walk home. Just after he left, a gang of young men and women crashed the Delgadillo party and assaulted the partygoers.

When he was far enough away from the Delgadillo home to be hidden in the shadows of tall trees and shrubbery, Díaz was attacked. Beaten with fists, struck over the head with a club, and stabbed twice in the stomach with an ice pick, he died at Los Angeles General Hospital later that morning without ever having regained consciousness.

Díaz's death initially attracted little media attention. However, the governor's office sent a memo to the law enforcement agencies of Los Angeles County ordering them to crack down on street violence and youth gangs. As a result, what ordinarily would have been a routine police investigation quickly took on heightened interest. In the weeks that followed the murder, the Los Angeles Police Department (LAPD)—which had a long tradition of heavily policing Latino communities—launched a highly publicized war on juvenile delinquency and turned the investigation into a major media event. Members of the LAPD conducted dragnets in the neighborhoods of Los Angeles, specifically targeting areas heavily populated by Mexican Americans. More than 600 young men and women were taken into custody. Within weeks of the crackdown, the police discovered that male and female Mexican American youths who lived in the vicinity of Thirty-eighth Street in Maywood had been attacked by a group of Anglo youths from the nearby town of Downey. For the Maywood group, such an attack constituted a challenge that demanded a response. Thinking that the Downey boys were at the Delgadillo party, a group of about forty Latino youths stormed the house.

Believing that the Maywood group constituted a criminal gang, the LAPD assumed that it had also been responsible for attacking Díaz. Although most of them had a police record, there was no evidence that any of them were involved in gang crime or other organized illegal activities. Using

beatings and other forms of coercion, the police forced confessions out of some of the Maywood group. Those who resisted were held incommunicado, even from their lawyers, until they came forward with information.

Indictment and Trial

The Díaz case, represented as a gang murder, went immediately to the Los Angeles County grand jury, which had already been convened to investigate the problem of youth gangs. Although there was clear evidence that the girls of Thirty-eighth Street had been involved in the fight at the Williams Ranch, the grand jury recommended that charges be brought only against the young men for murder. All of the Maywood men who had been in the vicinity of the Díaz attack were tried for conspiracy to commit murder; the young women who had been present were charged with the lesser crime of rioting. The case of *The People v. Zammora et al*, which came to be known as the Sleepy Lagoon Trial, began in early October 1942.

To support their contention that Mexican American youth gangs behaved little better "than wolf packs in the wild," the prosecution ordered that the jailed boys not receive a clean change of clothes or a haircut for almost three months prior to the trial, hoping to play on the racist sentiments of the jury—which was all Anglo. The defense attorneys protested in vain to the trial judge, with the prosecution arguing that the defendants' haircuts and clothing style were critical pieces of evidence.

After three months of testimony by dozens of witnesses, the state could not present enough solid evidence to support the charges. The most the district attorney's office could prove was that the Maywood group who went to Sleepy Lagoon did so with the express purpose of confronting the Downey gang and that some of the former were seen during the fight at the Delgadillo home. No direct connection to the Díaz murder was substantiated with evidence, and no weapon was ever produced.

The jury returned with a verdict after six days of deliberation. Five of the men—Joe Carpio, Richard Gastelum, Edward Grandpré, Ruben Peña, and Daniel Verdugo—were found not guilty. Henry

(Hank) Leyvas, José Ruíz, and Robert Telles were found guilty of murder in the first degree, with two counts of assault with a deadly weapon with intent to commit murder. Nine other men were convicted of murder in the second degree and two counts of assault with a deadly weapon with intent to commit murder. Five others were found guilty of assault. Stunned by the verdict, several of the boys wept openly as they were handed life sentences at San Quentin Prison.

Aftermath

During the trial, an East Los Angeles citizens group called the Committee for the Defense of Mexican American Youth began soliciting funds from the community to pay for an appeal of the expected convictions. Widely known as the Sleepy Lagoon Defense Committee (SLDC), the group also worked to alter the public perception of the case. Through parties, benefit concerts, and other events, it raised thousands of dollars to underwrite the legal costs of the appeal while generating publicity. In June 1944, the SLDC began a nationwide fundraising campaign by selling *The Sleepy Lagoon Mystery,* an account of the case by the well-known Hollywood screenwriter Guy Endore. A political tract designed to win sympathy for the defendants, the book blamed the newspapers for sensationalizing the trial and manipulating public opinion to increase circulation. The SLDC, meanwhile, emphasized the racial prejudice inherent in police handling of the case, the judicial proceedings, and public reaction. City newspapers began to rethink their sensationalistic coverage of the events and trial.

In October 1944, U.S. District Court of Appeals reversed the criminal court ruling in *People v. Zammora,* finding in favor of the defense in most cases. It concluded that a consistent pattern of bias on the part of the judge had unduly influenced the outcome of the trial. Not only had the community climate tainted the proceedings, but Judge Charles W. Fricke had effectively denied the defendants their constitutional right to consult with their lawyers. The appellate judges declared further that the state lacked sufficient evidence to convict the young men of either

conspiracy or murder and remanded the case. The state court conceded defeat and announced that all charges against the young men would be dropped. On October 28, 1944, Judge Clement Nye dismissed the case and ordered the men released and their records cleared.

The defendants, their families, and their community rejoiced at the outcome, but resentment over the handling of the case lingered, as did tensions between Latinos/as and Anglos in Los Angeles. Several episodes of racial violence, referred to as the Zoot Suit Riots, erupted again in the spring and summer of 1943. Not until decades later was the true murderer in the Díaz case (a man named Louie Encinas, who had since committed suicide) identified by his sister.

Caryn E. Neumann

See also: Gangs; Los Angeles; Zoot Suit Riots.

Further Reading

Endore, Guy. *The Sleepy Lagoon Mystery.* Los Angeles: Sleepy Lagoon Defense Committee, 1944.
Escobar, Edward J. *Race, Police, and the Making of a Political Identity: Mexican Americans and the Los Angeles Police Department, 1900–1945.* Berkeley: University of California Press, 1999.
Págan, Eduardo Obregón. *Murder at the Sleepy Lagoon: Zoot Suits, Race, and Riot in Wartime L.A.* Chapel Hill: University of North Carolina Press, 2003.

Soccer

Latinos/as have played a prominent role in the rise of soccer—*fútbol,* in Spanish—as both an organized competitive sport and a recreational pastime in the United States. In addition, their beloved game has provided an affirmation of heritage, a source of common interest and community bonding, and even, for some, a means of social mobility in U.S. society. Both as players and as fans, Latinos/as have contributed to the growth of soccer in America, especially since the early 1970s, even as long-held passions for favorite teams in the homeland—made increasingly accessible via Spanish-language media and new com-

Brazilian soccer legend Pelé teaches a young fan at his New York soccer academy in 1979. Pelé's participation in the North American Soccer League helped generate enormous—and heavily Latino—crowds during the 1970s. *(Adrian Taylor/ Keystone Features/Hulton Archive/Getty Images)*

munications technologies—have reaffirmed cultural ties and engendered friendly rivalries within and among immigrant communities.

Early Pro Soccer in America

Soccer is a relative newcomer on the American professional sports scene. It was not until the 1970s that fan interest supported a successful pro circuit—the North American Soccer League (NASL)—though its fortunes were in decline by the early 1980s. Before the NASL, and again until the 1990s, competition was confined largely to community youth leagues, high schools, colleges, and amateur immigrant groups with a fondness for the game. This made soccer in America a largely regional game, with hotbeds in New Jersey, New York, St. Louis, Southern California, and other areas with large Latino and European immigrant communities.

The first national professional leagues in America were established in 1967—the United Soccer Association (sanctioned by the International Football Federation, or FIFA) and the National Professional Soccer League. The latter had the advantage of a television contract with the CBS broadcast network, but viewer ratings for its matches proved disappointing. The two leagues merged the following year to create the NASL, with franchises in the United States and Canada. Team owners and league officials took extraordinary efforts to market the league and stimulate public interest in the sport, including the hiring of foreign stars. The legendary Pelé (Brazil), Franz Beckenbauer (Germany), and Giorgio Chinaglia (Italy) formed the multimillion dollar backbone of the New York Cosmos. For Latinos/as, the figure of Pelé, arguably the best player in the history of the sport, was especially attractive. The effect of the superstars was significant at the box office, at least for

Cosmos games. The club drew more than 40,000 fans per game, peaking at more than 78,000 for certain matches at their Giants Stadium home in northern New Jersey in the late 1970s.

The strategy of hiring former stars continued through the early 1980s, with Latin American imports coming from top teams in Mexico, Peru, Argentina, Paraguay, and Venezuela. The NASL also sought to increase the attendance of various cultural groups, including Latinos/as, by fielding teams in areas with a high density of those peoples. Teams particularly identified with Latino communities included the Los Angeles Aztecs (1974–1981) and San Diego Toros (1968).

Finally, however, the NASL failed to sell the sport to the U.S. public in a way that would guarantee its permanence. Attendance overall never averaged more than 15,000 fans per game, with some clubs never exceeding an average attendance of 5,000. Attempts to make the game more broadly appealing included "Americanizing" the rules, which may have discouraged fans from immigrant communities (including Latinos/as) that cared for the integrity of the traditional game as part of their cultural heritage. Additionally, the emphasis on big-name players at a high cost discouraged the development of local players who might have attracted more local fans—especially from minority communities. All of these factors, combined with the failure of the United States to win its bid to host the FIFA World Cup in 1986, led to a decline in fan interest and the demise of the NASL by 1984.

Renewed Growth and Latino Contributions

The selection of the United States as the site of the FIFA Men's World Cup in 1994 provided a boost for the sport at virtually every level, including professional. A new pro circuit called Major League Soccer (MLS) began competition with ten teams in 1996 and proved more commercially viable than it predecessors. Indeed, the founders of the MLS were meeting a commitment to FIFA to establish a premiere-level professional league in exchange for designating the United States as host of the World Cup. The MLS survived disappointing attendance in its early years

and underwent a resurgence in the 2000s. Already having expanded to fourteen teams, it was slated to increase to sixteen in 2010 and eighteen by 2012. Key to the growth and expansion of the league has been the burgeoning Latino/a population of the United States (and, in 2007, the arrival of another superstar, David Beckham of England). Indeed the MLS has become a source of cultural enrollment and social mobility for Latinos/as. The league today has strong programs of development, including several major soccer-dedicated stadiums across the country.

Latinos have achieved increasing prominence on the field as well, claiming league most valuable player (MVP) honors in five of the first seven seasons of the twenty-first century: Alex Pineda Chacón (Honduras) of the Miami Fusion in 2001; Carlos Ruíz (Guatemala) of the Los Angeles Galaxy in 2002; Amado Guevara (Honduras) of the New York/New Jersey MetroStars in 2004; Christian Gómez (Argentina) of D.C. United in 2006; and Luciano Emilio (Brazil) of D.C. United in 2007. The eleventh MSL franchise, added in 2004, was the Mexican-owned Chivas USA, based in Carson, California, and a sister team of the enormously popular Mexican first-division Club Deportivo Guadalajara. As of 2006, more than sixty Latin Americans competed in the MLS and were being specially marketed by Latino media as cultural representatives.

Friendly matches with visiting teams from Central America, South America, and Europe have attracted enormous crowds. The national teams of Mexico and the United States have played to full houses on both sides of the border in World Cup and Olympic qualifying matches, among others. Additionally, tournaments such as the Gold Cup—pitting national teams of the Caribbean, Central American, and North American federations—have made the United States a frequent site of competition. Finally, "friendly" matches with one or more visiting Latin American teams are now routinely scheduled in the United States because of the prospect of heavy attendance.

Among Latino/a immigrants in the United States today, fútbol plays a vital role in establishing social networks, reinforcing cultural identity, and helping people feel at home in an alien society.

Among the most popular voluntary organizations with which Latinos/as become involved are amateur soccer clubs, or leagues, in the communities where they settle. It has become commonplace in cities across the country to see Latinos playing informal or organized games of soccer in local playgrounds, schoolyards, and other open spaces. Spanish is normally spoken—itself a respite from the daily routine in society at large.

Another space in which soccer contributes to multiculturalism in the United States is the media. Spanish- and English-speaking television networks dedicate ever-increasing airtime to worldwide coverage of the sport. Television viewership of soccer in the United States began in the twenty-first century at an all-time high, but then continued growing each year, as more channels offered more coverage of the MLS and foreign competition. Corresponding growth is seen in Latino newspapers and radio stations, contributing to the increasing influence and commercial clout of the Latino media.

In response to this thriving market, and to help sustain it, the MLS in July 2007 created a Latin American Advisory Board (LAAB)—made up of a diverse cross-section of individuals from the Latino community, including former star players, coaches, media personalities, and members of the business community—to promote the growth of the MLS in particular, and the sport in general, in the United States. League officials, recognizing that the growth of the league depends on close contact with the Spanish-speaking community, mandated the new advisory board to disseminate information specifically to Latino groups and to act as a kind of sounding board for communications from it.

Latinas in U.S. Soccer

Whatever the cultural or national explanations, the emergence of women's soccer in the United States in recent years has been a result of its growth at the youth, high school, and college levels rather than the appeal of professional competition or highly paid imported superstars. And while girls growing up in America have taken inspiration from the success of the U.S. national team in the World Cup (championships in 1991 and 1999) and Olympic competition

(gold medals in 1996 and 2004) and while some foreign players have come to America to compete in women's college soccer, the development of female players has taken place largely in an environment less permeated by Latinas and Europeans. All in all, the participation of Latinas is marginal compared to that of Latino men, with relatively small percentages competing in major college programs or high amateur ranks.

Bernardo Aguilar-González

Further Reading

Foer, Franklin. *How Soccer Explains the World: An Unlikely Theory of Globalization.* New York: HarperCollins, 2004.

Kuper, Simon. *Soccer Against the Enemy: How the World's Most Popular Sport Starts and Fuels Revolutions and Keeps Dictators in Power.* New York: Nation, 2006.

Lever, Janet. *Soccer Madness.* Chicago: University of Chicago Press, 1984.

Markovits, Andrei. "The Other American Exceptionalism: Why Is There No Soccer in the United States?" *International Journal of the History of Sport* 7:2 (1990): 230–64.

Sugden, John, and Alan Tomlinson, eds. *Hosts and Champions: Soccer Cultures, National Identities and the USA World Cup.* Aldershot, UK: Ashgate, 1994.

Waddington, Ivan, and Martin Roderick. "American Exceptionalism: Soccer and American Football." *The Sports Historian* 16 (1996): 28–49.

Sosa, Sammy
(1968–)

While certainly not the first Latino to thrive in major league baseball, Sammy Sosa helped usher in a new era with his success as a power hitter, his popularity across the entire fan base of the American pastime, and his ability to remain connected to his Dominican roots. While paving the way for future generations of Latino ballplayers, Sosa also encountered controversies that tainted his reputation and otherwise remarkable record on the field.

Born on November 12, 1968, in San Pedro de Macorís—a village in the Dominican Republic that became known for producing major league baseball players—Samuel Peralta Sosa endured a childhood of poverty. Following the death of his father, seven-year old Sosa spent much of his time shining shoes to help his mother keep the family afloat. When not working, he pursued his dream of becoming a professional baseball player, one of the few available paths to economic solvency and upward mobility. Unable to afford a bat and glove, however, Sosa trained with homemade equipment: a glove made of empty milk cartons, a bat fashioned from a tree branch, and a ball made out of a ball of socks wrapped in tape.

Despite his crude equipment and undernourished frame, Sammy Sosa came to the attention of major league scouts. In 1985, the Texas Rangers signed him to a minor league contract with a $13,500 signing bonus, and by 1989 he had worked his way up to the major leagues. After a trade to the Chicago White Sox later that year and a trade to the Chicago Cubs before the 1992 season, Sosa emerged as one of the game's top power hitters. During the five-year period from 1993 through 1997, he averaged thirty-four home runs and 100 runs batted in (RBIs) per season.

It was in 1998, however, that Sosa achieved a new level of slugging prowess, joining Mark McGwire of the St. Louis Cardinals in a season-long home run hitting contest that saw both players break Roger Maris's single-season record of sixty-one homers in 1961. McGwire ended the campaign with a total of seventy round-trippers, to Sosa's sixty-six. In the excitement of the months-long home run race, American baseball fans embraced Sosa for his enthusiasm and vibrant personality no less than for his accomplishments. In addition to his home run total, Sosa's .308 batting average and league-leading 158 RBIs led the Cubs into the playoffs and ultimately earned him the National League Most Valuable Player (MVP) award for 1998. Nevertheless, many Latino fans and other observers noted the excessive praised bestowed upon McGwire at the expense of Sosa. Citing racism and xenophobia, more than a few commentators questioned why the humble, non-threatening minority player did not receive the same media attention as his white counterpart.

In addition to his accomplishments on the field, Sosa came to the aid of his home country, as Hurricane Georges in late September 1998 left hundreds of Dominicans dead and tens of thousands without food or shelter. Capitalizing on his popularity and financial status, Sosa donated large sums of money, water, and food, and used his celebrity to bring international attention to the plight of his homeland.

Back on the field, Sosa continued his blistering slugging over the next five seasons and more—averaging an amazing fifty-three home runs (including sixty-three in 1999 and sixty-four in 2001) and 130 RBIs from 1999 through 2003. Meanwhile, however, the popularity and media acclaim that came with the historic 1998 season began to erode. While the effort to chronicle his rags-to-riches story inspired many, it grew tiresome to others who knew many Latino players who had not been able to convert their talent into economic success. On a more direct, personal level, Sosa was increasingly plagued by questions concerning his age, background, injuries, and more serious matters.

His reputation wavered especially after a June 2003 incident in which a bat he used in a game shattered on the field and was found to be doctored—illegally hollowed out and filled with cork to propel the ball farther. Sosa was suspended for seven games for the infraction. And, despite becoming the first Latino player to hit 500 home runs in his career—a landmark reached early in the 2003 season—Sosa began to show signs of slowing down. Media commentators and fans began to question his success, wondering if his power at the plate was the result of performance-enhancing drugs.

That issue came to a head in 2005, in the wake of a book, *Juiced,* published by former baseball player José Canseco, in which he wrote about widespread steroid use in Major League Baseball. Accusations against Sosa, among others, became commonplace. Questions about his home run power, his physical transformation from skinny rookie to muscle-bound veteran, and his relatively rapid decline in productivity all contributed to the rumors. Compelled to testify before a U.S. congressional committee along with other players in March 2005, Sosa was unable to silence his critics, who despite his denials, continued to raise questions about the legitimacy of Sosa's success.

After retiring from the game in early 2006, Sosa returned to play for the Texas Rangers—the franchise with whom he had signed his first professional contract—in the 2007 season. Even as he slugged his six hundredth career home run—a plateau reached by only four other players in major league history—the rumors of past steroid use persisted. Tainted or not, Sosa's career ranked with those of such Latino greats as Roberto Clemente, Orlando Cepeda, and Tony Perez. It also coincided with the rise of a new generation of Latino players who thrived in the increasingly globalized world of professional baseball, constituting an ever-growing presence in the ranks of the major leagues.

David J. Leonard

See also: Baseball; Dominicans.

Further Reading

Christopher, Matt. *At the Plate with . . . Sammy Sosa.* Boston: Little Brown, 1999.

Malone, Julio. *Sammy Sosa in 9 Innings.* New York: Editorial Miglo, 2004.

Sosa, Sammy, and Marcus Breton. *Sammy Sosa: An Autobiography.* New York: Warner, 2000.

Sotomayor, Sonia (1954–)

A self-identified Nuyorican raised in a public housing project in the East Bronx, New York, fifty-four-year-old Judge Sonia Maria Sotomayor was nominated by President Barack Obama in June 2009 to become the third woman and the first Latino/a to serve on the U.S. Supreme Court. In introducing his nominee, President Obama underscored both Sotomayor's "sterling credentials in the law" and her "wisdom accumulated from an inspiring life's journey." The nomination easily won Senate confirmation in August.

Sotomayor was born on June 25, 1954, in the Bronx. Her father was a factory worker and her mother a nurse, both of whom came to the U.S. mainland from Puerto Rico during World War II. Sonia, who learned that she was a diabetic at age eight and lost her father at age nine, was a superior student who became interested in law and law enforcement from watching *Perry Mason* television shows and reading Nancy Drew mystery books.

After graduating from Cardinal Spellman High School in the Bronx in 1972, Sotomayor entered Princeton University on a scholarship—an experience she later likened to "a visitor landing in an alien country." She graduated summa cum laude in 1976 with a major in history and a prize-winning senior thesis on Luis Muñoz Marín, the first popularly elected governor of Puerto Rico. Then it was on to Yale Law School, where again Sotomayor was among a small minority of Latino students. An editor of the *Yale Law Journal* and an activist on behalf of minority issues, she earned her Juris Doctor degree in 1979 and was admitted to the New York Bar in 1980.

Her first job out of law school was as assistant district attorney in New York City, serving in that capacity from 1979 to 1984. After seven more years at a Manhattan law firm, where her work focused on commercial and intellectual-property litigation, she was recommended in 1991 by Senator Daniel Moynihan (D-NY)—and nominated by President George H.W. Bush—to serve as a federal district judge in the Southern District of New York. In 1997, President Bill Clinton named Sotomayor to fill a seat on the U.S. Court of Appeals for the Second Circuit; she easily won Senate confirmation the following year.

Sotomayor's written opinions as a federal appeals judge have been characterized as focused, analytically rigorous, and technically competent but not particularly colorful or imaginative. In her best-known case, she issued an injunction against Major League Baseball that barred it from hiring replacement players during a 1994 strike by union players; the ruling effectively ended the dispute. Despite her background in minority rights advocacy, her participation in such groups as the National Council of La Raza and the Puerto Rican Legal Defense and Education Fund, and the pride she expresses in her Latino background and community, observers note that Sotomayor has ruled repeatedly against claimants in minority discrimination cases on the federal bench. Nevertheless, as a Supreme Court nominee, she faced tough questioning by senators regarding her views on the relationship between personal experience and judicial philosophy.

Jeff Hacker

See also: History: 1965–Present; Nuyorican; Puerto Ricans; Women.

Further Reading

Lacayo, Richard. "Sonia Sotomayor: A Justice Like No Other." *Time*, June 8, 2009.

Sotomayor, Sonia. "A Latina Judge's Voice." *Berkeley La Raza Law Journal* 13:1 (2002): 87–93.

U.S. Court of Appeals, Second Circuit. http://www.ca2.uscourts.gov.

Southwest Voter Registration Education Project

Founded in 1974 by Willie Velasquez in San Antonio, Texas, the Southwest Voter Registration Education Project (SVREP) is a nonpartisan political organization devoted to voter research, registration, and litigation with the ultimate goal of increasing the electoral strength of Latinos, African Americans, and Native Americans. While its primary original goal was to increase voter participation among Mexican Americans in the urban areas of Texas, SVREP's focus expanded over the years to encompass much of the nation, helping to increase the political clout of Mexican Americans alongside other minority groups as well.

Beginning with a rudimentary but determined research agenda, Velasquez and SVREP targeted areas with low registration rates, canvassing from door to door and advertising their campaign in local Spanish-language media outlets. This approach not only resulted in increased registration, but also avoided undue attention from the Anglo establishment. SVREP made its greatest advances when it began to focus on rural registration drives in the years after 1975. Even in less populated areas, a small increase in registered voters could affect a virtual takeover of local government by a previously disfranchised population. Moreover, their research revealed a systematic watering down of Mexican American voting strength due to gerrymandering. From the late 1970s to the mid-1980s, SVREP teamed with the Mexican American Legal Defense and Education Fund (MALDEF) to launch a series of anti-gerrymandering lawsuits that helped to redraw jurisdictional lines in counties across Texas and the Southwest. The combined effects of these strategies were an increased political voice for Mexican Americans—the total number of Mexican American registered voters more than doubled from the mid-1970s to the mid-1980s—and reluctance on the part of political elites to continue gerrymandering for fear of retaliatory litigation. In fact, after the release of 1980 U.S. Census figures, 249 of Texas's 254 counties redrew jurisdictional lines on their own rather than wait for the inevitable onslaught of an SVREP/MALDEF challenge.

This level of success did not come without some complications, however, especially following the conservative resurgence that accompanied Ronald Reagan's victory in the 1980 presidential election. SVREP became the target of harsh attacks by conservative politicians and the Anglo press, which characterized it as racist, anti-democratic, and anti-American. In spite of this backlash, SVREP was able to complete one of its most successful voter registration drives in San Antonio in 1981, increasing the number of registered Mexican American voters by 40,000 to more than 150,000. As a result, Democrat Henry Cisneros won the mayoral election quite comfortably, becoming the first Mexican American to hold that office since the 1840s.

SVREP still had larger goals, hoping to increase the number of registered Latino voters in the United States from 3.4 million in 1980 to 4.4 million by the November 1984 elections. Such an undertaking required tens of thousands of volunteers and cooperation between groups in different parts of the country. If the drive were to be successful, Velasquez and SVREP felt that it would increase the political clout of Latinos/as exponentially. The original stated goals were unrealistic, however, and the drive was able to accomplish only half of its aim, registering just over half a million new Latino voters. While this represented a major leap in voter participation, it was not nearly enough to offset the overwhelming support for Reagan's reelection. Lost in coverage of his landslide victory was any recognition of the Latino vote.

Not discouraged, SVREP renewed its efforts after the 1984 registration drive. That same year, the research division of SVREP received its own charter as the Southwest Voter Research Institute (SVRI). The SVRI also serves as a public policy research institute that provides information and guidance to grassroots organizations dedicated to promoting full voter participation among Latinos/as. In addition, the SVRI entered into the realm of international politics in 1988 when it published a report critical of the Reagan administration's actions in Central America.

The SVREP suffered a major loss in 1988, when founder Willie Velasquez died of cancer at the age of forty-four. Velasquez shaped the organization in its early years and helped it grow into a true political force. During his tenure with the organization, the number of Latino registered voters in America more than doubled, the number of Latino elected officials more than doubled, and electoral maps across the Southwest were redrawn to truly represent Latino voting strength. Under President Antonio Gonzalez since 1994, SVREP has continued its voter registration, education, and research efforts. Velasquez's favorite saying remains the organization's motto: *"su voto es su voz"* ("your vote is your voice").

John Weber

See also: Mexican American Legal Defense and Education Fund; Politics.

Further Reading

Sepulveda, Juan A., Jr. *The Life and Times of Willie Velasquez: Su Voto es Su Voz.* Houston, TX: Arte Público, 2003.
Southwest Voter Registration and Education Project. http://www.svrep.org.

Spanglish

The officially unrecognized language known as Spanglish is a unique hybrid. Also known as *espanglish* or *espanglés,* it is a convergence of English and Spanish. Coinage of the term in the 1940s is attributed to the Puerto Rican writer Salvador Tió, who predicted that the popularization of Spanglish might result in the transformation of Spanish into patois (a provisional or transitional dialect) or Creole (pidgin French spoken in Louisiana). Today, the term Spanglish is also used to refer to the errors commonly made by Spanish speakers when they express themselves in English.

Phonetic translation—as in the coffee shop sign spelling of *donas,* for "doughnuts"—is one way in which Spanish and English are hybridized to create Spanglish. This unofficial language has become popular in mixed Latino-Anglo communities. *(Hector Mata/AFP/Getty Images)*

The origins of this speech, while unknown for certain, have been traced to 1513, when the first Spanish settlers of the state of Florida (meaning "Land of Flowers") founded St. Augustine. This city remains the oldest permanent European settlement on the North American continent and is considered the first common settlement by Spaniards and Native Americans. The contact between English and Spanish speakers that resulted from the U.S. annexation of Texas and its acquisition of California, Nevada, Utah, most of New Mexico and Arizona, and parts of Colorado and Wyoming proved to be fertile ground for the combination of languages, which was suitable for the creation of a new kind of language: Spanglish.

Today Spanglish is spoken in Latino communities (also known as "Hispanglos") that embody the confluence of Latino and Euro-American cultures in the United States. These bilingual communities are located primarily along the southwest border with Mexico (Arizona, California, New Mexico, and Texas), in Chicago, in Florida (especially the Miami area, where there is a large Cuban community), in New York City, in Panama, and in Puerto Rico. Although monolingual speakers of Spanish or English may be unable to speak or even comprehend Spanglish, its use in the media, popular music, and advertising have made it increasingly widespread. Thus, Spanglish is now commonly heard in Mexico, Venezuela, and countries of Central and South America.

As an unofficial language, Spanglish evolves on the basis of current, local vernacular and four basic processes:

(1) Literal translation, or what linguists refer to as "calque" or "loan translation." In this process, idiomatic expressions in either English or Spanish are literally translated into the other language. For example: "I'll call you back" becomes *te llamo p'atrás* in Spanglish.

(2) Adoption and adaptation, a process linguists refer to as "loanword" or "borrowing." Thus, English words are adopted and then adapted according to the rules of Spanish grammar. For example: The Spanish word for window is *ventana,* a feminine noun; the English counterpart, "window," is adopted into Spanish and adapted as *La windowa.* Borrowing is common in such areas as sports and computers. In baseball, for example, the fielders become *los filders* (rather than the literal *los jardineros*); in computers, to link becomes *linkear* (rather than *enlazar* or *ligar*). The caveat is that the loan process may produce false cognates or false friends. Thus, *ganga* in New York Spanglish refers to a gang, while in conventional Spanish it means *oferta,* or "good deal."

(3) Phonetic transcription. Since Spanish is a phonetic language (words are pronounced exactly as they are spelled), the same practice is oddly applied to English. Thus, "The United States" becomes *Los Unaited Esteits* in written Spanglish.

(4) Merging words or phrases in Spanish and English, a process linguists refer to as "codeswitching." Without making a distinction, words or phrases in Spanish and English are combined—as in, "Hey, where have you been? No te he visto all day."

Despite its widespread and growing use, Spanglish is not entirely accepted by the intellectual community. The Puerto Rican writer and journalist Salvador Tió predicted the decline of Latino culture because of *"vil-lingüismo"* (or "vile bilingualism"). For the Cuban critic Roberto González Echevarría, Spanglish poses a grave danger to Latino culture. He refers to it as *"una invasión del español por el inglés"* (an invasion of Spanish by English). The Mexican poet and literary critic Octavio Paz proposes, *"Ni es bueno ni es malo, sino abominable"* (It is neither good nor bad, but abominable).

Others, however, such as the academics Gloria Anzaldúa and Ilan Stavans, defend Spanglish as a creative production. Stavans himself wrote the first "translation" of the first chapter of *Don Quixote* in Spanglish. And, it is argued, the use of Spanglish by writers such as Rudolfo Anaya, Ana Lydia Vega, Pedro Pietri, Sandra María Estéves, Julia Alvarez, Sandra Cisneros, and Oscar Hijuelos, among others, recreates an oral and bilingual context that readily responds to a multicultural idea of the world.

While speakers of Spanglish are criticized by some because it is said to diminish the purity of both Spanish and English, others regard it as an inevitable expression of cultural identity with unique creative potential. Regardless of its detractors or supporters, Spanglish will no doubt remain a common—and controversial—form of communication.

Diana Castilleja

See also: Bilingualism; Conquest of the Americas; Spanish Language.

Further Reading

Morales, Ed. *Living in Spanglish: The Search for a Latino Identity in America.* New York: St. Martin's, 2002.

Roca, Ana, and John M. Lipski, eds. *Spanish in the United States: Linguistic Contact and Diversity.* Berlin, Germany: Mouton de Gruyter, 1999.

Silva-Corvalan, Carmen. *Language Contact and Change: Spanish in Los Angeles.* Oxford, UK: Clarendon, 1996.

Stavans, Ilan. *Spanglish. The Making of a New American Language.* New York: HarperCollins, 2003.

Spanish Language

Spanish is one of the Romance languages in the Italic subfamily of the Indo-European language family, with two major dialects in Spain: Andalusian and Castilian. Today, the Spanish language is the third most-spoken language in the world, with approximately 450 million native speakers. Castilian, or Castellaño, brings together the diverse idioms of peoples who inhabited the Iberian Peninsula over the course of 2,000 years, with modifications influenced by the Romans, Visigoths, and Arabs. Toward the end of the fifteenth century, with the union of the kingdoms of Castilla and Aragón and the extension of their dominion over the majority of the peninsula, the language of Castilla—Castellaño—gained ascendancy over the other idioms and dialects. The language crossed the Atlantic with the conquistadors, settlers, and missionaries of the New World, where elements of native languages such as Náhuatl (Aztec) and Quechua (Andean) were added.

Today, in the Western Hemisphere, Spanish is the official language of Argentina, Bolivia, Chile, Colombia, Costa Rica, Cuba, the Dominican Republic, Ecuador, El Salvador, Equatorial Guinea, Guatemala, Honduras, Mexico, Nicaragua, Panama, Paraguay, Peru, Puerto Rico, Uruguay, and Venezuela. In addition, it is widely spoken in the United States and Canada. Spanish dialects are spoken in diverse areas of North and South America, where unique "concoctions" of Spanish and other languages are spoken in particular regions or localities.

History

The Spanish language developed from Vulgar Latin, with major influences from Arabic during the culturally rich Andalusian period, and also from Germanic through the Visigoths. The Visigoths, Germanic tribes of Eastern Europe, invaded Hispania in the fifth century. Latin remained the official language of government and culture until the Moorish invasion in C.E. 719, when Arabic-speaking Islamic groups from Northern Africa completed their conquest of the region. Arabic and a related dialect called Mozarabic came to be widely spoken in Islamic Spain, except in a few remote Christian kingdoms in the north. When the Christian kingdoms began to reconquer Moorish Spain—in a process that lasted more than seven centuries—Vulgar Latin again became the dominant language, especially the Castilian dialect from the Northern Central plains.

There were three major periods in the formation of the Spanish language: the medieval period (thirteenth century to fifteenth century); the modern period (sixteenth century to seventeenth century); and the contemporary period (from the founding of the Real Academia Española in 1713 to today).

In the thirteenth century, King Alfonso X of Castile made Castellaño the official language of Castilla y León. In the late 1400s, during the reign of Isabella of Castile and Ferdinand of Aragón, the Castilian dialect gained wider acceptance as they unified the Iberian Peninsula under Christian rule. The more specific Castilian used in Toledo was made the kingdom's official dialect, adopted as the written and educational standard. Several other spoken dialects remained in use; the second-most commonly spoken dialect was Andalusian, spoken in the southern city of Seville in the Andalusia region.

With the founding of the Real Academia Española (Royal Spanish Academy) in 1713, the institution responsible for regulating the Spanish language, a process of standardization was begun. And while the language has continued to evolve over the centuries, especially in the Americas, the standardization has continued.

Colonial Roots of American Spanish

The Spanish language in the Americas has remained largely frozen—in terms of grammar and pronunciation—from the time it came over with the first explorers. The only significant changes have been the addition of contemporary words. Spanish explorers, conquistadors, and colonizers carried the Castilian and Andalusian dialects to the Americas. Castilian was used in administrative, religious, and cultural centers such as Mexico City, Potosí in Bolivia, and Lima in Peru. Andalusian became dominant in Argentina and Central America, areas remote from the administrative centers. Historians believe that Cristóbal Colón (Christopher Columbus) was also instrumental in bringing Sephardim (Jews of medieval Spain) to the New World, along with their language, Ladino—medieval Castilian with elements of Hebrew and other Eurasian languages. Ladino—still spoken by some descendants of Sephardic Jews who were expelled from Spain in the fifteenth century—added its own flavor to American Spanish.

Many indigenous languages have also influenced the Spanish spoken today in the Americas. Of the approximately 123 language families indigenous to the Americas, some with hundreds of languages and dialects, the most influential have been Náhuatl, Taíno, Maya, Quechua, Aimara, Guaraní, and Mapuche.

In 1565, Spanish conquerors and explorers established the first permanent European settlement in what is now the state of Florida, called Saint Augustine. During the 1600s and 1700s, often led by Sephardim from Mexico City who had escaped the Spanish Inquisition, explorers and settlers extended the Spanish language into present-day Arizona, California, Southern Colorado, New Mexico and Texas. When these areas were annexed by the United States after the Mexican-American War (1846–1848), many of the region's Spanish-speaking inhabitants remained, creating a distinct linguistic and cultural population in the American Southwest.

Contemporary Spanish

When, after the Spanish-American War (1898), the United States gained control of Cuba, Guam, the Philippines, and Puerto Rico, many of the Spanish speakers from these regions moved to the United States. They settled heavily in California, Florida, New York, and New Jersey, where they continued to speak and write in Spanish. Many Spanish speakers live in these same states today: 12.4 million in California, 3.3 million in Florida, 3 million in New York, and 1.2 million in New Jersey, according to the 2000 U.S. Census.

Legal and illegal immigration by Spanish speakers continued during the course of the twentieth century, especially from Mexico. Many came to work in agriculture and industry, while others fled political instability in Chile, Cuba, El Salvador, Guatemala, Honduras, and Nicaragua. The heavy influx of Spanish speakers, which continues into the twenty-first century, has influenced both the use and teaching of the language. In addition to being the most

widely spoken language after English, it is also the most commonly taught foreign language. Spanish is officially recognized by the state of New Mexico, where it is spoken by nearly 30 percent of the population. According to the U.S. Census Bureau in 2006, an estimated 34 million people over the age of five—or about 12 percent of the population—speak Spanish at home.

A number of states, such as California, Arizona, New Mexico, Texas, and New York, post signs and supply government documents in both Spanish and English. In Los Angeles County—where about 50 percent of residents are Spanish speakers—many business personnel are bilingual. And in states throughout the Southwest, the issue of bilingualism remains a source of tension between Latino and non-Latino residents.

In the twenty-first century, policy makers, school administrators, parents, teachers, and the academic community remain divided on the issue of bilingual education. Since the 1960s, and specifically since passage of the Bilingual Education Act in 1968, Spanish language and culture have gained increasing recognition and attention in the nation's schools. As a direct result of that legislation, combined with community activism and litigation by Spanish-speaking parents, bilingual and English as a Second Language (ESL) programs have been implemented in many elementary and some secondary schools throughout the United States. In addition, federal court rulings in such cases as *Lau v. Nichols* (1974) and *Castañeda v. Pickard* (1981) have mandated the availability of quality bilingual education in public schools, beginning with the principle that students with limited English-language proficiency are entitled to special assistance under the Civil Rights Act of 1964. Nevertheless, bilingual education remains controversial, as various opposition groups have fought for English-language dominance. In the 1990s, a bilingual policy movement called English Plus emerged in response to the English-only campaign but garnered relatively little public support and media visibility.

At the same time, however, the burgeoning of the nation's Spanish-speaking population has brought a rapid expansion of Spanish-language media. Circulation of Spanish-language daily newspapers increased from less than 140,000 in 1970 to more than 1.7 million in 2002—more than tripling since 1990 alone—according to the National Association of Hispanic Publishers. In television, two national Spanish-language networks, Telemundo and Univision, dominate the marketplace. Both were launched in the mid-twentieth century in an effort to reach the nation's growing Spanish-speaking population. The news media benefit from the fact that, in addition to culture, language defines their target demographic group. Latinos/as who trace their origins to many different countries all share Spanish as a common language; thus, Telemundo and Univision reach a large percentage of viewers even though they broadcast to an audience with varied national backgrounds—from New York's Puerto Rican community to Miami's Cuban community to Los Angeles's Mexican community. Univision's viewership totaled 3.1 million according to 2007 statistics, while Telemundo averaged just over 1 million prime-time viewers.

Vocabulary of Spanish America

Despite the ongoing process of standardization, the Spanish spoken in the Americas today differs somewhat from European Spanish because of words and phrases borrowed from indigenous tongues. Some words reflect natural features of the continent, such as plants and animals, derived from native terms. The words *tabacco* (originally *tabaco*), maize, *tomate*, coyote, pampa, condor, puma, and tapioca, for example, all come from indigenous languages. In addition, the lexicon also includes words from modern American culture and technology, such as *lonche, beisbol, chance, educación, radio,* and *computadora.*

English has also influenced the way some U.S. residents speak Spanish, giving rise to what is commonly called Spanglish—the substitution of English words for Spanish words. The use of "Spanishized" English words, a different kind of blending, takes a unique form called Frontera along the border between Alta California and Baja California. A similar but not identical phenomenon occurs in the border region between Mexico and Arizona, New Mexico,

and Texas. Each region reflects a distinctive mix of English and Spanish words and pronunciations. Thus, a typical Spanglish sentence might take the following form: *"Te llamaré, pues, cuando I get home,"* meaning "I'll call you later when I get home." By contrast, the use of "Spanishized" English in a single sentence is exemplified by the following: *"Voy a rentar un apartmento donde puedo parquear mi carro/auto afuera,"* meaning "I'm going to rent [correct Spanish, *alquilar*] an apartment where I can park [*estacionar*] my car [*coche* or *automovil*] outside." With many bilingual speakers, conversations may mix Spanglish and/or "Spanishized" English or "Englishized" Spanish in sentences of pure, grammatically proper English or pure Spanish. Speakers use the words or phrases that they feel will best convey what they wish to express; the result is a hybrid language. And so the Spanish language continues to evolve, just as cultures continue to evolve, including the old and the new of what was and is spoken in Spain, and what was and is spoken in the countries to which the language has been carried.

RuthAnne Tarletz de Molina

See also: Bilingualism; Conquest of the Americas; Education; Spanglish.

Further Reading

Castells, Matilde, Elizabeth Guzman, Paloma Lapuerta, and Carmen Garcia. *Mosaicos: Spanish as a World Language.* 4th ed. Upper Saddle River, NJ: Prentice Hall 2005.

Castillo, Carlos and Otto F. Bond. *The University of Chicago Spanish-English English-Spanish Dictionary.* New York: Pocket Books, 1987.

Pountain, C. *A History of the Spanish Language through Texts.* New York: Routledge 2000.

Spanish-American War

The Spanish-American War (April-July 1898) was a brief but intense conflict that led to radically reduced Spanish power, in both the Caribbean and the Pacific, and the emergence of the United States as a global imperialist power.

Background and Lead-up

By the latter part of the nineteenth century, the power and preeminence that had accrued to Spain with the "discovery" and settlement of the so-called New World was in conspicuous decline. Its remaining colonial holdings everywhere were few in number and fighting for their independence. Lacking the money and military prowess to contest guerrillas waging war in both the Philippines and Cuba, the Spanish government focused its attention on the latter, sending General Valeriano Weyler in 1897 to pacify the Cuban populace. Nicknamed "Butcher," General Weyler systematically quelled the island rebellion by means of violence on a massive scale, overseeing the murder of hundreds of thousands of Cubans, many of whom died in concentration camps. General Weyler had concluded that the only way to gain control over Cuba was to separate the rebels from the civilian population, sequestering masses of ordinary citizens in guarded compounds under harsh conditions. Many of the civilians died—roughly 300,000—as a result of disease and starvation. In addition, Weyler's forces systematically executed untold numbers of suspected rebels and individuals thought to be supporting their cause. As a result of ongoing battles between Cuban rebels and Spanish troops, the island's infrastructure, crops, livestock, and natural resources were effectively destroyed. By the end of 1897, Weyler had successfully gained control of Cuba's urban areas, while the rebels retained control of the countryside.

Given its geographic proximity to the United States, the events in Cuba elicited significant interest from U.S. politicians and the press, particularly the competing newspaper chains owned by William Randolph Hearst and Joseph Pulitzer, which sensationalized the conflict in their quest to secure readers. Although atrocities were committed on both sides, the American press exaggerated real events and fabricated whole events. The Hearst papers invoked especially alarmist and inflammatory language on a regular basis, characterizing the Spanish as cruel and inhumane while denouncing the Cubans as helpless and weak.

The editorial slant evident in the Hearst chain did not merely reflect its desire to out-duel its

Cuban rebels roast a pig at their jungle camp in 1896. The insurrection was quelled by the Spanish colonial regime, but Cuban independence came with the end of the Spanish-American War in 1898—only to be restricted by the United States in the ensuing years. *(Hulton Archive/Stringer/Getty Images)*

competitor for readers. It also reflected its owner's belief in an expansionist ideology under which the United States should extend its borders, spread democracy through military intervention, and fulfill a God-given mission of civilizing heathen peoples throughout the world. Republican President William McKinley resisted such an expansionist ideology, even though it had gained increasing support in the period leading up the war. Indeed, American expansion had been building since the end of the Civil War, with the acquisition of Alaska in 1867, rapid settlement of Native American lands on the Western frontier, and annexation of Hawaii in 1898. McKinley was clearly bucking the trend of dominant ideology by resisting expansion, as the principles of Manifest Destiny and Social Darwinism justified the spread of Christianity, democracy, and the American republic on grounds of divine providence and prevailing biological science, respectively. The corollary conviction in the superiority of Anglo-Saxon peoples further guided the debate about developments in Cuba and U.S. foreign policy as a whole.

Amid increasing calls for U.S. intervention on the behalf of the Cuban people, Tomás Estrada Palma, a Cuban revolutionary and later the island's first president, with the help of an American banker, offered $150 million in exchange for Cuba's independence from Spain. When the Spanish government refused the offer, Palma turned to the United States for assistance, bringing the cause of Cuban sovereignty before Congress.

In February 1898, two dramatic events pushed the United States into the conflict, joining the island rebels in their struggle for independence: the infamous Lôme letter of early February 1898 and the destruction of the battleship *Maine* in Havana Harbor the following week. In the first incident, Enrique Dupuy de Lôme, the Spanish minister in Washington, wrote a letter—which he intended to be private—to a friend and Spanish official living in Havana, Don José Canalejas, in which he described President McKinley as "weak and catering to the rabble, and, besides, a low politician, who desires to leave a door open to me and to stand well with the jingoes of his party." Cuban revolutionaries stole the letter from a Havana post office and subsequently released it to several American newspapers. Publication of the letter naturally outraged McKinley and angered the American people, helping turn public sentiment against the Spanish regime and in favor of the rebels. Less than a week later, on February 15, the U.S. battleship *Maine,* which had been sent to Havana to protect American lives and property, mysteriously exploded and sank, resulting in the death of 260 American sailors. While the facts remained unclear, the Hearst and Pulitzer papers seized upon the explosion to galvanize U.S. support for military intervention by blaming Spain for the bombing. Under the slogan "Remember the *Maine!* To hell with Spain!" public opinion became hostile and pro-war sentiment gained ascendancy.

Notwithstanding public opinion, President McKinley remained opposed to military intervention, instead taking a cautious approach in ordering an investigation of the *Maine* incident. Although Spanish officials and scientists concluded that the explosion was the result of a shipboard accident, a U.S. commission report rejected this assessment, concluding that the explosion was the result of an external force and most likely an act of war. (A 1976 study by U.S. scientists concluded that the explosion resulted from spontaneous combustion inside the ship's coal bunker. A 1999 study commissioned by the National Geographic Society challenged this finding, arguing instead that the explosion indeed had taken place in the coal bunker but that it had been caused by a mine.) President McKinley remained reluctant to initiate military action against Spain because of his concerns about the consequences of war on the nation's armed forces, its drain on the economy, and the prospective loss of life. In the end, however, public opinion and the conclusions of the *Maine* commission gave McKinley little choice but to take action. To the dismay of many, he opted first for the diplomatic route, demanding that Spain grant Cuba its independence. The regime in Madrid, which was reluctant to do battle with the United States but unwilling to give up its colony, offered autonomy for Cuba—one step short of full independence—which was insufficient to rebels on the island and to the United States.

The prospect of losing Cuba further revealed the shrinking power of the Spanish Empire, leaving Prime Minister Práxedes Mateo Sagasta and others worried about the long-term ramifications of Cuban independence. Such an eventuality would not only damage Spain's economy, but would also send a message to decolonization movements that Spanish hegemony could be challenged at this moment. Thus, fearing further erosion of Spanish global influence and power, Sagasta ultimately rebuffed the diplomatic efforts of the United States, arguing that Spain had the right to keep its overseas possessions; Spain had "discovered" these territories, the regime believed, which was a gift from God for conquering the Moors. Hoping to stave off a U.S.-led revolt, Spain sought diplomatic support from other European powers; it received none.

In mid-March, U.S. Senator Redfield Proctor (R-VT) took to the floor of Congress and, departing from the emotional and sometimes xenophobic arguments common at the time, offered a dispassionate assessment of the situation and concluded that America faced but one choice: war. With business and religious leaders now calling for U.S. military action, President McKinley appeared before Congress on April 11, 1898, at which time he asked for the authority to send U.S. troops to Cuba for the sole purpose of securing peace and independence.

On April 19, Congress passed resolutions demanding that Spain withdraw from Cuba and authorizing President McKinley to use appropriate military force to assist in the fight for national sovereignty. At the same time, Congress unanimously passed the Teller Amendment (named for its sponsor, Senator Henry Teller, R-CO), which stated that the United States had no intention of taking Cuba as a colony and that U.S. armed forces would not take permanent control of the island. In response, Spain severed diplomatic ties with the United States on April 23, leaving few to doubt the imminence of war. On April 25, Congress declared war against Spain but backdated the declaration to April 21 to legitimize certain military operations, such as the blockade of Havana.

Conduct and Consequences

For the United States, the war would begin with two decisive victories: without great opposition, Admiral William Sampson established an immediate blockade of Havana, while Commodore George Dewey destroyed Admiral Patricio Montoyo's small naval force in Manila Bay.

With the onset of fighting, the Spanish immediately dispatched Admiral Pascual Cervera to bolster Spanish forces on the island; on arrival, he docked his vessels in Santiago de Cuba. Admiral Sampson, meanwhile, made his way from Key West, Florida, and arrived in Cuba to blockade Cervera's vessels on June 1. In the days that followed, Major General William Shafter also transferred the Fifth Army Corps from Tampa, Florida, to the vicinity of Santiago de Cuba in preparation for the assault on Cervera's forces. The U.S. Army and Navy commanders disagreed, however, over the best strategy for securing victory against Cervera's forces. Ultimately, General Shafter concluded that Admiral Sampson's plan to capture the Spanish ships in Santiago Harbor would not work and organized an attack on the Spanish from both sides. Only July 1, some 15,000 U.S. ground forces—including Lieutenant Colonel Theodore Roosevelt and his regiment of cavalry volunteers, known as the Rough Riders—attacked some 1,200 Spanish troops in the Battle of El Caney and the Battle of San Juan Hill. With 200 soldiers killed and 1,200 wounded, U.S. casualties exceeded Spanish casualties, and Shafter's plan proved unsuccessful. Quickly abandoning the ground attack, U.S. commanders focused on a sea assault, and the efforts

of Samson and his naval forces secured victory for the United States.

On July 3, Admiral Cervera attempted to lead his ships out of the Santiago Harbor, at which time Admiral Sampson launched a five-hour campaign against the Spanish fleet that resulting in its complete destruction. The following day, Admiral Sampson sent a message back to Washington, in which he reported: "The fleet under my command offers the nation as a Fourth of July present, the whole of Cervera's Fleet." Participating in this battle as well was the future twenty-sixth president, Theodore Roosevelt.

Following the U.S. military successes in Cuba, as well as in the Philippines and Puerto Rico, President McKinley secretly informed Spain, through Great Britain and Austria, that the U.S, demands for peace had now changed. In addition to Cuba's independence, McKinley now sought a port in the Philippines, the island of Guam in the western Pacific Ocean, and the annexation of Puerto Rico, in exchange for monetary compensation. The president made it clear, moreover, that failure to accept these terms would force the United States to increase its demands.

The obliteration of Cervera's squadron effectively decided the outcome of the war, and Spanish military failures elsewhere led the Sagasta government to capitulate to U.S. demands and start peace negotiations. On August 13, as U.S. troops began advancing through Manila, Spanish forces there surrendered, the guerrillas were denied access, and the Americans occupied the city.

On August 12, less than four months after the U.S. Congress had declared war, the hostilities were officially halted with the signing of the Peace Protocol in Washington, D.C.

Having been soundly defeated militarily and with little global support, the Spanish could offer little resistance to the final terms of peace by the United States. On December 10, 1898, with the signing of Treaty of Paris, Spain ceded virtually all of its colonial possessions—the Philippines, Guam, and Puerto Rico—to the United States in exchange for $25 million. Under the provisions of the treaty, Cuba—which had no formal participation in the peace process—was granted independence. The Treaty of Paris was ratified on February 6, 1899, and went into effect on April 11. Two years later, however, as a condition of the withdrawal of U.S. troops, Congress passed legislation—called the Platt Amendment—that severely limited the autonomy of Cuba and made it a kind of de facto protectorate. Under its terms, Cuba remained politically and economically dependent on the United States

Although the Spanish-American War was not of great importance militarily or even an instance of significant global drama, it had major historical significance in international affairs. The United States had been emerging as an economic power through rapid industrialization and diversification in the latter decades of the nineteenth century, and the Spanish-American War signaled its arrival as a great military and diplomatic world power. With this came a more global vision of the U.S. role in the world and a new approach to foreign policy—an orientation variously characterized as expansionist and imperialist. Indeed it resulted in the acquisition of a number of nations and territories that would be directly and sometimes indiscriminately subjected to the policies of the United States, guided predominantly by national interests and ideologies. To the present day, debates rage among historians and other scholars as to whether or not 1898 was a unique moment of U.S. imperialism or the beginning of a long period of effective imperialism through economic domination.

Anita Damjanovic and David J. Leonard

See also: Cubans; Manifest Destiny; Military, Latinos in the.

Further Reading

Field, Ron. *Spanish-American War 1898.* Washington, DC: Brasseys, 1998.

Keenan, Jerry. *Spanish-American and Philippine-American Wars.* Santa Barbara, CA: ABC-CLIO, 2001.

May, Ernest R. *Imperial Democracy: The Emergence of America as a Great Power.* New York: Harcourt, Brace & World, 1961.

Nofi, Albert. *The Spanish-American War, 1898.* Conshohocken, PA: Combined Books, 1996.

Smith, Joseph. *The Spanish-American War: Conflict in the Caribbean and the Pacific 1895–1902.* New York: Longman, 1994.

Spirituality

In broad terms, Latino spirituality may be understood as the set of spiritual beliefs and practices associated with formal religious groups or, conversely, informal spiritual practices not affiliated with a particular church or denomination. Latinos/as living in the United States may choose to observe either form of practice, and many frequently engage in both varieties. What's more, Latinos/as sometimes meld spiritual practices associated with formal religious bodies into their informal rituals. This active "reconstruction" of formal spirituality is sometimes viewed as the result of larger social structural processes, such as globalization and economic marginalization, or, in certain cases, as an attempt by Latinos/as to maintain traditional, indigenous practices under the umbrella of larger, formal religious organizations. Latino spirituality is not a static, unchanging set of spiritual practices but a malleable process reflective of larger socially constructed and historical processes.

Indigenous Religious and Spiritual Practices

Although most Latinos/as today identify with formal religious groups, their participation in these religious groups is, in some ways, reflective of traditional, indigenous religious practices—practices that have been passed through the various cultures of Latin America for hundreds, if not thousands, of years. Examples of these indigenous-inspired religious practices include *Día de los Muertos*—a day corresponding to the Catholic All Saints Day on which Latinos/as engage in the rituals of wearing wooden skull masks, or *calacas,* and dancing to honor their dead relatives, whom they believe return from beyond to visit during this yearly celebration. It is a time for intensive ancestor worship and veneration, a key feature of indigenous religious practice. This ritual has a long history among Latin Americans; some suggest that it was part of Aztec religious tradition for over 3,000 years. Today, *Día de los Muertos* is no long celebrated as a stand-alone holiday but has been subsumed into All Saints Day in many communities. Despite these changes, the holiday retains many of the traditional indigenous elements of the early Aztec ritual.

The practice of *curanderismo* (folk healing) by some Mexican immigrants is another aspect of Latino spirituality with indigenous roots. *Curanderos* (folk healers) address illnesses associated with the mind, body, and spirit by utilizing herbal remedies, aromatherapies, and various ritual enactments. The infirm may be rubbed with herbal oils, while the curandero conducts ritual meditations. Practiced among modern Latinos/as, this ancient healing method has been increasingly acknowledged by Western medical professionals for its salutary effects. Surveys have shown that some Latinos/as will not engage conventional medical practitioners for the treatment of illness, but prefer to seek the assistance of curanderos. For many Latino immigrants, this is an especially salient feature of spiritual experience, particularly as the cost of conventional health care continues to rise and alternative wellness practices become more popular.

Another form of indigenous spiritual practice involves "informal sainthood." Many Latinos/as seek spiritual intervention and assistance from departed individuals whom they regard as capable of addressing their needs and intervening in a spiritual sense on their behalf—even though the departed are not officially designated saints by any formal religious organization. These informal saints, such as Rosario de Talpa de Jalisco, are important symbols of Mexican indigenous spirituality and remain prominent figures in the religious practices of Latinos/as in the United States.

Catholicism and the Latino Experience

Among the most enduring and influential legacies of Spanish colonialism is Latin American Catholicism. This is changing as well, however, as Evangelicals, Mormons, and various Protestant groups have begun to spread their messages throughout Latin America and the Latino immigrant communities of the United States.

Nevertheless, Catholicism certainly remains the most widely practiced formal religion among Latinos/as. Spiritual life is heavily influenced by Catholic symbols and cultural practices, as evidenced by the great number of Latinos/as who attend Catholic churches across the United States and the devotion that many express to prominent Catholic figures such as the pope. The formal Catholic influence remains powerful among Latinos/as in the United States. Most neighborhoods includes at least one Catholic church, which plays an active role in the community. The prominence of baptismal, first communion, and *quinceañera* ceremonies reflect the ongoing influence of Catholicism and its rituals on everyday Latino culture. By the same token, Latinos/as are having a profound impact on the face of Catholicism in the United States. Almost 80 percent of the growth of Catholicism in U.S. parishes is attributed to Latinos/as. In Los Angeles, for example, the largest Catholic archdiocese in the United States, nearly two thirds of all resident Catholics are Latino.

At the same time, the relationship of many Latinos/as with the Catholic Church is ambivalent, at least in part because the religion was originally forced upon Latin Americans by Spanish colonizers rather than freely and autonomously accepted. As such, even though millions of Latinos/as identify themselves as Catholic, many incorporate elements associated with indigenous roots into their spiritual practices. Moreover, the lack of religious infrastructure in rural colonial settings—many converts were forced to travel great distances to the nearest Catholic church or to wait many months for a priest's visit, if they were to receive the Holy Sacraments—prompted religious innovations that persist to the present day.

Protestantism and Evangelicalism

Though Catholicism's influence among Latinos/as is readily visible, a growing number of Latinos/as are embracing the evangelical or "born again" forms of Protestantism. Churches and temples associated with these groups, dispersed throughout Latino communities in cities such as Los Angeles and New York, are also beginning to appear in urban areas with smaller populations, such as cities in North Carolina and Georgia. During the late 1960s and the 1970s, U.S.-based evangelicals devoted extensive efforts to proselytizing in Latin American countries, particularly in Central America, to thwart the spread of liberation theology—a growing movement in the Catholic Church in the area. The movement advocated a reinterpretation of the Bible and the works of Jesus Christ in terms of their relevance to poor people. U.S. evangelicals, fearing the spread of communism and political unrest through liberation theology, funneled substantial financial and human resources into the region. This resulted in a dramatic shift toward evangelical spirituality among Latin Americans, especially those living in the war-torn regions of Central America. This, in turn, brought a rise in evangelicalism among Latinos/as living in the United States, as many of those who had converted during this period migrated to the United States and brought their evangelicalism with them.

Coupled with the influence of immigrant-based evangelicalism was the long-standing presence of Mexican American evangelicals, many of whom played an important role in the initial development of Pentecostalism—a popular variety of evangelicalism among Latinos/as. Mexican Pentecostals were also instrumental in the development of the Latin American Bible Institute (LABI), the Assemblies of God, the Vineyard, Victory Outreach, and other prominent Pentecostal groups in the United States.

Evangelicals engage in a variety of spiritual practices. These include speaking in tongues (glossolalia), in which the Holy Spirit is said to enter an individual's body and compel him or her to speak in a language decipherable to only a select few. Other practices include singing for extended periods to invoke the spirit of Christ, faith healing, extensive prayer at various times during the day, distributing religious tracts and evangelizing to people in public places, attending *escuela dominical* (adult Sunday school), and attending frequent religious services held at different times throughout the week. Not all evangelical groups engage in all of these practices; different churches and congregations incorporate various elements into their services, often reflecting specific socio cultural characteristics. Important to this aspect of evangelicalism is the fact that many Latinos/as congregate in small, storefront temples with modest congregations, sometimes with only five or ten members. Such small congregations are often comprised of individuals with similar experiences and needs—such as the elderly or young—and this allows the congregation to adopt practices that reflect their particular needs and interests.

All in all, the spiritual practices of Latinos/as are highly diverse and reflect a number of religious and cultural traditions. Indigenous religious traditions, Catholicism, Protestantism, and other religious bodies all have had a profound impact on the way Latinos/as practice their spirituality. As the tides of immigration continue to swell in the twenty-first century, it is certain that the face of Latino spirituality in the United States will change even while maintaining bits and pieces of its religious heritage.

Sarah Stohlman

See also: Día de los Muertos; Religion.

Further Reading

Broyles-González, Yolanda. "Indianizing Catholicism: Chicana/India/Mexicana Indigenous Spiritual Practices in Our Image." In *Chicana Traditions: Continuity and Change,* ed. Norma E. Cantú and Olga Nájera-Ramírez. Urbana: University of Illinois Press, 2002.

Sánchez-Walsh, Arlene. *Latino Pentecostal Identity.* New York: Columbia University Press, 2003.

Sterilization

Sterilization is an irreversible surgical procedure that renders men and women unable to reproduce. When performed on women, as it is in the majority of cases, the procedure usually involves the cutting, burning, tying, or removing of a portion of the fallopian tubes to prevent ova from reaching the uterus. Sterilization, both voluntary and involuntary, has been an issue of significant concern to Mexican and Puerto Rican women in the United States.

Voluntary Sterilization

Voluntary sterilization is the most common birth control method practiced by Puerto Rican women in both Puerto Rico and the United States. During the 1930s, the Puerto Rican government launched a program aimed at reducing the island's total population by encouraging birth control and migration. Government officials believed that such action would curb Puerto Rico's growing poverty and unemployment problems. Because it was irreversible and lacked the moral stigma of abortion, sterilization became the method of birth control preferred by both the government and general populace. In 1940, only 7 percent of the female island population was sterilized, but by 1965, a reported 34 percent of all married Puerto Rican women aged 20–49 had undergone the operation. Sterilization became so commonplace that women came to refer to the procedure simply as "*la operación*" ("the operation").

Puerto Rican women living in the United States today undergo sterilization at a much higher rate than any other ethnic group. Studies conducted on the Puerto Rican population of New York City found that while island-born residents were more likely to be sterilized than their mainland-born counterparts, the latter group still underwent sterilization at a significantly higher rate than white or African American women did.

There are a number of possible causes at both the structural and individual levels for the unusually high rate of voluntary sterilization among Puerto Rican women on both the island and the mainland. Structural causes include restrictive population policy, financial inability to provide for additional children, and lack of access to temporary birth control methods. Individual causes include familiarity with the procedure, the early average age of childbirth, a high rate of misinformation regarding the procedure, and sole female responsibility for birth control and child rearing.

Involuntary Sterilization

Involuntary sterilization became legal in the United States in the 1920s due to the enormous popularity and assumed scientific validity of the eugenics movement. Coined in 1883 by Charles Darwin's cousin, Francis Galton, the term "eugenics" derives from the Greek for "well-born." The movement gained popularity throughout the world, and its cause was championed by many of the great minds of the day, including Alexander Graham Bell and the Nobel laureate Thomas Hunt Morgan, whose work with fruit flies revealed the role of chromosomes in heredity.

Yet eugenics was a pseudo-science based on a fundamental misunderstanding of the laws governing genetic inheritance and evolution. Lacking the technology but not the will to support their claims, eugenicists asserted that genes determine not only physical traits, but personality as well. Personality traits such as criminality, promiscuity, deviance, and "feeble-mindedness," for example, were all believed to be genetically determined at birth. Thus, eugenicists sought to improve the human race by encouraging people with desirable traits to increase reproduction and by preventing the handicapped and those deemed "undesirable" from polluting the human gene pool through forced sterilization. In the United States, this label was applied disproportionately to Latinos/as, African Americans, and other stigmatized groups. The Nazi government's extermination of millions of Jews, Gypsies, homosexuals, and political prisoners during the Holocaust in World War II represents the most extreme case of eugenics theory put into action.

In 1897, Michigan became the first U.S. state to propose a sterilization law, but the measure failed to pass the state legislature. Ten years later, Indiana successfully passed sterilization legislation, but the state supreme court abolished the law in 1921. More than a dozen other states attempted to adopt their own sterilization laws but were opposed in the courts. By 1925, all state sterilization laws had been ruled unconstitutional except those of Virginia and Michigan. This changed in 1927 when the U.S. Supreme Court set the legal precedent for involuntary sterilization with their ruling in the case of *Buck v. Bell*.

When Virginia adopted its own sterilization law in 1924, doctors chose seventeen-year-old Carrie Buck as the first to be sterilized against her will. Like her mother before her, Buck had given birth to a child out of wedlock. Officials deemed her "feeble-minded" with "hereditary promiscuity" and committed her to a state institution. Buck's attempt to escape sterilization took her all the way to the U.S. Supreme Court. The justices ruled, 8–1, to uphold Virginia's sterilization law, claiming that the operation was in the best interest of the patient and society in general. Justice Oliver Wendell Holmes, Jr., writing for the majority stated, "three generations of imbeciles are enough. . . ." Ironically, Buck had not become pregnant for being promiscuous, but because she had been raped by a family member, her foster parents' nephew. The *Buck v. Bell* case legitimized involuntary sterilization, and in the wake of the ruling, twenty-seven states adopted sterilization laws. Over the next five decades, more than 60,000 people—disproportionately women of color—were sterilized against their will.

Involuntary sterilization continued in the United States following the defeat of Germany in World War II. The discovery of Nazi concentration camps caused some, having seen what it could lead to, to abandon the cause of eugenics altogether. For others, though, Nazi eugenics provided an extreme case against which the American brand seemed quite civil. Proposals for race-, class-, or disability-based sterilization continued to emerge during the postwar period. Many doctors and legislators continued to believe that involuntary sterilization was justified on the grounds that it could reduce poverty and hunger for future generations of Americans.

The low socioeconomic status of Mexican women living in the United States made them frequent victims of involuntary sterilization all the way into the 1970s. In 1978, ten women of Mexican descent brought a lawsuit against the Southern California-Los Angeles County Medical Center for sterilizing them against their will or without their knowledge. The prosecution argued that the doctors, who treated poor Latinas almost exclusively, regarded sterilization as necessary for population control, surgical practice for resident interns, and the "social good" of the patient.

The accused doctors had coerced the plaintiffs into agreeing to sterilization through a variety of means, including granting abortion requests contingent on acceptance of sterilization, presenting sterilization consent forms written in English as cesarean section releases, performing sterilization operations without the patients' knowledge immediately following delivery or abortion, claiming that California law required them to sterilize anyone who had undergone three cesarean section deliveries, and withholding pain killers during labor until consent was granted. Although the facts of the case illustrated that coercing Latina women into sterilization was standard practice at the medical center, the judge ruled in favor of the doctors, saying he could not blame them for cultural misunderstandings that resulted from language differences.

Sterilization Today

The 1970s saw the formation of the Committee to End Sterilization Abuse (CESA) for the purpose of monitoring the process by which poor minorities may be coerced, encouraged, or forced to consent to sterilization. Combining their efforts with those of other activist groups, the CESA successfully lobbied for legislation that defined informed consent and mandated that it be obtained at least seven days prior to any sterilization procedure.

In 2002, Virginia became the first state to issue a public apology for its participation in eugenics, with Governor Mark Warner calling the program "a shameful effort in which the state government never should have been involved." To date, no other state has apologized for crimes perpetrated in the name of eugenics. Today, eugenics continues in a more individualized form whereby parents can have their fetus checked for birth defects and choose to abort the pregnancy. While involuntary sterilization is no longer commonplace in the Latino community, voluntary sterilization continues to be the most popular method of birth control practiced by Puerto Rican women on the U.S. mainland and in Puerto Rico itself.

Bretton T. Alvaré

See also: Mexicans; Puerto Ricans.

Further Reading

Cogdell, Christine. *Eugenic Design: Streamlining America in the 1930s.* Philadelphia: University of Pennsylvania Press, 2004.

Del Castillo, Adelaida R. "Sterilization: An Overview." In *Mexican Women in the United States: Struggles Past and Present,* ed. Magdalena Mora and Adelaida R. Del Castillo. Los Angeles: Chicano Studies Research Center, University of California Press, 1980.

Hernandez, Antonia. "Chicanas and the Issue of Involuntary Sterilization: Reforms Needed to Protect Informed Consent." *Chicano Law Review* 3:3 (1976): 3 37.

Ordover, Nancy. *American Eugenics: Race, Queer Anatomy, and the Science of Nationalism.* Minneapolis: University of Minnesota Press, 2003.

Wehmeyer, Michael. "Eugenics and Sterilization in the Heartland." *Mental Retardation* 41:1 (2003): 57–60.

Taos Rebellion

The Taos Rebellion was a bloody fight between Hispano (Mexican and Indian) landowners in New Mexico and the U.S. Army in January 1847. The battle took place during the ongoing westward expansion of the United States and in the midst of the Mexican-American War, as Hispanos organized a popular insurrection against U.S. occupation of the territory. Although the Taos Rebellion was put down in a matter of a few weeks, it foreshadowed the struggles over land in the Southwest in the years to come.

In August 1846, after years of resistance to American settlers on the part of residents, New Mexico (then a Mexican province) was occupied by U.S. forces under General Stephen Watts Kearny. Governor Manuel Armijo surrendered to General Kearny at the Battle of Santa Fe, effectively ceding all of New Mexico to the Americans, without a shot being fired. Hispano residents deeply resented the foreign occupation but submitted to the vastly more powerful U.S. Army forces. Without direct resistance, Kearny and his troops soon departed Santa Fe for California, leaving New Mexico under the control of Colonel Sterling Price and newly appointed Governor Charles Bent.

Shortly after Kearny's departure, which left few troops inside New Mexico, several Hispanos devised a plan to attack and drive away Anglo American settlers in the province. The uprising, planned for Christmas Day 1846, was postponed after U.S. authorities got wind of the plot. Despite pleas by Governor Bent for domestic tranquility and peace between Hispanos and Anglo settlers, the insurrection broke out on January 19, 1847, as Hispano rebels under the leadership of Pablo Montoya and Tomasito, a Toaseña Indian, assassinated Governor Bent and his family. Several other Anglo officials in Don Fernando de Taos (present-day Taos, New Mexico), including Stephen Lee, the acting county sheriff, Cornelio Vigil, prefect and probate judge, and J.W. Leal, a circuit court attorney, were murdered as well. At the same time, a group of Anglo traders operating under the American flag were murdered while passing through the Mora area of New Mexico. In Aroyo Hondo, rebels laid siege to Simeon Turley's Mill, killing several Anglo employees. According to Colonel Price, "It appeared to be the object of the insurrectionists to put to death every . . . man who had accepted office under the American government."

The U.S. government responded with a major military offensive. Following a failed attack on the insurgents in Mora that resulted in the death of Captain Israel Hendley on January 24, Captain Jesse Morin led a cannon brigade into the area on February 1, 1847. Morin and his force of 200 succeeded in defeating the rebels, ultimately destroying the village of Mora and burning the surrounding ranches and fields. Meanwhile, Colonel Price led his troops into La Embudo Pass and Pueblo de Taos. In Taos, rebels retreated into an old Spanish mission church, leading to a two-day battle that resulted in heavy casualties for both sides; an estimated 150 to 200 Hispano rebels died in the fight. The Americans were clearly in command, reclaiming control of large territories with each succeeding battle. By February 7, the insurrection had been completely quelled.

The leaders of the Taos Rebellion were promptly put on trial, convicted, and publicly hanged in the Plaza at Taos. Over the next months, at least twenty-one other rebels were likewise tried and hanged for their role in the incident. Less than a year later, the worst fears of Hispano rebels became a reality, as New Mexico was acquired by the United States in the Mexican-American War and the Treaty of Guadalupe Hidalgo that concluded it. All nonnative inhabitants who did not leave the area within one year became U.S. citizens.

Jesse J. Esparza and David J. Leonard

See also: Mexican-American War.

Further Reading

Beck, Warren A. *New Mexico: A History of Four Centuries.* Norman: University of Oklahoma Press, 1962.

Durand, John. *The Taos Massacres.* Elkhorn, WI: Puzzlebox, 2004.

Ortiz, Roxanne Dunbar. *Roots of Resistance: Land Tenure in New Mexico, 1680–1980.* Los Angeles: Chicano Studies Center, University of California at Los Angeles, 1980.

Teatro Campesino, El

El Teatro Campesino (the Farmworkers Theater, or ETC) is an influential Mexican American performing arts organization located in San Juan Bautista, California, and founded as an extension of the United Farm Workers of America (UFW). The company was created in October 1965 by Luis Valdez and musician Agustín Lira, college-educated children of Mexican American migrant laborers, to recruit for César Chávez's fledgling farmworkers union, to draw attention to the plight of migrants, and to promote Chicano culture and identity. One of the first arts organizations dedicated to dramatizing the Chicano experience and working with Chicano performers, writers, and staff, ETC has played in some of the most acclaimed U.S. theaters, toured internationally, and won a number of mainstream theater awards. Its plays draw on traditional Mexican and Mexican American dramatic forms such as *carpas,* or tent shows; the Mexican comedian Mario Moreno Reyes's Cantinflas character (an urban farmworker bum); commedia dellarte; and religious, particularly Catholic, Aztec, and Mayan, ritual. In the 2000s, the group's performances seek to portray the Chicano experience in a context meaningful to all Americans.

Origins

The original troupe was made up entirely of migrant agricultural laborers and other members of Chávez's United Farm Workers of America. For most of the 1960s and 1970s, ETC members organized and performed as a collective: writing and improvising plays; creating costumes, props, and sets; and conducting publicity, fund-raising, and administrative work. Touring the bean fields and fruit orchards of central California, the troupe entertained migrant farmworkers and portrayed their experiences on flatbed trucks and makeshift stages. During Chávez's 340-mile (550-kilometer) march from Delano, California, to the state capitol in Sacramento in spring 1966 to draw national attention to the plight of farmworkers, ETC performed at nightly rallies to motivate farmworkers to join the union. Later it put on shows at weekly union meetings in Delano, usually a simple *acto* and a few songs. (*Actos* are short improvisational comic pieces satirizing difficult situations, employing Spanglish, miming, and slapstick, with few costumes and props. Placards were hung on the actors' necks to identify characters.)

During the course of the 1960s, ETC established its reputation as a quality theatrical troupe as well as a social activist organization. It began making the college circuit, hawking recordings, posters, scripts, and newsletters to pay travel costs. In 1967, ETC organized its first national tour to raise funds for striking farmworkers. Seeking to address a wider audience and set of concerns, the troupe became independent of the UFW and established El Centro Campesino Cultural (Farmworkers Cultural Center) in the town of Del Ray. It produced actos about the Vietnam War, indigenous culture, racism, equal education, and the growing Chicano civil rights movement—also known as *El Movimiento.* In 1969, ETC moved its base to Fresno; produced the film *I Am Joaquin: An Epic Poem,* a dramatization of Rodolfo "Corky" Gonzales's verse on Chicano history and culture; and created El Teatro Nacional de Aztlán (TENAZ), a national network of Chicano theater groups. TENAZ members would go on to plan national theater festivals throughout the western United States and cosponsor a major international theater festival in Mexico City in 1974.

Growth

In 1971, ETC moved to San Juan Bautista and began to follow a more consistent work schedule. Valdez began teaching drama at the University of California campuses at Berkeley and Santa Cruz from 1971 to 1974, drawing student members to ETC. In the early 1970s, ETC members studied with Aztec elder Andrés Segura and Mayan teacher Domingo Martínez Paredez, further enriching their knowledge of Mexican culture and ritual. Out of this emerged ETC's "Theatre of the Sphere," an aesthetic that emphasizes Mayan and Aztec spirituality. The troupe also began peforming *mitos* (myths), indigenous dance dramas that Valdez defined as "God's view of things." The mito *El Baile de los Gigantes,* for example, is an adaptation from the *Popul Vuh,* a Mayan sacred text. Also in 1971, ETC first presented the miracle play *La Virgen del Tepeyac* and, adapted with puppets, *La Pastorela: A Shepard's Tale.* The next year, it produced the nineteenth-century musical melodrama *Rose of the Rancho.*

In summer 1973, British stage director Peter Brook brought his International Centre of Theatre Research troupe to work with ETC. The two companies collaborated on a production based on an adaptation of the twelfth-century Persian poem *The Conference of the Birds,* which they performed at colleges and farmworker camps across California. The same year, ETC created its first collective full-length piece, *La Carpa de los Rasquachis* (The Tent of the Underdogs).

By the mid-1970s, ETC began moving toward more commercial productions, as evidenced by the designation of the group's *La Carpa* as an official U.S. Bicentennial event in 1976. Later that year, the Public Broadcasting Service (PBS) aired a film version of *La Carpa,* under the title *El Corrido.* In 1977, ETC members performed in the Richard Pryor comedy *Which Way Is Up?* (Valdez collaborated on the screenplay), further spreading awareness of the theater group. In 1978, ETC began to hold auditions for actors for the first time.

According to some critics, this was the point at which the collective nature and community theater focus of ETC began to dissolve into a more mainstream, hierarchical performing arts organization. ETC performed *Zoot Suit,* based on the Sleepy Lagoon murder trial and Zoot Suit Riots of the 1940s at the Aquarius Theatre in Los Angeles for forty-six weeks before moving to Broadway in 1979; as the

El Teatro Campesino, which began entertaining farmworkers with touring theatrical shows in the 1960s, has also sponsored other Latino groups and events. Culture Clash, a 1980s spin-off troupe, features political and social satire. *(Culture Clash Collection. Urban Archives Center. Oviatt Library. California State University, Northridge)*

first Chicano play to open on Broadway, it received mixed reviews and shut down after four weeks. As a result, the entire ETC ensemble was laid off for the first time in its history, and the original troupe was disbanded.

By the early 1980s, the ETC had rebounded. With an equal number of ensemble and auditioned performers, it received its first major National Endowment for the Arts grant and hired professional administrators for the first time. In 1981, the ETC opened a new theater facility—a transformed fruit-packing building from the 1940s—and presented *The Rose of the Rancho* and *Bandido.* The following year, it produced *Corridos,* a musical of Mexican and Mexican American narrative songs, at the San Juan

Bautista Playhouse and other theaters in the state. In 1987, PBS aired *Corridos: Tales of Passion and Revolution* starring Grammy Award–winning vocalist Linda Ronstadt. Valdez continued to write and direct throughout the 1980s; his film *La Bamba* (1987), the tragic story of Chicano rock and roll singer Ritchie Valens, met with critical success and launched the screen careers of actors Lou Diamond Phillips and Esai Morales.

The Next Generation

Although the company faced challenges in the mid-1990s, including bankruptcy and the laying off of most of its staff, ETC continued to stage new and revived works into the twenty-first century, with Valdez's three sons—Kinan, Anahuac, and Lakin—overseeing much of the day-to-day and creative work. In addition to its acclaimed and popular works of the past, such as *Zoot Suit,* and *Corridos,* it developed such new shows as the rock musical *The Fascinatrix.* Still based in San Juan Bautista, ETC holds yearly Christmas pageants, alternating annually between *La Virgen del Tepeyac* and *La Pastorela.* In addition, the group trains and mentors Third World directors, playwrights, and actors.

Vibrina Coronado

See also: Chávez, César; Migrant Workers; Performance Art, Solo; United Farm Workers of America; Valdez, Luis.

Further Reading

Broyles-González, Yolanda. *El Teatro Campesino: Theater in the Chicano Movement.* Austin: University of Texas Press, 1994.

El Teatro Campesino. http://www.elteatrocampesino.com.

El Teatro Campesino: The Evolution of America's First Chicano Theatre Company, 1965–1985. San Juan Bautista, CA: El Teatro Campesino, 1985.

Elam, Harry J., Jr. *Taking It to the Streets: The Social Protest Theater of Luis Valdez and Amiri Baraka.* Ann Arbor: University of Michigan Press, 2001.

Rose-Avila, Magdaleno. "Homegrown Revolution: Magdaleno Rose-Avila Offers a Historical Perspective on the Social Action Theater of Teatro Campesino—Protest & Art." *Colorlines Magazine: Race, Action, Culture* (Fall 2003).

Tejanos

Tejanos, an archaic Spanish spelling of Texanos, or Texans, refer to those Latinos/as in Texas who can trace their ancestry back to the original Spanish settlers of the state in the late eighteenth and early nineteenth centuries, when the territory that is now the Lone Star State was part of the Spanish empire. Most of these settlers were light-skinned and ethnically Spanish, as opposed to the largely mestizo, or mixed-Spanish and Amerindian, population of central and southern New Spain, which Mexico was called prior to independence. By the time of official Mexican independence in 1821, there were roughly 5,000 Tejanos in what is now Texas. Most identified with other Spanish colonists in Louisiana rather than with the inhabitants of central and southern Mexico. They generally were ranchers and farmers, though some lived in small settlements such as those at Nacogdoches and San Antonio.

During the 1820s and 1830s, large numbers of Anglo settlers, primarily from the southern United States, settled in Texas. By the early part of the latter decade, they outnumbered the Tejanos by about four or five to one. Unlike in California two decades later, the newly arriving Anglos and resident Tejanos generally got along well. There was intermarriage between the two groups as well as a shared political outlook. Both chafed under centralized rule from Mexico City, desiring instead a more federalist system of government in the country, with significant autonomy granted to far-flung provinces like Texas. And both were generally supportive of slavery, despite the fact that the new Mexican government had outlawed the practice. By the mid-1830s, both groups were in open revolt against the government in Mexico City and both played an important role in the revolution that led to Texan independence in 1836.

With independence came new tensions between Anglos and Tejanos. More affluent and more numerous, Anglo settlers began to seize Tejano land and cattle, forcing many to flee to Mexico, a dangerous decision given that authorities there considered them traitors for their participation in the Texan revolt. But many Tejano settlements survived and many Tejanos stayed on, laying the seeds of a culture that has survived in a much watered down form into the twenty-first century.

But over the years, the meaning of the term Tejano has shifted and now broadly includes almost any Latino/a who can trace his or her ancestry back to the nineteenth century, in contradistinction to the much larger population of Texan Mexican Americans who immigrated to the state in the twentieth century. Most Tejanos today identify with both their Spanish and Latin American heritage, with some celebrating African or Native American roots as well.

For the most part, Tejanos today, most of whom live in the southern part of the state, are well integrated into the larger Anglo population. Many do not speak Spanish at all, even as they claim a distinctive culture, much of it rooted in the celebration of a now largely lost vaquero (Spanish for cowboy) lifestyle and ethos. Aside from a distinctive style of cooking, known as Tex-Mex, with its emphasis on spiced and barbecued beef, Tejano culture is rooted in music. Tejano or Tex-Mex music is closely related to the sounds of northern Mexican styles, such as *norteño* or *ranchera*. Like the people who play it, contemporary Tejano music is a hybrid. Traditionally featuring accordian and *bajo sexto,* or an oversized, twelve-string guitar, but now incorporating saxophones and electric bass, Tejano music is a polkalike dance music—many Slavs and Germans settled in southern Texas in the nineteenth and early twentieth centuries—with the rhythms of U.S. big band swing music from the mid-twentieth century. The most popular recent purveyor of Tejano music and, arguably, the most famous Tejano musician of all time was the Grammy-winning Selena Quintanilla-Pérez, who was often referred to as the "queen of Tejano music," before her tragic murder in 1995 at the age of twenty-three.

James Ciment

See also: Identity and Labels; Music; Selena.

Further Reading

San Miguel, Guadalupe. *Tejano Proud: Tex-Mex Music in the Twentieth Century.* College Station: Texas A&M University Press, 2002.

Tijerina, Andrés. *Tejanos and Texas under the Mexican Flag, 1821–1836.* College Station: Texas A&M University Press, 1994.

Telemundo

Telemundo, a subsidiary of NBC Universal Media Group, is the second-largest Spanish-language television network in the United States. Based in Hialeah, Florida, it reaches 92 percent of Latino viewers though its thirty-six broadcast affiliates and nearly 700 cable affiliates. The NBC Universal Television Stations division also owns and operates fifteen Telemundo stations, as well as one independent Spanish-language television station.

Telemundo began as a single television station in Puerto Rico. On July 24, 1952, the Federal Communications Commission (FCC) granted the first permit for the construction of a commercial television station in a U.S. territory to El Mundo Broadcasting Company (founded by Angel Rámos), which also owned *El Mundo* newspaper and radio station WKAQ. Telemundo went on the air as WKAQ-TV on Channel 2 in San Juan on February 12, 1954.

On April 14, 1983, WKAQ-TV was sold to John Blair and Company, a U.S. broadcast sales firm that was subsequently acquired by Reliance Capital Group. Reliance already owned several Spanish-language television stations throughout the United States and, in 1986, shortly after purchasing Telemundo (WKAQ-TV), combined them to create the Telemundo television network. Thus, Telemundo of Puerto Rico became part of an ample network of Latino TV stations on the mainland.

Telemundo first went on the air in 1987, and from the outset emphasized U.S.-produced programming, primarily as a way of distinguishing itself from its main competitor, Univision. During its early years, Telemundo not only produced its own news and sports shows, but also offered *Cocina Crisco,* the first Spanish-language cooking show produced in the United States; *Angelica Mi Vida,* the first Spanish-language *telenovela* (soap opera) produced entirely on U.S. soil; and *Ocurrio Asi,* a tabloid news show with sensational stories from the United States and Latin America. By 1991, Telemundo was producing 54 percent of its programming in the United States.

The cost of creating in-house content during this period, however, proved far greater than the revenues the network earned through advertising sales.

In addition, many of the younger viewers the network had set out to capture viewed Spanish-language television as old-fashioned and rejected it in favor of mainstream youth-oriented programming, such as that offered by MTV. Thus, by mid-1993, Telemundo was in financial trouble and filed for bankruptcy under Chapter 11. After undergoing sweeping personnel and fiscal restructuring, the network finally emerged from bankruptcy in late 1994.

Wary of financial overexposure but determined to offer an alternative to Univision's telenovela-centered programming, Telemundo executives reached a production deal with Sony Pictures Entertainment in 1997. Under the terms of the deal, Sony re-created popular series from its archives of licensed TV shows in Spanish, including *Angeles* (*Charlie's Angels*), *Living En America* (*One Day at a Time*), and *Los Recien Casados* (*The Newlywed Game*). This new strategy was unveiled during the 1998 fall season in the hopes of attracting younger viewers who had lost interest in novelas. But young Spanish-speaking viewers had other ideas. During the 1998–1999 season, Telemundo's audience share plunged to an all-time low of 8 percent. By mid-1999, the network had returned to a telenovela-centric prime time schedule. Ironically, it was the acquisition of a Colombian telenovela, "Betty La Fea," that enabled Telemundo to surpass Univision's ratings in key markets during the 2000–2001 season.

In late 2001, the NBC Universal Media Group announced plans to acquire Telemundo Group Inc., and the deal was finalized in April of the following year. This transaction provided Telemundo with a vast programming library, an infusion of fresh capital, and access to all of NBC Television's national and local resources. Access to NBC Television's infrastructure gave a boost to Telemundo's news division. Many of its local and national news shows now beat Univision's in key markets, such as New York, Los Angeles, and San Antonio, Texas.

While Telemundo continues to compete directly with Univision by making telenovelas a central part of its programming strategy, the network's commitment to U.S.-produced content remains strong. All of the telenovelas shown on the network are made in the United States, a fact that Telemundo executives like to highlight while pointing out that Univision's novelas are produced abroad for foreign audiences. In 2004, Telemundo also launched Taller Telemundo, the first writers' workshop for aspiring telenovela writers. The four-month writing program is held in conjunction with Miami Dade College. After graduation, half the students enter an apprentice program at Telemundo to work on existing shows.

Telemundo has come a long way from its origins as a one-station network in Puerto Rico. Today it is a leading broadcaster in Puerto Rico and the second-largest Spanish-language television network on the mainland. While it has yet to catch up with Univision, it has been better able to compete against it thanks in large part to the resources of its parent company, NBC Universal Media Group. As the Latino/a community within the United States continues to grow—and as more and more second-generation viewers come of age—Telemundo executives hope their efforts to capture U.S.-born audiences with programming reflecting their unique experiences and concerns may enable it to challenge Univision's dominance.

Patricia Kim-Rajal

See also: Spanish Language; Television; Univision.

Further Reading

Noriega, Chon A. *Shot in America: Television, the State, and the Rise of Chicano Cinema.* Minneapolis: University of Minnesota Press, 2000.

Rodriguez, America. *Making Latino News: Race, Language, Class.* Thousand Oaks, CA: Sage, 1999.

Television

The history of Latinos and Latinas on North American television has both paralleled and lagged behind the experience of that immigrant group within society at large. Reflecting their relatively small numbers and rather low social profile in the United States in the first years of the medium, Latinos/as were rarely to be seen on the small screen. Those that were seen often were cast in the stereotypes that North Americans held of them. With the rise of Latino social activism in the 1960s came an end to the crudest of those stereotyped depictions, as well as the begin-

Cuban émigré Desi Arnaz played the role of orchestra leader Ricky Ricardo, husband of Lucille Ball in the hit television series *I Love Lucy* (1951–1957). The show's popularity made him the most familiar Latino face—and stereotype—in America. *(Leonard McCombe/Stringer/ Time & Life Pictures/Getty Images)*

nings of more rounded Latino characters. Still, through the 1970s and 1980s, there were few Latinos/as to be seen on national network television. The rapid growth of the Latino population finally began to have an impact on American television in two ways—more Latinos/as were featured in English-language series and more Spanish-language stations became available over the air and on cable.

Stereotypes in Early Television

The early depiction of Latinos/as on television was, not surprisingly, a legacy of Hollywood image-making. For decades, Latinos/as had been depicted in film largely as criminals, buffoons, or hot-blooded lovers, and so, in those incarnations, they showed up in early television. The most popular Latino star of early television was no criminal. But Desi Arnaz—who played Ricky Ricardo, the ever-suffering husband to Lucille Ball's Lucy Ricardo—did, say many media critics, embody the latter two stereotypes, a handsome Latin lover-

type forever flummoxed by his wife's antics and schemes.

For children, early television offered the cartoon character of Speedy Gonzalez, "the fastest mouse in Mexico." Speedy himself was no buffoon. The only stereotypical things about him were the audio and visual gags—he spoke with a heavy Spanish accent and wore an oversized sombrero, or traditional Mexican hat. But Speedy was repeatedly the odd man out in the cartoon, the hero who had to go in to rescue his fellow Mexican mice who, as stand-ins for stereotyped Mexican people, were depicted as lazy, hard-drinking womanizers.

In television advertising there was the Frito Bandito, mascot for Frito brand corn chips in the late 1960s and early 1970s. Singing the traditional Mexican tune "Canta no Llores," the Frito Bandito was, as its name implied, the cartoon incarnation of the stereotypical Mexican bandit. Packing two pistols and wearing a sombrero and bandaleros, the Frito Bandito spoke in a broken, Spanish-inflected English. He was also a character out of time, prompting much criticism from a newly politicized Mexican American community. At first, groups like the National Mexican American Anti-Defamation Committee (NMAADC) were only able to get the Bandito's worst features removed, such as his gold tooth and beard stubble. But it was the character itself that was offensive, and, finally, after much protest, Frito-Lay, the makers of the snack food, retired the Bandito for good.

Still, despite the fracas over the Frito Bandito, marketers' attempts to cash in on Latino stereotyping did not die in the early 1970s. Nearly a quarter century after the Bandito was retired, the national Mexican fast food chain, Taco Bell, aired its "Yo Quiero Taco Bell" ad campaign, featuring a talking Chihuahua, setting off new protests.

Efforts at Empowerment

Removing stereotypes was only one part of a larger effort in the late 1960s and early 1970s to improve the standing of Latinos/as on television. More important was the struggle to increase Latino access to television production, through training programs to develop future writers, directors, and editors; increased employment opportunities within the industry; and the creation of Latino-focused programming. And many in the community believed that with greater Latino presence on the production side of television, the depictions of Latinos/as would change as well. In 1969, the Equal Employment Opportunity Commission (EEOC) ran a series of hearings to explore what many considered to be the institutionalized racism and sexism in the television industry. The hearings exposed an industry that, critics said, systematically excluded women and minorities, including Latinos/as. Lacking power to litigate these cases, the EEOC merely provided a series of recommendations to the television companies and networks.

But this produced few substantive changes, leading several Latino activist groups, including Nosotros, a group founded by Mexican American movie and television actor Ricardo Montalbán, and NMAADC to lobby government agencies and congressional committees on the topic of stereotyping and the lack of Latino representation both in front of and behind the cameras. But for Latino activists, lobbying government agencies seemed a futile waste of time. Groups such as Justice for Chicanos in the Motion Picture and Television Industry (Justicia) utilized more militant tactics, including boycotting the Academy Awards and picketing local television stations, networks, and industry guilds to demand more positive representation and access to the media. Their threat to bring the militant and direct action–oriented Chicano organization the Brown Berets to industry offices unless changes were made had an immediate, though short-lived, impact in some cases. All three networks at the time, as well as the Public Broadcasting System (PBS), began to air more Latinos/as in their programming. Justicia's work had the most direct effect on television programming, and as a result, a number of Latino-created series were screened on all three networks and PBS.

The early 1970s saw a number of Latino-created and Latino-themed shows go on the air, albeit mostly on local stations rather than networks. These included, for Mexican Americans, ¡Ahora! (1969–1970), a news and public affairs show on KCET (the Los Angeles affiliate of PBS), which focused on the politics and culture of the Los Angeles Latino community; another California-based show, Unidos (1970–1971), which focused on the stories of average people in the Chicano community including welfare mothers and prisoners; and Acción Chicano (1972–1974), a weekly public affairs, culture, and arts series also on KCET. There were also specials, such as the Emmy Award–winning Los Vendidos (1972), a film version of Chicano playwright's Luis Valdez's drama of the same name.

All of these shows benefited from the federal Prime-Time Access Rule (PTAR), which stated that, because the public owned the airwaves, networks were obligated to provide public service information. By the 1970s, media activists had seized on the communal demands for access and visibility and the leverage provided by PTAR to facilitate greater Latino presence on American television. These shows not only brought the experiences of Latinos/as into American households, while demonstrating the financial significance of the Latino market to television executives, but provided the training ground for many Latino and Latina filmmakers, technicians, producers, and others. And the shows were varied: documentaries, discussions of social and political issues, art performances, and filmed conversations. Still, all the activity and activism had little effect on Latino media ownership. While there were zero television stations owned by Latinos/as in 1970, the figure in the early 2000s was still less than 2 percent.

Programming

Aired in 1969, I Am Joaquin, a dramatic reading of Rodolfo "Corky" Gonzales's poem "I Am Joaquin" ("Yo Soy Joaquín"), was the first Chicano film to appear on network television. The poem presented a celebration of Mexican history as a problematic combination of indigenous and Spanish cultures—an amalgam of conquered peoples and their conquerors—as a way to metaphorically represent the Chicano identity and experience. The poem and film ended in a call for community activism and resistance to American assimilation. Directed by Luis Valdez (in collaboration with his theater company, El Teatro Campesino), it constituted a combination of political activism and poetic consciousness, which became an important theme in the Chicano Movement of the period but had little effect on the presence of Latinos/as on television.

The first mainstream network show to feature a Latino lead character was *Chico and the Man,* which aired on the National Broadcasting Company (NBC) from 1974 to 1978. Although the star, Freddie Prinze, was actually of Puerto Rican background, he played a young Chicano mechanic working in an East Los Angeles garage. In the series, the Anglo owner, played by Jack Albertson, starts out as a bigot who spews anti-Latino slurs but eventually grows to accept Chico as a surrogate son and comes to accept the changing demographics of the neighborhood, as it transitions from a white working-class enclave to a large Chicago barrio. According to television historians, the program was troubled from the start. A Chicano activist was hired as a consultant, but his ideas were largely ignored by the show's writers and directors, while critics denounced the show for its exaggerated accents and the ubiquity of ethnic slurs used by the show's characters. It was also criticized for blurring distinctive Latino identities by casting a Puerto Rican to play a Mexican American; eventually the show's writers remade Chico's identity as half–Puerto Rican, half–Mexican American.

Flaws and all, *Chico and the Man* nevertheless proved to be ahead of its time. It would take nearly a quarter century—and the rising tide of Latino demographics—to get another successful Latino-

Mexican American actor and comedian George Lopez starred in and produced a weekly family sitcom, *The George Lopez Show* (2002–2007), with a nearly all-Latino cast. *(Mitch Haddad/Warner Bros./Getty Images)*

based series on national television. *The Brothers Garcia* ran on the cable channel Nickelodeon (2000–2003) and was billed as a comedy about a tight-knit "Hispanic-American" family in Texas. More successful was *The George Lopez Show* on ABC, premiering in 2002 and canceled in 2007. A more traditional family-based sitcom, the show was based loosely on the family and pre-entertainment work life of its main character, Chicano stand-up comedian George Lopez. Like the common portrayals of African Americans on television, Latino programs usually have been comedies, which, according to some critics, can continue to play off stereotypes even if the ethnic slurs are removed. In 2002, PBS aired the first successful Latino-based dramatic series, *American Family: Journey of Dreams.* Starring the Mexican American actors Edward James Olmos and Constance Marie, the series, as its name implies, offered the saga of a Mexican American family through the great events of the twentieth and early twenty-first centuries. The early 2000s also saw Latino characters incorporated into non-Latino–based programs, such as Gabrielle Solis, played by Mexican American actress Eva Longoria, the scheming and cuckolding wife on the ABC nighttime comedy soap opera *Desperate Housewives.*

Spanish-Language Stations

Spanish-language television in the United States began with individual entrepreneurs who developed Spanish-language programs for English-language stations, primarily in the Southwest, during the late 1940s and early 1950s. By the 1960s, it was not uncommon for programs created in Latin America to be sold to predominantly English-language stations and then aired during off hours, largely to tap into the growing Latino market in the Southwest.

Meanwhile, the year 1955 brought the first all-Spanish-language station in the country, KCOR-TV in San Antonio, Texas, though virtually all of the shows aired on the station were Latin American imports broadcast simultaneously over Spanish-language radio for the large number of Latinos/as who still could not afford a television set. During the late 1960s, however, everything changed with the arrival of three major Spanish-language networks: Spanish

International Network (which became Univision), Telemundo, and *Galavisión*. In addition to such other ventures as MTV Latin American and HBO *en Español*—which produces Spanish-language programming and films dubbed in Spanish—succeeding years also saw the spread of a Spanish-language audio option, Secondary Audio Programming (SAP), on most major mainstream networks.

While these stations and options have had a growing impact on the U.S. television landscape, Spanish-language programming remains dominated by imports, which present themes very different from those affecting the lives of Latinos/as in the United States, many of whom, especially in the second and third generation, speak little or no Spanish.

Ellen M. Gil-Gómez

See also: Identity and Labels; Popular Culture; Telemundo; Univision; *Yo Soy Joaquín.*

Further Reading

Albarran, Alan B., and David Fender. "Behind the Numbers: The Impact of Government Preference and Non-Preference on Minority Broadcast Ownership." In *ALANA: Ethnic Media in America,* ed. Guy T. Meiss and Alice A. Tait. New York: Kendall/Hunt, 2006.

Dávila, Arlene. *Latinos Inc.: The Marketing and Making of a People.* Berkeley: University of California Press, 2001.

Meiss, Guy T., and Alice A. Tait, eds. *ALANA: Ethnic Media in America.* New York: Kendall/Hunt, 2006.

Noriega, Chon, A. *Shot in America: Television, the State, and the Rise of Chicano Cinema.* Minneapolis: University of Minnesota Press, 2000.

Telles, Raymond
(1915–)

Although the city of El Paso, Texas, has had a high percentage of ethnic Mexican residents (both Mexican Americans and immigrants) throughout its history, their numbers rarely resulted in political power. Using tactics ranging from poll taxes to segregation, its Anglo community has historically imposed conditions that made it difficult for Latinos/as in this Southwestern city to enjoy basic civil rights, let alone control municipal government. Thus, the election of Raymond L. Telles as El Paso's first Mexican American mayor in 1957 marked a significant change in the city's history and for Latinos/as throughout the nation.

Telles was born on September 15, 1915, and grew up in a racially segregated El Paso on the city's north side—the area north of U.S. Highway 80, where a vast majority of the city's Anglo residents lived. Except for a few who resided in that area, a majority of ethnic Mexicans lived in El Segundo—or the Second Ward, the city's south side. Segregation thus defined the formative experiences of Raymond Telles growing up in El Paso, leaving a dramatic imprint on him. While Telles had a difficult childhood, his father's strict discipline encouraged hard work. A young Raymond contributed to the family income by doing odd jobs, such as shining shoes and selling newspapers. Following graduation from high school in 1933, Telles attended International Business College in El Paso. He completed his coursework in 1935 and was hired as an accountant by the U.S. Justice Department. In 1941, with the U.S. entry into World War II, Telles was drafted into the U.S. Army; the following year he transferred into the U.S. Army's Air Forces, becoming head of the Lend-Lease Program for Central and South America.

Upon the conclusion of his military service in 1947, Telles—who left with the rank of major—was immediately elected head of a local Mexican American veterans' organization. The next year, at the urging of his family and community leaders in El Segundo, Telles ran for county clerk. It was the first time anyone with a Spanish surname dared to run for a major county office, and his opponent played up the race issue to bring out the Anglo vote. The tactic failed, and Telles won; in the following eight years, he was reelected county clerk four times.

In 1957, sensing political trouble in City Hall, Telles decided to run for mayor against incumbent Tom Rogers. The election was highly contested, but Telles was able to amass citywide support, especially from the Latino community, and ultimately triumphed. As mayor, he quickly implemented a series of reforms and encouraged residents to meet with him regularly, just as he had done as county clerk. He often held neighborhood meetings on issues important to El Pasoans, both Mexican and Anglo. More

Mexican Americans were hired in city government than ever before, and his administration addressed the recurring problem of discrimination against African Americans by putting pressure on local businesses to stop the practice. In addition, Mayor Telles initiated a number of public works projects, including an upgrade of the city's flood control infrastructure and the creation of new parks. He was so successful during his first term that he went unchallenged on his reelection bid in 1959.

In 1961, amid efforts to secure a third term as mayor, Telles was named by President John F. Kennedy as the first Mexican American ambassador to a Latin American nation, Costa Rica. At first hesitant to leave El Paso with his work unfinished, he eventually accepted President Kennedy's diplomatic offer but only upon the completion of his mayoral term. He remained in Costa Rica for six years, leaving in 1967 to serve as head of the U.S.-Mexico Border Commission under President Lyndon B. Johnson.

Telles remained politically active for several years after his work with the Johnson administration. In 1969, he returned to politics in El Paso by challenging the three-term Democratic U.S. Congressman Richard White. While unsuccessful in his bid for Congress, Telles did return to Washington two years later, when President Richard Nixon appointed him chairman of the Equal Opportunity Employment Commission—making him responsible for eliminating job discrimination throughout the country. And when Jimmy Carter was elected president in 1976, Telles was named head of the Inter-American Development Bank in El Salvador.

The signature event in Telles's long career in public service, however, was his election as mayor of El Paso in 1957. He became the first Latino mayor of a major Southwestern city in the twentieth century, and his election helped to open up political opportunities for people of color throughout the United States, especially Mexican Americans.

Daniel Guzmán

See also: Politics.

Further Reading

Acuña, Rodolfo. *Occupied America: A History of Chicanos.* 6th ed. New York: Pearson Longman, 2007.

García, Mario T. *The Making of a Mexican American Mayor: Raymond L. Telles of El Paso.* El Paso: University of Texas at El Paso, 1998.

Tenayuca, Emma (1916–1999)

Known as "La Pasionaria de Texas" for her passionate support of Depression-era Mexican laborers in Texas, Emma Tenayuca was born on December 21, 1916, and raised in a Mexican barrio of San Antonio. The eldest of eleven children, she lived with her grandparents for most of her childhood to lighten the financial burden on her parents. Experiences with her grandparents, who were active in local and state politics, left a lasting effect on Emma's worldview and helped guide her life's work. Attending rallies at the Plaza del Zacate in San Antonio during her teenage years, she heard social activists discuss the Mexican Revolution, the plight of workers around the world, and the steps necessary to combat labor exploitation.

A dedicated student from childhood, Tenayuca read the works of Charles Darwin, Thomas Paine, and Karl Marx by the time she was fourteen. In 1934, as a high school senior, she organized a march of the unemployed on the state capitol in Austin. After graduating from Brackenridge High School, she took a job as an elevator operator and began organizing workers in San Antonio. By 1936, still only twenty, she had helped organize a local chapter of the International Ladies Garment Workers Union (ILGWU) in the city. Not content to organize exclusively among garment workers, however, she organized a strike of Mexican workers against the Finck Cigar Company that led to her own arrest.

Her exposure to Paine and Marx had not only inspired Emma's organizing efforts, but also contributed to her evolving sense of self. By the age of sixteen, she had rejected Catholicism because she believed it contributed to oppression of the poor. During the Finck Cigar strike, she was outspoken in her criticism of the church for not helping the striking Mexican American workers. Instead, she charged, local priests had used scare tactics by telling parishioners that all labor unions were communist.

Along with Mrs. W. H. Ernst, whom she had met while organizing the cigar workers, Tenayuca formed the Workers Alliance, an organization dedicated to protecting workers' rights. By 1937, she was general secretary for ten chapters throughout the Southwest. Vigorously protesting the beating and mass deportation of immigrants by the U.S. Border Patrol and advocating for a minimum wage, the right to strike, and equal rights for immigrant workers, Tenayuca and the Workers Alliance brought the issues of Mexican workers to public awareness. Convinced that communism represented the best opportunity for change for immigrant workers and the poor, Tenayuca joined the party ranks in San Antonio. Through her activities with the party, she met Homer Brooks, the chairman of the Texas Communist Party. They were married in 1938, and the following year she replaced him as chairman, serving until 1941.

With increased resources and the support of the national Communist Party, Tenayuca sought out bigger struggles. None was bigger than that represented by the pecan industry, which was extremely powerful in San Antonio at the time. A majority of the workers in the area's pecan fields were Mexican, most of them women who worked from sunrise to sundown in backbreaking conditions for extremely low wages. In January 1938, after management at the Southern Pecan Shelling Company lowered wages from five cents to three cents per hour, Tenayuca organized a strike by some 12,000 Mexican pecan shellers from 130 different plants. After daily threats from the company, outbreaks of police violence, and the arrest of Tenayuca and about 1,000 workers on trumped up charges, the five-week strike succeeded in securing significant improvements in working conditions and wages through arbitration. Although some 25 percent of pecan workers in San Antonio were fired the following year when operators decided to mechanize their plants, the strike served as an example of the power of labor organizing and the unwillingness of Mexican women to accept inhuman working conditions. "What started out as a movement for organization for equal wages," she later wrote, "turned into a mass movement against starvation, for civil rights, for a minimum-wage law, and it changed the character of West Side San Antonio."

For the fiery Tenayuca, however, the strike did not have a successful outcome, as she faced acts of violence, threats to her life, and eventual blacklisting. Unable to find work—she was forced out of her leadership position within the United Cannery, Agricultural, Packing, and Allied Workers of America (UCAPAWA)—she fled the city in 1939. After briefs stops in Houston and Los Angeles, she settled in San Francisco. She renounced the Communist Party, believing it had turned its back on the poor, and came to regard education as more important than labor organizing in combating injustice and promoting justice. In 1952, Tenayuca earned her teacher certification from San Francisco State College; in 1974, she obtained a master's degree in education from Our Lady of the Lake University in San Antonio. She worked as a reading teacher there until her retirement in 1982. Emma Tenayuca died on July 23, 1999, and was eulogized at her funeral with the following verse:

La Pasionaria, we called her, because she was our passion, because she was our heart— defendiendo a los pobres, speaking out at a time when neither Mexicans nor women were expected to speak at all.

Robert O. Marlin, IV and David J. Leonard

See also: Communist Party; Feminism Unions, Industrial and Trade.

Further Reading

González, Gabriela. "Carolina Munguía and Emma Tenayuca: The Politics of Benevolence and Radical Reform." *Frontiers: A Journal of Women Studies* 24:2 (2003): 200–29.

Tenayuca, Emma. *The Mexican Question in the Southwest.* N.p., 1939.

Tex-Mex

"Tex-Mex" is a colloquialism that refers to a general cultural experience lived by people of Mexican ancestry in the area reaching from central Texas to the Rio Grande Valley in the south. Tex-Mex also refers to specific cultural elements of experience, especially food, music, and language. The term is generally applied to individuals and families whose previous four or more generations were born and raised north of the Rio Grande, and whose presence in the region may date back to the early twentieth century, the mid-nineteenth century, or even the mid-eighteenth century. Their roots may date back to the Mexican Revolution, when many Mexican nationals settled north of the river; or to the period after the Mexican-American War (1846–1847), when the United States took control of the area north of the Rio Grande; or to the period of initial Spanish settlement of that area. In any event, Tex-Mex implies a long-term family presence within the current boundaries of Texas.

Nevertheless, since the borderlands are often characterized by fluid boundaries and flexible identity markers, the demographic meaning of Tex-Mex has widened. It is sometimes used in reference to Texans with immediate family members who were born south of the Rio Bravo, or were themselves born in Mexico but now live in Texas. The designation is applicable to the extent that they participate in features of Tex-Mex culture.

One defining element of the Tex-Mex experience is Spanish-English codeswitching, or the ability to move easily between the two languages in mid-sentence in a structured way. This skill is the result of lifelong learning and of a specific kind of bilingualism. An example of such codeswitching, in which words from each language are included in a single sentence, would be, "Compré un barbecue pit" (I bought a barbecue pit). Until recent decades, when Spanish or codeswitching was common among students in public schools, teachers would admonish, ridicule, or castigate them. Many older Texans recall being punished in school for Tex-Mex codeswitching. To the present day, codeswitching is targeted by both English and Spanish public school teachers who insist on ostensible language "purity." Despite these institutional efforts, this form of speech remains in daily use in south Texas. Tex-Mex codeswitching is more evident among long-term residents of Texas than among individuals with binational families who keep closer cultural ties with Mexico.

In musical terms, Tex-Mex is a folk genre most associated with the *conjunto,* a musical troupe incor-

porating the accordion. The music took form during the nineteenth and early twentieth centuries in central Texas, an area that had a well-established Tex-Mex influence stemming from Monterrey, Mexico, and was also home to accordion-playing Germans, Poles, and Czechs. The accordion element likely emanated from these European settlers. Conjuntos have also relied heavily on the guitar and/or *bajo sexto* (a kind of twelve-string guitar) in producing the dominant genres of *cumbia* music and Mexicanized polka. Lyrically, conjunto music often has a *corrido,* or ballad-like, quality, as well as a romantic flavor, brought forth differently by such artists as Narciso Martínez, Flaco Jiménez, and Los Tigres del Norte. Accounts of immigration travail and abuse by Mexican and U.S. authorities are common in later lyrics. Recent conjunto has been reinfused by elements from northern Mexico, including horns and electric keyboards, and in some cases is gravitating to a form known as Tejano music. Despite its working-class roots, conjunto music is now part of an expansive music industry.

Due to the ranching origins of the region dating back to 1749, the local cuisine favors beef, goat meat, and flour tortillas. These are most appreciated when prepared in an outdoor barbecue. In family settings, the offerings include *menudo* (tripe soup), *tripitas*

Barbecued meat—beef, goat, chicken, and almost any of their parts—is a staple of Tex-Mex cuisine. Beans, chili, salsa, melted cheese, tortillas, and combinations of them help fill the dinner platter. *(Karl Schatz/Aurora/Getty Images)*

(small intestines), and *mollejas* (sweetbreads). Especially prized is *barbacoa de cabeza* (head barbecue), made from an entire beef head cooked in a pit oven. In some parts of south Texas, a low-rising bread called *pan de campo* is still baked in campfires; everywhere, baked maize tamales are the Christmas meal centerpiece. Cooking competitions for foods like these are held in numerous South Texas communities and are a popular part of the Tex-Mex cultural landscape.

Other Tex-Mex cultural features recall rural traditions. Among these is the cattle-raising culture that launched the U.S. cattle industry. Folk religion, folk curing, and folklore are likewise outcomes of regional isolation, institutional scarcity, and narrative creativity. These evoke the relative remoteness of the region during much of its history and its inhabitants' need for self-sufficiency.

Servando Z. Hinojosa

See also: Foods and Beverages; Mexican-American War; Music; Spanish Language.

Further Reading

Alvarez, Robert R., Jr. "The Mexican-US Border: The Making of an Anthropology of Borderlands." *Annual Review of Anthropology* 24 (1995): 447–70.

Peña, Manuel. *The Texas-Mexican Conjunto: History of a Working-Class Music.* Austin: University of Texas Press, 1985.

Third World Liberation Front

The Third World Liberation Front (TWLF), a group of students at San Francisco State College (now San Francisco State University) and the University of California at Berkeley, went on strike in 1968–1969 to demand the institutionalization of ethnic studies at their respective schools. The organization, which formed separately on the two campuses in the midst of the civil rights movement, Chicano Movement, and the anti–Vietnam War protest movement, demanded freedom and self-determination for colonized people everywhere and an end to the war in

Southeast Asia. The strike remains one of the longest-lasting student protests in U.S. history.

The TWLF strike began on the San Francisco State campus in November 1968, made up primarily of African American, Mexican American, Asian American, and Native American students who demanded an education more relevant to communities of color on and off campus. The existing course of study, they contended, was being taught from a white, European point of view; the histories and present-day realities of people of color were said to be either missing from course content or distorted.

Students used various tactics in the context of a general strike, ranging from the occupation of campus buildings to a hunger strike. The university administration responded by ordering student arrests and suspensions. The strike officially ended in March 1969, with the administration retaining control of hiring and admissions but conceding the creation of the School (now College) of Ethnic Studies, the first in the nation.

At Berkeley, meanwhile, the TWLF was established in January 1969, when the Afro-American Student Confederation, the Mexican-American Student Confederation, and the Asian American Political Alliance joined forces. The group took the name Third World Liberation Front to express solidarity with the San Francisco State group and its global concerns. By the end of that month, the Berkeley group had gone on strike as well and had declared demands much like those at San Francisco State: curricular changes that would help to develop and enrich the cultural identities of students of color—a course of study that would allow students of color to explore their own histories and their struggles against colonization and oppression.

Specifically, Berkeley students made five demands to the administration: (1) a "Third World College" with separate departments devoted to Asian Americans, Black Americans, Mexican Americans, and Native Americans; (2) an increase in minority faculty, administrative, and staff appointments; (3) an increase in financial aid and work study for minority students; (4) minority control of programs pertaining to minorities; and (5) amnesty for strikers. By the end of February, after numerous violent encounters between police and strike participants,

California Governor Ronald Reagan ordered National Guard troops to the Berkeley campus. The guardsmen used tear gas on the protestors, and by early March, 150 students had been arrested and thirty-six suspended.

Also in March, however, the administration offered its proposal for a Department of Ethnic Studies, comprising the four areas of study demanded by the TWLF strikers. That fall, the new department offered its first classes—thirty-four in all—with a total of 990 students enrolled. In 1970, Afro-American studies was spun off from Ethnic Studies and became its own departmental unit. And in 1971, Berkeley introduced a program in comparative ethnic studies.

The events of 1968–1969 led to the creation of the first ethnic studies programs in the nation, which in turn led to ethnic studies offerings at many institutions nationwide, validating the role of student protestors and the TWLF. Thirty years later, on April 14, 1999, Berkeley students occupied the building that housed the Ethnic Studies Department to protest repeated budget cuts, discontinuation of courses, decline in faculty of color, and other signs of institutional disregard. Ultimately embracing the name of TWLF to link their struggle to that of the previous generation, the students began a hunger strike on April 29 and camped in front of California Hall, the site of the president's office. The administration ordered the arrest of the strikers, which inspired support from other students, faculty, and community members. The TWLF achieved most of its goals, and the 1999 strike came to be regarded as a prime example of successful collective action on the part of undergraduate students, graduate students, faculty, and community members to demand negotiation. The tactic of a hunger strike, in particular, signaled to the administration that the issues of concern and the future of ethnic studies were serious matters.

Despite the successes of the 1969 and 1999 student protests, the Third World Liberation Front was disbanded in the year 2000. According to an open letter from the group, the TWLF was becoming "an empty mockery of real dissenting voice" that "came to serve the purpose of knee-jerk conservative pundits and university officials as both scapegoat and smokescreen." The decision to disband the TWLF, while made by members themselves, thus may be recognized as an act of protest in its own right, in the spirit of its founders.

Mary K. Bloodsworth-Lugo

See also: Chicano Movement; Chicano Studies; Latino Studies.

Further Reading

Butler, Johnnella E., ed. *Color-Line to Borderlands: The Matrix of American Ethnic Studies.* Seattle: University of Washington Press, 2001.

On Strike! Ethnic Studies, 1969–1999. Video recording by Fifth Floor Productions; directed and produced by Irum Shiekh. San Francisco: NAATA Distribution, 1999.

Pulido, Laura. *Brown, Black, Yellow, and Left: Radical Activism in Los Angeles.* Berkeley: University of California Press, 2006.

Yang, Philip. *Ethnic Studies: Issues and Approaches.* Albany: State University of New York Press, 2000.

Thomás, Piri
(1928–)

Piri Thomás, a Puerto Rican–Cuban American writer, is the author of the critically acclaimed novel *Down These Mean Streets* (1967), an autobiography of his adolescence in "El Barrio" of New York City's Spanish Harlem during the Great Depression.

The first of seven children, "Piri" Thomás was born Juan Pedro Thomás on September 30, 1928, in the poor district of Spanish Harlem to John Thomás (originally Juan Tomás de la Cruz), a dark-skinned laborer, and Delores Montañez Thomás, a housemaid. By the age of fourteen, Thomás was struggling to survive in the streets of Spanish Harlem.

After a brief stint selling marijuana, he began committing armed robbery in order to sustain what had become a heroin addiction. The failed robbery attempt of a New York City nightclub in 1950, however, an event that ended in gunfire and the near death of Thomás and a police officer, dramatically changed his life. As a result of the nightclub incident, Thomás was convicted of attempted armed robbery in the first degree, carrying a sentence of fifteen years in prison.

After serving seven years in New York State's Sing Sing prison, Thomás was determined to reclaim his life. With a grant from the Rabinowitz Foundation, he began to put into writing his life growing up in the streets of New York. The result was *Down These Mean Streets,* a personal memoir of love and perseverance in a neighborhood plagued by racism, poverty, drugs, violence, and theft.

Leaving no topic untouched, the book explicitly details his sexual experiences (including homosexual encounters), his illegitimate child, his troubled relationship with his father, the death of his mother, and his addiction to drugs. Perhaps the most compelling aspect, however, is his honesty and his continuing struggles with issues of race and racism. In a series of thought-provoking chapters, Thomás seeks to understand his place in a society defined by black and white racial categories. Although he grew up identifying himself as a Puerto Rican male and speaking Spanish, American society categorized him as a black man because of the color of his skin. Thus, he discovered that being Puerto Rican did not exclude him from the prejudices suffered by African Americans in the United States. As a result, he came to recognize himself as both black and Puerto Rican. By identifying himself as a black Puerto Rican, or Afrorican, he was able to shed light not only on racial ideologies of blackness and whiteness in the United States but also on Puerto Rican definitions of whiteness.

His next work after *Down These Mean Streets* was an autobiographical sequel titled *Savior, Savior Hold My Hand* (1972), the story of his life after prison and his search for God; *Seven Long Times* (1974), a chronicle of his experiences in the New York State penal system; and *Stories from El Barrio* (1978), a collection of short stories for young readers about life in Spanish Harlem. Thomás has also recorded two albums of music and poetry entitled *Sounds of the Streets* and *No Mo' Barrio Blues,* both of which have garnered international recognition.

Today, Piri Thomás remains personally committed to the rehabilitation of drug addicts and the social empowerment of urban youths, regardless of skin color and economic status. Thomás also travels around the world lecturing and conducting workshops on the history of Puerto Rican literature. His creative writing workshop, Creations Without Hes-

itations, encourages participants to express the grief and happiness of their personal experiences through literature. His autobiography, *Down These Mean Streets,* remains a central text in Puerto Rican and Latino literature.

Brian Montes

See also: Identity and Labels; Puerto Rican Literature.

Further Reading

Thomás, Piri. *Down These Mean Streets.* New York: Alfred A. Knopf, 1967. New York: Vintage Books, 1997.
———. *Savior, Savior Hold My Hand.* New York: Doubleday, 1972.
———. *Seven Long Times.* New York: Praeger, 1974.
———. *Stories from El Barrio.* New York: Alfred A. Knopf, 1978.

Tijerina, Reies López (1926–)

A leading figure in the Chicano Movement of the 1960s, Reies Tijerina was known for his efforts to restore New Mexico land grants to the descendants of their rightful owners and for an armed raid on a New Mexico courthouse in 1967.

Reies López Tijerina was born on September 21, 1926, to a poor sharecropper family near San Antonio, Texas, and, as a boy, experienced the hardships faced by Mexican migrant workers. Throughout his childhood, Tijerina would be forced to move with his family in pursuit of seasonal crops, and the jobs that came with them, to Colorado, Wyoming, and Michigan. It was impossible for the boy to receive formal schooling. At the age of six, he lost his mother, which pushed the family even deeper into poverty. The boy was forced to look for food in garbage bins and hunt for dead rats in the fields.

As a teenager, Tijerina came to be admired by his friends for his skill as a religious orator, earning the nickname *el abogado sin libros* (lawyer without books). Although he was raised a Catholic, he enrolled at age eighteen in the Assembly of God Bible Institute in Ysleta, Texas, and, upon completion of his studies, dedicated himself to doing evangelistic work along the U.S.-Mexican border. Walking from town to town, he refused rides to emulate the sacrifice of Jesus.

By 1950, however, his credentials were revoked because of his "unorthodox ideas." After marrying fellow bible student Mary Escobar, Tijerina began his career as an itinerant Pentecostal preacher, carrying the message—again from town to town—for the next six years. He finally broke with the Pentecostal Church because he felt it had failed in its duty to the poor. As he later wrote in his autobiography, "I had fought with the church (with all religions) during ten long years, trying to get it to take the side of the poor in the struggle against the rich, but I failed."

While residing at the Valley of Peace, a commune he helped organize in Arizona in the early 1950s, Tijerina worked as a bail bondsman. The experience solidified his beliefs about American racism, as he witnessed firsthand the inordinate and unjust arrest of blacks, Latinos/as, and Native Americans. Because of a fight with the government over the land inhabited by Valley of Peace residents, Tijerina spent much of his time researching the history of the Treaty of Guadalupe Hidalgo of 1848, which ended the Mexican-American War, and Supreme Court rulings on Mexican American land disputes.

The commune was vandalized and finally destroyed by Anglo neighbors in 1957, and Tijerina moved to northern New Mexico. He spent his initial years there continuing his research into southwestern land grants and speaking out publicly about what he regarded as an ongoing, centuries-old injustice. Tijerina was convinced that virtually all the troubles faced by Mexican Americans could be traced back to the loss of their lands to Anglo settlers and the refusal of the U.S. government to uphold the land provisions of the Treaty of Guadalupe Hidalgo. In hopes of forcing the United States to return lands to its rightful Mexican and Indian owners, on December 12, 1959, he sent a letter signed by eighty families to President Dwight Eisenhower urging an investigation into the land claims. The Eisenhower administration would not take up the matter, prompting Tijerina and his supporters to turn to the Mexican government in hopes of exerting pressure on Washington to redress U.S treaty violations. Unsuc-

cessful in gaining Mexican support, Tijerina devised alternative plans.

In August 1962, Tijerina drafted a charter for the Alianza Federal de Mercedes (Federal Alliance of Land Grants), with the goal of forcing the U.S. and Mexican governments to uphold their obligations under the Treaty of Guadalupe Hidalgo. On February 2, 1963, the 115th anniversary of the signing of the treaty, the Alianza Federal de Mercedes—or La Alianza, as it became known—was officially incorporated. The organization stepped up efforts to force the return of lost lands to the heirs of the original owners, while working to foster Mexican American pride through demonstrations and cultural events. Tijerina found significant support, especially among poor and working-class Mexican Americans and Native Americans. By 1964, La Alianza had attracted more than 6,000 members, with an additional 14,000 signing up by 1966. Tijerina and the Alianza did not find support from all quarters, however, eliciting outrage for his incendiary rhetoric and radical positions from middle-class Latinos/as. By 1965, the media had dubbed him Don Quixote, equating his efforts to return the lost lands with the hapless tilting at windmills by the classical Spanish literary figure.

In October 1966, Tijerina and about 300 members of Alianza invaded and forcibly occupied a section of Echo Amphitheater Park in the Carson National Forest, located in northern New Mexico. Setting up an armed camp, Tijerina proclaimed the seized territory the "Republic of San Joaquín del Río de Chama," granting it to the descendants of the original settlers; the group went so far as to elect governing officials and grant visas to tourists passing through. Shortly after the takeover began, two forest rangers attempted to evict the occupiers from the park, only to face arrest by members of Alianza. In their newly formed criminal justice system, Tijerina's followers tried the rangers, convicted them of trespassing, gave them suspended sentences, and eventually released them. Less than a week later, Tijerina, along with five other members, was arrested and charged with assault on the rangers and illegal use of government property.

Fearing an escalation of Alianza activities following Tijerina's release on bail, District Attorney Alfonso Sánchez ordered the police to break up a

Chicano land-rights activist Reies López Tijerina speaks to visitors at his New Mexico ranch in June 2007, the fortieth anniversary of his armed raid on a New Mexico courthouse. *(AP Images/The New Mexican, Jane Phillips)*

scheduled meeting of the group on June 3, 1967. Tijerina eluded arrest, but eleven other members of Alianza were taken into custody. In response to what they regarded as an unwarranted and illegal arrest, Tijerina and a small band of *Aliancistas* initiated a raid on the county courthouse in Tierra Amarilla in an attempt to free those in custody and place District Attorney Sánchez himself under arrest. During the course of the raid, a prison guard and a sheriff's deputy both were shot; Tijerina and the others escaped into the mountains. The New Mexico National Guard launched a massive manhunt that tracked down Tijerina and forced his surrender the following week; he was promptly charged with fifty-four criminal counts, including kidnapping and armed assault. Later that year, Tijerina stood trial for his involvement in the occupation of Echo Amphitheater Park and, amid widespread protest for his release, won acquittal. In 1970, however, standing trial for his involvement in the Tierra Amarilla courthouse raid, Tijerina was found guilty and sentenced

to two years in prison. He was released from federal prison in Springfield, Missouri, on July 27, 1971, on five-year parole with a stipulation that he hold no position in the Alianza.

Although no longer the fiery activist, Tijerina continued to pursue his goal of securing the return of stolen land grants to their rightful owners. Renaming his organization the Alianza Federal de Pueblos Libres (Federal Alliance of Free Towns), Tijerina tried to reenergize the movement, but his conviction and time in prison weakened his leadership. When his parole was up, he resumed the presidency of a much-diminished Alianza. As the energy and activism of the Chicano Movement was beginning to decline, moreover, Tijerina took a less confrontational stance. His efforts to revive the Río Chama Republic during the 1980s proved unsuccessful. Tijerina's memoirs were published in 2000; today he lives in Mexico, across the border from El Paso, Texas.

Known as "King Tiger," a crude translation of his name, Tijerina stood with Corky Gonzales, César

Chávez, and José Angel Gutiérrez as one of the leaders of the Chicano Movement. At the same time, his emphasis on grassroots organizing, radical activism (including armed insurrection), and promotion of pride in Chicano/Indio identity set him apart from these other leaders. His decades-long mission, and all his efforts on its behalf, also reflected the importance he attached to Chicano/Latino history and rights. After all the arrests, charges, and convictions, and despite the waning activism throughout the country, his first and foremost objective remained the recovery of stolen land grants. No one else has been more determined in their efforts to assist displaced Mexican Americans.

Jesse J. Esparza and David J. Leonard

See also: Chicano Movement; Treaty of Guadalupe Hidalgo (1848).

Further Reading

Blawis, Patricia B. *Tijerina and the Land Grants: Mexican Americans in Struggle for Their Heritage.* New York: International Publishers, 1971.

Meier, Matt S. "King Tiger: Reies Lopez Tijerina." *Journal of the West* 27:2 (April 1988): 60–68.

Nabokov, Peter. *Tijerina and the Courthouse Raid.* Albuquerque: University of New Mexico Press, 1969.

Tijerina, Reies López. *They Called Me "King Tiger": My Struggle for the Land and Our Rights.* Trans. and ed. José Angel Gutiérrez. Houston, TX: Arte Público, 2000.

Tracking

Tracking is the educational practice of placing students into distinct academic, general, or vocational curricular paths. Schools use tracking or ability grouping to adjust instruction to the needs, abilities, and interests of different students. The practice can take a variety of forms: overt, when counselor and student select a particular class in a particular track; automatic, with test scores from one grade automatically determining a student's track for the following year; or, covert, with grouping done by a teacher and counselor with no indication in the master schedule that sections of one class are different.

Teachers and administrators who support tracking argue that it helps educators address the needs of students by effectively matching learning ability with specific educational content. Tracking in middle schools may take the form of block scheduling, whereby students are assigned to one class based on their ability, or assigned by ability to each subject separately (for example, science, mathematics). In high school, students may be assigned to academic, vocational, or general program tracks, or they may be assigned to separate ability-grouped courses within the curriculum track (for instance, advanced placement, honors, regular, and remedial courses). Typically, schools with high concentrations of minority and low-income students are located in large cities where it is not uncommon to offer a higher number of remedial courses in academic areas (often taught by less qualified or inexperienced teachers) and a reduced number of advanced courses.

Educational researchers suggest that students who intend to go to college, and their parents, often do not know when decisions have been made to move students out of college-preparatory science and math classes. In fact, research suggests that some teachers and school administrators may not want students and parents to know which courses are designed to prepare students for college. If they knew, more students would complain and demand better placement. Biology courses with titles such as "Ecology and You" or "Life on Earth" obscure the unfortunate reality that they will not prepare a student for admission to a four-year college or university. Likewise, students assigned to "business math" or other nonacademic courses will be unable to use those credits when they apply to a four-year college or university.

In the past two decades, research studies on tracking and ability grouping have called attention to the potentially harmful effects of these practices on Latinos/as, African American, and low-income students who are disproportionately represented in the lower tracks. Arguments against tracking center around the unequal educational opportunities afforded to students in different tracks. For example, researchers have found that students in the lower tracks receive fewer resources and are assigned teachers with lower standards and expectations. Other studies report that tracking actually widens the gap in achievement between students in the top and bottom levels over time. That is, students in the lower track are seldom able to catch up with their peers in the upper tracks.

Low expectations, combined with inadequate resources and persistent inequalities in the educational opportunities offered to Latino and other minority students, put those students at an even greater disadvantage in terms of their schooling and later in life. Most research indicates that ability grouping and tracking actually do more harm than good for the overall educational achievement and future prospects of Latino/a and other minority students. Evidence for this conclusion includes: (1) a lack of demonstrable improvement in employment opportunities; (2) a strong correlation between tracking and dropout rates; and (3) the stigma often attached to students who are grouped according to ability.

Gisela Ernst-Slavit and Catherine Carrison

See also: Education.

Further Reading

Gamoran, Adam. "American Schooling and Educational Inequality: A Forecast for the 21st Century." *Sociology of Education* (extra issue, 2001): 135–53.

Oakes, Jeannie. *Keeping Track: How Schools Structure Inequality.* 2nd ed. New Haven, CT: Yale University Press, 2005.

Secada, Walter G., Adam Gamoran, and Mathew Weinstein. "Pathways to Equity." In *Authentic Achievement: Restructuring Schools for Intellectual Quality,* by Fred M. Newmann and Associates. San Francisco: Jossey-Bass, 1996.

Stanton-Salazar, Ricardo D., and Sanford M. Dornbusch. "Social Capital and the Reproduction of Inequality: Information Networks Among Mexican-Origin High School Students." *Sociology of Education* 68 (1995): 116–35.

Treaty of Guadalupe Hidalgo (1848)

The Treaty of Guadalupe Hidalgo, signed on February 2, 1848, by the United States and Mexico, marked the official end of the Mexican-American War. With the treaty, Mexico ceded more than half its territory—525,000 square miles (1.36 million square kilometers)—to the United States, including all or parts of the present-day states of California, Arizona, New Mexico, Nevada, Utah, Colorado, Wyoming, and Texas.

The sovereignty of Texas had been in dispute since the Treaty of Velasco in 1836, when Mexico's president General Antonio López de Santa Anna granted it independence. The government of Mexico, however, did not accept the Treaty of Velasco. The ownership of Texas was thus an immediate cause of the war that broke out in April 1846 between Mexico and the United States. A year later, President James K. Polk appointed envoy Nicholas Trist to negotiate a peace treaty if the occasion arose. Trist traveled to Mexico with a draft copy of the proposed treaty, which included the cession of Mexico's northern territories to the United States.

After Santa Anna's troops were defeated at Churubusco in August 1847, an armistice was declared and Trist, fluent in Spanish, opened talks with Mexican officials. Santa Anna considered the demands for northern lands extortionate. He balked particularly at giving up New Mexico (then a large territory extending as a far north as Wyoming, and west to Nevada and Arizona) and at setting the country's border at the Rio Grande. Mexico also wished to keep its California territory south of Monterey. Trist had been advised to push for annexation of Baja California as well, but did not. As treaty talks broke down, armed fighting resumed.

Mexico City fell, and Santa Anna resigned the presidency. Now in a stronger bargaining position, President Polk and his cabinet wanted Mexico to give up Baja California as well as the northern territories. They regarded Trist's efforts as a failure and recalled him to Washington, but the letter of dismissal did not reach him until November. By that time, treaty negotiations were going well. Trist, driven by a sense of duty and the prospect of further bloodshed, stayed in Mexico, determined to deliver a treaty. Letters between the two countries could take more than a month to be delivered, so while Trist incurred the administration's wrath, officials in Washington could not effectively stop him.

After weeks of talks, the treaty was signed. Mexico ceded Alta California and the large New Mexico territory, and accepted the loss of Texas. The border between the two countries was set south of San Diego Bay and extended to the Rio Grande. Trist negotiated a payment of $15 million to Mexico in exchange for the territories, which was $5 million less than the maximum he had been authorized to pay. The treaty was signed in the Villa de Guadalupe, near the shrine of the Lady of Guadalupe in Mexico City. Guadalupe Hidalgo was the name of an old city, then a neighborhood in Mexico City, where the shrine was located. After the signing, Trist joined his hosts at a Catholic Mass in the basilica.

Journalist James Freaner carried the treaty to Washington, arriving on February 19, 1848. After Senate hearings, the treaty was approved on March 10 with a major change, requested by President Polk: the deletion of Article X, which guaranteed property rights for Mexicans and Indians living in the ceded territory being acquired by the United States. Debate over the deletion of Article X held up ratification by Mexico until late May 1848. The controversial Protocol of Querétaro was written to explain the loss of Article X and to ensure the land rights granted previously by Mexico in the ceded territories. U.S. courts have never recognized the protocol as binding.

Effects

For more than a century and a half, interpretation of the Treaty of Guadalupe Hidalgo has determined the voting rights, citizenship, property ownership, and civil rights of people in the American Southwest. Court cases have varied in their decisions over the years, and different courts have rendered opposite judgments. The treaty has been invoked successfully to grant citizenship to nonwhites at a time when the U.S. Constitution did not; to establish control of dam projects on the Colorado River; to protect communal ownership of land; and, conversely, to dispossess many tribal groups of their territorial possession. Of course, all these judgments could be—and sometimes were—overturned at later dates.

Article VIII of the treaty stated that all Mexican citizens who held property in the ceded territories would keep that property. Owners could stay on their land or move back to Mexico. If they stayed, they had to choose U.S. or Mexican citizenship within one year; failure to choose would result in U.S. citizenship by default. Either way, the property of these approximately 100,000 Mexicans would be "inviolably respected."

In actuality, however, many Mexican landowners lost their property, regardless of citizenship. As some Mexicans citizens were mixed race, and the new state of California extended citizenship only to white male Mexicans, many were stripped of their land rights. The New Mexico Territory (which included Arizona) similarly disenfranchised 8,000 Pueblo Indians as well as members of other tribes.

Even those granted U.S. citizenship were hard put to defend title to their property. Mexican land grants were often conflicting, inexact, or incomplete, relying on physical landmarks that changed over the years. In the New Mexico Territory, which did not have a state constitution or government, the U.S. Congress had to approve the decisions on landholdings made by politically appointed officials, who sometimes revoked previous decisions. Claims were delayed for years, and legal expenses forced some to give up their property. As late as 1891, a Land Claims court was set up in Colorado and New Mexico to decide cases left in doubt more than forty years earlier.

Texas

The U.S. Supreme Court ruled in *McKinney v. Saviego* (1856) that Texas, which had been specifically mentioned in Article X, was excluded from the provisions of the Treaty of Guadalupe Hidalgo. Since Texas had been admitted into the union in 1845, the court reasoned, it could not be part of the ceded territories. Nevertheless, the Texas legislature created commissions and passed laws into the twentieth century adjudicating both Spanish and Mexican claims. Few Tejano families had the economic resources to pursue their titles for so many years.

In 1923, the government of Mexico presented to the United States claims of $193 million on behalf of former citizens who had lost land in Texas after 1848. The United States and Mexico formed a joint commission to review more than 400 cases, and in 1941 the Mexican government took on the responsibility of reimbursing the heirs of legitimate claims. Payments were never made.

California

In Alta California, 40 percent of the land owned before the start of Mexican-American War was lost. Gold was discovered there early in 1848, and tens of thousands of gold seekers from across the United States, as well as from many other countries, flooded to the territory. Landowners found themselves dispossessed by a combination of unfamiliar laws, judicial systems, squatters, cultural differences, and the English language itself. Racism played a part as well; Mexicans were often brutally treated and not able to secure justice through the judicial system. Lynchings of Mexican landowners and outright fraud committed against them are documented in the diaries and memoirs of witnesses.

The California Land Act of 1851 gave a three-person commission authority to adjudicate property disputes stemming from the treaty. Appeals went to the state court system. Claims had to be filed within two years (later extended), and the procedure could prove expensive and draining. Decisions in California were also influenced by the tens of thousands of squatters—gold seekers who overran or built upon land they believed available. On average, land cases took seventeen years to settle. Even if an owner ultimately retained title to the land, he or she had to pay the squatters for any improvements and buildings they had erected while staying there.

Of the seventy-five land grant cases decided by California's Supreme Court between 1854 and 1930, half of the claimants were not Mexican, but Anglos who held Mexican land grants. Bankrupted by legal fees and other expenses, many Mexican landowners sold their property to Anglo speculators, who then pursued the cases in court—often at great personal profit, since the land increased in value.

Twentieth Century and Beyond

Controversy surrounding the treaty and its enforcement has not abated in the more than 150 years since its signing. Activist Reies López Tijerina paved the way for the Chicano militancy in the 1960s, organizing and demonstrating against historic abuses and promoting reclamation of lost lands. Tijerina and groups like the Brown Berets, along with Native American organizations, have focused international attention on the treatment of Latinos/as and Native people, using the Treaty of Guadalupe Hidalgo to prove the violation of rights. Through the year 2000, the U.S. Congress considered bills that would reopen claims by descendents of Mexican citizens whose rights or land, guaranteed by the treaty, were lost.

While some historians find that the treaty's language connotes respect and demands fair treatment of Mexican citizens, others believe that the treaty was so often ignored as to become a symbol of land grabs, swindles, and the disenfranchisement of Mexican Americans.

Vickey Kalambakal

See also: Aztlán; Mexican-American War; Tijerina, Reies López.

Further Reading

Drexler, Robert W. *Guilty of Making Peace: A Biography of Nicholas P. Trist*. Lanham, MD: University Press of America, 1991.

Griswold del Castillo, Richard. *The Treaty of Guadalupe Hidalgo: A Legacy of Conflict*. Norman: University of Oklahoma Press: 1990.

Trevino, Lee
(1939–)

The Mexican American professional golfer Lee Trevino, one of the most successful players on the men's professional tour during the 1960s and 1970s, has had an influence that extends well beyond the links. From an impoverished childhood in Texas, he changed the face of professional golf through the record of his success, flamboyant personality, and open discussion of the obstacles he overcame in succeeding in a sport that long excluded people of his ethnic background. Nicknamed the "Merry Mex" for his affable manner and the joy he brought to playing, Trevino attracted untold numbers of new fans to the game of golf and became an idol and role model for the Mexican American community.

Born on December 1, 1939, to parents of Mexican descent in Dallas, Texas, Trevino grew up in poverty. Raised by his mother, Erin Holst, and his grandfather, a gravedigger (he did not have a relationship with his father), Trevino spent his early years attending school and working. As early as the age of five, he labored in the cotton fields to contribute financially to the family. What little leisure time he had was spent playing golf, a game introduced to him by an uncle, who gave him a single rusty club and a few old balls. At the age of eight, his love of golf, the financial burdens facing the family, and the fact that he lived near a country club led Trevino to take up caddying. He was forced to drop out of school after the eighth grade to work full-time as a caddy and a shoe shiner, bringing home $30 per week between the two jobs. It was caddying that allowed him to develop his golf game, playing on the three practice holes available to caddies and hitting hundreds of balls per practice session.

In 1956, at the age of seventeen, Trevino joined the U.S. Marine Corps and spent four years in the military. Despite his military duties, he was able to spend a significant amount of time playing golf, especially during the last two years, shooting rounds with officers and participating in tournaments in the Far East. Upon his discharge in 1959, he dedicated himself to the game, working as an instructor and competing in tournaments. He won the Texas State Open in 1965 and joined the PGA (Professional Golfers' Association) Tour in 1967. In his second appearance at the U.S. Open Golf Championship that year, he finished fifth, only eight shots behind the winner, Jack Nicklaus. Although Trevino did not win a tournament during his rookie campaign, he finished forty-fifth on the PGA Tour money list, amassing $25,472 dollars in earnings. *Golf Digest* named him "Rookie of the Year."

Trevino won his first PGA major competition in only his second year on the tour, capturing the U.S.

Open title in 1968. Over the course of his career, he won a total of twenty-nine PGA tournament events, including six major titles. His best year was 1971, in which he won the U.S. Open, the Canadian Open, and the British Open, making him the only player to that time to win three national titles in the same year. He was also recognized as *Sports Illustrated*'s Sportsman of the Year and ABC's *Wide World of Sports'* Athlete of the Year. His success in 1971 and well into the next decade solidified his place as one of the top golfers of the era.

Throughout his career, which has included success on the Senior Tour since the 1990s, "Merry Mex" (also known as "Super Mex") Trevino has been known for his approachability, exuberance, and sense

Golfer Lee Trevino, known as the "Merry Mex," grew up in poverty and learned the game as a young caddy in Dallas, Texas. He went on to great success as a professional, winning six major championships and the adoration of the Mexican American community. *(Evening Standard/Stringer/Hulton Archive/Getty Images)*

of humor. In interviews, he often refers to his humble roots. As he said in a televised biography, "I showed that a guy from across the tracks, a minority kid with no education from a very poor background, can make it."

David J. Leonard and Carmen R. Lugo-Lugo

Further Reading

Kramer, Jon. *Lee Trevino (Overcoming the Odds)*. Orlando, FL: Raintree Steck-Vaughn, 1996.

Trevino, Lee, and Sam Blair. *The Snake in the Sandtrap (And Other Misadventures on the Golf Tour)*. New York: Henry Holt, 1987.

———. *Super Mex: An Autobiography*. New York: Arrow, 1983.

Unions, Industrial and Trade

Latino workers have formed an important part of the American working class since the early days of the republic and an important part of the organized labor movement from its inception. Latino workers first became members of the American working class as a result of the Mexican-American War of 1846–1847, which took half of Mexico and made U.S. nationals of about 100,000 residents. Between 1910 and 1930, riding the network of railroads that connected the two nations, more than 2 million Mexicans migrated into the United States as a result of the Mexican Revolution and the Cristero Rebellion. Most Mexican immigrants of that era settled in the Southwest, but some migrated as far as Illinois and Pennsylvania.

Throughout the early part of the twentieth century Mexican immigrants have typically found work in agriculture, food processing, construction, mining, and on the railroads, but some have also landed jobs in steel mills and auto plants. Mexican men became miners in Arizona, steelworkers in the Chicago area, autoworkers in Toledo, Ohio, and Detroit, and railroad workers in Pennsylvania. Some women worked in light industry such as garment manufacture or in food processing. During the Great Depression, an estimated 1 million Mexicans were driven out of the United States, only to be welcomed back for work with the outbreak of World War II. Beginning in 1942, the U.S.-Mexican Bracero Program brought 4.2 million workers to the United States, most working in agriculture, but some also on the railroads. Many other Mexicans also came to work in mining and manufacturing in the West and Midwest.

Latino immigrants from other countries joined the influx during the second half of the twentieth century. About 450,000 Puerto Ricans, already U.S. citizens, arrived on the mainland in the 1950s and another 200,000 in the 1960s. Most settled in New Jersey and New York, as well as a few in Ohio, becoming agricultural, industrial, and service workers. Following the Cuban Revolution, about 250,000 Cubans immigrated to the United States between 1959 and 1962, followed by another 300,000 in the "freedom flights" from 1965 to 1973. These were joined by another 100,000 Cubans following the Mariel Boatlift of 1980. Most settled in Florida and New Jersey. Some established businesses, but many others worked in manufacturing, service industries, and professions.

During the 1970s, civil wars in Guatemala, El Salvador, and Nicaragua led hundreds of thousands of Central Americans to migrate to the United States, settling in Los Angeles, Chicago, and Washington, D.C. Colombians, facing persistent political violence in that nation, also came to the United States. These Latino immigrants, of various nationalities and ethnicities—Mayan Indians, Honduran Garifunos, and Colombian Afro-Latinos, for example—found work in services, construction, and industry.

Beginning in the 1980s, the so-called Washington Consensus—that is, globalization and neoliberal policies—contributed to widespread economic dislocation in South America, leading hundreds of thousands of others to leave South America and migrate to the United States. These economic and trade policies also affected Mexico and Central America, which continued to hemorrhage their populations. Driven by political violence, criminal violence, and economic necessity, many migrated to the United States, often without legal documents.

Latino Union Experience before World War II

Latino immigrants have participated in all phases of the U.S. labor union movement from early on. Their status as a conquered people after 1847, Catholic religion, Spanish language, and nonwhite race (mestizo, Indian, Afro-Latino, for example) all led to discrimination. Many retreated into their own small communities and worked in isolation from Anglos. Latinos/as brought with them from Mexico mutual aid organizations, which were informal workers' insurance groups to help the sick and the injured and to bury the dead. These community-based mutual aid groups often included workers and members of the middle class. The Club Recíproca of Corpus Christi, Texas, founded in 1873, was one such organization. The Alianza Hispano Americana of Tucson, Arizona, founded in 1894, eventually expanded to 275 chapters.

The Knights of Labor, which exploded onto the American scene in the 1870s, spread during the 1880s into the West, where it attracted Mexican miners, railroad workers, and craftsmen. The only stable Latino workers' group of that period, however, was the Gorras Blancas of New Mexico that worked with the Knights.

During the early twentieth century, Mexicans faced discrimination from fledgling labor unions made up primarily of European Americans. Despite such opposition, Mexicans became members of the Western Federation of Miners (WFM), with which they would have a long association. The American Federation of Labor (AFL), whose local union by-laws often explicitly excluded black members, often barred Mexicans as well. Nevertheless, in some cases, Mexican workers succeeded in organizing within the context of the AFL. Around 1900, the AFL Federal Labor Union Local 11–1953 in Laredo, Texas, made up largely of miners and railroad workers, also included some 700 Mexican men and women, including barbers, bricklayers, painters, cooks, electricians, teamsters, seamstresses, maids, and female cigar workers. The union, led by Socialists, published its own weekly newspaper, *El Defensor Obrero* (The Workers Defender); one of its leaders was the writer and organizer Sara Estela Ramírez.

During the 1910s and 1920s Mexican workers participated in the AFL in other places as well, though racial exclusion often segregated them into Federal Labor Union affiliates. Other Mexican workers joined Industrial Workers of the World (IWW), a revolutionary syndicalist union that did not discriminate against black, Asian or, Latino workers. The Mexican Liberal Party (PLM), an anarchist political movement based in Mexico, and the Mexican consulate sometimes played the role of union on behalf of Mexican workers. Through these organizations, Mexican workers participated in organizing campaigns and strikes in mines and on railroads, and in other industries throughout the first two decades of the century.

With the Great Depression of the 1930s, Socialists, Communists, and Trotskyists led mass strikes throughout the United States. The AFL split, and John L. Lewis of the United Mine Workers led in the creation of the Congress of Industrial Organizations (CIO). Unlike the AFL, the CIO welcomed African American and Latino workers into its ranks. Some Mexican workers played leadership roles in the new federation. In 1938, for example, Emma Tenayuca of San Antonio, Texas, led a successful strike by the United Cannery, Agricultural, Packing, and Allied Workers of America (UCAPAWA-CIO), made up of workers who shelled pecans. In Chicago, Toledo, Cleveland, and Detroit, Mexican workers joined the United Steel Workers, the United Auto Workers, and other industrial unions of the CIO in the Midwest. Mexican workers were involved in the great strikes of the 1930s that won recognition for these unions and led to contracts, higher wages, improved working conditions, and later health and pension benefits. Puerto Ricans joined the International Ladies Garment Workers Union and other unions in New York and New Jersey. On their home island, Puerto Rican workers joined some AFL-CIO unions, while others joined independent unions.

Latino Union Experience since World War II

During the period of the 1940s and 1950s, American unions in general came under attack. The U.S. Congress passed the Taft-Hartley Act in 1947, provisions of which weakened unions' ability to express solidarity through sympathy strikes and boycotts. The law's anti-Communist clause also required union leaders to swear that they were not Communists, and the House Un-American Activities Committee

(HUAC) scrutinized unions for Communist ties. The right-wing political attack, in particular on the unions of the CIO, many of which were led by Communists, weakened the very unions that had been most beneficial to Mexican and other Latino workers. The Taft-Harley Act and the McCarran-Walter Act (Immigration and Nationality Act of 1952) were used, for example, to harass and persecute the International Mine, Mill and Smelter Workers' Union and the UCAPAWA, both of which had many Mexican American members.

Labor unions thus became more bureaucratic and conservative during the 1940s and 1950s, followed by a brief revival in the 1960s and early 1970s. The success of César Chávez of the United Farm Workers of America (UFW) in organizing agricultural workers in California provided a template as to how to organize Latino workers within other industries and unions. Some unions began to organize not only documented but undocumented workers as well. For example, the International Longshore and Warehouse Union (ILWU), the International Ladies Garment Workers Union, the United Electrical Workers Union, and the United Auto Workers Union all began to actively organize both documented and undocumented workers, as did the International Brotherhood of Teamsters years later. Within many of these unions, Latino workers began to play significant roles in positions of leadership as Spanish-speaking immigrants became an established part of the institutional life of the union.

American unions in general saw their power decline dramatically after 1979. The economic recessions of 1974–1975 and 1979–1981, combined with the election of conservative Republican Ronald Reagan and his firing of 13,000 members of the Professional Air Traffic Controllers Organization (PATCO) in 1980 had a disastrous impact on the entire labor movement. Government at all levels, as well as private employers, launched an offensive against unions across the board that adversely affected all workers, Latinos/as among them. At about the same time, corporations began to close older steel mills, automobile plants, and other industrial facilities throughout the Midwest and Northeast, a process called deindustrialization. Consequently, many Latino workers lost high-paying union jobs.

By the 1980s, Central Americans made up a large portion of the janitors who cleaned buildings in Los Angeles, of the restaurant and hotel workers in New York and Washington, D.C., and of the workers in meatpacking and poultry plants throughout the Midwest and the South. While some of these were union jobs, many more were nonunion and therefore became the target of organizing drives by the unions. During the 1990s, industrial unions tried to deal with the issue of declining membership and loss of power in their core industries by becoming general unions focused on organizing low-income workers, many of them Latinos/as.

By the twenty-first century, immigrants, most of them Latino/a, became central to the U.S. economy and the future of labor. Of the estimated 11.1 million undocumented immigrants in March 2005, 7.2 percent were employed, making up 4.9 percent of the U.S. workforce. The entire immigrant population—both legal and undocumented—made up 14 percent of the workforce and as much as 20 percent of workers in low-wage industries. Immigrants accounted for 17 percent of cleaning workers, 14 percent of construction workers, and 12 percent of food preparation workers. On average, they work for lower wages, have fewer benefits, and toil in substandard conditions. Most of these immigrants are Latinos/as and most of those are Mexicans.

During the 1990s, the AFL-CIO, particularly the Service Employees International Union (SEIU), UNITE-HERE, and the Laborers' International Union of North America (LIUNA), put much of their energy into organizing low-wage immigrant workers, documented or undocumented. The SEIU Justice for Janitors campaign won contracts with higher wages and health insurance for Latino janitors in cities throughout the country. In a dramatic shift, the AFL-CIO in 2000 passed a resolution calling for an end to sanctions against employers who hire undocumented immigrants and for a new amnesty program for immigrants without papers. With union membership still stagnant, Change-to-Win, founded in 2005 by SEIU and several other major unions, vowed to focus even more of its attention on organizing Latinos/as and other low-wage immigrant workers.

While no exact figures are available, Latino workers remain visible as both members and leaders within many unions today. SEIU, which organizes janitors and health care workers, has tens of thousands of Latino workers among its 2 million members. UNITE-HERE, which organizes hotel and restaurant workers, also has large numbers of Latino workers. The Teamsters have many thousands of Latino members who work in warehouses and food-processing plants. The United Food and Commercial Workers Union (UFCW) has significant numbers of Latino workers in meat and poultry slaughtering, processing, and packing plants. Latinos/as participate in significant numbers in the American Federation of Teachers (AFT) and the National Education Association (NEA), in cities and suburbs throughout the country. Many Latino public employees can be found in the American Federation of State, County and Municipal Employees (AFSCME). The building trades (carpenters, electricians, plumbers), which historically excluded African American, Asian, and Latino workers, as well as women, began in the 1990s to recruit some Latinos/as in the Southwest and Florida and in cities such as Chicago and New York. Where Latinos/as dominated a trade, such as drywall hangers in the Southwest, they have sometimes organized their own unions, struck, and won contracts and higher wages.

In the first decade of the twenty-first century, undocumented Latino immigrants were finding it harder to work in the United States and finding themselves facing deportation and criminal charges for using false Social Security numbers. Human Rights Watch found that whatever industry they worked in, Latino workers, like other American workers, found it harder to exercise their rights, to join labor unions, to strike, and to negotiate contracts throughout the early parts of the twenty-first century. Conditions were most difficult for workers in poultry and meat processing plants. Nevertheless, with the ongoing expansion of the immigrant population and labor pool, many unions see their future in the growing Latino working class.

Dan LaBotz

See also: Farah Strike; Justice for Janitors; Mariel Boatlift; United Farm Workers of America.

Further Reading

Compa, Lance. *Blood, Sweat, and Fear: Workers' Rights in U.S. Meat and Poultry Plants.* New York: Human Rights Watch, 2004.

Corona, Bert. *Memories of Chicano History: The Life and Narrative of Bert Corona.* Foreword by Mario T. García. Berkeley: University of California Press, 1994.

Fink, Leon. *The Maya of Morganton: Work and Community in the Nuevo New South.* Chapel Hill: University of North Carolina Press, 2003.

Gómez Quiñones, Juan. *Mexican American Labor, 1790–1990.* Albuquerque: University of New Mexico Press, 1994.

Stull, Donald D., and Michael J. Broadway. *Slaughterhouse Blues: The Meat and Poultry Industry in North America.* Belmont, CA: Wadsworth/Thomson Learning, 2004.

Vargas, Zaragosa. *Labor Rights Are Civil Rights: Mexican American Workers in Twentieth Century America.* Princeton, NJ: Princeton University Press, 2005.

———. *Proletarians of the North: A History of Mexican Industrial Workers in Detroit and the Midwest, 1917–1933.* Berkeley: University of California Press, 1999.

United Farm Workers of America

In 1962, César Chávez and Dolores Huerta founded the National Farm Workers Association (NFWA), which would later become the United Farm Workers of America (UFW), in California's Central Valley. The UFW, originally composed of organized Latino migrant farmworkers in the state, saw its membership grow from several hundred in the early 1960s to more than 50,000 today. Since its inception, the UFW has organized several successful field labor strikes, negotiated dozens of contracts with growers, and lobbied for fairer labor standards. The successes were hard fought, as UFW organizers encountered employer resistance ranging from legal battles to physical violence.

During the second half of the twentieth century, California agribusiness emerged as a multi-billion-dollar industry that relied on migrant farmworkers who moved up and down the state to pick cotton, strawberries, and grapes, hoe beets, separate lettuce, and harvest avocados. While the struggle for African American civil rights was taking place throughout the South, Chávez and Huerta worked

El Malcriado ("the ill-bred one" or "child who talks back to his parents") was the official publication of the United Farm Workers. UFW cofounders Dolores Huerta and César Chávez first published the underground paper in 1964. *(Rodolfo F. Acuña Collection, 1816–2007. Urban Archives Center. Oviatt Library. California State University, Northridge)*

tirelessly on the West Coast to provide social and economic justice by mobilizing farm laborers into an industrial labor union. The National Labor Relations Act (1935)—which reversed federal opposition to labor unions and guaranteed steel workers and manufacturing employees the right to join labor unions without fear of employer interference or punishment—excluded agricultural workers. Nevertheless, the NFWA petitioned farm employers for suitable housing, clean water, health care, decent wages, and limited usage of pesticides.

In 1962, there were few organized farm labor unions with dues-paying members. Activists assumed that a union of migrant farm laborers would be impossible because of their transient existence, high rates of illiteracy and poverty, language barriers, and diverse ethnic makeup. Yet the NFWA used multi-issue community organizing to incorporate the many needs (schooling, housing, and health care) of the migrant population. It also partnered with the mutual benefit associations of the Catholic Church, such as the National Catholic Rural Life Conference, to build trust, form alliances, and develop solidarity, training, and long-term commitment among its members. The NFWA was successful in recruiting large numbers of people at one time, using house meetings, grassroots mobilization, and portraying to the media obvious signs of worker solidarity.

Under the charismatic leadership of Chávez, the NFWA, based in Delano, California, functioned as a social service organization that offered counseling, a credit union, and a cooperative that made available language classes as an instrument of empowerment for farm laborers and their families. In 1965, with minuscule funding and several thousand members, the NFWA joined a strike against wine grape growers that had been initiated by the mostly Filipino American migrant workers of the Agricultural Workers Organizing Committee (AWOC), an affiliate of the American Federation of Labor–Congress of Industrial Organizations (AFL-CIO). The resulting Delano grape strike lasted over five years, with the strikers experiencing intimidation by individual growers in acts that included beatings, shootings, speeding vehicles near picket lines, and pesticide spraying. Regardless, 5,000 farmworkers remained off the job.

The NFWA evolved into a social movement when, in the spring of 1966, Chávez led a 300-mile march from Delano to Sacramento to publicize the strike and protest the injustices experienced by farmworkers. Committed to nonviolence, Chávez held a hunger strike in the winter of 1968 to dissuade workers from resorting to violence when assaulted by antiunionists. College students, labor leaders, civil rights and antiwar activists, environmental organizations, Chicano community groups, and religious leaders offered their support for NFWA's cause by participating in demonstrations alongside of field workers throughout California and by organizing volunteers in their own cities. External support from religious, political, and labor leaders allowed the NFWA to expand its tactics to include a consumer boycott of table grapes, and a national campaign convinced the public and ship cargo loaders to join the boycott.

The NFWA merged with the AWOC in 1966 to form the United Farm Workers Organizing Committee (UFWOC), and by 1970, five years from the start of the initial grape strike and with the help of more than 5,000 strikers, the UFWOC negotiated and signed union contracts. With more than 10,000 members and 150 contracts, the UFWOC had made significant progress from its uncertain beginnings. In 1972, the union accepted independent status with the AFL-CIO and became the United Farm Workers of America (UFW).

While the table grape boycotts and strikes ultimately proved successful, UFW leaders faced constant challenges. Agribusinesses stalled contracts, court rulings limited UFW activity, the political climate in California was constantly in shift, strikebreakers threatened the effectiveness of strikes, and the challenge to solidify an ethnically diverse and foreign-born workforce became increasingly more difficult. Farmworkers in California may have sympathized with UFW strikes, but, beset by poverty, many could not pass up earned wages compromised by participating in a strike. With the passage of the California Agricultural Labor Relations Act (ALRA) in 1975, collective farmworkers could legally organize boycotts, picket, march, and strike. Yet, while the ALRA did grant farmworkers the right to organize, it also hindered UFW organizing when agribusinesses ceased responding in the fields and instead took the fight to courtrooms, challenging the detailed tenets of the ALRA and slowing down negotiations in the process.

UFW's grassroots organizing declined in the 1980s as state workers failed to enforce the ALRA and the union faced internal organizational conflict over whether to concentrate efforts on either organizing in the field or attracting the support of the American public through direct mail campaigns. The UFW did see progress in the 1990s, however. Upon Chávez's death at the age of sixty-six in April 1993, his son-in-law Arturo Rodriguez succeeded him as a motivated UFW president. Rodriguez re-energized the UFW and launched a campaign in 1994 to organize in the field and negotiate new contracts. Success came in the mid-1990s, when the UFW finally settled a seventeen-year boycott with the lettuce grower Bruce Church and organized a massive campaign in California's central coast against shipping companies that employed more than 15,000 laborers and transported nearly half the strawberries grown in the United States. The organizing of strawberry workers led to two major contracts with leading producers.

Organizing immigrant farmworkers remains difficult, but many farmworkers' rights are a result of the early organizing efforts led by the NFWA and the UFW. Through decades of perseverance, the UFW has succeeded in building a broad base of support among farmworkers in the migrant community while also forging partnerships with businesses, religious institutions, immigrant rights groups, and Latino organizations. In the twenty-first century, the union continues to change the lives of laborers in rural California through organizing, contract negotiation, strikes, boycotts, political campaigns, and legislative reform.

Howell Williams

See also: Chávez, César; Grape Strikes and Boycotts; Huerta, Dolores; Kennedy, Robert F.; *Medrano v. Allee* (1972); Migrant Workers; Unions, Industrial and Trade.

Further Reading

Etulain, Richard W., ed. *César Chávez: A Brief Biography with Documents.* New York: Palgrave, 2002.

Ferriss, Susan, Ricardo Sandoval, and Diana Hembree, eds. *The Flight in the Fields: César Chávez and the Farmworkers Movement.* New York: Harcourt Brace, 1997.

Jenkins, Craig J. *The Politics of Insurgency: The Farm Worker Movement in the 1960s.* New York: Columbia University Press, 1985.

Univision

Univision Television Group is the oldest and most popular Spanish-language television network in the United States, reaching 98 percent of all Latino households. The network consists of twenty-six owned and operated (O&O) stations, sixty-six broadcast affiliates, and 1,834 cable affiliates. As large as it is, Univision Television Group is only part of Univision Communications' media properties, which also include another broadcast television network, a cable network, a radio network, a Latin music conglomerate, and an Internet portal that provides services such as e-mail and wireless communications. This makes Univision Communications Inc. the dominant force in Spanish-language media in the United States.

Univision began in 1961 in San Antonio, Texas, as the Spanish International Network (SIN), owned and operated by Telesistema Mexicano, Mexico's largest private broadcaster and the forerunner of Televisa, the largest Spanish-speaking media company in the world. The SIN stations, clustered along the U.S.-Mexico border, primarily broadcast Televisa content into the United States, though some attempts were made at creating local news programming. Facing no competition from other U.S.-based broadcasters for a Spanish-language audience, the network kept expanding; by 1982, it boasted sixteen O&O stations, 100 repeater stations, and more than 200 cable affiliates.

In 1986, the Federal Communications Commission (FCC) invoked section 310(a) of the Communi-

Univision Communications, Inc., the largest Spanish-language media company in the United States, includes two broadcast television networks, a cable television network, a radio network, and an Internet portal. Its headquarters are located in Los Angeles. *(Robyn Beck/AFP/Getty Images)*

cations Act of 1934, which restricted majority ownership of television and radio stations broadcasting in the United States to U.S. citizens, and forced Televisa's owners, the Azcárraga family, to sell SIN to Hallmark Cards, Inc. of Kansas City, Missouri. Hallmark executives changed the network's name to Univision and shifted its programming strategy from one that relied on *telenovelas* (serialized dramas similar to American soap operas) to one featuring more diverse content. This led to a period of declining ratings and a brush with bankruptcy. In 1992, Hallmark sold Univision to a consortium that included A. Jerrold Perenchio, Venevisa (a Venezuelan broadcaster), and Televisa (a Mexican broadcaster and former owner). At this point, Univision returned to its previously successful strategy of featuring telenovelas during the early afternoon and prime-time hours.

Univision Television Group has been the most watched Spanish-language network in the United States since its inception, due in large part to its exclusive access to Televisa's popular telenovelas. In 1992, with the creation the Nielsen Hispanic Television Index (NHTI), a service of Nielsen Media Research that surveys the viewing habits of U.S. Latino households, Univision was finally able to capitalize on its popularity. The new ratings system made it possible for Univision and others to convince advertisers to buy airtime, as the media companies were able to prove the size of their audiences. The Nielsen Hispanic Television Index (NHTI) has since come to be the standard data collection service for Latino television viewing.

Univision's financial fortunes improved dramatically following the creation of the NHTI. Shortly thereafter, Univision was recognized as the fifth–most watched television network in the country behind ABC, NBC, CBS, and FOX and began being publicly traded on the New York Stock Exchange. Univision's perennial popularity and record-breaking advertising revenues, at a time when most other broadcasters were seeing a decline in viewers, prompted network executives to expand the company's media portfolio and change its name to Univision Communications Inc. In addition to Univision Television Group, the company's holdings include:

- *Galavisión*—Univision's first acquisition, a cable television network. It now reaches 83 percent of Hispanic households and boasts 5.9 million subscribers.
- *Telefutura*—a broadcast television network launched in 2002 aimed at a younger, male-dominant Spanish-language audience. The network actively counterprograms telenovela-heavy Univision and features, instead, sports and movies.
- **Univision Music Group**—launched in 2001 and becoming the nation's top Latin music group. It is made up of three separate record labels: Univision Records, Fonovisa Records, and Disa Records.
- **Univision Online**—the most visited Spanish-language Internet site in the United States.
- **Univision Radio**—the company's latest venture. It was formed in 2002 when Univision acquired an existing Spanish-language radio network, the Hispanic Broadcasting Corporation, and changed its name. Since then, Univision Radio has aggressively expanded into new markets by buying English-language stations in large Hispanic markets and relaunching them as Spanish-language ones.

Univision Communications Group remains the leader in Spanish-language media in the United States. Its multiple operations allow it to cross-promote properties, helping to drive up its profits. For example, executives at Univision Music Group can boost sales by promoting its artists on Univision Radio networks and by scheduling appearances for them on Univision, Galavisión, and Telefutura programs.

Patricia Kim-Rajal

See also: Cisneros, Henry; Popular Culture; Spanish Language; Telemundo; Television.

Further Reading

Rodriguez, America. *Making Latino News: Race, Language, Class.* Thousand Oaks, CA: Sage, 1999.
Univision. http://www.univision.net.
Univision Portal en Español. http://www.univision.com.

Uruguayans

According to the U.S. Census Bureau, there were 18,804 Uruguayans living in the United States in the year 2000, comprising 0.10 percent of the Latino population. The small number reflects a history of relative stability in the home country. Uruguayans did not begin immigrating to the United States in any significant number until the 1960s, before which Uruguay experienced very little migration at all. The few who had left the country tended to stay away only temporarily, especially those who migrated to Argentina. The very few who did make their way to the United States before the mid-twentieth century did so in search of better educational and financial opportunities, only to return home after achieving their goals.

The history of Uruguay is one of relative political stability, economic prosperity, and social harmony, characteristics that also came to define the experience of Uruguayans living in the United States. A nation of only 3.5 million in 2008—more than 85 percent of whom are of white/European descent, 8 percent mestizo, and 6 percent black—Uruguayans have experienced little conflict and division based on race, ethnicity, religion, or social class compared to people in other countries. Moreover, its people have experienced a generally stable economy and accessible social welfare system, high rates of literacy, low levels of poverty, long life expectancy, and an overall high quality of life. Thus, the nation has seen scant migration for most of its modern history. The situation began changing in 1951, when the people of Uruguay approved a new constitution that abolished the office of the presidency, leading to an economic collapse. With alarming rates of inflation, a squeeze on social programs, and declining job prospects, the economic situation became dire by the early 1960s, resulting in a significant increase in immigration to the United States, Argentina, Australia, and Brazil, among other places. From 1963 to 1975, an estimated 180,000 Uruguayans left their country.

The mass exodus, especially in the professional and educated classes, contributed to the downward spiral of the economy, resulting in political upheaval and, in the early 1970s, the establishment of a military regime. Under the dictatorship, artists, intellectuals, politicians, and others who challenged official policies and ideologies faced persecution, leading to a significant wave of emigration, particularly among youth, professionals, and the educated. Most went to the United States. An estimated 68 percent of the 150,000 emigrants during this period were between the ages of fifteen and thirty-nine, resulting in additional financial strain for those who stayed behind. The loss of the professional and educated classes, and the further decline of economic prospects, continued to push other Uruguayans to emigrate.

Educated middle-class Uruguayans have not been the only group to take up residency in the United States, as members of the working-class have also found their way to U.S. shores seeking employment and a better life. Between 1963 and 1975, it has been estimated, some 48 percent of Uruguayans residing in the United States worked as skilled or unskilled workers and day laborers, compared to the 13 percent who found jobs as professionals, technicians, managers, and administrators. Another 28 percent were working as office employees and salespeople.

Uruguayan Americans have formed sizable communities in New York City, on Long Island (New York), and in New Jersey, with a smaller presence in Washington, D.C., and Florida. Although they comprise a small percentage of the Latino population, Uruguayans also comprise a distinctive community and contribute to the heterogeneity of those who are called "Latinos" in the United States.

David J. Leonard

Further Reading

Spear, Jane E. "Uruguayan Americans." In "Multicultural America." http://www.everyculture.com.

Taylor, Philip B., Jr. *Government and Politics of Uruguay.* Westport, CT: Greenwood, 1984.

Uruguayan American Chamber of Commerce. http://www.uruguaychamber.com.

U.S. Military
See Military, Latinos in the

Valdez, Luis
(1940–)

Having witnessed the hardships of his farmworking Mexican parents, who moved from harvest to harvest in California's Central Valley, the playwright and film director Luis Miguel Valdez has dedicated himself to showing the abuse and suffering endured by the tenacious migrant workers in the first half of the twentieth century. Since the early 1960s, Valdez has used his plays and movies to expose the blight experienced by the Latino community at the hands of Anglos residing in rural California, and to give voice to Latinos/as demanding improvement in their living and working conditions.

Born to Francisco and Armeda Valdez in Delano, California, on June 26, 1940, Valdez accompanied his father and mother on their travels as migrant farmworkers, until the family finally succeeded in settling down in San Jose, California. He attended a local public high school and San Jose State University (SJSU), where he majored in English and joined the college theater troupe to stage the experiences he had lived in his younger days. At SJSU, Valdez produced a one-act play titled *The Theft* (1961), which won a writing contest, and his first full-length play, *The Shrunken Head of Pancho Villa* (1963).

His immersion in the world of the arts helped Valdez discover the potential of using performance art to attract public attention to the social problems of the Latino population. Upon graduation in 1964, he worked for several months with the San Francisco Mime Group and then returned to Delano to join activist César Chávez and the United Farm Workers Association (UFWA) in their efforts to educate migrants and unionize farmworkers during the Delano grape strike of 1965. At the same time, he founded, wrote for, and directed El Teatro Campesino, an amateur theater troupe made up of harvesters, that toured the working camps to raise funds, spread news about the UFWA campaign, and perform humorous agitprop sketches (short morality plays) called *actos,* based on the current concerns of Mexican Americans. To increase political awareness among the community of Mexican laborers, many of whom were illiterate, the company used images of strikers and farmers suffering violent reprisal at the hand of police. Among his most popular productions were *Las dos caras del patroncito* (*The Two Faces of the Owner,* 1965), *Los Vendidos* (*The Sellouts,* 1967), *The Militants* (1969), *Bernabé* (1970), *Huelguistas* (*Strikers,* 1970), and *Vietnam Campesino* (*Vietnam Peasant,* 1970).

In 1967, Valdez left the union movement to broaden his horizons, expand the repertoire of his company, and extend the reach of his political message. With those goals in mind, he produced his first movie *I Am Joaquín* in 1969; created TENAZ (El Teatro Nacional de Aztlán), a national Chicano theater organization; and began a Chicano cultural center called El Centro Campesino Cultural in Del Ray, California (it later moved to Fresno and then to San Juan Bautista). Valdez's passionate and politically committed work inspired a new generation of Latino actors and producers, and gave rise to new theater groups throughout the United States. Meanwhile, he wrote, directed, and produced plays depicting the history of Latinos/as, including *La carpa de los rasquachis* (*The Tent of the Underdogs,* 1973), *El fin del mundo* (*The End of the World,* 1976), and especially *Zoot Suit* (1978), based on the famous trial of Henry Leyvas and eight other Latino youths in the 1942 Los Angeles Sleepy Lagoon case. After running successfully for two years in Los Angeles, *Zoot Suit* became the first theatrical production by a Mexican American ever to appear on Broadway.

Given the unexpected success of *Zoot Suit,* Valdez released a low-budget film version in 1982, casting

The founder of El Teatro Campesino in the 1960s and the writer-director of several major motion pictures in the decades since, Luiz Valdez—the son of migrant farm-workers—is recognized as the father of modern Chicano theater and film. *(Alan Levenson/Time & Life Pictures/Getty Images)*

(1973), three Los Angeles Drama Critics Awards (1969, 1972, 1978), and Mexico's prestigious *Orden del Águila Azteca* (1994), as well as honorary doctorates from Columbia University, San Jose State University, and the California Institute of the Arts. He has served as a member of the National Council of the Arts, which advises the National Endowment for the Arts. Widely acknowledged as the father of Chicano theater, Valdez teaches at the Teledramatic Arts and Technology Institute of California State University, Monterey Bay.

Jorge Abril Sánchez

See also: Film; Migrant Workers; Sleepy Lagoon Case; Teatro Campesino, El.

Further Reading

Babcock, Granger. "Looking for a Third Space: El Pachuco and Chicano Nationalism in Luis Valdez's *Zoot Suit.*" In *Staging Difference: Cultural Pluralism in American Theatre and Drama,* ed. Marc Maufort. New York: Peter Lang, 1995.

Barrios, Gregg. "*Zoot Suit:* The Man, the Myth, Still Lives. A Conversation with Luis Valdez." In *Chicano Cinema: Research, Reviews, and Resources,* ed. Gary D. Keller. Binghamton, NY: Bilingual, 1985.

Cárdenas de-Dwyer, Carlota. "The Development of Chicano Drama and Luis Valdez's *Actos.*" In *Modern Chicano Writers: A Collection of Critical Essays,* ed. Joseph Sommers and Tomás Ybarra-Frausto. Englewood Cliffs, NJ: Prentice-Hall, 1979.

Elam, Harry J., Jr. *Taking it into the Streets: The Social Protest Theater of Luis Valdez and Amiri Baraka.* Ann Arbor: University of Michigan Press, 2001.

Edward James Olmos as a street-smart *pachuco* (gang) leader unfairly arrested and convicted of a murder he did not commit. Although the film version of *Zoot Suit* was not as popular as the play, it received excellent critical reviews and some box-office profits while publicizing the issues of legal injustice, racial discrimination, and social rights.

Valdez's foray into film with *Zoot Suit* was just the beginning of his career as a moviemaker. In succeeding years he wrote and directed *La Bamba* (1987), with Lou Diamond Phillips as the Chicano rock and roll singer Richie Valens, and *The Cisco Kid* (1988), in which he also starred.

Valdez has been the recipient of numerous awards and honors, including an Obie (1968), an Emmy

Valenzuela, Fernando (1960–)

Arguably Mexico's most famous contribution to Major League Baseball, Fernando Valenzuela emerged as one of the sport's most colorful and successful pitchers during the 1980s. His passion for the game and popularity, especially among Latino fans, was a source of pride in his native country and in Mexican communities throughout the United States. In a total of seventeen seasons, most of them spent with the Los Angeles Dodgers, the left-hander compiled a record of 173–153, with a career earned run average of 3.53 and 2,074 strikeouts.

Valenzuela's age is somewhat of a mystery, although his birth date is officially listed by Major League Baseball as November 1, 1960. He was born and raised as the youngest of twelve children on a small farm in Navojoa (Sonora), Mexico. The Los Angeles Dodgers signed him to a major league contract in 1979, after watching him play for the Leones de Yucatán (Yucatán Lions) of the Mexican League. That same year, he pitched briefly for the Dodgers' Class A and AA minor league teams before being called up to the parent club late in the 1980 season. His brief appearance gave promise of great things to come.

Valenzuela's 1981 season was one of the most memorable—and exciting—by any pitcher in the modern era of baseball. He began the campaign with an unprecedented eight consecutive victories, including four shutouts and an opening day complete-game shutout over the defending Western Division champion Houston Astros. His early success gave birth to a phenomenon known as "Fernandomania," which was a function of his style and personal appearance as much as his on-the-field success. Valenzuela appealed to the ordinary fan with his short, portly physique and awkward pitching style. In the middle of his windup, he would look to the sky and then not look at the batter until he delivered the ball to the plate.

His debut came at an auspicious time: the Latino community in the United States, already one of the largest Spanish-speaking populations in the world, had expanded considerably during the 1970s. Now it found a hero in the person of Fernando Valenzuela. His humble beginnings and success on the field captured the imagination of Latino/as across the United States. Moreover, in a season shortened by a players' strike, Valenzuela helped maintain the popularity of the game for all fans. He helped the Dodgers defeat the New York Yankees in the World Series, and, when the season was over, he became the first pitcher ever to win Rookie of the Year honors and the Cy Young Award (as the league's top pitcher) in the same season. The accolades were justified, as Valenzuela finished the 1981 season as the National League leader in complete games, shutouts, innings pitched, and strikeouts.

The public's interest in Valenzuela went beyond wins and losses, with news reporters and television cameras following his every move. Games were sold out whenever he pitched. He had a greater impact on Major League Baseball than any Latino player since Roberto Clemente. His performance and popularity represented a breakthrough for Latinos/as in America. In a sport dominated by white and black athletes, Valenzuela represented the growing presence of a new culture and style of play in the major leagues. Playing in a city with a sizable Latino community heightened both his popularity and the appeal of the sport among Latinos/as. Consequently, there was a noticeable increase in Latino attendance at Dodger Stadium, and today Latinos/as represent a significant percentage of the fan base in Los Angeles and other cities with Major League franchises. The discovery of Valenzuela in Mexico and his rise to success helped demonstrate to other teams the importance of searching for players in small towns throughout Latin America—a scouting strategy teams practice today in great numbers. By the 2006 season, nearly 30 percent of players on major league rosters were Latinos or Latino Americans.

Valenzuela had his best full season with the Dodgers in 1986, reeling off career highs in wins (21) and strikeouts (242). His last great moment came on June 29, 1990, when he threw a 6–0 no-hitter against the St. Louis Cardinals. Although he would never again generate the excitement he did in 1981, Valenzuela remained a quality starter in the Dodgers' rotation throughout the 1980s. He pitched a total of eleven seasons with the Dodgers before moving on to brief stints with the California Angels, Baltimore Orioles, Philadelphia Phillies, and San Diego Padres.

In 2003, Valenzuela returned to Major League Baseball as a Spanish radio commentator for the Dodgers—the organization that paved the way for the black athlete (first and foremost, Jackie Robinson) in professional sports, and, to a lesser extent the Latino athlete as well. Valenzuela's debut in the United States coincided with a rapidly growing Latino population with increasing buying power. This proved to be a perfect market in which to promote the game of baseball and the mainstream American culture. Just as importantly, Fernandomania allowed that population to maintain its cultural identity and take pride in one of its own.

Frank DeLaO

See also: Baseball.

Further Reading

LaFrance, David. "A Mexican Popular Image of the United States Through the Baseball Hero, Fernando Valenzuel." *Studies in Latin American Culture* 4 (1985): 14–23.

Littwin, Mark. *Fernando!* New York: Bantam, 1981.

Regalado, Samuel. *Viva Baseball.* Chicago: University of Illinois Press, 1998.

Venezuelans

At the turn of the twenty-first century, according to the U.S Census Bureau, there were a total of 91,507 Venezuelans or people of Venezuelan descent living in the United States. As in the case of other South American communities, it is uncertain how many Venezuelans lived in the United States before the 1960s and 1970s. Although there is no definitive evidence of early migration, the overall number of U.S. immigrants from South America, combined with a history of European immigrants settling first in Venezuela and then moving to the United States, suggest a long-lived Venezuelan American community.

Whatever the uncertainties of quantity, it is well known that many Venezuelans came to the United States in search of educational opportunity, stayed on after graduation, and were reunited with relatives as part of family reunification (a cornerstone of U.S. policy after the Immigration Act of 1965). The pattern continued through the 1980s, with an increasing number of Venezuelan professionals immigrating to the United States in the wake of economic troubles at home. Like other South American newcomers, Venezuelan immigrants tended to settle in urban areas of the Northeast, as well as Miami, Chicago, and Los Angeles. By the 1990s, the U.S. Census reported that the highest concentrations were found in Florida (12,362), New York (5,559), Los Angeles (4,575), and Texas (3,295). While overwhelmingly

middle-class and urban, Venezuelan Americans are also diverse in many ways. Although the majority (70 percent) of middle-class Venezuelan Americans identify themselves as Africans, European, and Indian, some 21 percent identify exclusively as white, with 8 percent as black and 1 percent as Indian.

Notwithstanding the relatively small size of the community, Venezuelans have contributed significantly to America's cultural landscape in a range of areas. Notable members of the community include pop singer Mariah Carey, whose father is Venezuelan, and ballet dancer Iliana Veronica Lopez de Gonera, who has performed with the San Francisco Ballet, the Ballet Corps of the Cleveland Opera House, and the Miami City Ballet. Venezuelan Americans have had an especially strong presence in Major League Baseball—not surprisingly, given the popularity of baseball in the homeland. One of the earliest and most successful Venezuelan American players was shortstop Luis Aparicio, who was named Rookie of the Year in 1956, played on All-Star teams ten times during his seventeen-year career, and was inducted into baseball's Hall of Fame in 1974. Other Venezuelan stars have included Dave Concepcion, Andres Galarraga, Ozzie Guillen, Omar Vizquel, Edgardo Alfonso, Johan Santana, and Francisco Rodriguez. As of 2007, a total of 199 Venezuelans had played in Major League Baseball, serving as a source of great pride for the Venezuelan American community and Venezuelans throughout the world.

The influence of Venezuelans in the United States has not been limited to popular culture and sports, but is equally evident in the media. Reflective of the boom in Spanish-language television and newspapers, coverage regarding the experiences and news of Venezuelans and broadcasts of Venezuelan entertainment, news, and educational programming have become commonplace within Latino media.

Venezuelans have also brought their national cuisine to the American cultural landscape. Empanadas—fried turnovers made of cornmeal and stuffed with cheese, chicken, beef, or vegetables—have become staples of the American ethnic food scene, from the street corner vendor to the five-star restaurant. Less common but widely available in

Venezuelan American neighborhoods are *arepas,* tiny corn pancakes that can be stuffed with beef, shrimp, octopus, or avocado, among other things, and *tixana,* a mixed fruit drink.

Since the mid-twentieth century, Venezuelan Americans have shown an increasing interest in politics and other forms of civic engagement at both the local and national level. One notable example is that of Federico Morena, who immigrated to the United States from Venezuela in 1963, ultimately receiving his bachelor's degree in government from Notre Dame and his law degree from the University of Miami. After practicing law for several years in Miami and serving as a judge in Dade County, Florida, he was appointed to the U.S. District Court, Southern District of Florida. Ana María Distefano has achieved prominence as a government official, serving in high-level positions in the U.S. Department of Commerce and the Bureau of Census.

Political activities in the Venezuelan American community have often focused on the politics of the homeland, especially since the rise of President Hugo Chávez in 1998 and in the context of his virulent anti-American rhetoric. In December 2006, more than 800 Venezuelan Americans voted in the Venezuelan presidential election at a polling place in San Francisco, as did others throughout the United States. U.S. economic (oil) interests in Venezuela and the contentious relationship between Chávez and President George W. Bush underscored the importance of the election and U.S.-Venezuelan relations to the growing Venezuelan American community. Venezuelans thus provide an example of a relatively recent immigrant group that is striving to get ahead in their new homeland while maintaining tangible connections with the old one.

David J. Leonard

Further Reading

Hispanic Policy Development Project. *The Hispanic Almanac.* Washington, DC: Hispanic Development Project, 1984.

Meier, Matt S., with Conchita Franco Serri and Richard A. Garcia. *Notable Latino Americans: A Biographical Dictionary.* Westport, CT: Greenwood, 1997.

Walker, Drew. "Venezuelan Americans." *Multicultural America* Website. http://www.everyculture.com.

Vieques, Puerto Rico

Vieques is a small island—21 miles (34 kilometers) long and 5 miles (8 kilometers) wide—located less than 10 miles (16 kilometers) off the east coast of Puerto Rico, in the northeastern part of the Caribbean Sea. It has fewer than 10,000 residents. Politically, Vieques is a municipality of the island of Puerto Rico and a territory of the United States since 1898. Residents of Vieques (and Puerto Rico) have been citizens of the United States since 1917. Because of its strategic position, Vieques was under the control of the U.S. Navy from 1941 to 2003. The Navy purchased approximately two-thirds of the land area, building an ammunitions depot on the west side of the island and a military practice range on the east. Before long, it began using Vieques as a testing ground for weapons and the site of military exercises and maneuvers.

In the period leading up to World War II, the administration of President Franklin D. Roosevelt planned to build a Caribbean military base, similar to the one on Pearl Harbor, on the eastern shore of Puerto Rico. The result was the Roosevelt Roads Naval Station in Ceiba, a small town on the southern coast of Puerto Rico, and encompassing portions of the island municipalities of Vieques and Culebra. Roosevelt Roads eventually would become one of the largest naval facilities in the world, a remarkable fact given that it was built on the smallest of the Greater Antilles. In the course of developing Roosevelt Roads, the Navy confiscated a total of 25,440 acres in Vieques during the 1940s. By 1972, it owned 73 percent of the land in Vieques, becoming the largest landowner on the islet. According to military sources, land acquisitions forced the relocation of between 4,350 and 5,000 residents, or 40 to 50 percent of the population.

Social Conditions

After the Navy took possession, Viequenses were concentrated in the middle of the island; they were forced to endure the constant thunder of war games and lived in constant fear of a bomb or missile

Protestors against the U.S. target-bombing of Vieques set up dozens of camps on the island in defiance of the U.S. government and armed forces. The U.S. Navy finally withdrew in 2003, leaving behind widespread environmental damage and public health problems. *(Robert Sullivan/AFP/Getty Images)*

exploding in a civilian neighborhood. In addition, with the shutdown of local farms and plantations, socioeconomic conditions took an extreme turn for the worse. With 73 percent of its population living below the poverty line, according to one source, Vieques was, without a doubt, the poorest municipality in Puerto Rico. Almost half the adult population was unemployed. In addition to issues involving poverty (though perhaps related to them), Viequenses also suffered from myriad physical and mental ailments at rates astonishingly higher than in any other part of Puerto Rico or the United States. Among these were cancer, heart problems, hypertension, and diabetes.

Throughout the years, the residents of Vieques developed a relationship with the U.S. Navy marked by confrontation and altercation. Many of the incidents involved fishermen, who in the 1970s began protesting the Navy's seeming disregard for their livelihood. (It determined, for example, when and where the fishermen could fish according to the military practice schedule.) Reports filed by the police in Vieques also documented encounters between civilians and military personnel in Vieques's com-

munities. After a series of encounters between fishermen and the Navy in the early 1980s, a group of fisherman and Puerto Rican governor Carlos Romero Barceló filed a lawsuit in U.S. District Court. The suit was dropped when Governor Romero Barceló and then Secretary of the Navy James Goodrich reached an agreement known as the Memorandum of Understanding (MOU) in 1983. Among other things, the MOU promised "to increase safety, reduce bombing, protect endangered species, and create jobs."

April 1999 and Its Aftermath

Although the Navy did not keep the promises stated in the MOU, the document managed to placate Viequenses until April 19, 1999, when their fears of a military miscalculation materialized. On that day, while training for participation in the Kosovo conflict, two U.S. Navy planes were conducting war exercises off the coast of Vieques. At 6:49 P.M., the pilots were cleared to drop two five-hundred-pound bombs—but the airplanes were a mile and a half off course. The bombs were dropped on an observation post, killing a civilian security guard named David Sanes and injuring four others. The Navy called the incident a regrettable accident but offered no further explanation.

As a result of the accident, Puerto Rican protestors rallied under the slogan "not one more bomb." Hundreds of organizations and hundreds of thousands of individuals began protesting the actions of the Navy and pressuring the U.S. military to leave Vieques. The death of David Sanes helped create an unprecedented consensus, leading an entire people to make two specific requests: the immediate cessation of bombing on Vieques and the departure of the Navy from the islet. The resistance movement took different forms. By the end of 1999, ten protest camps had been set up on U.S. Navy grounds in Vieques. In addition, people and groups from the entire political landscape, including (at least at the outset) pro-statehood advocates, also joined in the quest to stop the bombing and get the Navy out. For the next four years, Puerto Ricans in Puerto Rico and the United States showed their support for Vieques in a variety of events and venues such as marches, gatherings, and rallies. Political figures on the mainland also joined Puerto Ricans in asking the government to get the Navy out of Vieques.

In the midst of the fight for Vieques, on January 31, 2000, Governor Pedro Rosselló delivered his State of Puerto Rico address, in which he announced that his administration had reached an agreement with the administration of President Bill Clinton that would "ensure peace for Vieques." Breaking from his "not one more bomb" position, Governor Rosselló reported that, "under the terms of the agreement, Puerto Rico would let the Navy resume training with dummy bombs in March." The agreement also allowed for military exercises (bombing practice) for ninety-three days out of the year and declared that the Navy would leave the island permanently after three years. As a result of the agreement, the Navy finally pulled out in May 2003. Although the island today is free of U.S. naval presence and constant bombardment, the military legacy in Vieques includes environmental degradation, a depleted population, dire economic conditions, and chronic public health issues.

Carmen R. Lugo-Lugo

See also: National Puerto Rican Coalition; Nationalism.

Further Reading

Barreto, Amílcar. *Vieques, the Navy, and Puerto Rican Politics.* Gainesville: University Press of Florida, 2002.
McCaffrey, Katherine. *Military Power and Popular Protest: The U.S. Navy in Vieques, Puerto Rico.* New Brunswick, NJ: Rutgers University Press, 2002.
Mullenneaux, Lisa. *¡Ni una bomba más!: Vieques vs. U.S. Navy.* New York: Penington, 2000.

Vietnam War

The Vietnam War marked a significant turning point for Mexican Americans in regard to the ways they thought about citizenship and patriotism. Since World War I, Mexican Americans had worked hard to demonstrate their patriotism so as to prove themselves worthy of full U.S. citizenship. In 1929, the League of United Latin American Citizens (LULAC), a Texas-based organization designed to promote the "American-ness" of Mexican Americans, began its efforts to promote assimilation through military service. Like the American GI Forum, founded in 1950, LULAC promoted military service as a marker of masculinity and U.S. citizenship.

Organizations such as LULAC and the American GI Forum thus supported the U.S. government and its military policies in the early years of the Vietnam War. In 1964, the Mexican American Political Association issued a statement of "unconditional support for President Lyndon Johnson's war in Vietnam." As the Johnson administration escalated troop levels in Southeast Asia in the mid-1960s, local chapters of the American GI Forum marched in support of U.S. forces and defended the U.S. goal of helping the "South Vietnamese remain free." Even after Rafael Guzman, a political scientist with the Ford Foundation, discovered in 1967 that Chicano soldiers accounted for 20 percent of all Vietnam casualties (compared with 6 percent of the general U.S. population), many members of the Mexican American community pointed to the findings as proof of patriotism. Opposition to the Vietnam War had not yet fully challenged the association between military service and citizenship.

A burgeoning social movement, however, was beginning to bring radical changes in Mexican American and Latino identity, and concerns about assimilation and social acceptance took a backseat to the need for empowerment and self-determination. The Chicano Movement eventually would organize some of the largest antiwar rallies within the larger anti–Vietnam War movement. Members believed that Chicanos should stay in their home communities and fight for Mexican American rights rather than fight and die in Vietnam. In 1970, Chicano activists organized the National Chicano Moratorium against the Vietnam War, a demonstration in East Los Angeles that drew between 20,000 and 30,000 people. It was the largest demonstration planned by members of the Chicano Movement.

Chicano antiwar sentiment focused especially on the military draft. Because most Chicanos did not attend college, few received draft deferments. In 1967, for example, only about seventy Mexican Americans attended the University of California, Los Angeles (UCLA), even though Los Angeles had the largest Chicano population of any city in the country. According to the 1960 U.S. Census, approximately half of the Chicano population had gone to school for less than eight years. In addition to the lack of access to draft deferments, few Mexican Americans sat on draft boards. The American GI Forum protests against the lack of Mexican Americans on draft boards in Texas aroused antiwar sentiment among Chicanos. In the San Francisco area, two women, Lea Ybarra and Nina Genera, founded Chicano Draft Help, which offered counseling to Mexican American draftees. Draft counseling organizations also appeared in New Mexico, Texas, and California.

The Chicano press paid scant attention to the war and often followed the patriotic ideology of groups like LULAC. The Houston newspaper *Compass* published lists of Mexican American winners of the Congressional Medal of Honor, while other papers focused their coverage on the progress of the war and stories of military heroism. Left-wing newspapers were more concerned with domestic issues such as education, unemployment, race relations, and allegations of police brutality. Two exceptions to the lack of coverage were *El Grito del Norte* and *El Grito,* both Chicano Movement publications. *El Grito del Norte,*

edited by Elizabeth Martinez, a civil rights activist, published a series of articles in 1969 on Vietnamese culture, and the following year it featured a story paralleling the experiences of Vietnamese peasants with those of Mexican farmworkers. Martinez went to Vietnam as a reporter and returned with stories about the geography of the country and the ways in which the war affected the mass of Vietnamese people. *El Grito* was published at the University of California, Berkeley, and edited by Professor Octavio I. Romano. One issue published in 1968 included an essay on the illegality of the Vietnam War according to international law. A year later, *El Grito* published a list of Latino casualties in Vietnam.

Anti–Vietnam War activism among Chicanos and Chicanas dwindled in the early 1970s, as the war began to wind down. The Brown Berets, which grew to fourteen chapters throughout the Southwest, disbanded in 1972. Chicano Draft Help closed its doors in 1972 as well, about a year before the draft was ended. In the years since, the publication of several books on the subject of Latino involvement in Vietnam War combat and protest, the release of a public-television documentary titled "Soldados: Chicanos in Viet Nam" (2003), and local efforts to memorialize the participation of Latino veterans and antiwar protestors all have raised the level of recognition in the historical record and public consciousness.

Heather Marie Stur

See also: American GI Forum; Chicano Movement; League of United Latin American Citizens; Military, Latinos in the; National Chicano Moratorium; Salazar, Rubén.

Further Reading

Mariscal, George. *Aztlán and Viet Nam: Chicano and Chicana Experiences of the War.* Berkeley: University of California Press, 1999.

Oropeza, Lorena. "Antiwar Aztlán: The Chicano Movement Opposes U.S. Intervention in Vietnam." In *Window on Freedom: Race, Civil Rights, and Foreign Affairs, 1945–1988,* ed. Brenda Gayle Plummer. Chapel Hill: University of North Carolina Press, 2003.

———. *Raza Si! Guerra No! Chicano Protest and Patriotism During the Viet Nam War Era.* Berkeley: University of California Press, 2005.

Trujillo, Charley. *Soldados: Chicanos in Viet Nam.* San Jose, CA: Chusma House, 1990.

Villaraigosa, Antonio
(1953–)

On May 17, 2005, Antonio Villaraigosa became the first Latino mayor of Los Angeles since Cristobal Aguilar in 1872, defeating incumbent mayor (and fellow Democrat) James Hahn in a run-off election. During his pathbreaking political career Villaraigosa has developed a reputation for orchestrating coalitions among people who normally do not work together.

Born Antonio Ramon Villar on January 23, 1953, in the East Los Angeles community of Boyle Heights, he began working at the age of seven shining shoes and selling newspapers to help the family make ends meet. Early in high school, he was diagnosed as having a spinal tumor that nearly paralyzed him. He eventually recovered and returned to high school, where he developed a reputation as a troublemaker. He was expelled from one high school and dropped out of another. In 1968, he graduated from Theodore Roosevelt High School and gained acceptance to the University of California, Los Angeles (UCLA).

While at UCLA, Villaraigosa turned his attention to politics and the struggle for Chicano rights, joining the Chicano student organization MEChA—Movimiento Estudiantil Chicano de Aztlán. In 1977, Villaraigosa graduated from UCLA with a degree in history and moved on to the People's College of Law in Los Angeles. While in law school, he met his future wife, Corina Raigosa; the couple combined their surnames to form "Villaraigosa."

Villaraigosa's life of public service began at age fifteen, when he did volunteer work with the United Farm Workers, led by the Mexican American civil rights leader César Chávez. Later he participated as a field representative and organizer with United Teachers Los Angeles (UTLA). His formal political career began in 1994, when he was elected as a California state assemblyman. In 1998, he was elected Assembly speaker—the first from Los Angeles in twenty-five years. While serving in Sacramento, Villaraigosa orchestrated the passage of several important measures, including a bond issue to help modernize the state's public schools, a bill prohibiting the sale of assault weapons, a measure to enhance urban neigh-borhood parks, and another law—known as "Healthy Families"—that sought to improve health care for all Californians.

In 2001, the popular Villaraigosa decided to run for mayor of Los Angeles. Despite a powerful coalition that included liberal whites and Latinos, he lost by 8 percent to fellow Democrat James K. Hahn. His failure to attract African Americans voters, who supported Hahn, ultimately decided the election.

In the wake of his election defeat, Villaraigosa spent two years at UCLA and the University of Southern California (USC) as a distinguished fellow, and wrote "After Sprawl," an influential article that addressed current urban issues. In 2003, he ran for and was elected to the City Council seat representing the Fourteenth District, defeating incumbent Lauro "Nick" Pacheco. In addition to attending to municipal affairs, Villaraigosa used his seat on the City Council to garner support and trust among African Americans. Upon declaring his intentions for a second run at the mayor's office, Villaraigosa received crucial endorsements from Congresswomen Maxine Waters, a prominent leader of the African American community, and Bernard Parks, the police chief who was fired by Hahn and later became a councilman. This gave Villaraigosa a decisive edge in the 2005 campaign, and he won 59 percent of the vote in the May 17 runoff.

During the course of the 2005 campaign, Villaraigosa had made a number of promises to the various factions in his coalition; early in his term, some supporters became frustrated that he did not address their issues quickly enough. While he was running, Villaraigosa had declared at least four major goals: raise the ethical standards of municipal government; take stronger control of the Los Angeles school system; add 1,000 police officers; and ease traffic congestion. His first acts as mayor were to require all city employees and government leaders to sign an ethics pledge and to remove all special-interest lobbyists from the city commission. Soon thereafter, he appointed a council of advisers to recommend improvements in public education; signed a directive that banned road construction during rush hour; increased trash fees through 2011 to pay for 1,000 more police officers; obtained funding to secure the city's ports and expand its freeways; and began an ambitious

Antonio Villaraigosa, a son of East Los Angeles, high school dropout, and Chicano rights activist of the 1970s, defeated incumbent James Hahn in May 2005 to become the first Latino mayor of Los Angeles since the 1870s. *(David McNew/Getty Images)*

program to fill 50,000 potholes in the city. Controversies have included the sale of public lands in the urban farm dispute of June 2006, and his veto of a lawsuit settlement that would have paid $2.7 million to an African American firefighter who claimed racial discrimination when some fellow firefighters fed him dog food (which they claimed was a simple prank).

In March 2006, Villaraigosa demonstrated with fellow Latinos/as in support of immigrant rights and against a controversial bill passed by the U.S. House of Representatives that would have made it a federal offense for immigrants entering the country illegally to remain. As his reputation has grown among Latinos/as, bipartisan progressive constituencies, and the Democratic Party, Villaraigosa has been mentioned as a prospect for higher office, including the governorship of California, in the future. Yet, in 2007, a personal scandal, resulting from his admission to a

romantic involvement with Los Angeles Telemundo newswoman Mirthala Salinas, cast some doubt on Villaraigosa's ability to achieve that goal.

Daniel Guzmán

See also: Los Angeles; Politics; United Farm Workers of America.

Further Reading

City of Los Angeles, Office of the Mayor, "Mayor's Biography." http://www.lacity.org/mayor/bi01.htm.

Murr, Andrew. "The Survivor's Story." *Newsweek* 145:22 (May 30, 2005): 32–34.

Nichols, John. "Progressive City Leaders." *The Nation* 280:24 (June 20, 2005): 18–19.

Viva Kennedy Clubs

Viva Kennedy Clubs were grassroots political organizations established to rally support for John F. Kennedy's 1960 presidential candidacy among Latinos/as, especially within Mexican American communities. The idea for the clubs originated with Carlos McCormick, a Kennedy staffer, and Héctor P García, founder of the American GI Forum (a Mexican American civil rights organization).

Following Kennedy's nomination at the Democratic National Convention in Los Angeles in July, McCormick set out across the country to set up local campaign organizations in Latino population centers. The movement soon gained grassroots momentum on its own, and Viva Kennedy Clubs were established across the Southwest, in California, throughout the Midwest, and as far east as Florida and Pennsylvania. García's involvement generated particular interest on the part of GI Forum members, whose publication served as the primary publicity vehicle. Once Viva Kennedy Clubs had been organized nationally, they developed a logo that depicted Senator Kennedy wearing a sombrero and riding a burro with the label "Viva."

The Viva Kennedy Clubs represented a significant development in Latino political history, marking the first time the community had organized an integrated political campaign, with a unified goal, across the country. The popularity of the clubs demonstrated the power of Latinos/as as an organized interest group seeking full integration into the body politic and society at large. The clubs also provided an early lesson in the struggle for civil rights, as Mexican Americans learned to work both inside and outside the political system to have their voices heard. The spirit of unity and empowerment helped spark the Chicano Movement of the late 1960s and the fight for rights and justice.

Although Viva Kennedy Clubs were located across the entire United States, the organization remained heavily influenced by local leaders and was largely run on the grassroots level. In Illinois and elsewhere, Puerto Ricans joined with Mexican Americans in organizing the clubs. Visits by prominent Latino politicians from other parts of the country, such as Texas state senator Henry B. Gonzalez and Alfredo Vidal, a Puerto Rican representative from New York, generated enthusiasm and promoted harmony. In other parts of the country, Viva Kennedy Clubs garnered support from Cubans and Central and South American Latinos/as, albeit in smaller numbers.

In such states as Texas and California, where the Latino population was especially large and established political networks made it easier to recruit members and coordinate operations, the Viva Kennedy Clubs focused their organizing efforts at a statewide level. In Texas, McCormick named Albert A. Peña, Jr., a San Antonio county commissioner and active Mexican American civil rights leader, as the state chairman. The Viva Kennedy Clubs proved especially popular in Texas and, relying on community fund-raisers, operated without help from Kennedy's national campaign. In California, where the Mexican American population was also large, McCormick appointed Congressman Edward R. Roybal, the most prominent Latino politician of the time, as the state cochair. In California, the Viva Kennedy Clubs overlapped with other influential Latino civil rights organizations, such as the Community Service Organization (CSO). The clubs proved highly successful in generating state support for the Kennedy candidacy, registering more than 100,000 voters. Southern California was especially fertile ground for recruiting Viva Kennedy members because of its sizable Latino population.

Following the 1960 campaign, the Latino community—and especially leaders of the Viva Kennedy movement—had high expectations for the Kennedy administration, hoping it would address issues important to them, such as civil rights, and appoint Latinos/as to positions of influence. They were generally disappointed, however, as major civil rights legislation was not forthcoming for several years and Latinos/as were offered relatively unimportant appointments, such as ambassadorships.

Nevertheless, the Viva Kennedy Clubs were so successful in organizing Latinos/as, that by 1961, the key organizers—including Roybal and McCormick—were intent on maintaining them as a political organization under a different name. Roybal and other Mexican Americans in California insisted that the national group take the name of the California organization—the Mexican American Political Association (MAPA)—because of its emphasis on Mexican American heritage and success in mobilizing support. No formal redesignation ever took place, but the MAPA continues to advocate for civil rights into the twenty-first century and share roots with the Viva Kennedy Club movement of 1960.

Despite their abbreviated existence, Viva Kennedy Clubs played a significant role in the election of 1960 and, more broadly, demonstrated the political potential of Mexican Americans, and Latinos/as in general, in the United States. For the first time in the nation's history, Latinos/as organized in large numbers to form a political movement and were instrumental in the outcome of a national election. Their unity demonstrated that the Latino community could be a major force in the political process.

Daniel Guzmán

See also: American GI Forum; Corona, Bert; Community Service Organization; García, Héctor P.; Mexican American Political Association; Peña, Albert A., Jr.; Politics; Roybal, Edward R.

Further Reading

Acuña, Rodolfo. *Occupied America: A History of Chicanos.* 6th ed. New York: Pearson Longman, 2007.

García, Ignacio M. *Viva Kennedy: Mexican Americans in Search of Camelot.* College Station: Texas A&M University Press, 2000.

West Side Story

West Side Story, a hit Broadway musical of 1957 and Academy Award–winning film of 1961, is set in New York City's Upper West Side and dramatizes the rivalry between two teenage gangs—one Puerto Rican and one white—and a love affair between members of their respective communities. The stage production, directed and choreographed by Jerome Robbins, with music by Leonard Bernstein and lyrics by Stephen Sondheim, ran for 734 performances on Broadway before going on tour and earning a Tony Award nomination for best musical (awarded instead to *The Music Man*). The film version, starring Natalie Wood and Richard Beymer, was one of the most popular musicals in Hollywood history and won a total of ten Academy Awards—including Best Picture; Best Director (Jerome Robbins and Robert Wise); Best Supporting Actor (George Chakiris), and Best Supporting Actress (Rita Moreno).

The story, a loosely based adaptation of William Shakespeare's tragedy *Romeo and Juliet,* focuses on the hostility between two rival gangs—the Jets, all-white second-generation Americans; and the Sharks, recent Puerto Rican immigrants. The dramatic tension revolves around the love relationship that develops between Maria, who is the younger sister of Bernardo, the leader of the Sharks, and Tony, who is a member of the Jets and best friend to Riff, the leader of the Jets.

Maria and Tony meet at a neighborhood dance. Although her family has already chosen a member of the Sharks, Chino, to be her husband, and in spite of the escalating enmity between the Sharks and Jets, Tony and Maria fall in love. Yet even as they profess their feelings for each other, Bernardo and Riff are setting plans for a rumble between the two gangs the following day. When Tony informs Maria of the impending showdown, she asks him to try to stop it;

he promises that he will. After a mock marriage ceremony that seals their lives together, Tony heads off to the rumble. He proves unable to reason with either side, however, and a knife fight breaks out in which Bernardo stabs and kills Riff. In an act of blind anger and revenge, Tony kills Bernardo.

Chino delivers the news to Maria. As she contemplates the death of her brother, Tony comes to her to explain how it happened. She forgives him, and the couple makes plans to escape together. Despite having been engaged to Bernardo, Maria's friend Anita agrees to help them escape. After being harassed by the Jets, Anita fails to reach Tony to tell him that Maria will meet him. In her anger and humiliation, she tells Tony's friends to tell him that Chino has killed Maria. This sets off the climactic chain of events: Tony begs Chino to kill him, too, but Tony soon discovers that Maria is in fact alive. As the two run toward each other, Chino appears from the shadows and shoots Tony. He dies in Maria's arms, at which point she delivers a heartrending speech to both gangs about hatred and racism and the damage they cause.

Aside from the central story of unrequited love and the theme of the dangers of racism, *West Side Story* includes a side narrative about the promise of the American Dream—the idea that all people of the United States can achieve their dreams through hard work and perseverance. The character of Anita, played by Puerto Rican actress Rita Moreno in the film version, serves as the voice of hope and faith in the American Dream. The sentiment is captured in the song "America": "I like to be in America! / O.K. by me in America! / Everything free in America / For a small fee in America."

Despite its critical acclaim, place in American popular culture, and groundbreaking representation of minority culture, *West Side Story* was criticized in some circles for certain prejudices. For one thing, it was pointed out, all of the main actors, including

American actor George Chakiris (center) plays Bernardo, the leader of the Sharks, a Puerto Rican street gang, in *West Side Story* (1961). The highly acclaimed film forged new ground for a musical with its portrayal of social conflict and minority culture. *(Authenticated News/Hulton Archive/ Getty Images)*

those who portrayed Puerto Rican characters, were white (with the exception of Moreno). A 2009 Broadway revival was noted for its efforts at cultural authenticity, including some song lyrics and portions of the dialogue in Spanish.

Lisa Guerrero

See also: Film; Gangs; Moreno, Rita; Popular Culture; Puerto Ricans.

Further Reading

Garebian, Keith. *The Making of West Side Story.* New York: Mosaic, 1998.
Shulman, Irving. *West Side Story.* New York: Pocket Books, 1990.

Women

By the early twenty-first century, Latinos/as had become the largest ethnic minority in the United States. At roughly 44 million in 2006, they constituted approximately 14.5 percent of the population, surpassing African Americans (39 million persons, or 12.9 percent). Of these 44 million Latinos/as, roughly 21 million were female.

Of all the major ethnic groups in the United States, the Latino population was the most gender-imbalanced. According to the 2000 U.S. Census, there were approximately 105.1 Latino males for every 100 females; for the population as a whole, there were roughly 96.1 males for every 100 females. (Unless otherwise indicated, all population and demographic statistics in this survey are from the 2000 U.S. Census.) This anomaly is not a new one in American history. Traditionally, ethnic groups that had a large immigrant component have been more heavily male, as men are more likely to immigrate in search of work. In addition, many Latino males in the United States come alone and leave their wives behind, working temporarily and sending some of their earnings to support their families back home.

As of 2000, despite the male bias in the Latino population, Latinas, like their counterparts in other U.S. ethnic groups, predominated among the middle-aged and seniors. In all age cohorts above 45, there were more Latino women than men; among cohorts over the age of 65, the ratio was 2–1 or higher. Even more pronounced than the female-to-male ratio was the relative youth of the Latino community compared to the American population as a whole. Whereas 25.6 percent of the entire U.S. population was under the age of 18, the figure for Latinos/as was 34.8. The percentage of Latinos/as over the age of 65 was 4.8, compared to 12.4 percent for the nation as a whole.

Given the large percentage of young Latinos/as, as well as the fact that there were so many more immigrants in that population, marriage rates tended to be lower among Latinos/as than in the population as a whole. While roughly 27.1 percent of the American population above the age of 15 had never been married, the figure for Latinos/as stood at 34.2 percent, or some 25 percent higher. But this figure varied among the different Latino immigrant groups. Among groups in which there was a higher percentage of recent immigrants, the percentage of those who had never married was also higher. Central Americans, for example, had the highest rate at 37.9; Cubans had the lowest, at 21.8. At the same time, Latinos/as were more likely to stay married than the rest of the population, a reflection, say some sociologists, of their more traditional values and Catholicism, which strongly discourages divorce. While some 18.5 percent of Americans over the age of 15 were separated, divorced, or widowed, the figure for Latinos/as was only 14.4 percent. This, too, varied significantly among different Latino groups, however, with Cubans having the highest rate at 22.9 percent and Mexicans the lowest at 12.1.

Latinos/as were also more likely to live in a household headed by a married couple than the American population as a whole, with the respective figures at 55.1 and 52.5 percent. Still, Latinos/as were significantly more likely to live in households headed by a female with no spouse present. While the figure for this kind of household was 11.8 percent among the population as a whole, it stood at 17.3 percent among Latinos/as, or nearly 50 percent higher. It was also more likely for Latinos/as to be living in households headed by a male with no spouse present. Some 4.1 percent of the population lived in such a household compared to 8.3 percent of Latinos/as. Again, this is due to the high number of single immigrants in the population, with many poorer Latinos/as sharing households with others of their sex and age. The only sector in which they lagged behind the U.S. population as a whole was that of nonfamily households. Whereas 31.5 percent of the American population as a whole lived in such households, the figure for Latinos/as was 19.3 percent, perhaps reflecting the fact that fewer Latino couples lived together without getting married.

Latino women were less likely to be working than their counterparts in the general population, a reflection perhaps of their higher marriage and lower divorce rates or the fact that many Latino women worked in the unofficial employment sector, where their numbers were less likely to be tabulated. While roughly 57.5 percent of all U.S. women over the age of 16 were officially in the labor force, the figure for Latino women was 53 percent; the figure for Latino men, 69.4 percent, was just 1.3 points below that for all American men. Labor force participation rates for Latino women depended somewhat on which subgroup they belonged to. For Cubans, generally wealthier and more often married than Latinos/as in general, the rate was 49.4 percent; among Central Americans, generally poorer and less often married, the figure was 57.9 percent.

Median earnings among Latino women lagged significantly behind those for Latino men and for U.S. women generally, though the gap between Latino women and men was smaller than that between men and women in the population as a whole. Overall, Latino women over the age of 16 in 1999 earned $21,634, compared to $25,400 for Latino men. In the U.S. population as a whole, the corresponding figures were $27,194 and $37,057. The smaller gap no doubt reflected the fact that both Latino men and women were more likely to work in unskilled positions, in which the gaps between traditionally male occupations and female occupations were smaller.

As in the case of labor force participation, median income earnings varied among Latino groups. The highest-paid Latino women were Cubans, at $26,254, perhaps reflecting the fact that Cubans generally tended to be better educated than Latinos/as as a whole. While more than 21 percent of Cubans over the age of 25 had a college degree, the figure for Latinos/as generally was just over 10 percent. At the other end of the spectrum, the lowest-paid Latino women were Central Americans, with a median annual income of just $18,588. Again, this was directly correlated with levels of educational achievement. At just 9.5 percent, Central Americans had the lowest rate of college graduates of any Latino subgroup, other than Mexicans. Oddly, Latino women were more likely to be represented in the ranks of management and the professions than Latino men. While just 14.6 percent of the latter worked as managers or professionals, some 22.9 percent of Latino women did so. The figures for the American population as a whole were 31.4 percent for men and 36.2 percent for women. But the Latino bias was counterbalanced by the higher percentage of Latino women in low-paying service occupations. While more than one-fourth of Latino women worked in that sector, less than 20 percent of Latino men did.

As indicated by these figures, the demographic profile of Latino women is mixed. While fewer Latino women were married than American women generally, fewer were separated or divorced. And while better represented in the professions than Latino men, Latinas were also more numerous in the lower-paying service sector. Finally, even though the gap in earnings between Latino men and women is smaller than that for the American population as a whole, both lag significantly behind the earnings of Americans generally.

James Ciment

See also: Family and Community.

Further Reading

U.S. Census Bureau. *We the People: Hispanics in the United States: Census 2000 Special Reports.* Washington, DC: U.S. Census Bureau, 2001.

Wrestling, Professional

Despite its critics, professional wrestling has been a financially viable form of popular entertainment in the United States for over a century. Although most people know that the outcome of matches is predetermined, professional wrestling cannot be entirely characterized as "fake," since many of the moves are potentially dangerous, especially if executed incorrectly. Some credit Vince McMahon Jr., owner of the biggest surviving national organization, World Wrestling Entertainment (WWE), with coining the phrase "sports entertainment" to describe wrestling, while others have referred to it as "performance art" or "simulated sport." Regardless, professional wrestling, and most notably WWE, continues to draw fans to both live events and pay-per-view telecasts. Over the past fifty years, Latino wrestlers have carved out a significant niche in the sport. While stereotypical and often racist representations have been justly criticized, the contributions of Latino wrestlers, both as individuals and collectively, have made a significant impact on the business.

Latinos in the Ring: A Brief History

In the 1950s and early 1960s, Miguel Perez was among the first Puerto Rican stars of WWE (known, until 2002, as the World Wrestling Federation, or WWF). In the early 1970s, Pedro Morales of Culebra Island, Puerto Rico, won the WWF championship as well as the Intercontinental title and the World Tag Team crown. Other Puerto Rican wres-

tlers, such as Carlos Colon and "The Unpredictable One" Johnny Rodz, were also regular performers in the WWF. In the western United States, particularly in California, Texas, and New Mexico, wrestlers from Mexico also earned names for themselves. Among the most notable were Pepper Gomez, Gory Guerrero, and the masked Mil Mascaras.

Many of the Latino names from the 1960s through the early 1980s were cheered as "faces" (good guys) even though nationwide surveys indicated that, in general, many Americans viewed Latinos negatively. Some authors credit this to the fact that socioeconomic status is a key factor in wrestling story lines, and working-class underdogs—many of whom were played by Latinos—often had the allegiance of fans. Not surprisingly, wrestling fans identified with the traditional working-class ideals as portrayed by the likes of Gomez, Morales, and Tito Santana, even as their origins were caricatured through the use of props and costumes—like the sombreros embroidered in Santana's tights. Characters like Santana, an Intercontinental champion in the early to mid-1980s, and later the WWE champion Eddie Guerrero attracted both Latino and white fans by calling attention to their Latino identities in scripted interviews, speaking partly in Spanish but refusing to escalate the racial conflicts instigated by "heel" (bad guy) characters. By the late 1980s, however, the WWF had become a world dominated by white wrestlers, such as Hulk Hogan, Greg Valentine, Paul Orndorff, and Randy "Macho Man" Savage, and the few remaining Latino wrestlers were largely confined to "jobber" status (losing one-sided matches to make other wrestlers look invincible).

In the mid-1990s, demographic shifts in the United States that significantly raised the national profile of Latinos/as and Latino culture were similarly reflected in professional wrestling. Although former Extreme Championship Wrestling (ECW) promoter Paul Heyman is credited for bringing wrestlers like Guerrero, Rey Mysterio, Jr., and Psicosis into the national spotlight in 1995, other promoters had long since used *luchadors* (wrestlers) in regional promotions. In general, the Lucha Libre athletes were significantly smaller than their counterparts in traditional U.S. wrestling. These cruiserweights relied less on pure feats of strength than on speed and agility, performing high-flying moves that larger wrestlers were not doing at the time and that few audience members had ever seen before.

Arguably, the moves that Lucha-style wrestlers brought to mainstream American wrestling promotions significantly changed the landscape of the sport. Today, for example, wrestlers of all races and ethnicities commonly use such daring moves as *huracarranas* (one opponent is caught in a headlock between the legs of the other wrestler then rapidly flipped away) and *pescados* (a flying crossbody dive) off the top rope of the ring. Some wrestling purists have been critical of the style, whether because of its emphasis on gymnastics-oriented, stylistic movements, or the greater potential danger of "high spots."

The son of a prominent Mexican wrestler in the early days of Lucha Libre, Eddie Guerrero became a star on the mainstream American circuit. He brought the Latino wrestling tradition into the twenty-first century with some old stereotypes and a new level of prestige. *(Peter Kramer/Getty Images)*

In addition to their characteristic style, Lucha Libre wrestlers in Mexico and the United States are noted for wearing face masks, which in Mexico is viewed as a symbol of pride. Of the masked performers who succeeded in the United States, Mil Mascaras and El Santo, and more recently the diminutive Ray Mysterio, Jr., stand out.

Eddie Guerrero, the Latin World Order, and Stereotypes

In the late 1990s, Latino wrestlers were brought into the WWF and the now defunct World Championship Wrestling (WCW) in greater numbers as the two organizations were engaged in a ratings battle, but they were mainly relegated to midcard status. In 1998, Eddie Guerrero spearheaded the formation of a group called the Latino World Order (LWO), a takeoff of the Hulk Hogan–led New World Order, the top faction in the WCW. Some observers regard this as a defining moment for Latinos in American professional wrestling because it was a story line, with a basis in reality that allowed Latinos to focus on a political and racialized agenda of empowerment. The LWO included several well-known Latino performers, including Mysterio, Jr., Psicosis, Juventud Guerrera, and Hector Garza, among others. In both their on-air promotions and behind-the-scenes talk, LWO members accused the people in charge of WCW, especially those booking the matches, of preventing Latino wrestlers from moving up the ladder to main event status. Some have suggested that the LWO angle ultimately failed because fans were unsure whether to treat the group as whining "heels" or as "faces," fighting against unfair treatment. Ultimately, the LWO's political agenda was undermined by the portrayal of members in an assortment of negative ways, from power-hungry individuals out only for themselves to depraved hedonists willing to accept bribes in exchange for giving up ties with the LWO.

Subsequently, Guerrero adopted the stereotypical "Latino Heat" gimmick in WWE, while Konnan, Guerrera, and Mysterio, Jr., were the key members of a group called the "Filthy Animals," portrayed as out-of-control, sexually hyped partiers. Although some Latino wrestlers claimed that they invented these racialized characters, others have contended that such characterizations are conceived by promoters and send negative messages to audiences, many of whom are young. Still others note that even stereotyped Latino characters allow diverse Latino groups to identify, in some measure, with the characters and to feel a sense of pride at being represented in popular culture.

The character of Eddie Guerrero provides a perfect example of the complex relationship between racial stereotypes and audience response. Guerrero had successfully played the heel numerous times in his career, including his successful pairing with a white tag-team partner, Art Barr, in 1994. Competing as Los Gringos Locos—wearing red, white, and blue attire, and taunting the audience with immigration-related gestures—the team elicited vigorous boos from predominantly Latino crowds in Los Angeles during their matches against well-loved Mexican stars El Hijo del Santo and Octagon.

In 2002, Guerrero, along with his real-life cousin, Chavo Guerrero, Jr., began appearing as the tag team Los Guerreros, whose stated motto was "We lie, we cheat, we steal." In a series of scripted vignettes, Los Guerreros were portrayed as getting the better of various white characters, whether hustling a man out of his money on the golf course, deceiving a "housewife" by posing as salesmen, or stealing from a baby. Although meant to be humorous, the vignettes did little to move Latino characters past blatantly stereotypical representations. That said, it became obvious in late 2003 that Latino audiences identified strongly, and positively, with Guerrero's character, as he was cheered fiercely at live shows, especially in areas with high concentrations of Latino Americans. This led the company to allow Guerrero to turn face again; in 2004 he became the second Latino champion of WWE by defeating Brock Lesnar before an audience at the Cow Palace in San Francisco that included several of Guerrero's family members.

Latino performers continue to be featured in relatively large numbers in WWE, especially in the SmackDown contests. Television ratings confirm that Latinos/as comprise one of the largest viewership segments of WWE television, and the SmackDown broadcasts are regularly rated among the top ten of all shows in U.S. Latino households. Story lines, however, continue to feature stereotyped racial images of Latinos/as. The buildup to Guerrero's win over Lesnar, for example, included an in-ring skit in which Lesnar wore a sombrero and mock-directed a Mariachi band. A relatively recent stable of Latino performers known as The Mexicools regularly featured Psicosis, Guerrera, and Super Crazy driving to the ring on "Juan Deer" tractors and carrying lawn maintenance equipment. Chavo Guerrero, Jr., a former cruiserweight and tag-team champion in WCW and WWE, was assigned a new character called Kerwin White, who denounces his Mexican heritage and exclaims, "If it's white, it's right!" among other racially insensitive remarks. While television cameras regularly focus on explicitly racist homemade signs in the audience, some might interpret these banners as indications of fan support.

There are few full-time women wrestlers in the major U.S. professional wrestling promotions, but recent years have seen Latinas such as Nidia and Melina Perez step out of their roles as valets to the male wrestlers and step into the ring themselves.

Finally, WWE pay-per-view events regularly include the "Spanish announcers table," with commentators Carlos Cabrera and Hugo Savinovich. Cabrera and Savinovich are also featured on "WWE en Espanol," the Spanish-speaking section of the WWE Web site.

In November 2005, after Eddie Guerrero was found dead in a Minneapolis hotel room from what was later ruled heart failure, the WWE Web site was flooded with thousands of e-mail messages from fans worldwide. Special tributes were held in the ring, and WWE Publishing released *Cheating Death, Stealing Life: The Eddie Guerrero Story,* a biography of the late wrestler. The tag team of Bautista and Mysterio elicited passionate cheers for their late friend—"Eddie! Eddie! Eddie!"—which served as a reminder of the longtime role of Latinos in professional wrestling and how their place within the business continues to be contested.

Ted Butryn

See also: Identity and Labels; Popular Culture.

Further Reading

Beekman, Scott. *Ringside: A History of Professional Wrestling in America.* Westport, CT: Greenwood, 2006.

Pope, Kristian, and Ray Whebbe, Jr. *The Encyclopedia of Professional Wrestling: 100 Years of History, Headlines & Hitmakers.* Iola, WI: Krause, 2003.

Reynolds, R.D., and Bryan Alvarez. *The Death of WCW.* Toronto, Ontario, Canada: ECW, 2004.

Sammond, Nicholas. *Steel Chair to the Head: The Pleasure and Pain of Professional Wrestling.* Durham, NC: Duke University Press, 2005.

Yo Soy Joaquín

The Chicano epic poem *Yo Soy Joaquín* (I Am Joaquín) was written by the Mexican American activist Rodolfo "Corky" Gonzales, the son of a Denver beet farmer, in 1965. Beginning with the lines *"Yo Soy Joaquín, / perdido en un mundo de confusion, / enganchado en el remolino de una/ sociedad gringa"* ("I am Joaquín, / lost in a world of confusion, / caught up in the whirl of a / gringo society"), the poem would become the most famous literary expression of the Chicano civil rights movement (also known as *El Movimiento*), inspiring and mobilizing Chicano people across America for decades. The creation of *Yo Soy Joaquín* marked a momentous year for Chicanos/as. As Chicana feminist scholar Gloria Anzaldúa wrote in *Borderlands* (1986), "Chicanos did not know we were a people until 1965 when César Chávez and the farmworkers united and *I am Joaquín* was published and *La Raza Unida* party was formed in Texas."

Yo Soy Joaquín was initially distributed in pamphlet form. It was later reprinted in several Chicano press newspapers; recited at Chicano rallies and consciousness-raising gatherings; reproduced by students and farmworker organizers; and published in English as *I Am Joaquín* by the Crusade for Justice in 1967 and in bilingual form by Bantam in 1972 under the title *I Am Joaquín, Yo Soy Joaquín: An Epic Poem*. In 1969, Chicano filmmaker and El Teatro Campesino director Luis Valdez dramatized the poem in a short film titled *I Am Joaquín: An Epic Poem*. More than forty years after it first appeared, the full text of the poem is cited extensively on the Internet, taught in literature classes, and included in the work of Chicano cultural leaders and artists.

Corky Gonzales died in April 2005. A former professional boxer and businessman, he had been a leader of the Viva Kennedy Clubs of Colorado (working for the 1960 presidential campaign of Democratic candidate John F. Kennedy), founded the Denver-based Chicano civil rights organization the Crusade for Justice in 1966, organized the first Chicano youth conference in 1969 in Denver, and was a keynote speaker at the 1972 convention of La Raza Unida Party, an alternative to the Democratic and Republican parties in Texas. In 1969, he founded Denver's Escuela Tlatelolco, the first all-Chicano elementary and secondary school in America. With his personal charisma and cultural vision, the author of *Yo Soy Joaquín* sparked interest, action, and a revolutionary spirit. His poem, like his personality and his annual conferences, motivated Chicano people to the cause. As reflected by the following translation excerpt, *Yo Soy Joaquín* served as a rallying cry for Chicanos/as, both urban and rural:

> And now the trumpet sounds,
> The music of the people stirs the
> Revolution,
> Like a sleeping giant it slowly rears its head
>   to the sound of
> Tramping feet . . .
>
> And in all the fertile farm lands,
> the barren plains,
> the mountain villages,
> smoke smeared cities
> We start to MOVE.
> La Raza! Mejicano!
> Español!
> Latino!
> Hispano!
> Chicano!
> or whatever I call myself,
> I look the same
> I feel the same
> I cry
> and
> Sing the same

I am the masses of my people and I refuse
to be absorbed.

I am Joaquín
The odds are great but my spirit is strong . . .

Yo Soy Joaquín begins with a detailed chronology of ancient Mexican and Chicano history, making references to Aztec legends, myths, and spiritual beliefs. It tells the story of colonization, of the mixing of Spanish and Indian blood, of resistance leaders such as Pancho Villa and Emiliano Zapata. Parallels are drawn with the struggles of contemporary Chicanos/as against poverty, unemployment, cultural assimilation, and war. All Chicanos/as, the poem says, are Joaquín. And as Joaquín fights to survive, so Chicano culture has and will continue to survive.

"Writing *I Am Joaquín* was a journey back through history, a painful self-evaluation, a wandering search for my peoples and, most of all, for my own identity," Gonzales wrote in the introduction of the Bantam edition. "The totality of all social inequities and injustice had to come to the surface. All the while, the truth about our own flaws—the villains and the heroes had to ride together—in order to draw an honest, clear conclusion of who we were, who we are, and where we are going."

Widely read in Chicano studies and literature courses in the twenty-first century, the poem stands as an important representation of both Chicano culture and the Chicano Movement of the 1960s and 1970s.

Nova Gutierrez

See also: Chicano/a; Chicano Movement; Film; Gonzales, Rodolfo "Corky"; Valdez, Luis.

Further Reading

Anzaldúa, Gloria. *Borderlands/Las Fronteras: The New Mestiza.* 1987. San Francisco: Aunt Lute, 2007.

Gonzales, Rodolfo. *I Am Joaquín, Yo Soy Joaquín: An Epic Poem.* New York: Bantam, 1972.

———. *Message to Aztlan: Selected Writings of Rodolfo "Corky" Gonzales.* Ed. Antonio Esquibel. Houston, TX: Arte Público 2001.

Young Lords

A short-lived, radical, grassroots organization made up primarily of Puerto Rican youth, the Young Lords emerged in the late 1960s and early 1970s as the progressive voice of Puerto Rican activists throughout the United States. From their storefront offices in New York City's Spanish Harlem, Chicago, and other cities with substantial Latino populations, they served the people of the economically challenged barrio neighborhoods, running clothing drives, day-care centers, and free breakfast programs. They also became known for their community-based revolutionary tactics, such as occupations of vacant land, hospitals, churches, and other social institutions to demand that city governments operate programs for the Puerto Rican and Latino poor. By attracting media attention, they forced city governments to make policy changes that benefited inner-city Latinos/as.

Founding and Growth

The New York City Young Lords Organization (YLO, later the Young Lords Party) was founded in Spanish Harlem in 1969 by a group of mostly Puerto Rican students from State University of New York (SUNY) campuses, Queens College, and Columbia University. Some of these like-minded, Latino student activists—including Miguel "Mickey" Melendez, Juan González, Felipe Luciano, David Perez, and Pablo "Yoruba" Guzman—formed the central committee. The group was inspired by the radical African American civil rights organization the Black Panther Party (BPP), national liberation struggles around the world, and the Cuban Revolution of 1959, which led to the implementation of social and economic programs for the Cuban people. The forerunner of the New York group was the Young Lords in Chicago, a former street gang founded in the 1950s that had gained national attention when it took over a local church in order to provide community-oriented programs for the poor.

After the founding of the New York chapter, Latino students and youth organized branches in Philadelphia, Boston, Milwaukee, San Diego, and

Los Angeles. Young Lords in these cities set up a variety of community projects, including free-breakfast programs for children, free health clinics, free clothing drives, and cultural events such as Puerto Rican history classes. Members lobbied for prison solidarity among convicted Puerto Ricans and for the rights of Vietnam War veterans. In New York, they proved that high numbers of barrio children living in public housing suffered from lead poisoning caused by paint and that a substantial number were infected with tuberculosis. In Chicago, Hilda Ignatin, Judy Cordero, and Angela Adorno led a subgroup in the Young Lords called Mothers and Others, organized around the broader women's rights movement of the 1960s. One of their goals was to educate both male Young Lords members and the community at large about how Latino women were underserved in their communities.

In October 1969, the Young Lords Party developed a 13-point program and platform that served as a guideline for community activism (revised in mid-1970). Points 1–4 proclaimed the group's desire for self-determination and an end to racism. Point 5 demanded community control over local institutions, such as hospitals, schools, and law enforcement. Point 6 called for all Puerto Ricans to learn Spanish and become familiar with their collective history. Points 7, 8, 9, 11, 12, and 13 demanded a socialist, nonviolent state. Point 10 highlighted the need for gender equity and an end to homophobia. The platform that accompanied the 13-point program emphasized the group's nationalistic approach. Much in the style of the Black Panthers, members of the Young Lords adopted a military dress code consisting of army field jackets, combat boots, and purple berets adorned with a YLO button.

Radicalism

The activities of the Young Lords Party that received the most attention involved the occupation of space in which Puerto Ricans had been subject to discrimination and abuse. One prominent example was the 1969 Garbage Offensive, which brought attention to the fact that Puerto Rican neighborhoods in upper Manhattan were being denied sanitation ser-

vices readily granted to middle- and upper-class white neighborhoods in the Bronx, Queens, and Brooklyn. After several weeks without garbage collection, trash had begun to accumulate on the sidewalks of East Harlem, leading the Young Lords to aid community members in sweeping the garbage onto the corners of neighborhood streets. After the New York City Sanitation Department continually failed to pick up the trash, the Young Lords pushed it into the middle of the streets and set it on fire, blocking major uptown thoroughfares. The incident received widespread media coverage and gained the attention of Mayor John Lindsay, whose administration added routes to the Department of Sanitation so that it regularly picked up garbage in East Harlem.

The physical health of the community was especially important to the Lords, and many of the group's actions were organized around securing better-quality health care services for Puerto Ricans in the United States. In East Harlem, the Young Lords organized a collective of party members, supporters, and doctors to go door-to-door and test barrio residents for tuberculosis and lead poisoning. When the city health department refused to station a testing vehicle in the community, the Lords seized a truck and tested hundreds of Harlem residents before the police attempted to recover it. As a result, the city began stationing tuberculosis-testing trucks in poor communities throughout New York City.

The 1970 seizure of Lincoln Hospital in East Harlem, carried out with the help of local Black Panthers, is perhaps the action for which the Lords are best remembered. The Lords and Panthers, along with hundreds of hospital workers and community members, set up a patient-employee complaint table at Lincoln Hospital and others in the area. When the hospital administration refused to address the hundreds of recorded complaints, the Lords occupied the building in the middle of the night. A coalition of community members, Young Lords, and Black Panthers set up a drug and alcohol detoxification center in the hospital auditorium, which became permanent after the occupation. The program set the standard for alternative methods of drug treatment, as the clinic utilized acupuncture instead of methadone in treating alcoholics and heroin addicts. Although the

Members of the Young Lords, a Puerto Rican community activist group, pose with a mobile chest X-ray unit they seized in New York's Spanish Harlem in 1970. The group was known for street-revolution tactics on behalf of the Latino urban poor. *(Meyer Liebowitz/Hulton Archive/Getty Images)*

center was discontinued by Mayor Ed Koch later in the 1970s, it succeeded in putting control of the community's health into the hands of the people.

Underlying the activities of the Young Lords was a philosophy that poverty and racism could not be eliminated unless monopoly capitalism was overthrown, bringing the economic extremes of wealth and poverty to an end. Group leaders argued that the ruling classes could not be brought down solely through nonviolent direct action, a tactic popularized by organizers of the civil rights movement in the early 1960s. Thus, the Young Lords did not limit their actions to what the law allowed and took increasingly violent measures in order to bring justice to their communities. These sometimes included the armed occupations of public places, such as East Harlem's First Spanish Methodist Church in 1970—dubbed the Second People's Church Offensive—during which Young Lords aimed to force city officials to negotiate prison reforms.

Demise and Legacy

Despite their achievements for the Latino community, the Young Lords were fractured by ideological differences and infiltration by the Federal Bureau of Investigation's (FBI's) covert antidissident program, COINTELPRO, which surveilled, harassed, and divided group members. The Lords disbanded around 1972, leaving a legacy of self-determination and political autonomy for Puerto Ricans. While their revolutionary program included armed struggle, the Young Lords' most effective and far-reaching efforts were their community-service programs. Former members continued to the fight for Puerto Rican rights—in 1977, for example, Melendez and others occupied the Statue of Liberty for eighteen hours, demanding the release of several Puerto Ricans imprisoned since the mid-1950s for attacks on Blair House and Congress. During the early part of the twenty-first century, other former members have demonstrated with Puerto Rican protesters who opposed the use of the island of Vieques as a target in U.S. military exercises. Others continue to speak out for Puerto Rican independence.

Jessica Hulst

See also: Nationalism; New York; Puerto Rican Revolutionary Workers Organization; Puerto Ricans; Vieques, Puerto Rico.

Further Reading

Flood, Richard. "Towards a Theory of Revolutionizing Street Nations." *Socialism and Democracy* 17:1 (March 31, 2003): 245.

Melendez, Michael. *We Took the Streets: Fighting for Latino Rights with the Young Lords.* New York: St. Martin's, 2003.

Young Lords Party and Michael Abramson. *Palante: Young Lords Party.* New York: McGraw-Hill, 1971.

Zapatistas

Just after midnight on January 1, 1994, the Zapatista Army of National Liberation (*Ejército Zapatista de Liberación Nacional,* or EZLN) entered seven towns in the poor southern state of Chiapas, Mexico, including San Cristóbal de las Casas, the region's principal market city. Here, leaders of the revolutionary guerrilla group—mostly Mayan Indians armed with a few AK-47 assault rifles, a number of smaller rifles, and several fake wooden guns—offered their Declaration of the Lacandon Jungle from the balcony of the government palace. A declaration of war, the statement put the Mexican government on notice that the nation's large population of indigenous peoples was unwilling to let the abuse and exploitation of their land and labor continue without an armed response. By calling themselves "Zapatistas," the EZLN claimed a historical and political connection to Emiliano Zapata, the legendary leader of the Mexican Revolution of 1910 against the dictatorship of Porfirio Díaz. In 1994, the Zapatistas of Chiapas declared that they were reviving the legacy of resistance to tyranny and injustice in the name of the peasants and indigenous populations of Mexico, as well as undertaking the contemporary global struggle against the forces of neoliberal capitalism and globalization. While the Zapatista rebellion of the 1990s has yet to achieve all of its revolutionary goals, it is widely considered an important catalyst to the growing influence of various political and social movements by minority communities in Latin America and elsewhere. The Zapatista example not only demonstrated that an underrepresented and oppressed group can organize an effective action against a dominating and hostile national government, but also showed how it could be done.

Revolution and Globalization

By claiming their rights as citizens of Mexico and as indigenous peoples who have suffered more than 500 years of racist and ethnocentric exploitation and violence, the Zapatistas proclaimed their awareness of the history of land expropriation and labor exploitation that has defined the experience of Indians in Mexico and throughout the Americas. The media-savvy EZLN immediately began using the Internet, cell phones, and other global outlets to disseminate their perception of the link between the legacies of European colonialism and its enslavement and abuse of indigenous peoples and the modern inequities of the globalization of local economies, agriculture, and labor. To further draw attention to their cause, the Zapatista declaration coincided with the formal implementation of the North American Free Trade Agreement (NAFTA) on January 1, 1994. The Zapatistas timed their armed uprising and media blitz both to derail NAFTA and to call attention to the plight of communities and regions "left out" of the economic and social benefits of the new world economy.

The two-pronged strategy of the initial uprising involved an armed insurgency that began in San Cristóbal de las Casas and included capturing the town hall there, an attack on a nearby military base, and the taking of seven towns. After the Zapatista army retreated back to its own bases in the surrounding jungle, the Mexican army put down the uprising with 15,000 troops that poured into Chiapas and, with helicopter gunships, attacked native villages, killing 150 people. With its violent response, the Mexican government soon found itself locked in a losing battle of words and a public relations nightmare in which the international community watched every move and countermove by the two parties. Furthermore, a key strategic and ethical component of the EZLN response since the initial armed uprising of January 1994 has been a consistent policy of nonviolent political and civil action, which has further highlighted the repressive tactics of Mexico's national government. In 1994, the speed with which news of the Zapatista struggle circulated and support for the uprising mobilized was largely the result of the EZLN's use of new technologies, such as the Internet and fax machines, to inform the public—both in Mexico and throughout the world—of the uprising and the government's response.

Technology and New Social Movements

A second strategy of the EZLN, equally influential and highly publicized, is the "communiqués" issued by the public face of the Zapatistas, a man known as Subcomandante Marcos. In the months and years following the uprising, Marcos became an internationally known figure, renowned for his witty and erudite messages to major media in Mexico, especially *La Jornada,* a leading daily newspaper, and electronic distribution channels worldwide. By taking advantage of one of the key features of modern globalization—information technologies that allow instant transnational communication—the Zapatistas rewrote the script for minority class and ethnic social movements. Marcos's communiqués were playful and ironic, using a variety of rhetorical strategies both to chide the Mexican nation and to attract the sympathy and solidarity of citizens who saw the justice of the Zapatistas' demands. This strategy demonstrated the great potential of global media to support the mobilization of groups who would seem to be greatly overpowered by national governments, international economic institutions like the International Monetary Fund, multinational corporate interests, and the apathy and ignorance of a world that had no idea Chiapas even existed.

The model of the Zapatista uprising thus suggested the possibility of successful minority movements around the world, including in the United States. For Latinos/as, the playful language and ironic tactics of Subcomandante Marcos resonated with the cultural politics of Latino theater groups and performance artists, such as Guillermo Gómez-Peña and Carmelita Tropicana. The intersection of cultural and ethnic identity with economic and state policy concerns also recalled the revolutionary efforts of César Chávez to organize migrant farmworkers in the United States during the 1970s and 1980s, as well as the Chicano Movement of the 1960s and 1970s. Beyond that, the Zapatistas have contributed to the growing importance of transnational indigenous social movements, such as those that led to the election in 2005 of the first indigenous president of Bolivia, Evo Morales. All of these connections reflect the importance of the Zapatista uprising and its political organization to a wide range of constituencies, including ethnic and minority communities seeking political, economic, and social equality in the United States. In following the separatist struggle of the Zapatistas, and supporting them through various nongovernmental organizations (NGOs) and other funding organizations, Latinos/as and Latino organizations in the United States believe that much can be learned from the Zapatista experience about political organizing on the local, national, and transnational levels.

Thus, the history of the Zapatistas is still unfolding. As the Mexican government was forced to engage with the EZLN on its demands, various congresses and official meetings with government representatives were organized in 1995 and 1996. Attending these meetings in their trademark face masks—an ironic commentary on their anonymity, a symbol of their solidarity as a group, and as protection from reprisals—the Zapatistas often left unsatisfied and frustrated by the official legalisms and refusals of their key demands for land and autonomy. Since the late 1990s, the indigenous peoples of Chiapas have developed autonomous zones called *caracoles*, where government officials and all traces of federal authority have been removed. These efforts at self-rule include their own political systems and institutions, educational systems, and direct engagement with various international NGOs that provide aid and support. The government in 1990 attempted to take back one of the autonomous zones in San Andrés, where police seized control of the town hall, but thousands of unarmed Zapatistas took it back in the days that followed.

Since December 1994, the Zapatistas have formed several autonomous municipalities, independent of the Mexican government, that have evolved into local government "juntas." By 2003, such *Juntas de Buen Gobierno* (Councils of Good Government) across the Chiapas region were largely responsible for organizing and implementing communitarian food-producing programs, health care, and school systems.

In the run-up to the Mexican presidential elections of 2006, the Zapatistas emerged from a period of silence and seclusion in Chiapas to announce a cross-country tour called *La Otra Campana* (The Other Campaign), covering thirty-one Mexican states, aimed at solidifying a left political coalition. The summer of 2006, however, was marked by a period of violence and protest, particularly in the community of Texcoco near Mexico City, associated with the EZLN. After a close and widely disputed vote count, conservative party candidate Felipe Calderón was declared the winner of the presidential balloting. Protests continued in Mexico City during August and September in support of Andrés Manual López Obrador, a left coalition candidate popular with Mexico's poorer communities. Calderón was confirmed as the winner by an electoral court and sworn into office on December 1, but the period of social and political unrest illustrated the continued influence of the Zapatistas and their model of social action—while leaving in doubt its pragmatic legacy in the politics and national policies of Mexico.

Katherine Sugg

See also: North American Free Trade Agreement.

Further Reading

Hayden, Tom, ed. *The Zapatista Reader.* New York: Thunder's Mouth, 2002.

Ross, John. *The War Against Oblivion: Zapatista Chronicles 1994–2000.* Monroe, ME: Common Courage, 2000.

Subcomandante Marcos. *Shadows of Tender Fury: The Letters and Communiqués of Subcomandante Marcos and the Zapatista Army of National Liberation.* Trans. Frank Bardacke, Leslie Lopez, and the Watsonville, California, Human Rights Committee. New York: Monthly Review, 1995.

Vodovnik, Žiga, ed. *Ya Basta! Ten Years of the Zapatista Uprising: Writings of Subcomandante Insurgente Marcos.* Foreword by Noam Chomsky and Naomi Klein. Oakland, CA: AK, 2004.

Zoot Suit Riots

A series of racial conflicts that took place in Los Angeles during World War II, the so-called Zoot Suit Riots pitted white U.S. Navy personnel against primarily Mexican American youth, known for their attire. The zoot suit, popular among Mexican American, African American, and Filipino youth during the 1930s and 1940s, diverged from mainstream style and signified a challenge to the calls for assimilation on the part of these communities. Characterized by a long coat with wide lapels and wide, padded shoulders (called the *carlango*), and wide-legged, tight-cuffed, or "pegged," trousers (called *tramas*), the zoot suit was regarded as more than a flashy fashion statement in the Latino community; it embodied the anti-American sentiment and outlaw spirit of Latino youth. The riots of 1943, in which U.S. Navy personnel attacked gangs of zoot-suiters, brought these feelings to a head.

Amid America's war efforts in Germany and Japan, Mexican Americans in Los Angeles faced all-too-familiar circumstances. Confined to poor neighborhoods that often lacked street lighting, police protection, or basic services, and prevented from attending integrated movie theaters, restaurants, or swimming pools, Mexican American youth had limited opportunity for social or economic advancement. Under these conditions, they began to organize neighborhood clubs, donning zoot suits as a way to differentiate themselves and express a defiant lifestyle known as *pachuco*, a unique Mexican American subculture defined by their distinctive clothes and street dialect, called *Caló*.

Following the bombing of Pearl Harbor in December 1941 and the systematic effort to intern Japanese Americans on the U.S. mainland, media and political figures also began targeting Mexican American youth, particularly the pachucos, as dangerous and criminal. To the Anglo mainstream, the zoot suit became a symbol of the noncompliant character of Mexican youth. Worse, it was perceived as a symbol of a lack of patriotism and respect for the United States, prompting random violence from both the police and military.

Los Angeles police arrested hundreds of Mexican American youths in June 1943 after a series of brawls instigated by U.S. Marines and sailors. The incident came to be called the Zoot Suit Riots, after the clothes worn by many of the Latinos. Only nine servicemen were taken into custody. *(Library of Congress)*

Outbreak

On May 31, 1943, a fight broke out between a group of U.S. sailors on leave and a group of Mexican Americans in East Los Angeles; one sailor was badly injured in the scuffle. The next evening, some 200 U.S. Navy personnel hired taxicabs to take them from the U.S. Naval Armory in Chávez Ravine to East Los Angeles. During the course of the evening, they cruised the streets by taxi, stopping to beat up Mexican youth, primarily those wearing zoot suits, and then proceeding on in search of additional victims. Upon returning to the armory, a petty officer who had led the rampage effort told law enforcement officers, "We're out to do what the police have failed to do. We're going to clean up this situation."

Over the next two nights, the sailors were joined by marines and other servicemen in the continuing mob action. Zoot-suiters were attacked on the streets and inside buildings. A group of musicians was assaulted leaving the Aztec Recording Company on Third and Main streets, as were black motorists and

street workers. A black defense worker had his eyes gouged out with a knife. The marauders stopped short of entering the city's "Negro district," aware that a violent defense had been organized, and returned to Mexican neighborhoods.

Without intervention by the police or military authorities, the rioting escalated and spread throughout East Los Angeles during the first week of June. Egged on by hysteria in the press, the worst of the rioting violence occurred on June 7, as soldiers, sailors, and marines from as far away as San Diego traveled to Los Angeles to seek out pachucos. Taxi drivers offered free rides to servicemen and civilians on their way to the riot areas. At the end of the night, approximately 5,000 civilians and military men gathered downtown.

In the final night of rioting, masses of civilians carried out the attacks against Mexican Americans. Thousands of Anglos ventured downtown after local newspapers publicized the times and locations at which Mexican American youth would be gathering. Many leaders of color, particularly those representing the African American and Mexican American communities, felt that the *Los Angeles Times,* the city's largest newspaper, represented the interests of the white elite and blamed the zoot-suiters for instigating the riots. The events of June 8, 1943, were described as follows:

> Thousands of servicemen joined by thousands of civilians last night surged along Main Street and Broadway hunting zoot-suiters. Chief of Police Horrall declared riot alarm at 10:30 P.M. and ordered every policeman on duty. More than fifty zoot-suiters had clothing torn off by servicemen, and civilians converged on bars, restaurants, penny arcades and stores in downtown areas searching for zoot-suiters. Streetcars were halted and theaters along Main Street were scrutinized for hiding zoot-suiters. . . . Police were handicapped by the tremendous crowds of civilians who apparently had listened to the police riot calls on the radio and had rushed into downtown.

Blocked by the crowds or not, the Los Angeles police did little to protect Mexicans from being attacked. Indeed, according to many in the streets, the police stood by and watched groups of sailors beat Mexican American youth. A number of zoot-suiters were arrested, however, including some found lying on the pavement with injuries.

Aftermath

By June 9, the violence had, for the most part, ceased. Prompted by mobilization of community groups and pressure from the federal government, senior military officials declared Los Angeles off-limits to all sailors, soldiers, and marines, insisting that the Shore Patrol arrest any disorderly personnel. Conversely, the Los Angeles City Council passed a resolution banning the wearing of zoot suits in public, punishable by a fifty-day jail term. Minority groups from throughout Los Angeles joined together to demand reform and justice.

The response to the Zoot Suit Riots underscored the increasing level of coalition-building and activism in greater Los Angeles. Black civil rights leaders took immediate action. The National Association for the Advancement of Colored People (NAACP) sought help from the federal government, sending telegrams to President Franklin Roosevelt and Governor Earl Warren urging them to launch an investigation of the incident. "Mayor Bowron and Chief of Police Horrall were asked for additional police protection," wrote the president of the Los Angeles branch of the NAACP. "It is my opinion that had the police functioned properly and taken the matter seriously, the situation would have not gone to the extent it did." The Urban League, fearing that unchecked racial violence put the black community in danger as well, also stepped up its coalitional efforts in the wake of the riots. Its leadership roundtable, a forum for municipal black leaders to discuss pressing issues, was expanded to include representatives from minority communities throughout Los Angeles.

In the annals of wartime America, the Zoot Suit Riots of 1943 provided another example of the racially hostile climate. Like Japanese internment and racial segregation, these actions targeted a particular group of people because of their racial/ethnic identify, because of their refusal to assimilate, and because of the willingness of the media and politicians to scapegoat people of color in a time of fear. At the same time, however, the riots were an impetus to political organizing on the part of an increasingly active Mexican American community, as well as the formation of activist coalitions among various minority communities.

David J. Leonard

See also: Carnalismo; Cholos; Gangs; Los Angeles; Mexican-American Movement; Pachuco; Sleepy Lagoon Case.

Further Reading

Leonard, Kevin Allen. "'Brothers under the Skin'?: African Americans, Mexican Americans, and World War II in California." In *The Way We Really Were: The Golden State and the Second Great War,* ed. Roger W. Lotchin. Urbana: University of Illinois Press, 2000.

Mazón, Mauricio. *The Zoot Suit Riots: The Psychology of Symbolic Annihilation.* Austin: University of Texas Press, 1984.

Pagan, Eduardo Obrego. *Murder at the Sleepy Lagoon: Zoot Suits, Race, and Riot in Wartime L.A.* Chapel Hill: University of North Carolina Press, 2003

Valdez, Luis. *Zoot Suit and Other Plays.* New York: Arte Público, 1992.

Chronology

1492 Italian explorer Christopher Columbus, sailing for King Ferdinand and Queen Isabella of Spain, lands on the present-day island of San Salvador in the Bahamas.

Spanish lexicographer Antonio de Nebrija publishes the first grammar of the Spanish language.

1493 Christopher Columbus, on his second voyage, finds Puerto Rico and the Virgin Islands. He establishes La Isabela, the first formal European establishment in the New World, on Hispaniola, the present-day island divided into Haiti and the Dominican Republic.

1498 Christopher Columbus embarks on his third voyage and explores the mainland of South America. Bartolomé de las Casas, who kept records of the explorer's travels, accompanies him. De las Casas later becomes a Dominican priest and settles in the state of Chiapas, Mexico.

1508 Spanish explorer Juan Ponce de León lands in Puerto Rico, where he establishes friendly relations with a native chieftain, Agueibana.

1509 Ponce de León is appointed governor of Puerto Rico. Spanish colonials enslave the indigenous Taínos to work in local mines.

1510 Spanish conqueror Diego Velázquez de Cuéllar conquers Cuba, establishing the cities of Santiago and Havana and directing explorations of the Gulf of Mexico.

1511 Velázquez becomes governor of Cuba, and the island's indigenous population is subjected to the *encomienda* system—soon to take over all of Spain's colonies—in which the Spaniards are given land and native slaves to work their plantations.

1512 The Laws of Burgos, the first European legal code for the colonies, are ratified in Burgos, Spain.

1513 Ponce de León encounters Florida, where he explores both the coastal regions and the interior.

1518 Spanish explorer Hernán Cortés sets sail from Cuba to explore Mexico's mainland.

1519 Spanish explorer and cartographer Alonso Álvarez de Pineda is the first European to see the Mississippi River. He charts the Gulf Coast region and disproves the theory of a sea passage to Asia.

Aztec king Moctezuma receives Hernán Cortés.

1520 On July 1, *Noche Triste* (Sad Night), the Spaniards are forced out of Veracruz by Cuitlahuac; Aztec king Moctezuma is killed.

1521 Hernán Cortés conquers Tenochtitlán, present-day Mexico City.

1524 King Charles of Spain establishes the Council of the Indies to oversee the development of Spain's colonies in the New World.

1539 Hernando de Soto sets sail from Havana, Cuba, for Florida and begins exploring the present-day southeastern United States.

1541 Francisco Vásquez de Coronado, leader of the first Spanish expedition to New Mexico, departs Spain to reach Quivira, the legendary Cities of Gold, in present-day Kansas.

1542 Portuguese sailor Juan Rodríguez de Cabrillo discovers the harbor at present-day San Diego, California.

Spanish explorer Alvar Nuñez Cabeza de Vaca publishes *La Relación,* which chronicles his shipwreck off the coast of Florida in 1536 and his subsequent journey to Mexico. He also documents the native peoples and flora and fauna he encounters.

1564 Spanish missionaries introduce grapes to California.

1565   Spanish admiral Pedro Menéndez de Avilés establishes the mission of St. Augustine, Florida, the oldest permanent settlement in the United States.

1570   One of the earliest Spanish missions is built in Virginia, thirty-seven years before the English established their colony at Jamestown.

1598   Portuguese sailor Juan de Oñate colonizes New Mexico and introduces livestock breeding—marking the beginning of the vaquero (cowboy) culture.

1610   Santa Fe, New Mexico, is founded as the capital city of the Spanish province of *Nuevo Mexico.* It is the oldest capital city in the United States.

1680   Under leader Popé, the Pueblo tribes of New Mexico revolt against the *encomienda* system established by the Spanish crown, killing twenty-one Franciscans and 380 Spanish colonists.

       The first royal *mercedes* (land grants) are awarded to Spaniards in northern Mexico, just south of the present U.S.-Mexico border.

1687   Italian Jesuit missionary Eusebio Kino establishes his first mission among the rural Indians of Sonora at Nuestra Senora de los Dolores in present-day Arizona. He goes on to found more than twenty missions, including the still-functioning Mission San Xavier del Bac in 1699. Across North America, these Catholic missions have dual roles: converting the indigenous populations and assisting the monarchy in maintaining order and rule over the native peoples.

1690   San Francisco de los Tejas, the first Spanish mission, is founded in Texas.

1691   Texas is made a separate Spanish province, with Don Domingo de Terán as its governor.

1693   The Spanish crown orders its colonizers to abandon Texas for fear of Indian uprisings.

1700   The Spanish settle Arizona.

1716   The possibility of French encroachment prompts the Spaniards to reoccupy Texas by establishing a series of missions. Of the missions, San Antonio, founded in 1718, is the most important and most prosperous.

1717   English and French slave trading companies bring African slaves into New Spain.

1738   The first free black community is established at Fort Mose in Spanish Florida.

1760   Large-scale cattle ranching in Texas begins with a grant by Captain Blas Maria de la Garza Falcón.

1767   King Charles III of Spain expels the Jesuits from the Spanish empire, allowing the Franciscans to become the primary missionaries in America.

1769   Catalan Franciscan missionary Junípero Serra establishes the first of a series of Spanish missions on the Pacific Coast, San Diego de Alcalá, in present-day San Diego.

1776   Explorer Juan Bautista de Anza, born in New Spain, establishes the presidio of San Francisco, Spain's northernmost outpost.

       The American colonies declare their independence from Great Britain, and the Revolutionary War begins. The war will end in 1783 with the signing of the Treaty of Paris; the national government of the United States will begin operating under the Constitution in 1789.

1803   The Louisiana Purchase is ratified, doubling the landmass of the United States.

1804   President Thomas Jefferson funds the two-year expedition of Lewis and Clark to explore the Louisiana Territory and the western frontier. Spain worries that the exploration foreshadows Anglo settlement of the West.

1810   Father Miguel Hidalgo y Costilla rings the bell of freedom, *El Grito de Dolores* (The Cry of Dolores), to usher in the Mexican War for Independence. The war lasts until 1821, when the Spanish crown recognizes the country's independence, ending 300 years of Spanish rule. Mexico acquires settlements in what is present-day California, southern Arizona, southern Texas, southern Colorado, and most of New Mexico.

       Soon after Mexico's independence, Anglo-American settlers begin to move into the Mexican territories of the present-day U.S. Southwest, including Texas.

1819   The Adams-Onís Treaty between the United States and Spain grants the former the present-day state of Florida and land surrounding the Gulf of Mexico.

1822   Joseph Marion Hernandez, a delegate from the Florida territory, becomes the first Latino in Congress.

1823   Erasmo Seguín, a Texas delegate to the U.S. Congress, helps pass a colonization act designed to attract Anglo settlers to Texas. Between 1824 and 1830, thousands of Anglo families enter East Texas, acquiring hundreds of thousands of acres of free and cheap land.

The Monroe Doctrine declares that European nations must not interfere in the activities of the Americas. The United States will reciprocate by not interfering in the affairs of Europe.

1824   Chumash Indians revolt against Franciscan missions in the Santa Barbara, California, area.

1829   The new republic of Mexico abolishes slavery.

1834   After 350 years, the Holy Office of the Inquisition, active in Spain and the Americas, is officially closed.

1836   Texas revolutionary forces led by Sam Houston battle the Mexican army, led by General Antonio López de Santa Anna, at the Battle of the Alamo.

Texas becomes an independent republic.

1845   The United States annexes the independent republic of Texas.

1846   The Mexican-American War begins, prompted by the U.S. annexation of Texas the previous year and a border dispute between the Mexican and American governments.

1848   The Treaty of Guadalupe Hidalgo ends the Mexican-American War. Signed by the United States and Mexico, the treaty calls for Mexico to cede 55 percent of its prewar territory not including Texas (which included all or parts of Arizona, California, Colorado, Nevada, New Mexico, Utah, and Wyoming) in exchange for $15 million and the assured safety of the property rights of Mexican citizens.

The California gold rush begins, bringing Anglo-Americans, Latinos/as, Native Americans, African Americans, and Chinese to the region.

1851   Los Angeles's first newspaper, the *Los Angeles Star* (*La Estrella de Los Angeles*), begins as a bilingual publication.

1853   President Franklin Pierce buys the Gadsden Purchase, the area from the Gila River region of Yuma, Arizona, to the Mesilla Valley of New Mexico, from Mexico. The United States plans to build a transcontinental railroad through the area.

A $5,000 reward is posted for the capture of Joaquín Murrieta, a folk hero known as the Mexican American Robin Hood. He is allegedly killed by California State Rangers.

1855   In the new American state of California, so-called greaser laws are passed to eliminate the customs of Mexican Americans (derogatorily called "greasers").

Editor Francisco Ramirez founds *El Clamor Público* (*The Public Outcry*), the first Spanish-language newspaper in Los Angeles.

1859   The first cigar factories are built in Florida, Louisiana, and New York. Many working-class Cubans come to the United States to work in the industry.

1861   The American Civil War begins when Confederate forces attack the U.S. military installation Fort Sumter in South Carolina. An estimated 10,000 Mexican Americans, plus thousands of other Latinos, fight on the two sides. U.S. Navy officer David Glasgow Farragut, the son of a Spanish-born ferry captain from Tennessee, is widely recognized as the war's most outstanding Latino serviceman.

1862   The Homestead Act is signed into law, allowing squatters to settle vacant land (often owned by Mexicans fighting legal battles for their ranches) upon the condition of improving it.

1864   Seaman John Ortega and U.S. Army corporal Joseph H. De Castro are the first Latinos to receive the Congressional Medal of Honor, for service in the American Civil War.

1865   The Medal of Honor is awarded to a third Latino, seaman Philip Bazar.

1868   Cubans depart for the United States en masse during the Ten Years' War, the island's first major attempt to gain independence from Spain.

1871   Esteban Bellán is the first Latino to play on a major league baseball team in the United States, the Troy (New York) Haymakers.

1872   María Amparo Ruiz de Burton publishes *Who Would Have Thought It,* the first known English-language book by a Mexican American author. Ruiz de Burton was one of the *Californios,* Mexicans who became U.S. citizens after California was ceded to the United States in the 1848 Treaty of Guadalupe Hidalgo.

1884 Helen Hunt Jackson publishes *Ramona,* a novel about a half–Native American orphan raised in Spanish *Californio* society. The book brings attention to the discrimination faced by indigenous and mestizo peoples in California.

1892 The first U.S. immigration station opens on Ellis Island, located at the mouth of the Hudson River in New York Harbor. By 1954, when the station will close, it will have processed more than 12 million immigrants.

1894 Alianza Hispano Americana, a fraternal benefit society (*sociedad mutalista*) is established in Tucson, Arizona, to provide social benefits such as insurance to Mexican Americans. It spread across the Southwest and became the biggest of these societies.

1895 Cuban independence forces, inspired by poet and activist José Martí, wage war against Spain.

Martí dies in battle and becomes an instant martyr. His oeuvre becomes a symbol for resistance and affirmation among Cubans and throughout Latin America.

1896 Puerto Ricans living in mainland United States form the Revolutionary Junta for Puerto Rican independence.

1898 On February 15, the U.S. battleship USS *Maine* explodes in the harbor of Havana, Cuba, killing 266 men on board and injuring many others. The event prompts the United States to declare war on Spain.

The Treaty of Paris, signed on December 10, ends the Spanish-American War. The treaty establishes the independence of Cuba, cedes Puerto Rico and Guam to the United States, and allows the United States to purchase the Philippines from Spain for $20 million.

1899 The United Fruit Company is founded when the Boston Fruit Company merges with other companies selling bananas in Central America, Colombia, and the Caribbean. The company's activity allows the United States to have an economic and political foothold in much of Latin America.

U.S. military rule in Cuba and Puerto Rico begins.

1900 The Foraker Act establishes a civilian government in Puerto Rico under U.S. dominance. The law allows for islanders to elect their own House of Representatives, but it does not allow the island to vote in the U.S. Congress.

1901 The Platt Amendment is passed, defining the terms of U.S.-Cuban relations. The United States withdraws its occupation troops; the act stipulates that Cuba may not sign treaties that threaten U.S. interests and grants the United States the authority to construct a naval base at Guantánamo Bay.

Mexican American outlaw Gregorio Cortez is captured in Texas.

Luis Muñoz Rivera founds the bilingual newspaper *Puerto Rican Herald* in New York City.

1902 The U.S. Reclamation Act is passed, funding irrigation projects for the arid lands of the American West and dispossessing many Latinos/as of their land through the exercise of eminent domain.

Cuba declares independence from the United States.

1903 The United States and the Republic of Panama sign the Hay-Bunau Varilla Treaty, granting the United States exclusive and permanent possession of the Panama Canal Zone. The canal, which will be completed in 1914, will connect the Pacific and Atlantic oceans and will facilitate the shipment of U.S. goods from coast to coast.

The University of Puerto Rico—today, the oldest and largest institution of higher learning on the island—is founded in Rio Piedras.

Japanese and Mexican beet workers go on strike in Oxnard, California, unified as the Japanese Mexican Labor Association (JMLA). The joint effort is heralded as a strong move toward interethnic labor cooperation.

1904 President Theodore Roosevelt's Corollary to the Monroe Doctrine declared the United States's right to intervene to stabilize the economies of small nations in the Caribbean and Central America if those nations are unable to pay their foreign debts.

1906 The U.S. Congress passes the Basic Naturalization Act, which establishes the Immigration and Naturalization Service and provides more uniform administrative procedures for processing naturalization applications. The law requires that aliens seeking naturalization speak the English language, among other requirements.

1907 United States and Mexico cosponsor the Central American Peace Conference in Washington, D.C., with delegates from Costa Rica, El Salvador, Guatemala, Honduras, and Nicaragua, in an effort to reduce the level of conflict between countries in the region.

1910 The Mexican Revolution begins in an effort to end the thirty-two-year dictatorship of Porfirio Díaz. Rebel leaders include Pancho Villa and Emiliano Zapata. The revolution causes hundreds of thousands of Mexicans to emigrate to the United States, particularly to the Southwest.

1911 The Mexican Protective Association, one of the earliest Mexican American labor organizations, which consists of tenant farmers, day laborers, and *braceros,* is founded in Texas. While of great consequence locally, the association does not have much regional or national effect.

1912 Racism against Latinos/as in the Southwest territories leads to lynchings in California and Texas. The Mexican ambassador formally protests.

1914 The Panama Canal opens to traffic.

1916 President Woodrow Wilson sends troops to the Dominican Republic amid general political instability in that country.

1917 President Woodrow Wilson signs the Jones-Shafroth Act, under which Puerto Rico becomes a commonwealth of the United States and all Puerto Ricans are granted U.S. citizenship. The measure also separates the executive, judicial, and legislative branches of Puerto Rican government; creates a locally elected bicameral legislature; provides civil rights to residents; and establishes English as the official language of Puerto Rico.

Congress passes the Immigration Act of 1917, which imposes a literacy requirement on all immigrants. The act is aimed at curbing the influx of individuals from southern and eastern Europe, but it ultimately reduces immigration from Mexico.

President Wilson signs the Selective Service Act, a military draft that encompasses Puerto Rico. Noncitizen Mexicans are required to register with their local draft boards, even though they are not eligible to serve.

During World War I, Mexican farmworkers, railroad laborers, and miners are allowed to enter the United States as temporary workers.

1921 The Order of the Sons of America (Orden Hijos de America), one of the first statewide Mexican American civil rights organizations in Texas, is founded in San Antonio to fight for equal citizenship rights.

1924 The U.S. Border Patrol is established to police the U.S.-Mexican frontier.

1926 *La Opinión,* the longest-running Spanish-language daily newspaper, is launched in Los Angeles, California.

Non-Latinos (primarily Irish, Italian, and Jewish immigrants) attack Puerto Ricans living in Harlem, New York. Competition for scare resources and jobs leads to what *The New York Times* described as "riots."

1929 The League of United Latin American Citizens (LULAC), a U.S. Latino political association, is founded in Corpus Christi, Texas.

Repatriation of Mexicans and Mexican Americans begins. Roughly 400,000 people, a large percentage of whom are legal U.S. citizens, are deported or "voluntarily repatriated" to Mexico. Repatriation will continue through 1937.

1930 Rafael L. Trujillo becomes dictator of the Dominican Republic (until 1961), and citizens begin to flee the island.

1931 The Lemon Grove (California) School Board tries to segregate Mexican students from whites by building a separate school. *Roberto Alvarez v. the Board of Trustees of the Lemon Grove School District* goes before the Superior Court of San Diego, which decides that Mexican children may not be discriminated against.

1933 President Franklin D. Roosevelt introduces the Good Neighbor Policy, by which he takes a stand to not intervene in the internal affairs of Latin American countries. During Roosevelt's administration, the U.S. government emphasizes cooperation and trade rather than military force to maintain stability in the Western Hemisphere.

The Roosevelt administration reverses the policy of English as the official language in Puerto Rico.

Mexican cotton workers in the Central Valley of California go on strike, supported by several groups of independent Mexican union organizers.

Cuban dictator Gerardo Machado is overthrown. Subsequently, General Fulgencio Batista revolts to overthrow newly installed President Carlos Manuel de Céspedes and becomes dictator of the Cuban provisional government.

1934 The Puerto Rican Communist Party is formed.

President Franklin D. Roosevelt annuls the Platt Amendment on U.S.-Cuban relations.

1935 President Franklin D. Roosevelt establishes the Puerto Rico Reconstruction Administration, charged with agricultural development, public works development, and electrification of Puerto Rico.

1936 The United States and Panama negotiate the Hull-Alfaro Treaty, in which the former relinquishes its rights to intervene and acquire land in the area.

Dionisio "Dennis" Chávez (D-NM) becomes the first Latino elected to the U.S. Senate.

1937 Anastasio Somoza García, formerly of the U.S. Marine–trained National Guard in Nicaragua, assumes the presidency of that country. His government is supported by the United States; he will rule as a dictator until his assassination in 1955.

1938 In San Antonio, Texas, young Mexican and Mexican American pecan shellers, mostly women, strike for better wages and working conditions.

Mexican president Lázaro Cárdenas expropriates U.S. and British oil companies, nationalizing the petroleum industry.

The Popular Democratic Party of Puerto Rico (Partido Popular Democrático, PPD) is formed under the leadership of future governor Luis Muñoz Marín. While it began as a nationalist party, under Muñoz Marín's leadership it adopted a pro-commonwealth (and generally antistatehood) position.

1939 In Los Angeles, labor and civil rights leaders Luisa Moreno and Bert Corona, among others, organize El Congreso de Pueblos de Habla Española (the Spanish-speaking Peoples Congress), America's first national Latino civil rights assembly.

1940 Bolstered by a coalition of political parties, including the Cuban Communist Party, General Fulgencio Batista is elected president in the first presidential election under the new Cuban constitution. In 1952, Batista will stage a military coup to take over the government.

President Franklin D. Roosevelt establishes the Office of Inter-American Affairs to improve U.S.–Latin American commercial and cultural relations.

1941 The United States enters World War II after the December 7 attack on Pearl Harbor. Latinos respond enthusiastically to the war effort, joining the U.S. Army, U.S. Navy, and U.S. Marine Corps as active combatants and serving on the home front in the defense industry. Approximately 375,000 Latinos will serve in the U.S. armed forces by the end of World War II in 1945.

1942 The Bracero Agreement is signed between the United States and Mexico, under which thousands of Mexican workers (*braceros*) enter the United States as guest workers to fill wartime labor shortages in agriculture and public works.

The Sleepy Lagoon murder takes place in southeast Los Angeles. Twenty-two Mexicans are convicted in a criminal trial; their conviction is overturned in 1944.

1943 The Zoot Suit Riots erupt in Los Angeles between World War II servicemen stationed in the city and Mexican American youth. The riots are named for the signature zoot suits worn by Mexican American teens and young adults.

1946 Civil rights lawyer and journalist Gilberto Concepción de Gracia forms the Puerto Rican Independence Party (Partido Independista Puertorriqueño, PIP) to end what he regards as U.S. colonialism.

President Harry S. Truman appoints Jesús T. Piñero as the first native Puerto Rican governor of Puerto Rico.

The U.S. Army School of the Americas, an institute for the training of Central and South American civilian, military, and police personnel in tactics of torture and warfare, is founded in Panama.

1947 The Community Service Organization is founded by Fred Ross and Edward Roybal in Los Angeles, to encourage voter registration and provide grassroots political support for Mexican Americans. Its most famous trainee is labor leader César Chávez.

Twenty airlines provide service between San Juan and Miami and between San Juan and New York, forging the first large migration by air in U.S. history.

In *Mendez v. Westminster School District,* a federal case that challenges racial segregation in Orange County, California, public schools, a circuit court of appeals rules that the segregation of Mexican and Mexican American students into separate Mexican schools is unconstitutional.

1948 Operation Bootstrap, a U.S. federal program designed to recruit Puerto Ricans to address labor shortages in the United States and promote the island's industrialization, begins.

President Harry S. Truman signs Executive Order 9981, establishing the President's Committee on Equality of Treatment and Opportunity in the Armed Services and ending segregation of U.S. armed forces.

In response to a Three Rivers, Texas, funeral home's refusal to bury a Mexican American soldier killed during World War II, Hector P. García forms the American GI Forum, a civil rights organization that provides health care and other benefits for Mexican American veterans.

1949 Luis Muñoz Marín takes office as the first elected governor of Puerto Rico. His tenure will end in 1965.

1950 The U.S. Congress upgrades Puerto Rico's political status from protectorate to commonwealth.

1951 Puerto Rican actor José Ferrer becomes the first Latino to win an Academy Award for his portrayal of Cyrano de Bergerac in the film of the same name.

The first episode of the television show *I Love Lucy,* starring Lucille Ball and Cuban-born bandleader Desi Arnaz, airs on CBS. It will run for 181 episodes and win four Emmy Awards.

1952 Congress passes the Immigration and Nationality Act of 1952 (also known as the McCarran-Walter Act). The act ends all racial restrictions on naturalization but maintains the quota system from 1924 and increases the government's power to exclude or deport immigrants suspected of communist sympathies.

1953 Mexican-born actor Anthony Quinn becomes the first Mexican American to win an Academy Award, for his performance as the brother of Mexican revolutionary Emiliano Zapata in *Viva Zapata!*

1954 The U.S. immigration station at Ellis Island closes.

Operation Wetback, a U.S. government program conducted with the cooperation of the Mexican government to deport undocumented workers, targets hundreds of thousands of Mexicans in Arizona, California, and Texas.

In *Hernandez v. State of Texas,* the U.S. Supreme Court determines that Latinos/as are entitled to equal protection under law by the Fourteenth Amendment to the Constitution, prompting Latinos/as to launch wide-ranging legal efforts to end all forms of discrimination. *Hernandez v. State of Texas* is the first U.S. Supreme Court case to be argued by Mexican American attorneys.

Brown v. Board of Education of Topeka, a landmark U.S. Supreme Court decision, outlaws racial segregation of schools, ending the "separate but equal" doctrine.

Four Puerto Rican nationalists—Lolita Lebron, Rafael Cancel Miranda, Irving Flores Rodríguez, and Andres Figueroa Cordero—enter the U.S. House of Representatives during an immigration debate. In the name of Puerto Rican independence, they shoot and wound five representatives.

1955 Raoúl Cortez launches KCOR-TV and KCOR-AM, the first Spanish-language television and radio stations, in San Antonio, Texas.

1957 Congress establishes the Civil Rights Commission to investigate whether citizens are being denied their right to vote based on nationality or ethnicity.

1959 In Cuba, Fidel Castro, Ernesto "Che" Guevara, and other guerrilla fighters lead a successful uprising against the dictatorial regime of Fulgencio Batista, who flees the island on New Year's Eve 1958. Within a few years, Castro will establish a Communist model of government, after which Cuban emigration to the United States will increase drastically.

Puerto Rican Juan Mari Brás founds the Pro-Independence Movement, grouping together supporters of Puerto Rican independence with socialist leanings. In 1971, the movement will become the Puerto Rican Socialist Party.

Eduardo Quevedo, Bert Corona, Francisca Flores, and others organize the Mexican American Political Association (MAPA) in Fresno, California, to support Chicano voting, political engagement, and civil rights actions.

1960 The U.S. government passes the Cuban Refugee Readjustment Act to assist islanders arriving in the United States as political refugees from Castro's Cuba.

1960s Beginning in the early 1960s, young Mexican Americans throughout the United States become involved in the larger civil rights movement and, through the burgeoning Chicano Movement (*El Movimiento*), seek to affirm a new sense of ethnic identity, cultural pride, and political empowerment.

1961 Teacher and activist Antonia Pantoja establishes ASPIRA (Aspire) to assist Puerto Rican children in advancing to higher education.

Dominican dictator Rafael Trujillo is assassinated.

In an attempt to overthrow the communist Cuban government, U.S. military officials and Cuban exiles join forces to invade the island in the Bay of Pigs invasion. The unsuccessful mission heightens tension between the United States, Cuba, and the island's advocate, the Soviet Union.

1962 César Chávez, Dolores Huerta, and other labor activists form the United Farm Workers Association in Delano, California, dedicated to organizing farmworkers in California's Central Valley.

The United States institutes an economic embargo against Cuba, prohibiting all trade with the island. *El bloqueo,* as it is called in Spanish, remains the longest trade embargo in modern history.

In a succession of events in mid-October referred to as the Cuban Missile Crisis, the United States blocks a Soviet plan to establish missile bases in Cuba. Soviet Premier Nikita Khrushchev finally agrees to withdraw the missiles if the United States declares publicly that it will not invade Cuba.

1963 Joan Baez, a folk singer and civil rights activist whose father was a Mexican immigrant, performs at the March on Washington in Washington, D.C.

John Rechy, a writer of Mexican-Scots descent, publishes *City of Night,* the first gay novel by a Latino.

1964 President Lyndon B. Johnson signs the Civil Rights Act, which prohibits racial discrimination in public places, provides for the integration of schools and other public facilities, and makes employment discrimination illegal.

The Economic Opportunity Act (EOA) is the centerpiece of President Johnson's War on Poverty. Programs for the poor include the Job Corps, the Community Action Program (CAP), and the Volunteers in Service to America (VISTA).

The Bracero Program, which began in 1942, officially ends. In succeeding decades, many out-of-work laborers are employed in low-wage jobs in factories, or *maquiladoras,* along the U.S.-Mexican border.

1965 To draw attention to the plight of migrant agricultural workers, Luis Valdez—later dubbed the "father of Chicano theater" and a leading film director—forms the civil rights–minded Teatro Campesino in Delano, California, to inform and entertain migrant farmworkers.

President Lyndon B. Johnson inaugurates "freedom flights" for Cuban refugees to fly to Miami. Some 300,000 Cubans take advantage of the program before Fidel Castro discontinues it in 1973.

Immigration and Nationality Act Amendments (also known as the Hart-Celler Act) end all quotas based on national origin and replace them with a system of preferences based on family relations to U.S. residents and labor qualifications. The amendments also establish a ceiling on Western Hemisphere immigration—120,000 per year—for the first time in U.S. history.

Former boxer and community organizer Rodolfo "Corky" Gonzales founds Crusade for Justice, a civil rights organization that aims to organize Chicanos in the Denver, Colorado, area.

César Chávez, Dolores Huerta, and others found the National Farm Workers Association, an event often cited as the beginning of the Chicano Movement. Over the course of the next decade, the Chicano Movement will push for better wages among migrant workers, a larger political representation in city and state leadership positions, and improved education.

1966 Grassroots organizer Reies López Tijerina and fellow Federal Land Grant Alliance members seize part of the Carson National Forest, in a protest to restore New Mexican land grants to the descendants of their Spanish colonial and Mexican owners.

Following the city's first downtown Puerto Rican Parade, allegations of police brutality and racial profiling trigger the Division Street Riots in Chicago.

1967 Piri Thomás, a New York writer and poet of Puerto Rican–Cuban descent, publishes his acclaimed memoir, *Down These Mean Streets.*

1968 The Brown Berets, Los Angeles students and community organizers from Young Citizens for Community Action, organize a series of East Los Angeles school walkouts—the so-called Chicano Blowouts—in which 10,000 students walk out of five area high schools to protest discrimination.

America's first Chicano studies program is established at California State University, Los Angeles.

The Mexican American Legal Defense and Education Fund (MALDEF), the most prominent Mexican American civil rights organization, is founded in San Antonio, Texas.

1969 El Plan Espiritual de Aztlán, a manifesto of Chicano activism and independence, emerges from the Chicano Youth Liberation Conference in Denver.

1970 The Chicano Moratorium in East Los Angeles protests the Vietnam War and the disproportionately high number of Chicano casualties in that war; 30,000 people march. A tear gas canister kills journalist Rubén Salazar.

According to the U.S. census, more than 80 percent of the "Hispanic" population of the United States lives in nine states, with the largest populations in California, New York, and Texas.

La Raza Unida Party, dedicated to improving the economic, social, and political life of the Latino community throughout Texas, wins city elections in Carrizo Springs, Cotulla, and Crystal City.

1971 Ramona Acosta Bañuelos becomes the first Latina treasurer of the United States.

Mexican American author and poet Tomás Rivera, later the chancellor of the University of California, Riverside, publishes his best known work, the novella *. . . y no se lo tragó la tierra* (*. . . the earth did not swallow him*).

1972 New Mexican novelist Rudolfo Anaya publishes his most famous work, *Bless Me, Ultima.*

The Labor Council of Latin American Advancement is founded to promote the interests of Latinos/as in U.S. organized labor.

1973 Puerto Rican baseball star Roberto Clemente becomes the first Latino elected to the Hall of Fame. Clemente had died in an airplane crash while on a relief mission to earthquake-ravaged Nicaragua on New Year's Eve 1972.

Pedro Pietri, Miguel Algarín, and Miguel Piñero found the Nuyorican Poets Café.

1974 In the case of *Lau v. Nichols,* the U.S. Supreme Court rules that school districts with children with little knowledge of English must establish bilingual services.

Fuerzas Armadas de Liberación Nacional (FALN), a Puerto Rican nationalist organization, begins its militant actions against the U.S. government. Between 1974 and 1983, it is responsible for 120 bombings.

Dramatist Miguel Piñero stages his most famous work, *Short Eyes,* in New York City. The play is nominated for six Tony Awards.

1975 Amendments to the Voting Rights Act of 1965 make permanent the national ban on literacy tests. Bilingual ballots are required in certain areas.

1976 An amendment to the Immigration and Nationality Act of 1965 sets a limit of 20,000 immigrants per country in the Western Hemisphere.

1977 U.S. President Jimmy Carter and Panamanian dictator Omar Torrijos sign the Panama Canal Treaty to turn the strategic waterway over to Panama by the end of the century. A peaceful transfer will occur on December 31, 1999.

1978 *Regents of the University of California v. Bakke,* a landmark U.S. Supreme Court decision on affirmative action, outlaws the use of quotas in university admissions but affirms the constitutionality of affirmative action programs for minorities.

1979 Civil war erupts in El Salvador. By the following year, civil war will break out in Nicaragua and Guatemala as well, forcing large numbers of Central American refugees to flee to the United States.

1980 The Mariel Boatlift, the mass migration of Cuban refugees from the port city of Mariel, brings more than 125,000 poor and working-class Cubans to southern Florida.

President Ronald Reagan maintains the U.S. cold war stance toward Latin America, believing that the Soviet Union will continue to support Marxist leaders across the Americas.

The Refugee Act establishes a permanent system and procedure for admitting refugees. Ceilings of 270,000 immigrants and 70,000 refugees were set for 1985.

1981   Cuban businessman Jorge Más Canosa creates the politically active Cuban American National Foundation to promote the transition from communism to democracy on the island.

Henry Cisneros is elected mayor of San Antonio, Texas, becoming the first Latino to hold this position in a major U.S. city.

1986   Congress passes the Immigration Reform and Control Act, creating a process through which undocumented immigrants can become legal immigrants by giving legal status to applicants who had been in the United States illegally since January 1, 1982. The law also makes it illegal for employers to knowingly hire undocumented workers.

1988   Lauro F. Cavazos becomes the first Latino to serve in the U.S. cabinet, as secretary of education.

1989   U.S. forces invade Panama in an attempt to overthrow military dictator Manuel Noriega, who had been indicted in the United States on drug trafficking charges and was accused of suppressing democracy in Panama.

1990   The Immigration Act increases the limits on legal immigration to the United States and institutes a lottery visa program.

Antonia C. Novello becomes the first woman and first Latina surgeon general of the United States.

Cuban American novelist Oscar Hijuelos becomes the first Latino to be awarded the Pulitzer Prize for Fiction, for his novel *The Mambo Kings Play Songs of Love* (1989).

1991   President George H.W. Bush signs the Cuban Democracy Act (also known as the Torricelli Bill), which bans trade with Cuba by foreign-based subsidiaries of U.S. companies and prohibits ships from docking in U.S. ports if they have visited Cuba.

1993   President Bill Clinton appoints Federico Peña as secretary of transportation, Henry Cisneros as secretary of housing and urban development, and Norma Cantú as assistant secretary for civil rights; all are the first Latinos/as to hold these positions.

Ellen Ochoa becomes the first Latina in space when she serves on the space shuttle *Discovery*.

In an effort to reduce the number of Mexican immigrants crossing the U.S. border illegally, the U.S. Border Patrol launches Operation Hold the Line in El Paso, Texas. With agents and technology concentrated in more remote areas, their efforts result in more apprehensions. The Border Patrol will later expand its immigration reduction efforts to San Diego, California.

The North American Free Trade Agreement (NAFTA), a comprehensive trade agreement between Canada, Mexico, and the United States, is signed into law by President Bill Clinton (the treaty had originally been agreed upon by George H.W. Bush of the United States, President Carlos Salinas de Gortari of Mexico, and Prime Minister Brian Mulroney of Canada). The treaty, which is to take effect on January 1, 1994, removes most barriers to trade and investment among the three countries, creating the world's largest free trade zone.

1994   California voters pass Proposition 187 in an effort to deny most publicly funded social services to undocumented immigrants and establish stricter penalties on individuals living in the state illegally. A federal judge later overturns the proposition.

1995   Latino groups organize a nationwide boycott of ABC-TV—with major turnouts in New York, Chicago, and Houston, Texas, and Los Angeles, San Francisco, and Fresno, California—to protest the network's failure to provide Latino-themed programming in its 1994 lineup.

1996   The Illegal Immigration Reform and Immigrant Responsibility Act increases border enforcement, raises restrictions on the admission of immigrants, and decreases the minimum offense required for deportation.

Californian voters pass Proposition 209, which amends the state constitution to prohibit using gender or racial preferences in public contracting, hiring, and education, effectively ending affirmative action programs in the state.

1998   California voters pass Proposition 227, a ballot initiative that abolishes most bilingual education in the state's public schools.

Bill Richardson is the first Latino to be appointed U.S. secretary of energy, by President Bill Clinton. Among other positions, Richardson will later serve as governor of New Mexico, and he will seek the Democratic nomination for president in 2008.

1999   President Bill Clinton grants clemency to twelve of the Puerto Rican Fuerzas Armadas de Liberación Nacional (FALN) political prisoners. Eleven are released and agree to renounce violence and sever ties with FALN; prisoner Oscar Lopez Rivera refuses to accept limited clemency.

The Clinton administration expands travel to Cuba for aid workers, relatives, athletes, scholars, journalists, and religious groups—but not to tourists.

Spanish-language Internet presence grows in 1999 and 2000. Spanish versions of AOL and Yahoo!, among other sites, are launched.

Protests reach a peak in the United States and Puerto Rico over the continuing use of the island of Vieques, a municipality of Puerto Rico and a territory of the United States, as a target bombing site by the U.S. Navy. Public opposition finally forced the U.S. Navy to depart the island in 2003.

Latino groups join the National Association for the Advancement of Colored People (NAACP) in protesting the lack of minority roles in prime-time television shows. Latino groups urge viewers to participate in a national brownout of ABC, CBS, Fox, and NBC during Hispanic Heritage Week in September. All four networks respond publicly to the protest and hire minority actors for add-on roles.

2000   U.S. Attorney General Janet Reno makes the controversial decision to send ten-year-old Cuban Elián González back to Cuba with his father. In 1999, the boy was rescued off the coast of Florida, after his mother and ten other people died trying to reach U.S. shores from Cuba.

California Governor Gray Davis declares March 31 César Chávez Day, a fully paid holiday for state employees.

As part of America's ongoing War on Drugs, President Bill Clinton initiates discussions with President Andres Pastrana of Colombia to increase U.S. aid to Colombia for counter-narcotics projects, sustainable economic development, and economic growth.

2001   Mexican-born Rosario Marin becomes the first foreign-born citizen to head the U.S. Department of the Treasury and the highest-ranking Latina in the George W. Bush administration.

2002   Speed skater Derek Parra becomes the first Mexican American to win a gold medal in the Winter Olympic Games, setting a world record in the 1,500-meter race. Speed skater Jennifer Rodriguez becomes the first Cuban American to compete in the Winter Olympic Games, winning two bronze medals.

2003   In *Gratz v. Bollinger*, a U.S. Supreme Court case regarding the University of Michigan's undergraduate affirmative action admissions policy, the justices rule that the school's points-based system is too mechanistic and therefore unconstitutional under the Equal Protection Clause of the Fourteenth Amendment.

Cuban-born playwright Nilo Cruz becomes the first Latino to win the Pulitzer Prize for Drama, for his play *Anna in the Tropics*.

The U.S. Census Bureau announces that Latinos/as constitute the nation's largest minority population.

2005   The U.S. House of Representatives passes the Border Protection, Antiterrorism, and Illegal Immigration Control Bill. Written to increase security of the U.S. border and provide more intense surveillance of immigrants entering the United States, the bill becomes the catalyst for U.S. immigrant rights protests across the country. The bill does not pass in the Senate.

2006   Large-scale protests over federal immigration policy sweep the country, uniting Latinos/as and immigration advocates.

The U.S.–Dominican Republic–Central America Free Trade Agreement (DR-CAFTA) is negotiated. The accord is designed to eliminate tariffs and trade barriers between the United States and Central America and to expand regional opportunities for workers, manufacturers, consumers, farmers, ranchers, and service providers of the countries.

President George W. Bush signs a series of laws to increase militarization and surveillance of U.S. borders. The Secure Fence Act of 2006 ensures funding for border security, including the construction of additional fencing and vehicle barriers along the U.S.-Mexican border.

2007   Univision, the most-watched Spanish-language television network, is sold for a reported $13.7 billion to a media and investment consortium. Later in the year, a show aired on the network became the first ever to exceed all English-language programs in viewer ratings that night.

2008   César Chávez Day is an observed holiday in eight states: Arizona, California, Colorado, Michigan, New Mexico, Texas, Utah, and Wisconsin.

Hispanic Heritage Month celebrates its fortieth anniversary.

In the presidential election, approximately two-thirds of Latino voters cast their ballots for Democratic nominee Barack Obama over Republican John McCain. About three-fourths of Latinos/as under the age of thirty support Obama, who becomes the first U.S. president of color.

2009   In May, President Barack Obama nominates Sonia Sotomayor, a federal appeals judge of Puerto Rican descent, to the U.S. Supreme Court. In August, the U.S. Senate confirms the nomination, making Sotomayor the first Latino to earn a place on the high court.

Erika Gisela Abad

Bibliography

Books

Abalos, David T. *The Latino Male: A Radical Redefinition.* Boulder, CO: Lynne Rienner, 2002.

Acosta-Belén, Edna, ed. *Adiós, Borinquen Querida: The Puerto Rican Diaspora, Its History, and Contributions.* Albany: State University of New York, 2000.

———. *The Puerto Rican Woman: Perspectives on Culture, History, and Society.* Westport, CT: Praeger, 1986.

Acuña, Rodolfo. *Anything but Mexican: Chicanos in Contemporary Los Angeles.* New York: Verso, 1996.

———. *A Community Under Siege: A Chronicle of Chicanos East of the Los Angeles River, 1945–1975.* Los Angeles: University of California at Los Angeles, 1984.

———. *Occupied America: A History of Chicanos.* New York: Pearson Longman, 2004; 2007.

———. *Sometimes There Is No Other Side: Chicanos and the Myth of Equality.* Notre Dame, IN: University of Notre Dame Press, 1998.

Aguayo, Sergio. *From the Shadows to Center Stage: Nongovernmental Organizations and Central American Refugee Assistance.* Washington, DC: Hemispheric Migration Project, 1991.

Aguirre, Adalberto, Jr., and Jonathan H. Turner. *American Ethnicity: The Dynamics and Consequences of Discrimination.* 4th ed. New York: McGraw-Hill, 2004.

Aguirre-Molina, Marilyn, Carlos W. Molina, and Ruth Enid Zambrana. *Health Issues in the Latino Community.* San Francisco: Jossey-Bass, 2001.

Ahern, Maureen, ed. *A Rosario Castellanos Reader: An Anthology of Her Poetry, Short Fiction, Essays, and Drama.* Austin: University of Texas Press, 1988.

Aitken, Thomas, Jr. *Poet in the Fortress: The Story of Luis Muñoz Marín.* New York: New American Library, 1964.

Alava, Silvio H. *Spanish Harlem's Musical Legacy, 1930–1980.* Charleston, SC: Arcadia, 2007.

Alba, Richard D., and Victor Nee. *Remaking the American Mainstream: Assimilation and Contemporary Immigration.* Cambridge, MA: Harvard University Press, 2003.

Albro, Ward S. *Always a Rebel: Ricardo Flores Magón and the Revolution.* Forth Worth: Texas Christian University Press, 1992.

Aldama, Arturo J., and Naomi H. Quiñonez, eds. *Decolonial Voices: Chicana and Chicano Cultural Studies in the 21st Century.* Bloomington: Indiana University Press, 2002.

Alexander, M., Jacqui Alexander, and Chandra Talpade Mohanty, eds. *Feminist Genealogies, Colonial Legacies, Democratic Futures.* New York: Routledge, 1997.

Algarín, Miguel, and Bob Holman, eds. *Aloud: Voices from the Nuyorican Poets Cafe.* New York: Henry Holt, 1994.

Algarín, Miguel, and Miguel Piñero, eds. *Nuyorican Poetry: An Anthology of Puerto Rican Words and Feelings.* New York: William Morrow, 1975.

Allsup, Carl. *The G.I. Forum: Origins and Evolution.* Austin, TX: Center for Mexican American Studies, 1982.

Almaguer, Tomás. *Racial Fault Lines: The Historical Origins of White Supremacy in California.* Berkeley: University of California Press, 1994.

Amnesty International. *USA: Appealing for Justice: Supreme Court Hears Arguments against the Detention of Yaser Esam Hamdi and José Padilla.* London: International Secretariat, 2004.

Anaya, Rudolfo, and Francisco Lomeli. *Aztlán: Essays on the Chicano Homeland.* Albuquerque: University of New Mexico Press, 1991.

Anton, Alex, and Roger Hernandez. *Cubans in America: A Vibrant History of a People in Exile.* New York: Kensington, 2003.

Antonio, Angel-Junguito. *A Cry of Innocence: In Defense of Colombians.* Plantation, FL: Distinctive, 1993.

Anzaldúa, Gloria. *Borderlands/La Frontera: The New Mestiza.* 1987. San Francisco: Aunt Lute, 2007.

Aparicio, Frances R., and Susana Chávez-Silverman, eds. *Tropicalizations: Transcultural Representations of Latinidad.* Lebanon, NH: University Press of New England, 1997.

Araton, Harvey. *Crashing the Borders: How Basketball Won the World and Lost Its Soul at Home.* New York: Free Press, 2005.

Archer, Christon, ed. *The Birth of Modern Mexico, 1780–1824.* Lanham, MD: Rowman & Littlefield, 2007.

Arguedas, José María. *Deep Rivers.* New York: Longitude, 2002.

———. *The Fox from Up Above and the Fox from Down Below.* Pittsburgh, PA: University of Pittsburgh Press, 2000.

———. *Yawar Fiesta.* New York: Longitude, 2002.

Arrarás, María Celeste. *Selena's Secret: The Revealing Story Behind Her Tragic Death.* New York: Fireside, 1997.

Arrendondo, Gabriela F., et al. *Chicana Feminisms: A Critical Reader.* Durham, NC: Duke University Press, 2003.

Arrizón, Alicia. *Latina Performance: Traversing the Stage.* Bloomington: Indiana University Press, 1999.

Babin, Maria Teresa, and Stan Steiner. *Borinquen: An Anthology of Puerto Rican Literature.* New York: Vintage Books, 1974.

Baeza, Abelardo. *Man of Aztlán: A Biography of Rudolfo Anaya.* Austin, TX: Eakin, 2001.

Baker, Colin. *Foundations of Bilingual Education and Bilingualism.* 4th ed. Clevedon, UK: Multilingual Matters, 2006.

Balderrama, Francisco, and Raymond Rodríguez. *A Decade of Betrayal: Mexican Repatriation in the 1930s.* Albuquerque: University of New Mexico Press, 2006.

Ball, Howard. *The Bakke Case: Race, Education, and Affirmative Action.* Lawrence: University Press of Kansas, 2000.

Bardach, Ann Louise. *Cuba Confidential: Love and Vengeance in Miami and Havana.* New York: Random House, 2002.

Barker, George C. *Pachuco: An American-Spanish Argot and Its Social Functions in Tucson, Arizona.* Tucson: University of Arizona Press, 1950, 1970.

Barnett, Alan W. *Community Murals: The People's Art.* Philadelphia: Art Alliance, 1984.

Barnett-Sanchez, Holly, and Eva Sperling Cockcroft, eds. *Signs from the Heart: California Chicano Murals.* Albuquerque: University of New Mexico Press, 1993.

Barrera, Mario. *Race and Class in the Southwest: A Theory of Racial Inequality.* South Bend, IN: University of Notre Dame Press, 1979.

Barreto, Amílcar. *Vieques, the Navy, and Puerto Rican Politics.* Gainesville: University Press of Florida, 2002.

Barrios, Luis, and David C. Brotherton. *The Almighty Latin King and Queen Nation: Street Politics and the Transformation of a New York City Gang.* New York: Columbia University Press, 2004.

Bart, Philip, ed. *Highlights of a Fighting History: 60 Years of the Communist Party, USA.* New York: International Publishers, 1979.

Bauer, K. Jack. *The Mexican War 1846–1848.* Lincoln: University of Nebraska Press, 1974.

Beck, Warren A. *New Mexico: A History of Four Centuries.* Norman: University of Oklahoma Press, 1962.

Beezley, William, and David Lorey, eds. *Viva Mexico! Viva la Independencia! Celebrations of September 16.* Lanham, MD: Rowman & Littlefield, 2000.

Bender, Steven W. *Greasers and Gringos: Latinos, Law, and the American Imagination.* New York: New York University Press, 2003.

Bennett, Herman L. *Africans in Colonial Mexico: Absolutism, Christianity, and Afro-Creole Consciousness, 1570–1640.* Bloomington: Indiana University Press, 2003.

Berg, Charles Ramírez. *Latino Images in Film: Stereotypes, Subversion, and Resistance.* Austin: University of Texas Press, 2002.

Beserra, Bernadete. *Brazilian Immigrants in the United States: Cultural Imperialism and Social Class.* New York: LFB Scholarly Publishing, 2003.

Bierhorst, John. *History and Mythology of the Aztecs: The Codex Chimalpopoca.* Tucson: University of Arizona Press, 1992.

Biesanz, Martin, et al. *The Ticos: Culture and Social Change in Costa Rica.* Boulder, CO: Lynne Rienner, 1998.

Bjarkman, Peter C. *Baseball with a Latin Beat: A History of the Latin American Game.* Jefferson, NC: McFarland, 1994.

Blawis, Patricia B. *Tijerina and the Land Grants: Mexican Americans in Struggle for Their Heritage.* New York: International Publishers, 1971.

Blea, Irene I. *U.S. Chicanas and Latinas Within a Global Context: Women of Color at the Fourth World Women's Conference.* Westport, CT: Praeger, 1997.

Bloom, Harold. *Hispanic-American Writers.* Philadelphia: Chelsea House, 1998.

Bost, Suzanne. *Mulattas and Mestizas: Representing Mixed Identities in the Americas, 1850–2000.* Athens: University of Georgia Press, 2003.

Boulais, Sue, and Barbara Mavis. *Tommy Nuñez: A Real-Life Reader Biography.* Hockessin, DE: Mitchell Lane, 1997.

Brackett, Virginia. *A Home in the Heart: The Story of Sandra Cisneros.* Greensboro, NC: Morgan Reynolds, 2005.

Brading, David A. *The First America: The Spanish Monarchy, Creole Patriots, and the Liberal State, 1492–1867.* New York: Cambridge University Press, 1991.

Bratt, Rachel G., et al. *Critical Perspectives on Housing.* Philadelphia: Temple University Press, 1986.

Bredeson, Carmen. *Henry Cisneros: Building a Better America.* Berkeley Heights, NJ: Enslow, 1995.

Briggs, Vernon M., Jr. *Mass Immigration and the National Interest.* Armonk, NY: M.E. Sharpe, 1992.

Brodie, Mollyann, et al. *2002 National Survey of Latinos.* Menlo Park, CA: Henry J. Kaiser Family Foundation; Washington, DC: Pew Hispanic Center, 2002.

Broid de Marek, Elizabeth. *Chicano Muralism.* El Paso: University of Texas Press, 1985.

Brown, E. Richard, et al. *Racial and Ethnic Disparities in Access to Health Insurance and Health Care.* Los Angeles: UCLA Center for Health Policy Research and Kaiser Family Foundation, 2000.

Broyles-González, Yolanda. *El Teatro Campesino: Theater in the Chicano Movement.* Austin: University of Texas Press, 1994.

Bruns, Roger. *Cesar Chavez: A Biography.* Westport, CT: Greenwood, 2005.

Burciaga, José Antonio. *Drink Cultura: Chicanismo.* Santa Barbara, CA: Capra, 1993.

Burgos, Adrian, Jr. *Playing America's Game: Baseball, Latinos, and the Color Line.* Berkeley: University of California Press, 2007.

Burkhart, Louise M. *The Slippery Earth: Nahua-Christian Moral Dialogue in Sixteenth-Century Mexico.* Tucson: University of Arizona Press, 1989.

Burkholder, Mark A., and Lyman L. Johnson. *Colonial Latin America.* New York: Oxford University Press, 1998.

Burnett, Christina Duffy, and Burke Marshall, eds. *Foreign in a Domestic Sense: Puerto Rico, American Expansion, and the Constitution.* Durham, NC: Duke University Press, 2001.

Burns, Allan F. *Maya in Exile: Guatemalans in Florida.* Philadelphia: Temple University Press, 1993.

Burns, Walter Noble. *The Robin Hood of El Dorado: The Saga of Joaquín Murrieta, Famous Outlaw of California's Age of Gold.* New York: Coward-McCann, 1932.

Buscaglia-Salgado, José F. *Undoing Empire: Race and Nation in the Mulatto Caribbean.* Minneapolis: University of Minnesota Press, 2003.

Butler, Johnnella E., ed. *Color-Line to Borderlands: The Matrix of American Ethnic Studies.* Seattle: University of Washington Press, 2001.

Byers, Ann. *Jaime Escalante: Sensational Teacher.* Springfield, NJ: Enslow, 1996.

Cabello-Argandona, Robert, ed. *Cinco de Mayo: A Symbol of Mexican National Resistance.* Encino, CA: Floricanto, 1991.

Cabeza de Vaca, Alvar Nuñez. *Adventures in the Unknown Interior of America.* Trans. and ed. Cyclone Covey. Albuquerque: University of New Mexico Press, 1997.

Cacheiro, Adolfo. *Reinaldo Arenas: Una Apreción Política.* Lanham, MD: International Scholars, 2000.

Calavita, Kitty. *Inside the State: The Bracero Program, Immigration, and the I.N.S.* New York: Routledge, 1992.

Camarillo, Albert. *Chicanos in a Changing Society: From Mexican Pueblos to American Barrios in Santa Barbara and Southern California.* Cambridge, MA: Harvard University Press, 1979.

Cameron, Maxwell A., and Brian W. Tomlin. *The Making of NAFTA: How the Deal Was Done.* Ithaca, NY: Cornell University Press, 2002.

Cantú, Norma, and Olga Nájera-Ramírez, eds. *Chicana Traditions: Continuity and Change.* Urbana: University of Illinois Press, 2002.

Carroll, Patrick J. *Felix Longoria's Wake: Bereavement, Racism and the Rise of Mexican American Activism.* Austin: University of Texas Press, 2003.

Castañeda, Jorge G. *Compañero: The Life and Death of Che Guevara.* New York: Alfred A. Knopf, 1997.

Castellanos, Jeannett. *The Majority in the Minority: Expanding the Representation of Latina/o Faculty, Administrators and Students in Higher Education.* Sterling, VA: Stylus, 2003.

Castellanos, Rosario. *Cartas a Ricardo.* Mexico City, Mexico: Consejo Nacional para la Cultura y las Artes, 1994.

Castells, Matilde, et al. *Mosaicos: Spanish as a World Language.* 4th ed. Upper Saddle River, NJ: Prentice Hall, 2005.

Castillo, Ana. *Massacre of the Dreamers: Essays on Xicanisma.* Albuquerque: University of New Mexico Press, 1994.

Castillo, Carlos, and Otto F. Bond. *The University of Chicago Spanish-English English-Spanish Dictionary.* New York: Pocket Books, 1987.

Castro, Max J., ed. *Free Markets, Open Societies, Closed Borders: Trends in International Migration and Immigration Policy in the Americas.* Coral Gables, FL: North-South Center, 1999.

Castro, Tony. *Chicano Power: The Emergence of Mexican America.* New York: E.P. Dutton, 1974.

Cesearetti, Gusmano. *Street Writers: A Guided Tour of Chicano Graffiti.* Los Angeles: Acrobat, 1975.

Chaney, Elsa M. *Supermadre: Women in Politics in Latin America.* Austin: University of Texas Press, 1979.

Chant, Sylvia, and Nikki Craske. *Gender in Latin America.* New Brunswick, NJ: Rutgers University Press, 2003.

Chávez, César. *The Words of César Chávez.* Ed. Richard J. Jensen and John C. Hammerback. College Station: Texas A&M University Press, 2002.

Chávez, Ernesto. *"¡Mi Raza Primero!" (My People First): Nationalism, Identity, and Insurgency in the Chicano Movement in Los Angeles, 1966–1978.* Berkeley: University of California Press, 2002.

Chavez, John R. *Eastside Landmark: A History of the East Los Angeles Community Union, 1968–1993.* Stanford, CA: Stanford University Press, 1998.

———. *The Lost Land: The Chicano Image of the Southwest.* Albuquerque: University of New Mexico Press, 1984.

Chavez, Leo R. *Shadowed Lives: Undocumented Immigrants in American Society.* 2nd ed. Orlando, FL: Harcourt Brace, 1998.

Chicano Coordinating Council on Higher Education. *El Plan de Santa Barbara: A Chicano Plan for Higher Education.* Oakland, CA: La Causa, 1969.

Christopher, Matt. *At the Plate with . . . Sammy Sosa.* Boston: Little, Brown, 1999.

Ciment, James. *Encyclopedia of American Immigration.* Armonk, NY: M.E. Sharpe, 2001.

Cisneros, Henry, ed. *Interwoven Destinies: Cities and the Nation.* New York: W.W. Norton, 1993.

Cockcroft, Eva, John Weber, and James Cockcroft. *Toward a People's Art: The Contemporary Mural Movement.* New York: E.P. Dutton, 1977.

Cockcroft, James D. *Latinos in the Struggle for Equal Education.* New York: Franklin Watts, 1995.

Cogdell, Christine. *Eugenic Design: Streamlining America in the 1930s.* Philadelphia: University of Pennsylvania Press, 2004.

Colón, Jesús. *A Puerto Rican in New York and Other Sketches.* New York: Mainstream, 1961.

Coltman, Leycester. *The Real Fidel Castro.* New Haven, CT: Yale University Press, 2003.

Compa, Lance. *Blood, Sweat, and Fear: Workers' Rights in U.S. Meat and Poultry Plants.* New York: Human Rights Watch, 2004.

Conniff, Michael L., and Thomas J. Davis. *Africans in the Americas.* New York: St. Martin's, 1994.

Conover, Ted. *Coyotes: A Journey through the Secret World of America's Illegal Aliens.* New York: Random House, 1987.

Cooney, Jerry W. *Paraguay: A Bibliography of Immigration and Emigration.* Longview, WA: J.W. Cooney, 1996.

Córdova, Gonzalo F. *Resident Commissioner, Santiago Iglesias and His Times.* Río Piedras, Puerto Rico: Editorial de la U.P.R., 1993.

Corona, Bert. *Memories of Chicano History: The Life and Narrative of Bert Corona.* Foreword by Mario T. García. Berkeley: University of California Press, 1994.

Cortes, Carlos E., ed. *Protestantism and Latinos in the United States.* New York: Arno, 1980.

Costo, Rupert, and Jeannette Henry Costo, eds. *The Missions of California: A Legacy of Genocide.* San Francisco: Indian Historian, 1987.

Couser, G. Thomas. *Altered Egos: Authority in American Autobiography.* New York: Oxford University Press, 1989.

Coyle, Laurie, Gail Hershatter, and Emily Honig. *Women at Farah: An Unfinished Story.* Oakland, CA: Coyle, Hershatter, and Honig, 1979.

Crane, Ken R. *Latino Churches: Faith, Family, and Ethnicity in the Second Generation.* New York: LFB Scholarly Publishing, 2003.

Crocker, Elvira Valenzuela. *MANA, One Dream, Many Voices: A History of the Mexican American Women's National Association.* Washington, DC: Mexican American Women's National Association, 1991.

Crosby, Faye J. *Sex, Race, and Merit: Debating Affirmative Action in Education and Employment.* Ann Arbor: University of Michigan Press, 2000.

Cruz, Celia, with Ana Cristina Reymundo. *Celia: My Life.* New York: Rayo, 2004.

Cruz, Wilfredo. *Puerto Rican Chicago (Images of America).* Charleston, SC: Arcadia, 2005.

Cuellar, Robert. *A Social and Political History of the Mexican American Population of Texas, 1929–1963.* San Francisco: R and E Research Associates, 1974.

Culture Clash. *Culture Clash: Life, Death and Revolutionary Comedy.* New York: Theatre Communications Group, 1998.

———. *Culture Clash in AmeriCCa: Four Plays.* New York: Theatre Communications Group, 2003.

Custodio, Álvaro. *El corrido popular mexicano: Su historia, sus temas, sus intérpretes.* Madrid: Júcar, 1975.

Cypess, Sandra Messinger. *La Malinche in Mexican Literature: From History to Myth.* Austin: University of Texas Press, 1991.

Dalton, Frederick John. *The Moral Vision of César Chávez.* Maryknoll, NY: Orbis, 2003.

Daniel, Cletus E. *Bitter Harvest: A History of California Farmworkers, 1870–1941.* Ithaca, NY: Cornell University Press. 1981.

Daniels, Roger. *American Immigration: A Student Companion.* New York: Oxford University Press, 2001.

———. *Coming to America: A History of Immigration and Ethnicity in American Life.* 2nd ed. New York: HarperCollins, 2002.

———. *Guarding the Golden Door: American Immigration Policy and Immigrants since 1882.* New York: Hill and Wang, 2004.

Daniels, Roger, and Otis L. Graham. *Debating American Immigration, 1882–Present.* Lanham, MD: Rowman & Littlefield, 2001.

Darder, A., and R. Torres, eds. *The Latino Studies Reader: Culture, Economy and Society.* Malden, MA: Blackwell, 2004.

Davidson, Theodore R. *Chicano Prisoners: The Key to San Quentin.* New York: Holt, Rinehart and Winston, 1974.

Dávila, Arlene. *Barrio Dreams: Puerto Ricans, Latinos, and the Neoliberal City.* Berkeley and Los Angeles: University of California Press, 2004.

———. *Latinos Inc.: The Marketing and Making of a People.* Berkeley: University of California Press, 2001.

Davis, William C. *Lone Star Rising: The Revolutionary Birth of the Texas Republic.* New York: Free Press, 2004.

Day, Frances Ann. *Latina and Latino Voices in Literature for Children and Teenagers.* Portsmouth, NH: Heinemann, 1997.

de Alba, Alicia Gaspar. *Chicano Art Inside/Outside the Master's House: Cultural Politics and the CARA Exhibition.* Austin: University of Texas Press, 1998.

De Anda, Roberto M., ed. *Chicanas and Chicanos in Contemporary Society.* Lanham, MD: Rowman & Littlefield., 2004.

De Genova, Nicholas P., and Ana Yolanda Ramos-Zayas, eds. *Latino Crossings: Mexicans, Puerto Ricans, and the Politics of Race and Citizenship.* New York: Routledge, 2003.

De Laguna, Asela Rodríguez, ed. *Images and Identities: The Puerto Rican in Two World Contexts.* New Brunswick, NJ: Transaction, 1985.

De Ruiz, Dana Catherine, and Richard Larios. *La Causa: The Migrant Farmworker's Story.* Austin, TX: Raintree Steck-Vaughn, 1993.

Del Castillo, Adelaida R., and Magdalena Mora, eds. *Mexican Women in the United States: Struggles Past and Present.* Los Angeles: University of California Press, 1980.

Del Castillo, Griswold, and Richard A. Garcia. *César Chávez: A Triumph of the Spirit.* Norman: University of Oklahoma Press, 1995.

DeStefano, Anthony M. *Gloria Estefan: The Pop Superstar from Tragedy to Triumph.* New York: Signet, 1997.

Díaz del Castillo, Bernal, and Maurice Keatinge. *The True History of the Conquest of Mexico, Written in the Year 1568 by Captain Bernal Díaz Del Castillo, One of the Conquerors, and Translated from the Original Spanish by Maurice Keatinge, Esq.; with an Introduction by Arthur D. Howden Smith.* New York: R.M. McBride, 1938.

Diaz-Stevens, Ana Maria, and Anthony M. Stevens-Arroyo. *Recognizing the Latino Resurgence in U.S. Religion: The Emmaus Paradigm.* Boulder, CO: Westview, 1998.

Dick, Bruce. *A Poet's Truth: Conversations with Latino/Latina Poets.* Tucson: University of Arizona Press, 2003.

Dick, Bruce, and Silvio Sirias, eds. *Conversations with Rudolfo Anaya.* Jackson: University Press of Mississippi, 1998.

Dietz, James L. *Puerto Rico: Negotiating Development and Change.* Boulder, CO: Lynne Rienner, 2003.

Dirks, Christopher. *The Gloria Estefan Scrapbook: A Celebration in Words and Pictures.* New York: Citadel, 1999.

Dixon, Daniel, and Julie Murray. *America's Emigrants: U.S. Retirement Migration to Mexico and Panama.* Washington, DC: Migration Policy Institute, 2006.

Doeden, Matt, and Pete Salas. *Lowriders.* Minneapolis, MN: Lerner, 2006.

Dolan, Jay P., and Allan Figueroa Deck. *Hispanic Catholic Culture in the U.S.: Issues and Concerns.* South Bend, IN: University of Notre Dame Press, 1994.

Dolan, Jay P., and Gilberto M. Hinojosa. *Mexican Americans and the Catholic Church, 1900–1965.* South Bend, IN: University of Notre Dame Press, 1994.

Drexler, Robert W. *Guilty of Making Peace: A Biography of Nicholas P. Trist.* Lanham, MD: University Press of America, 1991.

Drucker, M. *Frida Kahlo: Torment and Triumph in Her Life and Art.* New York: Bantam, 1991.

Duany, Jorge. *The Puerto Rican Nation on the Move: Identities on the Island and in the United States.* Chapel Hill: University of North Carolina Press, 2002.

Duncan, Patricia J. *Jennifer Lopez.* New York: St. Martin's, 1999.

Dunne, John Gregory. *Delano: The Story of the California Grape Strike.* New York: Farrar, Straus & Giroux, 1967.

Durand, John. *The Taos Massacres.* Elkhorn, WI: Puzzlebox, 2004.

Dzidzienyo, Anani, and Suzanne Oboler, eds. *Neither Enemies nor Friends: Latinos, Blacks, Afro-Latinos.* New York: Palgrave Macmillan, 2005.

Eastwood, Carolyn. *Near West Side Stories: Struggles for Community in Chicago's Maxwell Street Neighborhood.* Chicago: Lake Claremont, 2002.

Edwards, Jerome E. *Pat McCarran: Political Boss of Nevada.* Nevada Studies in History and Political Science. Reno: University of Nevada Press, 1982.

Einstein, Carol. *Claim to Fame, Book 2: Fourteen Short Biographies.* Cambridge, MA: Educators Publishing Service, 2000.

Eisen, George, and David Wiggins, eds. *Ethnicity and Sport in North American History and Culture.* Westport, CT: Greenwood, 1994.

El Teatro Campesino: The Evolution of America's First Chicano Theatre Company, 1965–1985. San Juan Bautista, CA: El Teatro Campesino, 1985.

Elam, Harry J., Jr. *Taking It to the Streets: The Social Protest Theater of Luis Valdez and Amiri Baraka.* Ann Arbor: University of Michigan Press, 2001.

Eleveld, Mark, ed. *The Spoken Word Revolution: Slam, Hip-Hop & the Poetry of a New Generation.* Naperville, IL: Sourcebooks MediaFusion, 2003.

Elizondo, Virgilio. *The Future Is Mestizo: Life Where Cultures Meet.* Rev. ed. Boulder: University Press of Colorado, 2000.

Elliott, John H. *Imperial Spain, 1469–1717.* New York: Penguin, 1963.

Embry, Jessie L. *"In His Own Language": Mormon Spanish-Speaking Congregations in the United States.* Provo, UT: Charles Redd Center for Western Studies, 1997.

Endore, Guy. *The Sleepy Lagoon Mystery.* Los Angeles: Sleepy Lagoon Defense Committee, 1944.

Escobar, Edward J. *Race, Police, and the Making of a Political Identity: Mexican Americans and the Los Angeles Police Department, 1900–1945.* Berkeley: University of California Press, 1999.

Esteva-Fabregat, Claudio. *Mestizaje in Ibero-America.* Trans. John Wheat. Tucson: University of Arizona Press, 1987.

Etulain, Richard W., ed. *César Chávez: A Brief Biography with Documents.* New York: Palgrave, 2002.

Etulain, Richard W., and Glenda Riley. *With Badges and Bullets: Lawmen & Outlaws in the Old West.* Golden, CO: Fulcrum, 1999.

Evans, Linda, and Eve Goldberg. *The Prison Industrial Complex and the Global Economy.* Boston: Kersplebedeb, 1998.

Fernández, Alfredo A. *Adrift: The Cuban Raft People.* Houston, TX: Arte Público, 2000.

Fernández, Mayra, and Rick Villarreal. *Antonia Novello, Doctor.* Cleveland, OH: Modern Curriculum, 1994.

Fernández, Roberta, ed. *In Other Words: Literature by Latinas of the United States.* Houston, TX: Arte Público, 1994.

Fernandez, Ronald, Serafín Méndez Méndez, and Gail Cueto. *Puerto Rico Past and Present: An Encyclopedia.* Westport, CT: Greenwood, 1998.

Fernandez, Ronald. *The Disenchanted Island: Puerto Rico and the United States in the Twentieth Century.* Westport, CT: Praeger, 1996.

———. *Los Macheteros: The Wells Fargo Robbery and the Violent Struggle for Puerto Rican Independence.* New York: Prentice Hall, 1987.

———. *Prisoners of Colonialism: The Struggle for Justice in Puerto Rico.* Monroe, ME: Common Courage, 1994.

Fernández-Kelly, Patricia, and Jon Shefner, eds. *NAFTA and Beyond: Alternative Perspectives in the Study of Global Trade and Development.* Thousand Oaks, CA: Sage, 2007.

Ferriss, Susan, and Ricardo Sandoval. *The Fight in the Fields: César Chávez and the Farmworkers Movement.* Ed. Diane Hembree. New York: Harcourt Brace, 1997.

Field, Ron. *Spanish-American War 1898.* Washington, DC: Brassey's, 1998.

Finbow, Robert G. *The Limits of Regionalism: NAFTA's Labor Accord.* Burlington, VT: Ashgate, 2006.

Fink, Leon. *The Maya of Morganton: Work and Community in the Nuevo New South.* Chapel Hill: University of North Carolina Press, 2003.

Fisch, Louise Ann. *All Rise: Reynaldo G. Garza, The First Mexican American Federal Judge.* College Station: Texas A&M University Press, 1996.

Fitzgibbon, Russell H. *Cuba and the United States, 1900–1935.* New York: Russell & Russell, 1964.

Fitzpatrick, Joseph P. *Puerto Rican Americans: The Meaning of Migration to the Mainland.* Englewood Cliffs, NJ: Prentice Hall, 1971.

Flores, Juan. *Divided Borders: Essays on Puerto Rican Identity.* Houston, TX: Arte Público, 1993.

———. *From Bomba to Hip-Hop: Puerto Rican Culture and Latino Identity.* New York: Columbia University Press, 2000.

Flores, William V., and Rina Benmayor, eds. *Latino Cultural Citizenship: Claiming Identity, Space, and Rights.* Boston: Beacon, 1997.

Flynn, Jean. *Henry B. Gonzalez: Rebel with a Cause.* Austin, TX: Eakin, 2004.

Foer, Franklin. *How Soccer Explains the World: An Unlikely Theory of Globalization.* New York: HarperCollins, 2004.

Fox, Geoffrey. *Hispanic Nation: Culture, Politics, and the Constructing of Identity.* Tucson: University of Arizona Press, 1996.

Francaviglia, Richard V., and Douglas W. Richmond, eds. *Dueling Eagles: Reinterpreting the U.S.-Mexican War, 1846–1848.* Fort Worth: Texas Christian University Press, 2000.

Franco, María Estela. *Rosario Castellanos: Semblanza psicoanalítica otro modo de ser humano y libre.* Mexico City, Mexico: Plaza y Janés, 1984.

Fregoso, Rosa Linda. *The Bronze Screen: Chicana and Chicano Film Culture.* Minneapolis: University of Minnesota Press, 1993.

Friedlander, Judith. *Being Indian in Hueyapan: A Study of Forced Identity in Contemporary Mexico.* New York: St. Martin's, 1975.

Fusco, Coco, ed. *Corpus Delecti: Performance Art of the Americas.* New York: Routledge, 2000.

———. *English Is Broken Here: Notes on Cultural Fusion in the Americas.* New York: New Press, 1995.

Galarza, Ernesto. *Barrio Boy.* South Bend, IN: University of Notre Dame Press, 1971.

———. *Farm Workers and Agri-Business in California, 1947–1960.* South Bend, IN: University of Notre Dame Press, 1977.

Gamio, Manuel. *The Life Story of the Mexican Immigrant: Autobiographic Documents.* New York: Dover, 1971.

———. *Mexican Immigration to the United States.* New York: Arno, 1969.

Gann, L.H., and Peter J. Duignan. *The Hispanics in the United States: A History.* Boulder, CO: Westview, 1987.

Ganz, Cheryl W., ed. *Pots of Promise: Mexicans and Pottery at Hull-House, 1920–40 (Latinos in Chicago and the Midwest).* Champaign: University of Illinois Press, 2005.

García, Alma M., ed. *Chicana Feminist Thought: The Basic Historical Writings.* New York: Routledge, 1997.

Garcia, Chris, ed. *La Causa Política: A Chicano Politics Reader.* South Bend, IN: University of Notre Dame Press, 1974.

Garcia, Chris, and Rudolph O. de la Garza. *The Chicano Political Experience.* North Scituate, MA: Duxbury, 1977.

García, Eugene E. *Teaching and Learning in Two Languages: Bilingualism and Schooling in the United States.* New York: Teachers College Press, 2005.

García, Ignacio M. *Chicanismo: The Forging of a Militant Ethos among Mexican Americans.* Tucson: University of Arizona Press, 1997.

———. *Héctor P. García: In Relentless Pursuit of Justice.* Houston, TX: Arte Público, 2002.

———. *United We Win: The Rise and Fall of La Raza Unida Party.* Tucson: University of Arizona Press, 1989.

———. *Viva Kennedy: Mexican Americans in Search of Camelot.* College Station: Texas A&M University Press, 2000.

Garcia, Juan Ramon. *Operation Wetback: The Mass Deportation of Mexican Undocumented Workers in 1954.* Westport, CT: Greenwood, 1980.

García, María Cristina. *Havana USA: Cuban Exiles and Cuban Americans in South Florida, 1959–1994.* Berkeley: University of California Press, 1996.

García, Mario T. *Desert Immigrants: The Mexicans of El Paso, 1880–1920.* New Haven, CT: Yale University Press, 1981.

———. *The Making of a Mexican American Mayor: Raymond L. Telles of El Paso.* El Paso: University of Texas at El Paso, 1998.

———. *Memories of Chicano History: The Life and Narrative of Bert Corona.* Berkeley: University of California Press, 1994.

———. *Mexican Americans: Leadership, Ideology, and Identity.* New Haven, CT: Yale University Press, 1989.

Garcia, Richard. *The Rise of the Mexican Middle Class: San Antonio 1929–1941.* College Station: Texas A&M University Press, 1991.

Garebian, Keith. *The Making of West Side Story.* New York: Mosaic, 1998.

Gaspar de Alba, Alicia. *Chicano Art Inside/Outside the Master's House: Cultural Politics and the CARA Exhibition.* Austin: University of Texas Press, 1998.

Gay, Kathlyn. *Leaving Cuba: From Operation Pedro Pan to Elian.* Brookfield, CT: Twenty-First Century Books, 2000.

Genat, Robert. *Lowriders.* Minneapolis: MBI, 2001.

George, Nelson. *Hip Hop America.* New York: Viking, 1998.

Gerace, Gloria. *Urban Surprises: A Guide to Public Art in Los Angeles.* Princeton, NJ: Architectural Press, 2006.

Gerhard, Peter H. *The North Frontier of New Spain.* Princeton, NJ: Princeton University Press, 1982.

Gerner, Fawn. *Hard Won Wisdom: Today's Extraordinary Women Mentor You to Find Self-Awareness, Balance, and Perspective.* New York: Berkeley, 2001.

Geron, Kim. *Latino Political Power.* Boulder, CO: Lynne Rienner, 2005.

Gibbs, Jewelle Taylor, and Teiahsja Bankhead. *Preserving Privilege: California Politics, Propositions, and People of Color.* Westport, CT: Praeger, 2001.

Gibson, Charles. *The Aztecs Under Spanish Rule: A History of the Indians of the Valley of Mexico, 1519–1810.* Stanford, CA: Stanford University Press, 1964.

Glazer, Nathan, and Daniel Patrick Moynihan. *Beyond the Melting Pot: The Negroes, Puerto Ricans, Jews, Italians and Irish of New York City.* Cambridge, MA: MIT Press, 1970.

Gómez Quiñones, Juan. *Chicano Politics: Reality and Promise, 1940–1990.* Albuquerque: University of New Mexico Press, 1990.

———. *Mexican American Labor, 1790–1990.* Albuquerque: University of New Mexico Press, 1994.

———. *Mexican Students Por La Raza: The Chicano Student Movement in Southern California, 1967–1977.* Santa Barbara, CA: Editorial La Causa, 1978.

———. *Roots of Chicano Politics, 1600–1948.* Albuquerque: University of New Mexico Press, 1994.

Gómez-Peña, Guillermo. *Dangerous Border Crossers: The Artist Talks Back.* New York: Routledge, 2000.

Gonzáles, César A., and Phyllis S. Morgan. *A Sense of Place: Rudolfo A. Anaya: An Annotated Bio-Bibliography.* Berkeley, CA: Ethnic Studies Library Publications, 2001.

Gonzales, Manuel G. *Mexicanos: A History of Mexicans in the United States.* Bloomington: Indiana University Press, 1999.

Gonzales, Rodolfo. *I Am Joaquín, Yo Soy Joaquín: An Epic Poem.* New York: Bantam, 1972.

———. *Message to Aztlán: Selected Writings of Rodolfo "Corky" Gonzales.* Ed. Antonio Esquibel. Houston, TX: Arte Público, 2001.

Gonzales, Sylvia Alicia. *Hispanic American Voluntary Organizations.* Westport, CT: Greenwood, 1985.

González, Alberto, Marsha Houston, and Victoria Chen, eds. *Our Voices: Essays in Culture, Ethnicity and Communication.* Los Angeles: Roxbury, 2004.

González, Fernando. *Gloria Estefan: Cuban-American Singing Star.* Boston: Houghton Mifflin, 2003.

Gonzalez, Gilbert G. *Guest Workers or Colonized Labor? Mexican Labor Migration to the United States.* Boulder, CO: Paradigm, 2007.

González, Juan. *Harvest of Empire: A History of Latinos in America.* New York: Viking, 2000.

González, Lisa Sánchez. *Boricua Literature: A Literary History of the Puerto Rican Diaspora.* New York: New York University Press, 2001.

González, Ray, ed. *Muy Macho, Latino Men Confront Their Manhood.* New York: Anchor, 1996.

Gonzalez-Pando, Miguel. *The Cuban Americans.* Westport, CT: Greenwood, 1998.

Gordon, Albert. *Intermarriage.* Boston: Beacon, 1964.

Gordon, Milton. *Assimilation in American Life: The Role of Race, Religion, and National Origins.* New York: Oxford University Press, 1964.

Graham, Otis. *Unguarded Gates: A History of America's Immigration Crisis.* New York: Rowman & Littlefield, 2004.

Griffith, Beatrice. *American Me.* Boston: Houghton Mifflin, 1948.

Griswold del Castillo, Richard. *La Familia: Chicano Families in the Urban Southwest, 1848 to the Present.* South Bend, IN: University of Notre Dame Press, 1984.

———. *The Treaty of Guadalupe Hidalgo: A Legacy of Conflict.* Norman: University of Oklahoma Press, 1990.

Grosfoguel, Ramón. *Colonial Subjects: Puerto Ricans in a Global Perspective.* Berkeley: University of California Press, 2003.

Gruzinsk, Serge. *The Mestizo Mind: The Intellectual Dynamics of Colonization and Globalization.* New York: Routledge, 2002.

Guajardo, Paul. *Chicano Controversy: Oscar Acosta and Richard Rodriguez.* New York: Peter Lang, 2002.

Guerin-Gonzales, Camille. *Mexican Workers and American Dreams: Immigration, Repatriation, and California Farm Labor, 1900–1939.* New Brunswick, NJ: Rutgers University Press, 1994.

Guerrero, Andrea. *Silence at Boalt Hall: The Dismantling of Affirmative Action.* Berkeley: University of California Press, 2002.

Guevara, Ernesto "Che." *The Motorcycle Diaries.* Trans. Alexandra Keeble. New York: HarperPerennial, 2004.

Guskin, Jane, and David L. Wilson. *The Politics of Immigration: Questions and Answers.* New York: Monthly Review Press, 2007.

Gutiérrez, David G., ed. *Between Two Worlds: Mexican Immigrants in the United States.* Wilmington, DE: Scholarly Resources, 1996.

———. *Walls and Mirrors: Mexican Americans, Mexican Immigrants, and the Politics of Ethnicity.* Berkeley: University of California Press, 1995.

Gutiérrez, José Angel. *The Making of a Chicano Militant: Lessons from Cristal.* Madison: University of Wisconsin Press, 1998.

Gutiérrez, Margo. *Sourcebook on Central American Refugee Policy.* Austin, TX: Central American Resource Center, 1985.

Gutiérrez, Ramón A., and Richard J. Orsi, eds. *Contested Eden: California Before the Gold Rush.* Berkeley: University of California Press, 1998.

Guy, Donna, and Thomas Sheridan. *Contested Ground: Comparative Frontiers on the Northern and Southern Edges of the Spanish Empire.* Tucson: University of Arizona Press, 1998.

Guzman, Ralph C. *The Political Socialization of the Mexican American People.* New York: Arno, 1976.

Haas, Lisbeth. *Conquests and Historical Identities in California, 1769–1936.* Berkeley: University of California Press, 1995.

Habell-Pallán, Michelle, and Mary Romero, eds. *Latino/a Popular Culture.* New York: New York University Press, 2002.

Hadley-Garcia, George. *Hispanic Hollywood: The Latins in Motion Pictures.* New York: Carol, 1993.

Hahn, Harlan, ed. *Peoples and Politics in Urban Society.* Beverly Hills, CA: Sage, 1972.

Hall, Charles, ed. *Quantifying Sustainable Development: The Future of Tropical Economies.* San Diego, CA: Academic Press, 2000.

Hamilton, Nora, and Norma Stoltz Chincilla. *Seeking Community in a Global City: Guatemalans and Salvadorans in Los Angeles.* Philadelphia: Temple University Press, 2001.

Haney-López, Ian F. *Racism on Trial: The Chicano Fight for Justice.* Cambridge, MA: Harvard University Press, 2003.

Hanratty, Dennis, ed. *Ecuador: A Country Study.* 3rd ed. Washington, DC: Federal Research Division, Library of Congress, 1991.

Hardin, Stephen. *The Alamo 1836: Santa Anna's Texas Campaign.* Westport, CT: Praeger, 2004.

Harris, Charles, and Louis Saddler. *The Texas Rangers and the Mexican Revolution: The Bloodiest Decade, 1910–1920.* Albuquerque: University of New Mexico Press, 2007.

Haslip-Viera, Gabriel, and Sherrie L. Baver, eds. *Latinos in New York: Communities in Transition.* South Bend, IN: University of Notre Dame Press, 1996.

Hassig, Susan. *Panama.* New York: Marshall Cavendish, 1997.

Hawxhurst, Joan C. *Antonia Novello, U.S. Surgeon General.* Brookfield, CT: Millbrook, 1993.

Hayden, Tom, ed. *The Zapatista Reader.* New York: Thunder's Mouth, 2002.

Healy, Nick. *Roberto Clemente: Baseball Legend.* Mankato, MN: Capstone, 2006.

Heizer, Robert F., and Alan F. Almquist. *The Other Californians: Prejudice and Discrimination Under Spain, Mexico, and the United States to 1920.* Berkeley: University of California Press, 1971.

Henao, Eda B. *Colonial Subject's Search for Nation, Culture, and Identity in the Works of Julia Alvarez, Rosario Ferré, and Ana Lydia Vega.* Lewiston, NY: Edwin Mellen, 2003.

Hernández, Carmen Dolores. *Puerto Rican Voices in English: Interviews with Writers.* Westport, CT: Praeger, 1997.

Hernández, José M. *Cuba and the United States: Intervention and Militarism, 1868–1933.* Austin: University of Texas Press, 1993.

Hero, Rodney. *Latinos and the U.S. Political System: Two-Tiered Pluralism.* Philadelphia: Temple University Press, 1992.

Herrera, Hayden. *Frida: A Biography of Frida Kahlo.* New York: Harper & Row, 1983.

Hill, Anne E. *Jennifer Lopez.* Philadelphia: Chelsea House, 2001.

Hing, Bill Ong. *Defining America Through Immigration Policy.* Philadelphia: Temple University Press, 2004.

Hispanic Policy Development Project. *The Hispanic Almanac.* Washington, DC: Hispanic Development Project, 1984.

Hitchman, James H. *Leonard Wood and Cuban Independence, 1898–1902.* The Hague, The Netherlands: Martinus Nijhoff, 1971.

Hoffman, Abraham. *Unwanted Mexican Americans in the Great Depression: Repatriation Pressures, 1929–1939.* Tucson: University of Arizona Press, 1974.

Holland, Clifton L. *The Religious Dimension in Hispanic Los Angeles: A Protestant Case Study.* Pasadena, CA: William Carey Library, 1974.

Hondagneu-Sotelo, Pierrette. *Gender and Contemporary U.S. Immigration: Contemporary Trends.* Berkeley: University of California Press, 2003.

Hoobler, Dorothy. *The Mexican American Family Album.* New York: Oxford University Press, 1994.

Horno-Delgado, Asuncíon, et al. *Breaking Boundaries: Latina Writing and Critical Readings.* Amherst: University of Massachusetts Press, 1989.

Horsman, Reginald. *Race and Manifest Destiny: The Origins of American Racial Anglo-Saxonism.* Cambridge, MA: Harvard University Press, 1981.

Hoyt-Goldsmith, Diane. *Celebrating a Quinceañera: A Latina's Fifteenth Birthday Celebration.* New York: Holiday House, 2002.

Ifekwunigwe, Jayne O., ed. *Mixed Race Studies.* New York: Routledge, 2004.

Ikas, Karin Rosa. *Chicana Ways: Conversations with Ten Chicana Writers.* Reno: University of Nevada Press, 2002.

Irwin, John. *Prisons in Turmoil.* Boston: Little, Brown, 1980.

Jacobson, David, ed. *The Immigration Reader: America in a Multidisciplinary Perspective.* Malden, MA: Blackwell, 1998.

Jenkins, Craig J. *The Politics of Insurgency: The Farm Worker Movement in the 1960s.* New York: Columbia University Press, 1985.

Jennings, Francis. *The Invasion of America: Indians, Colonialism, and the Cant of Conquest.* Chapel Hill: University of North Carolina Press, 1975.

Jeter, Sylvia. *The Quinceañera Planning Guide.* Frankfort, IL: Quinceanera-Boutique.com, 2002.

Jiménez, Carlos M. *The Mexican American Heritage.* Berkeley, CA: TQS, 2004.

Kamen, Henry. *Spain's Road to Empire: The Making of a World Power, 1492–1763.* New York: Allen Lane, 2002.

Kanellos, Nicolás. *Hispanic First: 500 Years of Extraordinary Achievement.* Stamford, CT: Gale Research, 1997.

Kanellos, Nicolás, and Bryan Ryan, eds. *Hispanic American Chronology.* New York: UXL, 1996.

Kanellos, Nicolás, and Claudio Esteva-Fabregat, eds. *Handbook of Hispanic Cultures in the United States: Literature and Art.* Houston, TX: Arte Público, 1993.

Kaplowitz, Craig A. *LULAC: Mexican Americans, and National Policy.* College Station: Texas A&M University Press, 2005.

Kawakami, Tim. *Golden Boy: The Fame, Money, and Mystery of Oscar de la Hoya.* Kansas City, MO: Andrews McMeel, 1999.

Keating, AnaLouise. *Women Reading Women Writing: Self-Invention in Paula Gunn Allen, Gloria Anzaldua and Audre Lorde.* Philadelphia: Temple University Press, 1996.

Keenan, Jerry. *Spanish-American and Philippine-American Wars.* Santa Barbara, CA: ABC-CLIO, 2001.

Keller, Gary, ed. *Chicano Cinema: Research, Reviews, and Resources.* Binghamton, NY: Bilingual Review Press, 1985.

Kellner, Douglas. *Ernesto "Che" Guevara.* New York and Philadelphia: Chelsea House, 1989.

Kevane, Bridget A. *Latino Literature in America.* Westport, CT: Greenwood, 2003.

Keyes, Cheryl L. *Rap Music and Street Consciousness.* Urbana: University of Illinois Press, 2002.

Kim, Sojin, and Peter Quezada. *Chicano Graffiti and Murals: The Neighborhood Art of Peter Quezada.* Jackson: University Press of Mississippi, 1995.

King, Elizabeth. *Quinceañera: Celebrating Fifteen.* New York: Dutton, 1998.

Kirsten, Peter N. *Anglo Over Bracero: A History of the Mexican Workers in the United States from Roosevelt to Nixon.* San Francisco: R and E Research Associates, 1977.

Kirwan, William E. *What Makes Racial Diversity Work in Higher Education: Academic Leaders Present Successful Policies and Strategies.* Sterling, VA: Stylus, 2003.

Klein, Alan M. *Sugarball: The American Game, the Dominican Dream.* New Haven, CT: Yale University Press, 1991.

Kramer, Jon. *Lee Trevino (Overcoming the Odds).* Orlando, FL: Raintree Steck-Vaughn, 1996.

Kreneck, Thomas H. *Mexican American Odyssey: Felix Tijerina, Entrepreneur and Civic Leader, 1905–1965.* College Station: Texas A&M University Press, 2001.

Krich, John. *El Beisbol: Travels Through the Pan-American Pastime.* New York: Prentice Hall, 1989.

Kuper, Simon. *Soccer Against the Enemy: How the World's Most Popular Sport Starts and Fuels Revolutions and Keeps Dictators in Power.* New York: Nation, 2006.

Kurian, George, ed. *Historical Guide to the U.S. Government.* New York: Oxford University Press, 1998.

LaBotz, Dan. *César Chávez and la Causa.* New York: Pearson/Longman, 2006.

Laird, Bob. *The Case for Affirmative Action in University Admissions.* Point Richmond, CA: Bay Tree, 2005.

Langham, Thomas C. *Border Trials: Ricardo Flores Magón and the Mexican Liberals.* El Paso: Texas Western Press, 1981.

Laó-Montes, Agustín, and Arlene Dávila. *Mambo Montage: The Latinization of New York.* New York: Columbia University Press, 2001.

Larralde, Carlos. *Mexican American Movements and Leaders.* Los Alamitos, CA: Hwong, 1976.

Latta, Frank Forrest. *Joaquín Murrieta and His Horse Gangs.* Santa Cruz, CA: Bear State, 1980.

Lattes, Alfredo E., and Enrique Oteiza, eds. *The Dynamics of Argentine Migration, 1955–1984: Democracy and the Return of Expatriates.* Trans. David Lehmann and Alison Roberts. Geneva, Switzerland: United Nations Research Institute for Social Development, 1987.

Lazarus, William. *Edward R. Roybal, Democratic Representative from California.* New York: Grossman, 1972.

Lederman, Daniel, et al. *Lessons from NAFTA for Latin America and the Caribbean Countries.* Washington, DC: World Bank, 2003.

Lemire, Elise. *Miscegenation: Making Race in America.* Philadelphia: University of Pennsylvania Press, 2002.

Leonard, Thomas M. *Fidel Castro: A Biography.* Westport, CT: Greenwood, 2004.

Lever, Janet. *Soccer Madness.* Chicago: University of Chicago Press, 1984.

Levine, Robert M. *Secret Missions to Cuba: Fidel Castro, Bernardo Benes, and Cuban Miami.* New York: Palgrave Macmillan, 2002.

Levine, Robert M., and Asis Moises. *Cuban Miami.* New Brunswick, NJ: Rutgers University Press, 2000.

Lewis, Oscar. *The Children of Sanchez: Autobiography of a Mexican Family.* New York: Random House, 1961.

———. *La Vida: A Puerto Rican Family in the Culture of Poverty—San Juan and New York.* New York: Random House, 1966.

———. *Life in a Mexican Village: Tepoztlan Restudied.* Urbana: University of Illinois Press, 1951.

Libal, Autumn. *Cuban Americans: Exiles from an Island Home.* Philadelphia: Mason Crest, 2005.

Lidin, Harold J. *History of the Puerto Rican Independence Movement.* Buffalo, NY: Waterfront, 1982.

Littwin, Mark. *Fernando!* New York: Bantam, 1981.

Lobo, RuthAnn, and Rebecca Lobo. *The Home Team: Of Mothers, Daughters, and American Champions.* New York: Kodansha America, 1997.

Lockhart, James. *The Nahuas after the Conquest: A Social and Cultural History of the Indians of Central Mexico, Sixteenth through Eighteenth Centuries.* Stanford, CA: Stanford University Press, 1992.

Lockhart, James, and Stuart B. Swartz. *Early Latin America: A History of Colonial Spanish America and Brazil.* Cambridge University Press, 1983.

London, Joan, and Henry Anderson. *So Shall Ye Reap: The Story of César Chávez and the Farm Workers' Movement.* New York: Thomas Crowell, 1970.

López, Adalberto, ed. *The Puerto Ricans, Their History, Culture and Society.* Cambridge, MA: Schenkman, 1980.

Lopez, Alfredo. *Doña Licha's Island: Modern Colonialism in Puerto Rico.* Boston: South End, 1987.

López, Ana M., and Chon A. Noriega, eds. *The Ethnic Eye: Latino Media Arts.* Minneapolis: University of Minnesota Press, 1996.

Lopez, Carlos U. *Chilenos in California: A Study of the 1850, 1852, and 1860 Censuses.* San Francisco: R and E Research Associates, 1973.

Lorca de Tagle, Lillian. *Honorable Exiles: A Chilean Woman in the Twentieth Century.* Austin: University of Texas Press, 2000.

Lotchin, Roger W., ed. *The Way We Really Were: The Golden State and the Second Great War.* Urbana: University of Illinois Press, 2000.

Loucky, James, and Marilyn M. Moors, eds. *The Maya Diaspora: Guatemalan Roots, New American Lives.* Philadelphia: Temple University Press, 2000.

Loza, Steven J. *Tito Puente and the Making of Latin Music.* Urbana: University of Illinois Press, 1999.

MacDonald, Victoria-María. *Latino Education in the United States: A Narrated History from 1513–2000.* New York: Palgrave MacMillan, 2004.

Macias, Reynaldo F. *A Study of Unincorporated East Los Angeles.* Los Angeles: University of California Press, 1973.

Maciel, David R., and Isidro D. Ortiz, eds. *Chicanas/Chicanos at the Crossroads: Social, Economic, and Political Change.* Tucson: University of Arizona Press, 1996.

Maciel, David R., Isidro D. Ortiz, and María Herrera-Sobek, eds. *Chicano Renaissance: Contemporary Cultural Trends.* Tucson: University of Arizona Press, 2000.

MacLachlan, Colin M. *Anarchism and the Mexican Revolution: The Political Trials of Ricardo Flores Magón in the United States.* Berkeley: University of California Press, 1991.

Madrid, Alejandro. *Sounds of the Modern Nation: Music, Culture, and Ideas in Post-Revolutionary Mexico.* Philadelphia: Temple University Press, 2008.

Maharidge, Dale. *The Coming White Minority: California's Eruptions and the Nation's Future.* New York: Times, 1996.

Mahler, Sarah J. *Salvadorans in Suburbia: Symbiosis and Conflict.* Boston: Allyn and Bacon, 1995.

Malavet, Pedro A. *America's Colony: The Political and Cultural Conflict Between the United States and Puerto Rico.* New York: New York University Press, 2004.

Maldonado, A.W. *Teodoro Moscoso and Puerto Rico's Operation Bootstrap.* Gainesville: University Press of Florida, 1997.

Maldonado, David. *Crossing Guadalupe Street: Growing up Hispanic and Protestant.* Albuquerque: University of New Mexico Press, 2001.

Malone, Julio. *Sammy Sosa in 9 Innings.* New York: Editorial Miglo, 2004.

Margolis, Maxine. *An Invisible Minority: Brazilians in New York City.* Boston: Allyn and Bacon, 1998.

———. *Little Brazil: An Ethnography of Brazilian Immigrants in New York City.* Princeton, NJ: Princeton University Press, 1994.

Marín, Christine. *A Spokesman of the Mexican American Movement: Rodolfo "Corky" Gonzales and the Fight for Chicano Liberation, 1966–1972.* San Francisco: R and E Research Associates, 1977.

Mariscal, George. *Aztlán and Viet Nam: Chicano and Chicana Experiences of the War.* Berkeley: University of California Press, 1999.

———. *Brown-Eyed Children of the Sun: Lessons of the Chicano Movement, 1965–1975.* Albuquerque: University of New Mexico Press, 2005.

Markuson, Bruce. *Roberto Clemente: The Great One.* Champaign, IL: Sports, 1998.

Marques, Rene. *The Docile Puerto Rican.* Philadelphia: Temple University Press, 1976.

Márquez, Benjamin. *LULAC: The Evolution of a Mexican American Political Organization.* Austin: University of Texas Press, 1993.

Marsh, Carole. *Antonia Novello: First Hispanic U.S. Surgeon General.* Peachtree City, GA: Gallopade International, 2002.

Martin, Philip L., and David A. Martin. *The Endless Quest: Helping America's Farm Workers.* Boulder, CO: Westview, 1994.

Martínez, Demetria. *Confessions of a Berlitz-Tape Chicana.* Norman: University of Oklahoma Press, 2005.

Martinez, Elizabeth, ed. *Five Hundred Years of Chicano History in Pictures.* Rev. ed. Albuquerque, NM: Southwest Organizing Project, 1991.

Martinez, Orlando. *The Great Landgrab: The Mexican-American War, 1846–1848.* London: Quartet, 1975.

Marzán, Julio, ed. *Inventing a Word: An Anthology of Twentieth-Century Puerto Rican Poetry.* New York: Columbia University Press, 1980.

Mason, Mauricio. *The Zoot-Suit Riots: The Psychology of Symbolic Annihilation.* Austin: University of Texas Press, 1984.

Massey, Douglas S., Jorge Durand, and Nolan J. Malone. *Beyond Smoke and Mirrors: Mexican Immigration in an Era of Economic Integration.* New York: Russell Sage Foundation, 2002.

Masud-Piloto, Felix Roberto. *From Welcomed Exiles to Illegal Immigrants: Cuban Migration to the U.S., 1959–1995.* Lanham, MD: Rowman & Littlefield, 1996.

Mathews, Thomas G. *Luis Muñoz Marín: A Concise Biography.* New York: American R.D.M., 1967.

Matthiessen, Peter. *Sal Si Puedes (Escape If You Can): Cesar Chavez and the New American Revolution.* Berkeley: University of California Press, 2000.

Maufort, Marc, ed. *Staging Difference: Cultural Pluralism in American Theatre and Drama.* New York: Peter Lang, 1995.

Mavis, Barbara. *Selena.* New York: Mitchell Lane, 2003.

May, Ernest R. *Imperial Democracy: The Emergence of America as a Great Power.* New York: Harcourt, Brace & World, 1961.

Mazón, Mauricio. *The Zoot-Suit Riots: The Psychology of Symbolic Annihilation.* Austin: University of Texas Press, 1984.

McCaffrey, James M. *Army of Manifest Destiny: The American Soldier in the Mexican War, 1846–1848.* New York: New York University Press, 1992.

McCaffrey, Katherine. *Military Power and Popular Protest: The U.S. Navy in Vieques, Puerto Rico.* New Brunswick, NJ: Rutgers University Press, 2002.

McCawley, William. *The First Angelinos: The Gabrielino Indians of Los Angeles.* Banning, CA: Malki Museum, 1996.

McWilliams, Carey. *North from Mexico: The Spanish-Speaking People of the United States.* 1949. Updated by Matt S. Meier. New York: Praeger, 1990.

Medina, Lara. *Las Hermanas: Chicana/Latina Religious-Political Activism in the U.S. Catholic Church.* Philadelphia: Temple University Press, 2004.

Meier, Matt S., and Feliciano Ribera. *The Chicanos: A History of Mexican Americans.* New York: Hill and Wang, 1972.

———. *Mexican Americans, American Mexicans: From Conquistadors to Chicanos.* New York: Hill and Wang, 1993.

Meier, Matt S., and Margo Gutierrez. *Encyclopedia of the Mexican American Civil Rights Movement.* Westport, CT: Greenwood, 2000.

Meier, Matt S., with Conchita Franco Serri and Richard A. Garcia. *Notable Latino Americans: A Biographical Dictionary.* Westport, CT: Greenwood, 1997.

Meiss, Guy T., and Alice A. Tait, eds. *ALANA: Ethnic Media in America.* New York: Kendall/Hunt, 2006.

Meister, Dick, and Anne Loftis. *A Long Time Coming: The Struggle to Unionize America's Farm Workers.* New York: Macmillan, 1977.

Meléndez, Edwin, and Edgardo Meléndez. *Colonial Dilemma: Critical Perspectives on Contemporary Puerto Rico.* Boston: South End, 1993.

Melendez, Miguel "Mickey." *We Took the Streets: Fighting for Latino Rights with the Young Lords.* New York: St. Martin's, 2003.

Mendoza, Vicente T. *El corrido mexicano.* Mexico City, Mexico: Fondo de Cultura Económica, 1954.

Meyer, Michael, William Sherman, and Susan Deeds. *The Course of Mexican History.* New York: Oxford University Press, 2007.

Miller, Debra. *Illegal Immigration.* San Diego, CA: Greenhaven, 2006.

Miller, Marilyn Grace. *The Rise and Fall of the Cosmic Race: The Cult of Mestizaje in Latin America.* Austin: University of Texas Press, 2004.

Minas, Anne, ed. *Gender Basics: Feminist Perspectives on Women and Men.* 2nd ed. Belmont, CA: Wadsworth/Thomson Learning, 2000.

Minkoff, Debra C. *Organizing for Equality: The Evolution of Women's and Racial-Ethnic Organizations in America, 1955–1985.* New Brunswick, NJ: Rutgers University Press, 1995.

Mirandé, Alfredo. *Hombres y Machos: Masculinity and Latino Culture.* Boulder, CO: Westview, 1997.

Mirriam-Goldberg, Caryn. *Sandra Cisneros: Latina Writer and Activist.* Berkeley Heights, NJ: Enslow, 1998.

Mitchell, H.L. *Mean Things Happening in This Land: The Life and Times of H.L. Mitchell, Cofounder of the Southern Tenant Farmers Union.* Montclair, NJ: Allanheld, Osmun, 1979.

Mohr, Eugene. *The Nuyorican Experience: Literature of the Puerto Rican Minority.* Westport, CT: Greenwood, 1982.

Monaghan, Jay. *Chile, Peru, and the California Gold Rush of 1849.* Berkeley: University of California Press, 1973.

Montejano, David. *Anglos and Mexicans in the Making of Texas, 1836–1986.* Austin: University of Texas Press, 1987.

Montes, Agustín Laó, and Arlene Davila, eds. *Mambo Montage: The Latinization of New York.* New York: Columbia University Press, 2001.

Montes, Segundo, Juan Jose, and García Vásquez. *Salvadoran Migration to the United States: An Exploratory Study.* Washington, DC: Georgetown University, 1988.

Moore, Burton, and Andrea A. Cabello, eds. *Love and Riot: Oscar Zeta Acosta and the Great Mexican American Revolt.* Mountain View, CA: Floricanto, 2003.

Moore, Joan. *Homeboys: Gangs, Drugs, and Prison in the Barrios of Los Angeles.* Philadelphia: Temple University Press, 1978.

Moore, Joan, and Harry Pachon. *Hispanics in the United States.* Englewood Cliffs, NJ: Prentice Hall, 1985.

Moraga, Cherríe. *Loving in the War Years: Lo Que Nunca Paso por sus Labios.* Cambridge, MA: South End, 2000.

Moraga, Cherríe, and Gloria E. Anzaldúa, eds. *This Bridge Called My Back: Writings by Radical Women of Color.* 1981. Berkeley, CA: Women of Color, 2002.

Morales, Ed. *The Latin Beat: The Rhythms and Roots of Latin Music from Bossa Nova to Salsa and Beyond.* Cambridge, MA: Da Capo, 2003.

———. *Living in Spanglish: The Search for a Latino Identity in America.* New York: St. Martin's, 2002.

Morales, Gabriel C. *Varrio Warfare: Violence in the Latino Community.* Seattle, WA: Tecolote, 2000.

Morales, Rebecca, and Frank Bonilla, eds. *Latinos in a Changing U.S. Economy: Comparative Perspectives on Growing Inequality.* Newbury Park, CA: Sage, 1993.

Morgan, John D., and Pittu Laungani, eds. *Death and Bereavement Around the World.* Vol. 2. Amityville, NY: Baywood, 2003.

Morin, Jose-Luis. *Latino/a Rights and Justice in the United States: Perspectives and Approaches.* Durham, NC: Carolina Academic Press, 2005.

Morley, Morris, and Chris McGillion. *Unfinished Business: America and Cuba after the Cold War, 1989–2001.* New York: Cambridge University Press, 2002.

Mujcinovic, Fatima. *Postmodern Cross-Culturalism and Politicization in U.S. Latina Literature: From Ana Castillo to Julia Alvarez.* New York: Peter Lang, 2004.

Mullenneaux, Lisa. *¡Ni una bomba más! Vieques vs. U.S. Navy.* New York: Penington, 2000.

Muñoz, Carlos, Jr. *Youth, Identity, Power: The Chicano Movement.* New York: Verso, 1989.

Murcia, Rebecca Thatcher. *Dolores Huerta.* Bear, DE: Mitchell Lane, 2003.

Musch, Donald J. *Balancing Civil Rights and Security: American Judicial Responses Since 9/11.* Dobbs Ferry, NY: Oceana, 2003.

Nabokov, Peter. *Tijerina and the Courthouse Raid.* Albuquerque: University of New Mexico Press, 1969.

Navarro, Armando. *The Cristal Experiment: A Chicano Struggle for Community Control.* Madison: University of Wisconsin Press, 1998.

———. *La Raza Unida Party: A Chicano Challenge to the U.S. Two-Party Dictatorship.* Philadelphia: Temple University Press, 2000.

———. *Mexican American Youth Organization: Avant-Garde of the Chicano Movement in Texas.* Austin: University of Texas Press, 1995.

———. *Mexicano Experience in Occupied Aztlan: Struggles and Change.* Walnut Creek, CA: Altamira, 2005.

Neal, Mark A., and Murray Furman, eds. *That's the Joint: The Hip-Hop Studies Reader.* New York: Routledge, 2004.

Negrón-Muntaner, Frances. *Boricua Pop: Puerto Ricans and the Latinization of American Culture.* New York: New York University Press, 2004.

Negrón-Muntaner, Frances, and Ramón Grosfoguel, eds. *Puerto Rican Jam: Rethinking Colonialism and Nationalism.* Minneapolis: University of Minnesota Press, 1997.

Newmann, Fred M., and Associates. *Authentic Achievement: Restructuring Schools for Intellectual Quality.* San Francisco: Jossey-Bass, 1996.

Ngai, Mae M. *Impossible Subjects: Illegal Aliens and the Making of Modern America.* Princeton, NJ: Princeton University Press, 2004.

Nieto, Sonia, ed. *Puerto Rican Students in U.S. Schools.* Mahwah, NJ: Lawrence Erlbaum, 2000.

Nofi, Albert. *The Spanish-American War, 1898.* Conshohocken, PA: Combined Books, 1996.

Norden, Deborah. *The United States and Argentina: Changing Relations in a Changing World (Contemporary Inter-American Relations)*. New York: Routledge, 2002.

Noriega, Chon A., ed. *Chicanos and Film: Representation and Resistance*. Minneapolis: University of Minnesota Press, 1992.

———. *Shot in America: Television, the State, and the Rise of Chicano Cinema*. Minneapolis: University of Minnesota Press, 2000.

Normark, Don. *Chávez Ravine, 1949: A Los Angeles Story*. San Francisco: Chronicle, 1999.

Norris, Marianna. *Father and Son for Freedom*. New York: Dodd, Mead, 1968.

Norsworthy, Kent, with Tom Barry. *Inside Honduras*. Albuquerque, NM: Inter-Hemispheric Education Resource Center, 1993.

Novas, Himilce. *Everything You Need to Know About Latino History*. New York: Plume, 2008.

———. *Remembering Selena: A Tribute in Pictures & Words*. New York: St. Martin's Griffin, 1995.

Oakes, Jeannie. *Keeping Track: How Schools Structure Inequality*. 2nd ed. New Haven, CT: Yale University Press, 2005.

Oboler, Suzanne. *Ethnic Labels, Latino Lives: Identity and the Politics of (Re)Presentation in the United States*. Minneapolis: University of Minnesota Press, 1995.

Ocasio, Rafael. *Cuba's Political and Sexual Outlaw: Reinaldo Arenas*. Gainesville: University Press of Florida, 2003.

O'Connell, Joanna. *Prospero's Daughter: The Prose of Rosario Castellanos*. Austin: University of Texas Press, 1995.

Odell, John S. *Negotiating Trade: Developing Countries in the WTO and NAFTA*. New York: Cambridge University Press, 2006.

O'Gorman, Edmundo. *The Invention of America: An Inquiry Into the Historical Nature of the New World and the Meaning of Its History*. Bloomington: Indiana University Press, 1961.

Ojito, Mirta. *Finding Mañana: A Memoir of a Cuban Exodus*. New York: Penguin, 2005.

Olson, James S., and Judith E. Olson. *Cuban Americans: From Trauma to Triumph*. London: Prentice Hall International, 1995.

Ordover, Nancy. *American Eugenics: Race, Queer Anatomy, and the Science of Nationalism*. Minneapolis: University of Minnesota Press, 2003.

Oropeza, Lorena. *Raza Si! Guerra No! Chicano Protest and Patriotism During the Viet Nam War Era*. Berkeley: University of California Press, 2005.

Ortiz, Roxanne Dunbar. *Roots of Resistance: Land Tenure in New Mexico, 1680–1980*. Los Angeles: University of California at Los Angeles, 1980.

Padilla, Felix M. *Latino Ethnic Consciousness: The Case of Mexican Americans and Puerto Ricans in Chicago*. South Bend, IN: University of Notre Dame Press, 1985.

———. *Puerto Rican Chicago*. South Bend, IN: University of Notre Dame Press, 1987.

Padilla, Yolanda C. Austin, ed. *Reflexiones 1998: New Directions in Mexican American Studies*. Austin: University of Texas Press, 1998.

Paerregaard, Karsten. 2008. *Peruvians Dispersed: A Global Ethnography of Migration*. Lanham, MD: Lexington.

Pagan, Eduardo Obrego. *Murder at the Sleepy Lagoon: Zoot Suits, Race, and Riot in Wartime L.A.* Chapel Hill: University of North Carolina Press, 2003.

Pagden, Anthony. *Spanish Imperialism and the Political Imagination: Studies in European and Spanish-American Social and Political Theory, 1513–1830*. New Haven, CT: Yale University Press, 1990.

Palermo, Joseph A. *In His Own Right: The Political Odyssey of Senator Robert F. Kennedy*. New York: Columbia University Press, 2001.

Pantoja, Antonia. *Memoir of a Visionary: Antonia Pantoja*. Houston, TX: Arte Público, 2002.

Pardo, Mary S. *Mexican American Women Activists: Identity and Resistance in Two Los Angeles Communities*. Philadelphia: Temple University Press, 1998.

Paz, Octavio. *The Labyrinth of Solitude; The Other Mexico; Return to the Labyrinth of Solitude; Mexico and the United States; the Philanthropic Ogre*. New York: Grove, 1991.

Pearlstone, Zena. *Ethnic L.A.* Beverly Hills, CA: Hillcrest, 1990.

Pedraza-Bailey, Silvia. *Political and Economic Migrants in America: Cubans and Mexicans*. Austin: University of Texas Press, 1985.

Peña, Manuel. *The Texas-Mexican Conjunto: History of a Working-Class Music*. Austin: University of Texas Press, 1985.

Penland, Paige R. *Lowrider: History, Pride, Culture*. Minneapolis, MN: MBI, 2003.

Perea, Juan F., ed. *Immigrants Out! The New Nativism and Anti-Immigrant Impulse in the United States*. New York: New York University Press, 1997.

Pérez, Emma. *The Decolonial Imaginary: Writing Chicanas into History*. Bloomington: Indiana University Press, 1999.

———. *Gulf Dreams*. Berkeley, CA: Third Woman, 1996.

Pérez, Laura. *Chicana Art: The Politics of Spiritual and Aesthetic Altarities (Objects/Histories)*. Durham, NC: Duke University Press, 2007.

Pérez, Louis A., Jr. *Cuba Under the Platt Amendment, 1902–1934*. Pittsburgh, PA: University of Pittsburgh Press, 1986.

Pérez y González, María E. *Puerto Ricans in the United States*. Westport, CT: Greenwood, 2000.

Pescatello, Ann, ed. *Female and Male in Latin America: Essays*. Pittsburgh, PA: University of Pittsburgh Press, 1973.

Pessar, Patricia R. *A Visa for a Dream: Dominicans in the United States*. Boston: Allyn and Bacon, 1995.

Peterson, Tiffany. *Cuban Americans*. Chicago: Heinemann, 2003.

Pineo, Ronn. *Ecuador and the United States: Useful Strangers*. Athens: University of Georgia Press, 2008.

Pitt, Leonard, and Dale Pitt. *Los Angeles from A to Z: An Encyclopedia of the City and County*. Berkeley: University of California Press, 1997.

Plummer, Brenda Gayle, ed. *Window on Freedom: Race, Civil Rights, and Foreign Affairs, 1945–1988*. Chapel Hill: University of North Carolina Press, 2003.

Poblete, J., ed. *Critical Latin American and Latino Studies*. Minneapolis: University of Minnesota Press, 2003.

Pollack, Sandra, and Denise D. Knight, eds. *Contemporary Lesbian Writers of the United States: A Bio-bibliographical Sourcebook*. Westport, CT: Greenwood, 1993.

Pope, Kristian, and Ray Whebbe, Jr. *The Encyclopedia of Professional Wrestling: 100 Years of History, Headlines & Hitmakers.* Iola, WI: Krause, 2003.

Portes, Alejandro, and Alex Stepick. *City on the Edge: The Transformation of Miami.* Berkeley: University of California Press, 1993.

Portes, Alejandro, and Robert L. Bach. *Latin Journey: Cuban and Mexican Immigrants in the United States.* Berkeley: University of California Press, 1985.

Portes, Alejandro, and Ruben Rumbaut. *Legacies: The Story of the Immigrant Second Generation.* Berkeley: University of California Press, 2001.

Pountain, C. *A History of the Spanish Language through Texts.* New York: Routledge, 2000.

Pulido, Laura. *Brown, Black, Yellow, and Left: Radical Activism in Los Angeles.* Berkeley: University of California Press, 2006.

Quinn, Rob. *Oscar De La Hoya.* Philadelphia: Chelsea House, 2001.

Quirarte, Jacinto. *Mexican American Artists.* Austin: University of Texas Press, 1973.

Quirk, Robert E. *Fidel Castro.* New York: W.W. Norton, 1993.

Raimon, Eva Allegra. *The "Tragic Mulatta" Revisited: Race and Nationalism in Nineteenth-Century Antislavery Fiction.* New Brunswick, NJ: Rutgers University Press, 2004.

Ramos, Henry A.J. *The American GI Forum: In Pursuit of the Dream, 1948–1983.* Houston, TX: Arte Público, 1998.

Ramos, Juanita. *Compañeras: Latina Lesbians.* New York: Routledge, 1994.

Regalado, Samuel. *Viva Baseball.* Urbana: University of Illinois Press, 1998.

Reimers, David M. *Still the Golden Door: The Third World Comes to America.* 2nd ed. New York: Columbia University Press, 2002.

Reisler, Mark. *By the Sweat of Their Brow: Mexican Immigrant Labor in the United States, 1900–1940.* Westport, CT: Greenwood, 1976.

Relethford, John. *The Human Species: An Introduction to Biological Anthropology.* 5th ed. New York: McGraw-Hill, 2002.

Restall, Matthew. *Seven Myths of the Spanish Conquest.* New York: Oxford University Press, 2003.

Reyes, Belinda I. *The Dynamics of Immigration: Return Migration to Western Mexico.* San Francisco: Public Policy Institute of California, 1997.

Reyes, Luis, and Peter Rubie. *Hispanics in Hollywood: A Celebration of 100 Years in Film and Television.* Hollywood, CA: Lone Eagle, 2000.

Reynolds, R.D., and Bryan Alvarez. *The Death of WCW.* Toronto, Ontario, Canada: ECW, 2004.

Ribes Tovar, Frederico. *Albizu Campos: Puerto Rican Revolutionary.* New York: Plus Ultra, 1971.

Ricourt, Milagros, and Ruby Danta. *Hispanas en Queens: Latino Panethnicity in a New York City Neighborhood.* Ithaca, NY: Cornell University Press, 2003.

Rivas-Rodriguez, Maggie, ed. *Mexican Americans & World War II.* Austin: University of Texas Press, 2005.

Rivera, Diego, with Gladys March. *My Art, My Life: An Autobiography.* New York: Citadel, 1960.

Rivera, Raquel. *New York Ricans from the Hip Hop Zone.* New York: Palgrave Macmillan, 2003.

Roberts, John Storm. *The Latin Tinge: The Impact of Latin American Music on the United States.* 2nd ed. New York: Oxford University Press, 1999.

Roberts, Randy, and James S. Olson. *A Line in the Sand: The Alamo in Blood and Memory.* New York: Touchstone, 2001.

Robinson, Charles M., III. *Texas and the Mexican War: A History and a Guide.* Austin: Texas State Historical Society, 2004.

Roca, Ana, and John M. Lipski, eds. *Spanish in the United States: Linguistic Contact and Diversity.* Berlin, Germany: Mouton de Gruyter, 1999.

Rodriguez, America. *Making Latino News: Race, Language, Class.* Thousand Oaks, CA: Sage, 1999.

Rodríguez, Clara E. *Changing Race: Latinos, the Census, and the History of Ethnicity in the United States.* New York: New York University Press, 2000.

———. *Latin Looks: Images of Latinas and Latinos in the U.S. Media.* Boulder, CO: Westview, 1997.

Rodriguez, Eugene, Jr. *Henry B. Gonzalez: A Political Profile.* New York: Arno, 1976.

Rodriguez, Luis J. *Always Running: La Vida Loca, Gang Days in L.A.* New York: Simon and Schuster, 2005.

———. *The Concrete River.* Willimantic, CT: Curbstone, 1991.

———. *Heart and Souls: Creating Community in Violent Times.* New York: Seven Stories, 2001.

Rodríguez, Victoria E., ed. *Women's Participation in Mexican Political Life.* Boulder, CO: Westview, 1998.

Rodríguez-Duarte, Alexis. *Presenting Celia Cruz.* New York: Clarkson Potter, 2004.

Rojo, Ricardo. *My Friend Che.* New York: Dial, 1968.

Romero, Maritza. *Jaime Escalante: Inspiring Educator.* New York: PowerKids, 1997.

Romero, Mary, Pierrette Hondagneu-Sotelo, and Vilma Ortiz, eds. *Challenging Fronteras: Structuring Latina and Latino Lives in the U.S.* New York: Routledge, 1997.

Romo, Ricardo. *East Los Angeles: History of a Barrio.* Austin: University of Texas Press, 1983.

Romotsky, Jerry. *Los Angeles Barrio Calligraphy.* Los Angeles: Dawson's Book Shop, 1976.

Rosales, F. Arturo. *Chicano! The History of the Mexican American Civil Rights Movement.* Houston, TX: Arte Público, 1996.

Rosales, Rodolfo. *The Illusion of Inclusion: The Untold Political Story of San Antonio.* Austin: University of Texas Press, 2000.

Rose, Tricia. *Black Noise: Rap Music and Black Culture in Contemporary America.* Lebanon, NH: University Press of New England, 1994.

Ross, Fred. *Conquering Goliath: César Chávez at the Beginning.* Keene, CA: United Farm Workers: Distributed by El Taller Grafico, 1989.

Ross, John. *The War Against Oblivion: Zapatista Chronicles, 1994–2000.* Monroe, ME: Common Courage, 2000.

Ruck, Rob. *The Tropic of Baseball: Baseball in the Dominican Republic.* Westport, CT: Meckler, 1991.

Ruíz, Vicki L. *From Out of the Shadows: Mexican Women in Twentieth-Century America.* New York: Oxford University Press, 2008.

Ruíz, Vicki L., and Virginia E. Sánchez Korrol, eds. *Latina Legacies: Identity, Biography, and Community.* New York: Oxford University Press, 2005.

Ruiz de Burton, María Amparo. *The Squatter and the Don.* 1885. Houston, TX: Arte Público, 1997.

Rumbaut, R., and A. Portes, eds. *Ethnicities: Children of Immigrants in America.* Berkeley: University of California Press, 2001.

Ryan, Bryan, ed. *Hispanic Writers: A Selection of Sketches from Contemporary Authors.* Detroit: Gale Research, 1991.

Said, Edward W., ed. *Convergences: Inventories of the Present.* Cambridge, MA: Harvard University Press, 2002.

Salazar, Ruben. *Border Correspondent: Selected Writings, 1955–1970.* Ed. Mario T. García. Berkeley: University of California Press, 1995.

Saldívar-Hull, Sonia. *Feminism on the Border.* Berkeley: University of California Press, 2000.

Sammond, Nicholas. *Steel Chair to the Head: The Pleasure and Pain of Professional Wrestling.* Durham, NC: Duke University Press, 2005.

Samora, Julian, Joe Bernal, and Albert Pena. *Gunpowder Justice: A Reassessment of the Texas Rangers.* Notre Dame, IN: University of Notre Dame Press, 1979.

Samora, Julian, with Patricia Vande Simon. *A History of the Mexican American People.* Notre Dame, IN: University of Notre Dame Press, 1993.

———. *La Raza: Forgotten Americans.* Notre Dame, IN: University of Notre Dame Press, 1966.

———. *Los Mojados.* Notre Dame, IN: University of Notre Dame Press, 1972.

San Miguel, Guadalupe, Jr. *Contested Policy: The Rise and Fall of Federal Bilingual Education in the United States, 1960–2001.* Denton: University of North Texas Press, 2004.

———. *"Let All of Them Take Heed": Mexican Americans and the Campaign for Educational Equality in Texas, 1910–1981.* Austin: University of Texas Press, 1987.

———. *Tejano Proud: Tex-Mex Music in the Twentieth Century.* College Station: Texas A&M University Press, 2002.

Sanchez, George I. *Concerning Segregation of Spanish-Speaking Children in the Public Schools.* Austin: University of Texas Press, 1951.

Sánchez, George J. *Becoming Mexican American: Ethnicity, Culture and Identity in Chicano Los Angeles, 1900–1945.* New York: Oxford University Press, 1995.

Sanchez, Reymundo. *My Bloody Life: The Making of a Latin King.* Chicago: Chicago Review Press, 2000.

Sánchez, Rosaura. *Telling Identities: The Californio Testimonios.* Minneapolis: University of Minnesota Press, 1995.

Sánchez Korrol, Virginia E. *From Colonia to Community: The History of Puerto Ricans in New York City.* Berkeley: University of California Press, 1994.

Sánchez-Walsh, Arlene. *Latino Pentecostal Identity.* New York: Columbia University Press, 2003.

Sandoval, Moises, ed. *Fronteras: A History of the Latin American Church in the USA Since 1513.* San Antonio, TX: Mexican American Cultural Center, 1983.

Santana, Déborah Berman. *Kicking Off the Bootstraps: Environment, Development, and Community Power in Puerto Rico.* Tucson: University of Arizona Press, 1996.

Santiago, Roberto, ed. *Boricuas: Influential Puerto Rican Writings—An Anthology.* New York: Ballatine, 1995.

Santiago Santiago, Isaura. *A Community's Struggle for Equal Educational Opportunity, Aspira versus Board of Education.* Princeton, NJ: Educational Testing Service, 1978.

Santillan, Richard. *La Raza Unida.* Los Angeles: Tlaquilo, 1973.

Schlesinger, Arthur, Jr. *Robert Kennedy and His Times.* Boston: Houghton Mifflin, 1978.

Schnabel, Tom. *Rhythm Planet: The Great World Music Makers.* New York: Universe, 1998.

Schwartz, Michael. *Luis J. Rodríguez.* Austin, TX: Steck-Vaughn, 1998.

Schwartz, Stuart B. *Victors and Vanquished: Spanish and Nahua Views of the Conquest of Mexico.* Boston: Bedford/St. Martin's, 2000.

Sepulveda, Juan A., Jr. *The Life and Times of Willie Velasquez: Su Voto es Su Voz.* Houston, TX: Arte Público, 2003.

Servin, Mauel P., ed. *An Awakened Minority: The Mexican Americans.* New York: Macmillan, 1974.

Shockley, John Staples. *Chicano Revolt in a Texas Town.* Notre Dame, IN: University of Notre Dame Press, 1974.

Shulman, Irving. *West Side Story.* New York: Pocket Books, 1990.

Silén, Iván, ed. *Los paraguas amarillos/los poetas latinos en New York.* Binghamton, NY: Bilingual Review, 1983.

Silva-Corvalan, Carmen. *Language Contact and Change: Spanish in Los Angeles.* Oxford, UK: Clarendon, 1996.

Simons, Geoff. *Cuba: From Conquistador to Castro.* New York: St. Martin's, 1996.

Sirias, Silvio. *Julia Alvarez: A Critical Companion.* Westport, CT: Greenwood, 2001.

Skierka, Volker. *Fidel Castro: A Biography.* Trans. Patrick Camiller. Malden, MA: Polity, 2004.

Sloane, Todd A. *Gonzalez of Texas: A Congressman for the People.* Evanston, IL: John Gordon Burke, 1996.

Smedley, Brian D., Adrienne Y. Stith, and Alan R. Nelson, eds. *Unequal Treatment: Confronting Racial and Ethnic Disparities in Health Care.* Washington, DC: National Academies, 2003.

Smith, Edward Lucie. *Latin American Art of the Twentieth Century.* London: Thames & Hudson, 1993.

Smith, Joseph. *The Spanish-American War: Conflict in the Caribbean and the Pacific, 1895–1902.* New York: Longman, 1994.

Sommers, Joseph, and Tomás Ybarra-Frausto, eds. *Modern Chicano Writers: A Collection of Critical Essays.* Englewood Cliffs, NJ: Prentice Hall, 1979.

Sosa, Sammy, and Marcus Breton. *Sammy Sosa: An Autobiography.* New York: Warner, 2000.

Spicer, Edwards. *Cycles of Conquest: The Impact of Spain, Mexico and the United States on Indians of the Southwest, 1533–1960.* Tucson: University of Arizona Press, 2003.

Spurgeon, Sara. *Ana Castillo.* Boise, ID: Boise State University, 2004.

Staten, Clifford L. *The History of Cuba.* Westport, CT: Greenwood, 2003.

Stavans, Ilan. *Bandido: The Death and Resurrection of Oscar "Zeta" Acosta.* Evanston, IL: Northwestern University Press, 2003.

———. *The Hispanic Condition: The Power of a People.* New York: HarperCollins, 2001.

———. *Spanglish: The Making of a New American Language.* New York: HarperCollins, 2003.

Stefoff, Rebecca. *Gloria Estefan.* New York: Chelsea House, 1991.

Stephanson, Anders. *Manifest Destiny: American Expansionism and the Empire of Right.* New York: Hill and Wang, 1995.

Stepick, Alex, et al. *This Land Is Our Land: Immigrants and Power in Miami.* Berkeley: University of California Press, 2003.

Sterling, Philip, and Maria Brau. *The Quiet Rebels: Four Puerto Rican Leaders: José Celso Barbosa, Luis Muñoz Rivera, José De Diego, Luiz Muñoz Marín.* Garden City, NY: Doubleday, 1968.

Stewart, Mark. *Alex Rodriguez: Gunning for Greatness.* Brookfield, CT: Millbrook, 1999.

Stone, Deborah. *Rita Moreno.* Castro Valley, CA: Quercas, 1990.

Stout, Glenn, and Matt Christopher. *On the Field with . . . Alex Rodriguez.* Boston: Little, Brown, 2002.

Striffler, Steve. *In the Shadows of State and Capital: The United Fruit Company, Popular Struggle, and Agrarian Restructuring in Ecuador, 1900–1995.* Durham, NC: Duke University Press, 2002.

Stull, Donald D., and Michael J. Broadway. *Slaughterhouse Blues: The Meat and Poultry Industry in North America.* Belmont, CA: Wadsworth/Thomson Learning, 2004.

Suárez-Orozco, Marcelo M. *Central American Refugees and U.S. High Schools.* Stanford, CA: Stanford University Press, 1989.

Suárez-Orozco, Marcelo M., and Mariela M. Páez, eds. *Latinos: Remaking America.* Berkeley: University of California Press, 2002.

Subcomandante Marcos. *Shadows of Tender Fury: The Letters and Communiqués of Subcomandante Marcos and the Zapatista Army of National Liberation.* Trans. Frank Bardacke, Leslie Lopez, and the Watsonville, California, Human Rights Committee. New York: Monthly Review, 1995.

Sudbury, Julia. *Global Lockdown: Race, Gender, and the Prison-Industrial Complex.* New York: Routledge, 2005.

Sugden, John, and Alan Tomlinson, eds. *Hosts and Champions: Soccer Cultures, National Identities and the USA World Cup.* Aldershot, UK: Ashgate, 1994.

Suntree, Susan. *Hispanics of Achievement: Rita Moreno.* New York: Chelsea House, 1992.

Taylor, Philip B., Jr. *Government and Politics of Uruguay.* Westport, CT: Greenwood, 1984.

Telgen, Diane, and Jim Kamp, eds. *Latinas! Women of Achievement.* Detroit: Visible Ink, 1996.

Tenayuca, Emma. *The Mexican Question in the Southwest.* N.p., 1939.

Thomas, David Hurst, ed. *Columbian Consequences.* Vol. 2. Washington DC: Smithsonian Institution, 1990.

Thomas, Evan. *Robert Kennedy: His Life.* New York: Simon and Schuster, 2000.

Thomás, Piri. *Down These Mean Streets.* 1967. New York: Vintage Books, 1997.

———. *Savior, Savior Hold My Hand.* New York: Doubleday, 1972.

———. *Seven Long Times.* New York: Praeger, 1974.

———. *Stories from El Barrio.* New York: Alfred A. Knopf, 1978.

Tichenor, Daniel J. *Dividing Lines: The Politics of Immigration Control in America.* Princeton, NJ: Princeton University Press, 2002.

Tijerina, Andrés. *Tejanos and Texas under the Mexican Flag, 1821–1836.* College Station: Texas A&M University Press, 1994.

Tijerina, Reies López. *They Called Me "King Tiger": My Struggle for the Land and Our Rights.* Trans. and ed. José Angel Gutiérrez. Houston, TX: Arte Público, 2000.

Tinker, George E. *Missionary Conquest: The Gospel and Native American Cultural Genocide.* Minneapolis, MN: Fortress, 1993.

Todorov, Tzvetan. *The Conquest of America: The Question of the Other.* Trans. Richard Howard. New York: Harper & Row, 1984.

Toor, Frances. *A Treasury of Mexican Folkways.* New York: Crown, 1947.

Torres, Andrés, and José E. Velázquez. *The Puerto Rican Movement: Voices from the Diaspora.* Philadelphia: Temple University Press, 1998.

Torres, Edén E. *Chicana without Apology: Chicana sin vergüenza.* New York: Routledge, 2003.

Torres, John Albert. *Sports Great Oscar De La Hoya.* Springfield, NJ: Enslow, 1999.

Torres, Lourdes, and Inmaculada Pertusa, eds. *Tortilleras: Hispanic and U.S. Latina Lesbian Expression.* Philadelphia: Temple University Press, 2003.

Torres, María de los Angeles. *In the Land of Mirrors: Cuban Exile Politics in the United States.* Ann Arbor: University of Michigan Press, 1999.

Trevino, Lee, and Sam Blair. *The Snake in the Sandtrap (And Other Misadventures on the Golf Tour).* New York: Henry Holt, 1987.

———. *Super Mex: An Autobiography.* New York: Arrow, 1983.

Trias Monge, Jose. *Puerto Rico: Trials of the Oldest Colony in the World.* New Haven, CT: Yale University Press, 1999.

Triay, Victor Andres. *Bay of Pigs: An Oral History of Brigade 2506.* Gainesville: University Press of Florida, 2001.

Trujillo, Carla, ed. *Chicana Lesbians: The Girls Our Mothers Warned Us About.* Berkeley, CA: Third Woman, 1991.

———. *Living Chicana Theory.* Berkeley, CA: Third Woman, 1998.

Trujillo, Charley. *Soldados: Chicanos in Viet Nam.* San Jose, CA: Chusma House, 1990.

U.S. Commission on Civil Rights. *Puerto Ricans in the Continental United States: An Uncertain Future.* Washington, DC, 1976.

United States Office of the Deputy Assistant Secretary of Defense for Military Manpower and Personnel Policy. *Hispanics in America's Defense.* Washington, DC: U.S. Government Printing Office, 1990.

Valdez, Carlos. *Justice for Selena: The State vs. Yolanda Saldivar.* New York: Trafford, 2005.

Valdez, Luis. *Zoot Suit and Other Plays.* New York: Arte Público, 1992.

Vargas, Zaragosa. *Labor Rights Are Civil Rights: Mexican American Workers in Twentieth-Century America.* Princeton, NJ: Princeton University Press, 2005.

———, ed. *Major Problems in Mexican American History: Documents and Essays.* New York: Houghton Mifflin, 1999.

———. *Proletarians of the North: A History of Mexican Industrial Workers in Detroit and the Midwest, 1917–1933.* Berkeley: University of California Press, 1999.

Varley, James F. *The Legend of Joaquín Murrieta: California's Gold Rush Bandit.* Twin Falls, ID: Big Lost River, 1995.

Vasconcelos, José. *La Raza Cósmica—Misión Iberoamericana—Notas de Viaje a América del Sur.* Barcelona, Spain: Agencia Mundial Ibrería, 1925.

Vásquez, Francisco H., and Rodolfo Torres, eds. *Latino/a Thought: Culture, Politics and Society.* Lanham, MD: Rowman & Littlefield, 2003.

Vélez-Ibáñez, Carlos. *Cultural Bumping: Mexican Cultures of the Southwest United States.* Tucson: University of Arizona Press, 1996.

Vento, Arnoldo. *Mestizo: The History, Culture and Politics of the Mexican and the Chicano.* Lanham, MD: University Press of America, 1998.

Vigil, Ernesto B. *The Crusade for Justice: Chicano Militancy and the Government's War on Dissent.* Madison: University of Wisconsin Press, 1999.

Vigil, James Diego. *Barrio Gangs: Street Life and Identity in Southern California.* Austin: University of Texas Press, 1988.

———. *From Indians to Chicanos: The Dynamics of Mexican-American Culture.* 2nd ed. Prospect Heights, IL: Waveland, 1998.

Vigil, Maurilio. *Chicano Politics.* Washington, DC: University Press of America, 1977.

Villarreal, Roberto E., and Norma G. Hernandez, eds. *Latinos and Political Coalitions: Political Empowerment for the 1990s.* New York: Greenwood, 1991.

Voces y Visiones: Highlights from El Museo del Barrio's Permanent Collection. New York: El Museo del Barrio, 2006.

Vodovnik, Žiga, ed. *Ya Basta! Ten Years of the Zapatista Uprising: Writings of Subcomandante Insurgente Marcos.* Foreword by Noam Chomsky and Naomi Klein. Oakland, CA: AK, 2004.

Wagenheim, Kal, and Olga Jiménez de Wagenheim, eds. *The Puerto Ricans: A Documentary History.* Princeton, NJ: Markus Weiner, 2002.

Walker, Paul Robert. *Pride of Puerto Rico: The Life of Roberto Clemente.* San Diego, CA: Harcourt Brace Jovanovich, 1991.

Walker, Thomas. *Nicaragua.* 4th ed. Boulder, CO: Westview, 2003.

Weber, David J. *The Spanish Frontier in North America.* New Haven, CT: Yale University Press, 1992.

Weber, Devra. *Dark Sweat, White Gold: California Farm Workers, Cotton, and the New Deal.* Berkeley: University of California Press, 1994.

Wells, Miriam J. *Strawberry Fields: Politics, Class, and Work in California Agriculture.* Ithaca, NY: Cornell University Press, 1996.

Wendel, Tim. *The New Face of Baseball: The One-Hundred-Year Rise and Triumph of Latinos in America's Favorite Sport.* New York: HarperCollins, 2004.

West, Gail, Navarre Perry, Doug Jacobs, et al. *The Lemon Grove Incident.* VHS. New York: Cinema Guild, 1985.

Whalen, Carmen Teresa. *El Viaje: Puerto Ricans of Philadelphia (Images of America).* Charleston, SC: Arcadia, 2006.

———. *From Puerto Rico to Philadelphia: Puerto Rican Workers and Postwar Economies.* Philadelphia: Temple University Press, 2000.

Whigham, Thomas, and Jerry W. Cooney. *A Guide to Collections on Paraguay in the United States.* Westport, CT: Greenwood, 1995.

Williamson, Joel. *New People: Miscegenation and Mulattoes in the United States.* New York: Free Press, 1980.

Wilson, Clint, II, Felix Gutierrez, and Lena Chao, eds. *Racism, Sexism, and the Media: The Rise of Class Communication in Multicultural America.* Thousand Oaks, CA: Sage, 2003.

Wolff, Nelson, and Henry Cisneros. *Mayor: An Inside View of San Antonio Politics, 1981–1995.* San Antonio, TX: San Antonio Express News, 1997.

Wollenberg, Charles. *All Deliberate Speed: Segregation and Exclusion in California Schools, 1855–1975.* Berkeley: University of California Press, 1977.

Wood, Michael. *Conquistadors.* Berkeley: University of California Press, 2000.

Worth, Richard. *Dolores Huerta.* New York: Chelsea House, 2007.

Wunnava, Phanindra V., ed. *The Changing Role of Unions: New Forms of Representation.* Armonk, NY: M.E. Sharpe, 2004.

Yang, Philip. *Ethnic Studies: Issues and Approaches.* Albany: State University of New York Press, 2000.

Yeager, Gertrude M. *Confronting Change, Challenging Tradition: Women in Latin American History.* Wilmington, DE: Scholarly Resources, 1994.

The Young Lords Party and Michael Abramson. *Palante: Young Lords Party.* New York: McGraw-Hill, 1971.

Zack, Naomi, ed. *American Mixed Race: The Culture of Microdiversity.* Lanham, MD: Rowman & Littlefield, 1995.

Zambrana, Ruth E., ed. *Understanding Latino Families: Scholarship, Policy, and Practice.* Thousand Oaks, CA: Sage, 1995.

Zavala, Iris M., and Rafael Rodriguez. *The Intellectual Roots of Independence: An Anthology of Puerto Rican Political Essays.* New York: Monthly Review, 1980.

Zendegui, Ileana C. *The Postmodern Poetic Narrative of Cuban Writer Reinaldo Arenas (1943–1990).* Lewiston, NY: Edwin Mellen, 2004.

Zentella, Ana C. *Growing Up Bilingual: Puerto Rican Students in New York.* Malden, MA: Blackwell, 1997.

Zolberg, Aristide R. *A Nation by Design: Immigration Policy in the Fashioning of America.* Cambridge, MA: Harvard University Press, 2006.

Web Sites

American GI Forum. http://www.agif.us.

ASPIRA: An Investment in Latino Youth. http://www.aspira.org.

Brothers to the Rescue (Hermanos Al Rescate). http://www. hermanos.org.

Center for American Progress. http://www.americanprogress. org.

Centro de Estudios Avanzados de Puerto Rico y El Caribe (Center for Advanced Puerto Rican and Caribbean Studies). http://www.ceaprc.org/.

Centro de Estudios Puertorriqueños (Center for Puerto Rican Studies–CENTRO). http://www.centropr.org.

Coalition of Cuban-American Women. http://coalitionof cubanamericanwomen.blogspot.com.

Countries and Their Cultures. http://www.everyculture.com.

Cuban American National Foundation. http://www.canf.org.

El Museo del Barrio. http://www.elmuseo.org.

El Teatro Campesino. http://www.elteatrocampesino.com.

Esmeralda Santiago Homepage. http://www.esmeraldasantiago. com/index.html.

Hispanic Americans in Congress. http://www.loc.gov/rr/hispanic/ congress/.

Hispanic Heritage Foundation. http://www.hispanicheritage. org.

Hispanic Tips. http://www.hispanictips.com.

ImpreMedia. http://www.impremedia.com.

La Opinión Digital. http://www.laopinion.com.

Latino Commission on AIDS. http://latinoaids.org.

Latino Nutrition Coalition. http://www.latinonutrition.org.

MALCS: Mujeres Activas en Letras y Cambio Social (Women Active in Letters and Social Change). http://www.malcs. net.

MANA, A National Latina Organization. http://www.hermana. org.

MEChA (Movimiento Estudiantil Chicano de Aztlán). http:// www.nationalmecha.org.

Mexican American Legal Defense and Education Fund. http:// www.maldef.org.

Mexican American Political Association. http://www.mapa.org.

National Alliance of Gang Investigators Associations. http:// www.nagia.org.

National Boricua Latino Health Organization. http://www. nblho.org.

National Conference of Puerto Rican Women. http://www. nacoprw.net.

National Congress for Puerto Rican Rights. http://www. columbia.edu/~rmg36/NCPRR.html.

National Council of Hispanic Women. http://www.nchwomen. org.

National Council of La Raza. http://www.nclr.org.

National Minority AIDS Council. http://www.nmac.org.

National Puerto Rican Coalition. http://www.bateylink.org.

National Puerto Rican Day Parade. http://www.national puertoricandayparade.org.

Nuyorican Poets Café. http://www.nuyorican.org.

Pew Hispanic Center. http://www.pewhispanic.org.

Prevenir es Vivir. http://www.contrasida-aids.org/.

Puerto Rican Studies Association. http://www.puertorican-studies.org.

Service Employees International Union. http://www.seiu.org.

Social and Public Art Resource Center. http://www.sparc murals.org.

Southwest Voter Registration and Education Project. http:// www.svrep.org.

United Farm Workers: http://www.ufw.org.

Univision. http://www.univision.net.

Univision Portal en Español. http://www.univision.com.

Uruguayan American Chamber of Commerce. http://www. uruguaychamber.com.

Index

Wyoming
  Mexicans *(continued)*
    Treaty of Guadalupe Hidalgo, 1:8,
      246; 2:477, 540, 589
  Peruvians, 2:423
  religion, 2:474
  Spanglish, 2:507

X

Xicanisma, 1:90, 101, 102
  See also Feminism
Ximenes, Vicente, 2:431

Y

. . . y no se lo tragó la tierra (. . . the earth did
  not swallow him, Rivera), 2:595
Yager, Arthur, 1:193
Yahoo!, 2:597
Yamada, Mitsuye, 2:350
Yañez, René, 1:153
Yarborough, Ralph, 2:430
Yarbro-Bejarano, Yvonne, 2:351
Ybarra, Lea, 2:562
Ybor, Vicente Martinez, 1:12
YCCA. *See* Young Citizens for Community
  Action
YCL. *See* Young Communist League
Year of Our Revolution, The: New and Selected
  Stories and Poems (Cofer), 1:126;
  2:461
Yekutieli, Adi, 1:62
Yepes, George, 1:302
Yerba Buena (Esteves), 2:461
YL. *See* Young Lords
YMCA. *See* Young Men's Christian
  Association

¡Yo! (Alvarez), 1:49
Yo Soy Chicano (1972), 1:187
Yo Soy Joaquín (*I Am Joaquín*, Gonzales),
  1:xxi, 208; 2:575–76
  chicanismo, 1:104, 105
  film, 1:187; 2:522, 528, 555, 575
  race, 1:104, 110; 2:426, 528, 576
  See also Gonzales, Rodolfo "Corky"
Yoruba faith, 1:54; 2:369
Young Citizens for Community Action
  (YCCA), 1:83; 2:595
Young Communist League (YCL), 1:129
Young Lords (YLs), 2:389, 390, 576–79
  Garbage Offensive (1969), 1:21; 2:577
  health and health care, 2:352, 389,
    577–78, *578*
  Morales, Iris, 2:351, 352
  National Conference of Puerto Rican
    Women, 2:380–81
  National Congress for Puerto Rican
    Rights, 2:381, 382
  Puerto Rican Revolutionary Workers
    Organization, 2:352, 463
Young Men's Christian Association
  (YMCA), 2:325, 326
Youth. *See* Blowouts; Children and youth;
  Gangs; Graffiti; Hip-hop; Sleepy
  Lagoon Case; Young Lords; Zoot Suit
  Riots
Youth, Identity, and Power (Muñoz, Jr.),
  1:107
Youth Force Coalition, 2:449
Yzaguerre, Raul, 2:385

Z

Zambos (mixed race), 1:38–39, 245; 2:360

Zammora et al v. People (1942). *See* Sleepy
  Lagoon Case
Zamora, Bernice, 1:102
Zamora, Pedro, 2:438
Zapata, Emiliano, 1:104, 139, 189, *280*;
  2:576, 581, 591, 593
Zapatistas, 1:266; 2:400–401, 581–83
Zapotecs, 2:365
Zaragoza, Ignacio, 1:117
Zayas, Alfredo, 2:428
Zia Summer (Anaya), 1:52
Zimmerman, Fred, 2:436
Zoo Risa (Galarza), 1:198
Zoot Suit (film, 1981; full release 1982),
  1:23, 187; 2:397, 555–56
Zoot Suit (play, Valdez), 2:523, 524, 555,
  556
Zoot Suit Riots, 2:583–85, *584*, 592
  assimilation, 1:115, 246; 2:327, 413,
    414, 583, 585
  carnalismo, 1:87
  cholos, 1:115, 199; 2:414
  film, 1:187; 2:397
  Mexican-American Movement, 2:327
  mural art, 1:61
  Opinión, La (Los Angeles), 2:412
  pachucos, 1:15, 87, 115, 199; 2:413–14,
    583, 584
  Sleepy Lagoon Case, 1:15, 187; 2:498,
    500
  Teatro Campesino, El, 2:523
Zorro, El, 2:368
Zubaydah, Abu, 2:415
Zvezda i smert' Khoakina Mur'ety (*The Star*
  and Death of Joaquín Murrieta, Grushko
  and Rybnikov), 2:368